How To Access Your Digital Forms

Included with your copy of this book is access to all its forms in digital format. So you can easily open and modify the forms, **we have replaced our jamesforms.com website and our old CDs with a convenient ZIP file of Word documents.**

Access is easy.
If you purchased this title on jamespublishing.com, a link to download the ZIP file should have already been delivered to your email inbox. Be sure to add customer-service@jamespublishing.com to your safe sender list so this message doesn't land in a spam folder. You can also access the download link at any time by **logging in at jamespublishing.com and clicking My Account** in the upper right-hand corner.

No account yet? No problem.
If you do not yet have a jamespublishing.com account, or you are having trouble, please contact customer support at **1-866-725-2637** or customer-service@jamespublishing.com. We will get you setup right away.

How to unzip the file:
Once you download the ZIP file, you need to extract the files onto your system. Typically, files are downloaded into your Downloads folder unless another directory was specified. Follow these steps to unzip:

1. **Double-click the ZIP file**. In Windows XP or newer and Mac OS X, you can double-click the ZIP file and it will open in a new window. You can then copy the contents to another folder. OS X will create a new folder next to the ZIP file when you double-click it, but may not open it automatically.

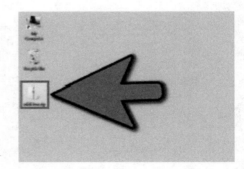

2. **Right-click the ZIP file**. In Windows you can right-click the ZIP file and select *Extract All…* or *Extract Here*. Extract All will allow you to set a path for the extracted folder to go, and Extract Here will decompress the folder and leave it in the same location as the ZIP file.

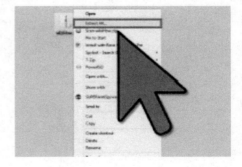

Can I share my digital forms with others?
No. Our forms are copyrighted, and they are licensed to a single individual book purchaser for his or her use only. It is unfair to our book authors if their forms are freely distributed, so please honor their hard work by not sharing their forms. Thank you for understanding.

(This page intentionally left blank.)

DEFENDING SPECIFIC CRIMES

Timothy E. Zerillo

James Publishing

Contact us at (866) 72-JAMES or www.jamespublishing.com

ABOUT THE AUTHOR

Timothy E. Zerillo has a criminal defense, personal injury, and complex civil litigation practice located in Portland, Maine. He practices in federal and state courts throughout the state.

Tim is a past President of the *Maine Association of Criminal Defense Lawyers* and is the Chair of the MACDL CLE Committee. He is a Delegate of the *National Association of Criminal Defense Lawyers*. Tim has been awarded the *President's Award* by the *Maine Association of Criminal Defense Lawyers*, which is an award given each year to the criminal defense attorney who best exemplifies the goals and values of MACDL and the legal profession. He has been elected to *New England Super Lawyers* for the years 2010 through 2018. Tim was elected to the *National Trial Lawyers Top 100* in 2014 and 2019. He regularly publishes articles focusing on criminal law issues in the *Maine Lawyer's Review*.

Tim is a frequent criminal defense lecturer having spoken on topics such as "Dealing With the DEA: How To Think Like Jay Z," "Winning the He Said/She Date Rape Case," "Attacking the Medical Evidence in Child Sexual Abuse Cases," "Ethical Issues in Opening Statements and Closing Arguments," "Using Written Jury Questionnaires to Win Your Case," "Defending Child Pornography Prosecutions," and "How to Prepare and Try a DV Assault Case."

Tim resides in Portland, Maine with his wife and two children.

ACKNOWLEDGMENTS

Many thanks to my wife, Shane, for her constant love and support. Additional thanks to Shane for not complaining (too much) as I toss and turn in bed before trial doing cross-examinations in my sleep.

Thanks to my mother, Meredith, father, John, sister, Holly, and my family at large for their love and support. (I know it is not always easy being related to a criminal defense lawyer). Thanks to my Editor, Donna Cole, for her wonderful job propping me up, and to Acquisitions Editor, Neil Stadtmore, for choosing me for this project. I also wish to acknowledge criminal defense lawyers everywhere. Thanks for all the inspiration.

To Siena and Anthony: no matter what you do in life, always find a way to fight for the little guy.

Timothy E. Zerillo

EDITORIAL STAFF

Managing Editor
Donna M. Cole

Production
Julie Anne Ines

Typesetter
Alexandru Oprescu

TABLE OF CONTENTS

EXPANDED TABLE OF CONTENTS

CHAPTER 4   THEFT OFFENSES

CHAPTER 5   BURGLARY AND ROBBERY

CHAPTER 7   DRUG CRIMES

CHAPTER 8   DRUNK DRIVING CASES

CHAPTER 9   FIREARMS OFFENSES: POSSESSION BY DISQUALIFIED PERSONS & OTHER FIREARMS CHARGES

CHAPTER 11   SEXUAL ASSAULTS AGAINST ADULTS

(Rev. 12/21/07) CC

Appearance

☐ State of Illinois

☐ City, Village, Town of _____

In the Circuit Court of Cook County, Illinois

Municipal Department, _____ District

_____

v.

_____ Plaintiff

No. _____

_____ Defendant

APPEARANCE

The undersigned enters the appearance of defendant _____.

Name: _____

Attorney for: _____

Address: _____

City/State/Zip: _____

Telephone: _____   Cook County Attorney Number ☐☐☐☐

DOROTHY BROWN, CLERK OF THE CIRCUIT COURT OF COOK COUNTY, ILLINOIS

CHAPTER 12   SEXUAL ASSAULTS AGAINST CHILDREN

CHAPTER 13　CHILD PORNOGRAPHY

INDEX

CHAPTER 1

CLIENT RELATIONS

(This page intentionally left blank.)

I.   CLIENT INTERACTION—YOU NEED TO BE A HERO (OR YOU WILL BE A GOAT)

§1:01   Defendants Talk

In no other area of the law is your reputation as a lawyer so constantly at stake as in criminal law. Defendants talk. They talk a lot. No place more so then in the jail.

Of course, there are those clients who will love you and think you walk on water, and those that will hate and resent you no matter what you do. In all likelihood, these are the extreme cases among those you represent. Try not to get too high on yourself or down on yourself depending on what the people at either fringe think.

The battle for your reputation is not played out at the fringes, but rather in the middle. Those people are in a bad spot when they come to you, but are also in a place where you can likely do some good. They are skeptical of lawyers, but will trust you if you prove yourself trustworthy to them. These are the people, like a swing vote in a presidential election, who will make or break your reputation. The "silent majority" of your clients will not stay silent when asked to give a thumbs up or thumbs down on you as a lawyer.

§1:02   Lower Client Expectations; Then Exceed them

Do not kid yourself; lawyers are sales people. We are highly educated sales people, but we are marketing ourselves with every client nonetheless.

As a result, we need to do what my father taught me early on: lower expectations, and then exceed them. When you exceed expectations constantly for a client, trust is built, and the client will be a future referral source for you. When you disappoint clients, the opposite will happen. It is that middle group of clients that you need to constantly exceed expectations with.

§1:03   Building Trust

Building client trust, like building trust in a relationship, is accomplished with the little things. Telling clients what to expect in a process where they feel blind is an enormous help. Keeping clients informed and following up is also important. Every time you do a little thing right, you take a step forward in building trust. Every time you don't do what you say you will do, and don't follow up the way you say you will, you take several steps backwards in the trust level your client has in you.

In short, you want to connect with the client. You have a difficult job to do, and you will either be viewed as a hero or a goat at the end of this process. Being a hero doesn't mean that you win every trial—it can mean that you exceeded expectations and guided the client through a very bad time with compassion and skill. If you do that consistently, you will serve both your clients and justice.

[§§1:04-1:09 Reserved]

II.   THE INITIAL CLIENT PHONE CALL OR EMAIL

Most of my potential client inquiries come either from my website, www.ZerilloLaw.com, or by telephone. Very few people walk in off the street, but it does happen, and it may happen to you more frequently than me depending on where your office is located.

§1:10   Responding to Email Inquiries

If the client contact originates from your website to your email, it is important to respond in kind as soon as you can. Some people are more comfortable finding out about the potential lawyer by email, so be prepared to sell yourself in writing.

To help with that, I have a template I use. I generally talk about the specifics of the potential client's case for a paragraph or two, then append these standard paragraphs to my email.

My belief is that people are impressed with the content and length of the response. I personalize my response in a paragraph or two, so they know it is not a stock email. A quick and thorough response projects knowledge and confidence.

Usually, good email contact will result in either a follow up phone call or a meeting. I find many clients are ready to skip the call and go straight to the meeting after an email exchange. If so, forward the email to whoever handles your calendar, and get the meeting scheduled right away.

§1: 11   FORM 1-10 Sample E-Mail Response

I am very sorry to hear about your recent charges of Class A Trafficking in Cocaine.

[Discuss specifics of client's case.]

To give you an idea of cost, you are likely looking at a cost of $_____. This represents a flat fee for pre-trial representation in your case.

For payment, we take all major credit cards, cash and check. I am more than happy to schedule a phone conference or meeting with you, if you are considering hiring us. Obviously, I don't want to schedule a meeting if you have no intention of hiring us, so I expect people to make these meetings in good faith.

Our practice is strictly litigation only. We do criminal defense (State and Federal), divorce and family law, personal injury and commercial litigation. We have significant experience and a very high success rate. If you haven't done so already, you can check out our website at www.ZerilloLaw.com. You can also view recent case results on my blog and YouTube channel.

We have a long history of successfully representing people involved in cases such as yours. I am the Past President of the Maine Association of Criminal Defense Lawyers. That is a position elected by the criminal defense community. I am a Delegate for the National Association of Criminal Defense Lawyers. I publish articles on Criminal Defense in the Maine Lawyer's Review. I also teach other lawyers about criminal defense topics in the State of Maine. I have represented everyone from local politicians, to doctors, to even other lawyers accused of crimes.

As you know, we do not enjoy an attorney-client relationship until I am retained (except preserving the privileged information you share with us). Until then, best wishes. I look forward to assisting you. ~Tim

§1:12   Telephone Inquiries

While web and email inquiries are popular, most of my new potential clients still come from the telephone. Client telephone contact is essential to a good attorney-client relationship. Building a good foundation for future success with that client means starting at the beginning, and that is with your staff.

In restaurant lingo, you have a front of the house and back of the house. The front of the house is the host or hostess, *maitre'd*, *sommelier* and wait staff. The back of the house is the head chefs, *sous* chefs and dishwashers.

If you own a restaurant, you can have the greatest chef in the world, but if he is not personable, you want to keep him behind closed doors. It doesn't mean he isn't valuable; it just means he is not for the front of the house.

You may have a great staff member or paralegal who is an excellent worker and productive, but subconsciously surly on the phone. Keep him or her off the telephone with new clients. This seems like common sense, but I experience downright nasty people on the phone when I call law firms all the time.

Friendliness on the phone is important. That said, you do not need to go over-the-top, either. Someone who is so friendly that they sound artificial doesn't help anything. Potential clients think that you are aloof and plastic when your staff over-extends their friendliness.

What you need is someone who can connect with the caller. Connecting is something largely that cannot be taught. It is your job to identify those on your staff who can best connect with clients the fastest. These callers are often distraught and frustrated. I want them hanging up the call with my office, even if they never spoke to an attorney, feeling warm and believing that progress had been made.

§1:13   New Client Questionnaires

One of the primary goals of the initial client call is to make sure that you have all essential client information and that conflicts have been checked before the call gets to an attorney.

Our New Client Questionnaire form gets basic contact information, case fact information and makes sure there are no conflicts of interest. Staff members are told to fill out the form while on the phone with the client, and ensure that it is entirely filled out.

§1:14   FORM 1-20 New Client Questionnaire

NEW CLIENT QUESTIONNAIRE CRIMINAL

Date: _____ Time: _____ Type of Case: Criminal

Name of Caller: _____ Relationship to Defendant: _____

Address: _____

Phone Number: (home)_____ (cell) _____

(work) _____ Email address: _____

Name of Client/Defendant: _____

Address: _____

Phone Number: (home)_____ (cell) _____

(work) _____ Email address: _____

Employer's Name and Location:_____

In Custody? _____ If so, where? _____

Alleged Victim: _____ Location: _____

Co-Defendants: _____ Location: _____

[PLEASE PLACE CALLER ON HOLD FOR CONFLICTS CHECK]

Court Information: Court/Location:_____ Docket No: _____

Pending Court Dates: _____ Type of hearing _____

Charges:

Count 1 _____, Class _____

Count 2 _____, Class _____

Count 3 _____, Class _____

Count 4 _____, Class _____

Count 5 _____, Class _____

What has the Defendant been accused of?

_____

_____

_____

_____

Initial Meeting: _____ Interview by:_____

§1:15   Checking Conflicts

You will note the conflicts provision here. I have inserted it in the form with a script for the telephone attendant for a few reasons.

First, the obvious reason is that the conflicts check should always be done. If you are in a small firm, this can be time consuming, but it is important. Simply set up a spreadsheet or word processing document and train your staff to fill it out in every case.

Second, you will note that I have the telephone attendant perform the conflicts check after the initial contact information and opposing party information have been given. The client has not provided any factual information at this point. This is so my office staff has not gained any client confidences or secrets from this initial information.

PRACTICE TIP: *Check conflicts early in call*

In Maine where I practice, client confidences and secrets are imputed to the attorney when my staff speaks to the potential client. Get the conflicts check with the caller done early to avoid conflicting you out of a present case you may be cultivating. You don't want to lose out on a big drug case because a co-conspirator called in and gave secrets to your paralegal.

§1:16   Talking to the Potential Client Yourself

Once the client reaches me on the phone, I want to be reassuring and informative (assuming it is a case I am interested in). As an attorney, you probably know how to charm the pants off of potential clients. (If you work for yourself, you won't last too long in the business, if you don't).

If you have cultivated your telephone skills, remember to connect. People are used to dealing with large multinational corporations where their calls are outsourced internationally. You have a major advantage over that miserable experience.

You need to personalize yourself and your practice in order to connect with callers. When the caller talks about how Officer Smith was a jerk and put the cuffs on too tight, let him know other clients of yours have complained about Officer Smith too (if true, of course). If the new client complains about the cops in a particular town or city, let the client know that you have dealt with them before too, and how difficult they can be. Not only does this convey your empathy, it also conveys your experience.

§1:17   Setting Up a Face-to-Face Meeting

Once you have established your interest in taking the case, set up a face-to-face meeting. Sometimes geographic distance prevents this from happening. In such instances, employ technology to get a virtual face-to-face meeting whenever possible. This is a little more personal than a phone call and connects you to the client when a face-to-face meeting isn't possible because of geography.

If a face-to-face meeting is possible, the transition between your phone conversation and the appointment set up should be handled seamlessly. In my office, my paralegal handles my schedule. I would introduce, or re-introduce, the potential client to my paralegal, who would then make the appointment over the phone. Train the person scheduling the appointment to make sure the potential client understands where the office is, where parking is and whether the client has any particular needs in the meeting. Make sure the staff person tells the client to bring any documents she has to the meeting.

§1:18   FORM 1-30 Letter Confirming Initial Client Meeting

After scheduling the initial client meeting, I send out the following letter:

Date

Joe Client
54 Samoset Way
New City, Everywhere 55555

Re: Meeting with Timothy Zerillo

Dear Joe:

It was a pleasure speaking with you on the phone today. This is to remind you that we have a meeting set up to discuss your case on April 1, 2019 at 1:00 pm. My office is located at 1250 Forest Ave, Suite 3A, Portland, Maine. Please call me or my paralegal if you have any questions. If you want further information about our firm, please feel free to check out our website at www.ZerilloLaw.com or my blog at www.ZerilloLaw.com/blog

Respectfully submitted,

_____

Timothy E. Zerillo
Attorney for Defendant
ZERILLO LAW FIRM, LLC

This letter reminds the client about the meeting time and location—which can be crucial. There are plenty of forgetful people out there. I always throw a business card or two in as a reminder. The letter is a nice touch toward starting a good relationship. Everyone likes to get mail that isn't a bill.

[§§1:19-1:29 Reserved]

III. THE INITIAL CLIENT MEETING

§1:30 Set the Stage for Trust Building

By the time of the initial client meeting, the potential client will already have researched you. She will have asked friends about you and looked you up on the internet. It is likely her impressions are good, otherwise she wouldn't be at the meeting to begin with. You want to bolster those good impressions with the initial client meeting and set the stage for trust building.

> **PRACTICE TIP:** *Put together a firm brochure*
>
> I don't know about you, but I hate waiting at the doctor's office. *People* magazine holds no interest for me, and I get bored in the waiting room pretty easily.
>
> I try to avoid that scenario with my clients, although it is easier said than done. To pass the time, I created a firm brochure for my clients to look at and take home when they leave. It covers several areas of interest, including sections about myself and the attorneys who work in my office. It includes articles I've written for periodicals and newspaper clippings of notable cases I've handled. Reading the brochure allows the potential clients to get to know me and my history and to pass the time if I'm running late. It can also be mailed to potential clients who haven't set up a meeting and are shopping around. It is very inexpensive to make and is a good conversion tool.
>
> Additionally, I would recommend hanging articles on your waiting room walls. I currently have hung four large plaques containing clippings of a few stories published about my legal victories. This serves the same purpose as the brochures, but, more often than not, I find potential clients wandering the room and reading the articles. Plaques are eye-catching and simple. While they can be expensive, newspapers provide great summaries and headlines that stick with the client.
>
> I know a personal injury law firm that has copies of hundreds of checks hanging on their reception wall representing settlements they received. It may be shameless self-promotion, but it also provides a bit of comfort to the client that they are in the right place.

§1:31 FORM 1-40 New Client Information Form

When clients arrive, have them fill out your New Client Form. This gives them something to do while they wait for your arrival. It also asks for immigration information and prior criminal convictions. I like to have this in the file in my client's own handwriting.

NEW CLIENT INFORMATION FORM

CRIMINAL CASE

NAME: _____

ADDRESS: _____

HOME TELEPHONE: _____ WORK TELEPHONE: _____

CELL TELEPHONE: _____ EMAIL AD: _____

IS THERE ANY NUMBER WHERE WE SHOULDN'T LEAVE MESSAGES? IF SO, WHICH NUMBER?

_____

EMERGENCY CONTACT NAME: _____ PHONE: _____

SOCIAL SECURITY NUMBER: _____

DATE OF BIRTH: _____

Since criminal charges have a variety of consequences, we ask some basic information about you. This is not meant to be intrusive, but is asked to help us better evaluate the potential consequences you face.

PLACE OF BIRTH: _____

If you were born anywhere other than the United States of America then please tell us what your alien/ immigration status is: _____

Please tell us about your prior criminal history, if any:

CRIMINAL CHARGE	WERE YOU CONVICTED?	DATE OF CONVICTION
1.		
2.		
3.		
4.		
5.		

(PLEASE CONTINUE ON REVERSE OF FORM, IF NECESSARY)

Take your time in the meeting itself. Take your time with whatever family arrives. Get a complete history. It is important to know your client, not just to know your client's case.

§1:32   Therapeutic Intervention

It is important to get the client involved in the appropriate therapy early and often. In individual chapters in this book you will hear me raise this issue again and again. It may be legal social work, but it is critical to your client's case and well being.

I tell my clients to consider that our defenses are proceeding on two different tracks. The first track is what they expect; active defense of the fact that they did not actually commit the crime alleged. The second track, which they sometimes do not expect, is the track where we make sure they are treated sufficiently for whatever could have caused the crime to have been committed. Proceeding on the second track is the client's choice. That said, I explain to them that if we run up against a roadblock on track one, track two allows us to switch gears effectively and plea bargain the case. Early therapeutic intervention can turn a case from a likely trial that is no more than a slow guilty plea into a positive negotiation.

§1:33   Retaining Experts

It is important to get experts involved early on if they can be helpful to your particular case. Explain to the client in advance that the expert's fee is in addition to your fee. Make sure the client knows that you are not getting any kickback from the expert to pad your own pockets. Make sure to provide that the client is responsible for expert fees in your fee agreement.

In some cases, experts are absolutely essential, in other cases they are not. This varies case-by-case. In virtually every child pornography case, for example, a computer forensic expert is needed, to consult with at the very least. This is not true for the garden-variety domestic assault, in which I rarely need experts.

Just be sure to explore the concept of an expert witness with the client regardless of whether he or she decides to retain one. If you identify the issue and properly explain the potential value of an expert to a client, you are doing your job. What you don't want is a post-conviction review in which the client is able to testify that he was not even aware that it was possible to get a chemist to dispute the results of an intoxilyzer at his drunk driving trial.

§1:34   Social Media

Which social networking sites are en vogue can change quickly. That said, I doubt mightily that social networking is going away any time soon. This means that people will continue to send and post incriminating statements and photographs of themselves.

Advise your clients to suspend their own posting, and in some instances, to shut down their pages. They won't like that, but the picture of your client with a joint in his mouth while he has sex with a blow up doll won't be great for sentencing.

We have taken to warning our clients about this in writing and verbally. At the start of our representation, we mail the client a letter with this warning, which is often very applicable in most cases.

§1:35   FORM 1-50 New Client Letter with Social Media Warning

Date

Client
Address

       Re: _____ v. _____
          Docket No.

Dear _____:

It was a pleasure to meet **(or speak)** with you. It is clear that you need an aggressive criminal defense to combat the _____charge against you. We have a proven track record of success in defending both State and Federal criminal matters. I am hopeful that we can achieve the best possible result in your case as well. This letter is sent as a brief introduction to go by as you navigate through rough waters.

One Simple Rule to Remember: SILENCE IS GOLDEN

One firm rule applies from now on related to your case: **do not discuss your case with anyone but your lawyer.** Anything you say can and will be used against you. This is true whether you talk to a police officer, a person you just met, or a "friend".

Bail (for use with STATE CASE)

You are out on bail. Please understand and abide by all bail conditions carefully. Take them seriously and literally. If you do not abide by your bail conditions, your bail may be violated and you may be re-arrested.

(for use with FEDERAL CASE)

RELEASE OR DETENTION

The first thing to worry about is whether you are going to be released while waiting for trial. There is no bond set automatically in federal court. Your family cannot simply pay a bondsman to get you out.

Court Appearance: If you are charged, you will soon appear before a United States Magistrate Judge. This is not the District Judge that will hear your trial. This Magistrate Judge will decide if there are any conditions that would allow your release.

Pretrial Report: In order to assist the Magistrate Judge, a Pretrial Services Officer will interview you and give the Magistrate Judge a written report about your background and criminal history. The Officer will not ask you about the facts of your case and you should not volunteer any information. If you lie to the Officer, it will hurt you later on.

Chance for Release: You are most likely to be released if you have little or no criminal history, if you have solid employment and family ties in your community, if you are a United States Citizen, and if you are not charged with a serious drug trafficking offense or crime of violence. Even if you are not a good risk for release, the Magistrate Judge must still hold a hearing and find reasons to keep you in custody. The only time this hearing is unnecessary is when you are being held in custody for other reasons -- such as a sentence in another case, a parole warrant, or a probation revocation warrant.

Your Rights

When people talk about "rights" in the criminal justice system, they are usually talking about the Fourth, Fifth, Sixth and Eighth Amendments to the United States Constitution. These rights include freedom from unreasonable searches and seizures, the right to remain silent, the right to legal counsel, due process of law, equal protection under the law, protection from double jeopardy, a speedy and public trial, the ability to confront one's accusers, subpoenas for witnesses, no excessive bail, and freedom from cruel and unusual punishment.

Not all of these rights apply in all cases, and there is a great deal of confusion about them. For example, if you never made a statement to the police, then it will not matter whether you were told of your right to remain silent. If you consented to a search of your car, then it will not make a difference whether the police had a search warrant (as long as the consent was valid).

Please raise all issues of your constitutional rights with us so we can determine if there is any legitimacy to claims that your rights were violated.

Initial Steps

The next step in the process is to evaluate the charges against you. This includes evaluating the Government's discovery, and doing our own investigation.

After the investigation, I may decide it is appropriate to file motions. There are a variety of criminal motions. Garden-variety motions include Motions for Discovery (to obtain missing or incomplete discovery from the Government) and Motions to Suppress (to attempt to exclude evidence which was obtained by Law Enforcement from a violation of Constitutional rights). I will discuss whether or not to file motions with you after I thoroughly review discovery.

RESOLVING YOUR CASE

Most cases are resolved by plea bargaining with the Government. I will plea bargain on your behalf throughout the course of your case. That said, you should almost never take a first offer from the Government (unless it involves an excellent deal or a dismissal) because offers generally get better as you get closer to trial. This is not always the case, but it is often the case.

Trial

In the event that you decide to go to trial, then you must be aware that there are inherent risks associated with trying any case. It is impossible to determine what a jury will do. Additionally, the Government will only try a case if they think they can win it. If you decide to go to trial, please remember the risks associated with trying your case. If you decide that you need to go to trial after balancing the risks and the offers you have received to resolve your case, we will be very pleased to represent you and attempt to achieve vindication for you against these charges.

Immigration Issues

If you were not born in the United States, please fill out the attached *Immigration Questionnaire*. This includes if you were born on a United States military installation oversees. This does not mean you will be deported, but we want to do our due diligence and check all these issues out for you before deciding how your case will proceed. **If you were born in the United States and do not have citizenship with any other country, you do not need to fill out the attached *Immigration Questionnaire*.**

<u>Fees</u>

To review our fee agreement, we have a flat fee in this case of $_____ ($_____ has been received—thank you). This fee includes all work up to trial, but does not include expenses for your cases, such as the employment of third parties like investigators or experts. Please see our Fee Agreement for greater detail on fee-related issues.

<u>Social Networking Sites Warning</u>

If you belong to a public social networking site such as Facebook, MySpace, YouTube, Twitter, Google Circles, LinkedIn, etc., PLEASE KEEP IN MIND THAT WHATEVER YOU POST IS NOT PRIVATE AND MAY BE SUBJECT TO DISCOVERY BY THE PROSECUTOR IN YOUR CASE.

Please take caution that whatever you write or post, or have written or posted, can fall into the hands of the Prosecutor. Generally, the information is obtained without your knowledge or permission. If you have a social media site you should immediately verify that all your settings are on PRIVATE (the highest setting possible) and nothing is public. Even with the highest privacy settings, you should write or post items with the assumption that it is open to the public.

We urge you to do the following regarding social media and electronic communication:
1. **Apply the highest privacy settings**.
2. **Be very selective about who you "friend" or link with**. Do not allow anyone to become a "friend" on an account unless you are absolutely sure you know that person.
3. **Refrain from using social media sites as much as possible while your case is pending**.
4. **Do not post anything about your case, do not answer questions about the facts**.
5. **Do not post anything about meetings with your lawyers or staff members**. This can result in a challenge to the attorney client privilege.
6. **Be very discreet about any photos that you post**.
7. **Think about what you post**: Do not post anything about your social life that involves drinking, doing drugs, partying or other activities that the Prosecutor may try to use to paint you in an unfavorable light to a jury.
8. **Do not send any emails regarding your case to anyone except your attorneys**. It is very important that you do not send emails to friends or family about your case. The Prosecutor may attempt to subpoena the e-mails from your friends or family members. If it is absolutely necessary for you to communicate with a friend or family member keep the communications to what is essential and generally try to communicate verbally. The people you communicate with could be subpoenaed to testify about your communications.
9. **Do not forward any emails from our office to anyone else**. Forwarding our e-mails or sharing our communications of any kind can result in waiver of the attorney client privilege.
10. **Do not participate in blogs, chat-rooms, or message boards if the content relates to your case**.

We have seen an increase in electronic surveillance. **You should assume that the Prosecutor looks for social media entries that might paint an unflattering picture of you.**

Be aware that the Prosecutor may be entitled to request all information contained within your home computers and laptop hard drives regarding the issues mentioned above. The Prosecutor may also be entitled to subpoena information directly from service providers.

Internet and social media security consultants recommend that you review the contents of your social network sites and that you review your "friends" or "connections" and keep only those that you know and trust.

KEEPING IN TOUCH

I will make every effort to keep you informed of the status of your case and I encourage you to call me or email me whenever you have questions or concerns. As you can imagine, I am often in Court, so please contact my assistant or send me an email if you cannot reach me by phone.

Thank you for putting your confidence in our firm. It is our objective to diligently handle your criminal case, keep you fully advised of its status and obtain a fair and just result for you.

I look forward to working with you on this matter.

Very truly yours,
Timothy E. Zerillo
ZERILLO LAW FIRM. LLC

Enclosure

IMMIGRATION QUESTIONNAIRE
ATTORNEY-CLIENT PRIVILEGED
ZERILLO LAW, LLC

What offenses might have immigration consequences? *Almost any* offense may have an immigration consequences for *some* non-citizens. Please fill out this form so we can analyze if a conviction has immigration consequences for your case:

Client's Name: _____

Where were you born? _____

How long have you been in the U.S.?_____

What is your immigration status?_____

What was your immigration status when you first entered the U.S.? _____

Have you ever been deported or removed from the U.S.? _____

What is your complete criminal history—including all felony, misdemeanor and municipal convictions and all deferred dispositions and prosecutions?

_____

_____

_____

Do you have a spouse or children that are U.S. citizens? _____

Which of the following do you want to Zerillo Law Firm, LLC to prioritize in your criminal case?
- ☐ getting a good immigration result

or
- ☐ getting a lesser criminal penalty?

Please contact Zerillo Law Firm, LLC with any questions about this form.

_____   _____
Client's Signature   Date

[§§1:36-1:39 Reserved]

IV.   FEE AGREEMENTS

§1:40   Flat Fee Agreements

Fee agreements are essential to good client communication and to the protection of your fee. It is exceedingly important that they are sent promptly, and signed by the client and a guarantor if at all possible. This is an administrative task that can be time consuming, but worth the effort.

We start, of course, with the proposition that no one likes to be charged any amount of money. As criminal lawyers, we charge large amounts of money, and clients can resent that. There are always some bad apple clients who will attack your fee. These clients cannot be eliminated, but can be neutralized by good, solid fee agreements. You can take away their ammunition if you are careful with those agreements and your communication.

Most of my criminal work is done on a flat fee basis. Flat fee criminal work is allowed in my neck of the woods, and I prefer it in criminal cases. It may not be allowed in your jurisdiction, so check your local bar rules.

I divide my flat fees in the categories of pre-charge, pre-trial, and trial fees. I don't include appeals in any of these fees at the outset. I credit the pre-charge fee, if any, against the pre-trial fee if the client is ultimately charged.

At the initial client meeting, I let the client know he or she will be receiving paperwork from us, including the fee agreement. The fee agreement should be mailed shortly after the meeting to maintain momentum in the process and to reinforce with the client that you do what you say you will do.

I also offer an hourly fee. I have drafted a Consolidated Fee Agreement where a staff member in my office can easily suit the fee agreement to the individual case.

§1:41   FORM 1-60 Fee Agreements

Date

Client

FLAT FEE RETAINER AGREEMENT

This agreement is entered into on the date indicated below between _____ (hereinafter referred to as "CLIENT"), and ZERILLO LAW FIRM, LLC (hereinafter referred to as "LAWYER").

The services for which LAWYER is being retained concern the following matters, charges and allegations: *Case caption and description of matter.*

The scope of LAWYER'S responsibilities and the scope of CLIENT's obligations are recited in detail below.

LAWYER agrees to represent diligently and zealously the interests of the CLIENT as regards to the criminal defense of allegations and complaints, which may arise out of the circumstances listed above.

In order to appropriately represent client, LAWYER will necessarily incur expenses. These expenses are different and separate from attorney's fees. These expenses include such items as fees for transcripts of court proceedings, investigators' fees and expenses, copying and binding fees for briefs, long distance telephone calls, fax charges at $1.00 per page, fees for service of process and other documents, costs of medical reports, costs of visual aids and demonstrative exhibits for use in court, costs of taking depositions, travel and lodging expenses, Xerox copying charges at $.25 per page, color copies $.50 per page, and extraordinary postage or Federal Express expenses. **CLIENT shall be responsible for all such expenses incurred in the representation of CLIENT.**

From time to time, LAWYER may find it necessary to employ outside parties to assist in the defense of CLIENT. Based upon the facts available to us now, these outside parties may either be **private investigators or expert witnesses**. It is expressly understood that LAWYER will act as a facilitator and to fully explain to all parties the reason for the retention of the investigator or the expert witness, as well as the risks and benefits of their retention, or of refraining from retaining such assistants. **CLIENT will be responsible for reasonable costs incurred to employ such investigators or experts, and will be solely responsible for payment of any fees incurred by such investigator. CLIENT will be billed directly by private investigator.**

The fees for representation by LAWYER of CLIENT in the above-captioned matter shall be as follows:

<u>Retainer:</u> $_____ as a "RETAINER". Payment of _____ has been received-thank you.

This RETAINER of $_____ represents a flat fee to secure LAWYER'S services.

CLIENT RELATIONS

[IF PAYMENT PLAN ON PRE-TRIAL FEE]

Retainer: $_____ as a "RETAINER." ($_____ has been received—thank you). The remaining $_____ will be paid in the following installments: _____.

For the pre-trial fee, LAWYER agrees to represent CLIENT in all **pretrial** stages of the proceedings, and to represent CLIENT in all criminal hearings up to the disposition of the case without trial.

[IF HOURLY FEE]

Initially, I will need an advance payment of $_____ ($_____ has been received—thank you). $_____ is now due. Please keep in mind the advance payment is not the full cost of legal services, which will depend solely on the amount of time spent on your case and the amount of disbursements incurred. Your advance payment will be applied against legal fees and disbursements on this matter. Our invoices to you will reflect the application of the advance payment and will set forth the balance remaining on the advance payment. In the case of monthly billings over the amount of the advance payment, you agree to pay any balance due thereon within fifteen (15) days after such billing. A late charge of 1/2 percent per month, compounding monthly, will be assessed upon any balance which remains unpaid for more than thirty (30) days from the date of invoice. You will be sent monthly itemized statements which you should carefully review. If you have any questions, please contact this office within 10 days of receipt or I will assume that you concur with these charges.

[IF RETAINER REFRESHER]

Refresher of Retainer:
After _____ of hours of attorney time spent on your case, a Retainer Refresher will be due.[1] This Retainer Refresher is employed because of the novelty of the case involved, and the uncertainty relating to the amount of time needed to defend these charges. The amount of the Retainer Refresher will be determined by the LAWYER. This Retainer Refresher cannot be set now, because neither LAWYER nor CLIENT currently know the amount of work remaining on the case at the time the Retainer Refresher will be due. There may be more than one Retainer Refresher.

Trial Fee:
Should the case proceed to Trial, CLIENT will be charged a Trial Fee. The amount of the Trial Fee will be determined by the LAWYER. The setting of the Trial Fee is not dependent on the number of hours of attorney time on the case. Rather, the Trial Fee is based on the pendency of trial and the necessity of LAWYER having to prepare for jury selection and trial. This Trial Fee cannot be set now, because neither LAWYER nor CLIENT currently know the length of time or work involved in trying this matter.

CLIENT recognizes that substantial work preparing for Trial and Jury Selection may be done by LAWYER in advance of Jury Selection and Trial. As a result, it is conceivable that a Trial Fee may be paid and thereafter CLIENT changes his or her mind about proceeding or continuing with Trial in advance of Jury Selection, or after Jury Selection but before Trial, or after a Trial has commenced. In such cases, CLIENT recognizes the significant work that goes into preparing for Jury Selection and Trial. Refunds of the Trial Fee in such a situations are up to the sole discretion of LAWYER. CLIENT acknowledges that the Trial Fee may be set without the need for a new Fee Agreement.

The RETAINER is the LAWYER'S property. **CLIENT acknowledges that this retainer is not excessive in CLIENT'S view, and is reasonable, in light of LAWYER'S experience and qualifications, and the difficulty and novelty of the case involved.**

The purpose of the RETAINER is to assure LAWYER's availability within the scope of representation recited above, and to enlist the LAWYER's diligence, skill and experience in efforts not only to secure favorable resolution of formal charges which may be, or have been, brought arising out of the above-recited circumstances, but to also utilize LAWYER's diligence, skill and experience in an effort to prevent formal charges from being brought.

Refunds: Refunds of all flat fees are at the discretion of the LAWYER in consultation with the Rules of Professional Conduct and Precedent. If LAWYER is forced to withdraw from representation of CLIENT, or if CLIENT

---

[1] This does not include paralegal, legal assistant or office manager time, but includes the time of lawyers associated with ZERILLO LAW FIRM, LLC.

hires other counsel, the issue of refundability of fees may come up. In a case in which there is an Engagement Fee, that fee is anticipated to be a **minimum** fee. The refundability of fees varies on a case-by-case basis. CLIENT acknowledges the following are relevant factors to refundability issues, and that the amount of time spent on the case is not the sole determining factor: (a) the nature, complexity and degree of difficulty of the work required in this retention of LAWYER for this case, (b) LAWYER'S agreement to perform all work necessary to effectuate the purpose of the retention; (c) LAWYER'S agreement to decline or defer other work if necessary to carry out his obligations to me pursuant to this Agreement; (d) if applicable, the novelty of the work and the special expertise and experience CLIENT believes LAWYER possesses to do the work to be performed; and (e) the urgency of the matter and inherent time limitations.

If, for any reason, we are compelled to commence collection efforts on any outstanding bill, then, in addition to the above, you agree to pay us actual attorney's fees and costs incurred (whether our own time or that of other attorneys is employed) in connection with that collection effort.

OTHER PROVISIONS TO THIS AGREEMENT

Withdrawal of Lawyer. Should CLIENT fail to cooperate with LAWYER's reasonable requests involving his/her defense, or abide by his/her financial agreement with LAWYER as set forth herein, or for any other reason as outlined in the Maine Rules of Professional Responsibility for the Conduct of Lawyers (The Bar Rules), LAWYER reserves the right to move to withdraw from representation of CLIENT. CLIENT should be aware that LAWYER may withdraw from representation in this matter only upon motion to and with the approval of the Superior Court. CLIENT retains the right to object to any motion to withdraw filed by LAWYER.

No Guarantee or Warranty. LAWYER warrants that the best efforts possible will be devoted to the representation of CLIENT's interests. However, LAWYER can make no guarantee of any result in pending matters; any decisions by prosecuting agencies as to indictment; decision by judges as to merits of cases; or decisions by any body, tribunal or court having jurisdiction over sentencing. **All LAWYER, or any attorney, can do is his or her best.**

LAWYER makes absolutely no warranty representation or guarantee of any type as to existence of any form of special relationship with any prosecutorial agency, law enforcement body, or court.

LAWYER cannot guarantee the outcome of your case. LAWYER will advise you of the recommended technical and legal tactical issues as they arise so that you may continue to evaluate whether and how you wish to continue the legal representation. However, lawyers are subject to independent ethical obligations and LAWYER is not obligated to pursue objectives or employ means simply because you may wish that LAWYER do so, especially if the LAWYER would be violating another duty by pursuing the requested action.

Privilege. Generally, the information you give to our firm is subject to the attorney-client privilege; however, lawyers are sometimes under an independent ethical duty to reveal privileged information, such as illegal or fraudulent acts committed by clients in the course of the attorney client relationship, the intention of the client to commit a crime or when the lawyer is required to divulge the information by law or court order.

[IF FLAT FEE]

Billing Records. CLIENT acknowledges that LAWYER may have limited or no billing records for work done by LAWYER on this matter. CLIENT consents to LAWYER not itemizing or documenting billing records for attorney's fees.

Not Contingency Agreement. This agreement is not a contingency agreement. The fee arrangement between LAWYER and CLIENT is exactly as discussed herein, and is not dependent upon any form of favorable result whatsoever. There is no premium or bonus for a successful result, nor is there contemplated any form of reduction, rebate or discount for an unfavorable result, or for a conclusion that is reached more swiftly than anticipated.

Appeal. This agreement does not include any appeals. If an appeal is either desired by the CLIENT or deemed advisable by LAWYER, a separate compensation agreement between LAWYER and CLIENT will be negotiated should client desire to retain the services of LAWYER as appellate counsel. CLIENT should be aware that LAWYER may withdraw from representation in this matter only upon motion to and with the approval of the Court. CLIENT retains the right to object to any motion to withdraw filed by LAWYER.

It is conceivable that during any legal proceeding arising out of the above recited facts, that an interlocutory appeal (or appeal in the middle of the proceedings) may be appropriate or necessary. In that event, LAWYER will explain the interlocutory appellate process, as well as the benefits and risks to the client of proceeding with such an appeal. If CLIENT desires to have such an appeal prosecuted on his or her behalf, additional compensation for such appeal, if any, shall be the subject of a separate, written agreement between LAWYER and CLIENT.

Other Lawyers. At the time this agreement is executed, there are seven (7) attorneys affiliated with LAWYER's office. From time to time, and in any proceeding up to and including trial, it may be appropriate for any or all of the attorneys affiliated with LAWYER's office to assist and to appear on behalf of CLIENT. The assignment of the attorney to assist or appear on behalf of the CLIENT is within the sole discretion of LAWYER with the following limitation:

A.   If there is a disagreement between CLIENT and a particular attorney, it is the responsibility of the CLIENT to communicate the disagreement and the problem, if any, with Lawyer's managing partner, Timothy E. Zerillo.

Other Cases. It is possible that a civil case or cases may arise out of the facts recited above which form the basis for CLIENT's retention of LAWYER. All parties expressly understand hereto that this agreement does not cover representation in any civil matter brought for compensation on behalf of any person or the estate of any person alleged to have been damaged by client. However, LAWYER will be available to consult with CLIENT's civil attorney of record concerning the applicability and appropriateness of CLIENT's assertion of any Fifth Amendment rights against self incrimination and to be present at CLIENT's deposition, if any, in any civil proceeding arising out of the facts recited above.

Funds Legitimate. I hereby further agree and assure my LAWYER that all funds which LAWYER is paid or to be paid under the Agreement of Representation will have been derived exclusively from legitimate sources and/or enterprises and/or earnings. Further, I affirm that no such funds will have originated in any illicit or illegal enterprise or activity of which I am aware or in which I have been, or have been alleged to have been, involved.

Files and Records. All of your original client materials will be returned to you, or you will have an opportunity to retrieve your client materials in an electronic format immediately upon the conclusion of representation. If you do not wish receive an electronic copy of your client materials within 12 months of the conclusion of your case they may be destroyed without further notice to you. If any notification is sent to you, it will be to the last current address we have on file for you. CLIENT consents to this file return policy.

CLIENT consents to LAWYER maintaining CLIENT's files with a cloud service provider. This is done to better organize CLIENT's files. LAWYER will provide reasonable security for CLIENT files.

If you have read the agreement and agree with its provisions, please sign this in the presence of a witness and return it to LAWYER if the enclosed self addressed stamped envelope. If you have any questions or concerns about the agreement, please contact LAWYER before signing.

The CLIENT acknowledges that he/she has carefully read this agreement and fully understands its contents. CLIENT acknowledges that he/she can have independent legal counsel review this agreement with CLIENT. If CLIENT chooses not to have this reviewed with independent legal counsel, that is solely CLIENT'S choice.

I HAVE READ THE ABOVE AGREEMENT BEFORE SIGNING IT.

Signatures:

_____   _____
Date   CLIENT

_____   _____
Date   LAWYER

§1:42   Guarantor Fee Agreements

Another thing that I think is important is a Guarantor Fee Agreement. Many of my client's fees are paid by relatives. You can get into a bit of an ethical stew if the guarantor thinks he or she gets to call the shots. I have the following language in my Guarantor Agreement and client Fee Agreement that makes it known that the Guarantor does not have decision-making abilities:

GUARANTEE OF PAYMENT

We, Mary and Joseph, as parents of JC, have read and understand the above fee agreement. We personally guarantee payment of the legal fees and costs outlined above from our own funds. We recognize that JC is LAWYER'S CLIENT, not us. We are paying the agreed to legal fee and related costs, but JC is the client and JC will have to make the ultimate decisions that affect his case whether we agree with his decisions or not.

Does that mean that every butinsky will be taken care of? No. It does, however, set a level of expectation that you can reference later when necessary.

§1:43   FORM 1-70 Guarantor Fee Agreement

Date

VIA U.S. MAIL
Guarantor Name
Address

      RE: Contract for Legal Services Regarding CLIENT
        Case Name:
        Docket No. XXXXX-XX-XXXX-XXXX

Dear _____ :

ZERILLO LAW FIRM, LLC (LAWYER) is pleased to represent _____ with respect to the above-referenced matter. We understand that you are in the unenviable position of paying for this representation. The purpose of this document is to confirm our agreement regarding the terms and conditions of our representation of _____.

This firm's representation of _____ (CLIENT) is limited to the terms of LAWYER'S fee agreement. It is our understanding, that you are acting as Guarantor of that payment.

ATTORNEY'S FEES

[IF FLAT FEE]

The fees for representation by LAWYER of CLIENT in the above-captioned matter shall be as follows:
Retainer: $_____ as a "RETAINER." ($_____ has been received—thank you).
This RETAINER of $_____ represents a pre-trial fee to secure LAWYER's services.

For the pre-trial fee, LAWYER agrees to represent CLIENT in all **pre-trial** stages of the proceedings, and to represent CLIENT in all criminal hearings up to the disposition of the case without trial.

The RETAINER is the LAWYER's property. You agree that securing the availability of ZERILLO LAW FIRM, LLC means that in consideration for taking on CLIENT's case and for the fee charged to you, that ZERILLO LAW FIRM, LLC, and its LAWYERS are rejecting other potential clients so that they may have an adequate amount of time to represent you. **GUARANTOR acknowledges that this retainer is not excessive in their view, and is reasonable, in light of LAWYER's experience and qualifications, and the difficulty and novelty of the case involved.**

The purpose of the RETAINER is to assure LAWYER's availability within the scope of representation recited above, and to enlist the LAWYER's diligence, skill and experience in efforts not only to secure favorable resolution of formal charges which may be, or have been, brought arising out of the above-recited circumstances, but to utilize LAWYER's diligence, skill and experience in an effort to PREVENT formal charges from being brought, when possible.

Refresher of Retainer: After _____ of hours of attorney time spent on your case, a Retainer Refresher will be due.[2] This Retainer Refresher is employed because of the novelty of the case involved, and the uncertainty relating to the amount of time needed to defend these charges. The amount of the Retainer Refresher will be determined by the LAWYER. This Retainer Refresher cannot be set now, because neither LAWYER nor CLIENT currently know

---

[2] This does not include paralegal, legal assistant or office manager time, but includes the time of lawyers associated with ZERILLO LAW FIRM, LLC.

the amount of work remaining on the case at the time the Retainer Refresher will be due. There may be more than one Retainer Refresher. **GUARANTOR agrees that this Retainer Refresher is the property of the LAWYER. GUARANTOR acknowledges that this Retainer Refresher agreement is reasonable in GUARANTOR's view, in light of LAWYER's experience and qualifications, and the difficulty and novelty of the case involved.**

Trial Fee: Should the case proceed to Trial, CLIENT will be charged a Trial Fee. The amount of the Trial Fee will be determined by the LAWYER. The setting of the Trial Fee is not dependent on the number of hours of attorney time on the case. Rather, the Trial Fee is based on the pendency of trial and the necessity of LAWYER having to prepare for jury selection and trial. This Trial Fee cannot be set now, because neither LAWYER nor CLIENT currently know the length of time or work involved in trying this matter. **GUARANTOR agrees that this Trial Fee is the property of the LAWYER. GUARANTOR acknowledges that these funds belong to the LAWYER and not the GUARANTOR. GUARANTOR acknowledges that this Trial Fee agreement is reasonable in their view, in light of LAWYER's experience and qualifications, and the difficulty and novelty of the case involved.**

GUARANTOR recognizes that substantial work preparing for Trial and Jury Selection may be done by LAWYER in advance of Jury Selection and Trial. As a result, it is conceivable that a Trial fee may be paid and thereafter CLIENT changes his or her mind about proceeding or continuing with Trial in advance of Jury Selection, or after Jury Selection but before Trial, or after a Trial has commenced. In such cases, GUARANTOR recognizes the significant work that goes into preparing for Jury Selection and Trial. Refunds of the Trial Fee in such a situations are up to the sole discretion of LAWYER.

Refunds: Refunds of all flat fees are at the discretion of the LAWYER in consultation with the Rules of Professional Conduct and Precedent. If LAWYER is forced to withdraw from representation of CLIENT, or if CLIENT hires other counsel, the issue of the refundability of fees may come up. In a case in which there is an Engagement Fee, that fee is anticipated to be a **minimum** fee. The refundability of fees varies on a case-by-case basis. CLIENT acknowledges the following are relevant factors to refundability issues, and that the amount of time spent on the case is not the sole determining factor: (a) the nature, complexity and degree of difficulty of the work required in this retention of LAWYER for this case, (b) LAWYER'S agreement to perform all work necessary to effectuate the purpose of the retention; (c) LAWYER'S agreement to decline or defer other work if necessary to carry out his obligations to me pursuant to this Agreement; (d) if applicable, the novelty of the work and the special expertise and experience CLIENT believes LAWYER possesses to do the work to be performed; and (e) the urgency of the matter and inherent time limitations.

[IF HOURLY]

Initially, I will need an advance payment of $_____ ($_____ has been received—thank you). Please keep in mind the advance payment is not the full cost of legal services, which will depend solely on the amount of time spent on your case and the amount of disbursements incurred. Your advance payment will be applied against legal fees and disbursements on this matter. Our invoices to you will reflect the application of the advance payment and will set forth the balance remaining on the advance payment. In the case of monthly billings over the amount of the advance payment, you agree to pay any balance due thereon within fifteen (15) days after such billing. A late charge of 1/2 percent per month, compounding monthly, will be assessed upon any balance which remains unpaid for more than thirty (30) days from the date of invoice. You will be sent monthly itemized statements which you should carefully review. If you have any questions, please contact this office within 10 days of receipt or I will assume that you concur with these charges.

For our services, you agree to pay us at our hourly rates, as now established or as modified in the future. The current attorney rates are as follows: Timothy Zerillo's current rate is $275 per hour. Stephen Sweatt's current rate is $90 per hour. Paralegal's current rate is $75 per hour, and general Legal Assistant hours are $40 per hour.

Please note that it is the policy of LAWYER'S office to ask for a refresher of your advanced payment in the event that the balance of your advanced payment dips below $1,500. At that point, LAWYER will ask you to refresh your advanced payment up to the amount of the initial advance payment balance. This is designed to prevent you from falling behind. As it is described, herein, your advanced payment will remain in LAWYER'S IOLTA trust account until LAWYER'S fees are earned or expenses incurred.

Services will be rendered and recorded in one-tenth of an hour increments. Client agrees to this method of recording and billing for attorney's time and fees.

If, for any reason, we are compelled to commence collection efforts on any outstanding bill, then, in addition to the above, you agree to pay us actual attorney's fees and costs incurred (whether our own time or that of other attorneys is employed) in connection with that collection effort.

You agree to be financially responsible for_____'s account. Other than financial responsibility, my understanding is that you will have no other involvement in this matter. Accordingly, I will discuss only billing matters with you, and no other attorney/client privileged information with you unless he/she would like me to.

EXPENSES

In order to appropriately represent CLIENT, LAWYER will necessarily incur expenses. These expenses are different and separate from attorney's fees. These expenses include such items as fees for transcripts of court proceedings, investigator's expenses, copying and binding fees for briefs, long distance telephone calls, fax charges, fees for service of process and other documents, costs of medical reports, costs of visual aids and demonstrative exhibits for use in court, costs of taking depositions, travel and lodging expenses, copying charges and postage or Federal Express expenses. **You shall be responsible for all such expenses incurred for LAWYER'S representation of CLIENT.**

THIRD PARTY OR EXPERT FEES

From time to time, LAWYER may find it necessary to employ outside parties to assist in your case. Based upon the facts available to us now, these outside parties may either be **private investigators or expert witnesses**. It is expressly understood that LAWYER will act as a facilitator and to fully explain to all parties the reason for the retention of the investigator or the expert witness, as well as the risks and benefits of their retention, or of refraining from retaining such assistants. **You will be responsible for reasonable costs incurred to employ such investigators or experts.**

GUARANTEE OF PAYMENT

I/We, (GUARANTOR NAME(S), as (Relationship to Client) of CLIENT NAME, have read and understand the above fee agreement. I/We personally guarantee payment of the legal fees and costs outlined above from our/ my own funds. I/We recognize that CLIENT NAME is LAWYER'S CLIENT, not me/us. I/We am paying the agreed to legal fee and related costs, but CLIENT NAME is the client and he/she will have to make the ultimate decisions that affect his/her case whether I/we agree with his/her decisions or not.

ACKNOWLEDGEMENT AND CONSENT

This is the entire agreement between the guarantor and LAWYER relating to the employment of ZERILLO LAW FIRM , LLC, its heirs, successors and assigns, by you, the Guarantor. It may not be modified or changed without the written consent of both parties. The Guarantor has had the opportunity to read this agreement and seek independent legal advice and understands all of its terms. By the attorney's and Guarantor's signatures to this letter agreement, they consent to the agreement and agree to abide by all of its terms and conditions.

If you are in disagreement with any of the above, please give me a call immediately. If not, please sign below the phrase "Seen and Agreed To," which indicates that you have read this letter and have agreed to the terms of my representation set out above. Please return the original to my office in the enclosed self-addressed, stamped envelope. If you have any questions, please do not hesitate to call.

Respectfully submitted,

_____
Timothy E. Zerillo
Attorney for Defendant
ZERILLO LAW FIRM, LLC

The Guarantor(s) acknowledge(s) that he/she/they has/have carefully read this agreement and fully understand the contents.

SEEN AND AGREED TO:

_____   _____
Guarantor   Date

§1:44   FORM 1-80 Fee Agreement Follow Up Letter #1

Getting Fee Agreements returned can also be a challenge. My staff calendars our first fee agreement follow up letter 20 days from sending the Fee Agreements. The New Client Follow Up Letter #1 goes like this:

Date

JC
50 County Way
Portland, ME 04101

     Re: Fee Agreement Letter

Dear JC:

We sent you a fee agreement letter for your case on January 2. We have not received your signature on that letter. Please sign and return the fee agreement letter at your earliest convenience. Thanks in advance for your assistance.

Respectfully submitted,

_____
Damian A. Ramsdell, Paralegal
ZERILLO LAW FIRM, LLC

§1:45   FORM 1-90 Fee Agreement Follow-Up Letter #2

If the client does not respond to New Client Follow Up Letter 1 within 20 days, we send New Client Follow Up Letter 2. The second letter is sent via certified mail, and is a little more strongly worded.

Date

JC
50 County Way
Portland, ME 04101

     Re: Fee Agreement Letter

Dear JC:

We sent you a fee agreement letter for your case on January 2. We sent a follow up letter to you on January 22. We still have not received your signature on that letter. Please send the signed fee agreement letter to us within 20 days or we will be forced to withdraw from your case. This is an action we would most certainly regret, but unfortunately, we have no choice. If you need a new copy of the fee agreement letter, kindly let us know and we will provide one. Thanks in advance.

Respectfully submitted,

_____
Timothy E. Zerillo
Attorney for Defendant
ZERILLO LAW FIRM, LLC

Obviously, if the client does not return the agreement, you might not want to do something as drastic as withdraw, so tempering the letter to the case is a good idea. In my jurisdiction, I don't need to have a client signature on the fee agreement, but it can be comforting, so I really try to get it.

[§§1:46-1:49 Reserved]

V.   WRAPPING UP THE CASE

§1:50   Leaving the Client Feeling Good About a Bad Situation

At the outset of this Chapter, I told you how important I think clear and timely information is to clients accused of crimes. They are at sea in a storm, and you are the beacon to the shore. Seeing the beacon while you are at sea doesn't make the storm any less rough. It gives you hope, however, and guides you to the other side.

This doesn't end when the case ends. You may have had a horrible case with a horrible result, but you handled it professionally, and guided your client admirably. Continue that as you close the file.

I developed a Client Closing Letter to help this process. It gives clients information about where they began, where they are at the moment, and what duties they have going forward. The letter can be modified to suit your practice.

Along with the Client Closing Letter, send a business card. Note in the letter what other areas of practice you engage in if you do more than criminal work. I like to include a magnet for their fridge too. Some clients are like annuities, so make sure they have your phone numbers readily at hand.

§1:51   FORM 1-100 Closing Letter

Date

Client Name
Address
Address

Re: State of Maine v. Client Name

Dear Client Name:

I am honored and pleased to have served you in defense of the above criminal matter. I was very pleased that we were able to get an excellent result for you in your case. If I can ever be of assistance to you in the future, please let me know. In addition to criminal defense, Zerillo Law Firm, LLC also handles complex personal injury, divorce and family law cases. I welcome and appreciate all referrals you may have for me. I have enclosed a card and magnet for your convenience.

The purpose of this letter is to reiterate the resolution of this matter for your understanding. As you know, the resolution of your charges is as follows: _____.

Case Dismissed by District Attorney—(w/o prejudice)

Your case has been dismissed by the District Attorney. This matter is now closed, but can be reopened at any time by the District Attorney's Office if more evidence is made available to them. It is in your best interest to no longer discuss what happened and not to admit to anyone that you committed the offense. That evidence may be used against you to reopen the case. Otherwise, the matter is closed and you should not have to worry about it.

Filing

Your case has been filed by the Court. It will automatically be dismissed in _____, as long as you abide by all the filing conditions. Please study those filing conditions and comply with them completely.

Deferred Disposition

You agreed to accept a Deferred Disposition of your matter(s). This means you pled guilty to the charge(s), but sentencing will be deferred for _____. You pled guilty to _____. If all the requirements of the Deferred Disposition are met, you will be able to _____.

As a regular part of a Deferred Disposition, there are standard requirements that must be met. You must appear in Court on the date and time you are notified to appear. **Your return to Court date is** _____ **at**

_____ **AM or PM.** Please make sure you have a copy of your Deferred Disposition at all times as you signed the form and are deemed to know all of the conditions. Please feel free to call with any questions you may have.

Case Dismissed after Successful Deferred Disposition

You have successfully completed your Deferred Disposition. The case is now dismissed and your criminal record will not show a conviction for this matter.

Stay of Execution—Report to Jail at later date

The Judge granted you a stay of execution and ordered you to report to _____ County Jail on _____, _____ at _____ AM or PM. The jail is located at _____. You can find more information about the jail at their website: _____. Please make sure you report no later than that day and time as failure to report to jail when ordered is a crime and the penalties can be significant additional incarceration. You are on bail until you report to the jail. Please study your bail conditions and make sure your follow them exactly. A violation of bail can result in a criminal charge with additional jail time likely. Please take these bail conditions seriously and do everything possible to be in compliance while you are waiting to serve your sentence.

Fine Payment—Initial Payment Due Date w/ monthly payments

You have been ordered by Court to pay a fine of $_____ plus surcharges. You have entered into a payment arrangement with the Court. Please ensure that every payment is made on time or appear in Court on the date and time the payment is due. When in Court you will have an opportunity to request more time to pay from the Judge. Requests are generally granted if good reason is provided.

For your convenience, fine payments can also be made online. To pay online, go to www.maine.gov/online/courtfines. Fine payments made online still must be paid on time. Save a receipt from your online fine payment as proof of payment.

If you fail to make an installment payment on any date a payment is due, OR you fail to pay the fine in full on the day the payment is due, you **must appear in court** for a contempt hearing on the date and time the installment payment is due or on the date and time full payment of the fine is due. At the hearing, you are obligated to show that your failure to pay is not attributable to a willful refusal to obey this order or to a failure to make a good faith effort to obtain the funds required for the payment.

If you fail to pay or appear as required you will be found in **CONTEMPT** and any license, certification, registration, permit, approval, or similar document issued to you by the State of Maine **WILL** be suspended without further notice. These include, but are not limited to, motor vehicle license, license to hunt, fish, or trap, engage in a profession, occupation, business, or identifying licenses issued by the Commissioner of Marine Resources and Inland Fisheries and Wildlife. In addition, you may be subject to a reasonable fine. Once suspended, these licenses each carry an individual reinstatement fee that will have to be paid in addition to the fine owed to the court before the license or other certification will be reinstated. Additionally, if the offense is a criminal offense, an arrest warrant will issue.

In addition, a late fee will be applied if your payment is late. **PAYMENT MUST BE RECEIVED AT THE COURT ON THE DATE THAT THE FINE PAYMENT IS DUE—PLEASE TAKE THIS INTO CONSIDERATION WHEN MAILING YOUR FINE PAYMENTS. BECAUSE THESE FEES ARE ASSESSED AUTOMATICALLY BY THE JUDICIAL BRANCH'S COMPUTER NETWORK, THERE WILL BE NO EXCEPTIONS TO THIS RULE. THE CLERK'S OFFICE HAS NO AUTHORITY TO OVERRIDE THE LATE FEES THAT ARE ASSESSED.**

License Suspension

Your license will be suspended / has been suspended by the Court or Bureau of Motor Vehicles (or both) for a period of _____. Do not drive a vehicle until you are properly licensed as the penalties are becoming increasingly more harsh, with jail time a strong possibility. You may owe fees to a Court or the Bureau of Motor Vehicles prior to getting your license back. The most important thing for you to do is continually update the Bureau of Motor Vehicles with your address. If the Bureau of Motor Vehicles sends you a letter that you don't receive and you can't prove you gave them an updated address, you will be deemed to have received that letter. The best approach is to go to a Bureau of Motor Vehicles location and determine your license status and the address on file for you. If you need to update your address, you should get proof of that update in writing and keep it in a safe place at home.

OUI Conviction

Because you were convicted of Operating Under the Influence, when your license suspension ends, you will be issued a conditional license according to 29-A M.R.S.A. § 2506. That is, you must not operate a motor vehicle with any amount of alcohol in your blood for the following period from the date your license was reinstated: on first conviction, one year; and on a 2nd or subsequent conviction, 10 years.

ASP—Alternative Sentencing Program

You are scheduled to participate in the alternative sentencing program on _____. You must call the telephone number in the paperwork provided to you and register with the program as soon as possible. Because of your decision to participate in this program, you must report at the time required, or if you decide not to do the program, you must report to the _____ County Jail located at _____, _____, Maine at the time the program is scheduled to begin. If you do not report to either the program or the jail no later than _____ on _____, _____, you can be charged with another crime for failure to report and those penalties can be significant additional incarceration. The fee for participation in the alternative sentencing program must be paid in advance.

Restitution

You have been ordered to pay restitution in the amount of $_____. This restitution is due no later than _____. Restitution must be paid to the District Attorney's Office. If you need more time to pay, the best course of action to take is to call your attorney or the District Attorney's Office and explain the situation. Failure to pay the restitution or contact anyone about the matter may result in another Court appearance and possible further penalties.

Felony Conviction

I have a form previously sent to you regarding the consequences of a felony conviction. I enclose that for your reference as an attachment to this letter. *See* **Effect of Felony Conviction Memo,** *attached.*

Probation

You need to understand that you have been sentenced to a partially or fully suspended sentence. That means you are sentenced to the full amount of time and you can serve that entire amount, regardless of the amount of time you must serve now (if any). A violation of a condition of probation can result in any amount of time up to the full amount remaining to be served. What may seem like an insignificant violation to you may be treated very harshly by a judge. A probation violation hearing cannot be heard by a jury, just one judge, and has a lesser standard of proof than that of a new crime. Any probation violation is likely to easily result in a significant amount of time remaining be served. Please make sure you have a copy of your probation conditions and you are familiar with them so that you may avoid violating them.

Administrative Release

You need to understand that you have been sentenced to a partially or fully suspended sentence with administrative release conditions for one year. That means you are sentenced to the full amount of time and you can serve that entire amount, regardless of the amount of time you must serve now (if any). A violation of a condition of administrative release can result in any amount of time up to the full amount remaining to be served. What may seem like an insignificant violation to you may be treated very harsh by a judge. An administrative release violation hearing cannot be heard by a jury, just one judge, and has a lesser standard of proof than that of a new crime. Any administrative release violation is likely to easily result in a significant amount of time remaining be served. Please make sure you have a copy of your administrative release conditions and make sure you are familiar with them so that you may avoid violating them.

. . .

We are closing our files for this matter and are removing the case from the active files list as we have completed our legal work in the matter. We believe that we have returned all original documents to you and that we are not in possession of any original documents or papers of yours. If you believe we are still in possession of an original document or document you provided to us that you would like, please let us know immediately so that we may look for it before we put the file in the closed files.

We will hold onto your file until _____, at which point it is scheduled for destruction pursuant to our Agreement. If you need anything before that time, please contact us.

Please feel free to call with any questions or comments you may have. It has been our pleasure to serve you.

Respectfully submitted,

_____

Timothy E. Zerillo
Attorney for Defendant
ZERILLO LAW FIRM, LLC

Enclosure

CHAPTER 2

STRATEGIES FOR ALL CRIMINAL CASES

STRATEGIES FOR ALL CRIMINAL CASES

I.   INVESTIGATION AND EVIDENCE PRESERVATION

A. Investigators

§2:01   Importance of a Good Investigator

In 2010, I asked F. Lee Bailey to speak at the Maine Association of Criminal Defense Lawyer's CLE. I was President of the organization at that time, and Mr. Bailey, like many wise people, was making Maine his home then.

When he expressed a willingness to speak, I asked him to pick his topic. Would he want to talk about Patty Hearst, Sam Sheppard or the Boston Strangler? Maybe he would like to relive his brilliant Mark Furman cross-examination from the O.J. Simpson trial?

No, he wanted to talk about the importance of your investigator. In fact, he titled his talk, "If Your Investigator is Good Enough, Most Any Lawyer Will Do."

Mr. Bailey's point is well taken. While I don't know that a good investigator can replace a good lawyer, a good investigator certainly can be very helpful. A good investigator can make or break your case.

Investigators will go places you can't go, don't want to go to, and don't have time to go to. Good investigators know the law and tiptoe up to the line without crossing it. They know how to walk the tightrope to get your client results, which you can then steal credit for. I had one particular investigator, now retired, that I used for a long time. I can't tell you how often I got her out of legal trouble herself as she investigated my cases.

I often involve investigators at the first client meeting. It makes the client happy and saves me from repeating information. Virtually all clients like the idea of a team working for them. Get the investigator on your team at the start of the case.

§2:02   Interviewing Victims

I often call upon my investigators to approach alleged victims. In Maine, tampering with a victim is a felony. The investigator must know what tampering is and is not. I have had cases with cops threatening to arrest my investigator until we educate them on what we can and can't do. I have even had the DA tell the cops to stop bothering my investigator and chilling my right to investigate.

Good investigators walk the line, but never cross it. They can get fantastic results in the process. As the lawyer, you can't walk the line. It is your job to make sure your investigator does not cross the line, but gets your clients the results they desperately need. I have had countless cases dismissed because the investigator got us a piece of information the police hid or didn't explore. This distresses prosecutors and detectives.

Very often victims will dispute their own statements to the police, which they will claim were a result of police coercion or their anger. Here is a good example. I was recently employed to handle a rape by compulsion case. An 18 year old high school student, my client, had sex with a 16 year old student in his car. This was all perfectly legal, except that the 16 year old said he forced himself on her.

Our client told the story as consensual sex. So, I had my investigator get her statement. The alleged victim told the police that she told my client "no," but he kept on engaging in sexual activity and then intercourse. She said she tried to fight him off, but couldn't. She gave a recorded and written statement to the police.

To our investigator, the alleged victim admitted that said that she may not have been saying "No" out loud. This may have only been her internal monologue. When I heard that, I told our investigator to get an affidavit. She did. The affidavit was great.

You often can't trust these alleged victims, however. I told the prosecutor I had the affidavit and to outright dismiss the case. He re-interviewed the alleged victim. When confronted, she told the prosecutor that my investigator had compelled her to sign the affidavit. Fortunately, my investigators record all meetings with witnesses. The recording showed that the alleged victim was not at all compelled to submit the affidavit. Twice bitten now by this victim, the prosecutor dismissed the case in its entirety.

§2:03   Hiring the Right Investigator

Hiring the right investigator is not an exact science. I started by looking for referrals, and then began trying investigators out on smaller cases. Some lawyers like to use ex-cops. I don't use ex-cops as a rule—sometimes they are still just police in disguise. But if you have an ex-cop who was reasonable as cop, he may make a good investigator. As with many things, you have to experiment to find the right person.

[§§2:04-2:09 Reserved]

STRATEGIES FOR ALL CRIMINAL CASES

B.   To Poly or not to Poly, That is the Question

§2:10   Never Agree to a Police Poly

Deciding whether to have your client take a polygraph can be a crucial question in your case. They can either be very useful, or of no use at all, depending on the situation that presents itself. One thing I can say, however, without question, is that clients should not agree to take the police poly.

I see this mistake occur quite frequently. The police poly is free, so that's nice, I guess. The defense lawyer's rationale is that the police polygraph examiner is, after all, still a polygraph examiner. He or she must provide objective findings as a result, right? Not necessarily.

Polygraph examinations are an inaccurate science. Police polygraph examiners come from a worldview that is different than yours and your clients'. Don't let them determine what the squiggle marks on your client's print out means!

§2:11   A Private Poly Can Be Useful, Though Inadmissible

Another reason not to allow the police poly is because you can't bury the results. If your client fails the police poly or it's inconclusive, it will say something to the detective and the prosecutor, even if the result is inadmissible in court. With a private poly, if I get a bad result, no one knows about it but me, the client, and the poly examiner. This is a clear advantage over police polygraphs.

Polygraphs are inadmissible in most places because the results are unreliable. *See Devries v. St. Paul Fire and Marine Ins. Co.*, 716 F.2d 939, 945 (1st Cir. 1983) (stating polygraph testing is of dubious scientific value and is irrelevant in federal courts); *United States v. Lea*, 249 F.3d 632, 640 (7th Cir. 2001) (stating results are inadmissible because the potential rate of error make it unreliable); *People v. Hinton*, 126 P.3d 981, 1020 (Cal. 2006) (rational to exclude polygraph results because the court has interest in barring unreliable evidence); *Capano v. State*, 781 A.2d 556,592 (Del. 2001) (polygraph results inadmissible because reliability not established). An exception to the general rule is found in New Mexico, where polygraphs are admissible if they meet certain standards for trustworthiness codified in New Mexico Rules of Evidence 11-707.

Just because they are inadmissible doesn't make them not useful, however. Polys can be exceedingly useful, especially in a case where a charging decision is in doubt. If the prosecutor or cop at all seems hesitant about the case, and your client maintains his or her actual innocence, see if a poly would be helpful to their decision making. Set up the poly privately and don't tell the prosecutor or cop it is being taken. If your client passes, share the results. If your client doesn't, bury the results. If law enforcement asks about it later, make something up (that doesn't violate your ethics rules).

Even when the prosecutor refuses to accept a good poly result, the poly can be a useful tool. This was well exemplified by my representation of a client named Jason.

Jason was referred to me after he lost a gross sexual assault trial where he was convicted of repeated sexual assault of his pre-teen daughter. His conviction was overturned on appeal, and I was hired for the retrial. From the outset, Jason was adamant with me that he was innocent, so I asked Jason if he wanted to take a poly. He had never been offered a poly before and he readily agreed.

Now, I had no idea if Jason would pass or fail. In fact, most of my clients fail or are inconclusive when they take a poly. In either situation, you learn something from the poly. A failed poly can be helpful with client control. A passed poly presents all sorts of possibilities.

Jason passed his poly. Then, he passed a police poly done with my polygraph examiner and myself present. I used that poly to get him out on bail. While the poly itself was inadmissible, the Bail Judge referenced Jason's willingness to take two polygraph exams as a factor in his release decision. Jason was bailed after nearly 4 years in prison. I am happy to report that he never went back. For more on Jason's case, see Ch. 12.

[§§2:12-2:19 Reserved]

C. Preserving Evidence from Destruction by Law Enforcement

§2:20 Combating Law Enforcement's Failure to Preserve Evidence

My clients and I have been burned by law enforcement's failure to preserve evidence far too often. Missing cruiser cams, rough notes of interviews and other relevant evidence go missing more often than we would like. Sometimes it is based on incompetence or sloppy work. Sometimes it is something more.

One of the ways I try to combat this issue is by providing written notice that we want law enforcement to preserve the evidence at the outset of the case. This is most useful in cases where charges have not yet been filed. Our Notice goes out on every case to the evidence officer for whatever law enforcement agency is involved as soon as we are hired. With this Notice sent in a timely fashion, it will be difficult for law enforcement to claim that they weren't aware the evidence was material or needed to be preserved.

Here is the Notice.

§2:21 FORM 2-10 Notice to Preserve Evidence

Date

Attn: Court Officer
Portland Police Department
Portland, ME 04112

RE: State v. Joe Defendant
Docket No. CR-12-2045

Dear Court Officer,

I represent Joe Defendant regarding a drug trafficking arrest by your department on or about [Date]. I am aware that certain items of evidence may be routinely disposed of prior to arraignment. To avoid any prejudice to my client and the potential inadvertent destruction of potentially exculpatory evidence, I ask that you take reasonable steps to preserve any audiotapes, videotapes, call logs, officers' notes or other notes or other items of evidence in the possession of your department. With regard to radio and telephone call tapes and logs, I ask you to preserve them from the time of the first call relating to my client to the time of his release from custody. For general surveillance tapes such as those of booking areas and interview rooms, etc., I ask that you preserve those that were taken while my client was present at the station.

Please note that this includes a request that you preserve all officer and law enforcement agent's rough notes or writing concerning our client, any co-defendants, or co-conspirators. Said rough notes and writings are discoverable by Defendant and subject to disclosure pursuant to Federal and State of Maine Rules of Criminal Procedure, and the principals announced in *Brady v. Maryland*, 373 U.S. 83, 87 S.Ct. 1194, 10 L.Ed. 215 (1963) and its progeny. The rough notes Defendant seeks to be retained may include impeachment information, exculpatory information, or information that may serve to mitigate punishment, notwithstanding that the notes may have been incorporated into official records.

Kindly pay particular attention to the cruiser cam and interview room video depicting the Defendant and all witnesses.

This is not a request that you provide me with these materials; I understand that I must go through the discovery process to obtain information. My goal is to preserve the items in the event they are needed in the defense of my client. By copy of this letter I am requesting that the District Attorney provide copies of all of the referenced materials to me as soon as possible. By copy of this letter to the arresting officer or detective assigned to this case, I am putting those individuals on notice of a duty to preserve the evidence described above.

Thank you for your anticipated cooperation.

Respectfully submitted,

_____

Timothy E. Zerillo
Attorney for Defendant
ZERILLO LAW FIRM, LLC

TEZ/ara
cc: Joe Defendant
Sgt. I. Gotcha
District Attorney I. Lockup

NOTICE

The preservation of potentially exculpatory information or information that is helpful to the defense is essential to the proper administration of justice. Please note that under *Arizona v. Youngblood*, 488 U.S. 51 (1988) bad faith on the part of law enforcement in the destruction of evidence exists when the police intentionally destroy evidence they know may be potentially useful to the defense. 488 US 51, at 58. By this letter, the Defendant here informs you that the above-requested information is potentially useful to the defense. Additionally, exculpatory evidence requires no bad faith for a violation by law enforcement to occur. The United States Supreme Court states: "We have held that when the State suppresses or fails to disclose material exculpatory evidence, the good faith or bad faith of the prosecution is irrelevant: a due process violation occurs whenever such evidence is withheld." *Illinois v. Fisher*, 540 U.S. 544, 547 (2004).

§2:22   Sanctions for Failure to Preserve Evidence

Back in the good old days, the good faith or bad faith of the police was irrelevant to the issue of whether the case should be dismissed for missing evidence. See *California v. Trombetta*, 467 U.S. 479 (1984). Then came *Arizona v. Youngblood*, 488 U.S. 51 (1988), which abrogated the *Trombetta* holding and required a showing of bad faith to get sanctions.

Youngblood, however, also allows you to skip over a showing of bad faith (which is a very difficult standard to meet), if the missing evidence is material. There have been some great cases on materiality in recent years. Below is a Motion to Dismiss for Failure to Preserve Evidence, a Post-Hearing Memorandum on the Motion to Dismiss and a Motion for Sanctions arguing these points.

§2:23   FORM 2-20 Motion to Dismiss for Failure to Preserve Evidence

STATE OF MAINE   UNIFIED CRIMINAL DOCKET
CUMBERLAND, ss   DOCKET NO. PORSC-CR-08-2614

STATE OF MAINE,   )
)
v.   )   DEFENDANT'S MOTION
)   TO DISMISS FOR FAILURE
JOE DEFENDANT,   )   TO PRESERVE EVIDENCE
)
Defendant   )

Now comes Joe Defendant, by and through Undersigned Counsel, and requests that this Honorable Court dismiss the above-referenced matter and submits the following memorandum in support of his motion to dismiss:

FACTUAL SUMMARY

On November 5, 2008, Joe Defendant was indicted on one count of Class B, Gross Sexual Assault. The Indictment stems from the allegation that on August 24, 2008, he engaged in a sexual act with Melody Victim, and that, at the time of the sexual act, Ms. Victim was unconscious or otherwise physically incapable of resisting and had not consented to the act.

On August 28, 2008, four days after the alleged assault, Ms. Victim reported the incident to Portland Police Department. She and her then boyfriend, Shawn Boyfriend, were interviewed by Officer Jay Incompetent of the Portland Police Department. The interview took place in the first floor interview room, number one, at the Portland Police Station. Only Officer Incompetent, Ms. Victim and Mr. Boyfriend were present during the interview. At some point during the interview, Officer Incompetent drafted witness statements for both Ms. Victim and Mr. Boyfriend, which the witnesses then signed before they left. These statements are almost identical to the official report Officer Incompetent drafted. In that report, Officer Incompetent states that "the entire conversation with Victim and Boyfriend was captured on the audio/video system in interview room #1."

When Mr. Defendant realized the investigation was occurring, he contacted Counsel's office. On September 15, 2008, Attorney Timothy E. Zerillo contacted Detective I. M. Unsympathetic of the Portland Police Department to make her aware Mr. Defendant was represented by Counsel. Attorney Zerillo spoke to Detective Unsympathetic on September 16, 2008 as well.

Mr. Defendant made a timely Motion for Discovery, on March 31, 2009 to the District Attorney, and filed that Motion for Discovery with the Court on September 10, 2009. At the Dispositional Conference on September 9, 2009, ADA Prosecutor mentioned to Counsel that the audio/video had not been preserved. She stated she had received an email from Detective Unsympathetic, dated September 3, 2009, stating the same. Counsel requested a copy of that email, but had not received it at the time of the hearing on Mr. Defendant' discovery motion, on September 22, 2009.

At the discovery hearing Undersigned Counsel again requested a copy of the email, and received it on September 23, 2009. *See* attached <u>Exhibit 1</u>. At the September 22nd hearing, ADA Prosecutor informed Undersigned Counsel that additional discovery was available and could be picked at her office. This additional discovery is evidence of Mr. Defendant meeting with Detective Unsympathetic to have a blood sample drawn. Like Officer Incompetent's conversation with Ms. Victim and Mr. Boyfriend, the meeting between Mr. Defendant and Detective Unsympathetic also took place in an interview room at the Portland Police Department. This interview was also captured on the interview room's surveillance system. Detective Unsympathetic properly provided a copy of this audio/video recording to the District Attorney's office, and it is available for review or copying by Mr. Defendant. *See* attached <u>Exhibit 2</u>.

Regardless of the timely discovery request, evidence of this nature is of the type that must be automatically provided by the State to the Defendant under Unified Criminal Docket Rules of Procedure, Rule 16(a). Therefore, the State was responsible for taking steps to preserve it.

ARGUMENT

A. The State's Failure to Preserve Known Exculpatory Evidence Was in Violation of Mr. Defendant' Fourteenth Amendment Due Process Rights.

The State's failure to preserve this properly requested audio/video that contained exculpatory evidence was is in violation of the Maine and United States Constitutions, pursuant to the Due Process Clause and the right to a fair trial. The Government is mandated to preserve and produce properly requested evidence that is exculpatory. The United States Supreme Court has held that "[t]he Due Process Clause of the Fourteenth Amendment, as interpreted in [*Brady v. Maryland* 373 U.S. 83 (1963)], makes the good or bad faith of the State irrelevant when the State fails to disclose to the defendant material exculpatory evidence." *Arizona v. Youngblood*, 488 U.S. 51, 57 (1988) (negligent failure of police to properly preserve evidence of assailant in a sexual assault case); see also *California v. Trombetta*, 467 U.S. 479 (1984). Under *Brady*, "the suppression by the prosecution of evidence favorable to an accused upon request violates due process where the evidence is material either to guilt or to punishment, irrespective of the good faith or bad faith of the prosecution." *Brady*, 373 U.S. at 87, 83 S.Ct. 1194. The duty to disclose applies even if the accused has made no request. *See United States v. Bagley*, 473 U.S. 667, 682, 105 S.Ct. 3375, 87 L.Ed.2d 481 (1985). The *Brady* rule also encompasses evidence "known only to police investigators and not to the prosecutor. *Kyles v. Whitley*, 514 U.S. 419, 438, 115 S.Ct. 1555, 131, L.Ed.2d, 490(1995).

A "true *Brady* violation" has three components: "[t]he evidence at issue must be favorable to the accused, either because it is exculpatory, or because it is impeaching; that evidence must have been suppressed by the State, either willfully or inadvertently; and prejudice must have ensued." *Strickler v. Greene*, 527 U.S. 263, 281-82 (1999).

In this case, the Defendant had properly requested the preservation of the audio/video. It is unknown whether the audio/video contains exculpatory evidence, but it is highly likely that it is impeaching for any of the three people present at the interview. The video has been inadvertently suppressed due to neglect on the part of the Portland Police Department. Thus, the State, through the Police Department, was at minimum negligent with regard to the duty it owes defendants according to *Brady*, and prejudice has ensued because of this negligence.

B. The State's Failure to Preserve Exculpatory Evidence Was in Violation of Unified Criminal Docket Rules of Procedure, Rule 16.

Alternatively, the State is required to preserve and produce evidence, "which [is] material to the preparation of the defense." UCD.R.Crim.P. 16(a)(1)(E). The audio/video at issue is vital to Mr. Defendant' defense. It is the only record of the interview of the complaining witness that was not created by Officer Incompetent. The video was timely and properly requested. The State is subject to sanctions for failure to obtain and preserve such evidence.

UCD.R.Crim.P. 16(d). Sanctions for failure to preserve evidence may result in the dismissal of the criminal action with prejudice or any other sanction deemed appropriate by this Court. *Id.*

Mr. Defendant avers that this case should be dismissed as the video evidence was properly requested and the State negligently failed to preserve the evidence.

C.　Conclusion

Based on the foregoing reasons, the Defendant requests that this Honorable Court dismiss this matter with prejudice.

Dated this ___ Day of _____, 20__ in Portland, Maine.

Respectfully submitted,

_____

Timothy E. Zerillo
Attorney for Defendant
ZERILLO LAW FIRM, LLC

§2:24　　FORM 2-30 Post-Hearing Memorandum on Motion to Dismiss for Failure to Preserve Evidence

STATE OF MAINE , SS	UNIFIED CRIMINAL DOCKET LOCATION: DOCKET NO. PORSC-CR-08-2614

STATE OF MAINE,	)	
	)	
	)	
	)	DEFENDANT'S POST-HEARING
v.	)	MEMORANDUM ON DEFENDANT'S
	)	MOTION TO DISMISS
JOE DEFENDANT,	)	
	)	
Defendant	)	

NOW COMES the Defendant, by and through Undersigned Counsel, and submits the following Memorandum on Defendant's Motion to Dismiss.

MEMORANDUM OF LAW PROCEDURAL HISTORY

Defendant, Joe Defendant, is charged with a single count of Gross Sexual Assault. Counsel requested discovery after being retained by Defendant. A portion of the discovery requested was the audio/video recordings of the interviews taken of the victim and another fact witness at the Portland Police Department. When Counsel learned these videos had been destroyed, he moved to dismiss this matter. A hearing was held on the same on November 24, 2009.

FACTS FROM THE HEARING

Two individuals testified at the November 24th hearing, Officer Jay Incompetent and Detective I. M. Unsympathetic. Officer Jay Incompetent testified that the interviews began on August 28, 2009 at 1946 hours (7:46 PM) and ended at 2200 hours (10 PM). The interviews were with Melody Victim, the alleged victim, and Shawn Boyfriend, a fact witness. Officer Incompetent hand-wrote the witnesses statements, which the witnesses signed. The entire interview, which was in excess of two hours, was recorded. The statements were 5 pages long in total.

Officer Incompetent gave his report to Detective Unsympathetic. Detective Unsympathetic received the report on August 29, 2008 and read it. Officer Incompetent's report clearly states that the interview was recorded. Officer

Incompetent thought that it was the Detective's duty to preserve the evidence. The Detective thought it was Officer Incompetent's duty. Neither preserved the evidence and it was destroyed.[1]

Officer Incompetent testified that he thought there was a standard of practice in the Portland Police Department that a detective secure the recording. Detective Unsympathetic said she was not aware of a Portland Police Department policy regarding the same. Both agreed that the audio/video of the interviews was useful evidence.

Officer Incompetent acknowledged that there were items not contained in his report or the statements that were discussed in the interview. He claims this was "small talk." Given that this interview was in excess of two hours, it is hard to believe that the Defendant is not deprived of impeachment information upon destruction of the video.

Additionally, it is clear that there are differences from Officer Incompetent's report and the statements. For example, the report states that the alleged victim had a few more drinks at Brian Boru's before going to the Defendant's house that night. Ms. Victim's statement is missing that information. Officer Incompetent's report states that Ms. Victim thought the pressure on her right groin was Bob Boyfriend, but her statement does not say that.

It is hard to imagine that the audio/video would not have contained dozens more of these inconsistencies. Obviously, Officer Incompetent got the extra information contained in his report, but not in Ms. Victim's statement, from the interviews. That can only lead us to one conclusion: the written statements are incomplete, and destruction of the audio/video evidence deprives Joe Defendant of Due Process of law.

ARGUMENT

Counsel noted in his oral argument that there are two standards at play here. The first standard is the standard of a *Brady* violation, which exists regardless of bad faith. The second standard is that of a *Trombetta/Youngblood* violation, for which bad faith is required. The clear differences between the two were described in the 2004 United States Supreme Court case of *Illinois v Fisher*, which held:

> We have held that when the State suppresses or fails to disclose material exculpatory evidence, the good faith or bad faith of the prosecution is irrelevant: a due process violation occurs whenever such evidence is withheld.

Illinois v. Fisher, 540 U.S. 544, 547 (2004).

The Supreme Court went on to describe the *Youngblood* analysis as a failure to disclose potentially useful information, which only violates due process if there is a showing of bad faith by the police. *Id*. at 547-548.

I.   THE *BRADY* VIOLATION MANDATES DISMISSAL

Brady v. Maryland, 373 U.S. 83 (1963) established that certain information must be disclosed by the prosecution regardless of a request by the defendant. That certain information that must be disclosed is material exculpatory evidence. *Illinois v. Fisher*, 540 U.S. 544, 547 (2004). In this case, the withholding or destruction of the videotapes is both material and exculpatory.

The United States Supreme Court has held that the prosecution has a due process obligation under the Federal Constitution to disclose material evidence favorable to a criminal defendant. *Brady v. Maryland*, 373 U.S. 83 (1963). Favorable evidence is quite broad. Arguably, favorable evidence can include anything reasonably positive to the defense. In *United States v. Bagley*, 473 U.S. 667 (1985), the Court held that regardless of the request, general or specific, favorable evidence is material, and constitutional error results from its suppression by the government, "if there is a reasonable probability that, had the evidence been disclosed to the defense, the result of the proceeding would have been different." *Id*. at 682.

A showing of materiality under *Bagley* does not require proof by the defendant that disclosure of the evidence would result in the defendant's acquittal. *Kyles v. Whitley*, 514 U.S. 419 (1995) (attached). All that is required is a "reasonable probability" that the information is necessary in order for the defendant to receive a fair trial, meaning a trial that results in a verdict worthy of confidence. *Id*. at 434.

In *Kyles*, the Defendant was accused of robbing and murdering a woman at gunpoint in the parking lot of a Schwegmann's Store in New Orleans, Louisiana. Id. at 423. There were six eyewitnesses, two with very different descriptions of the shooter. Id. at 423-428. Kyle's build, height and weight were contradicted, as was his hair style.

---

[1] Both officers testified that the audio/video is destroyed within 30 days if an order to preserve is not made.

Id. One witness, Beanie, tried very hard to implicate Kyles. *Id.* at 425. He gave four statements to the police, which were exceedingly inconsistent. *Id.* at 427.

Kyles was indicted for murder, and his counsel made a motion for exculpatory information. The State's response was there was "no exculpatory evidence of any nature." *Id.* at 428.

In the first trial, neither side called Beanie. *Id.* at 429. The jury hung. *Id.* After trial, the prosecutor re-interviewed Beanie. *Id.* In this fifth statement, Beanie was again significantly inconsistent in his version of events and implication of Kyles. *Id.* at 430. Beanie's statements were not disclosed to the defense. *Id.*

At the second trial, the defense blamed Beanie for the shooting, although they were still without Beanie's statements and other exculpatory items. Id. at 430. The State called Beanie as a rebuttal witness and Kyles was convicted. *Id.* at 430. He was later sentenced to death and Beanie was given $1,600 in reward money. *Id.* Kyles sought habeas corpus relief. The Fifth Circuit affirmed and the Supreme Judicial Court granted cert. *Id.* at 431-432. The Supreme Court held that the prosecutor's failure to disclose the above information resulted in a reasonable probability that there would have been a different result at trial, and reversed as a result. *Id.* at 419.

Ultimately, the decision in *Kyles* represents a major expansion of *Brady* and *Bagley*. Like the Court in *Bagley*, the Court in *Kyles* reaffirmed that impeachment evidence is exculpatory evidence. *Id.* at 433. Under *Kyles*, there is no difference "between exculpatory and impeachment information for *Brady* purposes...." *Id.* at 433.

This is crucial to the Court's decision here. ADA Deborah Chmielewski conceded that the destruction of the audio/video of the Victim and Boyfriend interviews deprived Defendant and Counsel of impeachment evidence. Under *Kyles* and *Bagely*, this impeachment evidence is exculpatory evidence. As a result, the State concedes that the Defendant is being deprived of exculpatory information due to the destruction of the videotape.

Since the destroyed audio/video is clearly and admittedly exculpatory, the only issue is whether it is material. Materiality is a low hurdle, however. If favorable evidence is not disclosed, the Defendant does not need to show that disclosure of the evidence would have resulted in an acquittal. Under *Kyles*, the issue is only whether there was a "verdict worthy of confidence." *Id.* at 434-435. This confidence is not necessarily related to the ultimate outcome, although it can be. *Id.* Materiality of the evidence is primarily related to the process and underlying fairness of the trial. *Id.*

The State has tried to argue that they have a strong enough case to proceed to trial. That is, of course, not the standard. The standard relates to the process and the fairness to the Defendant. It doesn't matter how strong the case is against the Defendant.[2] A verdict worthy of confidence is the appropriate standard, not sufficiency of the evidence. *Id.* at 434. Additionally, if a constitutional error under *Bagley* has occurred, there no harmless error review. Errors under *Bagely* are never harmless. *Id.* at 435.

II.   THE *TROMBETTA/YOUNGBLOOD* VIOLATIONS MERIT DISMISSAL

In *California v. Trombetta*, 467 U.S. 479 (1984), the Supreme Court devised a two part test for whether a good faith failure to preserve evidence violated due process:

1. The evidence "possesses an exculpatory value that was apparent before the evidence was destroyed..." at 489.
2. Evidence cannot "be of such a nature that the defendant would be unable to obtain comparable evidence by reasonably available means." at 489.

Regarding the first *Trombetta* standard, it is clear that the evidence possesses exculpatory value that was apparent. Officer Incompetent knew the evidence was needed as did Detective Unsympathetic. Regarding the second element, comparable evidence to the recordings is not available. These interviews were in excess of two hours long. Distilling those interviews down to 5 sheets of paper, written by a police officer, is not comparable to the tapes of the interview.

Arizona v. Youngblood, 488 U.S. 51 (1988) was decided after *Trombetta*, and added another element to the analysis. In *Youngblood* the failure of the State to preserve potentially useful evidence must be coupled with bad faith on the part of the police. Under *Youngblood*, bad faith exists when the police intentionally destroy evidence they know may be potentially useful to the defense. 488 U.S. 51, at 58.

Here, the police knew the audio/video was potentially useful. They both agreed with the same in testimony and it is apparent. As a result, law enforcement destroyed useful evidence, and violated *Youngblood*, in the process. This intentional destruction constitutes bad faith.

---

[2] While it doesn't matter how strong the case is against a defendant, the case against the Defendant here is very weak. Defendant is indicted for having intercourse with the alleged victim when she was incapable of resisting. The fact that the alleged victim had consensual intercourse with another individual 7 to 10 minutes before the alleged intercourse with the Defendant raises severe doubts as to the efficacy of this prosecution.

The State tries to walk a fine line by saying that the police did not destroy evidence, but merely failed to preserve it. Both officers were aware that failing to order the audio/video would cause its destruction. Both were aware that the tape recording existed, Detective Unsympathetic being aware within one day of the interview. Failing to order preservation is the same as destruction, even if it was a sin of omission rather than commission.

CONCLUSION

There is no remedy to satisfy these violations other than dismissal. The Court could certainly Order that Ms. Victim and Mr. Boyfriend not be permitted to testify at trial as a sanction, but that would be tantamount to dismissal, regardless. Counsel requests this Court Order that the violations admitted by the State would amount to a violation of Due Process if the case against Joe Defendant goes forward, and dismiss the matter with prejudice.

Dated this _____ day of _____, 20__, at Portland, Maine.

Respectfully submitted,

_____
Timothy E. Zerillo
Attorney for Defendant
ZERILLO LAW FIRM, LLC

§2:25   FORM 2-40 Motion for Sanctions for Failure to Preserve Evidence

STATE OF MAINE
, SS

UNIFIED CRIMINAL DOCKET
LOCATION:
DOCKET NO. PORSC-CR-08-2614

_____)
)
STATE OF MAINE)
)
v.)
)
JOE DEFENDANT)
Defendant)
_____)

DEFENDANT'S MOTION FOR
SANCTIONS PURSUANT TO
M.R.Crim.P. 16 WITH
MEMORANDUM OF LAW

NOW COMES the Defendant, Joe Defendant, by and through Undersigned Counsel, and hereby moves for Sanctions pursuant to M.R.Crim.P. 16 for the following reasons:

1. Counsel received discovery in this matter, which included police reports. Those police reports indicated that audio and video of nearly 2 hours of interviews at the Portland Police Department were taken of the alleged victim and an essential witness. This audio and video was not preserved and was destroyed.
2. Counsel brought a Motion to Dismiss (which was treated as a Motion to Suppress). An Order by Justice Yo Honor denying the Motion was entered on December 16, 2009. The denial was based on lack of bad faith by the police in the destruction of the video. In its Order, however, Justice Honor notes that the destruction of the audio/video has deprived Mr. Defendant of his full right of cross-examination, and, therefore, a fair trial.
3. The failure of the State to preserve and disclose the audio and video of the interviews requires an Order of Sanctions that Melody Victim and Shawn Boyfriend be restricted from testifying at trial, as supported by the attached and incorporated Memorandum of Law.

MEMORANDUM OF LAW

On August 24, 2008, there was a report of an alleged Gross Sexual Assault to the Portland Police Department. Officer Incompetent took the report on August 28, 2008. Officer Incompetent testified that the interviews began at 1946 hours (7:46 PM) and ended at 2200 hours (10 PM). The interviews were with Melody Victim, the alleged victim, and Shawn Boyfriend, an essential fact witness. Officer Incompetent hand-wrote the witnesses statements, which the witnesses signed. The entire interview, which was in excess of two hours, was recorded. The statements were 5 pages long in total.

Officer Incompetent gave his report to Detective Unsympathetic. Detective Unsympathetic received the report on August 29, 2008 and read it. Officer Incompetent's report clearly states that the interview was recorded. Officer Incompetent thought that it was the Detective's duty to preserve the evidence. The Detective thought it was Officer Incompetent's duty. Neither preserved the evidence and it was destroyed.[3]

Rule 16 of the Maine Rules of Criminal Procedure allows for the imposition of sanctions, including dismissal, for violations of the discovery rules. This requires that the State produce evidence, "material to the preparation of the defense." M.R.Crim.P. 16(b)(2)(A). This Court may sanction the state for its failure to obtain and preserve evidence. M.R.Crim.P. 16(d).

In addition to the protections imposed by the Rules of Criminal Procedure, the production and preservation of certain evidence is mandated by the Maine and United States Constitution as a matter of due process and the right to a fair trial. The United States Supreme Court has held that "[t]he Due Process Clause of the Fourteenth Amendment, as interpreted in *Brady,* makes the good or bad faith of the State irrelevant when the State fails to disclose to the defendant material exculpatory evidence." *Arizona v. Youngblood*, 488 U.S. 51, 57 (1988); see also *Brady v. Maryland* 373 U.S. 83 (1963); *California v. Trombetta*, 467 U.S. 479 (1984). The Law Court has found that a failure to disclose exculpatory evidence may result in a new trial. S*tate of Maine v. Rankin*, 666 A.2d 123 (Me. 1995). The United States Supreme Court case of *Illinois v Fisher* further explained:

> We have held that when the State suppresses or fails to disclose material exculpatory evidence, the good faith or bad faith of the prosecution is irrelevant: a due process violation occurs whenever such evidence is withheld.

Illinois v. Fisher, 540 U.S. 544, 547 (2004).

Here, Justice Honor's December 16, 2009 Order makes factual and legal findings that should have resulted in a dismissal under the law. Those findings are relevant to this Motion for Sanctions, regardless. Justice Honor found:

> Applying the first step, the State concedes that the destruction of the interviews deprived the defendant of **impeachment evidence**, and agrees that **impeachment evidence is exculpatory evidence**. See *Kyles v. Whitely*, 514 U.S. 419, 434 (1995). Applying the second step, there is no other way for the defendant to obtain comparable evidence; there is simply **no other comparable evidence** once the interviews were lost. Defendant **needs the interviews** to impeach the testimony of the State's key witnesses. (Emphasis added)

Justice Honor then went on to deny the Defendant's Motion because there was no bad faith regarding the destruction of the tape. Counsel argues that was an incorrect application of the law as it relates to admittedly exculpatory evidence. That said, Justice Honor's finding that the lost videotape is exculpatory and cannot be replaced is correct.

Going forward with trial without serious sanctions against the State, pursuant to Justice Honor's Order, is unfair. Doing so burdens Defendant with a Due Process violation while he is on trial. An Order of Sanctions excluding the trial testimony of Melody Victim and Shawn Boyfriend is the only appropriate remedy.

WHEREFORE, Undersigned Counsel respectfully requests that the Court order Sanctions against the State including exclusion of the testimony of Melody Victim and Shawn Boyfriend or any other Sanction the Court deems just.

Dated this ___ day of December, 20__ in Portland, Maine.

Respectfully submitted,

_____
Timothy E. Zerillo
Attorney for Defendant
ZERILLO LAW FIRM, LLC

---

[3] Both officers testified that the audio/video is destroyed within 30 days if an order to preserve is not made by the responsible officer.

§2:26 Preserving Grand Jury Testimony

I would like to see the current grand jury system abolished where I practice, and I am not the only one. We all know the prosecutor can indict a ham sandwich, but that is not the only problem with the Grand Jury process. At least in Maine, they don't routinely preserve and transcribe Grand Jury testimony. This means that the defense has no access to prior witness testimony that may be crucially important to the defense. It also means the prosecution has heard testimony that you have not. This gives the government a real edge in evaluating witnesses.

Hopefully, you practice in a state with more evolved rules of criminal procedure related to Grand Jury testimony. Those of you who don't, can sympathize with me, I'm sure.

Failing to record, preserve and transcribe Grand Jury testimony is tantamount to spoliation in my view. Laws concerning Grand Jury secrecy are often used to trump the rights of the accused. This is draconian.

That said, as painful as it is to continually lose the argument, keep making it. Ask at the outset simply to record and preserve the testimony. I do this by filing a motion to at least record and preserve the testimony. That way, at least it isn't lost forever, and you can argue that it should be disclosed later.

In Maine, to actually get the Grand Jury transcript, I need to meet the "particularized need" standard. This requires that I explain why I need the transcript without knowing what is in the transcript.

I first file the motion to record and preserve the grand jury testimony. In it, I argue that we have discovered inconsistencies in our investigation that necessitate at least recording and preserving the testimony now. I explain that I don't need to meet the particularized need standard because I am not asking for the transcripts to be released at that time. Later, at trial or once I can justify why the transcripts should be turned over, I file the particularized need motion.

[§§2:27-2:39 Reserved]

II. INITIAL CONTACT WITH PROSECUTOR

§2:40 The Two Points You Want to Make

There are two points to make in your initial contact with the prosecutor:
- First, you want to make sure that the prosecutor is aware that you are willing to work with him or her on charging decisions and other matters, such as your client surrendering without an arrest warrant being issued.
- Second, you want to leave a trail in writing showing you are the client's lawyer and directing the prosecutor to make sure his or her agents, meaning law enforcement, do not contact your client to get statements from him or her.

To that end, we have a form letter that may be modified, but is generally sent out as soon as we are retained. Obviously, you want to follow this letter with a phone call. It's good to start planting the seeds related to the disposition you want for your client early. Of course, if a charging decision has not yet been made it is even more important to get to the prosecutor fast.

Here is the letter.

§2:41 FORM 2-50 Initial Letter to Prosecutor

Date

District Attorney I.L. Lockuup
100 Federal Way
Legaltown, ME 04000

Re: Case
Docket No.

Dear DA Lockuup,

I write to inform you that I represent Joe Defendant with respect to this investigation. I ask that you direct all communications regarding this matter to me.

I hope to talk to you more about the investigation in the future. Of course, I trust that you will instruct your agents that they should have no direct communications with Joe Defendant. In the event that you have decided to charge Joe, please note that no warrants are necessary to secure his appearance. He will turn himself in if you deem it necessary.

Respectfully submitted,

_____

Timothy E. Zerillo
Attorney for Defendant
ZERILLO LAW FIRM, LLC

TEZ/ara
cc: Joe Defendant

[§§2:42-2:49 Reserved]

III.   BAIL ISSUES

§2:50   Bail Is Crucial in Most Cases

It is important to get your client out of jail in most situations if at all possible. On occasion, sitting in custody might be advantageous, so pressing for bail is not warranted. Those are the cases where your client is dead bang guilty and wants to accumulate time served, or cases in which bail is going to be so difficult, like a murder case, that you want your client to sit while you get your investigation started prior to making your bail argument.

In the vast majority of cases, however, getting your client out is crucial. Your client will feel better about you and his or her case if the client is released. The client will likewise be better able to assist in his or her own defense if out on bail.

§2:51   Your Bail Argument

A strong bail presentation is also a good way to showcase your legal skills and compassion to the client. Know the names of your client's mother, father, spouse and children. Be passionate about their case and their release. If you were stuck in jail, you would want a passionate argument from your lawyer.

Understanding your client, means talking to your client, as well as talking to your client's friends and family. These discussions are important, and they need to be thorough.

Below is a copy of my Bail Questionnaire. I take this form with me to the jail during my client interview. I use this form to point me to various issues I may want to raise in oral argument. Change it to suit your needs and the jurisdictional rules where you practice.

§2:52 FORM 2-60 Bail Questionnaire

BAIL QUESTIONNAIRE

Residential Information
- Where do you live?
- How long have you lived there?
- Do you rent or own?
- If you own your home, in whose name[s] is the deed?
- How much equity does the house have: when was it purchased, for how much down, and what is the balance on the mortgage?
- Who else lives there, and what is their relationship to you?
- If you cannot return to your home, where can you live? With whom? What is their relationship to you and their contact information?

Employment Information
- Where do you work, and for how long have you worked there?
- What are the hours?
- What is your job title?
- Who is your immediate supervisor, and how can he be contacted to confirm employment?
- If the job is recent, where did you work before?
- If bailed, will you be able to return to the job?

Who Does the Client Support?
- Remember to ask about not only spouse and children, but extended family—grandparents and grandchildren, aunts, uncles, nieces and nephews.
- If married, for how long?
- If divorced or separated or if your client has children from other relationships, does he pay child support; how frequently and how much?

Criminal Record
- All prior arrests, convictions and sentences.
- Bail status on the prior cases, and how many court appearances you made.
- If sentenced to probation or parole, how well did you comply with the conditions?
- History of FTA

Other
- Military service: branch, rank, where stationed and type of discharge.
- Immigration status.
- Is anyone willing to come to jail and post cash?

§2:53   Assignment of Cash Bail

Once you do a brilliant job at the bail hearing and get your client out of custody, remember the additional advantage of cash bail being set if you have a privately retained client. The cash bail component can likely be assigned to you to go toward your Counsel fees.

§2:54   FORM 2-70 Assignment of Cash Bail

STATE OF MAINE   SUPERIOR COURT
CUMBERLAND, ss.   DOCKET NO. CR-_____

STATE OF MAINE,   )
)
Plaintiff   )
)
v.   )
)
_____,   )
)
Defendant   )

ASSIGNMENT OF CASH BAIL

I, _____ , agree that the money on deposit with the Clerk of this Court, in the sum of $_____ , as bail for appearance of _____ before this Court, is hereby assigned to Timothy E. Zerillo, and I specifically authorize and direct the Clerk of this Court to pay said Timothy E. Zerillo the sum of $_____ .
     Dated at Portland, this _____ day of _____, 20____ .

_____

_____

Signed and acknowledged this _____ day of _____, 20____.

_____
Attorney at Law

ORDER OF ASSIGNMENT OF CASH BAIL

Cash bail in the amount of $_____ is hereby Ordered assigned to Timothy E. Zerillo for reimbursement of counsel fees.

Dated: _____

_____
Justice, Superior Court

§2:55   Bail Conditions

I really hate it when clients violate bail conditions. The prosecutor can really mess with them then. They can try to revoke bail, impose unreasonable bail, etc…To that end I try to warn people, both verbally and in writing, what their bail obligations are. I have a template bail conditions letter I use for this purpose.

§2:56   FORM 2-80 Bail Conditions Letter

Date

Client Name
Address
Address

Re: <u>State of Maine v. Client Name</u>

Dear Client Name:

I am honored and pleased that you have chosen me to assist you in defense of the above-captioned criminal matter. The purpose of this letter is to ensure you understand your bail conditions. As you know you were released on bail (under the condition that you promise to appear / in the amount of _____ to secure your appearance) at all future Court dates. You are also bound by the following conditions, which you agreed to, and which if violated could result in your being arrested and charged with an additional crime.

Please note that this letter is merely informative. If there is any conflict between this letter and your bail conditions, the bail conditions control. Please make sure you review your bail conditions and are familiar with them

<u>Appearance at Court</u>

You must appear for your initial appearance at _____ on _____.
OR IF MISDEMEANOR: I have entered my appearance and your not guilty plea, so we do not have to appear at your initial appearance on _____.

<u>No New Criminal Conduct</u>

You must not commit any new criminal conduct or violate any pending protection from abuse orders.

<u>Informing Court of Change in Contact Information</u>

You must immediately advise the Court of any change in your address or telephone number.

Waiver of Extradition

You have waived extradition to the State of Maine for prosecution of the charge(s) above.

No Use of Alcohol or Drugs

You are prohibited from using alcoholic beverages or illegal drugs.

No Possession of Alcohol or Drugs

You are prohibited from possessing alcoholic beverages or illegal drugs. The term possess in this context is construed liberally. You should not have ANY alcoholic beverages in your residence. Please call if you have questions about whether your contact with alcoholic beverages could be construed as possessing it.

No Possession of Weapons

You are prohibited from possessing any dangerous weapons, including, but not limited to firearms. The term possess in this context is construed liberally. You should not have ANY dangerous weapons in your residence. Please call if you have questions about this.

Additionally, no possession of firearms or weapons requirements could be extended to ammunition (even if the firearms are removed). Your best bet to avoid problems is to remove all ammunition as well as firearms and dangerous weapons.

Submit to Searches

The police are able to search you, your vehicle, and your residence and require you to submit to a chemical test, in order to determine whether you have violated any of these conditions. They may do so AT ANY TIME, without articulable suspicion or probable cause. OR They may do so if they suspect you have violated any of these conditions.

Prohibited Contact

You are prohibited from having any contact, direct or indirect, with _____, except is necessary for _____. You may not enter _____, except _____.

No contact means no direct or indirect contact. This provision will be liberally construed against you. The Maine Supreme Court found contact for the violation of a Protection from Abuse Order for a Defendant **observing** an alleged victim without having physical or verbal contact. See State v. Mark Elliott (Me. 2010). Please be very careful with no contact provisions of your bail.

Restriction on Driving

You are prohibited from operating a motor vehicle under any circumstances. OR You are prohibited from operating a motor vehicle unless lawfully licensed to do so.

Please feel free to call with any questions or comments you may have.

Respectfully submitted,

_____

Timothy E. Zerillo
Attorney for Defendant
ZERILLO LAW FIRM, LLC

[§§2:57-2:69 Reserved]

IV.   CO-DEFENDANTS

§2:70   Protect Yourself and Your Client

Cases with co-defendants in which other counsel is involved can be exciting. I say this as someone who labored by himself in practice for many years. They give you someone to bounce ideas off of, of course, to the extent that you trust the other lawyer.

I often see lawyers representing two co-defendants themselves, but that is not something I am in the practice of doing. In fact, I personally consider it dangerous. It's very difficult to tell when one of those co-defendants will turn on the other, even when they have aligned interests at the time of representation.

If you are one of two or more lawyers acting on a client's behalf who have aligned interests, please remember to protect yourself and your clients with a Joint Defense Agreement. This is something that is often overlooked. A

Joint Defense Agreement clearly spells out the nature of the confidentiality of discussions between yourself, and your co-defense attorneys and the co-defendants.

§2:71   FORM 2-90 Joint Defense Agreement

JOINT DEFENSE AND CONFIDENTIALITY AGREEMENT

This Agreement among the undersigned parties ("the Clients") and their counsel ("Counsel") memorializes understandings reached among counsel. The understandings concern the common defense of the clients in the matter of an investigation involving possible criminal, civil or administrative proceedings, which have been or may be initiated by the Department of Justice or any other investigative agency investigating possible violations of law that are being alleged against the clients.

Counsel believes that there is a common legal interest in a joint defense and representation of their respective clients in these proceedings. In this regard, the Defense Group wishes to continue to pursue separate but common interests and avoid any claim or suggestion of waiver of the clients' privileges. Accordingly, it is our intention and understanding that the communications among the clients and counsel are confidential and are protected from disclosure to any third party by the clients' attorney-client and attorney work product privileges.

The undersigned believe that such disclosures are matters of common legal interest and concern essential to the effective representation of our respective clients and, therefore, that such disclosures are covered by the joint defense doctrine recognized and explained at length in *In Re: Grand Jury Subpoenas 89-3, 89-4, John Doe 89-129*, 902 F.2d 244 (4th Cir. 1990); *United States v. Schwimmer*, 892 F.2d 237 (2d Cir. 1989); *United States v. McPartlin*, 595 F.2d 1321, 1336-37 (7th Cir. 1979); *Eisenberg v. Gagnon*, 766 F.2d 770, 787-88 (3rd Cir. 1985).

In order to accomplish the objectives of this Agreement, the undersigned agree that any and all of the following, no matter how disclosed to one another or to our respective clients, shall be covered by this Agreement: (a) witness interviews and statements, (b) memoranda of law, (c) briefing and debriefing memoranda, (d) summaries, (e) transcripts, (f) documents or conversations containing plans or theories for mutual, separate, or joint defense and representation, and (g) any documents or information that would otherwise be protected from disclosure to third parties under any theory.

No information obtained by any counsel to this Agreement as a result of this Agreement shall be disclosed to any third party without the express consent of the parties to this Agreement. Each party to this Agreement retains the right to determine what information in its possession it shall disclose to the other parties to this Agreement.

The parties agree that if any attempt is made by any third party to secure or obtain information covered by this Agreement, the other parties to this Agreement shall be promptly notified and shall be given copies of any writings or documents, including subpoenas, summonses and the like, which relate to the attempt by the third party to obtain the information.

It is further understood that all documents and information disclosed by and between the undersigned and their clients shall be treated as if protected by the attorney-client and attorney work product privileges, whether or not so identified or marked. The parties agree on behalf of their clients not to enter into any settlement with a third party which would require or result in disclosure of material covered by this Agreement.

If any party to this Agreement enters into negotiations with any third party for the purpose of resolving any or all of a client's potential liability, that client and his/her attorney agree (a) to inform all the other signatories to this Agreement of that fact; (b) to disclose the terms of any final settlement of the client's liability, including, but not limited to, the content of proffers and statements made by the client; and (c) to keep confidential and not disclose any information covered by this Agreement.

Upon final settlement of any client's potential liability, the member of the Defense Group representing that client shall disclose the terms of that settlement to the other members of the Defense Group and thereafter withdraw from the Defense Group, as provided below, if asked to do so by the other members.

Any member of the Defense Group may, on behalf of his client, withdraw from this Agreement at any time by giving written notice, hand delivered or by certified mail, upon all other members of the Defense Group, in which case this Agreement shall no longer be operative as to the withdrawing party, but shall continue to protect all communications and information covered by the Agreement and disclosed to the withdrawing party prior to the withdrawing party's notification of intent to withdraw. Immediately upon demand by any member of the Group, the withdrawing party and his counsel shall return all joint defense materials and copies thereof.

Each party waives the right to object to the continued retention by any other party of counsel or to seek the counsel's disqualification, on the ground that: (a) the counsel had access to the Joint Litigation Information pursuant to this Agreement; or (b) the counsel has a conflict of interest by reason of participation in joint litigation efforts under this Agreement. Each party waives any right to take testimony from counsel for another party based on that counsel's participation in joint litigation efforts.

Nothing contained herein shall be deemed to create an attorney-client relationship between any attorney and anyone other than the client of that attorney, and the fact that any attorney has entered this Agreement shall not be used as a basis for seeking to disqualify any counsel from representing any other party in this or any other proceeding; and no attorney who has entered into this Agreement shall be disqualified from examining or cross-examining any client who testifies at any proceeding, whether under a grant of immunity or otherwise, because of such attorney's participation in this Agreement; and the signatories and their clients further agree that a signatory attorney examining or cross-examining any client who testifies at any proceeding, whether under a grant of immunity or otherwise, may use any Defense Material or other information contributed by such client during the joint defense; and it is herein represented that each undersigned counsel to this Agreement has specifically advised his or her respective client of this clause and that such client has agreed to its provisions.

It is further understood and agreed that, to the extent that the parties have already been in communication with one another prior to the execution of this Agreement in relation to Joint Defense Matters, all previous privileged communications and all materials and information exchanged are subject to this Agreement.

This Agreement may be modified only in a writing signed by all parties. By signing this Agreement each attorney certifies that s/he has explained the contents of this joint defense agreement to his/her client and that each of us agree to abide by the understandings contained herein.

This Agreement shall remain in effect and be binding upon successor counsel in accordance with its terms and may be terminated by successor counsel only in accordance with its terms.

_____   Dated:
Defendant One

_____
Attorney for Defendant One

_____   Dated:
Defendant Two

_____
Attorney for Defendant Two

[§§2:72-2:79 Reserved]

V.   DISCOVERY ISSUES

§2:80   Prosecution's Obligation to Disclose Exculpatory Evidence

Discovery is a fertile ground for litigation. In your state practice, there are likely automatic discovery provisions in the Rules of Criminal Procedure. They often will require the prosecution to provide information that falls well short of constitutional requirements, however. Litigation over issues related to exculpatory evidence is the field you need to continue to plow in your practice, however.

The United States Supreme Court has held that the prosecution has a due process obligation under the Federal Constitution to disclose material evidence favorable to a criminal defendant. *Brady vs. Maryland*, 373 U.S. 83 (1963). Favorable evidence is, fortunately, quite broad. Arguably, favorable evidence can include anything reasonably positive to the defense.

§2:81   A "Verdict Worthy of Confidence"

In *United States vs. Bagley*, 473 U.S. 667 (1985), the Court held that regardless of the request, general or specific, favorable evidence is material, and constitutional error results from its suppression by the government, "if there is a reasonable probability that, had the evidence been disclosed to the defense, the result of the proceeding would have been different." *Id.* at 682.

A showing of materiality under *Bagley* does not require proof by the defendant that disclosure of the evidence would result in the defendant's acquittal. *Kyles vs. Whitley*, 514 U.S. 419 (1995) (prosecutor's failure to disclose contradictory witness statements describing shooter required reversal). All that is required is a "reasonable probability" that the information is necessary in order for the defendant to receive a fair trial, i.e., a trial that results in a verdict worthy of confidence. *Id.* at 434. It doesn't matter how strong the case is against the defendant. A verdict worthy of confidence is the appropriate standard, not sufficiency of the evidence. *Id.* at 434.

This confidence is not necessarily related to the ultimate outcome, although it can be. *Id.* Materiality of the evidence is primarily related to the process and underlying fairness of the trial. *Id.* at 434-435.

§2:82   *Bagley* Error Is Never Harmless

If a reviewing court finds a constitutional error under *Bagley* has occurred, there is no need for harmless error review, because such errors are never harmless. *Id.* at 435. This is something trial courts should be made aware of in ruling on discovery motions.

§2:83   Impeachment Evidence Must Be Disclosed

The Court in *Kyles* reaffirmed that impeachment evidence is exculpatory evidence. *Id.* at 433. Often defense lawyers think of exculpatory evidence as evidence that exonerates the Defendant, and nothing else. Under *Kyles*, there is no difference "between exculpatory and impeachment information for *Brady* purposes...." *Id.* at 433.

§2:84   Evidence Is Considered Collectively

Additionally, both *Kyles* and *Bagley* caution that the Government cannot escape the duty to disclose by arguing that each item of evidence should be considered individually in assessing the duty to disclose. *Id.* at 436. The evidence must be considered for its impact collectively. *Id.*

§2:85   Helpful Language from *Kyles*

Finally, *Kyles* provides fantastic language related to a prosecutor's duty to disclose evidence. While noting the prosecutor's discretion, the Court in Kyles states that "a prosecutor anxious about tacking too close to the wind will disclose a favorable piece of evidence." *Id.* at 439. A "prudent prosecutor will resolve doubtful questions in favor of disclosure." *Id.* at 439; *See also U.S. v. Agurs*, 427 US 97, 108 (1977). The *Kyles* Court goes on to note that the prosecutor's duty is not to win the case. *Id.* Rather, the prosecutor's duty is to seek the truth. *Id.*

This imposes a terrific duty on the prosecutor. Remind the prosecutor in your case of this duty to get what you need for your client.

[§§2:86-2:89 Reserved]

VI.   TRIAL OR PLEA? ADVISING THE CLIENT

§2:90   Setting Expectations and Covering Your Behind

As criminal defense attorneys, we have to recognize that many of our clients do not take responsibility for their own actions. That is often the reason why they ended up seeking our representation in the first place.

When a client who does not take responsibility for his actions loses at trial, he will most certainly cast blame. The most frequent target is his trial lawyer.

As a result, it's important to appropriately set expectations and cover your own behind as you prepare for trial. A client can not make an informed decision about trial unless he or she knows what trial entails. Spend time with the client, even if it is in custody. Explain burden of proof issues and the elements of your particular case. Certainly, this includes conveying in writing the risk of trial to your client and informing your client of the consequences, including the collateral consequences, of a conviction.

To do so, I have a trial risk letter that I send to clients when their cases appear in the trial list. It conveys the risk of trial, while still indicating that I'm pleased to go to trial for the client if the client wishes. See §2:92 Form 2-100 Trial Risk Letter. When the client is facing a felony conviction, I include a memo explaining the potential collateral consequences. See §2:93 Form 2-110 Memo on Effects of Felony Conviction.

If your client decides to go to trial after you have done your due diligence, then the choice will be an informed one and you have done your job.

§2:91   Collateral Consequences—the Constantly Shifting Landscape

Collateral consequences of a criminal conviction are constantly popping up in new and scary ways in the criminal defense world. They move on the tide of popular opinion that politicians like to try to surf. With our over-criminalization and over-punishment in the United States, it is no surprise that we overly-consequence the punishment so that you can get hit with a sucker punch that you never even saw coming after you think your case is over.

I can't begin to inform you of every collateral consequence of every crime, even if I knew them all (which I don't). The point, as usual, is that you don't need to know everything; you just need to know your client and do your homework. You don't need to know off the top of your head whether a drop down from a trafficking to a furnishing will disrupt your client's housing benefits. What you do need to do is identify the issue, and then research it.

One of the most notorious of the collateral consequences is the immigration consequence. I worked with an immigration lawyer in Boston while in law school. I learned from his practice that I know nothing about immigration law. It is a hyper-technical, rapidly-changing area of the law that you should not try to research yourself.

Thankfully, there are immigration advocacy projects everywhere now ready to help. Clear everything remotely suspicious through them. Remember, in *Padilla v. Kentucky*, 559 U.S. 356, 130 S. Ct. 1473 (2010), the Supreme Court of the United States held that counsel has a constitutional duty to inform a defendant of the risk that a guilty plea could result in his deportation. Since I am not willing to allow my clients to be subjected to my interpretation of the immigration statutes, I go to the immigration experts and you should too.

In §2:93 Form 2-100 Effects of a Felony Conviction Memo, which is sent with my Trial Risk Letter (§2:92 Form 2-100) I identify many collateral consequences. I urge you to create your own memo regarding collateral consequences so your clients are fully informed when making plea and trial decisions.

§2:92   FORM 2-100 Trial Risk Letter

Date

Joe Defendant
46 Not Guilty Lane
Nolo, ME 04044

RE: State v. Joe Defendant
    Docket No. CR-12-2045
    Trial Risk Letter

Dear Joe:

I understand that you are considering whether your case should proceed to trial. That choice is entirely yours. My job is to help you make the best decision for you, your family, and your case. I really enjoy jury trials—I would not be doing this type of work if I didn't. You can get some level of vindication at trial if you win. This is a great feeling, and I love to achieve a victory for my clients.

I would not be doing my job if I did not warn you of the dangers of proceeding to trial first, however. Trials are completely unpredictable, as are juries. There is never a way to determine with certainty what a jury will do with a case. By continuing to trial, you leave your fate in the jury's hands.

Proceeding to trial is entirely your choice. It may be that trial is a good decision for you either because you are morally or ethically unwilling to accept the deal offered by the Prosecutor, or simply because the deal isn't good enough for you to not risk trial That being said, as your attorney I need to warn you about potential pitfalls of jury trials.

Since your case involves a felony charge, I enclose a memo I have drafted titled "Effects of a Felony Conviction." Please review this Memo and consider it in making your decision whether or not to go to trial.

I will continue to prepare your case for trial unless I hear differently from you.

Respectfully submitted,

_____

Timothy E. Zerillo
Attorney for Defendant
ZERILLO LAW FIRM, LLC

§2:93　　FORM 2-110 Memo on Effect of Felony Conviction

EFFECTS OF A FELONY CONVICTION

The effects of a felony conviction are too numerous to document in this one memo. There is not one document that comprehensively describes all consequences of a felony conviction. In addition, laws change, and felony consequences change with them. I am drafting this memo to you to highlight some of the effects of a felony conviction.

1.　Possession of a Firearm

A felony conviction prohibits you from possessing a firearm. 18 U.S.C. §922(g)(1); 15 MRSA §393. Under Maine law, a "conviction" means "acceptance of a guilty plea or nolo contendere or a verdict or finding of guilt." 15 MRSA §.393(1)(D).

Possession of a firearm by a felon may be "actual or constructive." Constructive possession means the "power and intention to exercise control and dominion over a firearm." The person who has direct physical control over a thing over a given time is in legal possession of it. You can be in constructive possession over a firearm by exercising control over the firearm without actually possessing it. Possession can be sole or joint.

Needless to say, there are many ways a felon can be in possession of a firearm. The federal government takes possession of a firearm by a felon very seriously and will prosecute.

2.　Government Programs

You may become unable to participate in various federal programs as a result of a felony conviction. This can include student loans, federal housing, federally granted licenses, certain Social Security benefits and food stamps. The Government continues to add restrictions, so this is not an exclusive list.

3.　Voting Rights

Voting rights are governed by State law. There is no prohibition in the U.S. Constitution regarding voting rights. I am not aware of any Maine law prohibiting voting by felons. This is not true in every state, however, so if you are a resident of a state other than Maine, please check your home state's law on this issue.

4.　Travel Restrictions

My research does not reveal any travel restrictions imposed by the United States Government for a felony conviction. Other countries may restrict travel. Canada, for example, may restrict travel for any criminal conviction.

5.　Employment

The Maine Human Rights Commission and the EEOC interpret Title VII of the Civil Rights Act to prohibit employment policies that exclude people solely on the basis of their conviction. For certain jobs and professions, a felony conviction makes licensing difficult, however. For example, I think it would be very difficult for you to attain admission to the Bar, if you wanted to be an attorney. There are similar requirements for teachers, accountants, doctors, and other professions that are regulated. See 5 M.R.S.A. §5301–5303 precluding certain professional licenses for up to 3 years in some cases and 10 years in others after completion of sentence including probation. The same may be true regarding certain other jobs, particularly those which are government or military related, or require the individual to be bonded.

Please also consider the following:

- Convictions of offenses involving dishonesty, breach of trust, or money laundering disqualify an individual from working for institutions that are insured by the Federal Deposit Insurance Corporation. See 12 U.S.C. §1829.
- Federal laws bar certain classes of felons from working in the insurance industry without having received permission from an insurance regulatory official. See 8 U.S.C. §1033(c)(2).
- Certain classes of felons are barred, for 13 years after conviction or the end of imprisonment if sentenced for a term of longer than 13 years, from holding any of several positions in a union or other organization that manages an employee benefit plan, including serving as an officer of the union or a director of the unions governing board. See 29 U.S.C. §§504, 1111.
- Federal law also prohibits those convicted of certain crimes from providing healthcare services for which they will receive payment from Medicare. See 42 U.S.C. §1320a-7, or from working for the generic drug industry. See 21 U.S.C. §335a.
- A federal law that requires criminal history background checks for individuals who provide care for children. See 42 U.S.C. §13041. In addition, the Federal Child Protection Act, 42 U.S.C. §5119(a), authorizes states to enact statutes concerning the facilitation of criminal background checks of persons who work with children.
- Those in a state "licensed profession, trade or occupation" can be denied licensing. See 5 U.S.C. §§5301-5303. This covers a broad range of occupations so look carefully at the statute. Consideration of the conviction in an analysis of "fitness to practice" lasts three years from final discharge from the correctional system which generally means three years after completion of probation or supervised release. For those in the medical fields, the period is ten years.
- Since September 11, 2001, numerous efforts have been made to increase aviation security. Federal laws requiring background checks have been passed to ensure safety of travelers and airport employees. See 49 U.S.C. §§44935; 44936.

6. Credibility

In any future legal proceeding, civil or criminal, your felony conviction can be used to impeach your credibility. This is merely an evidentiary rule if you are ever called as a witness in any type of a court proceeding. This remains true for 15 years from the date of your conviction or 10 years from the date of your release under the Maine Rules of Evidence. The Federal Rule is limited to 10 years with some exceptions. The time period may be longer in other states.

7. Non-Citizens

If you are not an American citizen, you must carefully review 8 U.S.C. §1101 before any plea, trial or sentencing to see if a conviction or sentence might result in a mandatory lifetime deportation. An alien who has been convicted of an aggravated felony including but not limited to a "crime of violence" as defined in 8 U.S.C. §1101(a)(43) will be deported. Under current federal law a person is guilty of an "aggravated felony," for immigration purposes, if he or she is convicted of a "crime of violence" or any other crime listed in the statutory section for which he or she receives a sentence of at least one year. Note that the period of incarceration includes suspended portions as well as unsuspended, so anything more than 364 days will trigger mandatory deportation. This is a complex area and I suggest you get advice from someone who knows immigration law, for example, Immigration Legal Advocacy Project, 207-780-1593, www.immigrantlegaladvocacy.org, before you agree to anything.

8. Social Security Benefits

A felony conviction will result in the suspension of SS benefits (disability or retirement) during any term of imprisonment. The SS Act bars payment of SS benefits to incarcerated felons. The statute does not concern misdemeanors, so a misdemeanor conviction does not affect benefits, even during a jail sentence. Upon beginning supervised release or probation, you may have payments reinstated by presenting your release papers to an SS office. A fully suspended sentence or a sentence on probation, even following a felony conviction, does NOT affect your SS benefits. Once you have completed your sentence the felony conviction should not affect your future rights to social security benefits under current law. There is no way of knowing what laws Congress may try and pass in the future.

9. DNA Database

Convictions of certain crimes in Maine state courts require that the defendant provide a blood sample for DNA typing to be added to a law enforcement database. See 25 M.R.S.A. §1574. For convictions after October 1, 2001 a DNA sample must be provided following any felony conviction, as well as any misdemeanor "sex" crime such as unlawful sexual contact, visual sexual aggression against a child, sexual misconduct with a child under 14 years of age, or any lesser included offense of any crime of those listed if the greater offense is initially charged. "Lesser included offense" has the same meaning as in 17-A M.R.S.A. §13-A. This law has been upheld in both state and federal courts although it has yet to have been challenged in the Maine Law Court. DNA samples are being required of those convicted of almost all federal crimes as well.

10. Sex Offender Registration

Sex Offender Registration is mandatory after conviction of many Maine crimes and Federal crimes. If you are accused of a sex crime, this is a potential implication of a conviction for that crime. This is true for misdemeanor sex crimes as well.

11. Enhanced Future Sentences

Most states and federal law impose longer sentences on individuals with prior convictions. The amount of increase varies but has been getting longer. Some states have "three strikes" type laws that can result in sentences of up to life imprisonment. If you are convicted of a felony, it is more important than ever that you be sure not to become involved in conduct that could expose you to new criminal charges.

12. Denial of Student Loans

Under federal law (21 U.S.C. §862 and 862a), those convicted of certain drug related offenses may be ineligible for certain federal benefits. This can include grants, professional licenses or contracts but not Social Security, retirement or Veteran benefits. Benefits such as food stamps or student loans, however, can be lost.

13. Future Collateral Consequences

The courts have consistently ruled that even after the "punishment" portion of a criminal conviction is over, certain collateral consequences can apply, even if such consequences WERE NOT in existence at the time of the conviction. Unfortunately, we cannot predict what may happen here.

***

Please understand that while I have attempted to cover many areas, I cannot assure you that I have covered everything.

§2:94   The Guilty Plea

I really hate the guilty plea. It is like admitting defeat. But it is also important. I don't only represent the innocent, I represent the guilty.

When you have a case that cries out for a guilty plea that you believe is in your client's best interest, you need to handle it in as smooth a way as possible. That means setting expectations, and preparing for sentencing during the entry of the plea.

Knowledge is power

I write this section several hours after my client entered into a guilty plea on the federal charge of Possession of Firearms by a Prohibited Person. He had no significant criminal record, but he possessed 20 firearms including 2 AK-47's, which is a big problem (discussed further in the Ch. 9 Firearms Offenses).

Since he had a lack of a criminal record, it was really hard for him to understand that he could be guilty of a crime. Everyone knows that felons can't possess firearms, but someone with a restraining order?

Eventually, after many frustrating hours of explaining the process and the elements with him, light dawned over Marblehead. He was guilty.

So, now the trick is to alleviate any uncertainty I can. That is not easy because there's a lot of uncertainty!

The way most people stay the calmest through the process is to understand how the plea will go down. This is especially true of felonies, and isn't usually a big deal for misdemeanors. With felonies you should have some heavy duty inquiry from the court ahead of you into voluntariness and a factual basis for the change of plea. The client needs to understand all of the questions that will be asked of him or her and the correct way to answer them.

Some courts, especially Federal Courts, use plea scripts that individual judges have developed. If I have a Federal case, I make sure to get the plea script and go over it thoroughly with the client. Make sure he or she knows the importance of making a good impression of the judge who will sentence him. For more on sentencing, see §§2:150-2:153.

[§§2:95-2:99 Reserved]

VII. THE TRIAL

A. General Tips

§2:100   Prepare, Prepare, Prepare

There is nothing in this world that replaces hard work. That goes for the practice of criminal defense as well. It especially goes for preparing for trial. Although I don't try as many cases as many of you may, I prepare to try everything as seriously and thoroughly as I possibly can. I hear colleagues say that they prepare an hour or so for every one hour they are in trial. I would guess I prepare between 3 and 5 hours for every hour that I am in trial. If I could script the entire trial, I would. Obviously that's not possible. That said, I want to be prepared for every single contingency.

Maybe you're the type of person who can fly by the seat of your pants. If so, I congratulate you (as long as you are effective for your clients).

I am the type of person, on the other hand, who feels most comfortable if I have prepared as thoroughly as possible before the trial begins. As a result, trial preparation with me begins early. Everything I do, involving especially the review of discovery, is geared to possible trial issues.

I'm sure all of you have experienced the feeling that I have experienced, on a Sunday prior to a Monday Jury Selection with trial to begin immediately, thinking there is just not enough time. That is a horrible feeling, and I urge you to overly-prepare. The stakes are too high to do a merely competent job. Excellence is what we are striving for.

§2:101   Don't be Afraid to Lose

I am never horribly impressed with a prosecutor who has an amazing conviction rate. This is not a knock on prosecutors; it is merely to point out the obvious. That is, a prosecutor gets to choose which cases to take to trial and which not to try. If the prosecutor loses a trial, it's his own fault. Either he did not screen the case properly, or he did not perform well at trial.

A defense lawyer on the other hand, has to sometimes try cases that are losers. You may hear some veteran defense attorneys calling them "slow pleas." The fact that you are involved in a slow plea trial does not, in any way, remove your obligations to the client to provide a thorough and vigorous defense.

Don't be afraid to lose a case at trial. You can learn just as much from a loss as you can a victory. Often, you learn more. If your client has been well informed of the risks inherent in every trial, and the risks inherent in his or her particular case, then a losing attempt at trial is nothing to be ashamed of.

§2:102 Establishing Your Case Theory

One thing that is very important in the context of a trial is to establish your theory of the case. This needs to be something that you can put into a one or two sentence synopsis. It is often among the first things I will say in my opening. It may even border on argument, which may not be permitted in your jurisdiction, and isn't permitted in mine in opening.

A good case theory, however, established at opening and continued as a theory throughout the course of the trial, will bond you and the trial with the jury.

Let's say you are trying a complicated drug case. It involves drug trafficking in which a confidential informant was used to "middle" several drug transactions with your client. This confidential informant has a checkered past and had a girlfriend on probation and in some trouble during the time that he "middled" the transactions at issue.

There are probably tiny little details that will be important to you in this factual scenario. You will bring out these details at trial in attempting to impeach the confidential informant. You will use these little details to show how he is inconsistent with his statements to law enforcement. You will use those inconsistencies to prove him unreliable to the jury. But all of those smaller details are much too big for your trial theme. At opening in a case like this I would state the trial theme in a sentence or two, saying something like this:

> Members of the jury, the State has just given you a great opening statement about all the evidence that they think they have against my client. But all that evidence is based on the testimony of a rat. That rat can't be trusted, and we will show that their case can't be trusted as a result.

Obviously, you have to know your Judge. If "rat" is going to be too strong in front of a particular judge, then temper it. That said, you get the point. We have started our theme off immediately, "The State has evidence against the Defendant, but the evidence can't be trusted because it comes from a rat." That theme will continue throughout cross-examination and will take up a significant part of your closing argument. Keep revisiting this trial theme throughout the trial.

§2:103 Should Your Client Testify?

All I can say is be very careful putting your client on the stand. It is extremely dangerous, and often destroys the reasonable doubt you have been working so hard to create.

Before your client takes the stand, be sure to talk about the 5th Amendment. Make sure he knows, preferably in writing, that he cannot be compelled to testify. At the trial, have the judge take a break before the examination of the defendant, and warn your client on the record about the 5th Amendment protection. If he chooses to take the stand after all warnings, you have done your job.

I am reminded as I write this of a recent post-conviction case of a lawyer I know. He lost a trial where his client was accused of picking up a woman he didn't know in a car, taking her to a motel and raping her. He took the stand. The district attorney's first question on cross examination was, "How did you know she would want to go with you when you pulled up in your car?" His answer? "What woman wouldn't?" That is not a great answer.

After he was convicted of the rape, he brought a post-conviction review against defense counsel. He claimed he was never warned of the dangers of taking the stand. Make sure that you warn your clients of those dangers thoroughly.

§2:104 Experiment

A basic tactic that is often overlooked by lawyers is to experiment. You don't have to be tied to your desk or the courthouse all day. If the government claims that your client drove recklessly when he drove off the road striking and killing a pedestrian, go to the scene of the crash. Drive the area of the road yourself. Even better, get the same type of car and see how it handles there. Understand the road, the scene of the accident, the way the car handles, the way the road swells, and so on.

I did a rape case once where a young woman claimed that she was violently beaten and raped by two men in a motel room. The rape was so violent, she claimed, that they ripped the headboard off the wall. We decided to go to the motel. When we got into the room, we saw that the headboard was not anchored to the wall, but was merely screwed into some sheetrock. So, we did some experiments on how easily the headboard would fall, which did not take a lot of force, as it turned out. Then we bought the headboard from the motel owner and had it set up in the courtroom, ready to fall at the opportune time in the trial. For more on this case, see Ch. 11.

There are unlimited ways in which your experiments can discredit the government theories about your case. So don't forget to use your imagination and experiment.

[§§2:105-2:109 Reserved]

B. Tips for Opening Statements

§2:110   Beginning

I find the Opening Statement for me is much more difficult than the Closing Argument. That said, many jury consultants will tell you that the Opening is much more important than the Closing.

I am always concerned that I am bordering on argument in the Opening Statement. Maybe that means I am doing a good job while I am giving one. That being said, Openings certainly are important in setting the tone for your case.

I begin my Opening Statement with a stock phrase to get my mouth moving, sort of like this:

Your Honor, jury foreperson Smith, members of the jury may it please the Court. I am pleased and proud to represent Joe Defendant in this case. The single greatest thing I get to do as a lawyer is to address you in open court in a trial. That is because jurors, like you, who listen carefully and who make hard decisions, to apply the law of reasonable doubt are the most important people in our Court system. More on reasonable doubt later. For now, I want to tell you what this case is really about.

I think it is polite when you have new guests in your house (and the courtroom is YOUR house), to do an introduction. So, sometimes I will open like this:

This, ladies and gentlemen, is a criminal case. All criminal cases are serious, but this case is a Gross Sexual Assault, a rape. It is among the most serious of the criminal charges in our system. Criminal cases are different and more important than regulatory actions, then civil cases, and virtually every other type of case. Criminal cases involve the most serious type of government action. These cases strike at the heart of a person's freedom. There's just more at stake in a criminal case.

So, I think before I go further into this serious case, it is important to introduce some of the people you will see every day throughout this trial. My Mother always taught me it was polite to introduce people to others they don't know. So, let's do that here.

Over here is Judge Williams, you know him. He will give you instructions throughout the trial and when the trial is over. You might see him speak with the lawyers at sidebar from time to time. It is not our intention to be rude when we do this. It is just the way the trial process works.

Those two gentlemen over there are court officers. Their names are Bruce and John. They work all over this courthouse and have done so for many years.

The woman up front here taking down very skillfully everything I say is Doris. She is a court reporter. Her job is to take down an accurate record of everything said in this courtroom.

DA Stern has already introduced herself. Seated next to her is Bryan Brady. He's the detective in the case. The law allows the DA to have the investigating officer sit with them if they wish, and they have chosen to do that.

Most importantly, sitting here at my table is my Client, Matt. Now I am going to tell you about Matt in a second, but first I want you to use your imagination. As you know, Matt sits here before you today an innocent man accused of a very serious crime. You have all agreed in order to become jurors in this trial that you would follow the law of reasonable doubt and the presumption of innocence. So, when you see Matt sitting here, I want you to imagine a tube, plunked down over him. The tube sits over him and protects him throughout the entire trial. This tube is as strong as steel, but its translucent so you can see him sitting there in the courtroom. That tube never gets breached, it never gets broken, unless the State proves their case beyond a reasonable doubt.

§2:111   Theme

Now I want to launch back into my trial theme. This is a theme we want to have in a sentence or two that sums up your case.

Let's say that your client is charged with Unlawful Sexual Touching. He is charged with sneaking down in the middle of the night and touching the breasts of his sister-in-law, while she slept over on the couch in his house. She was asleep when the alleged breast touching took place. She was also on medication for Depression. She is the only witness to the incident. At trial, I might sum up the theme like so:

> The alleged victim had a dream that my client touched her and she wants to swear to it. I can't swear to what happened in my dreams, and I doubt that you can either. But Jennifer Victim swears she was touched while she was sleeping. She claims she can swear to it, despite the fact she was asleep and on Zanax.

§2:112   Facts, Presumption of Innocence, Burden of Proof

I will spend the rest of my Opening talking about facts that I will expect to come out at testimony. Be careful about this, however. If you aren't sure that something will be presented as evidence and you promise it will be at Opening the jury may make you pay for it. You also want to mention the burden of proof and presumption of innocence. I view the presumption of innocence issue as planting the seed in the Opening for all your reasonable doubt argument in Closing. I definitely do not hit reasonable doubt as hard at Opening as I will in closing, but it should be mentioned as well.

I usually try to make my point regarding the presumption of innocence by saying something like this:

> The fact that Joe was summonsed in this case doesn't indicate anything. The summons is only a means to activate the system of justice so that 12 of his peers can come in here and listen to the evidence. You determine guilt or innocence. The police officer doesn't determine it, the prosecutor doesn't determine it, and I don't determine it. Even the Judge doesn't determine it. You are the only ones to determine guilt or innocence.

> As a result of that, the burden in any criminal case rests solely with the prosecutor at that table. In this case, the State of Maine and that prosecutor over there have the entire burden of proving Joe's guilt. That burden never once shifts to this table. Joe doesn't have to do anything but sit there. He doesn't have to testify; his attorney doesn't have to cross examine anyone. He doesn't have to present evidence—he doesn't have to do anything. And if he does nothing, the law says that you cannot view that as an admission of guilt. The Judge will tell you so if you do not believe me.

> Why is that? Because the prosecutor has the opportunity to do all the advance investigation he wanted to do. He has every state government agency at his disposable, every police department at his disposal and your tax dollars to burn in creating this prosecution.

> Now he has to show you the case and prove to you that he spent your money wisely.

Or, perhaps try something like this to make your point:

> What is not evidence? The Indictment. The indictment is merely an accusation. It is made without the due process of the jury or a judge being present. It is merely a means to initiate the system of justice that brings you here today. It means nothing more.

> Can you see my hand here as I hold it up? (Hold up hand). You may say "Yes, Tim, I can see your hand."

> But you can only see one side of my hand. And it isn't until I turn my hand in this direction can you see both sides of my hand.

The Indictment, the accusation, only sees one side of things. You get to see both sides of things, and you get to judge them on the basis of whether the Government has proven its case beyond a reasonable doubt.

[§§2:113-2:119 Reserved]

C. Tips for Cross Examination

1. Law Enforcement Officers

§2:120   Setting Up the Officer's Cross

I always like to try to pin down the officer and his report as much as possible at the outset. I consider ordinary police officers to be semi-professional witnesses. They are usually quite skilled at testifying. Some law enforcement officers, like FBI and DEA agents, are fully professional witnesses. They are as smooth as you can get. Sometimes, they are dishonest as well.

The combination of a skilled, dynamic, and experience law enforcement officer can be powerfully dangerous to your case. As excellent criminal defense lawyer Cynthia Roseberry once said:

> We, as criminal defense lawyers, are forced to deal with some of the lowest people on earth, people who have no sense of right and wrong, people who will lie in court to get what they want, people who do not care who gets hurt in the process. It is our job—our sworn duty—as criminal defense lawyers, to protect our clients from those people.

Don't forget, the jury will generally like cop witnesses. They usually see them as honest. Don't kid yourself; if this is an old Western movie, you will be wearing the black hat and they will be wearing the white hat in the jury's eyes. The key is for the jury to mentally take that hat off them after the examination.

Since you will be often attacking the officer's competence, the quality of his investigation and the conclusions of the investigation, below I've provided a set up to your cross of the officer. You can use it in conjunction with the officer cross-examinations I've provided throughout this book.

§2:121   Officer's Training and Experience

I like to start by crediting the officer.

Q. How long have you been a police officer?
A. 15 years.
Q. Approximately how many traffic stops have you made?
A. I don't know, thousands.
Q. Performing traffic stops is a standard part of your job?
A. Yes.
Q. You do it almost every day you work?
A. Yes.
Q. You are very proficient at it?
A. Yes.
Q. You were trained as to how to stop a vehicle?
A. Yes.
Q. Approach a vehicle after a stop?
A. Yes.
Q. How to ask questions of a driver?
A. Yes.
Q. Your training was thorough, wasn't it?
A. Yes.
Q. You feel well qualified to work as a patrol officer?
A. Yes.

Q. You are well qualified because of your training and experience?
A. Yes.

§2:122   Officer's Reports

Since you will likely be attacking the officer's reports, I like to next pin the officer down on his or her report.

Q. In the course of your work you have to prepare police reports?
A. Yes.
Q. They are required, not optional?
A. Yes.
Q. They are part of your responsibilities as a patrol officer?
A. Yes.
Q. You are taught to write police reports in training?
A. Yes.
Q. Writing police reports is *important*?
A. Yes.
Q. You would agree with me that they are very important?
A. I guess I would.
Q. They are your *official record* of what happened?
A. Yes.
Q. You use them to refresh your recollection both *before* and *during* testimony?
A. Yes.
Q. Your supervisors use them?
A. Yes.
Q. Your supervisor signs off on the report after you write it?
A. Yes.
Q. Prosecutors use your reports too?
A. Yes.
Q. Defense counsel uses them?
A. Yes.
Q. You know that lawyers from both the prosecution and the defense will be reading them carefully?
A. Yes.
Q. So they are very important?
A. Yes.
Q. And we are dealing with important issues in this case before this jury?
A. Yes.
Q. We are dealing with serious charges?
A. Yes, we are.
Q. Did you write a report in this case?
A. Yes, I did.
Q. Your report in this case was accurate?
A. Yes.
Q. Your report in this case was thorough?
A. Yes.
Q. You wrote the report in the way you were trained to write it?
A. I did.
Q. Were there any errors in the report that you want to correct now?
A. I don't believe so.
Q. Are there any flaws in the report you would like to point out?
A. I don't think so.
Q. As far as you know, your police report is 100% correct?
A. As far as I know.

§2:123   Lack of Present Memory of Incident

Don't forget to pin the officer down a little further related to his lack of present memory of the incident as well. We want him to stick to the report we have just established is 100 percent correct (and will be not worth the paper it's printed on after you are done with the officer). We don't want him piping up later on in the cross examination that he now remembers something that explains an inconsistency or error in the report.

Q. One reason for reports is to help your memory.
A. Yes.
Q. You haven't seen my client since you arrested him until today, have you?
A. No.
Q. You have continued to work as a police officer since you arrested him, haven't you?
A. Yes.
Q. And you arrested him approximately 10 months ago, right?
A. That's right.
Q. You've been involved in dozens of cases in those 10 months.
A. That's true.
Q. Your memory at the time you arrested my client is better then it is now?
A. I think it is the same.
Q. Your memory does not get better as time goes on, does it?
A. No, but I remember the case.
Q. You remember your 10th birthday?
A. Yes.
Q. Do you remember the details today as well as you did when you were 10 years old?

The answer at this point doesn't matter much. If he keeps fighting you on this issue, he will lose the jury.

Now you are ready to attack the officer on the facts of your case. Attack the report, attack his procedure, attack everything. Every time you find a mistake the officer made, go back around to how he testified that his report is 100 percent accurate and his investigation completely thorough.

[§§2:124-2:129 Reserved]

2.   Children and Experts

§2:130   Cross Examination of Children

To me, an effective cross examination of a child witness is the hardest thing to do. They are naturally sympathetic—to both you and the jury. As a parent, I need to be careful that I don't put my own kids into the witnesses' shoes, which can also affect my cross.

I don't like cross examining kids, but that doesn't mean I don't do it thoroughly. In some cases, it is exceedingly important. Sometimes it is the entire case.

Lawyers act too sympathetic with kids on the stand. They act too chivalrous. Don't act like the child's parent no matter how cute and sympathetic he or she is. Don't offer a tissue when they are bawling. Forge ahead.

It is hard to follow this advice without seeming like a total ass. That said, you need to exercise control of this child. If you give an inch—by offering a tissue or asking if she is ok—she will take a yard. And the prison yard is where your client will be spending his free time.

There are a number of cross examinations of children in this book. Some of the most difficult and important are found in Ch. 12 Sex Crimes against Children.

§2:131   Cross Examination of Experts

Cross examination of experts can be particularly challenging. There is usually an unfair playing field when it comes to an expert cross examination. While you have the advantage over almost every other witness that you will examine, you may not have an advantage over an expert because of her highly technical and specialized knowledge.

I say that, of course, assuming that the expert has highly technical and specialized knowledge. Don't assume, however, that just because someone labels herself an expert in a particular area that she in fact is. Prepare yourself by understanding your jurisdiction's rules, and attack the admissibility of expert testimony *in limine*, and then later on via an offer of proof at trial. The best way to stop an expert is to knock her out of the case.

I know that doesn't happen that very often, so you are probably going to have to cross examine this so called expert. There are several cross examinations of experts in various areas in this book. I think the most important thing that I see missing from expert witness cross examination by defense counsel is research. When I see a weak cross examination of an expert, it's usually because the lawyer is deferring to that expert's opinion. You need to research the expert and the expert's credentials, and you need to research them thoroughly. This is a way in which the civil bar is well advanced ahead of the criminal defense bar. Websites like TrialSmith.com allow you to get expert information, including transcripts. These can be used in criminal cases, as well as civil. They are simply not used by criminal defense lawyers as often.

The Internet is the easiest way to do cheap and effective expert research. Everyone likes to toot her own horn, and experts are no different. You will probably find all sorts of good information about experts via a simple Google search.

Most importantly, however, is to research the subject matter. I once tried a 19 count Gross Sexual Assault case with a deep tear in the victim's hymen indicating penetration. The expert was a nationally renowned child sex abuse expert. He had crushed defense counsel all over New England. I did not want myself or my client to be crushed, and so I spent months learning about hymeneal anatomy and trauma. I drove my Associate nuts during this period, as I use to come into her office and tell her something new about the hymen every day.

Now you might say to yourself, "his client must have had unlimited funds to pay for all that research!" He didn't. I did the research because it needed to be done, not because I could be paid fully for it.

I am not suggesting that I research every expert for months at a time. I am suggesting that you need to research the area in which the expert is testifying so thoroughly that you become an expert yourself.

By the way, we hung that jury on the 19 count Gross Sexual Assault case.

[§§2:132-2:139 Reserved]

D. Tips for Closing Argument

§2:140 Return to Your Theme

As I mentioned earlier, I have an easier time closing then opening. The facts are in, and I feel like I can marshal those facts to make the best case for my client.

Remember to get back to that opening trial theme. This provides continuity for the jurors, and makes them think you have successfully proved a point you made at opening.

§2:141 Lack of Proof Arguments

If your theme is a lack of proof, you might want to reiterate that "they don't have it." You can do it something like this:

Sometimes jurors get a case and they know the state just doesn't have it. They haven't given them enough evidence. The evidence is faulty and insufficient.

And that hurts you as a juror, because you want to see justice done to people who have done wrong. You sort of wish it had been tied up in a bow so you could issue a guilty verdict that you could feel good about.

It is hard to actually follow the law. Saying they don't have it is hard when you are deciding a charge of gross sexual assault. But when they don't have it, you have to vote not guilty and they don't have it here.

There may come a time in your debate in the jury room when you get tired. You can't. There might be a time you may want to waiver. You can't. Your vote is too important. You cannot give up your belief when they don't have it—you must continue to vote not guilty.

And if you have a long debate about this is the jury room, you may want to consider this: the fact that you are even having the debate is because you have reasonable doubt! As much as it may hurt, the only way to do the right thing with that doubt is to vote not guilty, even if you hate to do so with a charge of gross sexual assault.

There's an old saying in show business that "when you've got it, you've got it." Well, it's also true that when you don't have it, you don't have it, and they don't have it here.

Continuing with the lack of proof theme is another argument I hear in various forms and I like to use as well:

People sometimes think of the role of a jury to find someone guilty or innocent. That is simply not accurate.

In Scotland, they have a 3 verdict system that describes this a little better.

A Scottish jury can come back, guilty, not guilty, or not proven. A not guilty finding would be a finding of what we think of as innocent. Not proven means the charges weren't proven beyond a reasonable doubt. Either one results in an acquittal.

In the U.S., we add not proven into not guilty. A vote for not guilty can mean you believe Joe to be innocent, or it can mean that you don't know if he is innocent, but that the Government has not proven the charge beyond a reasonable doubt.

§2:142   Calling a Witness a Liar

There probably will be times when you need to call a witness, and maybe the alleged victim, a liar. These things happen. When you do it, you can be vague and sort of elegant if it fits you in the case, saying something like this:

There's an old saying—"When a man points a finger at someone else, he should remember that 4 of his 5 fingers are pointing back at him."

Sometimes, blunt and to the point are better though. I was co-trying a case years ago when one of the lawyers gave a very nice 30 minute speech in closing about the problems with this young girl who was falsely accusing several men of forcible rape. He nicely pointed out her inconsistencies at trial revealed over long cross examinations.

My next Co-counsel got up for his closing and made the same point in a few seconds. He said, "Ladies and Gentleman of the jury. This alleged victim is a big fat liar."

The "big, fat liar" comment summed up in three words what co-counsel said in 30 minutes. Sometimes blunt and memorable is best.

§2:143   Reasonable Doubt Arguments

While I like to argue a lot of facts, you need to mix in the reasonable doubt analogies throughout the closing. They can be as short as something like this:

Beyond a reasonable doubt is a level of certainty upon which you would make the most important decisions of your life.

If you find that Joe is probably guilty, you have to let him go. Probably guilty is the same as not guilty.

There is also an often used reasonable doubt story related to the Irish, which I have heard others use as well, and I use like this:

The concept of reasonable doubt is credited with coming from the British, but it was really the Irish who made it up. England occupied Ireland at the time. The Irish were forced to apply English law when they sat on criminal juries. They finally got fed up, and said: "These are our clansman we judge. We have to go back and live with their families. They are in our community. The evidence against them must be so strong that it is beyond any reasonable doubt for us to be able to do that."

And the reasonable doubt standard was born. That is how they lived with themselves after finding a clansman guilty.

You see, reasonable doubt is for the defendant, but it's also for you, because you have to live with your decision.

If you convict Joe on the scant evidence before you, you will live with that doubt the rest of your life.

The doubt will be in your room.

The doubt will be in your mirror.

Don't let that doubt haunt you. Vote to apply the law of reasonable doubt and vote not guilty.

[§§2:144-2:149 Reserved]

VIII. SENTENCING ISSUES

§2:150 Preparing a Sentencing Memorandum

At sentencing, its time to put on the dog and pony show. In part, it is what many clients want. They simply want the Court to hear from them, and to hear about them. Maybe they know they are guilty, but they just want to explain their criminality. Or maybe they want to tell their life story. Either way, they usually like the dog and pony show.

At almost any contested sentencing, I like to spend a lot of time on my Sentencing Memorandum. See §2:151 Form 2-111.

The idea usually is to personalize the Client. I want my Sentencing Memorandum to be in the Sentencing Judge's hands a week or at least days prior to the sentencing. I want the proposals and my positive view of the Client planted like a seed in the judge's mind.

Attach to the Sentencing Memorandum a flood of letters of recommendation for your Client. They shouldn't be form letters, but they need to be personal. Especially effective if your Client faces a jail stay are letters from your client's children, if the children are old enough to write such a letter. Clear this with your Client first. I had a Federal drug case at sentencing once in which my Client's teenage daughter wrote a heartfelt plea to reduce her father's sentence. The Judge was obviously moved by the letter. He was lenient in his sentencing, and included in the sentence that my client be required to carry the letter with him and re-read it frequently.

§2:151 FORM 2-111 Sentencing Memorandum—Theft

STATE OF MAINE   SUPERIOR COURT
CUMBERLAND, ss.   PORTLAND
                                        DOCKET NO.CR-0*-****

STATE OF MAINE,)	
)	
)	
)	**DEFENDANT'S SENTENCING**
v.)	**MEMORANDUM**
)	
DIANA P,)	
)	
Defendant)	
)	

I. INTRODUCTION

Diana P faces one count of Theft by Unauthorized Taking or Transfer, a Class C felony.[4] It is expected that she will plead guilty to the same on May 14, 2007. Counsel and ADA _____ have agreed upon a 90 day cap for incarceration.

The purpose of this memorandum is two-fold. First, its primary goal is to assist the Court in arriving at a just sentence for Diana P, one that neither diminishes the severity of the offense for which she is charged, nor promotes disrespect for the law. At the same time, Counsel will identify significant mitigating and extenuating facts as they relate to Diana, the individual, which must be considered to arrive at a "just individualization of sentence(s)." 17-A M.R.S.A. §1151(6). Second, Counsel hopes to provide a framework for the kind of sentence that will serve society's interest in punishment, as well as enable Diana to continue as a valuable member of the community.

II. FACTUAL BACKGROUND

Diana P was born in New York and lived there until she was 9 years old when her mother moved her to New Jersey. Unfortunately, Diana did not experience the normal healthy childhood one might expect. Rather, she suffered extreme abuse in the form of molestation by her Father.

Despite possessing obvious talent and intelligence, the incest abuse took its toll. Diana survived her first suicide attempt her senior year of high school. She graduated from Academy of the Holy Angel despite suffering serious mental anguish concerning her Father's abuse of her. She went on to Upsala College in New Jersey where she graduated in 1982 with Bachelor Degrees in History and Political Science, as well as a minor in Economics. Diana was an emotional mess, despite her high level of intellectual functioning. She was hospitalized after surviving another suicide attempt.

After her release, she held down various jobs in New York's fashion district, including one at Lord and Taylor where she was selected for their management training program. Unfortunately, after college Diana started abusing drugs and alcohol to dull her emotional pain. In 1985, she was heavily abusing cocaine when she plead guilty of petit larceny. In New York, petit larceny is a Class A misdemeanor, for which Diana received and successfully served one year probation. Exhibit 1, Conviction Record and Criminal Code.[5] This misdemeanor is Diana's only prior criminal activity. The conviction is 22 years old. Diana has never done any jail time.

Diana continued abusing drugs and alcohol to self medicate for her emotional trauma until she hit bottom in 1990. She then joined various support groups and has been clean and sober since 1991.

Diana went on to receive an MBA from New York University. Diana had many prestigious and high level jobs after receiving her MBA, including a stint as the Marketing Director for the Technology Division of the Federal Reserve Bank. To acquire the position with the Federal Reserve Bank, Diana's criminal record was examined, she had to pass a lie detector test, and she was subjected to drug screening. Diana was able to put her past behind her, and she worked for the Federal Reserve Bank for a year until her step-father was diagnosed with cancer.

Diana quit her job with the Federal Reserve Bank to move to Limington, Maine to live with her mother and to help with her step-father's care. Diana quickly became a productive member of her new community. She worked at TriCounty Mental Health until it lost its funding. From there, she took a position at the Family Planning Association of Maine. She spent time working at Maine Public Broadcasting Network, and finally ended up at the Animal Refuge League (ARL) where she was the Executive Director until June 2006.

Counsel expects that Diana will admit that in May and June of 2006, that she directed ARL's payroll processor, Advantage Payroll Services, to overpay her $5,480.78. Also, in May 2006, Diana transferred $547.78 from ARL's checking account to her personal account. Diana will admit to improperly transferring these funds. She will pay full restitution, both for the amount misappropriated as well as the amount ARL spent on a financial audit.

---

[4]   17-A M.R.S.A. §353

[5]   Counsel has enclosed as Exhibit 1, the Conviction Record. The Code number for the offense committed, which is attached, suggests the conviction was dropped to the misdemeanor of petit larceny.

III. THE GENERALLY RECOGNIZED PURPOSES OF SENTENCING

The Maine Legislature has provided a framework of appropriate consideration in sentencing any criminal defendant.[6] The Court must consider all statutory objectives, which can generally be grouped into one of two categories: the nature of the offense and the background nature of the offender. While the Court must consider the deterrent effect of its sentence, 17-A M.R.S.A. §1151(1), as well as impose a sentence that does not diminish the seriousness of the offense, this Court must also individualize the basic period of incarceration. *State v. Hewey*, 622 A.2d 1151 (Me. 1993).

In the three-step process of sentencing, the trial court first determines the basic period of incarceration, by considering the particular nature and seriousness of the offense as committed by the offender. 17 M.R.S.A. §1252(c)(1); *State v. Hewey, supra*; *State v. Kehling*, 601 A.2d 620, 625 (Me. 1991). The mere classification of the charged offense does not automatically invoke the selection of the statutory maximum sentence as the basic period of incarceration. *State v. Gosselin*, 600 A.2d 1108, 1110 (Me. 1991). In evaluating the nature and seriousness of the criminal conduct to determine the basic period of incarceration the Court should review sentences imposed for similar conduct of other offenders convicted of offenses within the same classification. *State v. Corbett*, 617 A.2d 222, 224 (Me. 1992). The conduct is then placed "on a continuum for each type of offense to determine which act justifies the impositions of the most extreme punishment." *Id.*

A. Step 1: The Basic Period of Incarceration From Sentencing Data

Sentencing data is hard to come by in Maine. Counsel's office has tried to find reasonable, recent examples of Class C theft sentencing.

The Cumberland County case of *State v. Karnes*, CR-05-857 is relevant. *See* Exhibit 2, *State v. Karnes*, Judgment and Committment In that case, the Defendant was convicted of Negotiating a Worthless Instrument (Class C), and Theft (Class C). The Defendant was ordered to pay $5,000 in restitution and sentenced to 18 months, all but 30 days suspended, two years of probation. The Defendant in *Karnes* had a prior theft history. In that case, the Court took into consideration that Mr. Karnes' drug abuse had on his decision making, and his sentence was reduced due to his assertion that he would complete drug rehabilitation.[7]

The Defendant in *State v. Edwards*, CR-06-1545, was also convicted of Class C Theft by Unauthorized Taking. That Defendant was sentenced to only 7 days imprisonment and no probation. *See* Exhibit 3, *State v. Edwards*, Judgment and Commitment. *State v. Janelle Johnston*, (CR-05-854), also suggests that a short, straight time sentence may be appropriate for this type of crime. In *Johnston*, the Defendant was convicted of Class C Theft, and was given a straight sentence of 35 days with no probation. Exhibit 4, *State v. Johnston*, Judgment and Commitment.

The *Edwards* and *Johnston* matters suggest that the basic period of incarceration can be quite low for a Class C Theft. In this case, Counsel is suggesting that the Court actually load the Defendant with probation and time hanging over her head, and suggest a basic period of incarceration of one year as a result.

---

[6] 17-A M.R.S.A. §1151 provides as follows:

The general purposes of the provisions of this part are:

1. To prevent crime through the deterrent effect of sentences, the rehabilitation of convicted persons, and the restraint of convicted persons when required in the interest of public safety;
2. To encourage restitution in all cases in which the victim can be compensated and other purposes of sentencing can be appropriately served;
3. To minimize correctional experiences which serve to promote further criminality;
4. To give fair warning of the nature of the sentences that may be imposed on the conviction of a crime;
5. To eliminate inequalities in sentences that are unrelated to legitimate criminological goals;
6. To encourage differentiation among offenders with a view to a just individualization of sentences;
7. To promote the development of correctional programs which elicit the cooperation of convicted person; and
8. To permit sentences that do not diminish the gravity of offenses, with reference to the factors, among other, of;
    A. The age of the victim; and
    B. The selection by the defendant of the person against whom the crime was committed or of the property that was damaged or otherwise affected by the crime because of the race, color, religion, sex, ancestry, national origin, physical or mental disability or sexual orientation of that person or of the owner or occupant of that property.

[7] Information about the Karnes case was obtained from his Attorney, Vanessa Bartlett.

B.   Step 2: Matters of Mitigating and Extenuation Suggests That A Properly Individualized Sentence Will Include Minimal Incarceration

The second step in the sentencing process is to individualize the basic period of incarceration to determine the maximum period of incarceration based upon those factors peculiar to the Defendant. *State v. Hewey, supra* at 1154. In determining the maximum period of incarceration, the Court is to consider factors in aggravation and in mitigation that are appropriate to the case at hand.

i.   Aggravating Factors

Diana has one prior charge of petit larceny, a misdemeanor that occurred over 20 years before the incident at the Animal Refuge League. This prior indiscretion should not serve as a significant aggravating factor for this Court.

ii.   Mitigating Factors

Diana is a responsible member of society who has strong ties to friends and family in the community. She is a vital and concerned parent who is actively involved with her son, Joe's, education. This involvement is especially important because Joe has been diagnosed with ADHD, a condition that that makes it difficult for children to control their behavior. This interferes with Joe's ability to thrive in a traditional school setting. To that end, Diana has been in close contact with Joe's school and has been a voracious advocate for Joe when his needs are not being met. Barbara Harding Loux, a Social Worker at Joe's school, has written a letter to the Court concerning Diana at Exhibit 5. Joe's father has had little involvement in Joe's upbringing, as he lives out-of-state. Joe tried to live with his father in New York recently, but his father was unable to care for Joe because he suffers from severe liver problems. This leaves Diana as Joe's primary caregiver. It is certain that Joe will suffer emotionally, as well as scholastically, if Diana is removed from his life for any length of time.

Although it is reasonable to assume that any child would suffer at the incarceration of a parent, a child with ADHD is extremely vulnerable to the havoc wrecked by even slight transitions. Therefore, there is no doubt that Joe will be an unintended victim of any time Diana spends incarcerated.

iii. Matters in Extenuation

Numerous circumstances surrounding the commission of this offense do not amount to a defense or mitigation but are appropriate sentencing factors.

Diana suffered severe physical and emotional trauma a result of experiencing devestating and prolonged sexual and emotional abuse during her childhood. She was diagnosed with Post Traumatic Stress Disorder (PTSD), as well as a major depressive disorder, and has been hospitalized repeatedly because of her condition. Diana continues to battle this extreme mental anguish and is currently seeing Dr. Eliot Gruen for medication maintenance. Dr. Gruen notes that Diana suffers from PTSD and major depression, and that she takes medication and keeps appointments as directed. Exhibit 6, Dr. Gruen letter. She also regularly sees Ida O'Donnell, LCSW, who provides Diana with weekly psychotherapy treatment to manage and decrease her anxiety and depression.

It is the opinion of Ms. O'Donnell, as evidenced by her letter, Exhibit 7, that Diana's theft was a symptom of her stressful work environment triggering her PTSD symptoms. Diana was continuously humiliated and undermined by the Board of Directors of the ARL, which triggered survival functions of fight, flee, or freeze. Initially Diana fought the Board by trying to please it. When that did not work, she felt trapped and fought by stealing. Diana acted inappropriately by taking money, however, it was the way she felt she could regain control and feel safe. This is no excuse for her behavior, but rather an explanation of why she acted the way she did in her situation. This was not a thoughtfully crafted response to her position, but a base emotional response to her feeling threatened.

The community support for Diana is overwhelming. Exhibits 5-31 are all letters written in support of Diana and attesting to her good character. Such support suggests that Diana's likelihood of re-offending is low.

iv.   Conclusion Regarding Step 2

Diana's case involves matters in mitigation and extenuation that greatly outweigh any aggravating factors. These matters suggest that Diana should not be imprisoned for long, but should repay her debt to the community by being allowed to continue to work in the community. Far more harm will be done, to both Diana and her son, if Diana is incarcerated, than will occur if she spends no time in prison.

C. Step 3: Determining the Suspended Sentence and Probation

i. The Need For Incapacitation

It must be acknowledged that the Court will, and should, give significant consideration to the seriousness of the offense, the deterrent effect of the sentence, and a concern for public safety. 17-A M.R.S.A. §1151(1). While these factors are important, they are not determinative. They must be balanced with the other equally important purposes of sentencing. This is a situation where incapacitation will not meet the goals of either general or specific (individual) deterrence.

Jail-oriented sentencing is a frequent response to serious criminal offenses. All too often, jail sentences are imposed and society turns its back to the defendant and the condition of the prison system that she enters. While incarceration satisfies the public's thirst for retribution and, at least facially, the interest in public safety, the long term consequences of this type of sentencing on the individual and, eventually, the community, is strongly questioned.

Sentencing advocates and others involved in the failure of the current system have begun to seriously question whether incarceration is necessary to protect society where there is no history of violence. The reality of jail sentences is stark. A jail sentence can have a significant adverse impact on both the individual and society. Over thirty years ago the President's Commission on Law Enforcement and Administration of Justice warned that:

> Experts are increasingly coming to feel that the conditions under which many offenders are handled, particularly in institutions, are often a *positive deterrent to rehabilitation.*

> Life in many institutions is at best baron and futile, at worst unspeakably brutal and degrading. To be sure, the offenders in such institutions are incapacitated from committing further crimes while serving their sentence, but the conditions in which they live are the poorest possible preparation for their successful reentry into society, and often merely reinforce in them a pattern of manipulation or destructiveness.

The Challenge of Crime in a Free Society, 159 (1967) (emphasis added). Jail life carries with it the undertones of violence, peer pressure for acceptance of criminality and loss of self esteem which can turn a person not predisposed towards crime when she came into the system more likely to commit crime when she comes out. This will be especially damaging to Diana who already suffers from severe emotional distress. If incarcerated, she will be literally trapped, which will likely trigger the symptoms of her PTSD and cause her further psychological trauma. These factors must also be given serious consideration.

Diana is a first-time felony offender. Reliance on jail as a first choice sentence may fulfill the need for a retribution, but little else.

Moreover, there is little to suggest that Diana will re-offend without significant incarceration. The harshness of our jail system and the risk that it creates for Diana is real. While it does not negate the seriousness of the crime, it does substantially reduce the recognized need for incarceration to accomplish either rehabilitation or public safety.

ii. The Role of Deterrence

Deterrence as a sentencing rationale is subject to limitation. As the First Circuit states:

> The court's duty to "individualize" the sentence simply means that, whatever the judge's thoughts as to the deterrent value of a jail sentence, he must in every case reexamine and measure that view against the relevant facts and other important goals such as the offender's rehabilitation. Having done so, the district judge must finally decide what factors, or mix of factors, carry the day.

United States v. Foss, 501 F.2d 522, 528 (1st Cir. 1974). A balance clearly needs to be struck. The principle of limiting the role of deterrence is also set forth in the *American Bar Association Standards for Criminal Justice, Alternatives and Procedures*, where in the introduction to Chapter 18 it states that "[n]o one person or purpose, standing alone, can satisfactorily supply a comprehensive theory of punishment." The ABA standards correctly recognize that punishment should not be its own justification. *Id.*

The Court is urged not to focus its sentencing formulation on issues of general deterrence and protection of society as its singular guide-post in arriving at a just sentence for Diana: "Exclusive reliance upon these two general purposes of sentencing (deterrence and protection of society) will always lead inexorably to the maximum sentence and would negate the other purposes identified by the legislature." See, *State v. Saunders*, No. AD 82-43 (Me. App. Div., Oct. 18, 1983).

iii. The Proposal

A careful analysis of the aggravating and mitigating factors in this case supports a balancing of competing goals with a strong preference toward minimizing Diana's jail experience. The proposals to this Court take into account the severity of the criminal conduct, but also recognize the need for a just sentence. It is proposed that this Court sentence Diana P to the following: Theft by Unauthorized Taking (Class C), a sentence of one year, all but three days suspended, two years probation, 200 hours community service, and restitution of the money taken as well as an extra sum for the ARL to conduct an independent audit. This restitution should be paid within one week of sentencing.

The unsuspended sentence is designed as a shock sentence. Diana is a first-time felony offender and has never been incarcerated. She is a contributing member of the community. She is the caring and supportive mother of a son who has special needs and who's life will be significantly disrupted with grave consequences if Diana is jailed for a significant amount of time.

Justice must be tempered with mercy and an opportunity for one to right the wrongs of the past. Counsel urges the Court to weigh Diana's indiscretions against a personal history which strongly suggests the conclusion that the crime will never be repeated again. The sentence suggested herein would include a long period of probation and a significant amount of community service so as to require Diana to walk a straight and narrow path, as she had in the past, or to be incarcerated.

For the reasons set forth above, Counsel respectfully requests the Court sentence Diana P in accordance with the proposal set forth in this Memorandum.

Dated this the _____ day of _____ 20__, in Portland, Maine.

Respectfully submitted,

_____
Timothy E. Zerillo
Attorney for Defendant
ZERILLO LAW FIRM, LLC

§2:152   Sentencing Hearing

While I like to flood a Sentencing Memorandum with character letters, I like to limit my speakers at sentencing. Three or four short speakers plus my client is usually the most I want. I don't want the judge getting bored and the topic losing its effectiveness.

Don't be afraid to cut out a speaker who really wants to speak or to not include someone you would be expected to present. The litmus test is whether they fit your sentencing theme, and whether their presentation is likely to enhance your argument or not.

Finally, clear whatever your Client is going to say ahead of time. I urge Clients to write their statement down and for me to review it and approve it before a word is said. I don't want them going off the cuff in their sentencing. There is no winging it allowed.

Once I lost a trial on a sexual abuse of a minor case. The jury was out for two days on the issue of whether my client was aware the victim was 15 at the time they had sex. It was a close case that we ultimately lost, and it hurt.

My client's problem, in part, was that he was extremely arrogant. Although he hadn't taken the stand at trial, he was chomping at the bit to tell his story at sentencing. His story, however, was the same story the jury rejected—that he didn't know the victim's age.

I helped him write a statement to read to the court. It set a tone that allowed him to accept responsibility for his actions, and preserve appellate rights that he didn't do it.

At the sentencing, after several hours of the dog and pony show, my client stood to read our prepared statement. When I saw him get out his papers to read from, I noticed him pull out a different statement. I asked for a recess and tried to talk him out of reading his new statement—in which he spent 8 pages describing the victim as an under-aged lying whore.

He told me to pound sand. With all the venom he could muster at sentencing, he blasted the victim for 15 minutes. He did not do well at sentencing. I always tell my clients that story when they want to tell the truth about the victim to the sentencing judge.

§2:153   Get Creative

I urge you to think outside the box at sentencing as well. In all likelihood you are not subject to the traditional rules of evidence. Go crazy with creativity in both your presentation and proposals.

I was once handling a case in the York County Superior Court in Maine with a friend. We represented joint defendants in a felony case related to the molestation of lobster traps. Yes, that is the type of case we actually have in Maine.

As you probably know, lobstering is big business in Maine. There are constantly turf wars without turf, where the boundaries of the premier lobstering locations are fought over, year after year. Recently, there was a shooting over lobster traps in Downeast Maine. The jury acquitted the Defendant.

In this case, there had been a lobstering sting with the local game warden. Our clients felt betrayed by him, and it drove them out of a multi-generational family business.

In this case, our clients cut a lot of traps, and caused over $100,000 in damages. My friend and I took over the case from another attorney, got the felonies dropped down to misdemeanors, and received an agreed upon disposition on everything but a two-day jail sentence the prosecutor wanted. So we decided to have a sentencing.

I know what you're saying—two days in jail, who cares? Two days was everything to these people and their families. They really detested the idea of even one second of incarceration. It was also important to the victims, who were very vocal.

I spent time preparing my sentencing argument, drafting my Sentencing Memorandum, and preparing to pontificate at sentencing related to my client's liberty interest even over the two days in jail.

On the morning of Sentencing, in walks my friend. He walks in with the arresting Game Warden at his side. Turns out, my friend's sentencing preparation involved contacting the arresting officer to ask him if he thought our Co-Defendants should serve the two days. Interestingly, the Game Warden didn't think a jail stay was necessary. He told the Judge his reasons and spoke on the Defendant's behalf as a character witness at sentencing.

Our clients didn't get the two days—they walked out that morning. I think it had less to do with my pontificating and preparation of a polished sentencing memorandum then it had to do with my friend thinking outside the box and calling the arresting officer as our witness, however. Get creative.

CHAPTER 3

ASSAULT/BATTERY

Assault (or battery as the crime is called in many jurisdictions) comes in all shapes and sizes. These range from a bloody beating to merely offensive bodily contact without injuries. The domestic assault has taken on special significance in the criminal defender's world. Usually misdemeanors, the consequences of these assaults are more significant than one might expect. This chapter is designed to show you some ways to handle the various factual scenarios you might encounter.

ASSAULT/BATTERY

ASSAULT/BATTERY

(This page intentionally left blank.)

I.   SIMPLE ASSAULT/BATTERY

A. Elements and Common Scenarios

§3:01   The Elements

In Maine, where I practice, an assault occurs if the defendant (1) intentionally, knowingly, or recklessly (2) causes bodily injury or offensive physical contact to another person. 17-A Maine Crim. Code §207(1). In many other states, this crime is called battery.

In most jurisdictions, a simple assault (or battery) means that the victim suffered no permanent injuries and that a dangerous weapon was not used. It also means in most jurisdictions that the parties to the assault were not family or household members or former sexual partners. In many ways, the simple assault is the easiest assault to defend.

§3:02   The Bar Fight

Common with simple assaults (like many crimes) are alcohol and drug use among the combatants. A typical situation is the bar fight. The client comes to you charged with a simple assault. He was in a bar, and he sees some guy walk up to his girlfriend on the dance floor and ask for a dance. Your client, being chivalrous and marking his territory, approaches. Chivalry turns to hostility and a brawl ensues with your guy charged.

§3:03   The Self Defense Fight

Another common scenario is the self defense fight. Your client, a male in his early twenties, is out with friends from high school. They run into people they knew from high school who didn't like them then or now. Words are exchanged, and then they meet like the Jets and the Sharks in the parking lot of the bar. Your guy ends up charged because the police believe him to be the aggressor.

[§§3:04-3:09 Reserved]

B. Strategies and Tactics

§3:10   Interviewing Your Client

In the typical simple assault case, it is important to establish one of the following:
- Your client was not the aggressor,
- Your client and the victim were mutual combatants, or
- Your client was defending himself or herself or others.

To do this, you need to focus your initial questioning on the background between the client and the alleged victim. Were they long-time enemies? Had they threatened each other before? Had they fought before? Had there been threats against a loved one?

§3:11   Self Defense

The self defense theory is one of the more commonly and effectively used theories in a simple assault case. Centuries old, self defense theory allows for a person to reasonably defend himself or herself against physical harm. The reasonableness of the perceived harm and the reasonableness of the force used are generally the appropriate questions in a self defense case.

While all jurisdictions are different, there are two questions to ask yourself when evaluating a self defense case:
- Did your client have a reasonable belief that the circumstances required the use of force?
- Was the use of force required to prevent the client from suffering bodily harm? In other words, was the use of force the only option?

ASSAULT/BATTERY

Imagine a road rage incident. A man passes another man in his car. The man who was passed, speeds up to make the passing difficult. After finally completing the pass, the passing car operator gets out of his vehicle and runs at the driver of the other vehicle. If the driver of the passed vehicle gets out and beats the hell out of the other driver, can he win on a self defense theory?

It would be difficult. He has the opportunity to drive away. The circumstances did not require the use of force, but he used force anyway.

That is not to say you shouldn't attempt a self defense case that's weak. Sometimes it's all you have.

A good self defense case on the other hand, can save your client. The key is to establish the reasonableness of the use of force and the amount of force used. To do so properly, you need to establish the relationship and history of the parties. If someone knows that the person your client assaulted has a history of violence, then the justification for your client's use of force becomes much more reasonable.

§3:12   Defense of Others

Defense of others operates along the same line as self defense. The two questions to ask yourself when evaluating a defense of others case are:

- Did your client have a reasonable belief that the circumstances required the use of force?
- Was the use of force required to prevent another person from suffering bodily harm?

You can use this theory in creative ways as well. My associate had a case in which a couple was staying in a hotel on a long weekend. They got drunk and went back to their hotel where they ended up in an argument. The alleged victim said she was leaving. She was going to take the car and drive home that night. In a struggle for the keys, the client punched the alleged victim in the nose. The client called 911 in his stupor and told the operator (and the police later) that he struck the alleged victim.

My associate came to me saying, what can I do with this case? I thought about it a bit and said "Why don't you consider a defense of others as a theory?" If she drove, she could have killed herself or someone else. The police could testify as to how drunk the couple was. Our client needed to physically stop her from driving and injuring someone else.

Now, I realize this isn't the greatest defense of others case. The point, however, is that it gives us something to talk about. It may even allow for a little jury nullification to be mixed in, which never hurts a defendant.

§3:13   Defense of Premises

Defense of premises is another useful defense theory. Similar to other self defense and defense of others, the use of force must be necessary to protect the premises and the amount of force used must be reasonable.

I once handled an appeal to the Maine Supreme Court in the case of a dispute between neighbors. One neighbor came onto my client's land while having words with him. My client drew his weapon and threatened to shoot the neighbor. At trial, the request for a defense of premises instruction was denied. We won on appeal on that issue.

Again, your jurisdiction may be different. That said, if you have a criminal trespass on your client's land in which your client is charged with an assault, consider a defense of premises theory. If your client used non-deadly force to prevent or terminate a criminal trespass, that force may very well be justified.

§3:14   Lack of Injuries to Victim

Lack of injuries to the victim is an often overlooked area of inquiry in the simple assault case. The reason is usually that nearly all (if not all) jurisdictions allow proof of assault to be made by a mere showing of something like offensive bodily contact.

While offensive bodily contact may be proven easily with allegations of something like a shove, it doesn't mean a jury will like it. In fact, in many cases, lack of injuries becomes a nullification issue.

If you have a case involving minimal force, like a shove, make sure to bring lack of injury up in cross-examination. Ask questions about whether the victim sought medical treatment for the shove, and so on. Your sarcasm may ring true to the jurors who might give you nullification votes in the jury room.

§3:15   Therapeutic Issues

Like nearly all criminal cases, getting your client involved in therapy at the outset is an important thing to do. Many clients will not be receptive to this. I tell every client that his case will proceed along two different tracks at the same time. In the first track, we are contesting every issue, filing motions, and making arguments about the government's lack of a case. In the second track, we are preparing for negotiations with the government attorney and arguments at sentencing, if necessary.

In a simple assault matter, an anger management program is probably the best therapeutic intervention. Find a local provider who deals with anger issues. I prefer sessions that are not in a group setting to make sure privilege is preserved.

Have your client execute releases for the provider's records. After a couple of months of treatment, reach out to the provider. Usually, what you are looking for is a letter indicating the amount of treatment the client has gone through, the client's diligence in treatment, and a prognosis. You can then pull this letter out during negotiations with the prosecutor and/or during sentencing, as you see fit.

Many therapists will have no idea what you are looking for. Let them know when the client begins treatment what would help the client.

[§§3:16-3:19 Reserved]

C. Trial Themes

§3:20   Mutual Combatants

The mutual combatants theme is one I like to exploit in a simple assault case. It is a hybrid of self defense and a nullification argument. It also, in some jurisdictions, could be a consent defense.

The mutual combatants argument is really best reserved for the bar fight type of situation. For example, two guys really despise each other. They've hated each other since high school. This is a case of long time bad blood.

They meet out at a bar, and decide they will finally settle their disagreements in the parking lot. They square off. One fighter is more proficient, and the feud ends with the other fighter bloody in the parking lot. Often, the prize for the winner is an assault charge.

Mutual combatants is generally a nullification argument. Jurors don't like charges in this type of situation. Both guys squared up. Why should the better fighter get charged and convicted? Make sure to point out that the government didn't prosecute the loser.

§3:21   Defense of Others

In a simple assault, defense of others can often be raised, but rarely is. Imagine the typical fight over a woman in a bar. Let's say a young lady is dancing on the dance floor while her boyfriend watches. Another young man walks up to her, whispers something in her ear and starts to dance with her, quite aggressively. The client jumps in and punches the wanna-be Casanova in the face.

This situation could certainly develop into a good defense of others case. After all, the girlfriend couldn't get away from this guy. Perhaps what was whispered in her ear was rude. She might have perceived it as threatening. Defense of others in this context might provide a defense to the punch in the face.

§3:22   Size of Victim

Sometimes the size of the alleged victim provides good defense fodder as well. Juries react viscerally to people's size and shape. I have had a few cases where the alleged victim is oversized and my client undersized. In reality, obviously, this doesn't preclude an assault. In fact, what we know about Napoleonic Complexes probably would support an assault in many instances. That said, juries will sometimes eat this theory up. They look at a hulk of an alleged victim and they discredit his (or her) victimhood. Use that to your advantage.

ASSAULT/BATTERY

ASSAULT/BATTERY

§3:23 Hotheaded Victim

The hotheaded alleged victim can be very useful. This is why it is so important that you find out all you can about the alleged victim in your investigation. Have your investigator ask around. Does the alleged victim have a temper? Does he get into fights often? Is he easily flustered? An alleged victim who fights all the time can usually be easily baited on the stand. Further, the victim's temper explains why your client had reason to fear him or her, and folds in nicely to your self defense theory.

[§§3:24-3:29 Reserved]

D. Trial

§3:30 Jury Selection

While many of you have the right to individual voir dire in jury selection, in Maine, we do not. Like several jurisdictions, Maine has a system of excluding jurors, rather than including them. Therefore, I will not spend a tremendous amount of time on jury selection, since the rules vary so much by location.

Jury selection often forces you to rely on stereotypes. I don't like to accept stereotypes about anyone. They are often wrong and lead to prejudices. That said, with limited jury selection, stereotypes and a little biographical information are often all you have.

For example, I don't like teachers in assault cases. Teachers generally require order and respect a rule of law. In many assault cases, I am arguing that the rule that we don't hit other people doesn't apply to the facts of my case.

Generally, in a simple assault case of a bar fight, I like blue collar men and women. Manly guys. Macho guys. Women who like macho men. Women you could picture on the back of a motorcycle.

If I look at a potential juror and think there's a chance that the juror has never been in a physical fight, then he or she is out.

I'll give you an example. While I was in law school, my wife and I lived in Boston. After a long night out, we filed out of a local watering hole near the Boston Garden. In the crowd to get out the door, my wife was cut off by another woman. My wife muttered something about this woman to me.

The woman apparently heard what my wife said, because by the time we were out in the street, the woman grabbed my wife by the hair and started dragging her on her back down the road. I quickly extracted my wife from that situation, as she was helpless, like a turtle on its back.

Now, I certainly don't want to be married to the woman who grabbed my wife by the hair. I do want her on my assault jury, however.

§3:31 Sample Opening Statement—Mutual Combatants

Let's imagine, you have a bar fight case. I would probably hit some of the following notes in opening:

Good afternoon, members of the jury, my name is Tim Zerillo and it's a pleasure to represent Bobby Brawler in this assault case the State has brought against him.

When people go out at night after a hard day of work, they are often looking for something to drink and to blow off some steam. The same thing happened to my client on February 23, 2012 at the Drink-2-Much Tavern. He wasn't out to hurt anyone, just out for a good time with some friends.

But then he met Wendell Whiner. Let me tell you, the history between Bobby and Mr. Whiner goes back to High School. The evidence will show that they hated each other then and they hate each other now.

Well, after a couple of beers, words were exchanged. Both guys made a decision. They both decided to go out in the parking lot and settle this long time animosity between them once and for all.

The evidence will show that neither one of them was forced into that parking lot. The evidence will show that they both went there voluntarily because they hated each other.

In that fight, Bobby definitely got the better of Mr. Whiner, but punches were thrown by both sides. Of course, the police pursued charges against the winner of the fight only, and that is why we are here talking to you today.

Now, let's talk about a term you've all heard before: reasonable doubt....

For general tips on opening statements and sample language about the presumption of innocence and burden of proof, see Ch.2.

§3:32 Sample Cross-Examination of Disinterested Witness to Fight

With bar fight assaults, be sure to continue the mutual combatants theme. Even with an uninterested bystander witness, the same themes can be continued.

For tips on effective cross-examination, see Ch. 2.

Q. You were a witness to the fight in the parking lot?
A. Yes.
Q. You just testified that you witnessed my Client strike Mr. Whiner?
A. Yes, I did.
Q. Mr. Whiner wasn't on the ground when he was struck, was he?
A. No, he was standing.
Q. He was standing up, good. Was he standing up with his back toward my Client when he was struck?
A. No, he was facing him.
Q. Mr. Whiner was facing my Client when he was struck?
A. Yes.
Q. And Mr. Whiner's hands were up weren't they?
A. I'm not sure what you mean.
Q. His hands were up in a fighting stance weren't they?
A. Yes, like a boxer.
Q. Sometimes this is called squaring off. Have you ever heard that term before?
A. I believe so.
Q. Do you take squaring off to mean that 2 parties are facing each other in a fighting stance to get ready to fight?
A. Yes, that's what I think it means.
Q. And my Client and Mr. Whiner were squaring off here.
A. Yes.
Q. When the fight began, you saw that my Client got the better of Mr. Whiner?
A. He sure did.
Q. But Mr. Whiner threw punches at him, didn't he?
A. He tried to.
Q. Its true that you didn't know my Client or Mr. Whiner before this event, did you?
A. That's true.
Q. You don't know whether Mr. Whiner threatened my Client prior to the fight, do you?
A. No.
Q. You don't know if Mr. Whiner threatened my Client's wife prior to the fight, do you?
A. I do not.

§3:33   Sample Cross-Examination of Arresting Officer

The arresting officer probably didn't see the fight and knows nothing about it. This is obviously not a complete cross-examination, but here are a few areas to consider.

For more tips on cross examining police officers, see Ch.2

Q. Officer Smiley, you've handled a number of assault arrests.
A. Hundreds.

Q. You have the capacity to make decisions about who you arrest and who you don't, based on your investigation, right?

A. That's right, if there's probable cause.

Q. What you learned here when you arrived on the scene was that there had been a fight between Mr. Whiner and my Client, correct?

A. Yes.

Q. You learned that Mr. Brawler got the better of Mr. Whiner in the fight?

A. True.

Q. You learned that from speaking to a bystander witness, and from speaking with Mr. Whiner, correct?

A. Yes.

Q. From those interviews you learned that both parties decided to fight outside in the parking lot.

A. Yes.

Q. They both squared off to fight each other?

A. Yes.

Q. Neither party had weapons?

A. Not that I know of.

Q. Neither party sucker punched the other.

A. Not that I know of.

Q. They faced each other and fought.

A. Yes.

Q. And my client won that fight?

A. Yes.

Q. Mr. Brawler didn't appear hurt, but Mr. Whiner was hurt?

A. I didn't see it, but I'd say yes.

Q. You didn't arrest Mr. Whiner did you?

A. No, Mr. Brawler wasn't injured.

Q. But you know that you don't need injuries to have an assault, you simply need harmful or offensive bodily contact, isn't that true?

A. Yes.

Q. You knew Mr. Whiner punched Mr. Brawler, right?

A. I was told that, yes.

Q. But you didn't arrest Mr. Whiner?

A. No, I didn't.

Q. And that was because Mr. Brawler won the fight and Mr. Whiner didn't.

A. That's not right.

Q. Of those hundreds of assault cases you've been involved in, in how many have you arrested the person who was beat up?

A. I don't know, but it has happened.

Q. Tell me what cases it has happened in, so I can look them up.

A. I can't think of any right now.

Q. You can't think of any?

A. No.

Q. Are they infrequent?

A. Yes.

Q. Would you say they are very infrequent?

A. Yes.

Q. Despite their infrequency, you still can't remember any of them?

A. Not at the moment.

Q. You don't know if Mr. Whiner threatened Mr. Brawler before the fight here, correct?

A. I don't know what was said between them.

Q. Something led them both out to that parking lot to mutually fight, but you don't know what that was, do you?

A. No.

§3:34   Sample Closing Argument

At closing, I suggest you direct the jury to the general unfairness of these proceedings as they relate to your client. Focus on the people in the jury room who really can help you out. People who have been in fights before, and who aren't afraid to acquit your guy.

Here are some ideas. For further closing argument tips, see Ch. 2.

There is only one reason we are in this Courtroom today. There is only one reason we are having this trial, and there is only one reason I am delivering this closing argument to you right now. That reason is this: my client was a better fighter then Mr. Whiner.

When two guys have a long term beef with each other, like these two did, if you put them in the same small town long enough, something's going to happen. They are like ping pong balls bouncing off each other in one of those lottery machines.

These two ping pong balls decided they were going to settle things. And they did. Mr. Brawler got the better of Mr. Whiner.

It wasn't unfair. There was no cheating involved. It was a fair fight in which Mr. Brawler prevailed.

His prize is that he got charged criminally. And Mr. Whiner supports this prosecution. He decided he didn't want their beef to end it in the parking lot; he's continuing it. And he hasn't been charged because he lost the fight.

Why would you punish the guy who won the fight? There seems to me a lot of this type of attitude in our country and our community now. A lot of do-overs. Mr. Whiner didn't win a fight he agreed to so he wants a do-over in court. This isn't a video game; this is a court of law. You need to tell Mr. Whiner there aren't any do-overs, and find my client not guilty.

For sample language for burden of proof and reasonable doubt arguments, see Ch. 2.

[§§3:35-3:39 Reserved]

II.   DOMESTIC ASSAULT/BATTERY

A. Elements and Common Scenarios

§3:40   The Elements

The domestic assault situation is given significant weight in this chapter because it has become such a commonly charged crime. The ramifications of this crime for gun owners are very significant. Further, domestic assault allegations are, unfortunately, often used as a lever to gain an advantage in family law proceedings.

Although the specifics vary from jurisdiction to jurisdiction, domestic assault (or battery) is typically defined as: 1) intentional or knowing, 2) harmful or offensive bodily contact, 3) with someone the defendant is in a domestic situation with. The domestic relationship has been broadened over the years, and generally now will include not only immediate family, but also boyfriends, girlfriends and former sexual partners.

§3:41   The Drunken Night Out

A very common scenario in the domestic assault context is the drunken night out that got out of hand. Fortunately, these often also involve reluctant alleged victims. A simple scenario I see repeated over and over again involves a Friday night of drinking out at the local bar and grill. There is dancing; there is frivolity; there is fun. Until our client gets a text message from an unknown number that is intercepted by his wife. The text says something like "Miss you hot stuff."

ASSAULT/BATTERY

Our client denies knowing who this text came from, but the alleged victim has her suspicions. Shouting turns into pushing, shoving, tears and a call to the police.

Almost inevitably this call will result in an arrest for our client, at least in my jurisdiction. The police are taught here, and elsewhere, to arrest if there is a suspicion of domestic assault. Probable cause has gone by the wayside when it comes to domestic assault arrests.

§3:42   The Child Custody Dispute

Another common scenario you will see is a child custody dispute. There's been a decision by one party to either divorce or file a paternity proceeding to establish child custody. In the family matter action there is an allegation of abuse. This allegation is generally followed up by a restraining order.

Many DV allegations are true. Many are grounded in partial truths, or exaggerations. Some are complete fabrications. Complete fabrications and the faking of injuries does occur. These are harder to deal with than a truthful allegation in many ways. In a fabrication case, the alleged victim usually knows what she or he is doing, and has fabricated some injuries and allegations before.

[§§3:43-3:49 Reserved]

B.   Strategies and Tactics

§3:50   Client Interview

When you first meet with your client, it's important to get an idea about the whole of the relationship with the alleged victim. Some defense practitioners focus way too much, in my opinion, on the incident that precipitated the arrest. Rather, as it should be in most criminal law cases, the focus needs to be on the whole person. That includes the relationship with the alleged victim.

Establish at the outset not only what occurred on the date of the incident, but whether other incidents between the parties might be helpful to your client's defense. Was the alleged victim, for example, ever violent with your client in the past? Did he or she have a drug or alcohol problem? Did the victim have volatile relationships with his or her children or parents? Does he or she have a criminal record?

Your client will want to tell you all of this, of course. I have a case right now that I am picking a jury for in several days as I write this. In that case, my client does not have a great defense to the assault itself, but he was quick to point out that the alleged victim has fabricated various tax records for her small business over the years, and that he had proof of the same. Whether I can get this into evidence during the cross examination remains to be seen, and might be difficult. In some cases I have gotten such evidence in, usually when the judge or prosecutor is asleep. Not that cheating on your taxes means you can't be a victim of an assault. It does mean that you will falsely swear to something that isn't true, which you can relate to the false swearing in the victim's statement. I have a nearly hopeless case in front of me. The taxes give me something to talk about.

§3:51   Consider Firearms

A domestic violence assault conviction will usually result in a lifetime prohibition of firearm possession. 18 U.S.C. §922 prohibits possession of a firearm by persons subject to domestic assault convictions, protection orders, felony convictions, and a variety of other disqualifications.

When I was President of the Maine Association of Criminal Defense Lawyers, it was brought to my attention that many practitioners, some of whom have been practicing for a significant amount of time, were getting drop downs from domestic violence assault misdemeanors to simple assault misdemeanors and assuming that this would get their client around the Federal firearms prohibition. That is not the case.

When you get a drop down from a domestic assault to a non-domestic simple assault, the Federal government can look beyond the conviction and prohibit your client from possessing firearms for the rest of his or her life. Not such a great deal for gun owners.

In Maine, there is a long tradition of hunting. Families hunt together, and pass the tradition from generation to generation. This may or may not be a concern where you live, but in every domestic assault case I have I find out whether firearms are an important part of my client's life. You need to be aware that the drop down that might look like a good plea bargain could prohibit your client from possessing firearms for the rest of his or her life. And if you don't warn the client in advance of the plea, you are surely looking at a post conviction review, and perhaps a legal malpractice suit.

There may be drop down pleas in your jurisdiction that will not offend federal firearms laws. You need to be careful about checking the elements and matching them to the federal statute. When in doubt, ask an experienced federal practitioner.

> **PRACTICE TIP: *Request dismissal of the domestic case***
>
> When you enter a plea to a drop down and are trying to avoid federal firearms implications, I have something else I like to do if I can. Ask the prosecutor to dismiss the old domestic case in its entirety. Then re-file the new complaint with the plea bargained charge. That way you have a new docket number and no mention of the alleged domestic victim.
>
> Additionally, restoration of rights statutes are available in some states. The National Association of Criminal Defense Lawyers has compiled a state-by-state resource that is worth looking at.

§3:52 Making the Victim Your Witness

The alleged victim will often quickly become a defense witness in domestic assault cases. In a case of the drunken night with the reluctant victim, the hazy light of day often leaves the alleged victim exiled from her or his loved one. This is one hell of a hangover. This alleged victim should be contacted immediately.

Be very careful here. If your jurisdiction allows you to record conversations with the alleged victim, do so. Make sure that you are not tampering with the victim. Make sure that you tell the victim that she or he does not need to speak with you and is free to end the call at any time. If you can, take the call on speaker phone and have a witness in the room with you. If you take a meeting with an alleged victim, bring a witness and/or a recording device if your local ethics rules allow. Even better, if your client can afford it, have a private investigator complete the contact with the alleged victim on your behalf.

If you proceed cautiously, however, the reluctant alleged victim can give you some amazing information. Often, you can get the victim to provide you with an exculpatory affidavit. Even if the victim supports the prosecution but is willing to talk to you, the victim will likely provide you with a statement that is inconsistent with the statement you will ultimately receive in discovery. As a result, if you can speak with the alleged victim without violating the law or your local ethics rules, it is well worth the effort.

§3:53 Are They Domestic Partners?

One often overlooked defense is whether the government can prove that the relationship between your client and the alleged victim is covered by your jurisdiction's domestic violence statute. Typically they must be family, household members, or past or present sexual partners. Don't skip this step, because it can sometimes be fruitful ground for inquiry. For example, imagine that your alleged victim was struck at a bar by her boyfriend. She gave a statement to the police that her boyfriend struck her, and he was arrested.

When the case comes to trial, the alleged victim doesn't show up for court and is not subpoenaed. The court, over Confrontation Clause and hearsay objections, allows into evidence her statements to the police that her boyfriend struck her.

Forgetting about the ultimate issue in the case, it seems to me that the State would not have been able to prove, in Maine at least, that this was a domestic assault. The fact that the defendant was the alleged victims "boyfriend," without more, does not make this a domestic situation automatically. The term "boyfriend" does not mean there is enough to make them family or household members, or former sexual partners.

§3:54 Therapeutic Intervention

Don't forget to get therapeutic intervention for your client early on. I always tell my clients that these cases proceed along two different tracks. In one track of the case, we are advocates arguing every element and disputing every fact. In the second track, we need the defendant to do the right things in the event that advocacy fails. One of the right things to do in the domestic assault situation is get counseling. Anger management programs and batterer's intervention programs should be taken in anticipation of plea bargaining. They should be done privately so that they are privileged in the event that you head to trial. That said, you want a fail-safe to plea bargain with or to use at sentencing in the event that negotiation fails.

§3:55   Use the Restraining Order Hearing to Your Benefit

Very often the domestic violence assault charge comes with a restraining order. The defendant looks at the restraining order as another problem to deal with. The skilled criminal defense practitioner looks at the restraining order as free discovery.

I would urge everyone involved in domestic violence practice (if they are not already doing so) to attend restraining order hearings on behalf of your client. Your client should plead the Fifth and not testify, in almost all cases. That said, you should have a right to full cross-examination of the alleged victim. Make sure the hearing is recorded (many of them are not unless you request it) and make sure to fully cross-examine the alleged victim on all facts. Come prepared with case law related to your right to cross-examine in the event that you have a judge who sniffs out that this is merely a deposition for you as opposed to a real defense of the restraining order. Getting the alleged victim under oath in these cases is a potential goldmine.

[§§3:56-3:59 Reserved]

C. Bail and No Contact Order Considerations

§3:60   Bail Modification Tactics

In my jurisdiction, a no contact order is automatically issued against the alleged victim when bail is entered. This is a major problem. Often this means that husbands are removed from their homes to have no contact with their wives or children. This sets up potential bail violations if the no contact provisions are not modified.

Getting that bail modification is not easy. I counsel patience to defendants while I do a preliminary investigation, and determine if the alleged victim will be cooperative with us. I may even do a little judge shopping. If the alleged victim is cooperative with us, I want to bring her or him to the bail hearing to speak to the court. If the victim has provided an affidavit, I may use that at the bail hearing as well.

Be prepared to argue an alternative. Have counseling set up and argue that contact in the course of counseling should be allowed, or telephone and written contact, or supervised contact. I try to get full contact and often get it, but if I can't, I try to have alternatives prepared.

One of the best tactics in these cases, if you have a very willing alleged victim and money to burn, is to get that victim separate counsel. This is a move I often use and find to be very effective.

Domestic violence prosecutors and victim witness advocates believe always that reluctant victims can be turned. When I am hired to represent an alleged victim who wants no part in the prosecution, I can usually shut the prosecution down. Shutting down the government can usually be accomplished by telling the prosecutor that the alleged victim will no longer talk. The victim will only go to court if lawfully served with an appropriate subpoena. And if all that happens, the victim's testimony may not serve the state well. Or the victim may try to plead the Fifth.

Of course, while these tactics are generally successful, they are not always winning strategies. Overzealous prosecutors can threaten human services or child protective services involvement for victims who are mothers of minor children. I have had alleged victims arrested on material witness warrants. These are, however, worst case scenarios. I explain these types of worst case scenarios when my client is deciding how to proceed.

I can also go in as counsel for the alleged victim at the bail hearing and say very powerfully to the judge that the defendant will not be able to exert undue influence to convince the alleged victim to refuse to cooperate with the prosecution if the no contact order is lifted because the alleged victim has independent counsel.

§3:61   Motions to Amend Bail

One way to protect your client is with a motion to amend bail. I always have a reluctant victim case or two in my office. Perhaps the alleged victim has a child and home with the defendant. Now, the bail conditions restrict their contact, directly or indirectly, and restrict the client's ability to go to his own home.

Prosecutors understand that when the alleged victim is uncooperative with the prosecution, they need to dole out as much short term pain as they can. That means opposing motions to amend bail. They are virtually always opposed in my jurisdiction.

Judges have a different motivation. First, as you probably have noticed, many judges believe everything they read in a police report. Some judges are critical of police reports and victim statements, but most are not. Many judges never had criminal experience in private practice, and if they did, it was acting for the Government. They respect law and order. The police represent the law, and whatever the police concluded must be accurate.

The even bigger problem with motions to modify contact and judges is the unspoken fear. That judge's unspoken fear is that he or she will modify bail, and the defendant will kill the alleged victim after bail is modified.

A similar thing happened in Maine a few years ago. A man on a domestic charge had his bail lowered so he could get released. After he was released, he killed the victim in the domestic assault case.

The judge who lowered his bail was hammered by the press. Of course, the judge had done the appropriate thing. The bail review was appropriate, and was right in the heartland for bails set for similar cases. The judge, who was a fine jurist, couldn't predict the future. He got lambasted for his inability to do so in the local media, however.

This is the unspoken concern of many judges, no matter how the alleged victim supports the bail modification. You have to acknowledge that unspoken fear as you approach your bail argument.

§3:62   FORM 3-10 Motion to Amend Bail

STATE OF MAINE	SUPERIOR COURT
CUMBERLAND, SS	LOCATION: PORTLAND
	DOCKET NO.

STATE OF MAINE,   )
)
Plaintiff   )
)   DEFENDANT'S MOTION TO
v.   )   AMEND BAIL
)
,   )
)
Defendant   )

NOW COMES the DEFENDANT, by and through Undersigned Counsel, and Moves to Amend Bail as follows:

1. On _____, bail for Defendant was set with the following conditions relevant to this motion:
   _____.
2. Defendant now seeks amendment of bail as follows: _____.
3. This request to amend bail is appropriate in this matter…
4. ADA _____ (objects/has no objection) to this motion.

WHEREFORE, Counsel respectfully requests this Court grant this Motion to Amend Bail.

Dated this _____ day of _____, 20___, at Portland, Maine.

                                        Respectfully submitted,

                                        _____

                                        Timothy E. Zerillo
                                        Attorney for Defendant
                                        ZERILLO LAW FIRM, LLC

§3:63   Sample Bail Modification Argument

Here is a bail modification argument I did in a domestic assault case. My client, a 100 percent disabled veteran with post-traumatic stress disorder, allegedly assaulted his wife in a drunken rage. He did a pretty good number on her, and she had visible injuries to her face.

The alleged victim supported our motion. We got an affidavit from her with the helpful parts of her testimony, and then made a recommendation for a lawyer. Her lawyer attended the bail argument with her. Here is a portion of my argument:

Mr. Defendant is a father of two children and a step-father of two more children. He owns a home in Barrington, New Hampshire that he purchased in 2007. He resided with his wife, children, and step-children in that home prior to the alleged assault.

He has been married to Mrs. Victim for one year. She is represented in this matter. Attorney McLawyer is here for her. She supports this Motion, and Attorney McLawyer will discuss why at the appropriate time.

Mr. Defendant is a 100% disabled veteran. He served 425 days in Iraq. He was hit by shrapnel in a firefight and suffered a traumatic brain injury. He received a purple heart and was honorably discharged. He suffers from PTSD.

Mr. Defendant and his family subsist on his disability benefits as a veteran as a result of his PTSD.

He is not just sitting around collecting disability, however. He is a senior in college at the University of New Hampshire, majoring in Business Administration.

That was, at least, the situation before the incident. Now he is homeless as a result of these bail conditions, living in a borrowed truck. He can't pay for another rental and afford to pay the mortgage on his disability income, so he is on the streets or in the borrowed truck. And I don't have to tell you how cold this winter has been, your Honor.

His criminal history is scant. He has a 2003 drunk driving conviction, and no history of FTA's I'm aware of.

Since the time of his arrest, Mr. Defendant began a voluntary anger management program, and hopes to get into a counseling arrangement with his wife if his bail is modified.

We are asking the court to eliminate the no contact provision between Mr. Defendant and Mrs. Victim. There are a number of arguments supporting this.

First, Mr. Defendant has defenses to the fact that an assault took place as charged. All that said, it seems clear that any argument between the parties may have been caused by a mixture of alcohol and medications. The no alcohol use and possession provision will prevent a repeat of the same incident. Mr. Defendant is a Marine, your Honor. He will abide by your Order, including an order prohibiting alcohol.

Second, when the no contact provision is removed, the bench may be concerned that the defendant will exert influence over the alleged victim. Here, we have the unusual case where the alleged victim has her own counsel. She can certainly make her voice heard to her lawyer about her feelings concerning this matter. She can ask questions of her lawyer and her lawyer is certainly capable of representing her position.

Third, it is extremely important that this court amend these conditions. This family is torn apart. This is an opportunity for this couple to begin counseling and get their lives put back together, if that's what the parties want.

Fourth, I want to note that the prosecution made an offer to the defendant on Friday, which he has turned down, involving probation conditions. In that offer, he would have had contact with his wife. It is disingenuous for the State to now argue that there should not be contact.

PRACTICE TIP: Ask the prosecutor for an offer you can refuse

Note the last argument. This is a trick I figured out a few years ago. In advance of the bail argument, but after I have filed my bail motion, I ask for an offer from the prosecutor. The prosecutor knows that what the client wants is contact with the alleged victim. What the prosecutor wants, however is a conviction. So, often the prosecutor will float an offer that involves contact between the defendant and the alleged victim through probation, or something along those lines.

I never intend to accept these offers. A first offer is rarely a good offer. I just want to use it at the bail argument. If it would be safe for the defendant to plead guilty and have contact with the victim, why can the prosecutor take the position that it isn't safe if the defendant doesn't plead guilty? Some judges are receptive to this argument.

You will win some of these bail arguments and lose some. The important thing is to make the argument. Argue passionately for your client. Even in a loss, a client who sees a passionate argument will appreciate it greatly. And you can win a lot of them too.

See §3:62 Form 3-10 Motion to Amend Bail.

[§§3:64-3:69 Reserved]

D. Confrontation Clause Issues

§3:70　In Domestic Violence Cases

Confrontation Clause issues can be bewildering. Ever since *Crawford v. Washington,* 541 U.S. 36, 53-54 (2004), was decided, trial courts have issued various and sometimes conflicting or inconsistent rulings determining what evidence is testimonial and what evidence isn't testimonial for Confrontation Clause purposes. Lawyers presenting these cases have not been given clear guidance as they try to determine what is testimonial and what isn't.

The Confrontation Clause has taken on significance in the domestic violence assault cases. A Confrontation Clause issue in many domestic violence cases is whether an emergency exists to render statements given by the victim and/or witnesses at the scene of the incident non-testimonial.

§3:71　The *Crawford* Case

The U.S. Supreme Court began the revival of Confrontation Clause jurisprudence in *Crawford.* Crawford had been convicted of assault while armed with a deadly weapon. A statement from Crawford's wife, who was a witness to the assault on a third party, was admitted at trial.

Prior to *Crawford,* the admission of an out-of-court statement by a witness not subject to cross-examination at trial hinged on the issue of the reliability of the statement. *Ohio v. Roberts,* 448 U.S. 56 (1980). The *Crawford* Court rejected the reliability standard, and determined that the Confrontation Clause should prevail. Ultimately, the *Crawford* Court found that the Confrontation Clause bars admission of testimonial statements of a witness who did not appear at trial unless he or she was unavailable to testify, and the defendant had a prior opportunity for cross-examination. The Court found that out-of-court testimony is permitted "only if the witness is demonstrably unable to testify in person." 541 U.S. at 59.

The *Crawford* decision left open the issue of what were testimonial and nontestimonial statements to trigger the Confrontation Clause. Two cases, decided two years later as companions, *Davis v. Washington* and *Hammon v. Indiana,* 547 U.S. 813 (2006), further muddied the waters.

§3:72　The *Davis* and *Hammon* Cases

Davis was charged with violating a domestic no-contact order after police responded to a 911 call from his girlfriend, Michelle McCottrey. While on the telephone, McCottrey identified Davis as her assailant, and told the operator that Davis was using his fists to beat her, and that he had left her residence moments earlier.

McCottrey did not testify at Davis' trial. The Government submitted the recording of her 911 call as evidence linking Davis to McCottrey's injuries. The Supreme Court of Washington State held that the 911 call was not a testimonial statement under the *Crawford* analysis.

Mr. Hammon was charged with domestic battery after police responded to a call from Mrs. Hammon. While being questioned, Mrs. Hammon told an officer that her husband had thrown her to the ground and beaten her. Mrs. Hammon did not testify at Mr. Hammon's trial. The arresting officer was put on the stand to describe Mrs. Hannon's statements on the night of the incident. The trial court allowed this testimony over objection, and the Supreme Court of Indiana affirmed.

In *Davis*, the Supreme Court held that statements to police in the field are testimonial if they concern past events and are not made during an ongoing emergency. "When the ***primary purpose*** of the interrogation is to prove past events potentially relevant to a criminal prosecution, the statement is testimonial." *Davis* at 822 (emphasis added). The statements were properly admitted in *Davis* as non-testimonial as they related to the assault that was taking place during the call. In *Hammon*, the officer who interviewed Mrs. Hammon asked about past events. The officer was not asking "what is happening," but rather asked "what happened," rendering the statement testimonial.

§3:73   The *Bryant* Case

On February 28, 2011, the U.S. Supreme Court, with a majority opinion by Justice Sonia Sotomayor, expanded the scope of the ongoing emergency doctrine in the context of a murder trial. *Michigan v. Bryant*, 131 S. Ct. 1143 (2011).

In *Bryant*, the police were dispatched to a shooting and came across a gunshot victim at a gas station. The victim stated that the shooting took place several blocks away and identified the shooter before passing away. The statements by the decedent were admitted in the trial court over objection. The Michigan Supreme Court reversed on Confrontation Clause grounds, and certiorari was granted.

In *Bryant*, the U.S. Supreme Court held that a determination of the primary purpose of the investigation is an objective inquiry. In other words, the inquiry as to the primary purpose is not from the declarant's perspective. It is instead the declarant's purpose when viewed by reasonable participants after consideration of the circumstances in which those statements were made. So in *Bryant*, the US Supreme Court reversed the Michigan Supreme Court and held that the statements made by the declarant were admissible as non-testimonial because they were not made for the primary purpose of preparing for future prosecution. Therefore, the declarant's statements were admissible despite the Confrontation Clause.

While *Davis* was left untouched by this opinion, *Bryant* made clear that the ways in which a statement can be deemed nontestimonial pursuant to *Davis* and its progeny are not limited to those expressed in the *Davis* opinion.

The majority in *Bryant* highlighted, for example, that in *Davis* they considered the domestic violence context in which the statements were made. In doing so, they considered the continuing threat of harm was to the declarant of those statements only. As a result, they found that there was a "narrower zone" of potential victims in a domestic violence case than in a murder case where the public safety threat may be grander in scope.

The majority in *Bryant* also indicated that the type of weapon used may be relevant. In the domestic violence context of *Davis* and *Hammon*, the assailant used his fists. In *Bryant*, a gun was used. The Court found there is a greater risk of harm to general public safety from the use of a gun. That greater threat of harm was used as a justification for finding the statement non-testimonial.

Likewise, the *Bryant* Court disputed the lower court's position that the medical condition of the declarant was irrelevant. The majority in *Bryant* found that the medical condition was important to an examination of the primary purpose of the declarant's statements. The Court found that the declarant's medical condition may shed light on the ability of the declarant to have "any purpose at all in responding to the police questions and on the likelihood that any purpose formed would necessarily be a testimonial one."

In sum, the *Bryant* majority set up an expanded standard by which courts must now judge the testimonial or non-testimonial nature of statements that may implicate the Confrontation Clause. Courts must now determine the primary purpose of the interrogation, which requires an evaluation of the statements of the declarant in light of the circumstances in which the statements were made. While the existence of an emergency is an important determination a court can use in deciding whether a statement is testimonial, it is not the only deciding factor. In considering whether an emergency renders a statement testimonial or nontestimonial, a court should consider the actual existence and duration of the emergency, the type of emergency, the scope of danger imposed by the emergency, and whether that danger includes danger to the general public at large.

Not surprisingly, Justice Scalia issued a brutal dissent. He called the majority opinion a "gross distortion of the facts." He also noted that it is a "revisionist narrative in which reliability continues to guide our Confrontation Clause prudence, at least where emergencies and faux emergencies are concerned."

Despite Justice Scalia's dogged determination to hold onto a historic Confrontation Clause analysis, *Bryant* represents a shift in the Court's thinking. That the majority opinion was authored by Justice Sotomayor is consistent with this shift. Ultimately, *Bryant* moves us away from the emergency doctrine described in *Davis* and *Hammon*. Hopefully, this will not move us backwards to the Anti-Confrontation Clause reliability analysis of *Ohio v. Roberts*.

While Confrontation Clause issues are complex, they should always be raised. Remember, the Confrontation Clause trumps any hearsay exception.

[§§3:74-3:79 Reserved]

E. Investigation and Evidence Checklist

§3:80   Caution: Avoid Victim Tampering

Remember, it is crucial that you reach out to the alleged victim in the assault case, and most importantly, in the domestic assault case. If the victim is willing to talk to you, you need to be in touch with her or him, and soon. Even better, after the victim signs an affidavit for you suggesting that there should be no prosecution and retracting prior statements to the police or 911, try to arrange for the victim to get a private lawyer.

One needs to be extremely careful to not cross the line, here. Make sure you do not lean on the victim in the least. I constantly reassure, in writing and in recording of conversations, that the alleged victim does not need to speak to me. The conversation with me is entirely voluntary.

Don't threaten the victim or imply a threat. Don't tell the victim how tough you will be on her or him on the stand. Simply gather detailed facts. If the victim supports you in your attempt to torpedo the prosecution, work on drafting a helpful affidavit. If the victim doesn't want to end the prosecution but will still talk to you, get as many details as you can about the incident.

Remember to record the conversation with the alleged victim if the local bar rules allow it. If you cannot do so, have a witness with you for any conversation who takes copious notes.

§3:81   Ethical Rules—Recording Victim

As I alluded to above, recording the alleged victim is an essential if you talk to her or him. Before you do so, you need to find out if you can record and how you can do it.

Recording surreptitiously is possible in some jurisdictions depending on the location of the recording device. In other words, sometimes you can record over the phone, but not in someone's home. Sometimes you can record in person, other times you cannot. Get to know your local bar and criminal rules on the subject.

Of course, you can always tell the alleged victim you are recording. This is a second choice, only because most people will clean up what they say if they know they are recorded. If you have no choice in your jurisdiction, however, tell the witness you are recording.

I prefer to have these witness interviews done by my private investigator. Sometimes these cases develop so quickly, you need to get in before a private investigator is involved. If you can get a private investigator involved, make sure the investigator knows your jurisdiction's recording rules, as well as the elements of a tampering with a victim charge. Their errors may be imputed to you.

§3:82   Social Media

Make sure to scour the alleged victim and other witnesses' pages. You won't believe the wealth of information you can find. If the page is private, and it is allowed under your local rules, have your investigator friend the alleged victim to get access to his or her page and all its content.

On the other hand, advise your client to suspend posting and exercise extreme caution while using social media. For details, see Ch. 1, Form 1-50 New Client Letter with Social Networking Warning.

§3:83   Victim's Circle

Getting information from the alleged victim's circle of acquaintances is also a big potential help. I think this source of information is often ignored because it is assumed that the victim's friends won't talk to you or your private investigator. While it might be true that the alleged victim's closest pals will be reluctant to talk to you, his or her circle of acquaintances may be willing to talk. If they are, you and/or your investigator can get a wealth of information.

One domestic assault case I had occurred after the alleged victim picked my client up at a bar where he was singing in a band. My client had a local gig at a bar in Portland, and his girlfriend, the alleged victim, was his ride home. She showed up toward the end of the gig and gave him a ride.

Later in a protection from abuse (restraining order) proceeding, I cross-examined the alleged victim on this issue. She claimed she had only one margarita that night, because she was the designated driver for my client (who had been doing his customary drinking during his set).

My client said the alleged victim was drunk that particular evening, and that one margarita wouldn't do it for her.

So, you ask the basic questions: where does she hang out? Who does she hang out with? What does she like to drink?

It turned out my client knew that she frequented a local bar with friends when he was on stage. She had a regular bartender and friends she went with.

I assumed that the friends wouldn't give the alleged victim up. They were too tight, and had been friends since high school. But the bartender was an avenue.

So I interviewed him. He knew the alleged victim and remembered that night. She was knocking back not only multiple margaritas, but was preceding them with shots of Patron Tequila.

This little detail could have been critically important to the jury when we tried this case. As I always tell a jury, if the witness will lie about the small things, he or she will lie about the big things too.

We won that case. I don't know how significant the bartender's testimony was to the decision by the jury. We never know really what jurors are thinking. I do know, however, that details matter. To get them, you have to invade the alleged victim's social circle sometimes.

[§§3:84-3:89 Reserved]

F. Trial Themes

There are usually an abundance of trial themes to develop in domestic violence assault cases. Try a few of these ideas on for size, if it looks like they might fit your case.

§3:90   Good Relationship Gone Bad

Motivation to fabricate events usually provides you with significant cross-examination leeway. Perhaps you can spin the facts to present the domestic assault charge as a lever used by the victim for personal gain. Maybe it is used to get a good result in a divorce case, child custody case, or just to empty the joint home of its contents and sell the items on Ebay. Use those motivation to fabricate to your client's advantage.

There aren't many domestic assault cases where this argument can't be made. The easy cases to identify are the ones where the domestic assault is followed by the restraining order, the child custody case, or the divorce. The more subtle cases involve limiting your client's access to a shared home via a bail bond.

Don't assume the alleged victim is unsophisticated. It seems to me that many of the alleged victims I run into now clearly know what they are doing when they make a domestic assault call.

I took over a case just before jury selection, and was shocked when I learned what had happened since my client's arrest. He owned a home and his girlfriend and her son moved in. Things weren't going well, and he wanted to end the relationship. My client was a very soft spoken, non-confrontational gentleman, and let the woman and her son stay with him long after the relationship was over for him.

Finally, he officially ended the relationship. The woman threw a few items at him, and left with her son. She drove a few miles down the street, ran into a local business claiming she'd been assaulted, and they called 911 for her. Within an hour, my client was out of his own home, with an order that she was in control of the residence.

My client's former attorney did nothing about this. By the time I got involved, the home had been foreclosed on (because my client couldn't pay for two residences), and the woman lived there six months rent free.

We were able to get the case dismissed, but the damage was done to my client. And that damage, coupled with the blood sucking leach that alleged victim was, would have been exposed to the jury had the case been tried. Don't forget about these issues. It is not just about the alleged assault itself. There are strong motivations for the alleged victims to lie sometimes, and those motivations need to be highlighted to a jury.

§3:91   Victim Is Fabricating Injuries

I must admit, like anyone who has done more than a few domestic assault cases, I get jaded by the same old story. I hear it all the time in a case where there are visible injuries. The client always comes in and says something like, "She choked herself!" "I didn't do it!" "She punched herself in the face, it wasn't me!" "I watched her bite herself!"

Sometimes I roll my eyes at these comments. I know I shouldn't. I know alleged victims will go a long way to bring false allegations. However, these fabrication stories usually seem like reaching to me. Usually.

I was reminded recently not to discount these claims entirely. I have a client with a prior record of two domestic assault convictions in New Jersey who came to see me. He was from Texas, and was visiting Maine with a new girlfriend. He had three or four pending domestic charges in Texas on the current girlfriend. While in Maine, his girlfriend fled his car at a stop light, ran to a local 7-11, and started screaming that my client struck her and bit her in the arm. She had a welt on her head and bite marks on her arm.

My client claimed she made this up. I didn't believe him. The prior domestic convictions on other women; the pending charges in Texas on this girlfriend; the visible injuries all played against him.

I asked him to explain the visible injuries. He claimed she punched herself in the face and bit her arm before jumping out of the car at a traffic light. This seemed even more unlikely to me. I told him this seemed like a hard sell to a jury.

Then he told me that his girlfriend was essentially nuts, and that she threatened to fabricate these claims all the time. More importantly, he had proof. For a few months, he had been secretly videotaping her. He didn't have video tape of the incident he was charged for here, but he did have lots of other recent tapes of her. I reviewed the tapes. Here are some highlights from my notes on some of the videos (there are more, but you will get the idea):

> Victim: "I lie to drive you crazy"
> Alleged Victim is drunk
> She screams about money and Client not paying rent/utilities on time
> She claims Client scratched her, when tape shows her scratching herself.
> She said that she "fights like a man."
> She screams about scratches on her neck.
> Client appears to lean in to kiss her and she slaps him on the face.
>
> She threatens to file a report on Client because of some alleged damage.
> She wanted him out of the house 3 months ago: owes her $1400.00
>
> Says she "will testify against you in every case"
> She says the jury always decides for a "poor innocent woman." Says "I can prove mental stress."
>
> She's going to file an insurance fraud claim. Client asks if she would make something up like that? Her response:"I will say anything, I will f*** you over." "Now it's war."
>
> Alleged victim admits to being drunk.
> She calls Client various names: "fake," "pathetic," "ugly," "liar," "dumb," "turd" and "piece of shit."
> She wants Client to move out.
> She threatens to have Client beaten up.
> Client asks: "You would not lie?" She responds "You know me, I would. I will stab you in the neck."
>
> Alleged Victim admits to scratching herself.
> Client argues with her because she wants the keys to the car but she is drunk.
> She says "You hurt me, you scratched my throat."
> She follows up: "I punch, kick and fight like a man. I will f****** kill you."
> Client says "You just pushed me;" she responds "prove it."
>
> She starts arguing about the rent and utilities.
> She says "I hate you. I wish you were dead."
> Client says she just threw a pen at him; she responds by saying she thought he was a dart board.
>
> Client is being suffocated by alleged victim. He says that he is. She responds "if I could kill you, I would. I wish I could put you in the garbage disposal. I get close to you so that I can kill you. I am going to kill you."

Well, I suppose you can't really make this stuff up. Boy, was I wrong about underestimating the fabrication story. The district attorney, as you might imagine, dismissed the case. But there was no charge of filing a false report against the alleged victim, which would have been more satisfying.

Most of these fabrication cases are fruitless, and don't have videos that come along with them. Just don't doubt them entirely. Many fabrication cases are fabrications themselves. But some aren't. We need to keep an eye out for the fakers because they exist.

[§§3:92-3:99 Reserved]

G. Trial

1. Jury Selection

§3:100   Key Questions for Prospective Jurors

As I mentioned earlier, I am not focusing much on jury selection in this book, because the way jurors are picked varies so much by state. I do, however, want to focus on a few questions you may want to key on in a domestic assault selection.

You need to be sure you are asking a question about the potential juror's involvement in domestic assault organizations. I might ask (or request the court ask) a question along these lines: "Are you a member of any organization, such as the Maine Coalition to End Domestic Violence, whose primary purpose is to advocate for the prevention of domestic violence?"

Additionally, you need to make sure that the potential jurors are not, themselves, past victims of abuse. As people are unlikely to reveal this in front of a large group, they must be brought up to sidebar for further questioning. But how do you get them to sidebar? Try a question to the venire along these lines: "Have you or any of your close family members or close friends been the victim of any domestic abuse?" This allows the potential juror to go to sidebar without saying to the rest of the group that she or he was the one abused.

Once the juror is at sidebar, get all the details. Most of these people you want to strike. After you get the details, move to strike these folks for cause so you don't waste any of your peremptory challenges.

§3:101   FORM 3-20 Defendant's Proposed Voir Dire

STATE OF MAINE   UNIFIED CRIMINAL DOCKET
CUMBERLAND, ss   DOCKET NO.

STATE OF MAINE,	)
	)
Plaintiff	)
	)	DEFENDANT'S PROPOSED
v.	)	*VOIR DIRE*
	)
,	)
	)
Defendant	)

NOW COMES Defendant, _____, and respectfully requests that this Court give the following *voir dire*:

1. Are you, or are any of your family members, past or present employees of any law enforcement agency or organization?
2. Do you believe that law enforcement officers are more likely to tell the truth in trial than other witnesses?
3. Have you or any of your close family members or close friends been the victim of any domestic abuse?
4. Have any of you testified as a victim, or close family member of a victim, in a criminal trial, or spoken at a sentencing?
5. Have you ever been the victim of criminal conduct, either charged or uncharged?
6. Do you believe that if someone has been arrested that they have most likely committed the criminal conduct?
7. Are you a member of any organization, such as the Maine Coalition to End Domestic Violence, whose primary purpose is to advocate for the prevention of domestic violence?

8. This case involves the allegation of domestic violence between a married couple. How many of you feel that, because of the nature of the charges in this case, it might be difficult for you to sit as a juror?
9. How many of you believe that because Mr. Defendant was arrested and charged with a crime, that he is probably guilty of something, even if it is not what he is charged with in this case?
10. How many of you feel that you might have some difficulty presuming that Mr. Defendant is innocent of the charges against him in this case?
11. Have you or anyone close to you had an unpleasant experience or been a victim or witness to domestic violence?
12. Would any of you tend to give greater weight or consideration, no matter how slight, to the testimony of a law enforcement officer or a witness testifying for the state, merely because they are employees or testifying on behalf of the state?
13. Do any of you believe that a defendant in a criminal case should testify?
14. Does anybody on the jury panel know anybody else on the panel?

Dated this ___th day of _____, 20__, at Portland, Maine.

Respectfully submitted,

_____
Timothy E. Zerillo
Attorney for Defendant
ZERILLO LAW FIRM, LLC

[§§3:102-3:109 Reserved]

2. Opening Statement

§3:110 My Approach

Now let's turn to a brief Opening Statement. In this case, my client is accused of choking his wife, three times, including one time in which she passed out. She allegedly fled the residence and called 911. I don't really know what evidence is going to come out at trial. Sometimes, in cases like this, I want to deliver an effective opening statement while at the same time not saying much about the facts of this case. Here's how I might approach the opening in such a case.

§3:111 Sample Opening Statement

Good morning, my name is Tim Zerillo and I'm pleased to represent Ray Basher.

There are two sides to every story and it's no different here. When the police get involved in the private arguments people have in their private lives, sometimes only one side of the story emerges. When the evidence comes out here, it will show that there was an alleged altercation between two people. There were no other witnesses to that altercation. The police spoke to one of the two witnesses only, and this case came from that interview. But the beauty of the jury system is that you get to hear both sides of the story; you get to see both sides of the coin.

To properly do my job I need to supply you with some really boring, yet important, legal terms. First, as you've heard, the State must prove every element of crime of assault beyond reasonable doubt. A reasonable doubt is a doubt that would cause you to hesitate in a matter of importance in your daily affairs. If you hesitate when you are deciding this case, that hesitation is a reasonable doubt

Beyond a reasonable doubt is a level of certainty upon which you would make the most important decisions of your life. If you find that Ray is only probably guilty, you must let him go. I'll give you an example of this.

Some people like to skydive. I think it's crazy to jump out of a perfectly good airplane, but some people like it.

Imagine you are up in an airplane, the door is flung open, and someone you don't know hands you a parachute pack and says "jump." Would you feel comfortable with that?

The person who handed you the parachute was probably perfectly nice. You can imagine that the person who packed it may have been quite competent. But imagining that is not enough to make you comfortable.

You are going to want to check the parachute, check every strap, make sure every inch of thread is secure, watch the parachute get packed, and then check it again.

That is the care you would take with your life in your hands. That is also the care you must take with Ray's life in your hands.

The fact that Ray was arrested in this case does not indicate anything. The arrest is only a means to activate the system of justice so that 12 of his peers can come in here and listen to the evidence. You determine guilt or innocence—not the police officer and not the prosecutor—YOU.

As a result of that, the burden in any criminal case rests solely with the prosecutor at that table. In this case, the State of Maine and that prosecutor have the entire burden of proving Ray's guilt. That burden never once shifts to this table. As a result, Ray does not have to do anything except sit at the table. He doesn't have to testify, his attorney doesn't have to cross-examine anyone, he doesn't have to present evidence—he doesn't have to do anything. And if he does nothing, the law says that you cannot view that as an admission of his guilt. The Judge will tell you so.

Why? Because the prosecutor has the opportunity to do all the advance investigation she wanted to do. She had every state government agency at her disposal and she had your tax dollars to burn in creating this prosecution. Now she has to show you the case and prove to you that she spent your money wisely.

In this case the State must prove that: Ray intentionally, knowingly or recklessly caused bodily injury to Deborah Basher. Each of these elements must be proven beyond a reasonable doubt.

You need to listen very carefully to the facts of this case. On direct examination, Deborah will tell you that she was strangled by Ray three times. When you listen to the mechanisms of this strangulation, you will have questions. So I ask you to hold your opinion until after cross examination. Because after cross examination, you will have even more questions as to how this could have occurred. Your questions will be reasonable doubt.

Your job is to assess credibility of witnesses. There are credibility tools you can use as you judge credibility of a witness. Watch the witness's face, eyes, and body language. Does the witness appear truthful or evasive?

Often, you will see some of these physical cues during cross examination. Some famous lawyers have concluded that cross examination is the best tool on earth to get at the truth. You can be the judge of that too. You must judge the credibility of Deborah Basher and decide if her story makes any sense after cross examination.

If you find that Deborah has lied materially—at any time—that is a reasonable doubt. Once it is established that an alleged victim has lied materially, or repeatedly, that witness cannot be trusted—and reasonable doubt exists. If you find that she has been repeatedly inconsistent in her answers, you need to consider that as well, because you may find reasonable doubt from that alone.

From there, your only job is to be true to your oath as jurors, and render a not guilty verdict.

For general tips on opening statements and sample language about the presumption of innocence and burden of proof, see Ch.2.

[§§3:112-3:119 Reserved]

3. Cross-Examination of Alleged Domestic Assault Victim

§3:120   Key Points

Deborah Basher is on the stand. She is teary. She is upset. The prosecutor has done her job and left her a crying mess in the witness box. Offer no tissue. Do not withhold an inch of ground. The best way to stop a crying adult witness is to attack (or at least get her talking).

Key points to make with this witness are:
- She's cooperating with prosecutors, not the defense.
- She understands the importance of telling the truth and claims to have been truthful.
- Yet her story contains inconsistencies especially when she is pressed on details.
- She did not seek medical treatment after the alleged assaults.

For tips on effective cross-examination, see Ch. 2.

§3:121   Cooperation with Prosecutor

We need to establish whose side she's on up front:

Q. You met with the Assistant District Attorney prior to giving the testimony you just gave on direct?
A. Yes.
Q. You went through your testimony with her?
A. Yes.
Q. I called you, didn't I?
A. Yes.
Q. You didn't call me back?

§3:122   Importance of Telling the Truth

Now let's make sure she understands the importance of truth telling.

Q. You understand importance of telling the truth in making a police report?
A. Yes.
Q. You understand the importance of telling the truth in signing a statement?
A. Yes.
Q. You told the truth here to the police?
A. Yes.
Q. You told the truth to the 911 operator?
A. Yes.
Q. You told the truth in every written statement you made?
A. Yes.
Q. In every verbal statement you made you told the truth?
A. Yes.
Q. You told the truth because it is important to tell the truth?
A. Yes.
Q. Especially when you are making a very serious accusation like the one you are making here?
A. Yes.

§3:123   Inconsistencies in Victim's Story

In this case, there are several choking incidents alleged and some inconsistent statements.

Q. You testified today, that Ray choked you on April 30, 2010 a total of four times.
A. Yes, that's what I said.

Q. On April 30, 2010 you wrote a statement and described three choking incidents?

A. I don't remember that.

Q. [After showing her the statements on the record and pointing out all choking incidents]. Did I read your statement correctly?

A. Yes.

Q. And you described three choking incidents in your statement?

A. I guess I did.

Q. And you described four choking incidents today?

A. Yes.

Q. Which of these two statements were you wrong about?

A. I must have forgotten one of the times he choked me when I wrote that.

Q. But as you've told us before, you knew how important writing that statement was, didn't you?

A. Yes.

Don't shy away from the alleged violent act in a fabrication case. If there is some lying going on, I want the witness to give me details so she slips up.

Q. According to your April 30th statement, the first time he choked you, it was after you grabbed for his glass of soda?

A. Yes

Q. How long were you choked for?

A. I'm not sure. Five or 10 seconds.

Q. You wrote a statement on May 3, 2010 as well?

A. Yes.

Q. You said in the May 3rd statement "when he came close to me I held him back and pick up a glass with soda in it and told him to go away then he choked me until I dropped the glass."

A. Yes.

Q. Those statements are different, would you agree?

A. No, I think they are the same.

Q. In either event, you claim that he choked you so strongly that you dropped the glass.

A. Yes.

Q. That was a very hard choking?

A. Yes.

Q. After you dropped the glass you ran to get your phone?

A. Yes.

Q. Then you were choked until you dropped your phone?

A. Yes.

Q. There was significant force used?

A. Yes, very significant.

Q. You must have been scared of Ray at that point?

A. Yes.

Q. He's a big man?

A. He is.

Q. Your son was in the next room when these chokings happened?

A. Yes.

Q. Your son is 13 years old?

A. Yes.

Q. You must have been afraid that Ray had lost it, and would turn on your son?

A. I was definitely afraid for my son.

Q. So you left the house at that point to protect yourself and your son?

A. No.

Q. Actually, Ray went to the computer room?

A. Yes.

Q. That's because he was trying to get away from you?

A. No, he was trying to mess with my computer.

Q. You were in fact initiating the argument?
A. No, Ray was.
Q. You could have fled at that point with your son?
A. No, because all my stuff was there and Ray had my phone.
Q. After he choked you twice viciously as you described, you tried to follow him into the computer room?
A. I went into the computer room.
Q. You were choked for the third time in the computer room?
A. Yes.
Q. During the third time you claim to have been choked, you passed out?
A. Yes I did.
Q. That must have been a very hard choking?
A. It was.
Q. He choked you hard enough that you lost consciousness?
A. Yes.

§3:124 Failure to Seek Medical Care

I want to make sure that her post-choking actions match what most people would do if this actually occurred, which is call the police and seek medical treatment. It's not so here.

Q. After the last choking incident you left the house right away?
A. Yes.
Q. You took your son?
A. Yes.
Q. You went to the nearest store to you and borrowed a phone?
A. Yes.
Q. Only a few minutes elapsed between the time you called 911 and the time you left the house?
A. Yes.
Q. And the police responded quickly?
A. Yes they sure did.
Q. They were there within two or three minutes of your 911 call?
A. Something like that.
Q. You were able to call 911 after the strangulation where you lost consciousness?
A. Yes, I could talk.
Q. Along with the police came an ambulance?
A. Yes.
Q. You didn't request that, the 911 operator did?
A. That's right.
Q. The ambulance folks wanted to take you to the hospital, didn't they?
A. They said they wanted me to get checked out.
Q. And you went to the hospital?
A. No, I didn't.
Q. Despite being choked viscously three times, one time in which you were choked so hard you passed out, and you didn't go to the hospital?
A. No. I felt OK.
Q. How about a quickcare?
A. No, I felt fine.
Q. Did you follow up with your primary physician to check things out?
A. No.

[§§3:125-3:129 Reserved]

4. Cross-Examination of Arresting Officer in Bar Fight Case

§3:130   Key Points

The police have been called and told a woman was assaulted by her boyfriend at a bar. She doesn't show up at the trial, but the Court allows in her statements as an excited utterance and an exception to the Confrontation Clause requirement.

Key points to make with the arresting officer are:
- The officer's report is accurate.
- The officer's memory of the events was better when he wrote the report than now.
- The defendant and alleged victim were both drunk.
- The officer doesn't know how the victim's injuries occurred and whether they are recent or old.
- An alternative suspect could have been to blame for the assault.
- There were no witnesses to the alleged assault other than the defendant and victim.

For tips on cross examining police officers, see Ch.2

§3:131   Accuracy of Officer's Reports

First, let's establish the accuracy of the officer's reports in this case:

Q. In the course of your work you have to prepare police reports?
A. Yes.
Q. They are required, not optional?
A. Yes.
Q. They are part of your responsibilities as a police officer?
A. That's correct.
Q. You are taught to write police reports in training?
A. Yes.
Q. Writing police reports is important?
A. Yes.
Q. They are your official record of what happened?
A. Yes
Q. You use them to refresh your recollection both before and during testimony?
A. Yes.
Q. Your supervisors use them?
A. Yes.
Q. Prosecutors use them?
A. Yes.
Q. Defense counsel uses them?
A. I think you do.
Q. Did you write a report in this case?
A. Yes.
Q. Your reports are accurate and thorough?
A. Yes.
Q. Your investigation was thorough?
A. Yes.
Q. Were there any errors in the report that you want to correct now?
A. I don't think so.
Q. As far as you know it is 100% correct?
A. Yes.

§3:132   Memory Better When Report Written

We also want what is in the police report to control, so establish that the officer's memory was better at the time the report was written then at the time of testimony.

Q.   One reason for reports is to help your memory?
A.   Yes.
Q.   You've been involved in dozens of cases since April of 2010?
A.   That's correct.
Q.   Your memory does not get better as time goes on, does it?
A.   Not really.

§3:133   Both the Defendant and Victim Were Drunk

Now, I want to establish that both parties were drunk as skunks.

Q.   Bobby Boyfriend was very drunk when you found him, wasn't he?
A.   Yes.
Q.   He couldn't even stand up when you found him?
A.   No.
Q.   You had concerns that he knew where he was?
A.   True.
Q.   He had difficulty answering questions?
A.   Yes.
Q.   He had difficulty staying on point?
A.   Yes.
Q.   He constantly got sidetracked and asked if Gertrude was OK?
A.   Yes.
Q.   He was crying?
A.   Yes.
Q.   He was distraught?
A.   Yes.
Q.   You asked him how he got a bloody nose?
A.   Yes.
Q.   He said he didn't know how it happened?
A.   Yes.
Q.   He was so intoxicated you must have been concerned he didn't know what he was saying?
A.   Yes.
Q.   Gertrude Girlfriend also appeared very intoxicated?
A.   Very.
Q.   By all accounts, they both had been drinking all day and night?
A.   Yes, that's what was reported.
Q.   Have you spoken to Gertrude since the incident?
A.   No.
Q.   You cannot tell if her perception was accurate about that evening?
A.   I only know what she told me then.
Q.   And she was very drunk then, wasn't she?
A.   Yes, she was.

ASSAULT/BATTERY

§3:134   Source of Victim's Injuries Uncertain

Now let's get into where the injuries came from.

Q. You testified on direct that Gertrude was injured?
A. Yes.
Q. And that you could see those injuries?
A. Yes.
Q. You had never laid eyes on Gertrude before that call?
A. No, I never had.
Q. So you can't tell with any level of certainty if those were old or new injuries, can you?
A. She said they were new.
Q. But you don't know that, and she was very drunk?
A. She was very drunk.

§3:135   Alternate Suspects

Everyone at the bar was so drunk that an alternate suspect is plausible; so let's insert an alternate suspects line of questioning.

Q. There was another guy at the bar who started trouble that night too?
A. Yes.
Q. That was Steve from Nebraska?
A. Yes.
Q. He allegedly assaulted Bobby that night?
A. Yes
Q. Did you find Steve and talk to him?
A. No.
Q. Did you find out about Steve's assault on Bobby?
A. No, couldn't find him.
Q. Then you didn't find out if Steve assaulted Gertrude?
A. No.
Q. Bobby was beat up when you found him too?
A. Yes.
Q. That could have been from Steve assaulting Bobby?
A. It could have been. We couldn't find Steve to interview him.

Now I want to stretch out this Steve from Nebraska thing. Even if my Client hit Gertrude, he was so drunk, maybe he thought it was Steve?[1]

Q. Your investigation led you to believe that Bobby struck Gertrude?
A. Yes.
Q. Did you have concerns whether Bobby knew he was striking Gertrude given his level of intoxication?
A. I don't know how to answer that.
Q. Didn't you get information that the bartender had kicked Steve out from the bar?
A. Yes.
Q. Didn't you get information that Steve from the bar had threatened Bobby and Gertrude?
A. Yes.
Q. Maybe Bobby, if he did strike Gertrude, was so drunk he thought he was striking Steve?
A. I have no idea.

---

[1] In this case, the client admitted he struck the girlfriend, but we were able to get that confession suppressed.

§3:136   Lack of Witnesses

Assuming no one witnessed the assault, always bring that up as well.

Q.   You did not witness Gertrude getting assaulted?
A.   No.
Q.   Are you aware of any eyewitnesses to Gertrude getting assaulted?
A.   No.
Q.   So the only witnesses we have are Gertrude and Bobby who were both very drunk.
A.   Yes.

[§§3:137-3:149 Reserved]

5. Closing Argument

§3:150   My Approach

My client is an ex-marine. His girlfriend, and his ride from his concert, was a tiny woman. She alleged that she began driving the car. In the car, she claimed he began striking her. He got out of the car and she claimed that he slammed her head on the pavement. She had contusions to her head.

The prosecutor told me in advance of this case that I would never win it. Here is how I approached closing. We ultimately hung the jury.

For tips on closing arguments and sample language for burden of proof and reasonable doubt arguments, see Ch. 2.

§3:151   Sample Closing Argument

Allison Vick is a young lady with a problem. She hates Joe Client and she made up a story. But her story doesn't add up.

If you believe Joe Client's version of events is possible, then you must find him not guilty. You are going to make a hugely important decision today, and it needs to be made under the law.

The State must prove every element of the offense beyond a reasonable doubt. They must prove beyond a reasonable doubt that Joe Client intentionally, knowingly or recklessly caused bodily injury or offensive physical contact to Allison Vick.

If you find all of that beyond a reasonable doubt, then you must find that the state has not proven self-defense beyond a reasonable doubt.

The self-defense option is there because you could find that Joe had contact with her that caused her injuries, even though he was trying to hold her off of him.

A word about self defense…size doesn't matter…sex doesn't matter.

I myself am 6 feet tall and I weigh 195 pounds or so. Recently, my wife and I had a groundhog torturing our garden. My wife bought a have-a-heart trap, and I caught it. Of course, once I caught it, I thought, "what would I do with it?" I drove far away from my house with the animal in the trap. I drove it into the woods away from any other houses.

As I got ready to release it, I found a major flaw in the design of this trap. To open it and release the animal, you need to stand toward the trap exit.

As I was scratching my head trying to figure out how to let the animal go. Meanwhile, the groundhog is looking at me, hissing and growling. It looked as if it wanted to sink those sharp teeth into my neck. The fact that I was 10 times its size didn't matter. I was scared of it.

You heard from a number of witnesses in this case. Some witnesses really didn't tell you much of anything. You don't need to consider their testimony if you believe it isn't useful to you.

Allison's parents testified. They love their daughter. They are nice people. But they weren't there for this incident.

Even as adults do we tell our parents everything that really happened when something goes wrong in our lives? Or do we spin it so we sound good? Allison is on a bridge in a rural area without a ride. She needs to get a ride. She calls her parents. She needs to explain her condition. She doesn't want to say, I got drunk and attacked Joe, fell out of the truck, and attacked him again. So she says instead, Joe beat me up. And her parents, as parents would, believed her.

Otherwise, the parents don't provide much more insight. Rick L. does tell us that Joe wasn't slurring his words or stumbling when he spoke to him, so that blows Allison's theory out of the water that Joe was very intoxicated. We do know that.

The police officer Cheryl D. was not helpful. It wasn't her case. She took pictures of the injuries, but she doesn't know how her injuries occurred. The officer assigned to the case was never produced for you as a witness.

For the State, the only witness that matters is Allison Vick. And Allison was caught in some lies.

The first lie is that she only had one drink. We know for a fact that she had more than one drink. John Bartender testified. He remembered her having several margaritas and shots of tequila. Why would she lie about that?

Allison also gave a different version of the events to Jen M. and Betsy J. She met them at the Venus Bar after the incident. Jen and Betsy testified that Allison approached them after the incident and asked them how Joe was doing. She said she was surprised he hadn't called. Allison then launched into a story about the incident and excluded that Joe smashed her head into the pavement as she described to you.

You've seen the pictures of Allison and her bruising; you have them in evidence. Joe is a big man. If he smashed Allison's head into the pavement three or four times, as she testified on cross-examination, she would have had more than that bruise. Her injuries are inconsistent with her story. Thank God for those pictures.

Now a lot of the details are unclear as testified by Allison that night. I won't belabor all of them. But times, length of time at the bar are all confused, or fabricated. Likewise, she was confused as to whether her car door was open or closed, or whether her seatbelt was on or off.

But she does remember that Joe pulled her out of the car by her hair. Yet, after being pulled out by her hair, no hair fell out. Again, thank God for State's Exhibit 1. It shows her hair intact. She admitted it under cross examination that she didn't lose any hair. Use your common sense folks. Does it add up?

If Allison's story is probable, and Joe's story is only possible, you must find him not guilty.

Tom C. testified for Joe that he witnessed Allison have three drinks and that he did a shot of tequila with her. Allison lied. Maybe because she thought she was too drunk to drive, but she lied.

Betsy and Jen heard her give a whole different version of events. Allison lied.

You must judge the credibility of Allison Vick.

If you find that she lied materially—at any time—that is a reasonable doubt.

Once it's established that a victim has lied materially, or repeatedly, that witness cannot be trusted—and reasonable doubt exists.

Notice that Allison never gave you a reason for the fight she and Joe had in the car. She said that he just started calling her names and she didn't know why. Joe did give a reason. Allison was jealous of a girl named Amber who was a bartender at the club. She accused Joe of cheating on her.

Joe testified that Allison had made those accusations before. Gotten upset, hit him, pushed him. He had asked her to leave before and she refused.

This time he asked her to leave again, and Allison was pushed over the edge. Once she told the lies to her parents and then the police, she was stuck with them.

Allison lied.

The truth is that as they were on the bridge she began to strike him. She hit him three times. He wrestled the wheel. They ended up in the middle of the road just before the bridge. Joe got out of the car. He ordered her out. She lunged at him and fell. She got her injuries partially from that fall. She got up and attacked him. He held her off again. What happened while he held her off is unclear, but there may have been more injuries. Eventually she ran off to the side of the road and threatened suicide. Joe drove off. He returned when he realized she had no cell phone.

If Joe's version of events is possible, then you must find him not guilty.

Allison lied. Those lies are reasonable doubt.

[§§3:152-3:159 Reserved]

III.   FELONY AND AGGRAVATED ASSAULT

A. Elements and Common Scenarios

§3:160   The Elements

Generally, an assault is aggravated because it involved either permanent injuries, or because a dangerous weapon was used. Most of the defenses that can be used in the simple assault and domestic assault situation equally apply to aggravated assault and won't be repeated here. Issues of self-defense, defense or others and defense of property should be employed, consistent with the other examples used in this chapter.

§3:161   The Betrayed Husband/Boyfriend

Ordinary assault cases can be elevated to aggravated assault depending on the physical damage done to the alleged victim. I have seen this happen many times in the betrayed boyfriend/husband situation.

For example, an ordinary guy comes home from a day of work. All he wants to do is crack open a beer. It's been a hard week, and he knocked off work a little early.

When he gets home, he sees his wife in bed with another man. He flies into a rage and proceeds to kick the living daylights out of the other man. He does permanent damage to the man, and is arrested for an aggravated assault.

ASSAULT/BATTERY

§3:162   Assault with a Deadly Weapon

Another relatively common situation is the assault with a deadly weapon case. Virtually anything can be a deadly weapon, which allows prosecutors to upgrade these charges significantly.

I recently represented a woman who was charged with assaulting her boyfriend with a deadly weapon by hitting him with a frying pan. The assault was aggravated to a felony because it involved a deadly weapon.

Really, my client had been tortured by her boyfriend, and he was an abuser. The battered woman's defense can work well in these types of cases.

§3:163   Assault on an Officer

Many jurisdictions elevate a simple assault to a felony if it is committed on a police officer who is carrying out his or her official duties. This presents, of course, a significant opportunity for overcharging.

Just yesterday, as I write this, I resolved an assault on an officer case. In that case, I represented a tortured kid who was on bail for some truly stupid crimes. The local police had set up a sting operation for some car thefts. They used a bait vehicle full of electronics and a surveillance vehicle. My client, proving he wasn't any sort of master criminal, took a bottle of water out of the surveillance vehicle and ignored the bait vehicle full of electronics. He then proceeded to smoke marijuana with a friend out of a carrot, which the police enjoyed watching prior to arresting him.

Well, this got my client all sorts of attention, even national attention among some cable TV talking heads. In reality, however, what we had was a kid who was 18, with a lot of anxiety, but who was otherwise quite bright.

Although he was 18, he was still in high school. He had very good grades and a bright future. After the arrest for the theft of the water, coupled with a charge of burglary of a motor vehicle, my client stopped attending school and holed up in his room.

His mother reached out to his medical providers. One of these medical providers, who apparently didn't care to think this thing through, told my client's mother to call 911. The mom mentioned to 911 that my client had threatened to kill her, so when the police arrived they were thinking about an arrest, not about a well-person check.

The police officer stood in the doorway of my client's bedroom and agitated my client. My client was further agitated by his mother, on the other side of the police officer. Client and mom were trying to talk to each other through the big police officer blocking the door. Finally, my client moved the police officer aside to squeeze through the doorway, and he was arrested for an assault on an officer.

Assaults on an officer usually come up when your client has been a pain in the ass. He or she has flailed about during the arrest, and the officer caught a stray kick in the process. The officer might not be injured, but it is enough to trump up a charge.

[§§3:164-3:169 Reserved]

B.   Strategies and Tactics

The same strategies and tactics discussed earlier in this chapter, such as self-defense, defense of others and defense of property can be raised here. Some additional ideas to consider follow.

§3:170   Where Was the Assault?

Consider at first, where the assault took place. Assaults that take place outside of your client's home are certainly harder to defend, from a self-defense perspective. But if the assault takes place in your client's home, and the alleged victim doesn't live there, then there will likely be some justification you can use in defending the case.

§3:171   Lack of Serious Injury to Victim to Warrant Felony

At times, your case will be elevated to an aggravated assault because the alleged victim suffered permanent injuries. Don't just assume the injuries are permanent. It could be that injuries claimed to be permanent by the alleged victim are, in fact, not permanent. You might have to get your own doctor to testify as an expert on this issue, but I find that the Government is often unprepared for this argument. Imagine the case of a victim with a concussion as an injury. Is a concussion permanent? Well, it is certainly traumatic, but I don't know if it is permanent. A qualified neurologist might say it is not.

§3:172 Therapeutic Issues

For nearly all assault cases, I expect my clients to get involved in anger management therapy. I tell them to humor me and engage in the therapy not necessarily because they have a problem (although many do), but because I want to use this in plea bargaining with the prosecutor, or in the case of a sentencing, if needed.

Many clients resist treatment. They want nothing to do with therapy. It takes time, effort, money, and self-reflection. That being said, it is an important step in getting an appropriate plea bargain. Also, if they engage in the therapy, there is less of a chance they will get in trouble and violate bail as the case proceeds.

§3:173 Experts

For cases in which there has been a blood boiling anger inducing the assault, get experts to negate the *mens rea* of the event. In the case in which the man finds his wife in bed with another man, your client isn't exactly thinking clearly when he beats the holy hell out of the paramour.

While a jury may feel sympathy for your client, they need a reason to let him out of the assault. If a qualified shrink can explain that your client lacked the requisite *mens rea*, you might win points from the jury and give them the reason they need to justify a not guilty verdict.

Notice that I am not talking about an expert for a mental health defense other then negating mens rea. Obviously, in some cases, you have no choice but to raise mental health defenses related to competency and other issues. I once represented the Golden Gloves Heavyweight Boxing Champion for New England, who suffered from a delusion in which he thought God told him to beat up anyone who wouldn't give him a cigarette. Needless to say, you didn't want to bump into him that day if you were a non-smoker. We had no choice but to bring more traditional mental health defenses to aggravated assault charges there.

Traditional mental health defenses just don't work, in my experience. Jurors hate them. But if you can say that someone lost their mind temporarily, which everyone can relate to on some level, you might have something with a likeable defendant.

[§§3:174-3:179 Reserved]

C. Trial Themes

§3:180 Think Outside the Box

I urge you to think outside the box as you explore trial themes. The reality is that we are only limited by our own creativity. Sometimes we get stuck in a rut and can't get out of it. Try to break out of that rut with some new ideas.

Self-defense is an easy one. The first year attorney who gets a court appointed case can think of this. It's been discussed earlier in the chapter and I won't revisit it here, except to say, make it interesting to the jury in your argument.

§3:181 Defense of Others—Thwarting a Rape?

For example, imagine the case where the man comes home and finds his wife in bed with another man. He beats the living daylights out of the guy, but then smartly clams up when the police attempt to interrogate him.

How about this; the man came home and thought his wife was being raped? He had no reason to believe that she was cheating on him. She'd been a loyal wife as far as he knew, and he assumed a rape was occurring. He would have been justified, if he was right, to beat the holy hell out of the rapist.

Maybe that works for a fact pattern you have and maybe it doesn't, but don't be afraid to get creative.

[§§3:182-3:189 Reserved]

ASSAULT/BATTERY

D. Trial

§3:190 Sample Opening Statement

Let's imagine you're doing an opening on the case I described earlier with the frying pan. See §3:162. I might approach a portion of my opening this way.

Members of the jury, I am very pleased to represent Heather Pan in this case. That is not because I am thrilled to be involved in a criminal trial. I am thrilled to be involved in this particular case. And the reason for that is not only because I get to represent Heather Pan, but it's also because I get to describe to you her noble act of self defense against an abusive man.

Heather resides in an apartment in Biddeford, Maine. On October 10th, of this year, she invited her boyfriend over to her apartment after he finished work. When he arrived, he was drunk.

Heather had been in a relationship with her boyfriend, Burly, for a few months. That relationship was chaotic, and sometimes violent.

When he came over that night of October 10th, the abuse of Heather continued.

I don't want you to think that when I say abuse, that it always means that Burly was striking Heather. Anyone who has been in a relationship understands that the other person you are in a relationship with can learn how to push your buttons. And in this case, a drunk and agitated Burly continued to push Heather's buttons for the remainder of the evening.

He did so by degrading her. By telling her she was worthless, by telling her she was inadequate sexually. By doing anything he could do to offend and ridicule her.

Ridicule turned into screaming matches. And the screaming matches grew louder and louder. They continued to the wee hours of the morning. They drove Heather's roommate out of the house. The roommate left in the middle of the night to get away from the fighting. And Heather was left alone with Burly, who re-doubled his efforts after the roommate left.

Finally, Burly grabbed Heather's Apple computer and threatened to break it. Heather asked him to leave and to leave the computer alone. Burly would not do that. Mentally exhausted, Heather grabbed the heaviest object near to her that she could handle, which was a frying pan. Burly held her computer out as if he was going to drop it and allow it to smash on the ground. Heather asked him over and over again to leave and to leave her computer alone. She worked a long time to save money for that computer and he was threatening to destroy it. Burly knew that threatening to destroy the computer that she loved would push her over the edge. And it did. To get him to leave and drop the computer she struck him with the frying pan in the shoulder and neck area. Burly finally left, Heather's computer was, in fact, broken and Heather wept for the rest of the night until the police knocked on her door the next morning.

We have an aggravated assault here because the State has charged this as an assault with a dangerous weapon. The dangerous weapon was in fact the frying pan. In addition, Burly claims he has permanent injuries as a result of being struck by the frying pan.

I don't want to pretend that Heather did not strike him. She did. That's not the issue.

The issue for you folks to decide is whether striking him was justified. Hitting Burly with the pan can be justified in a variety of ways. The judge will tell you in the jury instructions that if Heather was reasonably using non-deadly force to defend her premises, her property, or herself, that she was justified in using that force. And you will note to yourself that after these hours and hours of anguish and fighting, that the only way Heather could get Burly to leave was finally to hit him. When you consider that when the evidence closes, you will also have to consider that the only appropriate verdict is a not guilty verdict.

ASSAULT/BATTERY

I'll get another chance to talk to you at the end of the case. Until that time, please keep your mind open to the possibility that Heather Pan was justified in using the force she used.

For general tips on opening statements and sample language about the presumption of innocence and burden of proof, see Ch.2.

§3:191   Sample Cross-Examination of Alleged Victim—The Cheating Wife

In this cross examination, I try to justify my client's use of force through his wife suggesting her husband could have believed he was thwarting her rape. See §3:161.

Q. You were married to Scott S. for 22 years, weren't you?
A. Yes.
Q. You had 2 children together?
A. Yes.
Q. They were grown by the time this incident occurred?
A. Yes.
Q. You didn't announce to Scott that you were having an affair with Robert?
A. No.
Q. That was a secret?
A. Yes.
Q. You did a good job keeping the secret up to that incident?
A. Yes.
Q. It is your understanding that Scott thought you were faithful to him?
A. Yes.
Q. When Scott came home early that day, he found you having sex with Robert?
A. Yes.
Q. You were face down during the intercourse when Scott came in?
A. Yes.
Q. Robert was on top of you?
A. Yes.
Q. Were Robert's hands on your arms?
A. I think so.
Q. From Scott's vantage point, it could have appeared you were being held down?
A. I wasn't being held down.
Q. I understand that. But in the split second Scott saw this, it could have appeared you were being held down?
A. I don't think so.
Q. In that split second, Scott might have thought you were being raped?
A. I don't think so.
Q. But if he gave you the benefit of the doubt, because you were always so loyal to him, that might have crossed his mind, right?
A. I suppose.
Q. And if you were being raped, you would have wanted him to act exactly the way he did, right?

For tips on effective cross-examination, see Ch. 2.

§3:192   Sample Cross-Examination of Officer Who Took the Report

Now, let's get back to the case in which our client hits her boyfriend Burly with a frying pan, which is based on an actual case of mine. See §3:162. Here is a cross of the cop who took the report.

Q. Officer Small, you arrived at my Client's house the morning after the alleged assault, didn't you.
A. Yes.
Q. My Client was there.
A. Yes.
Q. You spoke to her.

A. Yes.
Q. She was willing to speak with you.
A. Yes.
Q. She didn't appear evasive?
A. No.
Q. She was clearly upset?
A. Yes.
Q. She was tearful?
A. Yes.
Q. She fully cooperated with you?
A. Yes.
Q. Would you describe her physically as a small woman?
A. I would say she is pretty small.
Q. Had you spoken to Burly prior to speaking to my client?
A. No.
Q. Have you since?
A. Yes.
Q. Would you describe him as a large man?
A. Yes.
Q. The physical differences between Heather and Burly were not information you had when you originally interviewed Heather?
A. No.
Q. Heather told you she hit Burly with the pan?
A. Yes.
Q. But did she tell you what preceded that?
A. You mean the fighting?
Q. Yes. And the torturing. And the berating…
A. She told me they had been fighting and he threatened to break her computer so she hit him with a pan?
Q. Is that all you got out of it?
A. That was the gist.
Q. She didn't tell you she asked him to leave, repeatedly and he wouldn't?
A. I believe she did say that, yes.
Q. She told you he ignored her orders to leave?
A. Yes.
Q. Your investigation did not lead you to the conclusion that this was anyone's home other than Heather's?
A. Her roommates and Heather's, correct.
Q. And according to Heather, her order to leave was ignored by Burly?
A. Yes.
Q. Did she tell you that he threatened to break her computer?
A. Yes.
Q. And that she repeatedly asked him to put it down and he refused?
A. Yes.
Q. She told you she was scared to death of him?
A. She said she was scared, yes.
Q. When you arrested Heather, you were not considering any justifications for her use of force, were you?
A. No. I don't think that's my place.
Q. Right. You don't consider that, the jury does, right?
A. If they are instructed to.
Q. In other words, once you hear that force has been used, you don't go through an analysis to see if it is justified?
A. No.
Q. That is saved for another day and another venue?
A. Right.
Q. Like a trial?
A. Right.

For more tips on cross-examining police officers, see Ch.2

§3:193   Sample Closing Argument

Now a closing for our frying pan aggravated assault case. See §3:162.

My father taught me early on in life that you never went and looked for a fight. He taught me that it was always best to walk away.

He also taught me that when faced with a bully that the only thing they respond to, sometimes, is a punch in the nose.

Burly was a bully to Heather. In fact, he was more than a bully. He was a tormentor. He was a torturer.

I want you to imagine, those of you who are not female jurors, that you are female. I know the men on this jury are all men's men. You are all tough guys that can handle yourselves. You don't want to think of yourself as a woman, and I commiserate with that. But for this exercise you need to think of yourself as women. And you women on the jury, you don't have far to go to think about this.

Now as you picture yourself as a woman, I want you to picture yourself as a 19 year old girl alone in an apartment in Biddeford, Maine. You weigh 130 pounds. Your tormentor, your torturer, and your abuser, is a man. He weighs 200 pounds. You can not physically overpower him with your own strength and he has been torturing, tormenting and abusing you for five hours.

All you want is for him to leave you alone. All you want is for him to leave your apartment. And your one prized possession in the world, which he knows is your prized possession, your Apple computer, he is threatening to break. You don't have a lot of money. This computer is something you saved for. You use it every chance you can. It is more important to you than your car, than your TV, than your clothing... And Burly knows that.

So, it keeps getting worse and worse. He won't leave. And you can't make him leave-- unless you threaten to hit him with an object. So you grab a pan, which is the nearest object that you can find. You don't have any real weapons in the house. And you strike him with it, just once, and it works, and he leaves. And as soon as he leaves you run after him and lock the door, hoping to never see him for the rest of your life.

For any of you jurors who are picturing yourselves as Heather in this situation, are you able to say you would have done things differently?

Now I am going to make this exercise even more emotionally painful. Instead of yourself in Heathers place, I want you to put your daughter, or your sister, or your mother. Would you want them to grab that frying pan? I know that I would.

Heather Pan was justified in using the force that she used. That justification requires your vote of not guilty in this case.

For tips on closing arguments and sample language for burden of proof and reasonable doubt arguments, see Ch. 2.

(This page intentionally left blank.)

CHAPTER 4

THEFT OFFENSES

Theft cases encompass a wide variety of crimes. They range from simple shoplifting cases to the serious embezzlement felonies. There are those who make their living (or supplement their day job) with theft, and those who are compulsive about it. In this chapter, I explore some of the common types of theft cases you might encounter.

THEFT OFFENSES

I.   SIMPLE THEFT

A. Elements and Common Scenarios

§4:01   The Elements

The definition of simple theft, also known as larceny, varies somewhat from state to state but it generally has four elements. They are:
1.   The defendant unlawfully took
2.   Another person's property
3.   Without the owner's consent, and
4.   With the intent to deprive the owner of the property permanently.

§4:02   The Shoplifter

I have handled shoplifting cases with many different types of people. From the mother stealing food for her baby, to the mother who rolled up in her Mercedes and stole shoes that she could easily afford. People shoplift for a variety of different reasons.

I remember several years ago handling a theft for a law student. She was caught red-handed with three pairs of underwear from JCPenney. She was a bright young woman. She was driven. And she was caught and she confessed.

My initial reaction was that perhaps law school pressure was driving this impulse. But when I peeled back the onion even more, it was clear that she was in an abusive relationship with a controlling husband.

In a case like this, getting the client into therapy (see §4:10) and a shoplifting diversion program (see §4:15) can substantially improve your bargaining position with the prosecutor. An accord and satisfaction, if available in your jurisdiction, is an even better solution. See §4:13.

§4:03   The Professional Thief

Then you have the professional thief. These guys are great because they are an annuity for your practice. For every 100 things they steal, they are going to get caught a few times, and getting caught doesn't stop them. For them, thievery is an income supplement. They wish they could pull off an *Ocean's Eleven*-type job, but end up stealing copper piping from an abandoned house instead.

Generally these guys are easy to deal with, by the way. Unless they are complete jerks, they understand they are thieves and they understand they are guilty. Representing the guilty is a hell of a lot easier than representing the innocent.

When dealing with the professional thief, we don't want to put a silk hat on a pig. If your guy has a 20 year rap sheet for theft, it may be difficult to sell him to the prosecutor as an innocent who was caught running with the wrong crowd. I am generally looking for technical defenses to these cases, attempts to see if the victim wants to settle privately, or a quick plea bargain if there are no trial issues. Remember, if your guy is going to continue to steal, probation is no bargain. He will just do his time on an installment plan. Instead, if you are out of options, get the shortest non-probated jail sentence you can.

[§§4:04-4:09 Reserved]

B. Strategies and Tactics

§4:10   Therapy

One reason to discover if you are dealing with the professional thief or someone with a sudden bout of kleptomania is to determine what you want to do with the client as far as therapy goes. For clients who have been stealing things all their lives, therapy won't help because they aren't receptive to it. The purpose of therapy for them is to win brownie points with the DA. But unless you catch one of these guys at the start of his thieving career, the DA won't care much about the counseling anyway, because the client will inevitably have a long record.

THEFT OFFENSES

What about for the first or second offense shoplifter or small-time thief? Many mental health professionals will tell you that there is a correlation between shoplifting and depression. As a result, behavior modification therapy, often based on a diagnosis of obsessive compulsive disorder and depression, is a must.

Even with compulsive shoplifters, behavior modification therapy can be employed to change these behavioral patterns. Take a look at the article "Significance of Depression in the Mechanism of 'Compulsive' Shoplifting," G.H. Gudjonsson, *Medicine, Science and the Law*, Vol. 27, Issue 3 (July 1987). You can also explore the concept of masturbation in the context of shoplifting, surely a cure for depression, in "Kleptomania as risk-taking behavior in response to depression," Fishbain, David A., *American Journal of Psychotherapy*, Vol 41(4), Oct 1987, 598-603.

The link between shoplifting and depression makes sense. Otherwise, we need to wonder why celebrities and the well-off shoplift. Think of the names of female starlets caught shoplifting in the recent past: Winona Ryder, Lindsay Lohan and Megan Fox have all been nabbed.

I don't want to perpetuate a sexist myth that women are the only shoplifters. In fact, a 2008 study by the American Journal of Psychiatry indicated that men shoplift more than women. "Prevalence and Correlates of Shoplifting in the United States: Results from the National Epidemiological Survey on Alcohol and Related Conditions," *The Journal of Psychiatry*, July 2008, Vol. 165, No. 7.

It is appropriate for you to have a roster of therapists to deal with these issues for your clients. Since many therapists don't want to be involved in court proceedings, expectations need to be set up front. The client is engaging in therapy because he wants to change his behavior. That said, the therapist does need to be aware of the court case and how he or she is expected to assist you with it.

PRACTICE TIP: *Getting the client to the therapist*

Often, I will give the client a few names and phone numbers of good therapists and ask the client to follow up. Sometimes the client wants to check with his or her health plan to make sure the therapist accepts the client's insurance.

If the client is having issues that need immediate attention, I might call a therapist I know and trust at that initial meeting. For a client in crisis, having a meeting set-up by the time the client leaves your office can be a godsend.

§4:11   The Therapist and the Court Case

If I don't know the treating provider, I tell the provider up front what I am looking for. In most instances, I will want a letter from the therapist to the DA.

My general procedure for dealing with the therapist is to have the therapist contact me once therapy has begun. The client will need to sign a release first, of course. I tell the client to do this at the first meeting with the therapist. Then I make the therapist aware that I will need a letter from him or her at the appropriate time. In that letter I want the therapist to explain (1) my client's therapy-- what issues have been worked on, and the progress the client has made, (2) that the client understands and appreciates the bad behavior, (3) that the client has expressed remorse for the behavior, (4) the treatment plan going forward and, hopefully, (5) the therapist's view that the client presents a low risk of recidivism. The letter should be on letterhead, typed and hand signed. The appearance of professionalism is important.

If the therapist is hesitant, you should probably look elsewhere. There are other fish in the sea. The treatment your client needs is not the rocket science of therapy. Your client needs treatment probably for depression and obsessive compulsive disorders. You can always find someone else who is not afraid of court.

Of course, there are more reasons for shoplifting than depression and OCD. But treatment is usually key. Additionally, if you have a compulsive shoplifter, you may be able to argue that she did not have the appropriate *mens rea* to commit the theft through your mental health expert.

§4:12   FORM 4-10 Letter to Prosecutor Transmitting Letter from Therapist

[Date]

Cumberland County District Attorney's Office
142 Federal Street
Portland, ME 04101

    Re: State of Maine v. XXXXX
         Docket No. CR-1234

Dear ADA Doe,

Pursuant to our previous discussion, I enclose an updated letter from Dr. Ima Smarty, on behalf of my client, Ms. Krista Urge. The letter indicates that Ms. Urge had an adjustment disorder on the date of the incident causing her to act impulsively.

Also enclosed is an original copy of a letter from the Assistant Dean for Student Affairs regarding Ms. Urge. It indicates that she is currently enrolled and in good standing at the law school.

I appreciate you considering our request for a filing. Although Ms. Urge is without significant means, she has reserved $270 to pay JCPenney three times the value of the merchandise. This is a one-time incident from a successful law student, who deserves another chance.

I thank you for your consideration of our request. Please consider this letter and attachment an offer to compromise under the Maine Rules of Evidence.

                    Respectfully submitted,

                    _____

                    Timothy E. Zerillo
                    Attorney for Defendant
                    ZERILLO LAW FIRM, LLC

TEZ/dar
Enclosure

§4:13   Accord and Satisfaction or the Like

One of the goals I have in a shoplifting case is to get an accord and satisfaction for my client. Maine, like many other states, provides a statutory procedure for stopping the criminal process that allows the perpetrator in a misdemeanor case to compensate the victim who then can swear that she is satisfied with the repayment of what she's lost. See §4:14 Form 4-20 Accord and Satisfaction and Release.

These are great. I have seen prosecutors try to stop accord and satisfactions from being entered in court (I always wonder why they care). At least in Maine, the prosecutor generally has no luck. The argument is that the state does not have discretion under the statute to block the accord and satisfaction.

Unfortunately, in Maine we also have also a law that allows the victim to recover three times the value of the merchandise stolen. This means that my client will likely be paying a lot more than the value of the item to get that accord and satisfaction or dismissal from the DA.

§4:14   FORM 4-20 Accord and Satisfaction and Release

ACCORD AND SATISFACTION AND RELEASE

After being duly sworn, I, Javert, am counsel for French Revolution Foods and as an authorized agent do depose and state as follows:
1. I, Javert, am above the age of majority and of sound mind.
2. I am currently retained as counsel for French Revolution Foods in this matter and am authorized to speak on behalf of the company referencing this matter

3. I am aware and have knowledge that on or about January 1, 1815, Jean Valjean was accused of stealing a loaf of bread.

4. Jean Valjean has paid us 5 francs as part of a civil settlement and has justly and completely reimbursed us. It is our preference that this matter be resolved by way of this Accord and Satisfaction and we do not wish to further pursue this matter.

6. I hereby release Jean Valjean from any civil or criminal liability relating to the incident which occurred on or about January 1, 1815.

Signed under the pains and penalties of perjury this 31st day of December, 1832, Paris, France.

Javert
Counsel, French Revolution Foods

§4:15   Online Shoplifting Classes

Another way to impress the prosecution with a first or second offense shoplifter is through an online theft intervention program. There are many online shoplifting programs that your client can complete during the pendency of his or her case. Many people think that these programs must be ordered by the prosecutor before they are completed. This is untrue.

With a quick internet search you will find a number of shoplifting intervention programs. Examples are shoplifting.org, shopliftingprevention.org and shopliftingtheftclass.org. These classes can be done online after which the participant receives a certificate of completion. Completion of such a program, in combination with solid counseling, is a powerful bargaining tool.

My point is simple. I tell people that if they are serious about helping me help themselves get the best deal possible, they should jump through hoops. When we show up to plea bargain, the prosecutor will know that the defendant is committed to leading a law abiding life when the prosecutor sees that the defendant is in counseling and has completed a theft intervention course.

§4:16   "I Didn't Mean To" Defense

On occasion I run into the "I didn't mean to shoplift" defense. This is often the only escape for the shoplifter. After all, shoplifters are almost always caught with the merchandise on them. The only thing they have to attack is intent sometimes.

On occasion, these defenses are fruitful. I represented a woman several years ago, who was shopping for Christmas with her husband at L.L. Bean. Let's call her Stella Shopper. She was in Maine from Connecticut. She was a housewife, whose husband worked on Wall Street. She also had a son who was diabetic who was on this Christmas shopping trip.

She told me that she was walking around L.L. Bean with a series of tote bags. She intended to buy the tote bags, and was filling them with items she was also planning on buying.

In the midst of her shopping, my client got a call from her husband telling her that the son needed to take his diabetes medication, which was in her purse. His condition was severe, and Mrs. Shopper was vigilant, if not hyper-vigilant, about making sure he was healthy. She walked out an exit and was nabbed by the L.L. Bean loss prevention employees.

The L.L. Bean campus is fairly large, and there are a series of Bean buildings near each other on the campus. Her claim was that she never thought she was doing anything wrong by leaving the store because she was still in the complex, and that she was in a rush to meet her husband to give her son the medication.

Obviously, I have heard the "accidental" shoplifting story many times. If you have a compelling story like this one, it can be useful. Here, we got her into treatment not because we admitted she shoplifted, but rather to determine if she had panic issues or a panic disorder around her son's medication and diabetes. A doctor in Connecticut concluded that she did.

Then, we got the surveillance video. It was not terribly clear what was happening, but you could see her get a phone call and then quickly exit, lending credence to our theory.

It also helps in such a situation to establish that your client had the funds to pay for the merchandise. I think this is a less fertile ground than it used to be, however. With celebrity shoplifting stories, especially the Winona Ryder story, prosecutors, judges and juries know that people shoplift when they can afford an item.

For a cross-examination of the arresting officer in a case raising this defense, see §§4:40-4:44. For an excerpt from an opening statement and closing argument see §§4:30, 4:31 and §§4:50, 4:51.

§4:17   Suppressing Statements Made to Shopkeepers

I often wish I could suppress inculpatory statements made by clients in response to questioning by store employees. Shopkeepers detain suspected shoplifters, scare them, get confessions without *Miranda*, and generally do law enforcement's dirty work.

Perhaps there is a jurisdiction where a shopkeeper's detention and interrogation of a shoplifting suspect is considered to be state action. From my cursory review, it seems like most states make it difficult. New York has held:

> For state action to exist, it must be demonstrated that official participation in the investigation at issue preceded, or occurred contemporaneously with, the signing or utterance of an inculpatory statement. For example, when police officers have actively participated in defendant's apprehension, exerted official power to restrain defendant, escorted defendant to the site of interrogation, and awaited the outcome of the privately conducted interrogation in close proximity to the place of questioning, a custodial atmosphere of the nature *Miranda* was designed to alleviate has been created. (*see, People v. Jones*, 47 N.Y.2d 528, supra, 419 N.Y.S.2d 447, 393 N.E.2d 443) Under circumstances where police participation precedes or occurs contemporaneously with the private elicitation of inculpatory evidence, so as to create a coercive, custodial environment with the reasonable potential of infringing defendant's privilege against compulsory incrimination, the *Miranda* safeguards must be observed.

People v. Ray, 65 N.Y.2d 282 (1985):

The point here is that you may be able to hook in state action if you can find a way to attach the police work to the shopkeeper's Fourth Amendment violation. You may have an angle, for example, if there is a history of police practice allowing shopkeepers to detain and interrogate shoplifting suspects in order to circumvent the Fourth Amendment. Such history is difficult to determine. If you have practiced in an area long enough, however, you may find some shopkeepers with bad reputations for this.

If you have an illegal detention, even without state action under the Fourth Amendment, your client may have a civil claim against the store for false imprisonment and other torts. Obviously, it is not the same thing, but it may help your client exorcise her pique if she was treated horribly.

§4:18   Approach the Prosecutor Early

Especially in small-time theft and shoplifting cases, I like to approach the prosecutor early. Obviously, if I can ask the prosecutor to pump the brakes on the prosecution completely, that's great. But even if the prosecutor wants to have charges pending, asking for a continuance of court dates, and any other activity in the case, so your client can get treatment may be helpful. In any event, plant the seed early that your client is serious about getting treatment, avoiding further illegal activity, and making restitution.

Obviously, if you have triable defenses, you may not want to go this route. But if your case is lousy, and you want to try to find that one compassionate bone in the prosecutor's body, then this is a way to go.

Then, gather the helpful materials to your case. These include the therapist's letter (see §4:11), diversion certificate (see §4:15) and anything else that may be helpful. Sometimes I bring character letters with me stating what a nice person the client is. If my client is in school and doing well, I bring their report card in. Make a presentation that casts your client in a positive light.

When you are finally ready to approach the prosecutor about a final resolution, have all the paperwork in hand that supports your position that your client is on the path to being a productive member of society and not a recidivist.

[§§4:19-4:29 Reserved]

C. Trial—Accidental Shoplifting Defense

1. Opening Statement

§4:30   My Approach

For a summary of the facts on which this opening statement is based, see §4:XX As we open, my goal is simple. I just want to plant the seed that my client could have gotten confused in her rush to meet her husband and walked out of the store without thinking.

For general tips on opening statements, see Ch. 2.

§4:31   Sample Opening Statement

Like so many families do around Christmas, my client, Stella Shopper, came up to Maine to do some Christmas shopping at L.L. Bean. She wanted a beautiful time with her husband and son who came with her. What she didn't come up here to do was steal L.L. Bean tote bags.

We used to have this black lab named Brittany. My little sister, Holly, used to walk in the woods in the summer with Brittany near our camp on Little Sebago Lake. Holly was maybe 10 years old, and she would take those walks in the woods with Brittany.

Now one day Holly and Brittany come across a black bear in the woods. And this is a big, old black bear. It could tear you to shreds. And it starts to rear up when it sees them come around a corner.

Brittany does not run. She does not whimper. She jumps in between Holly and the black bear and goes on the attack. She jumps up as high as she can and tries to bite the bear in the face. A black bear! And the bear goes running.

Now I am not comparing my client to a dog. She probably wouldn't care for that too much. But what I am saying is that when you hear the evidence you will need to consider whether Mrs. Shopper intended to leave the L.L. Bean store without paying. Or did she just react to a medical issue with her son and react without thinking.

Because, see, Mrs. Shopper's son, Max, is severely diabetic. And Max was in another store across the street with his Dad. And in my client's purse was Max's insulin shot.

Now, you know L.L. Bean. It is several stores set over a large campus. They never close. They don't even have locks on the doors.

And there's Mrs. Shopper. In the middle of the Christmas mayhem. Tote bags over her arms, with merchandise in them she hadn't bought yet when she gets a call on her cell phone. Max needs his shot. And she immediately goes to the nearest exit and leaves. Until she is detained by security.

Was she like Brittany? Did she just react without thinking? One of the things you will need to determine here is did she intend to deprive L.L. Bean of their merchandise? If she did not intend to deprive them of their merchandise, then she has not committed a crime.

So you might then say to me, "OK, how are we supposed to judge what she is thinking?" Well, that's where the legal standard comes in. This is the State's case to prove. They have to prove her intent to steal beyond a reasonable doubt. If they don't, the law says you must find my Client not guilty. So, let's talk about reasonable doubt….

For sample arguments on burden of proof and reasonable doubt, see Ch. 2.

[§§4:32-4:39 Reserved]

2. Cross of Arresting Officer

§4:40   Key Points

Let's look inside the cross of the police officer in the L.L. Bean case, in which the client has the "I didn't mean to!" defense. For a summary of the facts, see §4:02. In this cross, I want to establish that:

- The L.L. Bean complex is large and houses several stores.
- Although the officer may know it well, shoppers can find it confusing.
- L.L. Bean is a little heavy-handed in how they attempt to stop shoplifting.
- Mrs. Shopper was putting merchandise in her tote bag, like an ordinary shopper.
- Mrs. Shopper told the officer she left because she got a call that her son needed his insulin shot and that she was disoriented.
- Surveillance video is consistent with Mrs. Shopper's story.
- The officer agrees that Mrs. Shopper did not commit a crime if she left the store without the intent to steal the merchandise and he does not know her intent.

For tips on cross-examining witnesses, see Ch. 2.

§4:41   Officer's Knowledge of Campus

Q. You've been a police officer in Freeport 19 years, right?
A. Yes.
Q. You've responded to many thefts at L.L. Bean?
A. Yes.
Q. Hundreds of them?
A. I would say so.
Q. Thousands of them?
A. No, not that many.
Q. Over a hundred but less than a thousand?
A. Yes.
Q. You are familiar with the L.L. Bean complex, the campus there?
A. Yes.
Q. You've been there many times?
A. Oh, yes.
Q. If I asked you to pick me up a fly rod, you don't need directions, you know right where to go?
A. I do.
Q. If I asked you to show me where the tents are, same thing, you know right where to go?
A. Yes sir.
Q. It is a fairly big complex there though isn't it?
A. Yes.
Q. You have a main store with a few floors, right?
A. Yes.
Q   And several other stores in the same L.L. Bean campus but which are separate.
A. Right.
Q. And there are parking lots and paths that go to those stores?
A. Yes.

§4:42   Typical Customer's Knowledge of Campus

Q. There are information desks throughout the main store, right?
A. Yes.
Q. People are often confused as to how they get somewhere or where they are, which is why the information desks are used?
A. I don't know why they are used really.

Q. Your department has gotten calls before of a child getting lost from his or her parent in the store?
A. Yes, that has happened.
Q. Have you ever had to come over when an adult has gotten disoriented in the store?
A. I remember a few years ago an elderly man getting disoriented.
Q. And there are signs all over the main store telling people where to go?
A. Yes.
Q. And that's because it is confusing to some people?
A. I don't know.

§4:43   Store's Extreme Efforts to Detect Suspected Shoplifters

Q. L.L. Bean is very interested in stopping shoplifting in its stores?
A. I would say so.
Q. That has been your experience?
A. They want to stop it.
Q. In fact, they are often quite aggressive in stopping it, right?
A. I don't know that I would say that.
Q. They are aggressive with their customers, right?
A. I don't think so.
Q. They have cameras all over the store, right?
A. They do have cameras.
Q. And they have employees with those cameras following people, right?
A. Yes.

§4:44   Defendant's Intent

Q. Mrs. Shopper had a tote bag she was carrying around, like this one, right?
A. Yes.
Q. And she was putting her merchandise in it, right?
A. Yes.
Q. While she was in the store she was doing this?
A. Yes.
Q. And she hadn't paid yet?
A. Right.
Q. Do you carry a tote bag yourself?
A. No.
Q. Me neither. But you know what they are for?
A. I would say to carry things.
Q. Right. Have you ever seen one of these (holding up a reusable shopping bag some stores have)?
A. Yes. Some stores give that to you to put your merchandise in while shopping.
Q. It isn't theft for a person to be shopping and put some items they plan to purchase in one of those shopping bags, right?
A. No.
Q. It also isn't theft to put your items in a tote bag before you pay?
A. Not until you leave the store with it.
Q. OK, I'll give you that. But you also need to leave the store with intent to steal the items, right?
A. That's right.
Q. Leaving the store with the items in the tote bag without intent to steal isn't a theft?
A. No.
Q. The tote bag I have here is open. Is that the way Mrs. Shopper's tote bag was?
A. Yes.
Q. You could see right into it?
A. Yes.
Q. You don't know if Mrs. Shopper intended to steal the merchandise do you?

A. I know she left with it in her bag without paying.
Q. And that, as you just said, is not a theft unless she intended to steal, right?
A. That's true.
Q. And you don't know that she intended to steal, do you?
A. No, just that she left.
Q. You questioned her, and she explained that she got a call that her son, who was a diabetic, needed an insulin shot?
A. Yes.
Q. And she told you she was disoriented?
A. Yes.
Q. And that she didn't mean to leave without paying?
A. Yes.
Q. And it is fair to say that you don't know one way or the other if that is true or untrue?
A. That's fair.
Q. But you did review the video surveillance here?
A. Yes.
Q. And it shows Mrs. Shopper receiving a call, right?
A. Yes.
Q. Just before hurrying off, right?
A. Yes.
Q. And that is when she exited without paying?
A. Yes.
Q. That surveillance video is consistent with what she told you?
A. Yes, it is.

[§§4:45-4:49 Reserved]

3. Closing

§4:50   My Approach

In closing I want to personalize the case for the jurors. While most jurors respect the law, they believe that the law should be applied to reach a fair result. If you can convince them that they might do the same thing your client is accused of if they found themselves in similar circumstances, you will be in good shape for acquittal.

For closing argument tips, see Ch. 2.

§4:51   Sample Closing Argument

… I know this case seems ridiculous. The theft of items in a tote bag from L.L. Bean. But this is a big deal to me and it's a big deal to my client. Theft crimes are very serious.

My client left the store without paying. There is no doubt of that. She doesn't dispute it and I don't dispute it. But that alone is not a theft. Ask the judge if you don't believe me. You also need the intent to steal.

Here, my client is putting things in the tote bag as she's in the store. She doesn't mean to steal them; she has the money for Christmas shopping in her purse. And she gets a call. It's from her husband. He and her son are on the other side of the L.L. Bean campus. He needs an insulin shot. He doesn't look so well. She has the shot. And she rushes into action as moms do. As she leaves the store, looking for them on another side of the campus, she is arrested by the L.L. Bean security.

This reminds me of a story. One time I was at Disney World with my wife and kids. A parades was coming down the street and as usual it's packed at Disney World. So my kids are up front so they can see, and my wife and I realize there are other kids behind us who can't see. I don't need to see the parade. I need a Tylenol. So I step to the back and let some other kids go up front. This is how it should be.

But there's a man who is lurking near the kids. I didn't even see him. My wife saw him though. Next thing I know, my wife springs into the crowd and knocks this guy on his rear-end because he was getting a little too close to my 12 year old daughter.

I should note that my wife is pretty small: 5′5″, maybe 108 pounds, she's a distance runner. This guy was a big guy, at least twice her size.

Now this guy was probably perfectly nice, and my wife may have just over-reacted. But she reacted. She didn't think of anything. She saw danger for her kid and she reacted.

Imagine the Marshall comes in here right now. He interrupts my closing. He whispers something to the judge. The Judge says "Excuse me Mr. Zerillo. Juror number 5. We've just received an urgent message. There is something wrong with your daughter. You need to leave right now and go to the hospital."

Would you remember if you grabbed all your things. Your keys? Your cell phone? Would you remember which exit you left from? Would you remember how you got to the hospital? The roads you took? The red lights you had to sit through? Or would it all be a dream until you knew your daughter was safe?

Mrs. Shopper didn't intend to steal anything. She got a call and she reacted. The tote bags were the furthest things from her mind until she helped her son.

For sample arguments on burden of proof and reasonable doubt, see Ch. 2.

[§§4:52-4:59 Reserved]

II.   EMBEZZLEMENT

A. Elements and Common Scenarios

§4:60   The Elements

Embezzlement differs from theft in that with theft, the initial taking must be illegal. By contrast, with embezzlement, (1) one person's property (often an employer's) (2) is entrusted to another person (often an employee) (3) who then fraudulently or unlawfully appropriates it.

§4:61   Padding Payroll

Padding the payroll is a fairly common way to embezzle money. If you are in a management position, you can inflate your hours, create bonuses, and manipulate your payroll in a host of other ways.

Diana was a very smart client of mine, who was emotionally fractured. A New Yorker, she moved to Maine as an adult. As a child, she had been molested by her father repeatedly.

Despite possessing obvious talent and intelligence, the incest abuse took its toll. Diana survived her first suicide attempt her senior year of high school. Inwardly, Diana was an emotional mess, despite her high level of intellectual functioning. She graduated college, and survived multiple hospitalizations and suicide attempts along the way.

After her release from her last hospitalization, she held down various jobs in New York's fashion district in a management training program. Unfortunately, after college Diana started abusing drugs and alcohol to dull her emotional pain. In 1985, she was heavily abusing cocaine when she pleaded guilty to petit larceny.

Diana continued abusing drugs and alcohol to self-medicate for her emotional trauma until she hit bottom in 1990. She then joined various support groups and has been clean and sober since 1991.

Diana went on to receive an MBA from New York University. From there, her career excelled and she held down various high level executive positions, including with the Federal Reserve.

Diana quit her job with the Federal Reserve Bank to move to Maine to be near family. She associated herself with various charities, and eventually with an animal shelter. Ultimately, she became the executive director of that animal shelter.

For some reason, which she could never explain to me, she began padding her payroll. She stole only around $6,000. This was not a Jean Valjean in *Les Miserables* situation. She had the money, but she padded the payroll anyway.

For a sentencing memorandum that proved effective in this case, see §4:75 Form 4-40. For guidelines for preparing a sentencing memorandum, see Ch. 2.

§4:62   Point of Sale Issues

Another embezzlement technique I've seen a few times in the restaurant industry. There, using point of sale terminals, embezzlers process fake refunds or comped items that they then manipulate into their tips. In one such case, my client, Barry, stole nearly $30,000 from his employer. We were able to resolve this case pre-charge by making a restitution agreement with Barry's employer. See §§4:71 Form 4-30 Release in Felony Embezzlement Case.

[§§4:63-4:69 Reserved]

B.   Strategies and Tactics

§4:70   Get to the Decision-Maker Before Client Is Charged

One of the differences between Barry's case and Diana's case is that I began to represent Barry before he was charged. Diana was charged and indicted by the time I got her case. She was going to be processed; the DA was not letting it go. I was constantly reminded by the DA, and even the judge, that I represented the woman who stole from the puppy dogs.

When you get a case where there has not been a charge, I like to do what they always tell salespeople to do: get to the decision-maker. In theft cases, the decision-maker is not the prosecutor, but the victim, typically an executive with the organization from which your client stole. I have had audiences with executives at all sorts of businesses: hotels, pubs, restaurants, real estate brokerages, law firms and so on. My sole goal once I have an audience is to grovel for a private solution.

Most of my clients have spent the money they stole, usually on something stupid. They are generally otherwise leveraged.

> **PRACTICE TIP:** *Always find out your client's financial situation*
> Who can he beg for money? Who will give him a loan? I would pay a lot to stay out of jail and most of my clients would too.

There is probably no single better time to have resources then pre-charge. You can sometimes stop these cases dead in their tracks, which is what I was able to do for Barry, if you have the resources. In reality, an ability to pay helps you anytime, even if you face a sentencing, however.

In Maine, like many states, a restitution order requires an ability to pay. When I used to do court-appointed work, I would often represent homeless people. The prosecutor would demand restitution. "What?" I'd say. "Good luck." Then we'd go in front of the judge, who I would remind that the court had already determined my client to be indigent, and no restitution would be ordered.

You can apply the same principle here. A friend of mine and I represented two lobsterman in a turf war where there was no turf—on the ocean. Lobster territories are not drawn on a map—they are handed down. Lines get blurred, and there is a constant ebb and flow to where one's territory begins and ends.

Our clients cut $100,000 of lobster traps in such a water war. They faced a number of felony charges that we had almost resolved with the prosecutor. Our only hurdle was the victim's difficult civil counsel who was pushing hard for restitution. We scheduled a meeting on a Saturday with a bright idea. We paid a renowned bankruptcy lawyer to review our client's finances. Someone civil counsel would know of. We'll call him Joe Bankruptcy.

Joe Bankruptcy spent a few hours with our clients and told us they were good candidates for bankruptcy. We called up civil counsel at our appointed time for the conference. We told him that our clients lost their heads. We wanted the case done. We could offer a nominal settlement, but no more. "Oh, and by the way, Joe Bankruptcy is here. He just spent a few hours with our clients going through their finances. He can talk to you about that if you want."

We heard nothing but crickets on the other end of the phone. Deal approved with the prosecutor, case closed.

THEFT OFFENSES

So, when I get to the decision-maker, I want to do three things without making any admissions on my client's behalf: 1) convey my sympathy to the decision-maker for the losses the business has suffered; 2) if possible, convey sympathy for my client's own circumstances; and 3) make it clear that the appropriate business decision involves keeping my client out of jail. This is often because it is hard to repay the victim from a jail cell, and because the court won't help with restitution if the client has no ability to pay.

To do this, you have to be prepared that you might get kicked out on your rear. That is OK. Some business people are so angry, they don't make good business decisions. Other times, you spare your client a felony conviction, jail time, shame, and all sorts of collateral consequences.

Such was the case with Barry. I begged and pleaded to get to the owner of the cinema chain that employed Barry to sit down with me. He agreed, begrudgingly. In the first meeting he told me he had already called the police, but hadn't met with them. I asked him not to. I told him he steered the ship now, but that once he started the process, another hand would take the wheel—the prosecutor. In that first meeting I just asked him to pause. Let me see if I could come up with a plan.

And that's what he did. My client was dead bang guilty of felony theft that they could prove totaling at least $30,000. The decision-maker agreed to a settlement of $30,000, in payments, and agreed not to call the police.

Now, in reality, I couldn't prevent him from calling the police. An ordinary Accord and Satisfaction wouldn't work in Maine because this was a felony level theft. That said, I drafted the release in §4:71 Form 4-30 that I hoped would encourage continuing this private resolution.

Obviously, all cases don't work out this way, but it is worth taking a shot. In this release, which is not binding for me on the criminal side of things, I am trying to take into account the alleged victim's desire to be made whole with my client's desire to be done with this mess. So I tried to build justifiable reliance into the release to protect my client the best I could.

§4:71   FORM 4-30 Release in Felony Embezzlement Case

RELEASE AND SETTLEMENT AGREEMENT

For consideration of the receipt of thirty thousand dollars ($30,000), I, _____ , and/or _____ , being of lawful age, hereby, for myself, my heirs, executors, administrators and assigns (hereinafter "Releasor"), release, acquit and forever discharge _____ [his/her] heirs, executors, administrators and assigns (hereinafter "Releasees"), of and from any and all actions, causes of action, claims or demands for damages, costs, contribution, indemnification, or any other thing whatsoever on account of, or in any way growing out of, any and all known and unknown injuries and other damages of whatever kind resulting or to result from claims of misappropriation and theft by Releasee of Releasor's money during the course of his employment with Releasor.

Payment of the thirty thousand dollars ($30,000) will be made by Releasee to Releasor according to the following schedule:

$15,000 upon execution of this document,

Installment payments of $5,000 per year on February 1 every year beginning on February 1, 2013 and ending on February 1, 2015, for a total of $15,000 in installment payments.

There shall be no penalty for Releasee's prepayment to Releasor.

Releasor hereby acknowledges and assumes all risk, chance or hazard that his or its damages may be or become permanent, progressive, greater, or more extensive than is now known, anticipated or expected.

Releasor understands that this settlement is the compromise of a doubtful and disputed claim, and that payment is not to be construed as an admission of liability on the part of any Releasee.

Since freedom from costs of future litigation represents an important item of consideration bargained for by the parties to this release, it is agreed that damages recoverable for breach of this settlement agreement shall include reasonable attorneys fees and other costs incurred as a consequence of such breach.

This "Release and Settlement Agreement" contains the ENTIRE AGREEMENT between Releasor and Releasees, with the exception of the Accord and Satisfaction Agreement, which is merged and incorporated herein. Its terms are contractual and not a mere recital.

Releasor further states that he has carefully read the foregoing "Release and Settlement Agreement" and knows and understands its contents and that he signs it as his own free act.

I hereby release _____ from any civil or criminal liability relating to theft of _____ funds during the course of his employment by _____ . I understand that all payments by _____ under the terms of this agreement are based on and in reliance of my statement that I will not pursue criminal prosecution against _____ for theft, or other civil charges, and that I will not cooperate with any prosecution of him for the same, as long as I am legally able to resist such cooperation. I make this statement as Releasor individually, and on behalf of _____.

Signed under penalty of perjury this day of _____, 20___, at _____.

_____,

individually and on behalf of

_____

§4:72   Forensic Accountants

Sometimes you may have a hard time resolving the case. You are headed toward litigation. Depending on the facts of the case, consider hiring a forensic accountant.

We use them with some frequency in civil cases, but they don't seem to be used as often criminally. If there is a question as to whether the numbers add up to prove that any funds were embezzled or if the amount of loss may be overstated, a forensic accountant should be a consideration.

§4:73   Client Set Up by Another Employee

In the rough and tumble business world, I also like the idea of finding a heel (as a last resort, of course). Perhaps your client has a business rival who set him or her up to climb the corporate ladder. Obviously, you need the right set of facts for this theory, but keep it in mind.

§4:74   Sentencing

Here's the time to let the teardrops fall. Our client Diana, who was "stealing from the puppy dogs," didn't seem too sympathetic until we told her story. We submitted our Sentencing Memorandum (see §4:75 Form 4-40), brought in witnesses and submitted letters of support from others, brought in her counselor and put on the dog and pony show (pun intended). In the end, she did a weekend in jail.

Sentencings can be opportunities. I don't like them. They are one of my least favorite things to do. But sometimes you can find sympathy for the alleged devil you represent.

For guidelines on preparing a sentencing memorandum, see Ch. 2.

§4:75   FORM 4-40 Embezzlement Sentencing Memorandum

STATE OF MAINE   SUPERIOR COURT
CUMBERLAND, ss.   PORTLAND
                                                    DOCKET NO.CR-0*-****

_____

STATE OF MAINE,   )
)
)
)   DEFENDANT'S SENTENCING
v.   )   MEMORANDUM
)
DIANA P,   )
)
Defendant   )
_____   )

I. INTRODUCTION

Diana P faces one count of Theft by Unauthorized Taking or Transfer, a Class C felony.[1] It is expected that she will plead guilty to the same on May 14, 2007. Counsel and ADA Julia Gulia have agreed upon a 90 day cap for incarceration.

The purpose of this memorandum is two-fold. First, its primary goal is to assist the Court in arriving at a just sentence for Diana P, one that neither diminishes the severity of the offense for which she is charged, nor promotes disrespect for the law. At the same time, Counsel will identify significant mitigating and extenuating facts as they relate to Diana, the individual, which must be considered to arrive at a "just individualization of sentence(s)." 17-A M.R.S.A. §1151(6). Second, Counsel hopes to provide a framework for the kind of sentence that will serve society's interest in punishment, as well as enable Diana to continue as a valuable member of the community.

II. FACTUAL BACKGROUND

Diana P was born in New York and lived there until she was 9 years old when her mother moved her to New Jersey. Unfortunately, Diana did not experience the normal healthy childhood one might expect. Rather, she suffered extreme abuse in the form of molestation by her father.

Despite possessing obvious talent and intelligence, the incest abuse took its toll. Diana survived her first suicide attempt her senior year of high school. She graduated from Academy of the Holy Angel despite suffering serious mental anguish concerning her Father's abuse of her. She went on to Upsala College in New Jersey where she graduated in 1982 with Bachelor Degrees in History and Political Science, as well as a minor in Economics. Diana was an emotional mess, despite her high level of intellectual functioning. She was hospitalized after surviving another suicide attempt.

After her release, she held down various jobs in New York's fashion district, including one at Lord and Taylor where she was selected for their management training program. Unfortunately, after college Diana started abusing drugs and alcohol to dull her emotional pain. By 1985, she was heavily abusing cocaine when she pleaded guilty to petit larceny. In New York, petit larceny is a Class A misdemeanor, for which Diana received and successfully served one year probation. *Exhibit 1*, Conviction Record and Criminal Code.[2] This misdemeanor is Diana's only prior criminal activity. The conviction is 22 years old. Diana has never done any jail time.

Diana continued abusing drugs and alcohol to self-medicate for her emotional trauma until she hit bottom in 1990. She then joined various support groups and has been clean and sober since 1991.

Diana went on to receive an MBA from New York University. Diana had many prestigious and high level jobs after receiving her MBA, including a stint as the Marketing Director for the Technology Division of the Federal Reserve Bank. To acquire the position with the Federal Reserve Bank, Diana's criminal record was examined, she had to pass a lie detector test, and she was subjected to drug screening. Diana was able to put her past behind her, and she worked for the Federal Reserve Bank for a year until her step-father was diagnosed with cancer.

Diana quit her job with the Federal Reserve Bank to move to Limington, Maine to live with her mother and to help with her step-father's care. Diana quickly became a productive member of her new community. She worked at TriCounty Mental Health until it lost its funding. From there, she took a position at the Family Planning Association of Maine. She spent time working at Maine Public Broadcasting Network, and finally ended up at the Animal Shelter where she was the Executive Director until June 2006.

Counsel expects that Diana will admit that in May and June of 2006, that she directed the Shelter's payroll processor to overpay her $5,480.78. Also, in May 2006, Diana transferred $547.78 from the Shelter's checking account to her personal account. Diana will admit to improperly transferring these funds. She will pay full restitution, both for the amount misappropriated as well as the amount the Shelter spent on a financial audit.

---

[1]   17-A M.R.S.A. §353

[2]   Counsel has enclosed as *Exhibit 1*, the Conviction Record. The Code number for the offense committed, which is attached, suggests the conviction was dropped to the misdemeanor of petit larceny.

III. THE GENERALLY RECOGNIZED PURPOSES OF SENTENCING

The Maine Legislature has provided a framework of appropriate consideration in sentencing any criminal defendant.[3] The Court must consider all statutory objectives, which can generally be grouped into one of two categories: the nature of the offense and the background nature of the offender. While the Court must consider the deterrent effect of its sentence, 17-A M.R.S.A. §1151(1), as well as impose a sentence that does not diminish the seriousness of the offense, this Court must also individualize the basic period of incarceration. *State v. Hewey*, 622 A.2d 1151 (Me. 1993).

In the three-step process of sentencing, the trial court first determines the basic period of incarceration, by considering the particular nature and seriousness of the offense as committed by the offender. 17 M.R.S.A. §1252(c)(1); *State v. Hewey, supra*; *State v. Kehling*, 601 A.2d 620, 625 (Me. 1991). The mere classification of the charged offense does not automatically invoke the selection of the statutory maximum sentence as the basic period of incarceration. *State v. Gosselin*, 600 A.2d 1108, 1110 (Me. 1991). In evaluating the nature and seriousness of the criminal conduct to determine the basic period of incarceration the Court should review sentences imposed for similar conduct of other offenders convicted of offenses within the same classification. *State v. Corbett*, 617 A.2d 222, 224 (Me. 1992). The conduct is then placed "on a continuum for each type of offense to determine which act justifies the impositions of the most extreme punishment." *Id.*

A. Step 1: The Basic Period of Incarceration From Sentencing Data

Sentencing data is hard to come by in Maine. Counsel's office has tried to find reasonable, recent examples of Class C theft sentencing.

The Cumberland County case of *State v. Doe*, CR-10-1111 is relevant. *See Exhibit 2, State v. Doe*, Judgment and Commitment In that case, the Defendant was convicted of Negotiating a Worthless Instrument (Class C), and Theft (Class C). The Defendant was ordered to pay $5,000 in restitution and sentenced to 18 months, all but 30 days suspended, two years of probation. The Defendant in *Doe* had a prior theft history. In that case, the Court took into consideration that Mr. Doe's drug abuse had on his decision making, and his sentence was reduced due to his assertion that he would complete drug rehabilitation.[4]

The Defendant in *State v. Edwards*, CR-11-1111, was also convicted of Class C Theft by Unauthorized Taking. That Defendant was sentenced to only 7 days imprisonment and no probation. *See Exhibit 3, State v. Edwards*, Judgment and Commitment. *State v. XXXXX Johnston*, (CR 05-111), also suggests that a short, straight time sentence may be appropriate for this type of crime. In *Johnston*, the Defendant was convicted of Class C Theft, and was given a straight sentence of 35 days with no probation. *Exhibit 4, State v. Johnston*, Judgment and Commitment.

The *Edwards* and *Johnston* matters suggest that the basic period of incarceration can be quite low for a Class C Theft. In this case, Counsel is suggesting that the Court actually load the Defendant with probation and time hanging over her head, and a basic period of incarceration of one year as a result.

---

[3] 17-A M.R.S.A. §1151 provides as follows:

The general purposes of the provisions of this part are:

1. To prevent crime through the deterrent effect of sentences, the rehabilitation of convicted persons, and the restraint of convicted persons when required in the interest of public safety;
2. To encourage restitution in all cases in which the victim can be compensated and other purposes of sentencing can be appropriately served;
3. To minimize correctional experiences which serve to promote further criminality;
4. To give fair warning of the nature of the sentences that may be imposed on the conviction of a crime;
5. To eliminate inequalities in sentences that are unrelated to legitimate criminological goals;
6. To encourage differentiation among offenders with a view to a just individualization of sentences;
7. To promote the development of correctional programs which elicit the cooperation of convicted person; and
8. To permit sentences that do not diminish the gravity of offenses, with reference to the factors, among other, of;

   A. The age of the victim; and
   B. The selection by the defendant of the person against whom the crime was committed or of the property that was damaged or otherwise affected by the crime because of the race, color, religion, sex, ancestry, national origin, physical or mental disability or sexual orientation of that person or of the owner or occupant of that property.

[4] Information about the *Doe* case was obtained from his Attorney.

B.　Step 2: Matters of Mitigating and Extenuation Suggests That A Properly Individualized Sentence Will Include Minimal Incarceration

The second step in the sentencing process is to individualize the basic period of incarceration to determine the maximum period of incarceration based upon those factors peculiar to the Defendant. *State v. Hewey, supra* at 1154. In determining the maximum period of incarceration, the Court is to consider factors in aggravation and in mitigation that are appropriate to the case at hand.

i.　Aggravating Factors

Diana has one prior charge of petit larceny, a misdemeanor that occurred over 20 years before the incident at the Shelter. This prior indiscretion should not serve as a significant aggravating factor for this Court.

ii.　Mitigating Factors

Diana is a responsible member of society who has strong ties to friends and family in the community. She is a vital and concerned parent who is actively involved with her son, Joe's, education. This involvement is especially important because Joe has been diagnosed with ADHD, a condition that that makes it difficult for children to control their behavior. This interferes with Joe's ability to thrive in a traditional school setting. To that end, Diana has been in close contact with Joe's school and has been a voracious advocate for Joe when his needs are not being met. Barbara L., a Social Worker at Joe's school, has written a letter to the Court concerning Diana at *Exhibit 5*. Joe's father has had little involvement in Joe's upbringing, as he lives out-of-state. Joe tried to live with his father in New York recently, but his father was unable to care for Joe because he suffers from severe liver problems. This leaves Diana as Joe's primary caregiver. It is certain that Joe will suffer emotionally, as well as scholastically, if Diana is removed from his life for any length of time.

Although it is reasonable to assume that any child would suffer at the incarceration of a parent, a child with ADHD is extremely vulnerable to the havoc wrecked by even slight transitions. Therefore, there is no doubt that Joe will be an unintended victim of any time Diana spends incarcerated.

iii.　Matters in Extenuation

Numerous circumstances surrounding the commission of this offense do not amount to a defense or mitigation but are appropriate sentencing factors.

Diana suffered severe physical and emotional trauma a result of experiencing devastating and prolonged sexual and emotional abuse during her childhood. She was diagnosed with Post Traumatic Stress Disorder (PTSD), as well as a major depressive disorder, and has been hospitalized repeatedly because of her condition. Diana continues to battle this extreme mental anguish and is currently seeing Dr. Eliot G for medication maintenance. Dr. G notes that Diana suffers from PTSD and major depression, and that she takes medication and keeps appointments as directed. *Exhibit 6*, Dr. G letter. She also regularly sees Ida O, LCSW, who provides Diana with weekly psychotherapy treatment to manage and decrease her anxiety and depression.

It is the opinion of Ms. O, as evidenced by her letter, *Exhibit 7*, that Diana's theft was a symptom of her stressful work environment triggering her PTSD symptoms. Diana was continuously humiliated and undermined by the Board of Directors of the Shelter, which triggered survival functions of fight, flee, or freeze. Initially Diana fought the Board by trying to please it. When that did not work, she felt trapped and fought by stealing. Diana acted inappropriately by taking money, however, it was the way she felt she could regain control and feel safe. This is no excuse for her behavior, but rather an explanation of why she acted the way she did in her situation. This was not a thoughtfully crafted response to her position, but a base emotional response to her feeling threatened.

The community support for Diana is overwhelming. *Exhibits 5-31* are all letters written in support of Diana and attesting to her good character. Such support suggests that Diana's likelihood of re-offending is low.

iv.　Conclusion Regarding Step 2

Diana's case involves matters in mitigation and extenuation that greatly outweigh any aggravating factors. These matters suggest that Diana should not be imprisoned for long, but should repay her debt to the community by being allowed to continue to work in the community. Far more harm will be done, to both Diana and her son, if Diana is incarcerated, than will occur if she spends no time in prison.

C.   Step 3: Determining the Suspended Sentence and Probation

i.   The Need for Incapacitation

It must be acknowledged that the Court will, and should, give significant consideration to the seriousness of the offense, the deterrent effect of the sentence, and a concern for public safety. 17-A M.R.S.A. §1151(1). While these factors are important, they are not determinative. They must be balanced with the other equally important purposes of sentencing. This is a situation where incapacitation will not meet the goals of either general or specific (individual) deterrence.

Jail-oriented sentencing is a frequent response to serious criminal offenses. All too often, jail sentences are imposed and society turns its back to the defendant and the condition of the prison system that she enters. While incarceration satisfies the public's thirst for retribution and, at least facially, the interest in public safety, the long term consequences of this type of sentencing on the individual and, eventually, the community, is strongly questioned.

Sentencing advocates and others involved in the failure of the current system have begun to seriously question whether incarceration is necessary to protect society where there is no history of violence. The reality of jail sentences is stark. A jail sentence can have a significant adverse impact on both the individual and society. Over thirty years ago the President's Commission on Law Enforcement and Administration of Justice warned that:

Experts are increasingly coming to feel that the conditions under which many offenders are handled, particularly in institutions, are often a *positive deterrent to rehabilitation.*

Life in many institutions is at best baron and futile, at worst unspeakably brutal and degrading. To be sure, the offenders in such institutions are incapacitated from committing further crimes while serving their sentence, but the conditions in which they live are the poorest possible preparation for their successful reentry into society.

Jail life carries with it the undertones of violence, peer pressure for acceptance of criminality and loss of self esteem which can make a person not predisposed towards crime when she came into the system more likely to commit crime when she comes out. This will be especially damaging to Diana who already suffers from severe emotional distress. If incarcerated, she will be literally trapped, which will likely trigger the symptoms of her PTSD and cause her further psychological trauma. These factors must also be given serious consideration.

Diana is a first-time felony offender. Reliance on jail as a first choice sentence may fulfill the need for a retribution, but little else.

Moreover, there is little to suggest that Diana will re-offend without significant incarceration. The harshness of our jail system and the risk that it creates for Diana is real. While it does not negate the seriousness of the crime, it does substantially reduce the recognized need for incarceration to accomplish either rehabilitation or public safety.

ii.   The Role of Deterrence

Deterrence as a sentencing rationale is subject to limitation. As the First Circuit states:

The court's duty to "individualize" the sentence simply means that, whatever the judge's thoughts as to the deterrent value of a jail sentence, he must in every case reexamine and measure that view against the relevant facts and other important goals such as the offender's rehabilitation. Having done so, the district judge must finally decide what factors, or mix of factors, carry the day. *United States v. Foss*, 501 F.2d 522, 528 (1st Cir. 1974).

A balance clearly needs to be struck. The principle of limiting the role of deterrence is also set forth in the *American Bar Association Standards for Criminal Justice, Alternatives and Procedures*, where in the introduction to Chapter 18 it states that "[n]o one person or purpose, standing alone, can satisfactorily supply a comprehensive theory of punishment." The ABA standards correctly recognize that punishment should not be its own justification. *Id.*

The Court is urged not to focus its sentencing formulation on issues of general deterrence and protection of society as its singular guide-post in arriving at a just sentence for Diana: "Exclusive reliance upon these two general purposes of sentencing (deterrence and protection of society) will always lead inexorably to the maximum sentence and would negate the other purposes identified by the legislature." *See State v. Saunders*, No. AD 82-43 (Me. App. Div., Oct. 18, 1983).

THEFT OFFENSES

iii. The Proposal

A careful analysis of the aggravating and mitigating factors in this case supports a balancing of competing goals with a strong preference toward minimizing Diana's jail experience. The proposals to this Court take into account the severity of the criminal conduct, but also recognize the need for a just sentence. It is proposed that this Court sentence Diana P to the following: Theft by Unauthorized Taking (Class C), a sentence of one year, all but two days suspended, two years probation, 200 hours community service, and restitution of the money taken as well as an extra sum for the Shelter to conduct an independent audit. This restitution should be paid within one week of sentencing.

The unsuspended sentence is designed as a shock sentence. Diana is a first-time felony offender and has never been incarcerated. She is a contributing member of the community. She is the caring and supportive mother of a son who has special needs and whose life will be significantly disrupted with grave consequences if Diana is jailed for a significant amount of time.

Justice must be tempered with mercy and an opportunity for one to right the wrongs of the past. Counsel urges the Court to weigh Diana's indiscretions against a personal history which strongly suggests the conclusion that the crime will never be repeated again. The sentence suggested herein would include a long period of probation and a significant amount of community service so as to require Diana to walk a straight and narrow path, as she had in the past, or to be incarcerated.

For the reasons set forth above, Counsel respectfully requests the Court sentence Diana P in accordance with the proposal set forth in this Memorandum.

Dated this the 7th day of May 2007, in Portland, Maine.

Respectfully submitted,

_____

Timothy E. Zerillo
Attorney for Defendant
ZERILLO LAW FIRM, LLC

[§§4:76-4:79 Reserved]

III.   COMMON FEDERAL THEFT OFFENSES

There are a number of federal theft-type offenses to consider as well. These aren't going to be minor thefts. They are often larger cases, like most federal cases are. A few to be on the lookout for are discussed here.

§4:80   Story Time: The EBay Scammer

Between April of 2003 and January 2004, Charles bought and sold merchandise over the internet, most often through eBay. A trust fund kid with a bad attitude, he loved to scam people, and most of these transactions were fraudulent. He would advertise a Rolex and ship the auction winner pornography. He would sell a bike and send a matchbox car. The Government presented evidence that the losses resulting from the fraud totaled over $421,000 and the victims from the fraud totaled approximately 321.

Charles pleaded guilty before my involvement, and I worked sentencing with co-counsel. Prior to his plea, Charles entered into a Plea Agreement with the government, which noted that his base offense level would be increased by twelve levels because the losses he intended were over $200,000, and by an additional four levels because his offense involved more than 50 victims. Also notable was a representation by the government that they would recommend to the court that the defendant be given a three point reduction for acceptance of responsibility.

During the half-day sentencing, in which the 10 most sympathetic victims came to Maine to testify (including a very sympathetic 9/11 first responder), our client lost his acceptance of responsibility. I think that came when, during the prosecutor's summation, my client stood up and yelled "I'm not a fucking thief!", grabbed the water pitcher at counsel table, and hurled it at the United States Attorney. Our client, who was a large man, was then tackled by several U.S. marshals, after which I was blessed with the view of his robust rear-end hanging out of his orange prison uniform. Our requests to continue sentencing for a mental health examination were summarily denied.

As you may imagine, the judge denied the defendant a three point reduction for acceptance of responsibility despite the government's original recommendation. This denial was officially as a result of the court's opinion that Charles had not been candid about his assets and because he had spent the majority of those assets. Likewise, the court did not sentence the defendant in accordance with the terms of his plea agreement related to the number of victims and amount of loss. Rather, the court found the defendant responsible for over $421,000 in losses from the fraud and for 321 victims. This enhanced his sentence by four levels above that negotiated in the plea agreement for amount of loss and number of victims and he received a 75 month sentence.

Welcome to federal theft work.

§4:81   Mail Fraud, Wire Fraud, Computer Fraud

Mail, fraud, wire fraud and computer fraud are often interrelated in federal court.

Mail fraud, 18 U.S.C. §1341 requires that the defendant devise or intend to devise a scheme to defraud (or to perform specified fraudulent acts), and that the defendant use the mail for the purpose of executing, or attempting to execute, the scheme to defraud. *See Schmuck v. United States*, 489 U.S. 705, 721 n. 10 (1989); *see also Pereira v. United States*, 347 U.S. 1, 8 (1954) ("The elements of the offense of mail fraud under … §1341 are (1) a scheme to defraud, and (2) the mailing of a letter, etc., for the purpose of executing the scheme.").

Wire fraud, 18 U.S.C. §1343, is very similar to the mail fraud statute. It adds the requirement of the use of an interstate telephone call or electronic communication made in furtherance of the scheme. See *United States v. Briscoe*, 65 F.3d 576, 583 (7th Cir. 1995) (*citing United States v. Ames Sintering Co.*, 927 F.2d 232, 234 (6th Cir. 1990) (per curiam)); *United States v. Frey*, 42 F.3d 795, 797 (3d Cir. 1994). According to *United States v. Profit*, 49 F.3d 404, 406 n. 1 (8th Cir. 1995), there are four elements of a wire fraud case: (1) that the defendant voluntarily and intentionally devised or participated in a scheme to defraud another out of money, (2) that the defendant did so with the intent to defraud, (3) that it was reasonably foreseeable that interstate wire communications would be used, and (4) that interstate wire communications were in fact used. The 10th Circuit and 5th Circuit finds that there are 2 elements: 1) a scheme or artifice to defraud, and 2) the use of interstate commerce to facilitate the same. *United States v. Hanson*, 41 F.3d 580, 583 (10th Cir. 1994); *United States v. Faulkner*, 17 F.3d 745, 771 (5th Cir. 1994). The 1st Circuit finds there are 3 elements to the crime: 1) a scheme to defraud by false pretenses, 2) knowing and willful participation in the scheme or artifice and 3) use of interstate wire communications. *United States v. Cassiere*, 4 F.3d 1006 (1st Cir. 1993).

If you find yourself defending one of these cases, you may wonder whether your client actually committed a fraud. What is it to defraud someone?

Unfortunately, the meaning is quite broad. "[T]he words 'to defraud' in the mail fraud statute have the 'common understanding' of '"wrongdoing one in his property rights by dishonest methods or schemes," and "usually signify the deprivation of something of value by trick, chicane, or overreaching."'" *Carpenter v. United States*, 484 U.S. 19 at 27 *quoting McNally v. United States*, 483 U.S. 350, 358 (1987).

There is a five year statute of limitations for wire and mail fraud. 18 U.S.C. §3282. Mail and wire fraud that affect a financial institution have a ten year statute of limitations. 18 U.S.C. §3293. Good faith is an available defense in a mail fraud and wire fraud prosecution. *See, e.g., United States v. Casperson*, 773 F.2d 216, 223 (8th Cir. 1985).

§4:82   Credit Card Fraud

There are a great many credit card fraud cases beyond the mail fraud area. They used to be prosecuted under mail fraud or wire fraud, but recent years has seen an expansion of statutes for credit card fraud. The statutes to be aware of are generally found at 18 U.S.C. §1029, and include trafficking or possession of counterfeit credit cards (called access devices), fraudulent production and use of the same.

An access device is a device that is capable of obtaining "money, goods, services, or any other thing of value." 18 U.S.C. §1029(e)(1). "[U]nauthorized access devices are a subset of access devices, and therefore must be capable of obtaining something of value." *United States v. Onyesoh*, 674 F.3d 1157, 1159 (9th Cir. 2012). The government must prove the devices are useable by a preponderance of the evidence. *Id.* at 1159-60.

EP, who was from New York, obtained some false credit cards with friends and decided to take a trip to Maine to buy video game systems and other electronics. In fact, he and his friends purchased $8,687.01 worth of toys, gift cards, video games and other electronics on several different fraudulent credit cards before they were caught. They had 314 fraudulent credit cards.

§4:83   Impact of Amount of Loss on Federal Sentencing Guidelines

Like many federal theft and fraud cases, the amount of loss is very important to sentencing. Let's look at the use of counterfeit credit cards (or access devices) for an idea of this.

For those of you who don't practice in Federal Court, the enhancements are absolute killers. The Federal Sentencing Guidelines have a Base Offense Level for every type of offense. Those base offense levels get significantly enhanced in almost every case. Take a case of Conspiracy to Possess a Counterfeit Access Device, for example.

Offense/Enhancement	Level
Conspiracy to Possess 15 or More Counterfeit Access Devices	6
Amount of Loss (actual loss $8,687)	+2
Possession of fraudulent identification feature (here a fake license)	+ 2 – if under 12, increase to Level 12.
Adjusted Offense Level	12
Acceptance of Responsibility	–2
Total Offense Level	10
Criminal History Category I, 6 to 12 months	

This isn't so bad, but don't let the amount of loss fool you. The actual loss is nothing under the special rule in U.S.S.G 2B1.1 comment n.3 F(i), which requires loss by the use of an unauthorized access device to be calculated at $500.00 per card, even if the card is unused. For round numbers sake, application of this rule would mean losses of $157,000. Let's watch how this swings the pendulum.

Offense/Enhancement	Level
Conspiracy to Possess 15 or More Counterfeit Access Devices	6
Amount of Loss ($157,000)	+10
Possession of fraudulent identification feature (here a fake license)	+ 2
Adjusted Offense Level	18
Acceptance of Responsibility	–3
Total Offense Level	15
Criminal History Category I, 18 to 24 months	

§4:84   Departure from Guidelines under Economic Reality Theory

In any cases in which you are dealing with intended losses that are large in comparison to actual losses, try to get the court to depart from the sentencing guidelines under an economic reality theory. In *U.S. v. McBride*, the United States Court of Appeal for the Sixth Circuit remanded the case to the district court to consider whether to depart downward under 2B1.1 where the intended loss "substantially overstated" the actual loss. *Id.* at 376-378. In support of its holding, the *McBride* court cited *U.S. v. Roen*, 279 F.Supp. 2d 986 (E.D. Wisc. 2003). *Roen* provides a sound argument to attack the intended loss amount to enhance sentencing.

In *Roen*, the defendant wrote several fraudulent checks from accounts that were closed. *Id.* at 986-987. The Presentence Investigation Report calculated his actual loss at $19,254.82 and his intended loss over $1.2 million. *Id.* The court held that "the amount of loss bore little or no relation to economic reality." *Id.* at 992. The court stated that "the discrepancy between the actual loss—$19,000—and the intended loss—over $1.2 million—was extreme." *Id.* In reaching its holding, the *Roen* court stated that "because the loss determination essentially dictates the severity of the sentence, it is this determination that will almost always be the subject of departure scrutiny." *Id.* at 990.

The *Roen* court noted three other departure reasons that may apply. The first departure could apply when "the amount of loss is determined to be the product of several sources, in addition to the defendant's conduct." *Id.* The second scenario is "when the defendant plays a limited role or inferior role in the scheme that bore little relationship to the amount of loss determined under the guideline." *Id.* at 991. The third situation occurs when the "defendant's effort to remedy the wrong merits considerations." *Id.*

Roen applies this "economic reality" principle." *Id.* Under this principle, "where a defendant devises an ambitious scheme obviously doomed to fail and which causes little or no actual loss, it may be unfair to sentence based on the intended (but highly improbable) loss determination from the [§2B1.1] table." *Id.* The court suggested two factors that are relevant in determining whether the "economic reality" principle applies: First, is there any reasonable possibility that the scheme could have caused the loss the defendant intended; second, whether the intended loss is grossly disproportionate to any actual loss. *Id.*

§4:85   FORM 4-50 Sentencing Memorandum—Credit Card Fraud, Federal

IN THE UNITED STATES DISTRICT COURT
FOR THE DISTRICT OF MAINE

UNITED STATES OF AMERICA,	)	
	)	
Plaintiff,	)	
	)	Case No. 2:11-cr-00100-GZS-3
v.	)	
	)	
EP,	)	
Defendant	)	

SENTENCING MEMORANDUM

On April 20, 2012, EP plead guilty to Conspiracy to Possess Fifteen or More Counterfeit Access Devices (18 U.S.C. §1029(b)(2),(a)(3) and (c)(1)(A)(i)) and Possession of Fifteen or More Counterfeit Access Devices (18 U.S.C. §1029(a)(3) and (c)(1)(A)(i)). He will be sentenced by this Court on August 15, 2012. EP submits the following Sentencing Memorandum for the Court's consideration.

I. FACTUAL BACKGROUND

A.   Case Background

On May 21, 2011, EP was arrested by local law enforcement for Aggravated Forgery and Theft by Unauthorized Taking or Transfer. He was released on bail on June 7, 2011. On June 21, 2011, the United States Attorney's Office filed an Indictment against EP, charging him with Conspiracy to Possess Fifteen or More Counterfeit Access Devices (18 U.S.C. §1029(b)(2),(a)(3) and (c)(1)(A)(i)) and Possession of Fifteen or More Counterfeit Access Devices (18 U.S.C. §1029(a)(3) and (c)(1)(A)(i)). EP traveled from New York and voluntarily appeared. Thereafter, he was released from detention. On April 20, 2012, Mr. EP conditionally pleaded guilty to both counts in the Indictment and has been incarcerated at the Cumberland County Jail, Portland, Maine since his guilty plea.

B.   Defendant's Personal Information

EP is a 28 year-old man. He is a lifelong resident of Brooklyn, New York. EP has a close relationship with both his parents, EP, Sr. and FC. Both parents live in New York. EP has a son who is 4 years old who resides in New York. EP also has a brother, who currently resides in New Jersey. EP is engaged to be married.

C.   Defendant's Criminal History

EP has no criminal history. He was charged in the Cumberland County Unified Criminal Docket for Aggravated Forgery and Theft by Unauthorized Taking or Transfer. However, the charges were dismissed in lieu of the Federal Prosecution.

D.   Evidence of Community and Family Support

Nine (9) letters of support for EP are attached to this Sentencing Memorandum as Exhibits 1-9. These letters paint another picture of EP that goes beyond the crimes he stands in judgment of. They speak of a man with a gentle spirit; a man with a good relationship with his son. They speak of a man who is caring and giving, but who made a mistake.

While I was impressed with EP's positive attributes as displayed in all the letters, I particularly note the letter contained in Exhibit 1, written by an inner-city educator and coach who met EP 18 years ago. He describes EP as a hard-working, determined, caring individual, who has never changed from the first day they met.

We ask this Court to strongly consider the positive and mitigating factors of EP's life as a Fiancé, Son, Friend, Father, and Brother contained in the attached letters.

E.   Defendant's Employment History

EP has primarily worked for his father's sprinkler company, Sprinklers-R-Us, as a licensed sprinkler installer in New York City, New York. He is a hard worker. His history of employment has been positive, and is a mitigating sentencing factor.

F.   Defendant's Educational History

EP graduated Canarsie High School in Brooklyn, New York in 2003. He attended Monroe College in New Rochelle, New York from September 2004 to November 2004. While incarcerated in the Cumberland County Jail, EP has enrolled in a Criminal Justice class.

G.   Defendant's Substance Abuse History

EP does not have a significant history of substance abuse. He considers himself a social drinker and admits to smoking marijuana fairly regularly prior to his arrest.

H.   Conduct After His Arrest

EP has committed himself to leading a law-abiding life since the time of his arrest. He did however admit to his supervising officer that he ingested a brownie that contained marijuana while on bail. No actions were taken by the supervising officer except for a drug test, which came back negative.

II. EP CONTINUES HIS OBJECTION THAT HE SHOULD BE CONSIDERED A MINOR PARTICIPANT IN THE ROLE OF THE OFFENSES CHARGED

The Sentencing Guidelines allow a defendant to obtain a mitigating role adjustment if he or she can show his conduct was less culpable than the Co-Defendants. U.S.S.G. §3B1.2. The Sentencing Guidelines allow a decrease of 4 offense levels if the defendant can prove he was a minimal participant; a decrease of 2 offense levels if the defendant can prove he was a minor participant; and a decrease of 3 offense levels if the defendant can prove his participation was between a minimal participant and minor participant. U.S.S.G. §3B1.2 (a) & (b). The determination of whether any of the adjustments apply is "based on the totality of the circumstances and involves a determination that is heavily dependent upon the facts of the particular case." U.S.S.G. §3B1.2 comment n.3(C).

EP is not suggesting that he was a minimal participant. To be a minimal participant, a person must have the "lack of knowledge or understanding of the scope and structure of the enterprise and of the activities of others." U.S.S.G. §3B1.2, comment n.4. Though EP had no idea where the credit cards came from, he was aware that the

Co-Defendants were not the people whose names were on the credit cards. He was also aware the credit cards were fraudulent.

However, EP was a minor participant in the offenses charged. A minor participant "is less culpable than most other participants, but whose role could not be described as minimal." U.S.S.G. §3B1.2, comment n.5. The First Circuit held that "to qualify as a minor participant, a defendant must demonstrate that he is less culpable than those with whom he acted and less culpable than the majority of those who participate in similar crimes." *United States v. Cirilo-Munoz*, 504 F.3d 106, 139 (1st Cir. 2007).

EP is less culpable than the Co-Defendants in this case. Co-Defendant MB and TC made repeated attempts to purchase items on the fraudulent credit cards. In fact, the Co-Defendants purchased $8,687.01 dollars worth of toys, gift cards, video games and other electronics on several different fraudulent credit cards. Co-Defendant MB admitted to Officer Kevin G. from the South Portland Police Department that he rented the vehicle they used to drive to Maine. There is no evidence that EP rented the hotel room, nor was there any evidence to suggest that EP had any knowledge of how the fraudulent credit cards were obtained or manufactured.

Counsel is under the impression that Co-Defendant MB is incarcerated in New York on similar charges as the case in hand. Co-Defendant TC was arrested and released on bail shortly before the charged offenses. At his Sentencing Hearing, his Attorney stated that the charges in New York stem from an incident that involved Co-Defendant MB's cousin. The Government is not alleging that EP was participating in activity similar to the charged offenses.

EP made one attempt to purchase an item on a fraudulent credit card. The credit card he used was declined and he promptly left the store without making a purchase. He did not make a single purchase on any of the one hundred and eighty-eight credit cards discussed in the Presentence Investigation Report. Unlike the Co-Defendants, EP never presented multiple fraudulent credit cards to the store clerks.

The majority of these types of cases involve defendants who seem to be more similarly situated to MB and TC than to EP. *See United States v. Sandoval*, 668 F.3d 865 (7th Cir. 2011) (Defendant stole credit card information from retail establishments and fraudulently ordered merchandise that the defendant sold, kept or returned for cash); *United States v. Blige*, 635 F.3d 668 (5th Cir. 2011) (Defendant stole customer's account information from cell phone providers and ordered cell phones that the Defendant would resell to other people); *United States v. Truong*, 587 F.3d 1049 (9th Cir. 2009) (Defendant stole unused gift cards, duplicated them and used the originals to purchase goods); *United States v. Prochner*, 417 F.3d 54 (1st Cir. 2005) (Defendant obtained credit card numbers online and would determine whether they were valid before using them to purchase goods or services)

Counsel submits that the majority of offenders in this type of crime are similar to EP's Co-Defendants. They have experiences with the planning and execution of these types of crimes. They have contacts to get their hands on false credit cards.

EP, while acting foolishly, did not mastermind this scheme. Rather, MB and TC, each with experiences committing the crimes here, were the leaders of this organization and the active participants of the scheme.

Should EP have controlled his own conduct? Yes. EP does not dispute his wrongdoing and he is remorseful for his actions. That said, EP's lack of criminal history, compared to the ample history of his Co-Defendants, suggests that he should be entitled to the two point minor participant adjustment.

III. EP OBJECTS TO THE GOVERNMENT'S ASSUMPTION THAT THE MINIMUM LOSS OF $500 PER ACCESS DEVICE APPLIES TO ACCESS DEVICES THAT ARE NOT USEABLE

An access device is a device that is capable of obtaining "money, goods, services, or any other thing of value." 18 U.S.C. §1029(e)(1). "[U]nauthorized access devices are a subset of access devices, and therefore must be capable of obtaining something of value." *United States v. Onyesoh*, 674 F.3d 1157, 1159 (9th Cir. 2012). The government must prove the devices are useable by a preponderance of the evidence. *Id.* at 1159-60.

In *Onyesoh*, the Defendant possessed 500 expired credit cards numbers. *Id.* at 1158. The Defendant argued that proof of usability of the expired numbers was required before the Government could apply the special rule imputing a minimum $500.00 intended loss to all access devices, including those without actual unauthorized charges. *Id.* The Government disagreed and argued that the expired card numbers could help a person create a credit history or open up new credit card accounts and no proof of usability was required. *Id.* The Court stated that "[n]o court, in this or any other circuit, has read usability out of the statute." *Id.* at 1159. The *Onyesoh* Court held that when the usability of an access device is not readily apparent, "some proof of usability is required when the defendant does not concede the fact or when the defendant challenges the sentencing enhancement." *Id.* at 1160.

In this case, the Government seized one hundred and eighty-eight cards from EP and the Co-Defendants. However, the evidence offered only proves that fifteen of those cards were used to make fraudulent purchases and the total cost of those purchases is $8,687.01. There is no evidence that the other one hundred and seventy- three cards were usable. Many of the cards were declined. As previously noted, the single card use attempted by EP was declined.

The Government calculated the actual loss in this case as $7,274.13 for the nine cards that were used to charge $500.00 or more. The Government calculated the loss attributable to the other one hundred and seventy-nine cards as $89,500.00 based on the special rule in U.S.S.G 2B1.1 comment n.3 F(i), which requires loss by the use of an unauthorized access device to be calculated at $500.00 per card. However, there is only evidence that six of those one hundred and seventy-nine cards were actually usable and, therefore, an access device. The Court should not apply U.S.S.G 2B1.1 comment n.3 F(i) to calculate the intended loss unless the Government can show that each of the one hundred and seventy-three unused credit cards was usable. No such evidence has been provided in discovery.

EP is requesting the total intended loss amount be recalculated as follows: actual loss amount for nine cards with unauthorized charges of $500.00 or more, $7,274.13, plus $3,000.00 for the other six usable cards, for a total intended loss amount of $10,274.13, which carries a four point Specific Offense enhancement pursuant to U.S.S.G §2B1.1(b)(1)(C).

IV. THE SENTENCING GUIDELINES *18 U.S.C. §3553(A)* ARE ADVISORY, NOT MANDATORY

The Sentencing Guidelines are advisory. That said, an appropriate sentence for EP is below the Guideline range.

The purpose of the Guidelines is for the Court to "impose a sentence sufficient, but not greater than necessary, to comply" with the purposes of sentencing set forth in the second paragraph of the statute. The United States Supreme Court has summarized factors set forth in the second paragraph of the statute: the "(1) offense and offender characteristics; (2) the need for a sentence to reflect the basic aims of sentencing, namely (a) just punishment (retribution), (b) deterrence, (c) incapacitation, (d) rehabilitation; (3) the sentences legally available; (4) the Sentencing Guidelines; (5) Sentencing Commission policy statements; (6) the need to avoid unwarranted disparities; and (7) the need for restitution." *Rita v. United States*, 127 S.Ct. 2456, 2463 (2007).

A.   EP REQUESTS THE COURT DEPART FROM THE GUIDELINE SENTENCE RANGE BECAUSE THE OFFENSE LEVEL SUBSTANTIALLY OVERSTATES THE SERIOUSNESS OF THE OFFENSE

EP argues above that his sentencing range should not be based on one hundred and seventy-three unused credit cards because the Government has not proven they were useable. However, if the Court agrees with the Government's calculations to determine intended loss and the offense level that stems from the same, EP should be granted a downward deviation because the offense level generated by that calculation substantially overstates the seriousness of the offense. U.S.S.G. §2B1.1 comment n.19(C).

A departure may be granted under the Sentencing Guidelines if "there exists an aggravating or mitigating circumstance." U.S.S.G. §5K2.0 (a)(1)(A). In cases similar to EP, courts have been encouraged to deviate from the Sentencing Guidelines. In *U.S. v. McBride*, the United States Court of Appeal of the Sixth Circuit remanded the case to the district court to consider whether to depart downward under 2B1.1 where the intended loss "substantially overstated" the actual loss. *Id.* at 376-378. In support of its holding, the Court in *McBride* cited *U.S. v. Roen*, 279 F.Supp. 2d 986 (E.D. Wisc. 2003). *Roen* provides an excellent analysis on departures based on the loss amount.

In *Roen*, the defendant wrote several fraudulent checks from accounts that were closed. *Id.* at 986-987. The Presentence Investigation Report calculated his actual loss at $19,254.82 and his intended loss over 1.2 million. *Id.* The court held that "the amount of loss bore little or no relation to economic reality." *Id.* at 992. The court stated that "the discrepancy between the actual loss—$19,000—and the intended loss—over $1.2 million—was extreme." *Id.*

In reaching its holding, the Court in *Roen* stated that "because the loss determination essentially dictates the severity of the sentence, it is this determination that will almost always be the subject of departure scrutiny." *Id.* at 990.

The Court in *Roen* noted three other departure reasons that may apply. The first departure could apply when "the amount of loss is determined to be the product of several sources, in addition to the defendant's conduct." *Id.* The second scenario is "when the defendant plays a limited role or inferior role in the scheme that bore little relationship to the amount of loss determined under the guideline." *Id.* at 991. The third situation occurs when the "defendant's effort to remedy the wrong merits considerations." *Id.*

THEFT OFFENSES

Roen applied the "economic reality" principle." *Id*. There, "where a defendant devises an ambitious scheme obviously doomed to fail and which causes little or no actual loss, it may be unfair to sentence based on the intended (but highly improbable) loss determination from the [§2B1.1] table." *Id*.

In *Roen*, the Court suggested two factors that are relevant in determining whether the "economic reality" principle applies: First, is there any reasonable possibility that the scheme could have caused the loss the defendant intended; second, whether the intended loss is grossly disproportionate to any actual loss. *Id*.

First, there is no evidence that one hundred and seventy-three unused cards were usable. Only fifteen credit cards provided were able to charge; none of which were used by EP. Even though EP made one attempt to purchase goods on an unusable credit card, the amount of loss in this case has no relation to the economic reality of EP's actions. Second, the discrepancy between the actual loss and intended loss are grossly disproportionate to one another.

There is at least an $80,000.00 dollar difference between the actual loss and intended loss in this case. Basic fairness should come into play when the Court considers whether to depart from the Guidelines as a result of the significant deviation between the actual loss and intended loss. *Roen* at 992. By adding the intended loss value, EP's offense level increases by 6 points pursuant to U.S.S.G §2B1.1. Without the 6 point increase, EP's Guideline Range would be 6 to 12 months, not 12 to 18 months as recommended in the Presentence Investigation Report.

The offense level substantially overstates EP's involvement. There is no evidence that each of the one hundred and eighty-eight credit cards were used or honored by any vendor on May 21, 2011. Though the Government can argue the cards were useable, there is no reasonable possibility that the EP would cause over $80,000 dollars in losses; especially, since the Co-Defendants made all the purchases in this case. As a result, a departure is requested and appropriate.

B.   EP REQUESTS THE COURT DEPART FROM THE GUIDELINE SENTENCE RANGE BECAUSE THE GUIDELINES PROVIDE A GREATER THAN NECESSARY SENTENCE

EP argues above that he is entitled to the minor participant adjustment because of his minor role in the charged offenses. However, if the Court agrees with the Probation's suggestion that EP is not entitled to the 2 point minor participant adjustment to his offense level, EP should be granted a downward deviation under 18 U.S.C. §3553(a)(6).

Here, we have a case involving three defendants who are charged with the same crimes. All of the purchases were made by the two Co-Defendants. Both Co-Defendants have a criminal record. In fact, TC admitted, through his attorney at his recent Sentencing Hearing, that he was on bail for similar charges in New York at the time he committed these offenses.

EP does not have a criminal record. He had never been arrested prior to May 21, 2011. There is no evidence that he manufactured the fraudulent credit cards. There is no evidence to suggest that EP was the mastermind of these offenses.

On July 24, 2012, a Sentencing Hearing was held for TC. Judge Singal ordered TC to serve 18 months in prison with 3 years of supervised release, to run consecutively with his current incarceration in New York. Co-Defendant MB has not been sentenced as of today's date.

Under the Guidelines suggested in the Presentence Investigation Report, EP's total offense level is 13, which has a Guideline range of imprisonment of 12 to 18 months (with a criminal history category of I). A sentence within that Guideline range would automatically satisfy the policy statements issued by the Sentencing Commission and would avoid sentencing disparity. Imposing such a sentence, however, would be to ignore the overarching mandate of §3553(a) that EP's sentence be no greater than necessary to comply with the purposes of sentencing set forth in §3553(a)(2). As §3553(a)(6) notes, it is not that all sentencing disparities are to be avoided, but only "unwarranted" sentencing disparities.

This young man made a terrible decision that he will have to live with the rest of his life. However, sentencing EP within the Guideline range is unwarranted because of his diminished role in this matter. Sentencing EP below the Guidelines with a term of supervised release would punish EP for the crimes he pleaded to. For the reasons set forth above, EP should be sentenced below the Sentencing Guidelines.

V. CONCLUSION

EP is a young man with a bright future. However, he has made mistakes. The mistakes that occurred in this case should not be the sole factors the Court uses to establish a fair and appropriate sentence. EP got caught up with the wrong crowd. He admitted his mistakes and is truly sorry for any harm his actions caused. His incarceration has been useful and has shown him to be taking his criminal convictions seriously.

EP is not attempting to minimize his conduct. Not only has his criminality impacted his own life, it has also impacted his family, including his son. EP is not making excuses for the poor decisions he made. He is truly sorry for his actions.

Counsel requests the Court grant him a minor role reduction. Additionally, the Government should be required to show that each of the one hundred and eighty-eight credits cards listed in the Presentence Report were usable under 18 U.S.C. §1029(e)(1) before an enhancement for unused cards is made. No such evidence has been received in discovery. Punishing EP for losses that could never occur because an access device was not useable is not only unjust, but it directly contradicts the Guidelines.

As a result of the above, Counsel suggests the Court impose the following sentence: in 2:10-CR-04-DBG, a sentence of six months of imprisonment, followed by one year of supervised release. Additionally, EP should receive credit for time served since he plead guilty on April 20, 2012.

Finally, the Defendant requests placement at MDC Brooklyn or MCC New York. This is, in part, because it will allow his family to visit him. Counsel knows that the Court's placement recommendation is not binding on the Bureau of Prisons, but asks the Court to kindly make it regardless.

Dated this 13th Day of August, 2012 in Portland, Maine.

Respectfully submitted,

_____

Timothy E. Zerillo
Attorney for Defendant
ZERILLO LAW FIRM, LLC

CHAPTER 5

BURGLARY AND ROBBERY

Burglary and robbery cases can be quite similar. Often what separates a burglary from a robbery is lack of use of a weapon or a violent act. They share many common traits and issues for the criminal defense practitioner, so I discuss them in the same chapter. So that I don't duplicate material, I discuss particular issues where they most often appear in my practice. Eyewitness identification issues, for example, appear in the robbery sub-section. That, of course, doesn't mean that eyewitness identification would not come into play in burglary cases or any number of other crimes.

BURGLARY
AND ROBBERY

I.   BURGLARY

A. Elements and Common Scenarios

§5:01   The Elements

Theft, burglary and robbery are close cousins. They often overlap.

The common law elements of burglary involved unlawfully entering a residence, at night, with the intent to commit a theft. These elements have been broadened subsequently. The forcible entry requirement is usually eliminated. All that is generally required is:

- Entry into a structure,
- With no legal grounds to do so and
- With intent to commit a crime therein.

As a result, a burglary can be committed usually without the intent to commit a theft. The intent to commit any crime will do.

§5:02   Dumb Kids

We tend to think that burglaries are committed by seasoned cat burglars. We imagine a caper film, with a group of guys using lasers to cut glass and doing elaborate acrobatics not to sound the alarm.

I've never represented one of those guys. But I have represented plenty of dumb kids who thought it was fun to break into a house. Usually, the decision to break into the house was helped along by alcohol or some other mind-altering drug. In either event, they break in, get caught, and suddenly have a felony on their hands.

I once represented a 19 year old kid who entered an acquaintance's house, to "borrow" a video game and gaming console. He had let the homeowner's son borrow one of his video games in the past, so he thought there was an open door policy. Boy, was he wrong! He was charged with a burglary felony. This is the type of dumb kid burglary case you may encounter.

§5:03   The Seasoned Cat Burglar

Seasoned cat burglars are usually not seasoned in the *Ocean's Eleven* sense of the word. There is no Danny Ocean mastermind and Reuben Tishkoff isn't financing the venture. More often than not, they are burglarizing because they are down on their luck or to feed a drug habit.

You do get the rare burglars who are actually quite skilled at their trade, and make a living at it. These guys are often the easiest to deal with. Getting pinched occasionally is part of the profession. They know what has to be proven and they know the risks. They usually take the best deal after negotiation.

[§§5:04-5:09 Reserved]

B. Strategies and Tactics

§5:10   No Burglars' Tools Found

One way to approach these cases if your clients were caught in the act or shortly thereafter, is to see if burglar's tools were found on or near your client.

This isn't a burglary case, but it makes the point. A frequent client of mine was caught with a friend and a Coke machine in the parking lot of the high school he then attended. The police happened by just as they were about to open the machine up. When they told the police their story, they said they found the machine on the side of the road and were returning it to the school. They were arrested.

All that said, they had no tools to open the machine up. How these two geniuses were planning on getting into the machine, I don't know. Since there were no burglar's tools found, it seemed to me that it was an argument to make to the prosecutor, and the prosecutor dropped the case.

The same goes for your clients caught in the act of breaking into a residence or commercial property. If they do not have burglar's tools, argue that there was no intent to forcibly enter. Each jurisdiction is different on this issue, but you may be able to paint the case as more criminal trespass than burglary.

If your client is caught with an entire tool belt full of tools at the scene, then you need to explain why. Maybe his job requires that he use those tools. Maybe he is remodeling his house. Whatever you do, don't leave that fact alone; explain it.

Always clarify for a jury what is meant by burglar's tools. The government witnesses will make burglar's tools sound so special and fantastic that they are beyond what they are: plain old tools available at any Home Depot. See §5:60 for a cross examination of a police officer on the burglar's tools issue.

§5:11   Dumb Kids: Get to Prosecutor Early

With the dumb kids cases, get to the prosecutor early (or cop, if it hasn't been charged yet), and try to get the case dumped or a favorable disposition early on. See §5:12 Form 5-10 Letter to Prosecutor; Dumb Kid Burglary Case.

I once had a case where my client claimed to have thought a house in his neighborhood was abandoned, so he let himself in to take a portable CD player. I had just resolved a case for him where he was accused of unlawful sexual contact. He got a misdemeanor assault deal for a year of probation and no jail time. While out on bail, he committed the burglary. But he was still a young, dumb kid.

I usually first approach the prosecutor with a letter and then follow up with phone calls, emails and knocks on the door. Below is the letter I wrote in this case. I followed this letter with emails, in person meetings and phone calls. The prosecutor was not very choked up by my client, especially in light of the fact that he committed this offense while on bail for the sex offense. That said, he was truly a dumb kid, and eventually the prosecutor came to our terms.

If your prosecutor has little sympathy for your client's attributes, consider filing a *de minimis* motion to dismiss. See §5:30 and §5:31 Form 5-20 *De Minimis* Motion to Dismiss.

§5:12   FORM 5-10 Letter to Prosecutor: Dumb Kid Burglary Case

ATTN: B. Kind, ADA
Cumberland County District Attorney's Office
142 Federal Street
Portland, ME 04101

    Re: State of Maine v. Joe Dumbkid

Dear ADA Kind,

I wanted to touch base with you on Joe Dumbkid's case which is up on the trial list for the end of this month. As you know Joe is charged with Burglary (Class B), Theft (Class E), and Criminal Trespass (Class D). The burglary charge involves an allegation that Joe entered a neighbor's house and took a portable CD player. Joe admitted he took the CD player, but stated that he thought that the house had been abandoned. The criminal trespass charge involves an apparent comedy of errors whereby Joe or another party went into the same neighbor's house while intoxicated and witnessed them having sex.

Joe is a young man with no prior criminal record, other than a misdemeanor assault he pled to earlier this year for which he got two years of probation. He was abusing alcohol and recreational drugs during this period of time and it certainly impaired his judgment. Joe has since left the area and moved to Augusta to live with his father. He has engaged in drug and alcohol counseling and has been clean and sober. I cannot stress enough how much I like Joe. He has made mistakes, but was honest about them. He has also done the appropriate things to keep those problems in check.

This case is way over-charged in my opinion. My pitch is for dismissal of the felony, plea to the misdemeanors for a one year deferred disposition, to result in dismissal if he stays out of trouble. He is already on probation, and is doing quite well. This incident, as you know, happened before he was on probation

Joe has acted like a dumb kid; that is for sure. But that is because he is, in fact, still a kid. He hit a bad patch in his life and made some stupid decisions. He is still young, and avoiding a felony here is crucial to his leading a productive life.

Thanks for your consideration.

                                  Very truly yours,
                                  Timothy E. Zerillo
                                  ZERILLO LAW FIRM, LLC

§5:13   Consent to Enter Residence

You will also see the occasional burglary where the defendant has a connection to the property at issue. Maybe it belongs to a friend of the family, an ex-spouse or girlfriend, or a neighbor. You may be able to raise the issue at the trial that there was an unwritten rule that the defendant could enter the premises.

I once represented a fellow who wandered into a neighbor's house, grabbed a bag of marijuana, and left. He was charged with a burglary. We argued that he had an open invitation into the house, and that, for these people, grabbing a small bag of pot was no more than grabbing a soda out of the fridge. Implied consent can be a powerful argument if raised properly.

§5:14   Property Recovery Issues

Again, don't overlook the obvious. This applies to property as well. If you assume that the property taken from your client by the police is also the property stolen in the burglary, you may be overlooking a fruitful area of inquiry.

I once had a long-term client with a bad drug problem. He had gone in and out of jail for all of his adult life. On one of the rare occasions he was out, he began burglarizing residences for money and other goods he could hawk to support his drug habit. He was pretty good at it actually, and wasn't caught for the vast majority of burglaries he did, which was in the hundreds from what I hear. He committed these burglaries around a small college town in coastal Maine, and the police were well aware of him and his activities.

He finally was nabbed on one. His probation officer did a random search of his residence and found some German currency from the early 20th century. The probation officer knew of a case in which German currency had gone missing. My client was arrested, and the police celebrated catching the guy who they believed was burglarizing dozens if not hundreds of area residences.

The client had been around the block, so he didn't say a word to the cops. There was no confession, but he also didn't have an alibi. So, I looked at the evidence. It seemed strange, of course, that my client had this fairly rare currency on him in coastal Maine. But who was I to say how rare it was?

So I contacted local coin and currency dealers to learn about it. Turns out it was a common type of German currency at the time it was issued. As a result, I argued that not only couldn't the State prove he burglarized the place by his mere possession, but the State could also not prove that the currency was the alleged victim's.

I can't remember the exact disposition, but it was ultimately favorable, especially in light of the client's long record. The moral of the story is don't assume the property recovered from your client is the actual property stolen in the burglary.

§5:15   Alternative Suspects

Don't forget to raise the issue of alternative suspects. I often have a tendency to consider alternative suspects in terms of specific individuals. Like Hannibal Lecter saying "It wasn't me, it was Buffalo Bill!" I think this stymies us, unless we have a specific person to point the finger at.

It doesn't have to be that difficult, however. I once handled a case where my client and his friend were charged with burglarizing a number of empty vacation camps on a lake. I had heard about other camps being burglarized on a lake not that far away. Raising the issue that the actual burglars were still at large proved useful.

PRACTICE TIP: *Make sure your client won't be blamed*

Only raise the issue of alternative suspects, such as in the camp burglary case above if you can do it in a way in which the jury won't blame the uncharged burglaries on your client too. For example, maybe there is a good alibi on the other charges that clears your client, and allows you to raise this issue.

[§§5:16-5:29 Reserved]

C. Motions

§5:30   Motion to Dismiss as *De Minimis*

When the prosecutor is unmoved by your "dumb kid" (see §5:11) client, you may find a receptive ear on the bench. Bend that ear with a *de minimis* motion to dismiss. In Maine, we have a statute that allows the court to dismiss a prosecution if the defendant's offense was trivial. Your jurisdiction likely has something similar.

Sometimes, a sympathetic judge will sway the prosecutor for you before the *de minimis* motion is even heard. Either way, pouting about the prosecutor's cold heart won't do anything, so file a motion.

For example, I had another case with a dumb kid, this one four months after his 18th birthday, that resulted in a charge of burglary of a motor vehicle. My client decided he was going to go to the local park in the affluent community in which he lived to smoke some pot. While there, my client and his friend, made conversation with a man in a passenger van.

The man was actually an undercover cop. The police, with nothing better to do, set up a sting in the park. There, a bait vehicle was filled with electronics and left unlocked. The van was the surveillance vehicle.

When the undercover officer saw my client coming, he left another officer to hide in the van, made conversation with my client, and left, leaving the van unlocked.

My client and his friend, thinking they were alone, then began the process of preparing to smoke marijuana. They decided it was a good idea to smoke it from a carrot. I'm not sure if they were trying to improve their night vision or if they just loved carrots. They had a coat hanger they fashioned for drilling a hole in the carrot.

It was a hot day, and my client noticed that there was a case of water bottles in the surveillance van. He decided it would be OK to help himself to one. He and his friend smoked the pot and he drank half the water. This was witnessed by the officer hidden in the surveillance van.

Neither my client nor his friend touched the bait vehicle.

If this fact pattern sounds familiar to you, it is because my client was lampooned for it on the national news. He was, essentially, called an idiot. In fact, he is a very bright guy who made bad choices.

Among other things my client was arrested for burglary of a motor vehicle for stealing the water.[1] Sounds like a case that would be emphatically thrown out as soon as it crosses a prosecutor's desk, right? Not this time.

The prosecutor, who also lived in this community, felt the need to teach this young man a lesson. She talked about a week in jail plus counseling. She wanted convictions. She wanted every heavy-handed thing you could think of.

This is the perfect case in which to file a *De Minimis* Motion to Dismiss. Since I couldn't get the prosecutor to toss the case on her own, I needed court intervention.

While you need to bring the *De Minimis* Motion with a straight face, it is possible it will never be heard. Here, for example, we conferenced the Motion and the judge leaned hard on the prosecutor. The judge made ground with the prosecutor that I had been unable to and the case was resolved that day.

File these motions strategically if you have a petty offense and the sympathy factor on your side. As the saying goes, if the law is on your side, argue the law. If the facts are on your side, argue the facts. If neither is on your side, pound the table.

§5:31   FORM 5-20 *De Minimis* Motion to Dismiss

STATE OF MAINE	SUPERIOR COURT
CUMBERLAND, SS	DOCKET NO. CR-11-1234

STATE OF MAINE,	)	
	)	
	)	MOTION TO DISMISS CHARGES
v.	)	AS DE MINIMIS INFRACTIONS
	)	AND MEMORANDUM OF LAW
BRIAN BURGLARY,	)	
	)	
Defendant	)	

---

[1] I raise this issue of the coathanger because the State claimed it was burglar's tools. Never mind the fact that the cars were both unlocked and the hanger had carrot all over it.

NOW COMES the DEFENDANT by and through Undersigned Counsel, and Moves to Dismiss the Charges against him as De Minimis Infractions as follows:

1. Defendant is charged with misdemeanor theft and burglary of a motor vehicle.
2. The charges at issue resulted when, on a hot August day, the Defendant reached into an unlocked vehicle and took a drink from a single bottle of water in a case full of water.
3. As is described in the facts and argument in the following Memorandum of Law, all charges in this matter must be dismissed as De Minimis.

MEMORANDUM OF LAW

On a particularly warm day in August, the Defendant, four months past his 18th birthday, went to the park in Falmouth with a friend. While there, they encountered a man in an unmarked van. The man asked them about the river near the park. The Defendant and his friend told the man about the river and the trail to get there.

The man walked toward the river. It was a hot day, and Defendant noticed there was a case of water bottles in the front seat of the van. The van was unlocked and its windows were partially open.

That van was actually a police surveillance vehicle. Next to the van was a bait vehicle, filled with electronics.

Defendant asked his friend if he thought it would be alright if he grabbed a water bottle because he was thirsty. The friend replied that he thought it was. Defendant then allegedly took a water bottle from the van and drank a portion of it.

Defendant and his friend ignored and never entered the bait vehicle. They never took any of the electronics from the bait vehicle, only the water from the surveillance vehicle. The crime of the century this certainly is not. Yet, Defendant is charged with Burglary of a Motor Vehicle and Theft.

Fortunately, the Maine Legislature has given Courts a mechanism to dismiss De Minimis infractions, such as the one here. Title 17-A MRSA s. 12 states:

1. The court may dismiss a prosecution if, upon notice to or motion of the prosecutor and opportunity to be heard, having regard to the nature of the conduct alleged and the nature of the attendant circumstances, it finds the defendant's conduct:
   A. Was within a customary license or tolerance, which was not expressly refused by the person whose interest was infringed and which is not inconsistent with the purpose of the law defining the crime; or
   B. Did not actually cause or threaten the harm sought to be prevented by the law defining the crime or did so only to an extent too trivial to warrant the condemnation of conviction; or
   C. Presents such other extenuations that it cannot reasonably be regarded as envisaged by the Legislature in defining the crime.

Here, a Motion to Dismiss as De Minimis is appropriate under all three of the potential grounds for dismissal of a De Minimis infraction, although subsections B and C are the most significant to this Motion.

Under Subsection B, if in fact that drinking of the water was a theft, it was done in such a way and "to an extent too trivial to warrant the condemnation of conviction." 17-A MRSA s. 12(b). Likewise, under Subsection C, it is likely that the Legislature did not envision that the crimes of Burglary of a Motor Vehicle or Theft would be committed by drinking water on a hot day.

This point is emphasized to a greater degree when you consider that the Defendant at issue, barely an adult at the time of the alleged offense, has a history of dehydration. Counsel is new to this case but is gathering the medical records now which should reflect that Defendant has a history of dehydration. In any event, he was thirsty, and it was a De Minimis infraction for him to take a drink.

Clearly this was not a wise move by Defendant. That said, he had just given directions to the person he thought was the owner of the car and the water. He thought they were on friendly terms. He thought it was acceptable to take the water to quench his thirst. This was certainly foolish, but it does not rise to the level of a burglary of a motor vehicle or a theft.

WHEREFORE, Counsel requests this Court to Dismiss this Matter as De Minimis.

Dated this __th day of _____, 20__, at _____

Respectfully submitted,

_____
Timothy E. Zerillo
Attorney for Defendant
ZERILLO LAW FIRM, LLC

§5:32   Motion to Sever Defendants

In a case with multiple defendants, the choice of attempting to sever the cases should be strongly considered. Usually, I decide if I want severance by determining whether my defendant looks better or worse than the other defendant(s). If I have the baby face in a group of hardened criminals, I want to move to sever. I don't want their stink on my guy. If I represent the hardened criminals, I want the more innocent guy around to make my clients look more credible and likeable.

This is, of course, a generalization. It is also a generalization that others don't agree with. Some would say that keeping the more innocent client tied to the more hardened criminals makes the innocent client look better by comparison. While I understand the theory, I don't agree with it. I think guilt by association is a pretty important intangible for jurors.

Of course, motions to sever occur in all sorts of criminal cases. I specifically include them here because burglaries often seem to have co-defendants. The more experienced burglars often work in tandem, think, the "Wet Bandits" from the great holiday movie, *Home Alone*. In addition, when dumb kids act dumb, they usually have friends with them to encourage their stupidity.

If you decide to pursue a motion to sever, judicial economy will be a strong argument for the government. The court wants to do anything it can get away with to eliminate cases on its docket.

§5:33   *Bruton and Its Progeny*

Remember to consider the constitutional implications of *Bruton v. United States*, 391 U.S. 123, 88 S.Ct. 1620, 20 L.Ed.2d 476 (1968). There, the appellant was tried with a co-defendant for an armed postal robbery. At trial, the court allowed the testimony of a witness who indicated that the co-defendant confessed to the crime and to having the help of Bruton in committing the crime. The court instructed the jury not to consider the confession by the co-defendant in determining Bruton's guilt. On appeal, the Circuit Court of Appeals upheld Bruton's conviction, and he challenged, on *certiorari*, his conviction in the Supreme Court. The Supreme Court held that the admission of a confession by a non-testifying co-defendant in a joint trial violates the Confrontation Clause of the Sixth Amendment.

Bruton has, of course, been the subject of significant litigation. In *California v. Green*, 399 U.S. 149, 158 (1970), the purpose of *Bruton* and the general purpose of confrontation was explained. Confrontation

> (1) insures that the witness will give his statements under oath – thus impressing him with the seriousness of the matter and guarding against the lie by the possibility of a penalty for perjury; (2) forces the witness to submit to cross-examination, the greatest legal engine ever invented for the discovery of truth; (3) permits the jury that is to decide the defendant's fate to observe the demeanor of the witness in making his statement, thus aiding the jury in assessing his credibility.

The ground gained in *Bruton* and *Green* was limited by the backwards holding in *Richardson v. Marsh*, 481 U.S. 200 (1987). *Richardson* provided an exception to *Bruton* when the co-defendant's confession is redacted to eliminate any mention of the defendant's name or existence, as long as the court issues an appropriate limiting instruction. It was held that when the statements do not refer directly to the defendant, there is no confrontation problem. In Footnote 5 to the opinion, the Court stated that "We express no opinion on the admissibility of a confession in which the defendant's name has been replaced with a symbol or neutral pronoun."

In *Gray v. Maryland*, 523 U.S. 185 (1998), the Supreme Court came back to its senses and answered the *Richardson* footnote problem it previously declined to rule on. In *Gray*, the Court found that a redacted confession with blanks or obvious redactions that infer the existence of another person is also a *Bruton* violation.

Imagine the scenario of two dumb kids, caught burglarizing their local boat yard. One confesses and implicates the other guy, and our guy doesn't say a word. I would certainly try to sever on *Bruton* grounds. See §5:34 for the motion to sever I might file in such a case.

§5:34   FORM 5-30: Motion to Sever Defendants

STATE OF MAINE		SUPERIOR COURT
KENNEBEC, ss		DOCKET NO. CR-12-11111

STATE OF MAINE,	)	
	)	
v.	)	DEFENDANT DUMBKID'S
	)	MOTION TO SEVER
IMA DUMBKID	)	DEFENDANTS
	)	
Defendant	)	

NOW COMES the Defendant, Ima Dumbkid, by and through Undersigned Counsel, and requests that this Court sever his case from Defendant Evendumberkid's case for the following reasons:

1. Mr. Dumbkid requests that his trial be severed from the trial of his co-Defendant in this case because he will be unduly prejudiced by the joint trial with Defendant Evendumberkid.

2. The allegations of the Indictment, make it impossible for Mr. Dumbkid to receive a fair trial. Joinder of the defendants in this case is prejudicial and will continue to be prejudicial during trial. As such, severance of joined defendants is necessary to avoid unfair prejudice in the event that one of the defendants would like to testify while the other defendant wishes to invoke his Fifth Amendment right.

3. During trial, statements that will be attributed to Mr. Evendumberkid may contain information about Mr. Dumbkid. Mr. Dumbkid's right to call Defendant Evendumberkid as a witness to contradict those statements or cross-examine him will be in direct conflict with Evendumberkid's privilege against self-incrimination. A joint trial of Defendant and Co-Defendant at which such statement is admitted would violate the Constitution, Bruton v. United States, 391 U.S. 123, 88 S.Ct. 1620, 20 L.Ed.2d 476 (1968).

4. Additionally, Mr. Dumbkid will be unduly prejudiced by evidence of Count Two of the Indictment, Possession of a Scheduled Drug, in which he is not charged. The nature of cocaine possession charges is such that if Mr. Dumbkid is tried with his Co-Defendant, there is a serious risk that the jury will be unable to make a reliable determination of his innocence or guilt, and that he will not receive a fair trial. Therefore, severance of the Co-Defendant's is mandated.

WHEREFORE, Counsel requests this Court grant his Motion to Sever Defendants.

Respectfully submitted,

_____

Timothy E. Zerillo
Attorney for Defendant
ZERILLO LAW FIRM, LLC

PRACTICE TIP: *Additional charges against co-defendant*

You will notice in the Motion to Sever Defendants that in addition to *Bruton* issues, that I mentioned the co-defendant's additional charges. Always look for that issue if the charges are different. The mere presence of additional charges may prejudice your client.

§5:35   Motion to Sever Counts

Sometimes you will come across a string of burglaries all charged in a single Indictment. That necessitates the filing of a motion to sever counts.

In a motion to sever counts, judicial economy concerns are working against you. As a result, you need to find a reason to trump the natural inclination of the court to clear its docket as quickly as possible.

I have found one very effective way to argue a motion to sever counts. The primary way in which I argue the case is not the prejudice suffered by the defendant if multiple crimes are charged together, although that should certainly be argued. Rather, the more moving argument is on Fifth Amendment grounds.

I always argue that my client has the election, in a multiple count trial alleging different criminal episodes, to testify related to some charges and not others. As a matter of course, my clients don't make the decision to testify until after the government has rested. As a result, I can't tell the court until we are through most of the trial whether or not my client will testify. If counts are tried together, and he chooses to testify related to one criminal episode but not the other, he faces a Hobson's choice that either violates his Due Process or Fifth Amendment rights.

§5:36　FORM 5-40 Motion to Sever Counts

STATE OF MAINE		SUPERIOR COURT
KENNEBEC, ss		DOCKET NO. CR-09-590

STATE OF MAINE,　　　　　　　　　)

v.　　　　　　　　　　　　　　　　　)　　　　　DEFENDANT'S

　　　　　　　　　　　　　　　　　　)　　　　　MOTION TO SEVER

MR. DEFENDANT,　　　　　　　　　)　　　　　JOINED COUNTS

Defendant　　　　　　　　　　　　　)

NOW COMES the Defendant, Mr. Defendant, by and through Undersigned Counsel, and requests that this Court sever Counts 1 and 2 of the Complaint in this matter, pursuant to M.R.Crim.P 8(d). As grounds therefore, Defendant states as follows:

1. A Complaint was brought against Defendant alleging an Assault in Count 1, with the alleged victim being Victim 1, and an Unlawful Sexual Touching in Count 2, with the alleged victim being Victim 2. These allegations involve similar facts, that is, that the Defendant laid down with each of the alleged victims when they were sleeping and touched them in an unwanted way.

2. M.R.Evid. 404(b) precludes the introduction of prior (or subsequent) "crimes, wrongs or acts… to prove the character of a person in order to show that he acted in conformity therewith." Therefore, evidence of the alleged "crimes, wrongs or acts" in Counts 1 is not admissible as to Counts 2, and *vice versa*.

3. Counts 1 and 2 do not arise out of the same "act or transaction" do not involve the same person, and are not part of a common scheme or plan. *See* M.R.Crim.P. 8(a). In fact, the cases involve different alleged victims. Accordingly, they should not have been joined in the Complaint in the first place. *Id.*

4. The Defendant is prejudiced by the joinder of these cases, on several grounds. First, the Defendant may elect to testify as to one of the claims, but not as to the other. Severance should be granted on that cause alone. *Cross v. U.S.*, 335 F.2d 987 (D.C. Cir. 1964).

5. The Defendant also contends that the jury may infer criminal conduct in Counts 1 from Counts 2 or *vice versa. United States v. Massa*, 740 F.2d 629 (8th Cir. 1984) (severance proper where jury could not be expected to compartmentalize evidence); *U.S. v. Lewis*, 787 F.2d 1318 (9th Cir.) (admissions of other crimes in one count prejudiced defendant on other joined count where evidence weak on second charge), *modified* 798 F.2d 1250, *cert. denied* 489 U.S. 1032 (1989).

6. M.R. Crim. P. Rule 8(d) allows the Court to sever Counts 1 and 2 as relief from prejudicial joinder. A joined trial would create the danger that the jury would use evidence admissible as to either of the counts "to infer a criminal disposition" on the part of the Defendant as to the other counts. *See United States v. Foutz*, 540 F.2d 733, 736-38 (4th Cir. 1976); *United States v. Gregory*, 369 F.2d 185, 189 (D.C. Cir. 1966), cert. denied, 396 U.S. 865 (1969). A joined trial on all counts against the Defendant creates a grave danger that the evidence as to each separate count will "cumulat[e] in the jurors' minds." Id.; *see United States v. Halper*, 590 F.2d 422, 430 (2d Cir. 1978); *United States v. Gregory*, 369 F.2d at 189. For each of these reasons, severance of Counts 1 and 2 is essential under Me. R. Crim. P. 8(d).

WHEREFORE, Counsel requests this Court grant this Motion to Sever Count 1 from Count 2 for the foregoing reasons.

Dated this the 9th day of October, 2009 in Portland, Maine.

Respectfully submitted,

_____

Timothy E. Zerillo

Attorney for Defendant

ZERILLO LAW FIRM, LLC

[§§5:37-5:49 Reserved]

D. Trial

1. Opening Statement

§5:50   My Approach

Let's imagine we're doing an opening in the case with the dumb kids who entered the residence to take the video game. I might approach a portion of the opening by recalling my own lack of judgment as a youth and encouraging jurors to do the same and then admitting that my client acted foolishly but not criminally.

Sometimes the dumb kid defense is the best way to go, especially if you are weak with the facts. Never underestimate the power of jury nullification for a sympathetic client.

PRACTICE TIP: *Prepare the client*

If you were going to attempt this type of opening in any case in which you are claiming that your client acted like an idiot but did not act in a criminal manner, always let the client know first. This sounds obvious, but I have heard of lawyers really pissing off their clients with this sort of approach and not clearing it first. I always say to my client, "Look this is the way I want to open, but I don't want to shock you and I don't want you to even think that anything I am saying I necessarily believe. I just want to sell it to the jury the best way possible. Are you ok with that?" I've never had a client refuse me.

For general tips on opening statements, see Ch. 2.

§5:51   Sample Opening Statement: "Dumb Kid" Defense

When I look back on how I was when I was eighteen years old, I can see now that I was virtually a complete idiot. You would laugh at some of the choices that I made. I was an adult, just like Micah is here. I was an adult within the meaning of the law, as is Micah. I could vote. So can he. I could sign up to fight in a war. So can he. But overall, I was really dumb.

And when I look back on the chances that I took and the things that I did, I shake my head. I wonder why in the world I thought it was wise to do such things? I know I would never do them now.

Perhaps when you look back on your own life, to the time when you were Micah's age, you feel the same way. Sometimes, I think that we begin to relive that feeling of our own stupidity at these ages through our kids. We shake our heads at them and wonder how they could be that stupid, when if we really reflected, we were probably just as stupid or more so.

Well, I won't dispute in this case that you are going to hear that Micah did some very stupid things. That he made a bad choice. And I would submit to you that if he reflects on it twenty years from now, he will agree with me that he was foolish.

But the major difference between the defense and the prosecution is this: the State believes the evidence shows that Micah's stupid act is criminal. The defense believes the evidence shows that Micah's stupidity is merely stupidity and that he should not be punished for the rest of his life by a criminal conviction.

[§§5:52-5:59 Reserved]

2. Cross-Examination

§5:60   Sample Cross-Examination of Officer Regarding Burglar's Tools

Here is a brief cross-examination regarding burglars tools. The point is to get the officer to admit that so called burglar's tools are just ordinary tools. The implication for the jury is that mere possession of the tools does not prove the defendant's intent to commit a burglary.

For tips on cross-examining cops and other witnesses, see Ch. 2.

BURGLARY
AND ROBBERY

Q. You testified on direct examination that Mr. Brakin Enter had "burglar's tools" on him when you found him at Mrs. Snipe's residence.
A. Yes.
Q. I want to go through this burglar's tools list, OK?
A. OK.
Q. You found a hammer?
A. Yes.
Q. You found a screw driver?
A. Yes.
Q. Philips head?
A. Yes.
Q. And a drill?
A. Yes.
Q. And a crow bar?
A. Yes.
Q. Those are the "burglar's tools?"
A. Yes.
Q. So burglar's tool aren't special tools, are they?
A. I don't know what you mean.
Q. When you say "burglar's tools," they sound like something really special, like a laser cutting through glass or something. You don't mean that do you?
A. No.
Q. These are normal tools.
A. I guess.
Q. Well, you have a hammer at home, don't you?
A. Yes, I do.
Q. And that's not a burglar's tool.
A. No.
Q. And you have a screwdriver?
A. Yes.
Q. Even a Philip's head like the one here?
A. Yes.
Q. And a drill?
A. Yes.
Q. And those aren't your burglar's tools, are they?
A. No, because I don't burglarize people.
Q. Right, and that's the point, isn't it? The tools on their own have no meaning related to whether Mr. Enter committed a burglary. (Answer doesn't much matter at this point)

§5:61   Sample Cross-Examination of Owner Regarding Implied Consent to Enter Premises

If there is an implied consent possibility, always cross examine the owner of the property on that issue. See Ch. 2 for cross-examination tips.

Q. Mr. Homebody, you testified that you have lived in the Whispering Pines neighborhood for 18 years.
A. Yes.
Q. You live there with your wife?
A. Yes.
Q. She knows Micah?
A. Yes, she does.
Q. Your wife co-owns the property with you?
A. Yes.
Q. Micah has come and gone from your house many times.
A. Yes.

Q. He is friendly with your son Tommy?
A. Yes.
Q. Micah is allowed to be on the property?
A. Not to steal video games.
Q. OK, but he can borrow video games?
A. He didn't borrow a video game.
Q. But you really don't know that, do you?
A. I know he didn't borrow it; he took it.
Q. That is because of what your son told you?
A. Yes.
Q. Didn't your son borrow a video game from Micah previously?
A. Yes.
Q. How do you know he didn't steal it?
A. He told me Micah let him borrow it.
Q. So your opinion about the burglary comes from your son entirely?
A. No.
Q. You don't have any independent knowledge of the facts at issue.
A. I believe I do.
Q. OK. Is your wife here to testify today?
A. No.
Q. You don't know if your wife gave Micah permission to enter and borrow the game.
A. No, she didn't.

[§§5:62-5:69 Reserved]

3. Closing Argument

§5:70   My Approach

Like many closing arguments, in the case above, I would simply focus on issues of reasonable doubt: when my client entered the house, he reasonably believed he had permission to do so and to borrow the video game
        For closing argument tips, see Ch. 2.

§5:71   Sample Closing Argument: Reasonable Doubt

You were supposed to have certain questions answered and they weren't, ladies and gentlemen. And when the questions aren't answered by the people required to answer them, the State, then you need to issue your vote of not guilty.

My client may have been foolish. He may have misapprehended the bounds of what he could do. He may not have carefully thought the process through, but he didn't commit a burglary. When he entered the house and took the video game, he thought he had permission and his thought was reasonable.

I have a grandfather who likes to grab a handful of nuts and raisins when he shops at the local grocery store. He calls that sampling; the store calls it theft; but it is common and it's ignored.

Imagine my grandfather shows up there one day and they aren't open yet, but somebody has left the door open. Grandpa wanders in, grabs his cart, starts shopping, and samples some nuts along the way.

Well, Grandpa thinks the store is open. He thinks sampling is OK. He hasn't committed a burglary even though the store is actually closed, because he thinks it's open. And he thinks taking the raisins and nuts is OK even though that may be wrong. Micah is no different here.

So let's take the actual facts, and now tie them to the heavy burden the State has to meet of proving this case beyond a reasonable doubt…

For sample arguments on burden of proof and reasonable doubt, see Ch. 2.

[§§5:72-5:79 Reserved]

II.   ROBBERY

A.   Elements and Common Scenarios

§5:80   The Elements

Robbery, unlike burglary, generally requires the use of force. While burglaries are often accomplished with no one around, robberies have active victims. Generally, robbery requires that the perpetrator have:

1. Taken something;
2. With intent to steal the thing that was taken;
3. Without a legal right to the thing that was taken;
4. Against the alleged victim's will; and
5. By force, intimidation or threat of force.

§5:81   Robbery on the Street

Here's a typical street robbery situation you might run across drawn from one of my cases. My client, Anthony Soprano III, and his "friend," Mr. Vic Tim, are walking down the street. They are only friends by virtue of the fact that they like to hang out in the same crack house and smoke and drink together.

It's about 11 in the morning, and they are walking up a street in Portland, Maine to get a money order. From there, the plan is to grab a few beers and start the day.

Vic Tim doesn't understand what is going on in Soprano's head. Soprano believes Vic took his wallet. He's been asking around the crack house and all the other crackheads, probably to diffuse suspicion from themselves, point to Tim as the culprit.

While walking up the street, Soprano's blood begins boiling just thinking about his wallet. He is convinced Vic took it. So, at the right time, Soprano reaches into Vic's rear pocket. Soprano isn't much of a pickpocket, so Vic resists. Soprano shoves him down, grabs the wallet, gives him a kick, and runs off.

Across the street, Mrs. Nearsighted is walking her dog. She sees Mr. Tim get thrown down and kicked, and calls 911. An ambulance and the police arrive, and the ambulance takes Mr. Tim to the hospital. Mrs. Nearsighted gives a statement to the police. Mr. Tim does as well, and identifies his friend from a photo array. Mrs. Nearsighted is not asked to identify Soprano from a photo array or line-up.

These types of situations raise all sorts of eyewitness identification and other issues, especially when the witness and the alleged perpetrator are of different races.

§5:82   Bank Robbery

While most of the burglary and robbery cases you handle will probably be state court cases, if you happen to catch a bank robbery case, you will be dealing with the feds.

Like many of these cases, with bank robberies you are dealing with desperate people. There are, of course, the more hardened professional "crews" that work bank robberies for a living. As the Ben Affleck movie *The Town* explained, in at least one fictional account, bank robbery and strong armed robbery in general is reputed to be passed down from father to son in Charlestown, Massachusetts. I don't know about you, but I don't see much of that expertise in bank robbery in my practice.

The professionals make up a small amount of the bank robbery cases. At the other end of the spectrum are the desperate, high and/or drunk, bank robbers who need the cash for a variety of different reasons.

All of them, professional and less than professional, end up in federal court. Any bank, credit union, or savings and loan association that operates under federal law and/or is insured by the Federal Deposit Insurance Corporation implicates federal jurisdiction. Plan on dealing with the FBI and the U.S. Attorney's office, therefore.

The particular challenges and problems that attend any federal prosecution should be explained to the client at the outset. Clients simply don't understand that federal court is an entirely different venue than state court. They don't understand the process unless they have been involved with it previously, and federal sentencing is a virtually indecipherable maze for them. Right off the bat, manage expectations.

Bank robbery cases are governed by 18 U.S.C. §2113. Under that section, it is a federal crime to take by force, violence or intimidation, money or any other thing of value from a bank, credit union or savings and loan. There is a significant sentencing difference depending on whether the robbery is armed or unarmed. Likewise, receipt or possession of money or property stolen from a bank is also a chargeable federal offense.

§5:83   Convenience Store Robbery

Of course, convenience store and corner store robberies are quite common. They are usually not very worthwhile jobs for the robber, because of the relatively small amount of cash kept on site. They are crimes of opportunity for the desperate. They almost always involve firearms, because the robber will assume that the store clerk has something under the counter for protection.

§5:84   Pharmacy Robbery

Pharmacy robberies are also crimes for the desperate that you might run into. The desperation, in this case, is usually a need for narcotics.

With the flood of drugs in the United States that are legally prescribed, comes a flood of addicts. In Maine, where I practice, we have one of the highest rates of residents in treatment for OxyContin addictions, and have experienced a spike in pharmacy robberies. HuffingtonPost.com, "Prescription Drug Spikes in Maine," April 21, 2011.

Maine is not alone, and I expect that pharmacy robbery will be an emerging practice area, if it isn't already, in your jurisdiction soon.

[§§5:85-5:89 Reserved]

B.   Strategies and Tactics

1.   Alibi

§5:90   Preserve Alibi Defenses with Proper Notice

Robbery defenses often hang on alibi and identification issues. It doesn't matter if it is a bank robbery, a street robbery or a pharmacy robbery, alibi issues are likely to rear their ugly head. To properly preserve alibi defenses, make sure you provide alibi notice in a timely and sufficiently detailed fashion.

If you have a bank robbery and are in federal court, be sure to follow the Federal Rules of Criminal Procedure along with your local rules on alibi notices. Likewise, in State court, make sure you are familiar with your notification requirements. You don't want to ruin a good alibi by missing the notice date.

In federal court, the government will send a request for the defense to provide alibi defenses. This request may routinely get sent to you with your initial batch of discovery, so watch for it. Under Federal Rules of Criminal Procedure 12.1, you have 14 days after the receipt of the government request for an alibi defense to comply.

Alibi disclosure must be made in writing. Your notice must also include:

(A) each specific place where the defendant claims to have been at the time of the alleged offense; and
(B) the name, address, and telephone number of each alibi witness on whom the defendant intends to rely.

F.R.Crim.P 12.1(a)(2).

Once you have issued an appropriate alibi notification, it is the government's turn. The government must then provide a notice of the witnesses they intend to call at trial that establish that your client was present at the crime scene, as well as the contact information for those witnesses. F.R.Crim.P 12.1(b)(1). This information must be served by the government no later than 14 days after the service of the defense alibi notice. F.R.Crim.P 12.1(b)(2).

Failure to give sufficient or timely notice may result in the exclusion of the alibi testimony. The court has broad discretion here. The court may grant an exception to the above notice requirements for good cause shown. F.R.Crim.P. 12.1(d). In determining the appropriate remedy for a defective notice, the court must consider whether the failure was tactical by the defense, or innocent. Further, the court should inquire as to whether the government has suffered any prejudice to its rights that cannot be cured. See generally, *Taylor v. Illinois*, 484 U.S. 400, 415 (1988).

§5:91   Verify Client's Alibi before Raising the Defense

The federal court notice requirements provide a tactical concern for the defense practitioner at the outset. Every defendant in a bank robbery case who hasn't already confessed by the time the case gets to you will claim to have an alibi. It may be a really bad alibi, or it might be good. Explore these alibis and check them out. Don't take your client's word for it that he was with his baby mama at the time of the bank robbery. Call the baby mama and see what she says. Or, better yet, have your investigator take her statement. Does she sound credible or is she reciting a story they previously rehearsed? Has the FBI already spoken to her? If so, what was the story then?

The point is that the alibi defense can be useful, but only if it is credible. If your alibi notice is going to be easily broken down by the government as lacking in a shred of truth, then don't use it. If the client insists it be used even though it is ridiculous, make sure to warn the client sufficiently about what can happen.

[§§5:92-5:99 Reserved]

2. Eyewitnesses

§5:100   Always Consider Potential Identification Flaws

The science of eyewitness identification is a field of study far too broad for this Chapter. It is an important and evolving intersection of science and law that is often ignored by the criminal practitioner in evaluating a client's potential defenses. We get an armed robbery case, a witness identifies our guy out of a photo array, and we think we're toast. You may, in fact, be toast, but don't assume you are until you thoroughly consider potential identification flaws.

Imagine the convenience store robbery situation. It's 10 at night in a local convenience store. There is a white female in her mid-twenties behind the counter, and a white male trucker in his mid-fifties gassing up for the night with some fuel and coffee.

In walks a black male. He demands the money from the register. He brandishes a firearm. Then, as quickly as he is there, he is gone into the night.

If your client gets picked up on this, assuming there are no other witnesses, the cashier at the register and the trucker are likely to view your client in a line-up or a photo array (or both). How these witnesses identify your client, a stranger to them, is likely the key to your case.

§5:101   Misidentification: Single Greatest Cause of Wrongful Conviction

The simple fact of the matter is that eyewitness identifications are often wrong. Time after time, DNA exonerations of defendants point to eyewitness identification as flawed. According to the Innocence Project, "eyewitness misidentification is the single greatest cause of wrongful convictions nationwide, playing a role in more than 75% of the convictions overturned by DNA testing." www.InnocenceProject.com.

It is not only the Innocence Project that has found the correlation between wrongful conviction and misidentification. *See*, Atul Gawande, "Under Suspicion: The Fugitive Science of Criminal Justice," *The New Yorker*, Jan. 8, 2001, (noting that a study of 63 DNA exonerations of wrongfully convicted people involved 53 mistaken identifications); Gary L. Wells et al., "Eyewitness Identification Procedures: Recommendations for Lineups and Photospreads," 22 Law & Hum. Behav. 603, 605-08 (1998) (study of 40 cases involving wrongfully convicted people who were convicted of serious crimes and served time in prison. Thirty-six of the 40 cases involved eyewitness identification in which one or more eyewitnesses falsely identified the person); U.S. Department of Justice Office of Research Programs, "Convicted by Juries, Exonerated by Science: Case Studies in the Use of DNA Evidence to Establish Innocence After Trial" (1996) (Twenty-eight cases studied based on wrongful convictions later cleared by DNA evidence. All 28 cases involved eyewitness identification.).

§5:102 Stress as a Reason for Misidentification

There are a number of theories about what causes mistaken identification, but none of them have been conclusively established. Some theorize that the stress of being involved in a crime decreases cognitive functioning to a level that it becomes impossible for an accurate identification to be made. *See* Elizabeth F. Loftus & James M. Doyle, *Eyewitness Testimony: Civil and Criminal* § 2.08 (2d ed. 1992).

In addition to the stress implicit by being involved in a crime, don't forget also the stress imposed by the police. Police procedures can distort the witnesses' perspective when making the identification. Subtle rewards and punishments offered by the police can influence the ability of the witness to make an accurate identification, as well. *See* Loftus & Doyle, *Eyewitness Testimony: Civil and Criminal, supra*, §§ 3.04, 3.06, 3.10-11.1. Further, some people are massively intimidated by the police, even if they aren't the ones being accused. That intimidation could skew the identification.

§5:103 Cross-Racial Identification

Let's also not forget the issues inherent in identifying someone of another race. Cross-racial identification issues should always be raised when a member of one race identifies another, such as in our convenience store robbery example. There, a white male and female are identifying a black male. Raise cross-racial identification issues in a Motion to Suppress, if applicable, and then at trial. See §5:132 and §5:133 Form 5-60 Motion to Suppress and Dismiss.

Don't just assume that because there are two eyewitnesses that your client has no hope. Numerous studies on cross-racial identification show that people are less adept at accurately identifying strangers of other races and better at accurately identifying people of their own race. *See e.g.*, "They All Look Alike; The Inaccuracy of Cross-Racial Identification," 28 *AM J.Crim.L.* 207 (2001); "Perspectives on the Impact of Lineup Composition, Race and Witness Confidence on Identification Accuracy," 4 *L. & Hum. Behav.* 315 (1980).

Remember that issues of cross-racial identification and suggestive identification apply not only to lay witnesses, but also to police witnesses. *Manson v. Brathwaite*, 432 U.S. 98 (1977) expanded the concept of suggestive identifications to law enforcement. Due process still applies whether the witness is a lay witness or law enforcement. Whenever the cop is the one making the identification, raise these same issues as you would with a lay witness. Deconstruct the myth that the cop has special powers of identification that normal people do not possess.

§5:104 Reliability of Identification

The United States Supreme Court in *Neil v. Biggers* established a balancing test of factors to be used in determining the reliability of the identification. "The factors to be considered in evaluating the likelihood of misidentification include the opportunity of the witness to view the criminal at the time of the crime, the witness' degree of attention, the accuracy of the witness' prior description of the criminal, the level of certainty demonstrated by the witness at the confrontation, and the length of time between the crime and the confrontation." *Neil v. Biggers*, 409 U.S. 188, 199-200 (1972).

Reliability of the procedure and the identification must be the lynchpin of any identification. Reliability arguments are largely factual, but be sure to make them. Even if the police procedure was not suggestive, the identification may not be reliable for a number of reasons. Is the witness biased? Was he high when the identification was made? The possibilities are too numerous to list. Suffice it to say, if something occurs with the identification that raises your eyebrow, bring it up.

§5:105 Use of Suggestive Procedures

State v. Cefalo, 396 A.2d 233 (Me. 1979) holds that "upon finding that the state used an unnecessarily suggestive procedure, the trial judge must determine whether the witness' out-of-court or in-court identification of the defendant has a basis independent of the suggestive effect of the defective confrontation." *Cefalo, supra* at 236.

BURGLARY AND ROBBERY

Whenever you have a photo array or a live line up you need to determine whether or not the police procedures used were at all suggestive. The Supreme Court has acknowledged that suggestive police procedures "increase the likelihood of misidentification." *Neil*, 409 U.S. at198. As a result, the reliability of the police procedure is in issue in every case in which an identification has been made. *See e.g. Manson*, 432 U.S. at 114 ("Reliability is the linchpin in determining the admissibility of identification testimony …").

Photo arrays, like line-ups, must not be impermissibly suggestive. Watch out for the obvious issues associated with photo arrays, like mixing up people of different races when the witness says the robber at issue was black. Those issues are fairly easy to pick out, but sometimes we think about the more obscure issues so much, we miss the obvious ones.

The less obvious issues with photo arrays should also be considered. Look at the background of the photos. Are some of the photo backgrounds different than others? Does the background difference subtly suggest that your client should be picked out of the array? Do the hairstyles suggest something? Does the angle of the photo suggest something?

§5:106   Other Angles of Attack

Further, don't forget to pick out the things the police didn't do that they should have done related to eyewitnesses. Often we focus on breaking down what the police did, instead of what they should have done. Look for witnesses the police should have provided line ups or photo arrays to. If you have a police incompetence theme at trial, the failure to have eyewitnesses properly identify your client will fit in quite nicely.

In addition to the eyewitness issues raised above, get creative. You are not tied to what other people have done. Criminal defense is not cookie cutter. While you shouldn't forget to question witnesses about their vision correction issues, that also should not be the end of your inquiry.

Examine lighting conditions to determine how that might affect identification. Lighting experts can be retained to explain how the different types of lighting can change the human eye's ability to adequately identify. Further, you can hire surveyors to adequately gage distances of observation and determine whether there were any obstructions to the witnesses' claimed identification. The possibilities are only limited by your creativity.

[§§5:107-5:119 Reserved]

3.   When Drugs or Alcohol Are Involved

§5:120   Drug Treatment

Drug treatment is essential in any pharmacy robbery case, or any other case in which drugs and alcohol played a role. Get your clients in with an experienced licensed drug and alcohol counselor for treatment. Avoid treatment in a group setting if at all possible, because of privilege issues.

Make sure the therapist knows the deal. You will be calling on him or her to write letters and/or testify for your client. Some treatment providers don't want to be involved in cases involving lawyers. Unless your client already has a long term therapeutic relationship established, that is not the provider you want. You don't want to be fighting the provider for testimony if you have a sentencing.

With robbery cases, if they are serious enough, your client may be incarcerated. Part of the hypocrisy of criminal law is that often the people who most need good treatment are in jail and can't get it.

Just because you can't get your client ideal treatment, however, does not mean that you can't get good treatment. If your client is incarcerated and can't make bail or get it lowered, try to bail him or her directly to an inpatient treatment program. If that doesn't work, try to arrange counseling in the jail. It isn't perfect, but you may find dedicated individuals there who will give you client a hand.

Getting your client involved in treatment serves two purposes: the client's health and help with plea bargaining or a sentencing argument with the court. Tell your clients that no matter how heavy the evidence is against them, that honest and ambitious participation in treatment is never negative and is almost always positive.

[§§5:121-5:129 Reserved]

C. Motions

§5:130   Motion to Strike Aliases

In robbery cases, I often see aliases listed in the Indictment. It is exceedingly easy to overlook these. When in doubt, move to strike aliases before you get to trial. See §5:131 Form 5-50 Motion to Strike Aliases.

In federal court, a motion to strike aliases is really a motion to strike surplusage. Under Federal Rule of Criminal Procedure 7(d), the court can strike surplusage from the indictment on the defendant's motion. The purpose of the rule is to prevent prejudice to the defendant from implications in a name that are neither material nor relevant.

In essence, your best chance of getting an alias struck is if you can relate it to a prejudice the defendant will suffer if the alias is uttered in front of the jury. Aliases that have no obvious relationship to the charge will usually be allowed. For example, if your client is accused of a bank robbery and his nickname is "Slim," he probably is not terribly prejudiced by that alias. Bring the motion anyway, though. It is worthwhile to argue that the fact that the defendant has any street name whatsoever is prejudicial just by virtue of the fact that he has a street name. Of course, if the street name alias is "Killer," then the defendant will almost certainly suffer prejudice if the jury hears that is his nickname.

If the government is using the alias to identify him, then that is a different story. They will have a very strong argument then. If it is relevant for identification purposes, it is probably getting admitted.

§5:131   FORM 5-50 Motion to Strike Aliases

UNITED STATES DISTRICT COURT
FOR THE DISTRICT OF MAINE

UNITED STATES OF AMERICA,	)	
	)	
Plaintiff,	)	
	)	
v.	)	Criminal No. 12-1234
	)	
ROY ROY,	)	
	)	
Defendant.	)	

MOTION TO STRIKE ALIASES

The Defendant, Roy Roy, by and through Undersigned Counsel, brings this Motion to Strike Aliases as follows:

1. Defendant is accused of robbing the First National Bank on August 1, 2017. The indictment charging this alleged bank robbery lists Defendant's given name, as well as an alleged alias, namely, "Killer"
2. Allowing the Indictment for an alleged crime of violence in which the Defendant is called "Killer" is extremely prejudicial to the defense.
3. Under Federal Rule of Criminal Procedure 7(d), this Court can strike surplusage from the Indictment on the Defendant's Motion. The purpose of this rule is to prevent prejudice to the Defendant from implications in a name that are neither material nor relevant.
4. The name "Killer" contains an extremely strong negative connotation, especially in a case in which the Defendant is alleged to have held up a bank at gunpoint. If the Government is allowed to call Defendant "Killer" in the Indictment, it is as if they are providing information that the people who know Defendant well enough to give him a nickname, think of him as a killer. This negative connotation is, of course, extremely prejudicial to the Defendant.

WHEREFORE, Counsel respectfully requests this Court strike the surplusage from the Indictment in which Defendant's alias is listed as "Killer."

Dated this __ day of _____, 20__ in Portland, Maine.

                                                               Respectfully submitted,

                                                               _____
                                                               Timothy E. Zerillo
                                                               Attorney for Defendant
                                                               ZERILLO LAW FIRM, LLC

§5:132   Motion to Suppress Identification

It is almost always worth trying to move to suppress the identification of your client by eyewitnesses. Even relatively strong identifications should be challenged as long as you have a straight-faced argument. Here is a version of one I drafted where I was pretty well grasping at straws.

In our street robbery case, we left Mr. Soprano, knocking his victim down in the street and fleeing. An eyewitness, Mrs. Nearsighted, calls the case in. She describes Mr. Soprano as 5′5″ white male with dark hair, mid 30's. This is a pretty accurate description of Mr. Soprano.

The police, down the street, hear the description over their radio just as Mr. Soprano charges around the corner. He matches the description and has blood on his clothes.

The police pat him down and detain him. He refuses to answer questions. They seize the clothes with blood on them for DNA analysis. They don't find the stolen wallet and let him go.

They create a photo array where everything looks good. There are six photos, all white males, all the same age. The hairstyles are largely the same. The background of the photos is too. There is only one argument I can come up with on the suggestibility of the array. For an example of the motion I would bring, see §5:133 Form 5-60 Motion to Suppress and Dismiss.

I will likely lose the motion to suppress on the identification issue, but I want the cop on the stand. I want his testimony. The motion to suppress, even if lost, will likely be worth it from that perspective. I also want Mrs. Nearsighted on the stand and her testimony as well.

§5:133   FORM 5-60 Motion to Suppress and Dismiss

STATE OF MAINE   SUPERIOR COURT
CUMBERLAND, ss.   DOCKET NO. CR-11-8512

STATE OF MAINE,   )
)
)
v.   )   DEFENDANT'S MOTION
)   TO SUPPRESS AND
ANTHONY SOPRANO III   )   DISMISS
)
Defendant   )

The Defendant, Anthony Soprano III, by and through Undersigned Counsel, moves this Honorable Court to suppress all physical objects, statements of the Defendant, tests results, and out-of-court and in-court eyewitness identifications of the Defendant on the following grounds:

1.   All evidence seized from Defendant was the result of an illegal stop, search and seizure in violation of the Fourth, Fifth, Sixth and Fourteenth Amendments to the United States Constitution and Article 1, Sections 5 and 6 of the Constitution of the State of Maine.

2.   All statements made by the Defendant were in violation of *Miranda* rights.

3.   The police officer who detained the Defendant lacked reasonable, objective grounds for detaining the Defendant. See *Florida v. Royer*, 460 U.S. 491, 498 (1983) (An individual "may not be detained even momentarily without reasonable, objective grounds for doing so.") and *Terry v. Ohio*, 392 U.S. 1 (1968) (Officers may stop a person only if they have reasonable and articulable suspicion that criminal activity is afoot). The detention of the Defendant by the state agent violated the Fourth Amendment of the United

States Constitution applicable to the States through the Fourteenth Amendment and Article I, section 5, of the Maine Constitution.

4.   The police seized Defendant's hat and shirt because they claimed they had blood on them. The search of the Defendant was conducted without consent and without a warrant or probable cause. The search of the Defendant by the State agent violated the Fourth Amendment of the United States Constitution applicable to the States through the Fourteenth Amendment and Article I, section 5, of the Maine Constitution. In a criminal case where the accused "moves to suppress evidence seized without a warrant in violation of the Fourth Amendment, the government bears the burden of proving that the warrantless seizure falls within one of the narrow exceptions to the warrant requirement of the Fourth Amendment." *United States v. Reith*, 66 F. Supp. 2d 52, 55 (D.Me. 1999) quoting, *United States v. Ramos-Morale*, 981 F.2d 625, 628 (1st Cir. 1992). Seizure of these items was without probable cause.

5.   A photo array was used by the police in identifying Defendant. This photo array was unnecessarily suggestive. The police were well aware that Defendant was on the shorter side; he was identified as being 5′5″ tall. His mug shot included in the photo array, shows his head only at the bottom of the image. All the other images fill the photo box. Defendant's does not. This suggests he is a shorter man, especially when compared with the other images included. The Supreme Court has acknowledged the powerful impact that law enforcement procedures can have on the accuracy of eyewitness identification. In *Neil v. Biggers*, the Supreme Court disapproved the use of suggestive procedures "because they increase the likelihood of misidentification," and it is the admission of testimony carrying such a "likelihood of misidentification which violates a defendant's right to due process." 409 U.S. 188, 198 (1972). The admissibility of identification testimony, therefore, is to be determined by whether the identification is reliable, with particular attention being paid to the procedure itself. *See, e.g., Watkins v. Sowders*, 449 U.S. 341, 347 (1981) ("it is the reliability of identification evidence that primarily determines its admissibility"); *Manson v. Brathwaite*, 432 U.S. 98, 114 (1977) ("reliability is the linchpin in determining the admissibility of identification testimony …").

WHEREFORE, the Defendant moves that all physical objects, statements of Defendant, identifications, test results and any other evidence obtained as a result of the search and seizure of Defendant be excluded as evidence and the case dismissed.

Dated this ___th day of _____, 20___ at Portland, Maine.

Respectfully submitted,

_____

Timothy E. Zerillo
Attorney for Defendant
ZERILLO LAW FIRM, LLC

[§§5:134-5:139 Reserved]

D. Trial Themes

§5:140   It Wasn't Me

Like the singer Shaggy and his song you might remember from the early 2000s, the most common theme in a robbery trial is the "It wasn't me!" defense. Like Shaggy, many robbery defendants have some pretty bad "it wasn't me" defenses. Always evaluate the "it wasn't me" defense by honestly evaluating the eyewitnesses at the scene, and the alibi the defendant presents.

In my opinion, you should present no witnesses as opposed to putting on crazy and unbelievable alibi witnesses. The jury is skeptical of any non-independent witnesses anyway. So, if your client's mother testifies your defendant was with her all day picking out window treatments, and you doubt it, the jury will too.

You have to be really careful here. If the defendant wants you to put on his mom for the window treatment alibi, then you need to warn your client about the ramifications. Those ramifications are, of course, that everyone

BURGLARY AND ROBBERY

will think your client is a liar, and his or her mother is too. These are the type of warnings to carefully phrase in writing to protect both your client and yourself.

Of course, good alibi witnesses can be a fantastic help. They are just few and far between.

§5:141   It Was My Property To Begin With!

There may be a defense that your client could not have stolen what was already his or hers. Consider my client, Anthony Soprano III, who seems likely to have beaten his friend to take his wallet. See §5:81. He believes the wallet, however, to be his. This presents two points to make at trial.

First, is the issue as to whether the wallet was his. Can the government establish beyond a reasonable doubt that Anthony Soprano didn't own the wallet? Second, even if it is clear that he didn't own the wallet, it may not be clear whether he *believed* he owned the wallet. You may be able to attack the intent to steal as a result.

§5:142   I Needed to Stop a Crime

My client, a hunter, was hunting on his property in Buxton, Maine. He hears shots and goes to investigate. He comes upon four men dragging a large buck from his property to the border of another piece of property.

He does what any good Mainer would do. He fires three shots, not at the men, but in their general direction. The men freak out, one calls 911, and my client is charged with a criminal threatening with a dangerous weapon and a robbery.

The robbery threw me for a loop, but it met the definition in the Maine Robbery Statute.[2] In thinking about this, it occurred to me that we could argue that the force here, the firing of the shots, was to prevent the occurrence of a crime. It was arguably his deer, it was his land, and he was using non-deadly force to prevent a theft of *his* property. As you may have guessed, this case was ultimately dismissed.

§5:143   Defenses That Generally Don't Work But Might Be All You Have

Criminal defense lawyers can only play the cards they are dealt. We aren't prosecutors who get to pick and choose (that's why a prosecutor with a great trial record isn't terribly impressive to me). Sometimes you are only left with bad defenses that generally don't work. Here are a few that scrape the bottom of the barrel. Hey, sometimes you can catch lightning in a bottle!

Entrapment

A tough defense to robbery. An entrapment defense would require an inducement to commit the robbery by another person, of course. The defense would need to be prepared to confront the argument that the defendant was predisposed to commit the robbery to begin with.

Intoxication

Voluntary intoxication is generally a defense that has been written out of the law. Perhaps you can exploit an argument that your client did not have the requisite *mens rea*, but that's usually about it.

Involuntary intoxication gives you a better shot. Of course, it is a rarer shot, factually. Involuntary intoxication is a defense to most crimes, including robbery.

Duress

Duress defenses can be interesting, especially if there was a robbery with multiple persons involved, and you represent the weakest appearing of the bunch. A duress defense generally requires strong proof that your client was

---

2 "The actor threatens to use force against any person present with the intent:
(1) To prevent or overcome resistance to the taking of the property, or to the retention of the property immediately after the taking; or (2) To compel the person in control of the property to give it up or to engage in other conduct that aids in the taking or carrying away of the property." 17A MRSA s. 651.

forced to commit the act, but in some situations it can fit. Imagine the girlfriend of a bad dude drug dealer who says he'll kill her if she doesn't rob a rival dealer. The duress defense may be a winner there.

I currently represent a team of young, foolish drug addicts. One, a young lady, appears to have set the stage for entry into various residences to commit robberies by saying her car is broken down and asking to use the phone. When her two male compatriots enter the residence behind her, significant violence ensues.

Perhaps the young lady has a viable story, however. Perhaps her own life is threatened unless she does the men's bidding. Perhaps she has been abused her whole life by violent men. That may have the making of a potential duress defense.

Just like in law school, issue spotting potential defenses based on the facts of your case is the key.

[§§5:144-5:149 Reserved]

E. Trial

§5:150   Jury Selection

You want a diverse jury in a robbery case, especially if cross-racial identification is in issue. As usual, I am looking for blue-collar people generally. We want to stay away from the law and order types. Since robbery cases are about planting the seed of doubt usually, we want people who are skeptics, and anyone, really, who is a non-conformist.

§5:151   Sample Opening Statement

Here is part of an opening statement from the facts of the robbery case we discussed earlier. See §5:83. This is the convenience store robbery with an eyewitness identification. Our client is a black male and the two eyewitnesses are white, one female and one male.

Ladies and gentleman of the jury, my name is Tim Zerillo and I represent this man here, Mr. Dash. As you just heard, he is accused of robbing the 11-7 convenience store on April 9, 2012 just before midnight. You heard how that robbery took place. You heard how the robber was armed with a gun. And you heard that there were two witnesses to the robbery, Mr. Trucker and Mrs. Clerk. And that's all horrible.

But Mr. District Attorney left out a few details that I'll bet you will think are important. He left out the fact that when the police came to visit Mr. Dash, they never found a weapon. They never found a gun. He left out the fact that Mr. Dash has an alibi for where he was on that evening and you're going to hear more about that alibi throughout the trial. He left out the fact that forensics like fingerprints don't show Mr. Dash in the 11-7 convenience store. He left out the fact that they have no video surveillance of this robbery.

When you take everything he left out, what we're left with is two eyewitness identifications of Mr. Dash. One of the identifications is by Mr. Trucker. The other is by Mrs. Clerk. He also left out evidence related to white people identifying black people.

This evidence that we're going to raise might make you uncomfortable. You've heard people say before when talking about other people of another color that "they all look alike to me." And maybe you've said it. And that might, in some respect, deep down inside of you, make you feel uncomfortable.

While some people who are racist might say that, there are plenty of people who are not racist who are merely speaking the truth from their experience when they say "they all look alike." When it comes to eyewitness identification, it's actually true.

We will show you evidence that eyewitness identification, which is all that you have here, is extremely flawed. We will show you evidence that eyewitness identification is even more flawed when it involves identifications of people of a race other than your own. In other words, as a white man, it is harder for me to identify accurately a black man. We will also present evidence that it is even harder if you are attempting to make an identification across both racial and gender lines. Meaning that not only is it hard for me to accurately identify a black man over a white man, but that it is even harder for me to accurately identify a black woman than either a white or black man.

Anytime we're dealing with issues of race it makes us all uncomfortable. But the evidence you will evaluate in this trial holds Mr. Dash's life in the balance. So I've got to talk about these uncomfortable things. And I expect you will be true to your oath as jurors and evaluate the uncomfortable things when you're back in the jury room. And if you do, I believe your vote will be that Mr. Dash will be not guilty.

Now, let's talk about the burden of proof...

For general tips on opening statements and sample language about the presumption of innocence and burden of proof, see Ch. 2.

§5:152   Sample Direct Examination of Alibi Witnesses

Maybe you have a decent alibi witness in your case. Let's place that in context of a robbery. Make sure to establish the credibility of that witness by connecting him or her to the community as well as your client.

Q. Sir, please state your name for the record.
A. Mr. Al I. By.
Q. OK Mr. By, thanks. Have you ever testified in a trial before?
A. No.
Q. Are you nervous?
A. A little bit.
Q. That's normal. I'm going to ask you some questions, then the prosecutor will, and you just answer those questions as best you can.
A. OK.
Q. You know Mr. Soprano?
A. Yes.
Q. How?
A. He's my brother in law.
Q. OK. Where do you live, Mr. By?
A. Right in Portland, in North Deering.
Q. Good. Do you work?
A. Yeah, probably too much.
Q. Don't we all! Where do you work?
A. At the Maine Hospital.
Q. The one right in town?
A. Yes sir.
Q. What do you do there?
A. I am a nurse.
Q. Great. Been there a long time?
A. About 14 years.

PRACTICE TIP: *Tie witness to community*

Depending on the judge I am in front of, I will try to tie my witness to the same community the jury is in. It relates well to closing, in which you can place great importance on truly using the reasonable doubt standard to judge the people in the community in which the jurors live.

If the judge barks at you as you go down that line, back off and get to the point. If the prosecutor objects, it is almost welcome. They look like horses asses and you can shrug your shoulders to the jury as if to say, "You see how unreasonable these people are?"

That said, don't bore the jury to death with this. A little biographical data is good, but an entire biography is not.

Q. Mr. By, I am wondering if you can tell the jury where you were on July 5, 2012.
A. Sure. I was at my Father's camp on Little Sebago Lake in Gray.
Q. And how long were you there?
A. All day.
Q. How is your memory of that day?
A. I feel it is quite good.
Q. Why is that?
A. Well, I had just worked four days in a row and had to work on the 4th of July. So I got out to the camp on the 4th of July by midnight, went to sleep, and when I woke up the next day, my brother-in-law was there.
Q. When did you wake up on July 5th?
A. Around 10.
Q. And did your brother in law, the Defendant here, leave at all that day?
A. No, he was there the whole time.

§5:153   Sample Cross-Examination of Cop Who Failed to Conduct Lineup or Photo Array

Take, for example, our client who is accused of robbing his "friend" in the street. The alleged victim is given a photo array at the hospital and identifies our client. The witness who viewed the robbery from across the street is never given a photo array to review or a line-up.

This is just sloppy police work, but it is not unusual. The police had the identity of the perpetrator from the alleged victim, so they didn't bother with the independent eyewitness. The independent eyewitness is completely disinterested in the prosecution, and it would have been a fruitful area for the police to pursue. Don't let the jury forget their sloppiness at trial.

Q. Officer Rookie, you studied at the Academy.
A. Yes, I did.
Q. You were pleased with that training?
A. Yes, it was very thorough.
Q. You believe it prepared you well for the job you are doing today?
A. I believe it did, yes.
Q. One of the things that you were taught to do was to arrange a line up?
A. They taught us that.
Q. And to arrange a photo array?
A. They taught us that as well.
Q. In this case, Mr. Vic Tim was in the hospital when you showed him the photo array?
A. He was.
Q. Had he not been in the hospital, you might have done a line up instead?
A. That would really depend on a number of factors.
Q. It would be something you would have considered?
A. Yes, I would have considered a lineup if Vic Tim wasn't in the hospital.
Q. And because of that, you opted for the photo array.
A. Yes.
Q. I want to get back to that shortly, but before I do, I want to ask you about Mrs. Nearsighted.
A. OK.
Q. Mrs. Nearsighted allegedly saw the robbery from across the street.
A. Yes.
Q. You viewed her as an important witness.
A. I did.
Q. Did you do a line up with her then?
A. No, we did not.
Q. She wasn't in the hospital was she?
A. Not that I know of.
Q. You went to her apartment to interview her?
A. Yes.

Q. She never refused to cooperate with you?
A. No.
Q. But you never asked her to identify my client in a line up?
A. No.
Q. So, you must have shown her a photo array to identify him?
A. Is that a question?
Q. Let me try again. You never showed Mrs. Nearsighted a photo array?
A. No.
Q. You never showed Mrs. Nearsighted a line up?
A. No, I didn't.
Q. You never had this important witness identify the Defendant?
A. No.
Q. You ignored your training?
A. No, I didn't ignore my training.
Q. Well, you just forgot it then?

> **PRACTICE TIP:** *Your attitude with the officer*
>
> How smarmy you get with a police officer witness really depends on the judge you are in front of, the type of witness and your own personality. I know lawyers who, at trial, absolutely abuse cops on the stand. It works for them and fits their personality. I know others who try to be very heavy with cops and it comes off as contrived and sleazy. I play it by ear. Is the jury going to be receptive to me fully hammering the cop, asking objectionable questions just so the jury hears them, and generally putting on a show? It really may depend on how likeable the cop is, and how he is playing with the jury. It also depends on the type of case you are defending. You need to make those calls on a case-by-case basis, doing your best to read the jury and the judge.

For more tips on cross examining police officers, see Ch. 2

§5:154   Sample Cross-Examination of Cop on Photo Arrays vs. Line Ups

If the witness has been shown a photo array and not a line-up, and a line-up was available, follow that line of questioning as well.

Q. It is important to you that the identification in this case is accurate?
A. Of course.
Q. So, you want to do the best you can do to make sure it is right?
A. Yes.
Q. We already said that you showed Mr. Vic Tim the photo array because he was in the hospital?
A. Yes.
Q. But Mr. Tim was only in the hospital for one day, wasn't he?
A. Yes.
Q. And you never did a line up anyway?
A. We had our identification through the photo array, which is my policy.
Q. It is your policy not to do line ups?
A. It's not how I normally proceed.
Q. Is it your policy, or department policy?
A. It is not really a policy. It's just my own way of investigating these charges that I think is most effective.
Q. So, your own policy is to use a photo array. Would agree with me that a lineup is a more accurate way of identifying someone then a photo array?
A. I wouldn't agree with that.
Q. A photo array is just head and shoulder pictures?
A. Yes.
Q. You can see more then just heads and shoulders with a line up, right?
A. Yes, you can.

Q. You can see how heavy or thin someone is in a line up?
A. Yes.
Q. But not in a photo array?
A. I think you can tell that from their face.
Q. You can't tell their body shape from the shoulders down in a photo array, can you?
A. No, as I said, it is head and shoulders only.
Q. You can't tell how someone stands from a photo array.
A. No.
Q. You can't hear their voice from a photo array.
A. No.
Q. You don't give them profile pictures so you can't see their profile from a photo array.
A. No you can't.
Q. You can't see their walk from a photo array?
A. No, I guess you can't.

For more tips on cross examining police officers, see Ch. 2

§5:155   Courtroom Exhibits

One way to bolster "it wasn't me!" defense is with records that corroborate the story. This is largely an over-simplification, but juries tend to believe records over witnesses who may not be disinterested or may have a bias motive.

Telephone records for landlines and mobile phones can be very helpful. Try to get all incoming and outgoing calls, which may prove difficult, depending on the carrier.

Each phone carrier has different subpoena requirements, and you will need to research the subpoena requirements of that carrier. Additionally, the carriers get hundreds if not thousands of phone record subpoenas each day, meaning the processing of the request can be slow. A hint is to send a request, and then a follow up marked "2nd Request," two weeks later, and then another marked "3rd Request" two weeks after that. It seems to speed up the process marginally. Sprint will actually fax the records to you for an additional $50 expedite fee.

Each carrier has different fees it charges for records as well. They can get costly, but are often well worth it.

Also consider the social networks your client belongs to. Some of these social networks tag where you are when you update. At the time I write this, Twitter records the location of your tweets, unless you disable your settings from doing so.

Likewise, ask about your client's technology. Many phones and tablets, such as the Iphone and Ipad, record your locations. That data could be useful.

You will note that I am asking for cell sector and site locations in the subpoena. While these records are not necessarily as accurate as GPS, they are a way in which you may be able to determine the location from which a call was made.

§5:156   FORM 4-70 Subpoena for Phone Records

STATE OF MAINE   SUPERIOR COURT
CUMBERLAND, ss.   CRIMINAL ACTION
                                                    DOCKET NO:

STATE OF MAINE   )
)
v.   )   SUBPOENA
)   (M.R.Crim.P.17)
TONY SOPRANO JR.   )

TO: AT&T
        National Compliance Group
        PO Box 24679
        West Palm Beach, FL 33416-4679

Fax: 888-938-4715

You are hereby commanded to produce certain records detailed below in connection with the above-captioned matter on or before _____ at _____. *Production by email to* _____ *or via fax to* _____ *is preferred.*
   You are commanded to produce cell phone records and a certification that the records are kept in the ordinary course of your business, including, but not limited to, call history as well as cell site/sector location at call origination and call termination, for the period _____ through _____, for the following phone number:

**FAILURE TO COMPLY WITH THIS SUBPOENA
MAY SUBJECT YOU TO BEING HELD IN CONTEMPT OF COURT**

Dated this __th day of _____, 20__.

Respectfully submitted,

_____

Timothy E. Zerillo
Attorney for Defendant
ZERILLO LAW FIRM, LLC

§5:157   Sample Closing Argument

Again, it's all about reasonable doubt in our convenience store robbery case.

Sometimes jurors get a case and they know the State just doesn't have it. They haven't given them enough evidence, or the evidence presented is faulty and insufficient.

And maybe that hurts you as a juror. Because you want to see justice done to people who have done wrong. You sort of wish it had been tied up in a bow so you could issue a guilty verdict that you could feel good about.

What the State doesn't have here is stunning. They don't have fingerprints. They don't have a surveillance video. They don't have a confession. They don't have the stolen goods. They don't have the gun.

They have, instead, two eyewitnesses to a robbery. Those eyewitnesses were scared. They were frightened. It was late at night. They were tired. They feared for their lives.

This is a very dangerous case. It is dangerous because each and every one of you want to do the right thing. You want to bring the robber to justice. You want to put that person behind bars. And this case is dangerous because, maybe, my client looks like a robber to you. Maybe his cornrows are offensive to you. But you can't judge a book by its cover.

The hard work is actually following the law. Saying the State doesn't have it is hard when you are deciding a charge of robbery. But when they don't have it you have to vote not guilty, and they don't have it here.

There may come a time in your debate in the jury room when you get tired. You can't. There might be a time you may want to waiver. You can't. Your vote is too important. You cannot give up your belief that they don't have it; you must continue to vote "Not Guilty."

And if you have a long debate about this is the jury room, you may want to consider this: the fact that you are even having the debate in the first place is because you have reasonable doubt! As much as it may hurt, the only way to do the right thing with that doubt is to vote not guilty, even if you hate to do so with a charge of robbery.

BURGLARY
AND ROBBERY

There's an old saying in show business that "when you've got it, you've got it." Well, it's also true that when you don't have it, you don't have it, and they don't have it here.

Now, let's talk about how the State hasn't met their standard of proof in the legal elements of a robbery case. …

For tips on closing arguments and sample language for burden of proof and reasonable doubt arguments, see Ch. 2.

BURGLARY
AND ROBBERY

(This page intentionally left blank.)

CHAPTER 6

CRIMINAL THREATS

What happens if I say to you "If you don't read my book, I'll kick your butt." This is, of course, a threat. But is it a criminal threat? Is it conditional or future threat? Are there other defenses if I'm charged? These are all areas we will explore in this chapter.

I. ELEMENTS AND COMMON SCENARIO

§6:01   The Elements

The elements of criminal threatening, as well as the name of the crime, vary by jurisdictions. Also called criminal harassment or assault by threat, criminal threat statutes typically require an intentional or willful threat to cause death or serious injury to another person or member of the person's family that causes the person threatened to reasonably fear for his or her safety or the safety of a family member. For example, the Maine statute provides that a person is guilty of criminal threatening if he intentionally or knowingly places another person in fear of imminent bodily injury. 17A Maine Criminal Code §209A. Federal law makes it a crime to transmit in interstate commerce "any communication containing any threat … to injure the person of another." 18 U. S. C. §875(c).

§6:02   Misdemeanor or Felony?

The more significant criminal threatening cases usually involve the use of a weapon.

In most states, the use of a dangerous weapon accompanying the threat is the distinguishing factor between felonies and misdemeanors. In Maine in 2011, a Representative in the Maine Legislature was actually charged with criminally threatening someone at a local Dunkin Donuts. Since the threat involved the use of a gun, it was charged as a felony. That doesn't mean that the weapon was used after the threat, just that it was used as a part of the threat.

The use of a dangerous weapon in Maine includes the situation in which the weapon is threatened to be used in a manner capable of producing death or serious bodily injury. 17-A M.R.S.A. S. 2(9). So, if my client says to a person, "I am going to kill you and your whole family with this Glock," all the while with his hand on the Glock in his waistband, he can be charged with the felony without pointing the weapon in the direction of the victim.

On the surface, the criminal threatening case commonly presents itself as a machismo contest, with both sides puffing out their chests. In reality, the party who first draws the weapon or threatens its use is usually not the toughest one, but the one who is acting the toughest.

The most effective way to attack the case is by exploring what caused your client to draw or brandish that weapon.

§6:03   Conditional and Future Threats

When the word "if," or something similar appears in the language of the threat, it is likely a conditional or future threat. Imagine an exchange where an alleged victim steps toward the defendant in a way that makes the defendant uncomfortable. The defendant says: "Don't move. Take another step and I'll blow your head off." The threat is conditional; the condition precedent is the alleged victim taking another step.

Imagine the same scenario and the alleged victim retreats. The defendant calls out to him: "If I ever see you on my property again, I'll kill you with my trusty shotgun, Bessie." This is a future threat.

In some jurisdictions, conditional and future threats are not a crime. The defendant would be in trouble in other states, however. In California, for example, a conditional threat is a crime if:

1. The defendant willfully threatened to use force on another person unless that person immediately did an act that the defendant demanded.
2. The defendant intended to use force immediately to compel the other person to do the act.
3. The defendant had no right to demand that the other person do the act.
4. When the defendant made the threat, he had the present ability to use force on the other person.
5. The defendant placed himself in a position to compel performance of the act he demanded and took all steps necessary to carry out his intention.

Judicial Counsel of California Criminal Jury Instructions, Cal Crim 916; *see, e.g.*, *People v. Bolin*, 18 Cal. 4th 297 (1998).

The key, of course, is to research the law where you practice. If your case is in a jurisdiction where conditional or future threats are not criminal threats, then you need to carefully analyze the language of claimed threat.

The defendant's threat may have been issued in response to a threat from the victim. Whether the victim's threat is a conditional or future threat has implications for whether the defendant can successfully raise self-defense as a defense to the criminal threat charge. See §§6:10-6:12.

§6:04 Criminal Threatening and the Domestic Violence Case

Maine was one of the first states to add a domestic violence crime to its ordinary criminal threatening statute. Given the trend in the law to further criminalize the domestic violence area, other states may follow.

Maine's domestic threatening crime, called "domestic violence criminal threatening," adds collateral consequences if a family or household member is the target of the threat. It also bumps a misdemeanor criminal threatening not involving a weapon up to a felony if there are domestic predicate prior convictions. *See generally* 17-A M.R.S.A §209-A.

Ohio also has a criminal threatening element in its domestic violence statute. *See generally* ORC Ann. 2919.25(c). The Ohio statute enhances the threats based on priors, and based on issues such as whether the alleged victim was pregnant at the time of the offense. *Id.*

Consider the collateral consequences, discussed in Ch. 3, if a domestic violence criminal threatening conviction occurs. In the right circumstances, many lifetime consequences could flow from a mere threat on a household member or former sexual partner.

§6:05 Scenario: the Neighborhood Dispute

My primary hypothetical in this chapter comes from a case that I took over after my client lost his trial. We appealed and were successful. This scenario raises many issues that can come up in criminal threatening cases. Here are the facts.

One sunny afternoon, our client, Trig R. Happi, was at his home on in Windham, Maine. Happi was on his property with a neighborhood teenager, Michael Incredible. Incredible and Happi were sitting at a steel table outside Happi's garage. Happi's garage is approximately 75 feet from Lake Drive.

Incredible was having trouble with his all-terrain vehicle and had come over to Happi's property to ask for help with it. While Happi was engaged in a conversation with Incredible, an auto pulled into Happi's driveway. The auto blocked the mouth of Happi's driveway, and was parked parallel to Lake Drive. The occupants of the auto were Clyde Dean and Bonnie Dean.

Clyde Dean lived about a quarter of a mile away from Happi. To get to their property, the Deans had to pass by Happi's property on Lake Drive. Lake Drive has a 15 mile per hour speed limit.

Happi had installed a speed bump in front of his house. Happi said this was done at the request of the Lake Drive Road Association. Dean believed the speed bump was there to slow him down as he drove in front of Happi's house. Dean was upset because his Chevy Beretta got slightly damaged when it bottomed out going over the speed bump.

On the afternoon in question, Dean claimed to have seen Incredible in Happi's driveway while passing the Happi property. Dean did not know Happi at the time of the incident. He did know Incredible, however. Dean claimed that he rolled down the window, and engaged Incredible in a conversation. Ultimately, he entered Happi's property and had a conversation with Happi. The conversation escalated to the point where Happi went to his shed and retrieved a handgun.

Dean testified to the following: Dean requested that Happi remove the speed bump and Happi refused. Dean got ready to leave the property and said that if it happened again - in other words, if his car got damaged again, "there is going to be some type of problem." Happi replied, "What type of problem is that?" Dean then said, "We will probably end up getting in a fist fight." Dean said that he began to leave.

Dean's self-serving statements painted a rosy picture of his own actions. In Happi's view, Dean came onto Happi's property looking for trouble.

Incredible testified that Dean entered Happi's property with an "attitude type walk" and that he "looked mad." Dean was "shaking his head looking at the ground …" Dean told Happi "me and you are gonna' go at it."

Happi took that to mean that if he didn't do what Dean wanted him to do, Dean would beat him up. Happi did not consider whether this was a conditional or present threat. Happi excused himself, entered his shed, and retrieved a handgun. Happi came out of the shed with the hand gun and ordered Dean to leave. Dean refused to leave. Happi shoved Dean toward the end of the driveway. According to Happi, the gun was in Happi's right hand

and behind him, out of Dean's reach, with the barrel pointed at the ground. Incredible verified that the gun was always pointed at the ground.

Happi stated that Dean shoved him and pointed the barrel of the gun toward him. He claimed great fear at this action.

Bonnie Dean was waiting in the car at the mouth of Happi's driveway while this was occurring. Bonnie Dean said that Happi pushed Clyde Dean out toward his car and began waving the gun around. Bonnie Dean testified that no voices had been raised until the point when Happi pulled the gun. At that point, she stated that Happi started screaming, "Get out of here! I'll kill you!" No one but the Deans heard Happi threaten to kill anyone.

Mike Incredible said that Dean told Happi on several occasions to drop the gun and they would fight. Dean said on three or four occasions, "If you drop your gun, I'll fight you. I'll wreck you." Happi also said that Dean threatened him with physical harm if he dropped the gun. Happi stated that Dean said, "If you didn't have that gun, I would kick your ass." Dean denied making those statements.

Happi was charged with two counts of criminal threatening with a dangerous weapon, which are felony charges.

[§6:06-6:09 Reserved]

II.   STRATEGIES AND TACTICS

A. Affirmative Defenses

§6:10   Self-Defense in the Face of an Imminent Threat

Self-defense standards vary by jurisdiction. That said, a person is usually justified in using reasonable non-deadly force on another person in order to defend himself from an imminent threat of physical harm.

Self-defense is something you can easily overlook in a criminal threatening case. We usually relate self-defense to the use of physical force to repel an attack. It can be used in the criminal threatening context with success, however.

The first step is to determine if self-defense is an issue in your case. Let's use our case with Trig R. Happi. Happi testified to the following:

Q. You say that Mr. Dean made threats. What threats did he make to you?
A. "We'll get into it" was one, and there were two more before he left the property.
Q. Is that all he said is "we'll get into it?"
A. It was preceded by something about if I hit a speed bump again, we are gonna' have a problem, something to that effect. I asked him, really, what kind of problem are we going to have? And he said "we are going to get into it."
Q. What did you take it to mean when he said "we are gonna' get into it?"
A. I took it to mean he was, if I didn't do what this person wanted, he was threatening to beat me up. His threatening conduct, his threatening statement, I interpreted that as, well, he is behaving like a bully saying that I am going to do what I am told or else, and I certainly had no intention of doing as I'm told by this person, so I guess he's gonna' have to carry out his threat.

Here, the threat on Happi could be considered a conditional threat rather than an imminent threat, because it was conditioned on Dean not hitting the speed bump in the future. See §6:03 on conditional and future threats. We argued that Happi believed the threat was imminent since he had no intention of complying with Dean's demands to remove the speed bump.

§6:11   Gestures as an Imminent Threat

You may be able to establish a threat of imminent bodily injury to justify a self-defense instruction because of gestures alone. Have witnesses testify about how the aggressor puffed out chest, his aggressive walk, and whether he was using his hands in a way that said, "Come On! Let's Go!"

I have a good friend I won't name, because he is now a successful person in the financial industry. When I was in college with him, fist fights followed him wherever he went. And he would throw down with anyone.

My friend wore glasses. You could always see a haymaker coming from him, however, when he grabbed those glasses and tossed them away. Everyone familiar with him knew a fight was coming when the glasses came off.

To someone familiar with my friend's *modus operandi*, the tossing of the glasses would have made the threat of harm imminent. No words needed to be spoken. The tossing of the glasses spoke enough.

Explaining how these non-verbal cues create sufficient imminence is the trick. The devil is in the details. Try to have your witnesses put into words how exactly the non-verbal cues were actual imminent threats of harm.

§6:12   Previous Threats May Help Establish Imminence

Part of your investigation needs to go to the issue of previous history between your client and the alleged victim. In addition to threats made to your client on the day of the incident, also consider past threats that may impact your client's state of mind. Performing a complete investigation is crucial in the defense of every criminal matter. Perhaps there are witnesses who will testify that the alleged victim previously threatened your client. If so, he might be justified in uttering his own threats and drawing a weapon.

Imagine in our factual scenario here that Happi heard from others in the Lake Drive Association that Dean was mad at him. In fact, Dean was overheard telling someone that he was going to "teach Happi a lesson."

A genuine imminent threat might appear benign out of context. In context, it is a genuine threat. Consider this exchange:

Defendant: I don't have your money, man.

Alleged victim: What did I tell you last time would happen if you don't have it?

Defendant: I don't have your money because I spent it on this Glock 18. Get the hell away from me or I'll unload the clip into your skull.

Without context we don't know that there is a threat to be imminently fearful of. With context, defendant may testify the alleged victim told him that if he didn't have the money he would kill him the next time he saw him. Or, maybe the defendant wasn't even told of the death threat directly. Perhaps the alleged victim told a third party that he would kill the defendant the next time he saw him if he didn't have his money.

This is, of course, potentially useful evidence at trial. If Happi heard from a third party that Dean threatened him, you will probably overcome the hearsay exception ("It's not offered for the truth of the matter asserted, but rather for the effect on the listener, Your Honor"). The effect of that statement on Mr. Happi, of course, is that it would cause him to fear an imminent attack by Dean, therefore justifying pulling the weapon.

§6:13   State May Need to Disprove Self-Defense

Once self-defense is at issue, many jurisdictions require that the court determine if the state has disproved self-defense beyond a reasonable doubt on every single element of the charges against defendant. In other words, once you have put self-defense at issue, the burden shifts to the State to disprove self-defense beyond a reasonable doubt. A determination as to whether the issue has been generated sufficiently is up to the judge. Each jurisdiction is different, but usually all that is required are sufficient facts to make the self-defense case plausible.

On cross examination of Happi, Prosecutor Will Getcha tries to disprove self-defense. Happi testifies on cross as follows:

Q. Now eventually things take a turn for the worse I guess when he indicates that if he has a problem with the speed bump again, I think your words were, " We will get into it?"

A. I believe that's what he said.

Q. And you responded, "What does that mean" or words to that effect?

A. Something to that effect, yes, sir. No, no. Excuse me, "we will have a problem. What kind of problem?" Something to that effect, "Yes, we will have a problem. What kind of problem? We are going to get into it."

Q. Okay. So "We will have a problem." You inquire what kind of problem. "He says we will get into it?"

A. Yes.

Q. Now you took that to mean if he is driving in the future? I mean he had already driven over the thing right now at that point in time heading on his way out, correct?

A. I took it to mean a threat, sir.

Q. Well, let me just ask you. He had already driven over the speed bump, was heading past your house in the other direction, right?

A. Yes, sir.

Q. So if he was going to have a problem with the speed bump again, then it's going to have to happen on a return trip at some point?

A. I didn't really consider that at the time, sir.

Happi's testimony on cross examination is that he did not consider whether the threat was conditional at the time the threat was made. He took the threat as putting him at an immediate risk.

PRACTICE TIP: *If your client testifies*

If you are raising self-defense in a criminal threat case and your client insists on taking the stand, remind your client that a conditional threat could sink his defense.

Of course, Happi's testimony was contradicted by the testimony of the victim, Clyde Dean. Dean said on direct examination that he made a conditional threat. Dean testified that he had said if he rode by and it happened again (that his car bottomed out on the speed bump again) that "we will probably end up getting into a fist fight."

Dean's testimony conflicts with Happi's perception that there was a present threat. That is not the issue, however, if the government in your jurisdiction is required to disprove self-defense beyond a reasonable doubt. As a result, it is not Dean's perspective that is in issue; it is Happi's. That perspective will likely be subject to a reasonableness test, however. Whether the reasonableness test is objective or subjective depends on your jurisdiction.

§6:14   Defense of Premises

Along with self-defense, consider defense of premises as a possible avenue of relief. In most jurisdictions, defense of premises is a defense to criminal threats. It usually requires that the defendant be in possession or control of the premises. If he was, the use of non-deadly force is justified if the defendant reasonably believed the force was necessary to prevent or terminate the commission of a criminal trespass or other crimes.

Therefore, if the criminal threats were made on your client's property, consider requesting a defense of premises instruction. The Maine Jury Instruction Manual does a good job of spelling out the requirements for defense of premises in my jurisdiction:

> If you find that sufficient facts have been introduced to raise a question of whether the Defendant was acting to prevent or terminate a criminal trespass, the State must prove beyond a reasonable doubt either (1) that the Defendant was not acting to prevent or terminate a criminal trespass; or (2) that the Defendant's beliefs that led to his actions, when viewed in light of the nature and purpose of the Defendant's conduct and the circumstances known to the Defendant, were a gross deviation from what a reasonable and prudent person would believe in the same situation.

Maine Jury Instruction Manual, 4th Ed., §6-60.

The reasonableness of the defendant's beliefs is often at issue. If permitted by the jurisdiction, argue that objective reasonableness is not the standard. The defendant's subjective belief, unless that belief grossly deviates from what a reasonable person would believe, should be sufficient.

In Happi's case, we know that Dean came onto his property. We know that Happi felt the need to pull his firearm, whether or not he actually pointed it at Bonnie or Clyde Dean. We know he felt threatened by the Deans' appearance on the property.

The defense of premises to repel a criminal trespass was appropriate in this instance. Drawing a firearm is non-deadly force, at least in Maine. Happi used the presence of the firearm to repeal Dean from the property.

In the Happi matter, the trial court gave a jury instruction on defense of premises that focused on reasonableness. The trial court instructed the jury that it must consider whether it was a reasonable defense of premises. We objected consistent with the above instruction. Ultimately the Maine Supreme Court reversed the convictions, holding that the trial court's instructions on the reasonableness of the defense of premises were erroneous.

The defense of premises can be a great tool if the facts support defense of your client's property.

§6:15　Defense of Others

Just like self-defense and defense of premises, defense of others is a possible consideration if the threat can be linked to the protection of another person. Generally, a person is justified in using force to protect a third party from unlawful use of force by an aggressor to the extent that the third party would be justified in acting in self-defense.

Defense of others implicates the "alter ego" rule, which may be somewhat outdated. In earlier common law, for the alter ego rule to apply, the third party had to, in fact, have been justified in self-defense, irrespective of how the situation would have appeared to a reasonable person. Most jurisdictions today take the view that the use force is justified if it reasonably appears necessary for the protection of the third party from the aggressor.

§6:16　First Amendment Issues

Since criminal threat cases usually involve speech, you should consider the rare case in which you can claim First Amendment protection. The First Amendment prohibits states from punishing people based upon the content of their speech. Only "true" threats are outside First Amendment protection. See *Watts v. United States*, 394 U.S. 705 (1969) (Petitioner's remark during political debate at small public gathering that, if inducted into Army (which he vowed would never occur) "the first man I want to get in my sights is L.B.J.," held to be crude political hyperbole which, in light of its context and conditional nature, did not constitute a knowing and willful threat against the President). So, political hyperbole, for example, will likely be protected.

If you think your client's speech might fall under First Amendment protection, then you need to consider the two most general exceptions to the First Amendment that you may encounter: the fighting words doctrine and the true threats doctrine.

The primer for the fighting words doctrine is found in *Chaplinsky v. New Hampshire*, 315 U.S. 568 (1942). *Chaplinsky* holds that the fighting words doctrine takes speech outside First Amendment protection if: 1) the speaker addresses his words to a specific person, 2) the words were expressed in person, 3) the words would likely provoke violence in the average person under the circumstances; and 4) the threat of violence is imminent.

The true threats doctrine is also an exception to First Amendment protection. True threats must be genuine threats, not exaggerations or jokes. *Watts v. United States*, 394 U.S 705 (1969). Unlike fighting words, true threats do not have to be made in person to be an exception to the First Amendment.

If you have speech, absent an exception, you might want to consider coverage of the First Amendment. At least it will make for an interesting and memorable argument.

[§6:17-6:29 Reserved]

B.　Negating the Elements

§6:30　Consider the Mens Rea

The Anthony Elonis case reminds us to consider mens rea in the context of a criminal threat. *Elonis v. United States*, 575 U.S. ___, 135 S. Ct. 2001; 192 L. Ed. 2d 1. Anthony Elonis or "Tone Dougie," posted his own rap lyrics containing graphically violent language related to his wife, co-workers, a kindergarten class, and state and federal law enforcement. His employer fired him for threatening co-workers, and his wife sought and was granted a restraining order against him. Elonis claimed that his lyrics were "fictitious" and not intended to depict real persons. Elonis was charged with five counts of violating 18 USC §875(c), which makes it a federal crime to transmit in interstate commerce any communication containing any threat to injure the person of another.

The crime at issue was silent as to the *mens rea* required for the threat. At trial, the District Court gave a juror instruction, over Elonis' objection, that was akin to a negligence standard. Elonis was convicted and the Third Circuit affirmed.

Writing for the Court, Chief Justice Roberts held that the district court's jury instruction erroneously employed a "reasonable person" standard "inconsistent with 'the conventional requirement for criminal conduct — *awareness* of some wrongdoing.'" The Chief Justice began with the text of §875(c): a communication must be transmitted and that communication must contain a threat. That said, the statute itself does not indicate a required mental state.

Faced with statutory silence on the required *mens rea*, the Chief Justice turned to a familiar maxim: "[W]rongdoing must be conscious to be criminal." This background principle of criminal law means the Court "interpret[s] criminal statutes to include broadly applicable scienter requirements, even where the statute by its terms does not contain them."

This presumption in favor of scienter is not limitless, of course. Roberts pointed out that a court may only graft onto a criminal statute the mental state "necessary to separate wrongful conduct from 'otherwise innocent conduct.'" Since the only element of §875(c) that separates "wrongful" from "innocent" conduct is "the threatening nature of the communication," a defendant must possess some mental state regarding "the fact that the communication contains a threat." As to this "crucial element," the Third Circuit's mistaken standard was akin to civil liability in tort law, which "reduces culpability on the all-important element of the crime to negligence." The Court has "long been reluctant to infer that a negligence standard was intended in criminal statutes." As a result, SCOTUS reversed.

Keep *mens rea* in mind when looking at the criminal threatening statutes in your own cases.

§6:31   Get the Accuser Talking on the Record

I urge you to speak to the alleged victim (or better yet, have your investigator do it) in almost every case. In the context of criminal threatening cases, I find it quite important. The exact language and circumstances of the alleged threat are crucial. Pin down the alleged victim in a recording (or deposition, if allowed where you practice) to ensure a positive spin on the alleged threat for your client.

In our scenario, for example, Dean may feel foolish or that he overreacted. Maybe Happi's lowering the speed bump will be enough to satisfy Dean and then he might ask the prosecutor to drop the charges or cease cooperating.

I always tell my investigator that I don't care if the alleged victim has forgiven and forgotten. I just want him talking. If he starts talking about the incident in a recording, he may bury himself somewhere.

§6:32   But Beware of Accuser and Witness Tampering Accusations

That said, in every case in which you speak to an alleged victim, you need to be careful you don't end up with an allegation of victim tampering thrown back in your face. In a case where the alleged victim has already claimed threatening by the defendant, alleging tampering by you will be no great leap. Take ordinary precautions and use a well-trained investigator whenever possible.

§6:33   Sufficiency of Evidence That Threat Was Made

Sometimes we miss the really obvious stuff. For example, what is the evidence that the threat was made in a criminal way? Could the words have been taken out of context? Was the alleged victim's perception off for some reason? Perhaps he was too angry to hear properly. Or, maybe he has hearing loss. Does he have a bias or motivation to make up the threat?

Don't forget the small stuff.

§6:34   Does Client's History Explain Why He Pulled a Weapon

I am not going to play psychologist here, but understanding why your client pulled a weapon is just as important as the facts. The trick is to peel back the layers of reasons with your client, who, very often, will not understand himself, why he pulled the weapon, or made the threat.

I met Mr. Happi after he had already lost his initial trial and had been remanded to custody. I spoke to him, of course, about the facts of the case described already in this Chapter. In addition to those facts, I also wanted to know why he pulled the gun, even if he never pointed it at Dean. He didn't know why himself. But we explored his personal history, and came up with ideas.

Eventually, Happi told me about two past traumas in his life that became very important in his case. The first involved a series of incidents of horrible physical abuse perpetrated on him by his father, who was the same man who taught him about guns. Later, as an adult, he was subject to a carjacking in which the carjacker was armed. His trial counsel did not know, or ask about, any of these incidents.

The amateur psychologist in me said, "Hey, my client might suffer from PTSD!" So I went to the DSM IV to look up Post Traumatic Stress Disorder and it seemed to apply (not surprisingly). My amateur diagnosis was used just as a way to understand my client, and to get him in the right professional hands.

Now I had identified a reason why my client had pulled the gun, instead of calling the police or even punching Dean in the face. But how does this help?

Once you have identified the potential issue, it is time to get an expert on the line. You need to have your client diagnosed with PTSD (and perhaps other co-occurring disorders). From there, you need an expert to testify that someone in Happi's situation has an enhanced fight or flight response because of past trauma.

This may or may not be a good issue for trial. You need to decide if you think these facts could negate *mens rea*. If it does not help with *mens rea*, it may still help you if you end up at sentencing. The PTSD should be a mitigating factor. In Happi's case, we used the information related to his past trauma to get him out of jail and a reasonable sentence, and then filed an appeal (which, I am happy to report, we won on the most important issues).

PRACTICE TIP: *Consider a psychiatric expert*

If your client has trauma in his past around violence and abuse, a psychiatric expert may be able to provide information to negate *mens rea*, or at least present good sentencing information.

Remember forensic psychology and psychiatric treatment pre-trial are crucial in almost every criminal case. If your client resists, tell him it is a contingency in the event that things go badly at trial. Some of the more manly men will accept treatment if they think it is mere legal posturing.

---

§6:35   Did Client Point Weapon at Victim?

If there is a weapon involved, make sure you investigate its location, and whether or not it was actually brandished or pointed at the alleged victim. There is a difference between a gun that is shown to someone in a holster and one pointed at your head. The same goes for knives and other weapons.

At times, such as in Happi's case, the weapon is drawn so that the aggressor knows it is there, and for no other real reason. The weapon may not be pointed at a person. If it is not, there is an argument that there was no use of a deadly weapon. As discussed earlier in the chapter (see §6:02), brandishing a weapon may not be needed for your client to threaten use of the weapon, however. Even if you can escape the use of a dangerous weapon enhancement, you still may have a criminal threat to deal with.

[§6:36-6:39 Reserved]

III.   TRIAL

A. Jury Selection

§6:40   Jurors to Keep

As I mentioned earlier, I am not focusing much on jury selection in this book because the way jurors are picked varies so much by state. Unfortunately, in Maine, we are very limited in our jury selection and do not have individual *voir dire*.

I want to make a few points related to the jury selection in the Happi case. What you are looking for are people with something to lose: people with families; people with property.

You don't need guys who belong to the NRA, although that wouldn't hurt in this factual circumstance. Likewise, you don't have to eliminate gun control advocates necessarily, but you should be careful with anyone who cannot abide by any circumstance where a gun may be used.

I don't care for guns myself. That said, I have a family and a home, and I would pull a gun in the right circumstances to protect myself, my family, or my home. If you have jurors who feels the same way, then Trig R. Happi should survive that jury.

§6:41   Jurors to Avoid

Also, I know this is sort of hard to explain, but I would avoid people who don't do anything for themselves—the type of person who would never get his own hands dirty. These people are more likely to call 911 than take the Dean threat head on. And someone like that will have trouble understanding Happi's protective instincts. The difficulty is identifying such people. You do know who these people are not: people who are doers. People who would push your car out of a ditch in a snowstorm. People who pitch in when the going gets rough. Those are my people. If I feel like a potential juror wouldn't bother to throw me a life vest if I was drowning, I'll strike him or her.

[§6:42-6:49 Reserved]

B. Opening Statement

§6:50   My Approach

Here, I try to paint a simple picture. Dean is the aggressor. Our client is enjoying a beautiful summer day in Maine and is interrupted by this irrational and aggressive neighbor. I try to put the jury inside my client's head so they relate to him throughout the case.

§6:51   Sample Opening Statement Excerpts

Here are some excerpted ideas from the case of State v. Trig R. Happi:

Good morning, ladies and gentlemen of the jury. My name is Tim Zerillo and I am proud to represent this man right here, Trig R. Happi of Windham Maine.

Now, I know most, if not all of you, have never been on a jury before. I can imagine that, earlier this morning, you were having a cup of coffee and reading the paper thinking "Hmm, I'm on a jury today; I wonder what I'll have to do?'"

And the natural answer to that question might be "I guess I'll just keep an open mind and make my decision based on the facts of the case." That sounds very reasonable in fact, doesn't it?

But you cannot have an open mind. You must realize that my Mr. Happi is innocent. He is innocent unless and until this prosecutor gives you enough credible facts to allow you to allow you to have an open mind. Until that time, you must, if you are true to your oath, consider him right now to be innocent.

We are going to begin with using our imaginations. Imagine you are on your property on a nice sunny day. There is a neighbor who is on your property, an invited guest, and he is asking your help with something or other. It is a nice, lazy summer day.

It's a nice picture isn't it? I bet you can almost smell the charcoal from the barbecue.

Unfortunately, that pretty picture is going to suddenly be torn in two when Clyde Dean drives his car onto your property and blocks the mouth of your driveway. Since your property is on a lake, that driveway is the only way in or out. He charges up to you and demands to know why you've put a speed bump in the road. You tell him you were asked to do it, but he doesn't accept that. He does not appear rational to you. He appears to look like someone who has lost control. And on the inside of your body, you are scared. You try not to look that way on the outside of your body, but on the inside, you are shaking like a leaf.

So you ask Dean to leave. But this makes him more aggressive. He's up in your face. Now you are even more scared. You are fighting your body not to show your fear. And then you remember your firearm in your shed.

Now you may admit to yourself that you aren't thinking your clearest in this moment of stress and anxiety. You are, however, in charge of the part of your brain that is telling you that you need to remove Dean from the property.

So you remember your firearm in your shed. You grab the firearm and tell him to leave. You don't point it at him. You don't threaten to kill him. You keep it behind your body, but make sure Dean knows it's there. And in doing this, you get him off the property.

The evidence in this case will reveal that this happened to Mr. Happi. Mr. Happi isn't denying he grabbed his weapon. The evidence will show, however, that it was reasonable for him to grab his weapon. And I believe if you use your imaginations and put yourself in that same place as you hear the evidence, that your will agree that it was reasonable.

Now, Dean will testify that the gun was waved around at him. His wife Sandra, who was in the car, will try to back that up. But the neighbor on Mr. Happi's property will tell you no such thing happened. This neighbor, Mike Incredible, is a disinterested witness. He has no dog in this fight, and I expect him to discredit the Deans.

If you find Mr. Incredible's testimony to be credible, then you have some real issues to consider. Because if you find that the Dean's lied materially—at any time—that is a reasonable doubt. Once it has been established that an alleged victim has lied materially, or repeatedly, that witness cannot be trusted—and reasonable doubt exists.

So let's talk about reasonable doubt compared to the elements of the offense the State needs to prove in this case. ...

For general tips on opening statements and sample language about the presumption of innocence and burden of proof, see Chapter 2.

[§6:52-6:59 Reserved]

C. Cross-Examination

1. The Accuser

§6:60   Key Points

Let's take a look at how to approach a potential cross examination of Mr. Dean. Key points to make with him are:
- Dean and Happi were not friends.
- Happi did not invite Dean onto his property.
- Dean was the initial aggressor.
- Dean refused to leave.
- Dean's aggression and refusal to leave made it reasonable for Happi to draw his weapon.
- The gun was not pointed at Dean.

§6:61   Accuser and Defendant Were Not Friends; Victim Was Trespassing

Q. Mr. Dean, you had never met my client before that day on his property.
A. No.
Q. You don't get together for dinner?
A. No.
Q. You don't barbecue?
A. Not hardly.
Q. You're not friends with Mr. Happi?
A. Absolutely not.
Q. You were driving by, your car hit the speed bump, and you decided to go talk to him about it?
A. I didn't like my car bottoming out on his speed bump.
Q. But you had never met him before that day, right?

A. No.
Q. And you didn't call him before you came over?
A. No. I was right there.
Q. You didn't ask permission to come on his property?
A. No, I walked to where he was to talk to him.
Q. You weren't invited on that property.
A. I don't know what you mean by that, there were no signs telling me to stay out.
Q. That's what you need to stay off someone's property, a "stay out" sign?

§6:62   Accuser Was the Aggressor

Let's talk now about how Dean came onto the property. We want to establish that he is the aggressor, and that his aggression made it reasonable for Happi to draw his weapon. The witness will never, of course, say he was the aggressor. The idea then is to give the jury some facts that make them believe he was the aggressor, despite his claims.

Q. Mr. Dean, after your car hit the speed bump, you were angry, weren't you?
A. No.
Q. You liked your car bottoming out on that speed bump?
A. No.
Q. So you were angry?
A. No, I didn't like it, but I wasn't angry.
Q. You were upset then?
A. No, I wasn't really upset. Maybe a little bit though.
Q. OK. So you hit the speed bump, you didn't like it, and you were a little upset. Is that fair?
A. Yes.
Q. And you decided that you were going to go onto Mr. Happi's property.
A. Yes.
Q. So you pulled your car off of the speed bump and into the mouth of Mr. Happi's driveway, right?
A. Yes.
Q. This blocked in Mr. Happi's cars, didn't it?
A. I think he could have gone around me.
Q. Gone around you on the lawn?
A. Yes, maybe one side of his tires on the lawn.
Q. Did your wife Bonnie Dean ask what you were doing?
A. I don't remember.
Q. You don't remember because you were more than a little upset, weren't you?
A. No.
Q. So, you got out of your car and walked up to Mr. Happi and Mike Incredible.
A. Yes.
Q. You were walking with a purpose?
A. I don't know what you mean?
Q. You had your chest puffed out?
A. I was just walking.
Q. You were walking fast, too.
A. I was just walking normal.
Q. You got to Mr. Happi and said to him, "What the hell do you think you're doing putting that speed bump there?"
A. Something like that.
Q. You didn't introduce yourself first?
A. I don't remember that.
Q. You didn't say "Excuse me" or "Pardon me"?
A. I don't remember.
Q. Did you even say "Hello" or "Hi"?
A. I don't remember.

Q. Could it be that because you were a little upset you just got straight to the point?
A. Could be.
Q. Mr. Happi didn't ignore you and continue his conversation with Mike Incredible?
A. No.
Q. He answered you that the Association told him to put that speed bump up?
A. Yes.
Q. When he said that, he didn't have any firearm that you could see?
A. No, he got that later.

§6:63   The Threats

Now let's get him to talk about the threats.

Q. Ultimately, you asked Mr. Happi to take down the speed bump and he refused.
A. Yes.
Q. And you told him "Me and you are gonna' go at it."
A. If the speed bump wasn't removed.
Q. He already told you he wasn't removing the speed bump right?
A. Right.
Q. So, if you were telling the truth about going at it with him, you were going to actually have to "go at it."
A. I don't understand.
Q. When you say "go at it," you mean to fight?
A. Yes.
Q. You told him you were going to "go at it," meaning fight, if he didn't take down that speed bump?
A. Yes.
Q. And he told you he wasn't taking that speed bump down.
A. Yes.
Q. So you were going to fight before he drew that weapon.
A. I don't think we were going to do it right then and there.
Q. It could have been taken that way though.
A. I don't know how he took it.
Q. My father taught me how to defend myself in a fight when I was a kid, did your father teach you?
A. Yes.
Q. And what did he tell you about taking the first punch.
A. That if I knew a fight was definitely coming to take the first punch.
Q. Same thing I was taught. How do you know for sure that a fight is coming before it happens?
A. You can never know for sure.
Q. That's right.

§6:64   Accuser Refused to Leave

We want to make it clear to the jury that not only was Dean the initial aggressor, but that he refused to leave. This should help us with our argument that drawing the weapon was reasonable.

Q. After he refused to lower the speed bump, you left the property voluntarily?
A. No, he drew a gun and waved it around, scaring me and my wife half to death.
Q. He drew the weapon because he asked you to leave and you refused?
A. No.
Q. You came onto his property to start something with him, then you refused to leave, and he had to draw his weapon to get you off his property.
A. That's not true.
Q. Well, you agree with me that you weren't invited onto the property?
A. Yes.
Q. And you agree that you didn't leave until he drew a weapon, right?

A.   I didn't leave until after his gun was drawn.

Q.   And even then, he needed to shove you off the property?

A.   Yes, he pushed me.

Q.   You didn't leave on your own because you were so angry that you were seeing red?

A.   No.

Q.   You think you were seeing clearly?

A.   Yes.

Q.   Someone pulls a gun on me, I would run. You just stood your ground.

A.   So?

Q.   Either one of two things is happening here—either you are so angry that you didn't care about the gun or you weren't afraid that the gun was really a threat to you—which is it?

A.   I don't know.

§6:65   The Gun

I also want to create reasonable doubt about the gun aspect in this case:

Q.   When Mr. Happi grabbed the gun, he put it behind him?

A.   Initially, but he started to wave it around later on.

Q.   When he put it behind him, the barrel was pointed at the ground, right?

A.   I don't know; I couldn't see it.

Q.   You couldn't see it because it was behind his back?

A.   Right.

Q.   He pushed you off his property because you refused to leave?

A.   He did push me, yes.

Q.   He used one hand to push you?

A.   I believe so.

Q.   And the gun was behind his back in one hand while he pushed you with his other hand?

A.   I think so.

[§6:66-6:69 Reserved]

2. The Responding Officer

§6:70   Key Points

Now let's cross examine the responding police officer. Unless the cop has actually witnessed the threat, he doesn't know a heck of a lot. He can be a useful way to keep your client off the stand and still get in his statements (if you want them in that is). Key points to make are:
- The officer did not witness the incident.
- He knows only what the participants have told him.
- He does not know what threats Dean may have made to Happi and whether self-defense by Happi was required.
- He does not know whether Happi pointed the weapon was pointed at Dean

For tips on cross examining police officers, see Ch.2

§6:71   Officer's Knowledge Limited to Participants' Statements

Q.   Officer Notmuch, you already described on direct examination responding to a call at Lake Drive.

A.   Yes.

Q.   That call came in from Clyde Dean?

A.   I believe that is what he told 911.

Q.   You didn't know Dean before this day?

A.   No.

Q. And you didn't know Happi either?
A. No.
Q. So you met with Dean at his house?
A. Yes.
Q. And you met with Happi at his house?
A. Yes.
Q. And they both gave you statements?
A. Yes.
Q. Did you take a statement also from Mike Incredible?
A. Yes.
Q. And he largely supported Happi in his statement to you, didn't he?
A. I would say so.
Q. And you took a statement from Bonnie Dean?
A. Yes.
Q. So your knowledge of this matter is really limited to those 4 statements, isn't it?
A. I'm not sure what you mean.
Q. You didn't find any physical evidence.
A. We took the gun.
Q. Well, Happi gave you the gun didn't he?
A. Yes.
Q. You didn't really find it; he gave it to you?
A. OK.
Q. Are you telling me you found other evidence? What other evidence was that?
A. That's all I can think of.
Q. So the evidence was the 4 statements, and the gun that Happi stipulated he pulled out of the shed.
A. Yes.
Q. You weren't there when the incident happened?
A. No.
Q. You don't have any independent knowledge about the incident?
A. No.
Q. You didn't canvas the neighborhood for other witnesses.
A. There were no other witnesses.
Q. How do you know? Did you canvas the neighborhood?
A. No.
Q. Did you find out about the relationship between the parties by interviewing the neighborhood people?
A. No.
Q. And you didn't find any physical evidence other than the gun?
A. No.

§6:72   Officer Did Not Witness Incident

Q. Since you didn't witness anything personally, you didn't see how Dean approached Mr. Happi.
A. Not other then what they said.
Q. And what they said was different?
A. I guess.
Q. Mike Incredible told you Dean came on the property with an "attitude type walk," right?
A. That's how he described it.
Q. You don't know what Dean had said to other people would be the consequences if Happi didn't lower that speed bump?
A. No.
Q. You don't know if my Client was scared of Dean?
A. He told me he was.
Q. And he told you he got his gun because of that fear?
A. Yes.

§6:73   Officer Does Not Know Whether Defendant Pointed Weapon at Accuser

Q. Officer Notmuch, you don't know for certain whether Mr. Happi ever pointed the weapon at Dean, do you?

A. Not for certain.

Q. That's because there are 4 statements you have taken, and half the statements contradict the other half of the statements.

A. Right.

Q. And you weren't there?

A. Right.

Q. So you couldn't know for certain?

A. No.

Q. You arrested my client in this case?

A. Yes.

Q. When you arrested him, you used a probable cause standard, didn't you?

A. That's what we are taught to use, that's correct.

Q. You didn't have to use the standard of beyond a reasonable doubt to arrest Mr. Happi, did you?

A. No, we are taught to make sure we have probable cause to arrest.

Q. And that is a lower standard then beyond a reasonable doubt, isn't it?

A. Yes.

[§6:74-6:79 Reserved]

D. Closing Argument

§6:80   Sample Closing Argument

Here are some Closing Argument thoughts for the Trig R. Happi case.

In the movies, when someone is threatened and they finally stand up for themselves, pull a gun on the bad guy and say "get off my property," we cheer. We like that because it goes to a very fundamental urge in human beings, to protect ourselves, our home and our loved ones when we are under attack.

That is primal. It doesn't require a lot of thought. It is an instinct.

Here, the instinct by Mr. Happi to protect himself and his property might not have been the most thought through thing he has ever done. It may not even have been smart. But it was not criminal. It was self-protection.

I am not a gun guy. But as I think of this case, I can tell you with absolutely certainty, that there are situations in which I would take the gun out of the shed and have used it in the same way that Happi did, to repel Dean from my property.

And even if you don't like guns like me, you would have to be honest in telling yourself that there are situations in which each one of you would grab that gun out of the shed. Maybe it would take more for you than it did Happi, but I don't think it would take much more.

If your home was threatened, you would do it. If a loved one was threatened, you would do it. If you were threatened yourself, you would do it. You don't have to like guns or be a gun owner to understand fight or flight as an instinct.

Mr. Happi's instinct was to fight as opposed to retreat. He's probably not proud of it, and maybe he would have done it differently. But going on an instinct to protect yourself and your property is not criminal.

In fact, it is written into our criminal code as a justification. You are justified to use non deadly force, which this is, to protect yourself and your property. Drawing a gun in Maine law is non-deadly force.

Mr. Happi's actions were justified. You don't have to like them; that's OK. But they were justified and they were not a crime.

For those of you who are gun owners, and there are a whole lot of you in Maine, what were you taught when you were little? You use your weapon to defend yourself. To defend your home. To defend another person. I would argue that what Mr. Happi did was entirely consistent with that approach.

Now let's talk about the burden of proof which the State has not met in this case. …

For tips on closing arguments and sample language for burden of proof and reasonable doubt arguments, see Ch. 2.

CHAPTER 7

DRUG CRIMES

Drug cases involve people in all walks of life. Compared to other areas of my practice, my clients with drug cases seem to be among the most diverse. I've represented doctors, lawyers and politicians accused in drug crimes. You can, at the same time, have very hardcore drug traffickers facing life sentences in federal court, and a soccer mom facing a drug felony because she got hooked on some pain pills after a back injury. Your clients can range from extremely violent, to weak and very passive. They are sometimes sophisticated and knowledgeable when it comes to court and dealing with the police, and sometimes they really don't have a clue.

Like an actor with range, the lawyer needs to be multiple characters to his or her clients from the drug world. For some, you need to be tough, filing motions, contesting every piece of evidence and pounding the table. For others, you need to be the shoulder to cry on and an advocate for the weak and addicted.

In either situation, drug cases can be exciting and frustrating at the same time. They present opportunities to deal with diverse areas of law and science, all in a very high stakes game.

Before I begin highlighting various areas in drug practice, I want to mention the issue of treatment. In every case (virtually) I recommend drug treatment for my client. Even if someone used marijuana one time and got caught with it that one time, I recommend treatment. The types of treatment depend on the case, but drug treatment can never hurt your case.

Remind your clients to be careful in group settings. If they want to try AA or NA, that is fine, but it is of limited use to their case. You need them in a privileged treatment setting. The intensity of that treatment really depends on the addiction and the facts of the case.

I.   A WORD ABOUT PRE-TRIAL DIVERSION AND FEDERAL COURT

§7:01   Will Humanizing the Defendant Help?

There are a great many wonderful texts about federal drug defense cases. While I reference federal criminal cases throughout this book and this chapter, I don't exclusively concentrate on them. I do want to make one brief note about federal court specifically, however.

Those of us who practice in federal court often get bogged down in the nuts and bolts of proof and sentencing. While the Sentencing Guidelines are no longer mandatory, where I practice, they are almost always followed.

Even more damaging is the lack of charge bargaining. Those of you in state courts charge bargain all the time. You look to drop down felonies to misdemeanors, and so on. This doesn't happen in federal court practice generally, at least in my neck of the woods.

All of this serves to strip away the importance of the human qualities of our clients that we often want to highlight to the prosecutor. Don't abandon all hope, even in federal court, that you can capture some of that humanity. It is essential that we find our client's soul. In some cases, that requires a lot of digging. In other cases, like the one referenced in the next sectioned, the soul can be easy to capture.

§7:02   My Favorite Federal Case

My favorite federal case never involved me stepping foot inside of any courtroom. I received a call from the mother of my future client who was a soldier. He had just returned home from his first tour of duty in Afghanistan, when he was arrested on a federal warrant out of Maine. I spoke to my future client and his mom, and found his story remarkable.

He had been living in California and got mixed up with some very dangerous people. One of them wanted to ship more than a kilogram of cocaine to Maine. My client hooked his friends up with others who had the cocaine, and they shipped it together to Maine. Once the cocaine was in Maine, it was like watching the Three Stooges attempt a drug deal, and they were caught pretty easily.

Shortly after mailing the cocaine from California, my client decided he had hit rock bottom, and tried to clean up his life. He returned to his home in Colorado, intent on changing his life. He moved back in to live with his parents. He made inquiries with the Army to determine whether he was too old to enlist (he was in his early to mid-30's at the time). He was trying to make a final decision as to whether to enlist or go to a local college when the FBI approached him regarding the drug deal. He cooperated with them, admitted his conduct, and they left him.

The FBI meeting took place on a Friday. That weekend, there was a family gathering in Vail. My client attended the family gathering. His cousin, who had been deployed overseas in the Army, and his uncle who served in Vietnam, were both there. He spoke to them about his idea to join the Army. They encouraged him to enlist.

The final decision was made after my client saw his godson. My client had recently become godfather to his brother's baby son. His brother's family was at the family gathering from Denmark.

My client looked at his godson and decided that he wanted to do something to make his godson proud of him. He felt that living a clean life himself was not enough; that he had to atone for his past mistakes with something bigger.

On the drive home from Vail, my client told his father he was enlisting in the Army and that he would be going overseas. That Monday, he called the recruiter and started the enlistment process. Ultimately, he was deployed, and engaged in the very dangerous job as a forward observer in Afghanistan.

While my client was fighting in Afghanistan, the other two individuals involved in the drug deal went to trial in Federal Court in Maine and they lost. They were sentenced while my client was away.

When my client returned to his base in Colorado, he was arrested. Talk about a homecoming! The war hero (and he was a hero) came home and was arrested for federal cocaine distribution and conspiracy.

Worst of all, he was dead bang guilty. He had already confessed his conduct to the FBI. At the same time, he was a guy who had completely rehabilitated himself by making a great sacrifice for the United States.

§7:03   Can Pretrial Diversion Be a Solution?

I thought that if I was ever going to attempt a federal pretrial diversion, this was the case.

The major objectives of pretrial diversion as described in the U.S. Attorneys Manual ("UAM"), Chapter 9-22.010 are:

- To prevent future criminal activity among certain offenders by diverting them from traditional processing into community supervision and services.
- To save prosecutive and judicial resources for concentration on major cases.
- To provide, where appropriate, a vehicle for restitution to communities and victims of crime.
- The period of supervision is not to exceed 18 months, but may be reduced.

Eligibility for Federal diversion programs is governed by UAM 9-22.100:

The U.S. Attorney, in his/her discretion, may divert any individual against whom a prosecutable case exists and who is not:

1. Accused of an offense which, under existing Department guidelines, should be diverted to the state for prosecution;
2. A person with two or more prior felony convictions;
3. An addict;
4. A public official or former public official accused of an offense arising out of an alleged violation of a public trust; or
5. Accused of an offense related to national security or foreign affairs.

§7:04   The Outcome

I am thankful to report that my client's case was completely diverted. It remains one of my favorite cases because my client was such an extraordinary guy, and the results matched his extraordinariness. He completed a second tour in Afghanistan and was promoted to Sergeant and Tank Commander. He is now a Drill Sergeant.

While it does not happen very often in federal court, we can't lose sight of the possibility of diversion.[1] Redacted letters I wrote in support of diversion in this case are below.

I understand that you are handling federal cases that are far from diversion cases. They have horrible facts and horrible laws applied to those facts. Keep on fighting them though. Occasionally, while scouring the ocean you find the oyster that made the pearl. You never find it, however, if you don't look. So look hard.

§7:05   FORM 7-10 Letter #1 in Support of Diversion

October 28, 2009

U.S. Attorney's Office
100 Middle Street
6th Floor, East Tower
Portland, ME 04101

     Re: <u>United States v. Clint Client</u>
         Case No.

Dear AUSA:

This letter is written pursuant to FRE 406, and is intended to be a plea discussion communication within the meaning of that Rule.

I am writing this letter in the hopes that you will divert Mr. Client's case. The reasons for the requested diversion are set forth below. I understand that this would represent an extraordinary step on your part. When the facts of the case are compared to Mr. Client's admirable record of service to our country and rehabilitation, I believe diversion is appropriate.

The major objectives of pretrial diversion are as described in the U.S. Attorneys Manual ("UAM"), Chapter 9-22.010 are:

To prevent future criminal activity among certain offenders by diverting them from traditional processing into community supervision and services.

---

[1] I know that in some jurisdictions, federal diversion happens more regularly. In Maine, it had been six years or so since there had been a diversion before this case, and that one didn't work out very well. It also involved a less serious charge.

To save prosecutive and judicial resources for concentration on major cases.

To provide, where appropriate, a vehicle for restitution to communities and victims of crime.

The period of supervision is not to exceed 18 months, but may be reduced.

Mr. Client enlisted in the Army on September 6, 2007. He recently re-enlisted for an additional five years.

Mr. Client was deployed to Afghanistan from July 3, 2008 through June 13, 2009. His "Enlisted Record Brief" is attached at <u>Tab 1</u>.

He was engaged in a very dangerous job in Afghanistan, that of Forward Observer. A Forward Observer proceeds ahead of an infantry unit and finds the enemy. He then directs munitions to the enemy's location. This includes adjusting artillery/mortar rounds to the location of the enemy. He also calls in attack helicopters and fixed wing aircraft for attack.

While in-country, he was involved in over 100 patrols, and over 150 fire missions. Prior to his arrest, Mr. Client signed up for his next deployment, which was set to occur in the Summer of 2010. His current rank is Specialist E-4.

Mr. Client has been given many impressive commendations by the Army. Attached at <u>Tab 2</u> is the NATO Medal of Service. Attached at <u>Tab 3</u> is Mr. Client's Army Commendation Medal. Attached at <u>Tab 4</u> and <u>Tab 5</u> are the Army Achievement Medals for bravery above and beyond the call of duty in his capacity as Forward Observer. Attached at <u>Tab 6</u> is the "Order of the Spur" awarded to Mr. Client.

Also attached at <u>Tab 7</u> is a letter from Charles Heroic. Mr. Heroic served with Mr. Client in Afghanistan. Mr. Heroic indicated that Mr. Client's service in Afghanistan saved the lives of U.S. soldiers and Afghan civilian.

Eligibility for Federal diversion programs is governed by UAM 9-22.100:

The U.S. Attorney, in his/her discretion, may divert any individual against whom a prosecutable case exists and who is not:

1. Accused of an offense which, under existing Department guidelines, should be diverted to the State for prosecution;
2. A person with two or more prior felony convictions;
3. An addict;
4. A public official or former public official accused of an offense arising out of an alleged violation of a public trust; or
5. Accused of an offense related to national security or foreign affairs.

Looking at these factors, it is clear that Mr. Client would be a good candidate for diversion:

This offense, under current Department guidelines, would not otherwise be diverted to the State for prosecution.

Mr. Client does not have two or more felony convictions. It appears that he does not have any prior criminal record, save a public intoxication (which may not even be criminal. I am not sure at this point.)

It is unlikely that Mr. Client is an addict. Although he may have used drugs in the past, there is no evidence that he has any addiction problems. As a member of the U.S. Army since 2007, he is subject to random urinalysis testing for illegal drugs. Mr. Client has been drug tested 24 or 25 times since enlisting. There have been no positive tests. It is also improbable that he would have access either to illicit drugs or the opportunity to regularly ingest them while serving in Afghanistan. Further, it is impossible that Mr. Client could have operated at the level at which he did, earning so many distinctions in combat operations, if he were addicted to drugs.

Mr. Client is not a public official or former public official, nor is this an offense arising out of a violation of public trust.

Mr. Client's is not an offense relating to national security or foreign affairs.

It strikes me that Mr. Client's impressive record should be a significant factor in determining how to proceed. He has clearly rehabilitated himself. He puts his life on the line every day in combat. If he is willing to continue to do a very dangerous job that he is quite good at, we should find a way to keep him doing it. I look forward to hearing from you.

Respectfully submitted,

_____

Timothy E. Zerillo
Attorney for Defendant
ZERILLO LAW FIRM, LLC

TEZ/ses

Enclosures
cc: Clint Client

§7:06   FORM 7-20 Letter #2 in Support of Diversion

November 9, 2009

U.S. Attorney's Office
100 Middle Street
6th Floor, East Tower
Portland, ME 04101

　　　Re: <u>United States v. Clint Client</u>
　　　　 Case No.

Dear AUSA:

　　　Kindly consider this a supplement to my October 28, 2009 letter requesting diversion of Mr. Client's case. As you know, I attached several tabbed documents to my October 28th letter (Tabs 1-7). These documents were various commendations and achievements received by Mr. Client while engaged in active combat operations in Afghanistan.

　　　In supplement to those documents, I attach Tabs 8-11. These include 3 award recommendations and approvals, as well as an award announcement. I include these because they provide some additional detail as to why the commendations and awards previously provided were given to Mr. Client. They detail Mr. Client engaging in more than 80 dismounted combat patrols in the Hindu Kush Mountains of Afghanistan, and directing munitions against attacking forces (Tab 8). They discuss his display of command and leadership for his fellow soldiers while advancing through small arms fire (Tab 8). They evidence his bravery and leadership as a Forward Observer, in the face of overwhelming peril (Tab 9).

　　　Mr. Client even built a 30 foot by 70 foot roof over an Army radio station. This is detailed in Tab 10. He tells me that while this may not sound as dangerous as the fire fights and work as Forward Observer, that it was actually one of the most dangerous jobs he did while deployed. The enemy was constantly discussing blowing up that radio station, and yet Mr. Client and one fellow soldier built this 30 foot by 70 foot roof, while open targets, because the Army needed it done.

　　　I could not be more impressed with Mr. Client. I am sure you feel the same. I understand deferment is an extraordinary measure. That said, I cannot imagine a time when I have ever had a client who has taken such amazing steps to rehabilitate himself.

　　　I look forward to discussing deferment with you, or any other member of your office, at your earliest convenience.

　　　　　　　　　　　　　　　　　　　　Respectfully submitted,

　　　　　　　　　　　　　　　　　　　　_____
　　　　　　　　　　　　　　　　　　　　Timothy E. Zerillo
　　　　　　　　　　　　　　　　　　　　Attorney for Defendant
　　　　　　　　　　　　　　　　　　　　ZERILLO LAW FIRM, LLC

　　　TEZ/ses
　　　Enclosures
　　　cc: Clint Client

§7:07   FORM 7-30 Letter #3 in Support of Diversion

December 14, 2009

U.S. Attorney's Office
100 Middle Street
6th Floor, East Tower
Portland, ME 04101

　　　Re: <u>United States v. Client Client</u>
　　　　 Case No.

Dear AUSA:

　　　I am writing to answer the questions you and the United States Attorney had in considering our requested deferment for Clint Client. At the outset, I want to express my appreciation for the consideration that you and the United States Attorney are giving this matter.

Question 1: Does Mr. Client have a criminal record?

Answer 1: No. Mr. Client does not have any criminal record and no juvenile record. The drinking in public we referenced earlier turned out to be a civil offense.

Question 2: Did Mr. Client express an interest in the Army prior to the FBI visit?

Answer 2: Yes and no. Mr. Client insists that nothing but the absolute truth be expressed in my communications with you, so as easy as it would be for me to answer that he had already signed up for the Army prior to the FBI visit, but that is not entirely true.

Mr. Client returned to Colorado intent on changing his life on June 18, 2007. He returned to Colorado to live with his parents. He made inquiries about the Army to determine whether he was too old to enlist. He was trying to make a final decision as to whether to enlist or go to a local college when the FBI approached him. He learned that he could enlist.

The FBI approached him August 3, 2007. He told them everything he knew and believed he was a cooperating witness for the Government.

That meeting took place on a Friday. That weekend there was a family gathering in Vail. Mr. Client attended the family gathering. His cousin who had been deployed overseas and his uncle who served in Vietnam were both there. He spoke to them about his idea to join the Army. They encouraged him to enlist.

The final decision was made after seeing his godson. Mr. Client had recently become godfather to his brother's baby son. His brother's family was at the family gathering from Denmark.

He looked at his godson and decided that he wanted to do something to make his godson proud of him. Mr. Client felt that living a clean life himself was not enough; that he had to atone for his past mistakes with something bigger.

On the drive home from Vail he told his father he was enlisting in the Army and that he would be going overseas. That Monday he called the recruiter and started the enlistment process.

I can see how it could appear that Mr. Client was trying to run away, but he was not. He came clean to his parents about the situation. He told them that if the FBI did come to look for him that they should explain that he enlisted.

The FBI did, in fact, come to see his parents in 2008. Mr. Client's parents told the FBI that their son was overseas fighting in Afghanistan, and asked if they should attempt to contact him. The FBI told them not to contact him.

One more quick point on this topic. Mr. Client was not trying to hide in any way shape or form. If he was trying to hide from the federal government, it would seem foolish for him to enlist in the Army. When he returned from deployment this year, and before he knew there were charges against him, he re-enlisted for another five years and volunteered to re-deploy. He is currently set to deploy for another tour in Afghanistan this summer.

I want to close this letter by being a little corny. I was watching my favorite holiday movie, *It's a Wonderful Life,* with my wife and kids recently. I could not help thinking of Mr. Client while watching it. As you recall, in the very beginning of the movie the protagonist, George Bailey, saves his little brother Harry Bailey's life as he falls through the ice. George loses his hearing in one ear and cannot enlist in World War II. Harry fights and receives the Medal of Honor for saving the lives of those aboard a transport carrier that was about to be destroyed. As Clarence the Angel reminds George Bailey in George's greatest moment of despair, Harry was only able to save those men because George saved him when he was a boy.

I think of Mr. Client's case as our own *It's a Wonderful Life* moment. The highest and best use for him is in the hills of Afghanistan protecting our lives while he risks his own. It is my hope that your office will be kind enough to allow him to continue to do so.

Enclosed as Tab 14, is a letter from Mr. Client's parents. The letter describes the events surrounding Mr. Client's entry into the army.

Respectfully submitted,

_____

Timothy E. Zerillo
Attorney for Defendant
ZERILLO LAW FIRM, LLC

TEZ/ses
Enclosures
cc: Clint Client

[§§7:08-7:19 Reserved]

DRUG CRIMES

II.   DRUG POSSESSION

A. Elements and Common Scenarios

§7:20   The Elements

Possession statutes typically require the state to prove (1) the defendant knowingly had (2) a controlled substance (3) on his or her person or under his or her control (e.g., the drug was in the defendant's car or home or storage unit).

§7:21   The Weekend User—"Whose Vial Is That Anyway?"

The weekend warrior drug user presents the low end of the totem pole of serious drug charges. While they may not be the most serious cases on the docket, they should be unbelievably serious to you because they are serious to your client.

> **PRACTICE TIP:** *The weekend warrior as a source of repeat business*
>
> The weekend warrior presents a great opportunity for you to build your practice. Do a good job on the case and one of two things will happen. The client will either clean up and stay out of trouble, which is good for society, and good for you, or the client will re-offend and come back to you for help. Either way, you benefit, so do a nice job.

The weekend warrior isn't quite a serious drug addict. He or she likes to party a bit with "social" drugs: marijuana, cocaine, ecstasy, etc. Weekend warriors hold down good jobs or are students, and just got searched by the cops at the wrong time.

A typical fact pattern I see all the time goes like this: some friends are out partying, and they are driving to their next stop on a Saturday night. A cop pulls the car over for a brake light being out. As the officer approaches, he smells the odor of marijuana in the car, and sees a roach in the ashtray. He orders everyone out, and searches your client's purse, where he finds a small bag of pot. The search of the car in the backseat reveals an eight ball of cocaine.

The client presents in your office as hysterical. She's been charged with a misdemeanor for the pot and felony possession for the coke. She has only a prior drunk driving conviction. She's a weekend warrior, but she's got a criminal problem.

§7:22   The Addict

The addict presents slightly differently than the weekend warrior. Those differences may be subtle, but they exist. The addict may also have been out partying, even with social drugs. But ask what other drugs the client uses. Has she ventured into opiates? Does she ever do drugs alone? What is her record?

You should ask your client these questions to differentiate the types of treatment needed and the steps to be taken. Remember, addicts are great liars. You need to gain their trust and get to the bottom of things. To do so, you need to think critically of your client. You need to ask questions. And you need to evaluate whether the answers to your questions square with what you see.

Let's imagine the exact same factual scenario as above with our weekend warrior. The client admits to the marijuana, but says the cocaine isn't hers. She has a good job, and everything seems fine on the surface. This is her colloquy with me on drug history.

Attorney: There are a lot of things going on here that we need to address. We need to see if the stop was good and if you have standing to bring claims for a bad stop. Whether the search of your purse was good. Whether the government can prove the drugs are real. But before we get into that, I need to understand your drug history to help you. You have to remember we are in an attorney-client privileged setting, and I want to help you, so be honest with me, OK?

Client: OK.

Attorney: When did you first use anything? Probably pot?

Client: Yes. I was 12 years old.

Attorney: OK. Who'd you get it from?

Client: My older brother was a dealer.

Attorney: Does he still?

Client: No, he was killed a few years ago.

Attorney: I'm sorry. Did your parents use?

Client: My mother did. Used crack. She's sober now.

Attorney: Great. Your father?

Client. He died when I was little.

Attorney: Was that drug related?

Client: I don't know.

Attorney: I'm asking you all these questions not because I'm nosy and not because I'm judging, I just want to understand you and how I can help. It sounds like you had a rough childhood.

Client: Yes. Very rough.

Attorney: So, you moved onto harder stuff from pot when?

Client: 15 years old I took some oxy's.

Attorney: How?

Client: I just took them. In the pill form.

Attorney: Someone show you to crush them up and snort them?

Client: Later on.

Attorney: How old were you?

Client: 16 years old. Then I stopped that shit. Almost OD'd.

Attorney: Ouch. Did you get into a program?

Client: They sent me to a drug counselor.

Attorney: Nothing inpatient?

Client: No. Did an IOP once.

Attorney: 20 days?

Client: Uh huh.

Attorney: What else have you used?

Client: You name it. Blow, weed, e, shrooms, vikes.

Attorney: Heroin?

Client: Not for a while.

Attorney: Are the opiates to party, or is that on your own?

Client: I don't use that shit now.

Attorney: But when you did?

Client: Usually alone.

Attorney: When did you last do that?

Client: Like a year ago.

Attorney: So, the IOP was when?

Client: Right after I last used opiates.

So, this is the addict, disguised as the weekend warrior. It isn't rocket science, but to get a better understanding of the client and the client's case and overall wellness, you need to look beyond the current charges. You need to ask questions and understand just how deep the illness goes.

This client is either lying to me about her current use of opiates or she is on a very slippery slope toward opiate relapse. You can't be an opiate addict hanging out with guys with cocaine and having marijuana in your purse without major problems coming your way. I am going to have to have a really hard talk with my client after this colloquy about what I see and the need for inpatient rehab occurring right away.

[§§7:23-7:29 Reserved]

B. Strategies and Tactics

§7:30   Drug Counseling

As previously noted, I recommend my clients engage in drug counseling in almost every case. I don't care if they are arrested for the first joint they've ever smoked in their life, I still recommend they get into counseling. It is part of the game we need to play. Explain to your drug clients that they cannot change the facts that caused them to come to your office, but they can change what happens between the charge and disposition.

The type of drug counseling depends on the addiction. This is one reason to figure out when someone is an addict pretending to be the weekend warrior.

For the Weekend Warrior

For the true weekend warrior, I would likely suggest a substance abuse evaluation to start. It will likely show a minimal problem. The client should then follow up with a licensed drug and alcohol counselor.

It is very important, if you are going to do drug cases, to understand who the good people are who can craft carefully worded and thoughtful substance abuse evaluations. You find these people by networking, but it is important to find them.

I had a client who was charged as a college student with drug possession. She was completely guilty. There were no defensible issues I could see. She was a weekend warrior client, and we got her a beautiful deferred disposition. All she needed to do was stay out of trouble for six months and get a substance abuse evaluation.

Three days before the end of her deferred disposition she realized she had completely forgotten to get the substance abuse evaluation. She freaked out, and tried to get it on her own. The places she called in the phone book had six week waits and she had only three days. She called me.

I knew someone. I called him. He evaluated her the day after my call, faxed me his report the day after that and the case was over.

This was not because I did anything special. I didn't know anything special. The only thing I knew was who to get her to, and because of my connection to this person, we went to the front of the line.

Whenever you can do it for your client, use those connections. In *Goodfellas*, Henry Hill walks in through the back door of the Copa into a full house and they snap out a table for him in the front of the stage. Impressive, huh? Well, it worked on Karen in *Goodfellas,* at least.

You have connections too. Whenever you can use them to let your clients feel special, feel like you pulled strings for them, do it. They won't forget it.

You also need to make connections with good licensed drug and alcohol counselors, psychologists, and psychiatrists. You need respected people in the field. They also need to know how to write a good letter to your prosecutor. Getting your people to the right professionals can make the small difference between a winning and losing result for your client.

For the Addict

Now, if you discover that you have an addict masquerading as the weekend warrior, then I would take a different tact, although treatment still needs to be a component. I wouldn't send the client for the substance abuse evaluation. With his history, I think it is clear there is a problem. Instead, get him into an inpatient treatment program. This can be easier said than done depending on your client's financial and insurance situation. If it is possible to do, get it done, however. A licensed drug and alcohol counselor isn't enough.

Follow up should be to an outpatient program that is acceptable to you and your client's providers. It is important that the client be set up to succeed. Do everything you can to put the client in the best position possible for not only the case, but for life.

§7:31   Point to an Alternative Suspect in a Possession Case

One common (and sometimes effective) way to approach the possession case is to point the finger at someone else. While possession is liberally construed in general, the government often cannot meet its burden of proof.

In the example in §7:21, above, the marijuana is in our client's purse and there is cocaine in the car. If she doesn't own the car, then you blame the car owner or whoever was in the backseat. If your client was in the backseat with the coke and she didn't cop to it, then the argument is it was dark out and she didn't know it was there, or that the front seat people tossed it in the backseat when the cops pulled them over. There are many possibilities to explore.

§7:32   Hire a Chemist

Although not terribly common in the possession case, you may argue that the drugs at issue were not actually the drugs charged. This happens especially in the cocaine context in my experience. There, the state probably used a gas chromatography mass spectrometer (GCMS) machine. It's an instrument designed to detect minute or microliter substances. Since the cocaine is usually a solid, the chemist generally adds methanol to put it into a liquid form. From there, the GCMS machine can analyze the substance.

If you have concerns about the calibration of the machine, the process used or the credentials of the expert, hire your own chemist. The chemist can at least give you information as to how to cross-examine the state's expert, but also may provide valuable testimony regarding the defects in the chemical analysis.

§7:33   Drug Dog Tactics

Drug dogs are often used to trick people. They are used in a fake auto stops for civil violations. The occupant or driver of the car, thinking he or she has no choice and is only stopped for a traffic violation, allows the so-called "free air sniff" by the canine. When the dog alerts, the police have cause for a search.

Establishing the reliability of the drug dog is critical to the constitutionality of the search. If the drug dog is unreliable, the reasons underpinning the search of the car are unconstitutional. *Florida v. Harris* 133 S.Ct. 1050 (2013) explored this topic. In summary, *Harris* simply endorses the following methodology:

If the State has produced proof from controlled settings that a dog performs reliably in detecting drugs, *and the defendant has not contested that showing*, the court should find probable cause. But a defendant must have an opportunity to challenge such evidence of a dog's reliability, whether by cross-examining the testifying officer or by introducing his own fact or expert witnesses. The defendant may contest training or testing standards as flawed or too lax, *or raise an issue regarding the particular alert. Id*. at 1052, *emphasis added.*

For the canine search to be constitutionally protected, the canine must be reliable. The Supreme Court in *Harris* rejected the idea that a canine's field performance hits and misses be recorded and automatically discovered. *Id*. at 1056-1057. Records of hits and misses in the field are less reliable than records of hits and misses in a properly controlled setting. *Id*. The underlying decision in *Harris* was overturned primarily because Florida had ruined the fluid concept of probable cause by creating "…a strict evidentiary checklist, whose every item the State must tick off…" in order to admit drug canine evidence. *Id*. at 1056.

The fluidity of the probable cause concept supports the request for canine discovery. While the evidence of real world hits and misses of the dog may not be discoverable under *Harris*, the methodology of the canine's training and the reliability of the dog in general should be discovered. In addition, the Second Circuit has interpreted *Harris* to mean that field performance records, while not required in all cases, may be relevant in some cases. *United States v. Foreste*, 780 F.3d 518 (2d Cir. 2015). As the Second Circuit points out in *Foreste*, the *Harris* case would be entirely stripped of its holding if there were no opportunity to challenge a drug dog's reliability and to discover evidence upon which to base that challenge. *Id*.

Robust discovery practice on this topic is essential. It is equally important, whenever it can be afforded, to have a canine expert to at least consult with during the discovery, suppression and trial process.

Additionally, pay particular attention to the timing of the stop. If you have a sham stop for a traffic infraction, the pretext may give way to an unconstitutional search if the police are not prompt with their canine search.

In *Whren v. United States*, 517 U.S. 806 (1996), the Court held that an officer's actual motivation in making a stop (for example, to investigate for drugs) is generally irrelevant if the officer has probable cause for the stop and could have stopped the person for that reason anyway (for example, the person committed a traffic violation). However, in *Rodriguez v. United States*, 135 S.Ct. 1609 (2015), the Supreme Court abrogated that government argument in the context of drug dog searches.

In *Rodriguez*, a law enforcement officer with a narcotics canine stopped a vehicle for swerving. *Id*. at 1612. The officer asked the driver for license, registration and proof of insurance. *Id*. at 1613. The officer then issued a written warning to the driver for swerving. *Id*.

After issuing the warning, the officer asked the driver if he could walk his drug canine around the vehicle. *Id*. The driver refused. *Id*. The officer walked his canine around the vehicle anyway, and the dog alerted half-way through his second pass. *Id*.

The time from the issuance of the warning ticket in *Rodriguez* to the completion of the dog sniff search was seven to eight minutes. *Id.* The District Court, followed by the Eighth Circuit, denied Rodriguez's Motion to Suppress under the theory that the intrusion was *de minimis* and that it "was not of constitutional significance." *Id.* at 1613-1614.

The Supreme Court reversed. They found that a dog sniff is not an ordinary accoutrement to a traffic stop. *Id.* at 1615. The stop may not be prolonged unless there is reasonable suspicion to justify holding an individual beyond the time necessary to complete the stop. *Id.* The length of additional time is inconsequential. "The critical question then, is not whether the dog sniff occurs before or after the officer issues a ticket...but whether conducting the sniff 'prolongs'—i.e., adds time to—'the stop... .'" *Id.* at 1616.

[§§7:34-7:39 Reserved]

C. Discovery and Suppression Motions

§7:40   Suppressing Evidence Found During Search of Vehicle Incident to Arrest

The U.S. Supreme Court case *Arizona v. Gant*, 129 S. Ct. 1710, 556 U.S. 332 (2009), may prove helpful in getting the drugs and other evidence suppressed, especially when they are discovered as a result of a vehicle stop. *Gant* significantly narrowed the search incident to a lawful arrest exception to the warrant requirement. Search incident to lawful arrest was discussed in dicta as early as 1914 in *Weeks v. United States*, 232 U.S. 383 (1914). The exception was expanded as time went on.

Chimel v. California, 395 U.S. 752 (1969) clarified the reasoning for the exception by focusing on (1) officer safety and (2) destruction of evidence. Later cases expanded *Chimel*'s philosophy. *United States v. Robinson*, 414 U.S. 218, 235 (1973) allowed for search incident to arrest based on a traffic stop, without distinguishing how the traffic stop related to the *Chimel* factors. In *Belton v. New York*, 453 U.S. 454 (1981), a police officer conducted a search incident to lawful arrest of the passenger compartment of the subject vehicle after the occupants had exited the vehicle. The logical argument by Belton, which the Court at that time did not agree with, was that by being outside of the car, any weapons were also outside of his reach. So, after *Belton* and until *Gant*, an arrest of an individual in a car also allowed a search of the car and its compartments automatically.

Rodney Gant was arrested in Tucson, Arizona for driving with a suspended license. The police searched the car incident to a lawful arrest while Gant was out of the car, and they found drugs and a gun, charging him with those items as well. Coming to its senses in an opinion authored by Justice Stevens, the Supreme Court held that a search of a vehicle incident to lawful arrest does not meet probable cause and is not an exception to the warrant requirement unless 1) there is an opportunity for the suspect to enter the car during the execution of the search, or 2) the vehicle contains evidence of the offense for which the suspect has been arrested. *Gant* is a great case to use if your clients, like mine, get pulled over for stupid things like a license plate light being out while they are transporting a kilo of cocaine.

§7:41   Suppressing Statements in Case of Unlawful Detention

Once the police have your client out of the vehicle, they will be looking for confessions. This, of course, raises *Miranda* issues you shouldn't ignore.

Miranda stands for the well-known proposition that the prosecution cannot offer any statements made by a defendant in times of custodial interrogation "unless the use of procedural safeguards effective to secure the privilege against self-incrimination have been demonstrated." *Miranda v. Arizona*, 384 U.S. 436, 479 (1966). Those procedural safeguards are, of course, *Miranda* warnings.

Since *Miranda* usually requires custody and interrogation, custody usually being the sticking point, your job is to establish at the motion hearing as coercive and intimidating an atmosphere as possible. Don't leave anything out that could serve to intimidate your client, including any show of force by the cops, the number of officers, your client's lack (hopefully) of prior police involvement, his familiarity with the surroundings, the size of the room, the number of exits, the tone employed by the officers, and so forth. Again, you are only limited by your imagination. See §7:44 Form 7-40 and §7:46 Form 7-60 Motions to Suppress with *Miranda* arguments.

§7:42   Suppressing Evidence Found as Result of Illegal Stop of Vehicle

The stop of a vehicle can seem almost impossible to contest, given the difficult standard of reasonable and articulable suspicion. Contest bad stops anyway, whenever possible.

The Fourth Amendment prohibits unreasonable search and seizures of a person by law enforcement. *United States v. Arvizu*, 534 U.S. 266, 273 (2002). These protections extend to brief investigatory stops of a vehicle. *Id.* at 273. An investigatory stop requires some objective manifestation that the person stopped is or is about to be engaged in criminal activity. *Id.* at 273. In determining whether the government has reasonable articulable suspicion for an investigatory stop, the courts look at the "totality of the circumstances" of each case to determine whether the officer has a "particularized and objective basis" for suspecting crime is afoot. *Id.* at 273. However, a mere "hunch" is insufficient to justify a stop. *Id.* at 273; *United States v. Foster*, 634 F.3d 243, 246 (4th Cir. 2011).

Further, argue that reasonable suspicion requires reliability "in its assertion of illegality." *United States v. Johnson*, 620 F.3d 685, 693 (6th Cir. 2010), (citation omitted). Likewise, no matter how long the officer has been on the beat, argue that "blind deference is not owed," despite the experience and knowledge of a law enforcement officer. 325 F.3d 63, 68 (1st Cir. 2003). This is especially true if the officer is proceeding on "inchoate unparticularized suspicion or 'hunch' of criminal activity." *Id.* at 68.

Here is one more arrow for your quiver in this area. Consider that an officer must do more than label behavior "suspicious" to validate a stop. *United States v. Foster*, 634 F.3d 243, at 248 (4th Cir. 2011). In *Foster*, a detective saw a young black male talking to himself in a parked SUV followed by another black male popping up in the seat who the detective recognized as a "bad person." *Id.* at 245 After speaking with these individuals briefly, the cop left and watched their vehicle from across the street until he made the decision to block in the SUV. *Id.* The court held that these factors were not sufficient to validate the stop because the officer was acting on a hunch. *Id.* at 249.

For passengers, consider *Brendlin v. California*, 551 U.S. 249 (2007). Brendlin was stopped for a car registration issue, and, low and behold, drugs and meth manufacturing equipment were found in the car. The issue for the Court was whether a passenger in a vehicle is detained when a car is stopped so as to contest the validity of the stop. The case is significant, because it represents the first time the Supreme Court recognized that all the parties are seized when a car is stopped. For your possession cases in which you represent a passenger, now you have clear standing to contest the stop, and probably any seizure. See §7:46 Form 7-60 Motion to Suppress with illegal stop arguments.

§7:43   Suppressing Evidence Found During Entry into Home Based on Plain View

Like plain view sightings of roaches in the ashtray of a car, the cops will sometimes claim the plain view of drugs in a residence. This is an attempt, yet again, to get around the warrant requirement and to avoid doing actual police work.

This usually happens with the knock and talk. The cops knock on the door of a residence, the door is answered, and they force their way in based on a claimed view of drugs or paraphernalia in plain view. Bring motions to suppress in those cases. They are hard to win, but not impossible. See §7:44 Form 7-40 Motion to Suppress with illegal entry arguments.

§7:44   FORM 7-40 Motion to Suppress: Entry into Home Based on Plain View, Miranda Violation

IN THE UNITED STATES DISTRICT COURT
FOR THE DISTRICT OF MAINE

UNITED STATES OF AMERICA,	)	
	)	
Plaintiff,	)	
	)	
v.	)	Case No. 05-11111
	)	
	)	
HENRY BUD,	)	
	)	
Defendant	)	

DRUG CRIMES (side tab)

MOTION TO SUPPRESS EVIDENCE WITH INCORPORATED MEMORANDUM OF LAW

NOW COMES, the Defendant, Henry Bud, by and through Undersigned Counsel, and moves the Honorable Court to suppress all physical objects obtained pursuant to the unlawful entry into his home and the subsequent search and arrest of the Defendant, as well as all statements made by the Defendant. Specifically, the Defendant requests that this Court suppress all the items, including narcotics, seized in the search of his home on or about December 30, 2004, and that this Court suppress all statements made by the Defendant after law enforcement officer's entry into his home.

STANDING

The seizure of narcotics and other evidence at issue in this Motion took place in the apartment the Defendant shared with his girlfriend, Hattie Coker, at the Shady Lane Apartments. Although Ms. Coker told law enforcement officers that the apartment was rented in her name, there seems to be no disagreement that the Defendant resided in that apartment as well. As a result, the Defendant had a reasonable expectation of privacy in the seizure of narcotics and other items in his apartment.

FACTUAL BACKGROUND[2]

On December 30, 2004, Drug Enforcement Agency (hereafter "DEA") agents, acting in conjunction with the Needless Police Department, had a Confidential Source (hereafter "C.S.") place a series of recorded phone calls to Tim Ratley. That day, the CS purchased 1/8th ounce of cocaine from Ratley. Ratley was arrested thereafter.

Also, on December 30, 2004, Ratley was interviewed by DEA Special Agents (hereafter "S.A.") Wolf and Boucher. Ratley indicated that he had picked up the cocaine ultimately delivered to the C.S. at Henry Bud's apartment. Ratley indicated that the cocaine was obtained from Lucas Luckless, but was picked up at the Bud residence. The law enforcement officers continued surveillance of Bud's apartment. Meanwhile, MDEA S.A. Rose drafted an Affidavit and Application for a Search Warrant.

During the surveillance of the apartment, the agents observed Lucas Luckless leave the apartment in a vehicle usually driven by Hattie Coker. Luckless was then arrested by law enforcement for Operating after Suspension.

The agents performing surveillance allege that the auto Luckless was driving then returned to the Bud apartment complex. A male unknown to the agents was driving the car. DEA S.A. Iforgot then followed this male to the door to the apartment. The male knocked on the door, and S.A. Iforgot claims to have identified himself at that point. S.A. Iforgot then alleges that he could see through the doorway, in plain view, a marijuana smoking pipe on a table. S.A. Iforgot then claims to have entered the apartment to perform a protective sweep.

This description of the entry into the Bud apartment will be significantly contradicted by defense witness testimony. These witnesses will testify that S.A. Iforgot, along with S.A. Tagalong and another law enforcement officer pushed open the door to the Defendant's apartment and forced their way in. They entered the apartment after Hattie Coker's father, George Coker, came to the door. The officers ran after Mr. Coker as he walked to the Defendant's door. Mr. Coker knocked on the door and Bud answered. As the door opened, the three officers pushed their way into the apartment. When the officers were asked to display a search warrant, the officers said they didn't need one. Additionally, George Coker will testify that there was no marijuana pipe in plain view from the doorway.

The officers did not read *Miranda* warnings to the Defendant. The agents told the Defendant that they would not arrest Hattie Coker if he gave them the narcotics. Ultimately, the Defendant disclosed the location of some cocaine, said to weigh 12 grams. The agents arrested the Defendant and Hattie Coker. [3]

A search warrant for the Bud residence was signed on December 31, 2004 at 12:36 am. The illegal entry and search of the Bud residence was conducted between 9:00 pm and 10:00 pm on December 30, 2004.

LAW AND ARGUMENT

A. Illegal Entry Into The Defendant's Home

Warrantless entries by law enforcement officers into a private home are presumptively unreasonable. *Payton v. New York* 455 U.S. 573, 100 S.Ct. 1371 (1980); *United States v. Samboy*, 433 F.3d 154 (1st Cir. 2005). The police

---

[2] Counsel notes that this factual recitation is based on the reports provided to Counsel at this time. The police reports are incomplete and do not contain information regarding crucial witnesses, such as DEA S.A. Iforgot.

[3] Coker is not indicated in the current conspiracy and the state charges against her have been dismissed.

have a heavy burden of demonstrating an urgent or exigent need to justify a warrantless arrest in a private home. *Minnesota v. Olson*, 495 U.S. 91, 110 S.Ct. 1684 (1990). Even if law enforcement officers had probable cause to believe that a crime has been or is being committed, "the constitutional protections afforded to an individual's privacy interest in his own home outweigh the government's interest in crime prevention." *Samboy, supra* at 158, *citing Payton, supra* at 588-589, 100 S.Ct. 1371.

The police may make warrantless entry into a person's private home if there are exigent circumstances. The government bears the burden of proving exigent circumstances. *Samboy, supra* at 158, *citing U.S. v. Balbacchino*, 762 F.2d, 176 (1st Cir. 1985). Here, there are no exigent circumstances that would have necessitated entry into the Defendant's home. There was no indication that Bud knew the officers were outside his home. By all accounts, the drugs were Luckless's, not Bud's. There was no evidence that Bud would dispose of the drugs even if he knew the officers were there.

The reality is that the police did not make entry into the Bud home based on exigent circumstances anyway. Rather, S.A. Iforgot claims that he observed the marijuana pipe from the plain view of the Bud doorway. No such marijuana pipe could have been observed from the doorway, and a plain view exception does not apply.

The government cannot meet the burden of proving that there were exigent circumstances to enter the Defendant's home and commit a warrantless search, nor were any other exceptions to the warrant requirement present. The Defendant's arrest was unlawful and all physical evidence seized or obtained as a result of his unlawful arrest should be suppressed as "fruit of the poisonous tree." *Wong Son v. United States*, 371 U.S. 471, 487 thru 488, 83 S.Ct. 407 (1963).

B.   Suppression of Statements

Mr. Bud is asserting that all statements law enforcement obtained from him should also be suppressed. First, the statements should be suppressed because they are a result of an illegal entry and arrest pursuant to the Fourth Amendment as they constitute "fruits of the poisonous tree." *Wong Son v. United States*, 371 U.S. 471 (1963).

Second, the statements were obtained in violation of the Fifth Amendment, Self-Incrimination Clause, as well as the Fourteenth Amendment, as the statements were involuntary. The Defendant was not apprised of his *Miranda* rights after the agent's illegal entry into his home. *Miranda v. Arizona*, 384 U.S. 436 (1966). Clearly the Defendant was in custody and interrogated as a result of the agent's forced entry into the Defendant's home. Further, the Defendant was promised that his girlfriend, Hattie Coker, who was pregnant with his child at the time of the incident, would not be arrested if Bud showed the agents the narcotics. As a result, Bud gave the officers a packet of cocaine.

After illegally entering Bud's home, the agents failed to apprise the Defendant of his *Miranda* rights. Moreover, in an effort to encourage him to make statements and eventually to cooperate, the agents informed Bud that they would not charge Hattie Coker with any crime if he turned over narcotics to them. Based on the failure to give the Defendant *Miranda* warnings despite custodial interrogation, and the agent's attempt to render his statements involuntary, all statements by the Defendant should be suppressed. Since the statements led the agents to discover the cocaine, the seizure of the cocaine should likewise be suppressed as fruit of the poisonous tree.

CONCLUSION

For the above-stated reasons the Defendant is requesting an evidentiary hearing on the issues contained in this Memorandum and prays this Court suppress all evidence obtained pursuant to the unlawful entry into Henry Bud's apartment in accordance with the Fourth Amendment. Further, any statements obtained or evidence seized after the unlawful entry must be suppressed as fruit of the poisonous tree.

Finally, all statements obtained from the Defendant should be suppressed as they violated the Fifth Amendment Self-Incrimination clause and were involuntary pursuant to the Fourteenth Amendment. Since the Defendant's statements lead to law enforcement's discovery of narcotics, the seizure of those narcotics should also be suppressed.

Dated this 13th day of February, 2006 in Portland, Maine.

Respectfully submitted,

_____
Timothy E. Zerillo
Attorney for Defendant
ZERILLO LAW FIRM, LLC

DRUG CRIMES

§7:45   FORM 7-50 Motion for Discovery: Drug Dog, Lengthy Detention, Miranda, Consent

UNITED STATES DISTRICT COURT
DISTRICT OF MAINE

UNITED STATES OF AMERICA	)	
	)	
v.	)	Crim. No.
	)	
ADAM W.	)	
Defendant	)	
	)	

DEFENDANT'S MOTION FOR DISCOVERY

NOW COMES the accused party herein, ADAM W, by and through his undersigned Counsel pursuant to Federal Rules of Criminal Procedure 12, 16, *Brady v. Maryland*, 373 U.S. 83 (1963) and *Giglio v. United States*, 405 U.S. 150 (1972) and respectfully moves the Court for an Order requiring the Government to provide Counsel for Defendant with the following information:

1. The Defendant seeks two types of discovery that the Government has indicated it will not provide absent a Court Order compelling production.
2. Defendant was pulled over in the context of a complex operational plan involving at least three law enforcement agencies. Law enforcement's plan was to have a drug detection dog available when they pulled the Defendant over. The drug dog here, named Aros, alerted on the passenger door of the Defendant's vehicle. He did not alert when he walked around the driver's door of the vehicle on three occasions, and only alerted on his fourth time by the door.
3. Defendant requested discovery and received Aros's training and certification records. There were no videos recorded of Aros's training. There were no records received related to the length of time or the number of times it takes Aros to alert on a contraband substance.
4. Defendant will file a Motion to Suppress related to the dog sniff search in this matter. He seeks information in this Motion for Discovery that is relevant to that Motion to Suppress.
5. Counsel requested that AUSA Michael C. provide records of Aros's other cruiser cam videos from the sniff searches and Trooper Adam F.'s (Aros's handlers) training records for his previous drug dog, Caro. *See Exhibit 1, Attorney Zerillo Letter to AUSA C.*. In the Letter to AUSA C., similar arguments are made to those made herein, and will not be repeated as a result.
6. AUSA C. issued a response letter to the Undersigned denying the request for Aros's other cruiser videos and the Caro records. *See Exhibit 2, AUSA C. Letter to Attorney Zerillo*. In his denial, AUSA C. indicates that there are no less than 30 cases in which videos of Aros may be found, and that some of the cases are open cases or involve targets. *Exhibit 2.*
7. The Defendant's potential drug dog expert is Steven N. An *Affidavit of Steven N* is attached as *Exhibit 3*. Mr. N will opine that the dog's actions during the stop and sniff did not create a positive alert and generally reflect inadequate training of the dog. *Id.* at ¶¶ 10-14, ¶ 26. The items sought in this motion are relevant to this opinion.

MEMORANDUM OF LAW

REQUIREMENTS UNDER *BRADY* AND PROGENY

The United States Supreme Court has held that the prosecution has a due process obligation under the Federal Constitution to disclose material evidence favorable to a criminal defendant. *Brady vs. Maryland*, 373 U.S. 83 (1963). Favorable evidence is quite broad. Favorable evidence can include anything reasonably positive to the defense. In *United States v. Bagley*, 473 U.S. 667 (1985), the Court held that regardless of the request, general or specific, favorable evidence is material, and constitutional error results from its suppression by the Government, "if there is a reasonable probability that, had the evidence been disclosed to the defense, the result of the proceeding would have been different." *Id*. at 682.

The U.S. Supreme Court has continued in its case law to reemphasize the importance of Government disclosure to the Defense:

> In *Brady*, this Court held that the suppression by the prosecution of evidence favorable to an accused upon request violates due process where the evidence is material to guilt or to punishment, irrespective of the good faith or bad faith of the prosecution. We have since held that the duty to disclose such evidence is applicable even though there has been no request by the accused, and that the duty encompasses impeachment evidence as well as exculpatory evidence. Such evidence is material if there is a reasonable probability that, had the evidence been disclosed to the defense, the result of the proceeding would have been different. Moreover, the rule encompasses evidence known only to police investigators and not to the prosecutor. In order to comply with *Brady*, therefore, the individual prosecutor has a duty to learn of any favorable evidence known to others acting on the government's behalf in [a] case, including the police.

Strickler v. Greene, 527 U.S. 263, 280-81 (1999) (*citations and quotation marks omitted*).

The protections of *Brady* stem from the requirement of due process and the right to a fair trial. *Bagley* at 675. A showing of materiality under *Bagley* does not require proof by the defendant that disclosure of the evidence would result in the defendant's acquittal. *Kyles vs. Whitley*, 514 U.S. 419 (1995). All that is required is a "reasonable probability" that the information is necessary in order for the defendant to receive a fair trial, meaning a trial that results in a verdict worthy of confidence. *Id*. at 434.

In *Kyles*, the Defendant was accused of robbing and murdering a woman at gunpoint in the parking lot of a Schwegmann's Store in New Orleans, Louisiana. *Id*. at 423. There were six eyewitnesses, two with very different descriptions of the shooter. *Id*. at 423-428. Kyles' build, height and weight were contradicted, as was his hair style. *Id*. One witness, Beanie, tried very hard to implicate Kyles. *Id*. at 425. He gave four statements to the police, which were exceedingly inconsistent. *Id*. at 427.

Kyles was indicted for murder, and his counsel made a motion for exculpatory information. The State's response was there was "no exculpatory evidence of any nature." *Id*. at 428.

In the first trial, neither side called Beanie. *Id*. at 429. The jury hung. *Id*. After trial, the prosecutor re-interviewed Beanie. *Id*. In this fifth statement, Beanie was again significantly inconsistent in his version of events and implication of Kyles. *Id*. at 430. Beanie's statements were not disclosed to the defense. *Id*.

At the second trial, the defense blamed Beanie for the shooting, although they were still without Beanie's statements and other exculpatory materials. *Id*. at 430. The State called Beanie as a rebuttal witness and Kyles was convicted. *Id*. at 430. He was later sentenced to death and Beanie was given $1,600 in reward money. *Id*. Kyles sought habeas corpus relief. The Fifth Circuit affirmed and the Supreme Court granted certiorari. *Id*. at 431-432. The Supreme Court held that the prosecutor's failure to disclose the above information resulted in a reasonable probability that there would have been a different result at trial, and reversed as a result. *Id*. at 419.

Bagley requires that the undisclosed evidence be material when determining whether an error has occurred. In other words, if favorable evidence is not disclosed, the Defendant does not need to show that disclosure of the evidence would have resulted in an acquittal. Under *Kyles*, the issue is only whether there was a "verdict worthy of confidence." *Id*. at 434-435. This confidence is not necessarily related to the ultimate outcome, although it can be. *Id*. Materiality of the evidence is primarily related to the process and underlying fairness of the trial. *Id*.

This means that the strength of the Government evidence is not an issue. What is in issue is fairness in the process. Here, that includes the process related to a Motion to Suppress (*see* Section II, *infra*).

The prudent course for the Government is to disclose the evidence to the defense. Here, they have refused. *Exhibit 2*. The Court in *Kyles* states that "a prosecutor anxious about tacking too close to the wind will disclose a favorable piece of evidence." *Id*. at 439. A "prudent prosecutor will resolve doubtful questions in favor of disclosure." *Id*. at 439; *see also U.S. v. Agurs*, 427 US 97, 108 (1977). It should be noted additionally that discovery errors under *Kyles* and *Bagely* are never harmless. *Id*. at 435.

BRADY AND PROGENY APPLY TO MOTIONS TO SUPPRESS

Brady applies to the disclosure of information relevant to pretrial constitutional motions, such as motions to suppress. *See Gaither v. United States*, 759 A.2d 662 (D.C. 2000), *mandate recalled and opinion amended by*, 816 A.2d 791 (D.C. 2003) (remanding for an evidentiary hearing, *inter alia*, to determine if *Brady* information had been withheld regarding suggestive procedures used in the identification process). In *United States v. Gamez-Orduno*, 235 F.3d 453, 461 (9th Cir. 2000) , it was a violation of *Brady* when the Government failed to disclose a report that would have demonstrated that defendants had Fourth Amendment standing to challenge a search. The Ninth Circuit noted that "[t]he suppression of material evidence helpful to the accused, whether at trial or on a motion to suppress, violates due process if there is a reasonable probability that, had the evidence been disclosed, the result of the proceeding would have been different." *Id.* at 461.

In *Smith v. Black*, 904 F.2d 950, 965-66 (5th Cir. 1990), the nondisclosure of *Brady* information related to eyewitness identification may have affected the fact-finder's findings at the suppression hearing. The Fifth Circuit found that "timing is critical to proper *Brady* disclosure, and objections may be made under *Brady* to the state's failure to disclose material evidence prior to a suppression hearing." *Id.* at 965, *citing cases omitted*; *see also Nuckols v. Gibson*, 233 F.3d 1261, 1266-67 (10th Cir. 2000) (*Brady* violation when Government failed to disclose allegations of theft and sleeping on the job of police officer whose testimony was needed related to the admissibility of a confession).

THIS MOTION IS CONSISTENT WITH THE HOLDING OF *FLORIDA V. HARRIS*

Florida v. Harris, 568 U.S. 237, 133 S.Ct. 1050 (2013) is instructive here. There, a canine officer was on patrol with his drug dog, Aldo. Harris' truck was pulled over with an expired license plate. *Id.* at 1053. The canine handler walked Aldo around the exterior of the car, where he alerted on the driver's side door. *Id.* at 1054. The subsequent search did not find drugs, but revealed items related to the cooking of methamphetamine. *Id.*

Harris moved to suppress the dog sniff as insufficient probable cause. He won at the state court level, and Florida found that "[T]he State must present . . . the dog's training and certification records, an explanation of the meaning of the particular training and certification, field performance records (including any unverified alerts), and evidence concerning the experience and training of the officer handling the dog, as well as any other objective evidence known to the officer about the dog's reliability." *Id.* at 1055.

The Supreme Court reversed. It did not appreciate such a rigid reading of probable cause, or the imposition of "a strict evidentiary checklist, whose every item the State must tick off." *Id.* at 1056. The Court found that a dog's satisfactory certification may "provide sufficient reason to trust his alert." *Id.* at 1057. Further, the Court was concerned that field test data results would skew the accuracy of the dog's testing because of a variety of reasons. *Id.* at 1056-1057.

This does not mean that we should assume that any drug dog that is certified provides probable cause with his sniff. The Court went on to say:

> A defendant, however, must have an opportunity to challenge such evidence of a dog's reliability, whether by cross-examining the testifying officer or by introducing his own fact or expert witnesses. The defendant, for example, may contest the adequacy of a certification or training program, perhaps asserting that its standards are too lax or its methods faulty. So too, the defendant may examine how the dog (or handler) performed in the assessments made in those settings. Indeed, evidence of the dog's (or handler's) history in the field, although susceptible to the kind of misinterpretation we have discussed, may sometimes be relevant, as the Solicitor General acknowledged at oral argument. See Tr. of Oral Arg. 23-24 ("[T]he defendant can ask the handler, if the handler is on the stand, about field performance, and then the court can give that answer whatever weight is appropriate"). And even assuming a dog is generally reliable, circumstances surrounding a particular alert may undermine the case for probable cause-if, say, the officer cued the dog (consciously or not), or if the team was working under unfamiliar conditions. *Id.* at 1057-1058.

This "correct approach" demanded by the Supreme Court is consistent with the approach it has espoused by lower courts related to their probable cause findings:

> Under the correct approach, a probable-cause hearing focusing on a dog's alert should proceed much like any other, with the court allowing the parties to make their best case and evaluating the totality of the circumstances. If the State has produced proof from controlled settings that a dog performs reliably in detecting drugs, and the defendant has not contested that showing, the court should find probable cause. But a defendant must have an opportunity to challenge such evidence of a dog's reliability, whether by cross-examining the testifying officer or by introducing his own fact or expert witnesses. The defendant

may contest training or testing standards as flawed or too lax, or raise an issue regarding the particular alert. The court should then consider all the evidence and apply the usual test for probable cause-whether all the facts surrounding the alert, viewed through the lens of common sense, would make a reasonably prudent person think that a search would reveal contraband or evidence of a crime.

Id. at 1052-1053.

The discovery requested here is consistent with this standard.

THE NINTH CIRCUIT RECENTLY AFFIRMED
THE IMPORTANCE OF THE TYPES OF REQUESTS MADE HEREIN

United States v. Jonathan Michael Thomas, decided by the Ninth Circuit on August 8, 2013, represents an affirmation of the type of discovery requested here. There, at a Border Patrol stop, a drug dog began to demonstrate alert behavior according to the Government. The driver and his passengers were asked out of the car, and the dog alerted on a toolbox, where 150 pounds of marijuana was seized.

Thomas filed a Motion to Suppress, alleging that probable cause was not established by the alert, and that his receipt of heavily redacted training and performance records on the dog violated *Brady*. The District Court found that the limited disclosures were sufficient under Federal Rule of Criminal Procedure 16. Thomas went to trial, lost, and appealed the Motion to Suppress (among other issues).

The training logs and performance records of the dog in *Thomas* were redacted, however. Those redactions would have shown the training methodology and commentary related to the team's performance. The Ninth Circuit found it error to not disclose these records.

The Government in *Thomas*, like here, claimed a privilege related to these records. This call for privilege was quickly, and with vast common sense, rejected. The Ninth Circuit said:

> Second, the government cites law-enforcement privilege. But, neither the magistrate, nor the district court, relied on that doctrine as a justification for withholding the records. Furthermore, our caselaw calls for an *in camera* evaluation by the trial court of the government's claim to privilege if the defendant goes beyond "mere suspicion" that the undisclosed evidence will be helpful in his criminal case. As we have nothing but a bare assertion of sensitivity, and because there has been no *in camera* review, we cannot approve of the limited disclosure on this ground. *Id.*, citations omitted.

DISCOVERY AS IT RELATES TO THE FACTS OF THIS CASE

Steven N's Affidavit is attached at *Exhibit 3*. His credentials in this field are impeccable. He has in excess of 30 years of experience as a dog trainer for police service work, and later as an expert. *Exhibit 3*, at ¶ 2, 3. He has trained canines for law enforcement use. *Exhibit 3* at ¶ 3. He has been designated as an expert in dog sniff search cases 85 times. *Exhibit 3* at ¶ 2.

Mr. N has reviewed the cruiser camera video of the stop in question, the report of the canine handler, Trooper Adam F and the Aros training records. *Exhibit 3* at ¶ 8. The canine training was not video recorded. While Mr. N can conclude that there are errors in the sniff as described in *Exhibit 3*, he also indicates that it would be useful to his opinion to see the items requested herein. *Id.* at ¶ 26. The Government's reasons for denying that request are not compelling, especially in light of the *in camera* review process that could be employed. Additionally, the videos in issue could be redacted to remove identifying information or could be subject to a protective order related to their dissemination. This would accomplish the goal of giving the Defendant the required materials while protecting the law-enforcement privilege concerns of the Government.

WHEREFORE, the Defendant requests this Court grant this Motion for Discovery.

Dated this 27th day of August, 2013, at Portland, Maine.

Respectfully submitted,

_____

Timothy E. Zerillo
Attorney for Defendant
ZERILLO LAW FIRM, LLC

§7:46   FORM 7-60 Motion to Suppress: Illegal Stop; Extended Detention; Involuntary Consent; Miranda Violation; Drug Dog; Search Warrant

UNITED STATES DISTRICT COURT
DISTRICT OF MAINE

UNITED STATES OF AMERICA	)	
	)	
v.	)	Crim. No.
	)	
ADAM W.	)	
Defendant	)	

MOTION TO SUPPRESS AND DISMISS WITH MEMORANDUM OF LAW

The Defendant, ADAM W, by and through Undersigned Counsel, moves this Honorable Court to suppress evidence seized from the Defendant and all statements of the Defendant on the following grounds:

- There were no grounds to stop the Defendant's vehicle.
- The extended detention of the traffic stop was illegal and invalidated consent.
- Any consent by Defendant was produced by illegal police trickery.
- All statements made by the Defendant were in violation of *Miranda* rights.
- The canine sniff search of Defendant's vehicle lacked probable cause.
- The search warrants lacked probable cause.

Due to the constitutional infirmities described herein, the statements of the Defendant, and the evidence seized as a result of the statements of the Defendant, are fruit of the poisonous tree, and must be suppressed.

WHEREFORE, the Defendant moves that all statements of Defendant be suppressed and excluded as evidence, and that the search and the items found in the search of Defendant's automobile, home and electronics equipment be suppressed.

MEMORANDUM OF LAW

Counsel presents the following Memorandum of Law to the Court to attempt to expand on the suppression issues described above.

STATEMENT OF FACTS

The facts underlying this Motion are derived from the Indictment, the reports of the officers, and the audio and video of the cruiser camera capture of the stop of Defendant by Law Enforcement Officers. This audio/video will be made available to the Court by the Defendant in advance of the hearing if the Court would like to review the cruiser camera materials in advance.

A confidential source began providing the authorities information that Adam W was distributing cocaine. On February 12, 2013, Special Agent (hereafter "SA") Seth P issued an Operational Plan.[4] The plan listed the involvement of seven Maine Drug Enforcement Agency (hereafter "MDEA") Special Agents (hereafter "SA"). The plan indicated that a confidential source gave information that Defendant had been re-supplied with cocaine. The plan was for the confidential source to make a call for the contraband to be delivered and for the Defendant's car to be intercepted in route. The State Police were assigned to intercept the Defendant's vehicle and to use a canine "to gain entry" into the vehicle.

In the afternoon of February 12, 2013, several agents were watching the Defendant's residence in Falmouth. At approximately between 2:40 PM to 2:45 PM, SA Andrew H and SA Jake H were asked by SAP to conduct

---

[4] Facts drawn from the Operational Plan of SA Seth P., 2.12.13.

surveillance on the Defendant's vehicle, a Cadillac.[5] They followed the Cadillac from a distance. They followed the Cadillac from Falmouth to Portland. As they proceeded past the Lyman Moore Middle School, SA Jake H claimed to visually estimate the Cadillac's speed to be 20 to 25 miles per hour in a 15 miles per hour zone. The Agents did not use radar to clock the speed of the vehicle.

Meanwhile, the MDEA had pre-arranged a stop with Officer Mark K. of the Portland Police Department. Officer K was "asked to stop" the Defendant's vehicle, and did so on Stevens Avenue in Portland.[6]

The stop was, in actuality, a ruse. Officer K did not randomly stop the Defendant. Nor did he stop the Defendant for a traffic violation. Rather, he stopped the Defendant at the behest of the MDEA and their plan to gain entry into Defendant's vehicle. He did not let the Defendant in on this secret, however.

Officer K intercepted the Defendant's vehicle on Stevens Avenue in Portland and stopped it. Before stopping the Defendant's vehicle, Officer K was told over the radio "the dog will be supplied and over shortly." [7] The MDEA had arranged not only for Officer K, but also a State Police Trooper and canine handler to be present for the ruse traffic stop.

Officer K. stopped the vehicle on Stevens Avenue in Portland. He approached the subject vehicle, containing the Defendant driving and an adult female passenger. He took the driver's license and registration from the Defendant driver and his female passenger.[8] Counsel's view of the cruiser camera recording is that the license and registration documents were not returned to Adam W during the course of his stop and ultimate arrest.

Officer K. told Defendant that the stop was legitimately based on speeding in a school zone. He did not in any way make it appear that there was anything more to the stop than an ordinary traffic stop.[9] Officer K. returned to his vehicle to run Defendant's license and registration. Everything appeared to be valid with the license and registration. Officer K. then waited for the drug dog to arrive. The Defendant remained in his vehicle as ordered.

Trooper Adam F, a Police Trooper with the Maine State Police, arrived with his canine, Aros. Officer K told Trooper F that there was "apparently some stuff in the car."[10] Officer K asked Trooper F if he wanted him "to throw him (Adam W) a line" about a new dog needing to run around the car for training purposes.[11] In sum, Officer K offered to continue to deceive Defendant.

That is precisely what was done. Officer K approached the car with Trooper

F and indicated that "this officer has a brand new dog he wants to run around the car."[12] The Defendant was told to stay in his automobile.

The Defendant tried to object and Officer K re-assured him by indicating that this was a random occurrence. Officer K even told Defendant he wouldn't receive a traffic ticket for being cooperative:[13]

W: "I mean, is this really necessary? I mean, I'm just getting pulled over for a traffic violation."
K: "I understand, what happens is they have to get a certain number of, like, reps in, like the dogs walking around the car. So usually, they team up with us, guys who do a lot of traffic. So, they have the dog kind of team up with us sometime –"
W: "Yeah, that's fine."
K: "-So when I stop a car usually he'll come in and run his dog around the car-"
W.: "Cool."
K.: "-and it's usually pretty random."
W: "Yeah that's cool."
K: "Alright?"
W: "Alright."
K: "No big thing."
W: "That's fine."
K: "I'll tell you what, I'll even cut you slack on the ticket just for being cooperative."

5   Facts drawn from the 2.13.13 Report of SA Andrew H. and the 2.14.13 Report of SA Jake H..
6   Facts drawn from Officer Mark K. Report dated 2.12.13.
7   Facts drawn from cruiser camera video, approximately 4:08.
8   Facts drawn from cruiser camera video, approximately 5:00 to 7:06.
9   Facts drawn from cruiser camera video, approximately 5:00 to 7:06.
10 Facts drawn from cruiser camera video, approximately 11:14.
11 Facts drawn from cruiser camera video, approximately 11:34.
12 Facts drawn from cruiser camera video, approximately 11:50.
13 Facts drawn from cruiser camera video, approximately 12:05.

Trooper F began taking canine Aros around the subject vehicle.[14] After one lap around the vehicle, Aros did not appear to alert. Aros proceeded back around the subject vehicle a second time and still did not alert. Aros was taken around the driver's side door a third time and did not alert. On his fourth pass by the driver's door, Aros appeared to alert.[15] The Defendant was then ordered out of the vehicle.

Defendant was handcuffed.[16] He was not read his *Miranda* warnings. The Defendant issued a variety of incriminating statements that there were guns in the car, drugs on his person and in the car. Cocaine was allegedly seized from Defendant's person and the trunk of the vehicle.

SA Seth P applied for a search warrant for Defendant's house, car and cell phones after the stop. The warrant was signed February 12, 2013 at 6:25 PM by Maine District Court Judge Paul E. A search was executed thereafter of Defendant's house yielding additional suspected cocaine and another firearm.

ARGUMENT

THERE WAS NO REASONABLE SUSPICION TO STOP THE SUSPECT VEHICLE

The Fourth Amendment prohibits unreasonable search and seizures of a person by law enforcement. *United States v. Arvizu*, 534 U.S. 266, 273 (2002). These protections extend to brief investigatory stops of a vehicle. *Id.* at 273. An investigatory stop requires some objective manifestation that the person stopped is or is about to be engaged in criminal activity. *Id.* at 273. In determining whether the Government has reasonable and articulable suspicion for an investigatory stop, the Courts look at the "totality of the circumstances" of each case that the officer has a "particularized and objective basis" for suspecting crime is afoot. *Id.* at 273. However, a mere "hunch" is insufficient to justify a stop. *Id.* at 273, *United States v. Foster*, 634 F.3d 243, 246 (4th Cir. 2011).

The motor vehicle stop in this case was a ruse. The MDEA created an operational plan that included a pre-arranged stop by Officer Mark K of the Portland Police Department. Their goal was to gain entry into this vehicle, recover narcotics and arrest Mr. W. The production of this plan was of movie quality. With SA Seth P acting as the director, he instructed his actors (i.e, MDEA agents, Portland Police Officers and Maine State Troopers) how to act and proceed to ensure the show went off without a hitch.

The one wrinkle in SA P's plot plan was how to stop the vehicle? Stopping the vehicle when Mr. W entered his vehicle could have damaged their investigation and revealed their confidential informant. Arguably, no reasonable and articulable suspicion existed at that point. The MDEA needed some basis to stop the vehicle because they could not be sure that narcotics existed in the vehicle. As a result, SA Jake H alleged that Mr. W was speeding based on his visual estimate of speed.

The visual estimate of speed described by SA H does not give rise to reasonable articulable suspicion as defined in *Terry v. Ohio*, 392 U.S. 1, 21 (1968). SA H alleges in his Investigative Report that based on his visual estimates of speed, Mr. W was traveling 25 miles per hour (hereafter "mph"), which was approximately 10 mph over the speed limit. Based on SA H's representations, Officer K was ordered to make a traffic stop. Officer K never observed any erratic driving or speeding.

In *United States v. Sean Sowards*, the United State Court of Appeals of the Fourth Circuit held that an officer lacked probable cause to initiate a traffic stop based exclusively on an officer's visual estimate without an "appropriate factual foundation and necessary indicia of reliability" to be an objectively reasonable basis to initiate the stop. 690 F.3d 583, 594 (4th Cir. 2012). In *Sowards*, the officer relied exclusively on visual estimates. *Id.* at 585. The officer alleged that the Defendant was going traveling 75 mph in a 70 mph zone. *Id.* at 585. The Fourth Circuit stated that "where an officer estimates that a vehicle is traveling in only slight excess of the legal speed limit, and particularly where the alleged violation is at a speed difficult for the naked eye to discern, an officer's visual speed estimate requires additional indicia of reliability…." *Id.* at 592.

As in *Sowards*, no additional indicia of reliability exist in this case. This is not a case where Mr. W was allegedly operating his vehicle significantly higher than the speed limit. It is not clear how fast Mr. W's vehicle was traveling. An SA can be heard on the audio recordings claiming the speed to be 20 to 25 mph.[17] The speed limit was 15 mph. Not only does this range of speed call into question SA H's ability to visually estimate speed, it diminishes the reliability of the test. SA H's vehicle was not equipped with radar, nor was there any evidence to suggest that

---

[14] Facts drawn from cruiser camera video, approximately 13:20.
[15] Facts drawn from cruiser camera video, approximately 14:30.
[16] Facts drawn from cruiser camera video, approximately 16:02.
[17] Facts drawn from dispatch recording (file 13-1155.mp3), approximately 1:12 and from cruiser camera video, approximately 2:00.

SA H paced Mr. W's vehicle to confirm his estimate. There is also no evidence that Officer K observed any activity that gave rise to reasonable and articulable suspicion to stop Mr. W's vehicle. In fact, Officer K's cruiser was equipped with radar, but he made no references in his investigative report that he used it to confirm Mr. W's speed.

This bellies the underlying point. The plot plan of the agents was to get into the W vehicle. A sham visual estimate of speed was used as the mechanism to do so. This justification, however, lacks believability and should be rejected.

Based on the forgoing facts, there was no reasonable articulable suspicion to stop the vehicle. As a result, any evidence obtained from the stop should be suppressed.

THE EXTENDED DETENTION OF DEFENDANT IN THE TRAFFIC STOP WAS ILLEGAL AND RESULTED IN AN INVALID CONSENT AND UNCONSTITUTIONAL SEARCH

A traffic stop is a seizure within the meaning of the Fourth Amendment. *Delaware v. Prouse,* 440 U.S. 648 (1979). The Supreme Court has viewed the typical traffic stop to "resemble, in duration and atmosphere, the kind of brief detention authorized in *Terry v. Ohio,* 392 U.S. 1, 88 S.Ct. 1868, 20 L.Ed.2d 889 (1968)." *Berkemer v. McCarty,* 468 U.S. 420, 439 n. 29, 104 S.Ct. 3138, 82 L.Ed.2d 317 (1984). Here, the detention for the traffic stop was prolonged to justify a search of the Defendant and his vehicle.

The case of *Florida v. Royer,* 460 U.S. 491 (1983) significantly limited the scope of a *Terry* stop. There, the Supreme Court observed that "the scope of the detention must be carefully tailored to its underlying justification." *Id.* at 500. As Justice Powell noted in his concurrence, "The scope of a *Terry*-type 'investigative' stop and any attendant search must be extremely limited or the *Terry* exception would swallow the general rule that Fourth Amendment seizures [and searches] are reasonable only if based on probable cause. In my view, any suggestion that the *Terry* reasonable suspicion standard justifies anything but the briefest of detentions or the most limited of searches finds no support in the *Terry* line of cases." *Id.* at 510-511, Justice Powell, concurring, *citations omitted*.

It is not only the scope of the intrusion, but also the duration that must also be considered. Again, *Royer* held:

> The predicate permitting seizures on suspicion short of probable cause is that law enforcement interests warrant a limited intrusion on the personal security of the suspect. The scope of the intrusion permitted will vary to some extent with the particular facts and circumstances of each case. This much, however, is clear: an investigative detention must be temporary and last no longer than is necessary to effectuate the purpose of the stop. Similarly, the investigative methods employed should be the least intrusive means reasonably available to verify or dispel the officer's suspicion in a short period of time. It is the State's burden to demonstrate that the seizure it seeks to justify on the basis of a reasonable suspicion was sufficiently limited in scope and duration to satisfy the conditions of an investigative seizure.

Id. at 500, *citations omitted.*

In *United States v. Perkins,* 348 F.3d 965 (11th Cir. 2003), a motorist was pulled over late at night for swerving in his lane of travel. He was given a warning for an improper lane change. *Id.* at 968. The officer, however, finding the motorist nervous, continued to detain him and called a canine unit. *Id.* The motorist consented to a search and showed law enforcement where narcotics were hidden. *Id.* Since these actions were based on a hunch, the evidence was suppressed. The Eleventh Circuit found that "the continued detention of Perkins and Scott beyond the issuance of the traffic citation...was unlawful. Since Perkin's consent to the search of the car was the product of an unlawful detention, 'the consent was tainted by the illegality and was ineffective to justify the search.'" *Id.* at 971, *quoting Florida v. Royer,* 460 U.S. 491, 507-508, 103 S.Ct. 319 (1983). The Sixth Circuit has come to the same conclusion on similar facts. *U.S. v. Smith,* 263 F.3d 571 (6th Cir. 2001).

The Tenth Circuit considered a similar issue in *United States v. Trestyn,* 646 F.3d 732 (10th Cir. 2011). *Id.* at 736. There, a couple was pulled over for not displaying a front license plate. The Officer asked them questions about where they were going to and coming from. *Id.* He found their story suspicious. *Id.* The Officer called for a canine sniff and the dog alerted on the minivan, where ecstasy was seized. *Id.* at 737.

In *Trestyn,* the Tenth Circuit asked whether the Fourth Amendment intrusion was related to the traffic stop and found that it was not. *Id.* at 742. The Court noted that the Officer's questions to the Defendants about their travel plans and the request for their licenses exceeded the scope of the underlying justification for the stop. *Id.* at 744. The Tenth Circuit found that "An officer may not extend a traffic stop beyond a reasonable duration necessary to accomplish the purpose of the stop unless the driver consents to further questioning or the officer has reasonable suspicion to believe other criminal activity is afoot." *Id.* at 742, *citing U.S. v. Rice*, 483 F.3d 1079, 1083-84 (10th Cir. 2007).

Here, the traffic stop was presented to Defendant as a routine traffic violation. Officer Keller secured the Defendant's license, registration and insurance papers. He assured Defendant that this was a minor matter, and asked him questions concerning where he was going and where he was coming from. He then returned to his police cruiser with the Defendant's license and other papers.

Under Maine law, when Officer K. took the Defendant's driver's license, registration and insurance papers, he seized the Defendant. *State v. Garland*, 482 A.2d 139 (Me. 1984); *State v. Gulick*, 759 A.2d 1085 (Me. 2000). The Defendant was not free to leave.

Officer K. had abundant time to write a ticket and release Defendant. Instead, he held Defendant's license and then, after seizing Defendant, talked him into consenting to the dog sniff search.

By prolonging the detention, he continued to seize the Defendant without probable cause. All statements made by Defendant, including the alleged consent to search, should be suppressed as a result of the illegal seizure.

THE SEARCH OF THE SUSPECT VEHICLE WAS A RESULT OF ILLEGAL POLICE TRICKERY RENDERING THE CONSENT TO THE CANINE SNIFF SEARCH INVOLUNTARY

Pursuant to Fourth Amendment jurisprudence, evidence obtained after an illegal investigation is tainted by the illegality and inadmissible, notwithstanding consent, unless the taint is somehow purged.

Consent to search must be, under the totality of the circumstances, voluntarily given. *Schneckloth v. Bustamonte*, 412 U.S. 218, 248-49, 93 S.Ct. 1943, 36 L.Ed.2d 702 (1973). It is the government's burden to prove that consent was voluntary. *Bumper v. North Carolina*, 391 U.S. 543, 548-49, 88 S.Ct. 1788, 20 L.Ed.2d 797 (1968). The government's burden of establishing voluntary consent "cannot be discharged by showing no more than acquiescence to a claim of lawful authority." *Bumper v. North Carolina*, 391 U.S. 543, 548-49 (1968).

Officer Mark K. tricked and coerced Mr. W. into consenting to a drug canine search of his vehicle. The government bears the burden of proof by a preponderance of the evidence that any consent was "uncoerced." *United States v. Vázquez*, 724 F.3d 15, 18 (1st Cir. 2013) *(citation omitted)*. Whether coercion existed "is a question of fact based on the totality of the circumstances, including the consenting party's knowledge of the right to refuse consent; the consenting party's possibly vulnerable subjective state; and evidence of inherently coercive tactics, either in the nature of police questioning or in the environment in which the questioning took place." *Id.* at 18-19. The courts must also consider "any evidence that law enforcement officers' ... misrepresentation prompted defendant's acquiescence to the search." *Id.* at 19.

Mr. W's vehicle was allegedly pulled over for speeding. This, of course, was a ruse. The MDEA planned for the vehicle to be stopped and searched in hope to discover narcotics. Once Officer K. stopped the vehicle, Officer K. informed Mr. W that he was speeding. Officer K gathered Mr. W's license, registration and insurance and returned to his cruiser. When Officer K returned, he asked Mr. W if a drug canine could search his vehicle. In order to try to gain consent, Officer K stated "I'll tell you what, I'll even cut you slack on the ticket just for being cooperative."[18]

As previously described, this was all a hoax. There was a drug canine on standby according to the operational plan by SA P. Officer K was informed to pull over Mr. W and wait for the drug canine to arrive on scene.[19] Before speaking to Mr. W about consenting to the canine search, Officer K can be heard communicating with SAs about waiting for the drug canine and what type of "line" he was going to give to Mr. W to obtain consent."[20] "When government agents seek an individual's cooperation with a government investigation by misrepresenting the nature of that investigation, this deception is appropriately considered a part of the totality of circumstances in determining whether consent was gained by coercion or duress." *United States v. Harrison*, 639 F.3d 1273, 1278-1279 (10th Cir. 2011).

In *United States v. Harrison*, the United States Court of Appeals for the Tenth Circuit affirmed the district court's decision to suppress the defendant's consent to search his apartment because it was not voluntary. *Id.* at 1281. In *Harrison*, Alcohol Tobacco and Firearm (hereafter, "ATF") agents suspected Harrison of illicit activity, but did not have probable cause to search his home. *Id.* at 1275-1276. Two ATF agents decided to knock on Harrison's door and inform him that anonymous an phone call indicated that there were drugs and bombs in his apartment. *Id.* ATF agents had no information that bombs existed in the apartment. *Id.* When Harrison denied the existent of

---

[18] Facts drawn from cruiser camera audio approximately 12:05.
[19] Facts drawn from cruiser camera video, approximately 4:08.
[20] Facts drawn from cruiser camera video, approximately 8:30 and 11:35.

bombs, one ATF agent explained that their boss made them investigate bomb allegations to ensure there was no threat to society. *Id.* Eventually, after some coaxing from the ATF agents, Harrison consented to the search of his home, which revealed a gun hidden in the wall. *Id.*

Mr. W.'s case is similar to the facts in *Harrison*. In both cases, law enforcement created a ruse to gain consent. In fact, as in *Harrison*, Officer K told Mr. W that for being so cooperative, he would not write him a speeding ticket.[21] As in *Harrison*, Mr. W was fed lines from an agent of the Government to gain consent. When "police misrepresentation of purpose [for consent] is so extreme that it deprives the individual of the ability to make a fair assessment of the need to surrender his privacy ... the consent should not be considered valid." *Id.* at 1280 (*citing* 2 Wayne R. LaFave et al., Criminal Procedure § 3.10(c) (3d ed. 2007)).

The conduct by MDEA and local law enforcement agencies in Mr. W's case was so extreme that it deprived Mr. W of the ability to voluntarily consent. The Government did not have probable cause to search the vehicle prior to consent. Otherwise, Mr. W's consent, or a warrant, would not be necessary. It is one thing to simply investigate a case by asking questions; however, it is a whole different thing to create an extremely detailed ruse to illicit consent in an effort to seize contraband and establish probable cause for future warrants, which was the case here. This egregious conduct cannot be tolerated; as a result, the consent should be held involuntary and any evidence seized as a result of the search must be suppressed.

DEFENDANT WAS NOT ISSUED HIS *MIRANDA* WARNINGS DESPITE CUSTODIAL INTERROGATION

A person who is in custody and subject to interrogation must be advised of the rights referred to in *Miranda v. Arizona*, 384 U.S. 436 (1966), in order for statements made during the interrogation to be admissible against him or her at trial. *State v. Bridges*, 829 A.2d 247, 254 (Me. 2003). *Miranda* stands for the well-known proposition that the prosecution cannot offer any statements made by a defendant in times of custodial interrogation "unless the use of procedural safeguards effective to secure the privilege against self-incrimination have been demonstrated." *Miranda v. Arizona*, 384 U.S. 436, 479 (1966). Those procedural safeguards are, of course, *Miranda* warnings. "[A] *Miranda* warning is necessary only if a defendant is: (1) in custody; and (2) subject to interrogation." *State v. Higgins*, 796 A.2d 50, 54 (Me. 2002) (citation and quotation marks omitted). Defendant submits that *Miranda* warnings should have been read to the Defendant as soon as the Defendant's license, registration and insurance were obtained by law enforcement and the Defendant was seized. In the alternative, as soon as the Defendant was ordered out of the vehicle and handcuffed, *Miranda* warnings should have been issued.

Defendant's License, Registration and Proof of Insurance

This was no ordinary traffic stop. As is argued throughout this entire Motion, this elaborate ruse, orchestrated by the MDEA, was designed to detain and arrest Mr. W. As soon as Mr. W was pulled over, Officer Mark K requested his driver license, registration and proof of insurance. "[A] person questioned by law enforcement officers after being 'taken into custody or otherwise deprived of his freedom of action in any significant way' must first" be given *Miranda* warnings." *United States v. Hughes*, 640 F.3d 428, 434 (1st Cir. 2011) (*emphasis added*).

The Defendant was deprived of his freedom the moment his license was taken away from him. He was seized from that moment as well. *Garland, supra*; *Gulick, supra*. Defendant's driver's license, registration and insurance papers were never returned during the traffic stop. Instead of returning Mr. W's license, Officer K began to plot, with the assistance of the MDEA, how to manipulate Mr. W into consenting to the search of his vehicle and to making incriminating statements.

Of course, the seizure of his license and other papers made it impossible for Defendant to legally drive away. The nature of the encounter would not cause a reasonable person in the same circumstances to feel free to leave.

The entire *Miranda* analysis boils down to two questions: 1. whether a reasonable person in the circumstance would feel free to terminate the interrogation and leave; and 2. would those circumstances be likely to coerce the suspect to engage in questioning by the police. *United States v. Rogers*, 659 F.3d 74, 78 (1st Cir. 2011), *citing Thompson v. Keohane*, 516 U.S. 99 (1995) and *Berkemer v. McCarty*, 468 U.S. 420 (1984). Here, it is apparent that Defendant could not leave, and that a reasonable person would not feel free to refuse to speak with the police.

---

[21] In *Harrison*, an ATF agent told Harrison that they were not there to "bust" him for a "small bag of weed." *Id.* at 1276.

Defendant Ordered Out of the Vehicle

Should the Court not be persuaded by the above argument, Defendant argues that the he was in custody and subject to interrogation the moment he was ordered out of his vehicle. This is evident in the cruiser video from Officer Keller's police cruiser.

Defendant was ordered out of his vehicle shortly after the initial traffic stop.[22] Initially, there appears to have been at least three law enforcement officers on the scene from two different police departments. The reason why Defendant was ordered out of the vehicle was that the drug canine allegedly "hit" on the vehicle. Once Mr. W was removed from his vehicle, he was patted down for weapons while being placed in handcuffs.[23] Officer K physically held Mr. W for the entire time thereafter (approximately 9 minutes) until he was placed in another Portland Police cruiser, by another uniformed officer, where he remained. When Mr. W asked to use his cell phone to call his lawyer, Trooper Adam F said "not at the moment."[24]

Mr. W was clearly not free to leave. This was a formal arrest at the point he was removed from the vehicle. At no point on the recording did a law enforcement officer read *Miranda* after this arrest.

The issue here is whether *Miranda* warnings should have been given to the Defendant before his incriminating statements were made after being ordered out of the vehicle. This issue turns entirely on whether the Defendant was subject to custodial interrogation at the time the statements were made. In the simplest terms possible, if a custodial interrogation took place, *Miranda* had to be given. Based on the facts described above, Mr. W. was, in fact, subjected to a custodial interrogation.

That said, should the Court consider this an ordinary traffic stop, the First Circuit has held that a investigatory stop can "escalate into custody for *Miranda* purposes where the totality of the circumstances shows that a reasonable person would understand that he was being held to 'the degree associated with a formal arrest'." *United States v. Fornia-Castillo*, 408 F.3d 52 (1st Cir. 2005). Here, the only conclusion is that a reasonable person would believe that he was being held to the degree associated with a formal arrest, and the statements he issued to the police must be suppressed as a result. Likewise, the consent to search that he allegedly gave to search the vehicle is invalid, because it was obtained through improper circumvention of *Miranda*.

THE CANINE SNIFF SEARCH LACKED PROBABLE CAUSE AND WAS NOT SUPPORTED BY PROPER TRAINING STANDARDS

Florida v. Harris, 568 U.S. 237, 133 S.Ct. 1050 (2013), decided in February of 2013 may have limited some arguments related to canine sniffs, but it is still a live issue. To be certain, the case at bar raises many of the issues the Supreme Court has indicated that this Court should be cognizant of.

In *Harris*, a canine officer was on patrol with his drug dog, Aldo. Harris' truck was pulled over with an expired license plate. *Id.* at 1053. The canine handler walked Aldo around the exterior of the car, where he alerted on the driver's side door. *Id.* at 1054. The subsequent search did not find drugs, but revealed items related to the cooking of methamphetamine. *Id.*

Harris moved to suppress the dog sniff as insufficient probable cause. He won at the State Court level, and Florida found that "[T]he State must present . . . the dog's training and certification records, an explanation of the meaning of the particular training and certification, field performance records (including any unverified alerts), and evidence concerning the experience and training of the officer handling the dog, as well as any other objective evidence known to the officer about the dog's reliability." *Id.* at 1055.

The Supreme Court reversed. It did not appreciate such a rigid reading of probable cause, or the imposition of "a strict evidentiary checklist, whose every item the State must tick off." *Id.* at 1056. The Court found that a dog's satisfactory certification may "provide sufficient reason to trust his alert." *Id.* at 1057. Further, the Court was concerned that field test data results would skew the accuracy of the dog's testing because of a variety of reasons. *Id.* at 1056-1057.

This does not mean that any "certified" drug dog presents automatic probable cause. The Supreme Court went on to say:

---

[22] Mr. W. provided Officer K. with his license, registration and insurance during his initial contact. Officer K. never returned his license, registration or insurance as he ordinarily would had this case been about speeding and not suspected drug possession/trafficking.

[23] Facts drawn from cruiser camera video, approximately 16:48.

[24] Facts drawn from cruiser camera video, approximately 23:30.

A defendant, however, must have an opportunity to challenge such evidence of a dog's reliability, whether by cross-examining the testifying officer or by introducing his own fact or expert witnesses. The defendant, for example, may contest the adequacy of a certification or training program, perhaps asserting that its standards are too lax or its methods faulty. So too, the defendant may examine how the dog (or handler) performed in the assessments made in those settings. Indeed, evidence of the dog's (or handler's) history in the field, although susceptible to the kind of misinterpretation we have discussed, may sometimes be relevant, as the Solicitor General acknowledged at oral argument. See Tr. of Oral Arg. 23-24 ("[T]he defendant can ask the handler, if the handler is on the stand, about field performance, and then the court can give that answer whatever weight is appropriate"). And even assuming a dog is generally reliable, circumstances surrounding a particular alert may undermine the case for probable cause if, say, the officer cued the dog (consciously or not), or if the team was working under unfamiliar conditions.

Id. at 1057-1058.

This "correct approach" demanded by the Supreme Court is consistent with the approach espoused by lower courts related to their probable cause findings:

Under the correct approach, a probable -cause hearing focusing on a dog's alert should proceed much like any other, with the court allowing the parties to make their best case and evaluating the totality of the circumstances. If the State has produced proof from controlled settings that a dog performs reliably in detecting drugs, and the defendant has not contested that showing, the court should find probable cause. But a defendant must have an opportunity to challenge such evidence of a dog's reliability, whether by cross-examining the testifying officer or by introducing his own fact or expert witnesses. The defendant may contest training or testing standards as flawed or too lax, or raise an issue regarding the particular alert. The court should then consider all the evidence and apply the usual test for probable cause-whether all the facts surrounding the alert, viewed through the lens of common sense, would make a reasonably prudent person think that a search would reveal contraband or evidence of a crime.

Id. at 1052-1053.

Here, Defendant alleges a significant number of incurable ills in the canine sniff search. Aros did not alert on the driver's side door of the automobile until his fourth pass around the vehicle.[25] This indicates that the canine did not detect contraband drugs.

Further, the Defendant argues that there could have been cuing of the dog by his handler. Since the dog did not alert on its first pass, but was continuously reintroduced to the same area, the dog may have been cued to alert. This cuing could have been intentional or unintentional. Defendant will argue, however, by having the dog encounter an area four times before an alert was made, the handler here increased the possibility that he was cuing the dog.

Finally, the training records received and the real world performance by Aros indicate that the canine's training was insufficient. The training documentation is inadequate, as are the training procedures and record-keeping procedures.

WITH THE FRUIT OF THE TRAFFIC STOP SUPPRESSED, THE AFFIDAVIT IN SUPPORT OF THE SUBSEQUENT SEARCH OF THE DEFENDANT'S RESIDENCE AND CELL PHONE IS NOT SUPPORTED BY PROBABLE CAUSE

The Affidavits to search the Defendant's Falmouth residence and the cell phone located in the truck are heavily dependent on the fruits of the traffic stop. If the fruits of the stop are suppressed, SA P's Affidavits do not support probable cause to search. The fruits of an illegal search cannot be cleansed by their use in an affidavit to obtain a legal search. *United States v. Grandstaff*, 813 F.2d 1353, 1355 (9th Cir. 1987) (the government cannot insulate an illegal warrantless search by including the product of that search in a warrant affidavit). Pursuant to Fourth Amendment jurisprudence, evidence obtained after an illegal investigation is tainted by the illegality and inadmissible, unless the taint is somehow purged. *Wong Sun v. United States,* 371 U.S. 471, 491, 83 S.Ct. 407, 9 L.Ed.2d 441 (1963).

---

[25] Facts drawn from cruiser camera video, approximately 14:30.

The Affidavit issued on February 12, 2013 by SA Seth P contains 13 paragraphs of non-boilerplate information.[26] The first five paragraphs indicate that a Confidential Informant (hereafter "CI") purchased cocaine from Defendant in controlled buys on two occasions. The first was in June of 2012 and the second was in December of 2012. The CI gave the authorities information, according to the Affidavit, that W. received his shipments of cocaine on Thursdays before the weekend. It is indicated that he made sales by using his car and that he stored the remainder at his house.

There is no information in the Affidavit as to the source of the knowledge of the CI or the reliability of the CI.

According to the same Affidavit, on February 12, 2013, the CI told SA P that the Defendant had been re-supplied with a large amount of cocaine, and that he would be coming to Portland with the cocaine. The remaining paragraphs of the Affidavit of February 12, 2013 (paragraphs 7-13) relate to circumstances of the traffic stop.

When the circumstances of the stop are excised from the Affidavit, probable cause is lacking. All that remains are two stale controlled buys; the most recent one to the stop was two months prior. This is not sufficient probable cause.

Likewise, the Affidavit of February 19, 2013 should also be suppressed. This Affidavit relied nearly entirely on the fruits of the traffic stop and the search of the Defendant's residence. For the same reasons as cited above, this search is tainted, and the fruits of it must be suppressed.

WHEREFORE, Defendant requests this Court GRANT his Motion to Suppress.

Dated this 6th day of January, 2014, at Portland, Maine.

Respectfully submitted,

_____
Timothy E. Zerillo
Attorney for Defendant
ZERILLO LAW FIRM, LLC

[§§7:47-7:59 Reserved]

D. Trial: Drugs Found During Traffic Stop

Possession cases often do not go to trial. If your client has been caught with heroin in his pocket along with a syringe his defenses at trial may be few. Sometimes you end up in a trial in these cases, however, and you need to be ready when you do. Here are some issues you may encounter in a case such as that for our weekend warrior (see §7:21) in the backseat of the car with the cocaine sitting next to her.

§7:60   Sample Cross-Examination of Cop—Lack of Knowledge of How Drugs Got in Vehicle

In addition to your normal cross of cop stuff; sloppy investigation, etc., add in lack of knowledge about how the cocaine got in the back seat. For tips on cross examining police officers, see Ch.2

Q. Officer, you went through your credentials on direct examination, and I heard them as did the jury. Very impressive.
A. Thank you.
Q. You have seen quite a bit in your career, haven't you?
A. You could say that.
Q. If I remember my research, you were a corrections officer before you became a police officer with your current department?
A. That's right.
Q. When you came upon the car that night, you didn't have suspicions as you approached the vehicle that you were in the middle of a drug stop?
A. No.
Q. You thought this was just a traffic stop?
A. Yes.
Q. Then you smelled marijuana and ordered out the driver and passengers?
A. Yes.
Q. Including my client, Wendy Warrior?

---

[26] Facts related to the 2.12.13 Search Warrant of Seth P. are drawn from the Search Warrant and Affidavit.

A. Yes.

Q. And you ultimately searched her purse?

A. Yes.

Q. And you found some marijuana?

A. Yes.

Q. She told you that was hers?

A. Yes.

Q. When you searched the back of the vehicle, you found some cocaine?

A. Yes.

Q. Next to where she was sitting in the backseat?

A. Yes.

Q. And she denied that it was hers?

A. She did.

Q. Right away?

A. Yes.

Q. She didn't hesitate?

A. No.

Q. You believed that she ditched the cocaine in the backseat when you ordered her out of the car?

A. I did believe that, yes.

Q. But you would agree that you don't know that for sure?

A. I don't know anything for sure.

Q. Nothing?

A. No.

Q. Wow. Okay. When the police come, people who are holding drugs try to get rid of them?

A. In most cases.

Q. And in this case, the guys in the front seat could have tossed the drugs in the back seat, couldn't they?

A. I suppose it's possible, but not likely. It was sort of shoved in the crack of the seat and I don't think they would have had time.

Q. But you don't know for sure right?

A. I don't.

Q. Because you know nothing for sure.

A. That's true.

Q. You know nothing for sure because you've seen some crazy things in your career?

A. Yes.

Q. You've had lots of suspects toss drugs before being arrested?

A. I suppose so.

Q. You've seen people do wild things to avoid being detected with drugs by law enforcement.

A. I have.

Q. When you were a corrections officer, there were drugs in the jail, weren't there?

A. Yes, unfortunately they do get in.

Q. While you were there, people were caught sneaking drugs in their rectum, weren't they?

A. Yes, that happens.

Q. You caught people yourself with drugs in their rectum?

A. Not in jail.

Q. Where then?

A. A gentleman I arrested was holding there once.

Q. You would agree that people will do a lot not to get caught with their drugs?

A. I would.

§7:61   Closing Argument—Point the Finger at Other Vehicle Occupants

Here are some closing ideas for the Wendy Warrior case.

There's an old saying that when a person points a finger at someone else, that person should remember that the other 4 fingers are pointing back at him.

Here, Bobby Bad and Jimmy Junk are pointing the finger at Wendy Warrior. But they are the guilty ones. They should be the ones sitting here, not Wendy.

Let's imagine that you wanted to try an experiment. You have a cat and a mouse. You put them both in a box. You tie the box up tight. After a while, you go back and look in the box. Only the cat is in there. That would be circumstantial evidence that the cat ate the mouse.

Let's put the cat and mouse back in the box. You go back after a while, untie the box and look in. The cat is alone in there. But in the corner, on a far wall of the box, you see a hole. That tiny hole would be reasonable doubt as to whether the cat ate the mouse. Just a tiny hole is all it takes.

You don't need to be a drug user to know that people will do everything and anything to get rid of drugs when the cops come calling. As the officer said, he's discovered people inserting drugs into their rectums so they go undetected. Simply the fact that the cocaine was next to Wendy is irrelevant. There were two other people in the car, and the drugs could have come from any of them. That's right. I said it; the drugs could have come from Wendy, or Bobby or Jimmy. And if they could have belonged to any of the three of them, then the state hasn't proven its case that Wendy is guilty. Now, let's talk some more about reasonable doubt to explain what I mean. ...

For tips on closing arguments and sample language for lack of proof and reasonable doubt arguments, see Ch. 2.

[§§7:62-7:69 Reserved]

III.   DRUG SALE AND TRAFFICKING

A. Elements and Common Scenarios

§7:70   The Elements

In general, drug sale or trafficking requires (1) that the defendant actually or constructively possessed (2) a controlled substance (3) with the *mens rea* to distribute the controlled substance. Actual distribution may or may not be required.

§7:71   The Addict

Addict sellers are no different than addicts in a possession case. See §7:22. They have just taken the extra step. Maybe they don't have the money to buy any more so they have become drug mules. They are couriers. They get a taste for a little work. These are often the saddest cases for me.

§7:72   The Full-Time, For Profit, Seller

These are the considerably less sympathetic guys. They are simply in it for a buck. If they don't use themselves, they are even less sympathetic.
These are the most dangerous people to deal with. The drug world represents a competitive business. You have to crawl over some bodies to get to the top. Be careful when dealing with kingpins.

§7:73   Selling and Furnishing in General

Often, I get trafficking cases that are really furnishing cases. The distinction can make quite a difference depending on where you practice. My jurisdiction distinguishes between furnishing drugs and trafficking drugs.

Trafficking is exchanging drugs for money or some other consideration, while furnishing is providing the user with the drug for no consideration.

In Maine, trafficking means to make or create, to sell, barter, trade for consideration or exchange for consideration. 17-A MRSA §1101(17). You probably have a similar definition where you practice. Furnishing, on the other hand, is to "give, dispense, administer, prescribe, deliver or otherwise transfer to another." 17-A MRSA §1101(18).

Be careful that your case is not overcharged as trafficking when it should be furnishing. For example, one of my clients shipped seven pounds of marijuana from Colorado to Maine. He admitted he shipped the pot to himself and was charged with a felony level trafficking.

How will the state prove that my client intended to traffic? He could have been planning to go into the woods and smoke seven pounds of pot for all I know. In fact, he told the cops that he planned to give some of the pot away, and smoke some of it. As a result, we have an overcharged trafficking case. Watch your definitions.

§7:74   School Zones and Safe Zones

A common factual hybrid that complicates life representing drug dealers is the school zone/safe zone issue. Chances are, if your clients are like mine, they aren't terribly cognizant of whether they are within a 1,000 feet of a school zone when they pass crack to a buyer on the street. School is the last thing on their mind.

School zone and safe zone laws are generally applied in one of two ways. Drug crimes committed in these zones can be separate from garden-variety drug trafficking or distribution. More commonly, however, sales in these zones have elevated punishments associated with the ordinary trafficking or distribution sentences.

One thousand feet is the most common distance used in the zone statutes. Jurisdictions vary, however. Minnesota, North Carolina and Rhode Island have a distance of only 300 feet. Other states have expanded the school zone beyond 1,000 feet, but none have approached Alabama, which has a three mile zone around schools and all public housing. That's 15,840 feet.

[§§7:75-7:79 Reserved]

B. Strategies and Tactics

§7:80   Identifying Snitches

Let's talk a bit about the snitch, otherwise known as a "confidential source," "source of information," "confidential informant," "cooperating defendant," and the like. Snitches are great fodder for fun in your case. Potentially devastating to your client, they represent the opportunity for you to attack and discredit an often easy target.

To do so, you need to find out who they are, the earlier the better. Often your client will know who the snitch is. If the client has suspicions, start beating the bushes with your investigator early. We want the snitch to know that we are around and gunning for him or her.

If your client has no idea who the snitch is, file motions to reveal the informant's identity. Most jurisdictions have a statute and case law that protects the snitch's identity. It is not impossible to get over those hurdles, however. Federal Court provides its own problems, as usual, with the Jencks Act. 18 U.S.C. § 3500 (statements of government witnesses cannot be subpoenaed or discovered until after witness has testified on direct).

Many of the statutes and rules protecting snitches are based on *Roviaro v. United States*, 353 U.S. 53 (1956). *Rovario* sought to justify the protection of confidential information. The U.S. Supreme Court noted in *Roviaro*, however "that no fixed rule with respect to disclosure is justifiable." *Id.* at 62. We can argue from *Roviaro* that where the disclosure of an informant's identity is relevant and helpful to the defense of an accused, or is essential to a fair trial, the government's privilege to withhold disclosure of the informant's identity must give way. *Id.* at 60-62.

Your own jurisdiction will have interpretations of *Rovario* for you to argue. The point, of course, is to file motions and find out who the snitch is so you can get to work on him or her.

§7:81   FORM 7-70 Motion to Disclose Confidential Informant

STATE OF MAINE		SUPERIOR COURT
SOMERSET, ss.		DOCKET NO. CR-11-11111

STATE OF MAINE,   )

)

)

v.   )   DEFENDANT'S MOTION

)   TO DISCLOSE CONFIDENTIAL

TOMMY TRAFFIKA   )   INFORMANT

)

Defendant   )

NOW COMES the Defendant, Tommy Traffika, by and through the Undersigned Counsel, and hereby respectfully moves this Honorable Court to order the state to disclose identifying information of the confidential informant, pursuant to Maine Rule of Criminal Procedure 16, Maine Rules of Evidence 509, the United States Constitution, and the Maine Constitution, and states as follows:

1. Defendant is indicted for trafficking in cocaine.
2. Discovery reveals that the cocaine charge was based on a single drug sale to a confidential informant. This sale was not recorded in any way, and the only witness to the alleged sale was the informant.
3. Maine Rule of Evidence 509 allows an exception to the privilege related to confidential informants. If "there is a reasonable probability that the informant can give relevant testimony," the identity of the informant should be revealed. See also, for example, *State v. Devlin*, 618 A.2d 203 (Me. 1992).
4. Maine Rule of Evidence 509 is built chiefly from the teachings in *Roviaro v. United States*, 353 U.S. 53 (1956). The Court noted in *Roviaro* "that no fixed rule with respect to disclosure is justifiable." *Id* at 62. It can be further concluded from *Roviaro* that where the disclosure of an informant's identity is relevant and helpful to the defense of an accused, or is essential to a fair trial, the government's privilege to withhold disclosure of the informant's identity must give way. *See generally Roviaro* at 60-62.
5. In *State v. Devlin*, the Court noted that the confidential informant "was the sole witness present throughout the transaction, other than the accused, who could amplify or contradict the testimony of the state's witness…". *State v. Devlin*, 618 A.2d 203, 204 (Me. 1992).

WHEREFORE, the Defendant, by and through Undersigned Counsel, for the above mentioned reasons, hereby respectfully moves this Honorable Court to order the state disclose the identity of the confidential informant named in the discovery, and order further relief as justice so requires.

Dated this __th day of _____, 20__ at Portland, Maine.

Respectfully submitted,

_____

Timothy E. Zerillo
Attorney for Defendant
ZERILLO LAW FIRM, LLC

§7:82   Representing Snitches

You may have the opportunity to represent a snitch. Of course, we don't call them snitches then; now they are "clients."

When representing the informant, your primary role is to protect his rights while he spills his guts. In doing so, you really need to first determine your client's level of expectation concerning the cooperation. Depending on the jurisdiction, the cooperation may help, but may not go far.

If you are in federal court, make sure your client understands this intimately. In federal court, your client's cooperation may get a downward "departure" from the sentencing guidelines. In only the rarest cases will the charge actually go away. However, many clients think cooperation will get them off the hook.

Federal cooperation is governed by the following policy statement:

Upon motion of the government stating that the defendant has provided substantial assistance in the investigation or prosecution of another person who has committed an offense, the court may depart from the guidelines.

(a) The appropriate reduction shall be determined by the court for reasons stated that may include, but are not limited to, consideration of the following:

(1) The court's evaluation of the significance and usefulness of the defendant's assistance, taking into consideration the government's evaluation of the assistance rendered;

(2) The truthfulness, completeness, and reliability of any information or testimony provided by the defendant;

(3) The nature and extent of the defendant's assistance;

(4) Any injury suffered, or any danger or risk of injury to the defendant or his family resulting from his assistance;

(5) The timeliness of the defendant's assistance.

Federal Guidelines Manual §5k1.1 (policy statement).

This policy effectively means that your client can lay everything on the line to help the government, including risking his life, and the government can only move for a downward departure. You can have the greatest plea agreement in the world, and the court solely determines the amount of the departure, generally in a percentage, off the sentence. So, if your client participated in some controlled buys, and provided lots of information to the government and generally risked his neck, you are probably going to get a large departure. But that large departure is 40 or 50 percent. I have seen them as large as 60 percent, and I have heard about them being higher, but it really depends on the judge. Those massive departures are sort of like searching the ocean for Moby Dick.

When representing cooperating individuals, your initial talks with the government may be governed by a proffer agreement. It should expressly allow your client to speak freely and allow the government to evaluate what the client has to say. If the client's cooperation is of interest to the government, a cooperation agreement may be employed. If your client gets deeper into cooperation, an immunity agreement may be necessary, which will require that you understand the complexities of immunity law. Suffice it to say, all immunity is not created equal, and if you find yourself in such a situation, make sure you understand exactly what is being offered to you and its limits. Remember also, the state's offer of immunity to your client does not bind the federal government.

§7:83   FORM 7-80 Proffer Agreement

PROFFER AGREEMENT

This Agreement sets forth the terms that will govern the meeting between Joe Blow ("Client"), who is represented by Timothy Zerillo, Esq., and A.USA, Assistant United States Attorney for the District of Maine that will take place on January 22, 2014.

(1) **THIS IS NOT A COOPERATION AGREEMENT.** The Client has agreed to provide the Government with information, and to respond to questions, so that the Government may evaluate Client's information and responses in making prosecutive decisions. By receiving Client's proffer, the Government does not agree to make a motion on the Client's behalf or to enter into a cooperation agreement, plea agreement, immunity or non-prosecution agreement. The Government makes no representation about the likelihood that any such agreement will be reached in connection with this proffer. The parties understand that the purpose of this agreement is to provide the Government with an opportunity to assess the information which the Client can provide so that the Government can make appropriate prosecutive decisions with respect to him.

(2) In any prosecution brought against Client by this Office, except as provided below, the Government will not offer in evidence in its case-in-chief, or in connection with any sentencing proceeding for the purpose of determining an appropriate sentence, any statements made by Client at the meeting, except in a prosecution for false statements, obstruction of justice or perjury with respect to any acts committed or statements made during or after the meeting or testimony given after the meeting. The parties understand, however, that in the event of a prosecution of Client, the Government will provide to the Court

the information which Client provides pursuant to this Agreement. The parties understand that, while the Government will not introduce Client's statements in evidence except as permitted in this agreement, the Government cannot bind the Court as to its appropriate use of such information and that the Court will use such information to the extent permitted by law.

(3) Notwithstanding item (2) above: (a) the Government may use information derived directly or indirectly from the meeting for the purpose of obtaining leads to other evidence, which evidence may be used in any prosecution of Client by the Government; (b) in any prosecution brought against Client, the Government may use statements made by Client at the meeting and all evidence obtained directly or indirectly therefrom for the purpose of cross-examination should Client testify; and (c) the Government may also use statements made by Client at the meeting to rebut any evidence or arguments offered by or on behalf of Client (including arguments made or issues raised sua sponte by the District Court) at any stage of the criminal prosecution (including bail, all phases of trial, and sentencing) in any prosecution brought against Client.

(4) The Client understands and agrees that in the event of a criminal prosecution in which Client seeks to qualify for a reduction in sentence under Title 18, United States Code, Section 3553(f) or United States Sentencing Guidelines, Sections 2D1.1(b) (11) or 5C1.2, the Government may offer in evidence, in connection with the sentencing, statements made by the Client at the meeting and all evidence obtained directly or indirectly therefrom.

(5) Client waives the application of Fed. R. Evid. 410, and Fed. R. Crim. P. 11(f), as to any statement that he/she makes pursuant to this agreement and which the government is otherwise entitled under this agreement to introduce in evidence.

(6) It is further understood that this Agreement is limited to the statements made by Client at the meeting and does not apply to any oral, written or recorded statements made by Client at any other time. No understandings, promises, agreements and/or conditions have been entered into with respect to the meeting other than those set forth in this Agreement and none will be entered into unless in writing and signed by all parties.

(7) The understandings set forth in paragraphs 1 through 6 above will remain in effect during any additional sessions of the meeting. However, in the event that the parties should enter into a cooperation agreement, the provisions of such cooperation agreement will supersede the provisions of this Proffer Agreement and will govern the subsequent dealings between the Government and Client. Further, in the event that the parties should enter into a cooperation agreement, and such cooperation agreement is thereafter deemed not binding on Client, the terms of this Proffer Agreement shall nevertheless remain binding on Client.

(8) Client and Attorney acknowledge that they have fully discussed and understand every paragraph and clause in this Agreement and the consequences thereof. Client's decision to enter into this Proffer Agreement is voluntary.

Dated:

                                        UNITED STATES ATTORNEY

_____   By:_____

Client   Assistant United States Attorney

_____   _____

Attorney for Client   Supervisory Assistant U.S. Attorney

Dates of Continuation   Initials of counsel, Client, AUSA,

_____   _____ _____ _____

_____   _____ _____ _____

DRUG CRIMES

§7:84   School Zones, Safe Zones and Surveyors

The safe zone/school zone issue can be a real bear to deal with. Most states, and the feds, significantly aggravate drug crimes that take place in a safe zone or school zone. This can cause not only a higher level of charge for you client, but it can also cause mandatory minimums to kick in.

I think practitioners often see the safe zone/school zone allegation and attack only the drug allegation. They skip the issue entirely. Don't assume that the school zone/safezone issue is locked up.

First, find out how your jurisdiction calculates the distance. Most statutes require that it be calculated as the crow flies. That's not good for your client. But perhaps the statute in your jurisdiction doesn't describe how the distance is measured, and you can argue that an alternative measurement is possible, or that the statute is unconstitutionally vague.

So, how does the government prove the drug buy took place within a prohibited distance? In *United States v. McCall*, 553 F.3d 821 (5th Cir. 2008), the Fifth Circuit discussed evidentiary options that may be considered in proving a distance. There, the distance from a drug transaction and the school was proven (or attempted to be) by aerial photograph. The photograph did not indicate scale, however. The Fifth Circuit noted that an aerial photograph without scale was useless. The Court went on to expound upon ways in which distance to a school zone from a drug transaction could have been proven:

> The myriad ways that the government easily and simply could have proved the static, objective fact of the distance between the elementary school and McCall's house unavoidably influences the content that we give to the concept of what a reasonable juror must see and hear to know a distance beyond a reasonable doubt. For example, the government could have offered testimony from a witness who measured the distance, or who could authenticate the circle (marked on the photograph) as accurately superimposing a 1000-foot radius on the aerial photograph, or introduced a witness who knew how the aerial photograph was confected and knew its scale. Or, the government could have tendered, *inter alia*, a map with scale, or a certified copy of a public record of the distance, or an official publication of the distance. It also could have emulated the successful prosecutor in *United States v. Sparks*, 2 F.3d 574, 579-80 (5th Cir. 1993) by having a qualified official testify. The circle, far more sufficient evidence of the distance, was excluded on the first day of a trial that continued for a second day; and the government did not rest until six more witnesses had testified. Yet at no point after its preferred method—the photo with the circle on it—was excluded, did the government bother to seek leave to obtain and offer probative evidence of the distance; and nothing in the record reveals an impediment to it having done so."

McCall, 553 F.3d at 834.

However, in *United States v. Henderson*, 320 F.3d 92 (1st Cir. 2003), the court said:

> Be that as it may, Henderson neglects the fact that the proper way to determine whether a sale was 1,000 feet or less from a school is by measuring a straight line, rather than a pedestrian travel route. *See United States v. Soler*, 275 F.3d 146, 155 n. 6 (1st Cir. 2002) (explaining that "the schoolyard statute envisions straight-line rather than pedestrian-route measurements"). Here, the government introduced into evidence, without objection, a map of the Elm Park Community School area which provided a detailed illustration of the distance between 27 Wachusett Street, where the drug transactions took place, and the school. This map demonstrated that each of the drug transactions occurred within 1,000 feet of the school; the government, in closing argument, pointed out as much to the jury. We do not hesitate to find that this evidence was sufficient to support the verdict.

Id. at 103.

The proof required of the school zone distance is often quite low, as you can see. There are opportunities in some cases, however.

In borderline cases, you may be able to argue that the government needs to prove beyond a reasonable doubt where the drug sale took place within a building. This can work in large apartment buildings and houses, where some of the building is within the school zone/safe zone, and some is not.

I once had a case where my client allegedly engaged in a number of drug buys with a long time snitch. The charges were aggravated because the sales occurred inside a school zone, according to the government, in a single family residence.

I drove by and questioned the school zone issue. The police claimed it was within the 1,000 feet of the school and provided me this map from the City of Portland with their measurements.

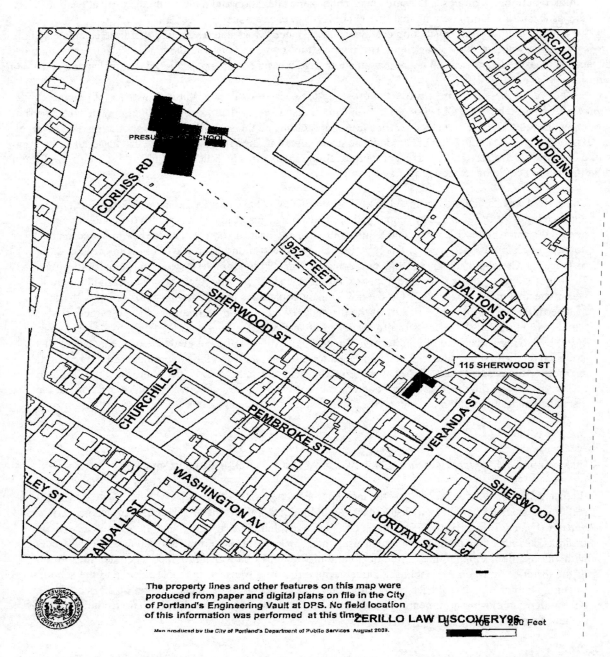

The property lines and other features on this map were produced from paper and digital plans on file in the City of Portland's Engineering Vault at DPS. No field location of this information was performed at this time. ZERILLO LAW DISCOVERY96

Map produced by the City of Portland's Department of Public Services August 2009.

So, this was certainly enough for me to take notice. Another 48 feet and this case isn't aggravated. There are no mandatory minimums. What do you do?

What I did was hire a surveyor. Here is what my surveyor came up with:

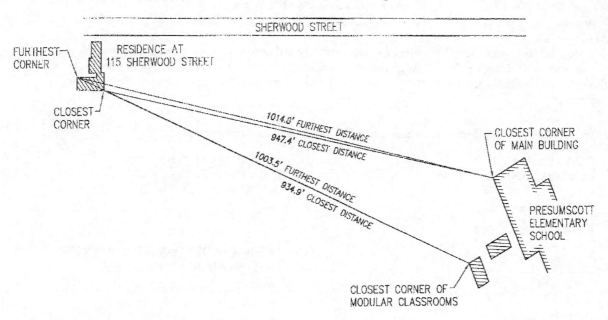

So, the police were correct that the building was inside the 1,000 feet of the school zone, but they were also wrong too. Part of the building was outside the 1,000 feet of the school zone. So what do you do with that?

The snitch testified the transaction took place in the house, but didn't say where. We argued that the snitch couldn't testify effectively to where the transactions took place in the house, and therefore, could not provide evidence beyond a reasonable doubt that our client was within the 1,000 feet.

I'm not the first person to try this type of approach. In *United States v. Soler*, the First Circuit noted:

[T]o convict under [the federal schoolyard statute], the government must prove beyond a reasonable doubt that the distance from a school to the actual site of the transaction, not merely to the curtilage or exterior wall of the structure in which the transaction takes place, is 1,000 feet or less. ... Precise measurements may be unnecessary in some cases where the spatial leeway is relatively great and the gap in the chain of proof is relatively small. ... [citing cases with spatial leeway as small as 326 feet]. In such extreme instances, common sense, common knowledge, and rough indices of distance can carry the day. When the spatial leeway is modest, however, and personal liberty is at stake, courts must examine the government's proof with a more critical eye.

United States v. Soler, 275 F.3d 146, 154 (1st Cir. 2002)

§7:85   Cross Racial Identification

Don't forget cross-racial identification issues in drug cases as well. The problems with eyewitnesses in general are only enhanced when a person of one race identifies a person of another race.

This is quite common in the context of drug sales. In such cases, the only witnesses are either confidential sources (aka snitches) or drug agents posing as drug addicts. Often, defense counsel misses this issue.

Your client is charged with drug trafficking. He is a large black male, with the street name "Bigs." A white undercover officer is introduced to a group of drug users. He makes several drug buys for crack of a man he claims was identified to him as Bigs. He later identifies Bigs in a driver's license photo and your client is arrested. The discovery also identifies your client as being clean shaven.

Your client claims that he didn't sell to the undercover. He doesn't have an alibi and he won't plead. He is, frankly, not very believable, but he is insisting you try the case.

In addition to raising the ordinary issues related to the perception of the drug agent, you also need to raise cross-racial identification. If you have the resources, hire an expert to discuss why misidentification is more prevalent in the cross-racial identification context. If you don't have those resources, cross-examine the officer on this issue. Raise it *via* a motion to suppress and dismiss as well as in trial.

Imagine our case of the identification of Bigs. At the suppression hearing, put the agent on the stand and go after him or her.

Follow up at the suppression hearing or immediately thereafter with a memo to hammer home the points you feel you made at the suppression hearing. This memo needs to be timely, but doesn't need to be book-length. It is designed to reinforce with the court the work you've already done. In Bigs' case, I wrote the following motion to suppress.

§7:86   FORM 7-90 Motion to Suppress Eyewitness Identification

STATE OF MAINE	SUPERIOR COURT
CUMBERLAND, SS	LOCATION: PORTLAND
	DOCKET NO. CR-07-1234

STATE OF MAINE,	)	
	)	
	)	
v.	)	MEMORANDUM ON DEFENDANT'S
	)	MOTION TO SUPPRESS
	)	
JIM SLIM,	)	
	)	
Defendant	)	

NOW COMES, JIM SLIM, by and through Undersigned Counsel, and makes his Memorandum on Defendant's Motions to Suppress and Dismiss.

Manson v. Brathwaite, 432 U.S. 98 (1977) expanded the concept of suggestive identifications to law enforcement. Due process still applies whether the witness is a lay witness or law enforcement. The issue here is not really whether MDEA Agent Paul Hewson's identification was impermissibly suggestive, because a single photo must be, but whether that identification taints Hewson's in-court and out-of-court identifications of Slim.

State v. Cefalo, 396 A.2d 233 (Me. 1977), squarely placed the burden of proving a Constitutional identification on the state. *Cefalo* is appended to this Motion for the Court's review. While acknowledging *Manson v. Braithwaite, supra*, the Law Court held:

> We believe that placing the burden on the state to prove that an unnecessarily suggestive identification procedure did not create a substantial risk of misidentification best expresses the balance the Supreme Court struck between the twin due process concerns. No identification will be excluded solely because the police employed an unnecessarily suggestive pretrial identification procedure. Reliability is the key to admissibility. **However, if the police ignore the frequent warnings of this court and continue to use defective confrontation procedures, the state will run the risk of being unable to establish independently the reliability of the identification.** This approach assures that reliable and probative identifications will be admissible, while deterring the police from employing unfair procedures that violate norms of governmental fair play and create the risk of misidentification.

State v. Cefalo, supra at 238 (emphasis added).

With the burden resting with the state, the Law Court went on to recite the standard:

> Accordingly, we hold that once a defendant, as the movant in the suppression hearing required by *State v. Boyd, supra*, proves by a preponderance that a pretrial identification procedure was unnecessarily suggestive, the burden shifts to the state to show by clear and convincing evidence that the corrupting effect of the suggestive procedure is outweighed by the reliability of the identification as measured by the factors set forth in *Neil v. Biggers*....

State v. Cefalo, supra at 238-239.

The United States Supreme Court in *Neil v. Biggers* established a balancing test of factors to determine the reliability of the identification. "The factors to be considered in evaluating the likelihood of misidentification include the opportunity of the witness to view the criminal at the time of the crime, the witness' degree of attention, the accuracy of the witness' prior description of the criminal, the level of certainty demonstrated by the witness at the confrontation, and the length of time between the crime and the confrontation." *Neil v. Biggers*, 409 U.S. 188, 199-200 (1972).

These identification standards continue to the in-court identification of the Defendant. *Cefalo, supra* holds that "…upon finding that the state used an unnecessarily suggestive procedure, the trial judge must determine whether the witness' out-of-court or in-court identification of the defendant has a basis independent of the suggestive effect of the defective confrontation." *Cefalo, supra* at 236.

Here, the issue is not that the identification was unnecessarily suggestive. Clearly, an identification from a single photo is as suggestive as it gets. The issue for the Court is whether in addition to suppressing the evidence of the photo, whether the Court should suppress the in-court identification of the Defendant by Agent Paul Hewson. The gravamen of this question falls on the reliability of the identification.

Here, Hewson's identification of Slim as "Bigs" is unreliable. He states that Slim is a black male who is in his mid-twenties. Slim is in fact, thirty-six. He states that Slim was clean-shaven, when, in fact, he had a beard. He states that Slim weighs 260 pounds, then says he is 240 pounds, when, in fact, he is well over 300 pounds. He states that there was another person he spoke to on the phone, going by the name "Migs," as opposed to "Bigs". Finally, numerous studies on cross-racial identification show that people are less adept at accurately identifying strangers of other races and better at accurately identifying people of their own race. See e.g., "They All Look Alike; The Inaccuracy of Cross-Racial Identification, "28 *AM J.Crim.L.* 207 (2001); "Perspectives on the Impact of Lineup Composition, Race and Witness Confidence on Identification Accuracy," 4 *L. & Hum. Behav.* 315 (1980).

These factors require the Court to suppress the out-of-court and potential in-court identifications of Slim by Paul Hewson and dismiss the indictment.

Dated this 7th day of February, 2014, in Portland, Maine.

Respectfully submitted,

_____

Timothy E. Zerillo, Esq.
Attorney for Defendant
ZERILLO LAW FIRM, LLC

PRACTICE TIP: *Get a record*

No matter what happens in your motion to suppress, make sure it is recorded and transcribed. At the very least, you now know something about how the agent will testify at trial and hopefully are aware of some weaknesses you can press on.

[§§7:87-7:99 Reserved]

C. Trial

§7:100   Sample Opening Statement—Reasonable Doubt Re Cross-Racial Identification

Let's take a look at an Opening in Bigs case (see §7:85). In that case, I approached the Opening as follows:

There may be a person in Portland who is selling drugs named Bigs, but it is not the man who sits next to me at this table.

The evidence will prove nothing but one fact-- that Jim Slim was in the wrong place at the wrong time with the wrong skin color. And once you hear how thin the government's evidence is, you will agree with me that a proper application of reasonable doubt can only result in one finding—that Jim is not guilty.

Jim sits here, presumed innocent. If you believe Jim to be guilty right now, you are not obeying your oath. You have not heard any evidence yet. He is to be presumed innocent as he sits here during this trial.

DRUG CRIMES

The fact that Jim was arrested in this case does not indicate anything. An arrest is only a means to activate the system of justice so that 12 of his peers can come in here and listen to the evidence. You determine guilt or innocence—not the police officer and not the prosecutor—YOU.

The burden in any criminal case rests solely with the prosecutor at that table. In this case, the state of Maine and that prosecutor have the entire burden of proving Jim's guilt. That burden never once shifts to this table. Jim does not have to do anything except sit here. He doesn't have to testify; his attorney doesn't have to cross-examine anyone; he doesn't have to present evidence; he doesn't have to do anything. And if he does nothing, the law says that you cannot view that as an admission of his guilt. The Judge will tell you so.

Why? Because the prosecutor had the opportunity to do all the advance investigation she wanted to do. She had every state government agency at her disposal and she had your tax dollars to burn in creating this prosecution. Now she has to show you her case and prove to you that she spent your money wisely.

Spending the money wisely means proving the case beyond a reasonable doubt. Anything less is a waste.

So what is reasonable doubt? We know that the state must prove every element of a crime beyond reasonable doubt. That includes proving beyond a reasonable doubt that Jim Slim sold crack cocaine to Agent Paul Hewson. If there is a reasonable doubt that Jim sold crack to Paul Hewson, then you must acquit him.

But what is reasonable doubt? Reasonable doubt is a doubt that would cause you to hesitate in a matter of importance in your daily affairs. Beyond reasonable doubt is a level of certainty upon which you would make the most important decisions of your life.

If you hear the state's case and decide that it's plausible, then you hear the defense case and decide that it's possible, that possibility is a reasonable doubt.

And that heavy burden on the state applies to each and every step in the case beyond a reasonable doubt. There is no rest from this. The state never shifts that burden to this table. It is always their burden to carry.

Here, the state must prove beyond a reasonable doubt that Jim Slim sold crack cocaine to Agent Paul Hewson. Hewson's job in the street is to gain the trust of drug dealers and get them to sell drugs to him. He is no stranger to testifying. His job here is to get your trust.

He will look a lot different in court than when he is on the street. He will be in a suit and tie and look very pressed and perfect. And that is part of the job of convincing you.

But don't be distracted from the actual evidence. The evidence will point to the fact that the police have the wrong man. Hewson's identification of the man who sold him drugs was that he was a black male in his mid-20's, weighing 250 pounds and clean shaven.

That description does not match Jim. The evidence will be that Jim is over 300 pounds, 38 years old and has a beard. You will wonder then, do they have the right black male?

The state's entire case hangs on the identification of Jim Slim by Agent Paul Hewson. You will find that Hewson's ID of Jim is riddled with inconsistencies, so much so that it sounds like he is identifying the wrong person.

And then, here's the icing on the cake. When Jim was arrested, this alleged drug dealer didn't have any drugs on him! There were no drugs on his person, no drugs in the apartment he was in, but they arrested him anyway, as Bigs. And the officer who ID'd him as Bigs, Paul Hewson, wasn't even there for the arrest!

All of these facts will lead you to the conclusion that reasonable doubt exists in this case.

If you find that there is a question as to Hewson's ID; if you believe that it is possible that Jim Slim is not Bigs; if you believe there was an improper investigation, then you will have reached the point where you have found reasonable doubt.

We hope you will be true to your oath. And, at the end of this trial, enter a not guilty verdict.

For general tips on opening statements and sample language about the presumption of innocence and burden of proof, see Ch.2.

§7:101   Sample Cross-Examination of Undercover Cop in a Drug Sale on Identification

Let's look at a cross-examination in the trial of Bigs. See §7:85. This may have not been the greatest case to try, I'll admit it. We have a DEA agent conducting multiple drug buys with an individual he can readily identify. That said, you don't get to choose all the trials you have, and this is how I approached the cross of the agent here. For tips on cross examining police officers, see Ch.2

Report Accurate; Memory Better Then Than Now

Q. Agent Hewson, you have had extensive training in law enforcement investigation techniques?
A. I have.
Q. You were trained to write reports?
A. Yes.
Q. You were trained that it is important for your reports to be accurate and thorough?
A. Yes.
Q. You know your reports may be used in court.
A. Yes.
Q. You wrote a report in this case.
A. Yes.
Q. Your report was accurate.
A. Yes.
Q. And thorough.
A. Yes.
Q. You also believe your investigation was thorough.
A. I do.
Q. One reason you thoroughly write reports is to help your memory later on.
A. I'm not sure I understand that one.
Q. You've been involved in dozens of cases since 2007
A. Sure.
Q. Your memory of the drug buys in this case at the time of the drug buys was better than it is now.
A. I would say so.
Q. Your memory does not get better as time goes on, does it?
A. No.
Q. Neither does mine.

Investigation Was Shoddy

I want to weave in the theme of a shoddy, sloppy and lazy investigation throughout the cross-examination.

Q. In all of your experience, have you ever run into anyone else with the street name Bigs?
A. I don't believe so.
Q. You don't know all the street names out there, do you?
A. Not even close.
Q. Did you check with Portland Police on that?
A. No.

Q. Did you check with the DEA for anyone else with that street name?
A. No.
Q. Did you do a search in the computer system for people with the alias Bigs?
A. No.

Agent Is Experienced and Was Prepared by Prosecutor

I also want to establish that this isn't Mr. Hewson's first rodeo.

Q. You go undercover on drug buys as part of what you do?
A. I do.
Q. That's dangerous sometimes, right?
A. It can be.
Q. You need to be trained in how to handle a controlled buy.
A. Yes.
Q. They call it a "controlled buy," but it's dangerous because you can't control everything.
A. You can't.
Q. One of the ways to take out some of the danger is to gain the trust of the dealer.
A. That helps.
Q. And you were trained how to gain the trust of the drug dealer.
A. Yes.
Q. That requires a certain skill.
A. Yes.
Q. On the other hand, you are also trained in how to testify.
A. I don't know if I'd say I'm trained to testify. I tell the truth when I testify.
Q. Of course you do. But there is DEA training related to testifying before juries and judges that you have been through, isn't there?
A. I suppose so.
Q. You testify in front of juries frequently?
A. I'm not sure I would say frequently.
Q. You testify before juries often?
A. OK, I would agree with often.
Q. You work with Assistant Attorney General here frequently?
A. Yes.
Q. She spent time with you preparing the case for trial.
A. Yes.
Q. She met with you.
A. Yes.
Q. She discussed her direct examination of you?
A. Yes.
Q. You discussed strategy with her?
A. That's up to her.
Q. She even discussed what I might ask you?
A. She did.

Attacking Agent's Identification of Defendant: The First Buy

We want to attack the identification in part by breaking down the drug buys. Here is the first buy:

Q. You've claimed that you engaged in four drug buys with my client, Jim Slim, correct?
A. Yes.
Q. I want to go through them one by one with you. The first time was 2.21.07, right?
A. Yes.
Q. It took place at 7:45 PM.

A. Yes.

Q. Its dark out at 7:45 PM in February in Maine, isn't it?

A. Yes.

Q. And it was dark out after you made that first buy?

A. Yes.

Q. The buy took place outside an apartment building, near the entrance?

A. Yes.

Q. And the entrance light didn't work?

A. Not at the time, no.

Q. At the time of this buy, you had never met the person named Bigs before?

A. No.

Q. You didn't have an identity for him?

A. No, we just knew he was called Bigs.

Q. Did you have a picture of him?

A. No.

Q. Did you do any surveillance beforehand to try to ID him?

A. No.

Q. Since you were really trying to identify him the first time, you really tried to pay attention to what he looked like?

A. Yes.

Q. And you made note of all the physical traits you observed in your report?

A. I tried to, yes.

Q. Did think you were successful in that?

A. I think so.

Q. The report date for that buy is 2.14.07?

A. Yes.

Q. You wrote the report seven days before the drug buy took place?

A. That must be wrong. It's a typo.

Q. OK, what is the correct report date?

A. I don't know for certain, probably several days after the buy.

Q. But you don't know for sure?

A. No.

Q. Are you sure that the drug buy date is correct?

A. Yes.

Q. Couldn't the report date be accurate but it's the drug buy date that's wrong?

A. I don't believe so.

Q. Is there anything else wrong with the report?

A. I don't believe so.

Q. You got in touch with Bigs on 2.21.07 through Migs.

A. Yes.

Q. Did you ever ID Migs?

A. Yes.

Q. Migs told you he couldn't help you and to call Bigs.

A. Correct.

Q. When you saw Bigs, he was wearing a cap?

A. Yes.

Q. So you didn't get a look at his hair?

A. No.

Attacking Agent's Identification of Defendant: The Next Two Buys

Let's set the table with the next two buys.

Q. Second buy was 4.3.07?

A. Yes.

Q. It was at 7:28 PM.?
A. Yes.
Q. It was dark out just like the first time?
A. It was.
Q. This time, the deal took place with Bigs in a car.
A. Yes.
Q. You were outside the car.
A. I was. I kneeled outside the passenger window.
Q. And Bigs was in the passenger seat?
A. Yes.
Q. Could you identify the driver?
A. No.
Q. What did the driver look like?
A. He was black, in his twenties I'd guess. A male.
Q. Anything else?
A. Not that I recall.
Q. The interior lights in the car were not lit.
A. No, they weren't.
Q. You ran the plates for that car, later?
A. Yes.
Q. The car wasn't registered to Jim Slim was it?
A. It wasn't.
Q. This total deal took approximately one minute.
A. Yes.
Q. You didn't stare at him for the full minute, did you?
A. No.
Q. You had to act as though you could get caught for the deal to look authentic.
A. I guess.
Q. And people get uncomfortable in a drug deal when you spend a lot of time staring at them.
Objection: Your honor, he's calling for the agent to speculate.
Court: Attorney Zerillo?
Zerillo: Your honor, the state laid this tremendous groundwork on direct to try to establish that this agent is an extremely well-credentialed drug officer, with intimate knowledge as to how to operate a controlled drug buy. He has also claimed to be able to identify my client. On cross, I should be allowed to inquire if it is commonplace or considered suspicious in the context of drug sales for staring to occur.
Court: Overruled for that one question.
Q. Agent, in the context of drug deals, is it your experience that the people involved in the deal get uncomfortable when you stare at them for periods of time?
A. I don't know.
Q. You don't know because you don't stare at the drug dealer during controlled drug buys?
A. I don't stare, no.
Q. So, when you look at the drug dealer, it is in glimpses?
A. Not really glimpses, but I don't stare at him either.
Q. The third time is May 2, 07?
A. Yes.
Q. The deal takes place in the building stairwell that time?
A. Yes.
Q. Also at night?
A. Yes.
Q. How was the lighting?
A. The stairwell was fully lit.
Q. Another black male other than Bigs did the transaction for Bigs, right?
A. Yes.
Q. Was this Migs?

A. No.
Q. Migs is another black male?
A. Yes.
Q. Was this another black male named Popeye?
A. No.
Q. This was an unknown black male?
A. Yes.
Q. And you were told that Bigs sent him.
A. Yes. He said Bigs asked him to come downstairs and sell to me.
Q. Could have been a different Bigs then?
A. I don't think so. It was in the same place as before.
Q. Did you ever ask around if there were others with the street name Bigs?
A. No.
Q. And so, the only times you dealt with Bigs directly were on February 21st and April 3rd?
A. Yes.

Attacking Agent's Identification of Defendant: Defendant's Current Appearance vs. Agent's Observations

I want to compare my client's appearance in court with the agent's observations of Bigs.

Q. Today, you are identifying that gentleman at defense table as Bigs?
A. Yes, he is.
Q. Does he look the same today as he did on February 21, 2007?
A. I would say so.
Q. Does he look the same as he did on April 3, 2007?
A. Yes.

Let's raise the idea of a faulty identification.

Q. After the initial buy on February 21 you were shown a black and white photograph?
A. Yes.
Q. That was provided to you by Agent Dave Evans?
A. Yes.
Q. It was a DMV photo from Massachusetts of Jim Slim?
A. It was.
Q. And you were able to identify Jim Slim as Bigs from that photograph?
A. Yes.
Q. You've conducted photo arrays, haven't you?
A. Yes.
Q. You have been trained as to how to assemble a photo array?
A. I have.
Q. There are procedures you follow to make sure the photo array isn't faulty?
A. Yes.
Q. If the photo array isn't set up properly, it could be suggestive?
A. It could.
Q. Meaning that it could suggest to the eyewitness what the answer should be.
A. Right.
Q. Setting up a photo array is something you have done many times.
A. I have.
Q. You've studied the Maine Law Enforcement Officer's Manual, haven't you?
A. Yes.
Q. That was part of your training, wasn't it?
A. Yes, it was.
Q. The Maine Law Enforcement Officer's Manual tells you how to set up a photo array, doesn't it?

A. It does.
Q. It doesn't tell you to set up a photo array with a single photo does it?
A. No.
Q. It suggests you use six photos, right?
A. Yes, that's what it suggests.
Q. And the photos need to be of similar looking people?
A. Yes.
Q. So if the witness was identifying a black man, you would include pictures in the photo array of six similar appearing black men?
A. Right.
Q. You wouldn't include five white guys and a picture of one black man would you?
A. No.
Q. And that is because doing that could suggest to the witness what the answer was?
A. It could.
Q. You were only given one picture, weren't you?
A. I was shown a copy of one license photo.
Q. In black and white.
A. Yes.

In the first drug buy, the agent noted in his report what Bigs looked like. Now, we want to pick those observances apart.

This first instance came from the wire recording of the first buy. As he was walking away from the buy, the agent noted various things about the physical appearance of Bigs. In doing so, he noted that Bigs was "clean shaven." At our suppression hearing, he answered my description of Bigs by, in part, saying he had a "five o'clock shadow."

Q. On 2.21.07 you were wired.
A. Yes.
Q. You recorded the buy so that you could create a record of what happened?
A. Yes.
Q. And you also noted on the recording some physical characteristics you observed from Bigs?
A. Yes.
Q. That was so your recollection was recorded?
A. Yes.
Q. And you could look back on it later if you needed to?
A. Yes.
Q. At the time you made this recording, you hadn't identified Bigs?
A. No, I had not.
Q. So you noted everything you could think of that would help you identify him?
A. Well, I said what came to mind.
Q. What came to mind right after meeting him for the first time?
A. Yes.
Q. One of the things you noted that he was "clean shaven."
A. I did.
Q. Those were the words you used specifically; "clean shaven?"
A. Yes.
Q. And you noted on the wire other various physical characteristics of Bigs.
A. Yes.
Q. In May, we had a hearing and we discussed that first meeting with Bigs, right?
A. Yes.
Q. I asked you at that time how Mr. Slim looked in that first drug buy in February, and you told me he had a five o'clock shadow, correct?
A. I don't remember that.

Q. [Showing him Transcript]. I'm showing you the May Transcript. Take a look at this please Agent. Question,"What did Bigs look like?" Answer, "He was a black male, in his mid-twenties, heavy set, he had a 5 o'clock shadow…" Did I read right, Agent Hewson?

A. You read it right.

Q. And you gave that testimony under oath, didn't you?

A. Yes.

Q. And you said at that time that Bigs had a 5 o'clock shadow?

A. Yes.

Q. So which is it; did he have a 5 o'clock shadow or was he clean shaven?

A. He had stubble, but he was clean shaven.

Q. OK. He never had a beard, right?

A. No. He was clean shaven, but he had some stubble.

Q. You were a military man, right?

A. I was in the Army.

Q. When you were in the Army, clean shaven meant shaved with a razor without stubble, right?

A. It depends

Q. When you went into the Army, you were given an IET Soldier's Handbook?

A. Yes.

Q. They are very precise about your appearance in that Handbook.

A. They were.

Q. Clean shaven to the Army means shaved with a razor without stubble, doesn't it?

A. To the Army, but there is more than one version of clean shaven.

Q. So you don't use the Army definition?

A. Not since I left the Army.

Q. And clean shaven to you can mean with stubble?

A. It can.

Q. Would you describe me as clean shaven?

A. Yes.

Q. Would you describe the judge as clean shaven?

A. I would.

Q. How about Jim Slim?

A. Not as clean shaven as you or the Judge, but yes.

I made sure to have client not shave for a day before this. He was the type of person whose beard grew fast, so he only needed to show up for court with stubble on one day. That said, this was effective here, because it illustrated my point. No one would have called my client clean shaven at the time. The agent, however, was painted into a corner, and we knew he would try to fight his way out that way.

Let's pick on some other inconsistencies between our client and the Bigs description.

Q. On 2.21.07 you said Bigs weight was 250 or 260 lbs.

A. Yes.

Q. That was an accurate?

A. I believe so.

Q. If I represented to you that Jim Slim weighed around 350 pounds in 2007 would that surprise you?

A. That's heavier than I thought, but it wouldn't surprise me.

Q. It would be inconsistent with your ID wouldn't it?

A. It would be higher than my estimate.

Q. So your estimate would have been wrong then?

A. If he actually weighed that much, yes.

Q. You also estimated his age?

A. Yes.

Q. And this was based on your view of him in that first controlled buy?

A. It was.

Q. And you estimated that Bigs was in his mid-twenties.

A. Yes.
Q. But when you arrested Jim Slim, he was 35 years old, right?
A. Yes.
Q. If Jim Slim was in fact Bigs, your estimate of his age must have been wrong?
A. Mr. Slim is Bigs, and yes, I was wrong about his age.

In this case, the Agent claimed that he could identify Jim Slim as Bigs, and also that Bigs took the crack out of his mouth. I want to try to tie this to the identification if I can.

Q. You observed Bigs take crack out of his mouth on February 21?
A. Yes.
Q. And you were able to identify Jim Slim as Bigs at that first encounter.
A. After I was shown a photographe, I identified the individual in the photograph as Bigs.
Q. You have also told us that the lighting was sufficient for that identification, right?
A. Right.
Q. When he opened his mouth, you were able to observe his teeth?
A. Yes.
Q. Did he have any crowns?
A. I don't remember.
Q. Braces?
A. I don't remember.
Q. Fillings?
A. I don't know.
Q. Did you do DNA testing on the bag that came out of his mouth?
A. No.

Attacking Agent's Identification of Defendant: Others in Drug World Who Match Defendant's Description

Further attack the identification by pointing out others who match his description who are around in the drug world.

Q. On 2.21.07 you spoke to someone named "Migs?"
A. Yes.
Q. Did you ever meet Migs?
A. Yes.
Q. Migs is a black male?
A. Yes.
Q. Migs is a heavyset black male?
A. Yes.
Q. He is approximately the same age as Jim Slim?
A. Yes.
Q. Migs is clean shaven?
A. I believe so.
Q. On 5.8.08 you did a buy that was supposed to be done with Bigs, but it was with another black male name Popeye?
A. Yes it was.
Q. On 5.2.07 when you went to try to do a buy, an unknown black male answered the door.
A. Yes.
Q. He was also heavyset?
A. Yes.
Q. That was another black male who was not Bigs?
A. No, he was not.
Q. And you never identified that other heavyset black male?
A. No.

§7:102   Sample Cross-Examination of Snitch

Crossing snitches is fun. Approaches to crossing these "special" witnesses have been covered in hundreds if not thousands of books, and I will not devote tremendous time to the subject. Again, the only limit is your imagination.

Here's a generic snitch cross. I don't even need to provide you many details; he is just a plain old drug snitch. The same concepts apply to your cases universally.

The easy part of a snitch cross is to go through the plea agreement. The harder part is to really paint the picture with your words. To do so, you need to know what this snitch is about. What he is giving up if he goes to jail. I want to be arguing at closing that this guy is going to be missing driving his Escalade and his daughter up unless he points the finger at my guy.

Q. Mr. Snitch, you used to be a drug dealer, right?
A. Yeah.
Q. It's a dangerous business?
A. Yeah.
Q. You need to do what you have to do to survive, don't you?
A. Yeah.
Q. You had to carry a gun, right?
A. Yes I did.
Q. You had more than one gun?
A. Sometimes.
Q. You needed those guns to protect yourself?
A. Yeah.
Q. To protect your cocaine?
A. Yeah.
Q. To protect your cash?
A. Yeah.
Q. It was something you needed to survive?
A. If you was smart, yeah.
Q. But you got caught, didn't you?
A. Yes.
Q. And that was the end of your drug dealing career?
A. Yeah.
Q. And you were put under indictment?
A. Yeah.
Q. And you were guilty of the charges in that indictment?
A. Yes.
Q. And you worked out a deal with the government?
A. Yes.
Q. You became what is commonly known as a snitch?
A. I guess so.
Q. You found out that the sentence you faced had a mandatory minimum associated with it?
A. Yeah.
Q. You were looking at 10 years, right?
A. Yeah.
Q. You're not looking at that now, are you?
A. I don't know yet.
Q. You're hoping for a lot less because of your testimony in this case?
A. I am.
Q. You've been out on bail since you made your deal?
A. Yes.
Q. You drive a nice car, don't you? A 2010 Cadillac Escalade?
A. Yeah.
Q. You like it?

A. Yeah.

Q. You have a girlfriend?

A. Yes.

Q. She's nice looking?

A. Yeah.

Q. Attractive?

A. Yeah.

Q. She lives with you?

A. Yeah.

Q. You have friends?

A. Yeah.

Q. They come over to your house?

A. Uh huh.

Q. Speaking of houses, you have a nice house?

A. Pretty nice.

Q. 3 bedrooms, 2 baths, Contemporary Cape.

A. Right.

Q. That sounds nice.

A. It's pretty nice, I guess.

Q. You have a daughter too, don't you?

A. Uh huh.

Q. She's 10?

A. Yep.

Q. You share custody of her?

A. Yes.

Q. She must be the love of your life?

A. She is.

Q. She means a lot to you?

A. She means everything to me.

Q. You've been to jail before?

A. Yeah.

Q. They give you a cell.

A. Yeah.

Q. Usually with a roommate?

A. It depends. Usually.

Q. It's a tiny little room.

A. Yeah.

Q. And if you were in jail or prison, you'd be done driving that Cadillac?

A. Yes.

Q. You'd be done living in that nice house?

A. Yeah.

Q. That little jail cell would be your house?

A. Yeah.

Q. You'd be done seeing your girlfriend, except during visiting hours?

A. Yeah.

Q. You'd be done seeing your daughter except in visiting hours?

A. Yes.

Q. You get 10 years, you'd miss her high school graduation, wouldn't you?

A. Probably, yeah.

Q. You'd miss teaching her to drive?

A. Yup.

Q. You'd miss a lot, right?

A. Yup.

Q. Let's go through your plea agreement now…

§7:103   Sample Closing Argument—Reasonable Doubt

Let's consider now the closing in the Jim Slim/Bigs case. See §7:85. This was a difficult trial, but we did our best to defend the client and attack the primary government witness, the DEA agent Paul Hewson. Now it's time to bring that all together in closing and pray for a sympathetic juror.

It's not good enough. What they've given you is not good enough. The ID is wrong. The investigation is shoddy. Not good enough.

The state's entire case hangs by a thread of Paul Hewson's career. The state's theory is that because he has been in law enforcement so long, he must be right. But we know that longevity doesn't ensure accuracy.

Judge Proper asked you a question in jury selection way back before this case began. He asked you if you believed that law enforcement officers are more likely to tell the truth than any other witness. You all said no. You all said you didn't give their testimony more weight than anyone else's. You all said they should be treated the same. And you were right when you said that.

But now the state wants you to treat Paul Hewson's testimony differently. They want you to say that he's more credible than our alibi witnesses. They want you to say he's more credible than our witnesses who told you that there are several people in the area with the street name of Bigs. Their case is not good enough.

We brought in two witnesses for you. Remember, the defense has no burden to do anything, let alone bring in witnesses. But we brought in two witnesses for you. Both of them said that in 2007, at the time that Jim Slim was allegedly involved in this drug deal, he had a beard. He was not clean shaven. We have provided pictures to you. Pictures from throughout 2007 that showed Jim Slim with a beard.

And yet, Agent Paul Hewson attempts to get away from his initial report that Jim Slim was clean shaven in that first February drug deal. He said he was clean shaven, now he says he had stubble. Ask yourself if an army man saying clean shaven meant with a beard or stubble. I don't know exactly what's going on here, but Agent Hewson is not being honest. He is trying to win. And you might like him, but your job isn't to declare a winner. It is to follow the law related to this case. In fact, that is the only way anyone wins. If you properly apply reasonable doubt to the facts of this case, everyone wins.

It is arguable that Agent Hewson later found out Jim Slim has a beard. But he has already said on tape that he was clean shaven. So he's stuck with it. And he knows he's stuck with it.

This is a military man. Clean shaven means clean shaven. He is allegedly so close to Bigs that he can see this man pull crack out of his mouth; they are right next to each other. That he didn't identify him properly when he said he was clean shaven makes no sense at all. Now he says "clean shaven" meant "well maybe it was stubble." What??? And we know from our witnesses presented to you and from photographs that Jim Slim had a beard at that time.

But the state got their agent to say on the stand that he was 100% positive that Jim Slim is Bigs. A wiser man than me once said "to be positive about something is to be mistaken at the top of your voice." And it's just not good enough.

In addition to the mistaken identification, we've got other heavyset black males running around the drug world not identified by Agent Hewson. We've got Bigs, we've got Migs, we've got Popeye and we've got another unknown black male never identified. The prosecution never properly identifies who any of these people are, but yet they will prosecute my client. It's not good enough.

The evidence against the Jim Slim is weak at best. The state wants to make it as easy as pie for you. But it isn't. There are no drug sales to anyone other than Hewson. There are no pictures by surveillance. There is no video of Jim Slim. There is no DNA on the bags allegedly taken out of Jim Slim's mouth.

There are no fingerprints taken from Jim Slim. Jim Slim is not clean shaven. There is no proof beyond a reasonable doubt.

Sometimes people think the role of the jury is to find someone guilty or innocent. That is not your role and that is not accurate. In Scotland they have a three verdict system that describes this a little bit better.

In Scotland a jury can come back guilty, not guilty, or not proven. Not guilty in Scotland would be a finding of what we think of as innocent; not proven means the charges weren't proven beyond a reasonable doubt. Either one results in an acquittal.

In the United States we add not proven into not guilty. A vote for not guilty can mean you believe Jim Slim to be innocent or it can mean that you don't know if he is innocent, but the government has not proven the charges beyond a reasonable doubt. And that is the only logical conclusion you can come to here.

There may be someone in Portland with a street name Bigs who is dealing drugs, but that person is not Jim Slim. What they've given you is not good enough to get beyond a reasonable doubt. What they've given you is just not enough.

For tips on closing arguments and sample language for burden of proof and reasonable doubt arguments, see Ch. 2.

[§§7:104-7:109 Reserved]

IV. CONSPIRACY

A. Strategies

§7:110   The Elements

What is a drug conspiracy? It is simply a meeting of the criminal minds.

Under 18 U.S.C. 371, it is a separate federal crime to conspire or agree with someone else to do something, which, if actually carried out, would be a separate federal crime. The essence of the conspiracy charge is an agreement, followed by some overt act. The goal of the conspiracy need not be accomplished for a person to be guilty of a conspiracy in federal court, however. Your own state undoubtedly has a similar conspiracy law.

Conspiracy charges can come up in any number of types of criminal cases, but in the drug world, you often see them as a tag along to the trafficking and sale case. As a result, many of the approaches to defending the conspiracy charge are similar to the defense of the trafficking or sale of drugs charge.

§7:111   Downward Sentencing Adjustments for Small-Time Players

What people don't understand often is how a conspiracy charge can really bite them in the back side. This is especially true if they played a minor role in the conspiracy. I always tell potential clients charged with conspiracy that when they join the conspiracy, they are like a spoke on the wheel of a bike. The rider of that bike takes them from place to place, and even though they don't control the bike, they are responsible for whatever trouble they get for all the places they go.

This hard fact is difficult for people to accept. Perhaps they muled drugs one time to support their habit. Or their boyfriend is a dealer and they delivered a package on one occasion. How can they be responsible for the entire drug conspiracy?

Setting these expectations up front is exceedingly important. In federal law, the limited role your client played in the conspiracy can be considered. Additionally, if your client was the ringleader of the conspiracy, look out.

If your client was a small player in a drug conspiracy, try to get the court to accept some of these mitigating role adjustments. If your client was a minimal participant and your case is in federal court, you can get a four level decrease. US Sentencing Guidelines §3B1.2. If your client is a minor participant, you can get a two level decrease. *Id.* The defense bears the burden of proof by a preponderance of the evidence that the client deserves a minor or minimal participant finding by the court. *See United States v. Carpenter*, 252 F.3d 230, 234 (2d Cir. 2001); *United States v. Brubaker*, 362 F.3d 1068, 1071 (8th Cir. 2004); *United States v. Posada-Rios*, 158 F.3d 832, 880 (5th Cir. 1998).

In deciding whether your client played a minor or minimal role, the court first determines if your client was substantially less culpable than the average participant in the conspiracy. US Sentencing Guidelines §.3B1.2, Application Note 3(A). The average participant can be related to the participants in the conspiracy at hand, as well as to other similar conspiracies. *See e.g. United States v. Santos*, 537 F.3d 136, 142 (1st Cir. 2004) ("[A] defendant must prove that he is both less culpable than his cohorts in the particular criminal endeavor and less culpable than the majority of those within the universe of persons participating in similar crimes."); *United States v. Rahman*, 189 F.3d 88, 159 (2d Cir. 1999) ("A reduction will not be available simply because the defendant played a lesser role than his co-conspirators; to be eligible for a reduction, the defendant's conduct must be 'minor' or 'minimal' as compared to the average participant in such a crime.").

Once it has been established that your client is sufficiently less culpable than the average participant, the court determines what adjustment is in order. Adjustments for minimal participants are " intended to cover defendants who are plainly among the least culpable of those involved in the conduct of a group." US Sentencing Guidelines §3B1.2, comment. (n.4). Minor participants, on the other hand, are "less culpable than most other participants, but whose role could not be described as minimal." US Sentencing Guidelines §3B1.2, comment (n.5).

While the general rule is that a small player in the conspiracy owns the entirety of the criminal conduct, you should argue otherwise. If your client was simply a drug mule, argue that she should be responsible only for the quantity of drugs she couriered or stored as her relevant conduct. US Sentencing Guidelines §1B1.3.

Of course, if you are in state court without sentencing guidelines, your opportunities are limitless. You should put on the whole dog and pony show at sentencing. If your client walked an old lady across the street when he was 10, bring it up.

§7:112   Withdrawal from the Conspiracy

Since forming a conspiracy means a meeting of the minds and a singular overt act in furtherance of the conspiracy, you can also withdraw from a conspiracy. "Withdrawal" from a conspiracy requires that the conspirator take affirmative action to disassociate from the other conspirators. *See United states v. Gonzalez*, 797 F.2d 915 (10th Cir. 1986). Of course, withdrawal is only really effective if your client completed the withdrawal prior to the overt act of the crime. *United States v. Heckman*, 479 F.2d 726, 279 (3d Cir. 1973), n. 10. Withdrawal from conspiracy, therefore, may be a partial blessing if there has been long term criminal activity and your client has only withdrawn from portions of it.

§7:113   Upward Sentencing Adjustments for the Head Honcho

If you represent the head honcho in the conspiracy, you face upward adjustments from the Sentencing Guidelines in federal court. These upward adjustments can be devastating in some cases.

Aggravating role adjustments are found generally in US Sentencing Guidelines §3B1.1. If your client was the organizer or leader of the enterprise, it is a four level adjustment. *Id*. A manager or supervisor gets a three level adjustment. *Id*. These both pre-suppose there are five or more participants in the conspiracy. If there are fewer than five or more participants, a leader, organizer, manager or supervisor gets a two level increase.

Distinguishing an organizer or leader from a manager or supervisor is another fact-bound inquiry made by the court. Here is the non-exhaustive list of factors the court is to consider:
- The exercise of decision making authority;
- The nature of participation in the commission of the offense;
- The recruitment of accomplices;
- The claimed right to a larger share of the fruits of the crime;
- The degree of participation in planning or organizing the offense;
- The nature and scope of the illegal activity; and
- The degree of control and authority exercised over others.

US Sentencing Guidelines §3B1.1, Comment (n.4).

[§§7:114-7:119 Reserved]

B.   Motions

§7:120   Motion for Bill of Particulars

Of course, you can bring a Motion for a Bill of Particulars in any case in which you think it is needed. In the drug case context, they seem to come up for me more often than not in the conspiracy charge. The reason for this is simple: the defendant needs to understand how his alleged role in the conspiracy relates to the charges filed.

Simply bring a motion for a bill of particulars to determine this. When doing so, ask for particular findings to be made in the indictment. This is done to provide you information and to hem in the government.

Imagine the case in which I represent Nick Narco. He is accused in a federal indictment of conspiracy to distribute heroin. In my motion for a bill of particulars, I might request the following:

    a)   How Nick Narco is alleged to have conspired with other individuals to accomplish the aforementioned acts;

    b)   The identity of each of those other individuals who supposedly conspired with Nick Narco;

    c)   The overt act(s) done by Nick Narco to initiate the alleged conspiracy;

    d)   When the initial act was done and what parties were privy to it;

    e)   Any and all facts to be relied upon by the government in proving the conspiracy alleged herein;

    f)   What, if any, physical evidence seized by the government constitutes an illegal substance for the purpose of the charge alleging Count I of the Indictment and the total weight of any illegal substance supposedly used or attempted to be used by the parties charged herein in furtherance of the conspiracy.

Of course, you need to know the law in your jurisdiction related to your burden on the motion. In federal court, F.R. Crim. P. 7(f) applies. In almost every case, the argument for the Bill of Particulars revolves around prejudice to the client. Prejudice to the defendant occurs when he or she cannot intelligently and effectively mount a defense without the requested particulars. *See United States v. Valenzuala-Bernal*, 102 S.Ct. 3440 (1982).

§7:121   FORM 7-100 Motion for Bill of Particulars

IN THE UNITED STATES DISTRICT COURT
FOR THE DISTRICT OF MAINE

UNITED STATES OF AMERICA,	)	
Plaintiff,	)	
	)	
v.	)	Case No.
	)	
SMACK SMITH,	)	
STEVE STONER,	)	
and	)	
NICK NARCO,	)	
Defendants.	)	

MOTION FOR BILL OF PARTICULARS AND MEMORANDUM OF LAW

NOW COMES the accused party herein, Nick Narco, by and through his counsel, Timothy E. Zerillo, and respectfully moves the Court pursuant to the Federal Rules of Criminal Procedure 7(f), for an order requiring the Government to file a Bill of Particulars setting out the specific details of each crime alleged against the accused party herein. Specifically, the accused is interested in the order directing the Government to set out with specificity the following information:

    1.   As to Count I of the Indictment, charging Nick Narco with conspiracy to knowingly and intentionally possess with intent to distribute and to knowingly and intentionally distribute 500 grams or more of a mixture or substance containing a detectable amount of cocaine, a Schedule II controlled substance, and 100 grams or more of a mixture or substance containing a detectable amount of heroin, a Schedule I controlled substance, and to aid and abet the commission of those crimes in the State of Maine, the accused party would respectfully request the Government to set out with specificity:

a) How Nick Narco is alleged to have conspired with other individuals to accomplish the aforementioned acts;
b) The identity of each of those other individuals who supposedly conspired with Nick Narco;
c) The overt act done by Nick Narco to initiate the alleged conspiracy;
d) When the initial act was done and what parties were privy to this;
e) Any and all facts to be relied upon by the Government in proving the conspiracy alleged herein;
f) What, if any, physical evidence seized by the Government constitutes an illegal substance the purpose of the charge alleging Count I of the Indictment and the total weight of any illegal substance supposedly used or attempted to be used by the parties charged herein in furtherance of the conspiracy.

MEMORANDUM OF LAW

F.R. Crim. P 7(f) provides that the Defendant may direct the filing of a Bill of Particulars upon the Defendant's Motion. A Bill of Particulars provides details of the charges so the Defendant may mount a defense to avoid prejudicial surprise and to protect against the threat of a second prosecution on the same facts. *United States v. Chavez*, 845 F.2d 219 (9th Cir 1988).

If a Motion for a Bill of Particulars is not granted in a case in which there is a lack of particularity in the Indictment, prejudice will occur. Prejudice to the Defendant occurs when he or she cannot intelligently and effectively mount a defense. *See United States v. Valenzuala-Bernal*, 102 S.Ct. 3440 (1982). Here, the Indictment lacks the particularity that an order granting this Motion can cure.

Dated this 10th day of February, 2014, at Portland, Maine.

Respectfully submitted,

_____
Timothy E. Zerillo
Attorney for Defendant
ZERILLO LAW FIRM, LLC

[§§7:122-7:129 Reserved]

C. Trial

Most of the trial components related to an ordinary drug trial will relate to the conspiracy trial. That said, you will also have other issues related to the alleged formation of the conspiracy, and sometimes with withdrawal from the conspiracy. Consider our friend Nick Narco's heroin trafficking ring. Imagine Nick decides to take the stand.

§7:130 Client May Have No Choice Other Than to Testify

Often, there is really no choice but for the client to get on the stand, and withdrawal from a conspiracy may be such a situation. You may be left with a factual situation in which your client cannot establish withdrawal from the conspiracy without taking the stand. Ask the court to again remind the client before taking the stand that there is a Fifth Amendment right to silence and that he or she cannot be forced to testify. This warning should be on the record and outside of the presence of the jury.

PRACTICE TIP: *Warn the defendant*

Always warn the defendant in writing of the benefits and detriments of taking the stand. I think that it is often malpractice to not strongly warn of the dangers of taking the stand. I have actively talked clients out of taking the stand in the middle of trial, sometimes with the help of other defense counsel who watched the evidence come in.

§7:131 Sample Direct Examination of Defendant Regarding Withdrawal

Q. Mr. Narco, how are you doing today?
A. I've been better.
Q. I imagine. Have you ever testified before?

A.   No.
Q.   You have heard the testimony given about the drug conspiracy the government alleges?
A.   Yes.
Q.   Were you a part of that drug conspiracy?
A.   Sort of. I was and then I wasn't.
Q.   Are you a drug user?
A.   Yes I am. Well, I was. I am a drug addict.
Q.   So you acknowledge possessing illegal drugs?
A.   Sure. Many times. I am a drug addict.
Q.   What kind of drugs are you addicted to?
A.   Heroin. Opiates.
Q.   You know a man named Smack Smith?
A.   Yes.
Q.   How do you know him?
A.   He used to deal me H.
Q.   What's H?
A.   Heroin.
Q.   How long did he deal you H?
A.   Almost a year.
Q.   He charged you for it?
A.   He did, and then he stopped.
Q.   Why?
A.   Because he wanted to go into business with me and Stoner.
Q.   Who's Stoner?
A.   An old friend of mine I used to get high with.
Q.   What was this business?
A.   Smack knew a guy in Rhode Island who had a bunch of H. He wanted Stoner and me to go down to Rhode Island, pick up the H, and bring it back?
Q.   What was your cut supposed to be from this?
A.   Ten grams for the delivery and more when we distributed.
Q.   Same deal for Stoner?
A.   Yes.
Q.   Who was paying for the heroin you were supposed to pick up?
A.   Smack.
Q.   You had no money in this?
A.   No.
Q.   How much heroin were you supposed to be picking up.
A.   I don't know exactly, like, 1000 or so grams.
Q.   Did you ever pick up that heroin?
A.   No.
Q.   Why not?
A.   Because I backed out.
Q.   Why?
A.   I got nervous. He was dealing with these Italians in Rhode Island that were very scary, and there were some Dominicans involved, and I freaked out.
Q.   When were you scheduled to go to Rhode Island?
A.   May 24, 2012.
Q.   When did you freak out?
A.   The night before.
Q.   Had you brought up any other drugs to Smack at this point?
A.   No, I never did; this was going to be the first time.
Q.   How did you back out?
A.   I just didn't show up.
Q.   Didn't show where?

A. I was supposed to meet up with Smack and Stoner that night of the 24th to go down and I didn't show.

Q. Did anyone go down?

A. Stoner did. He was pinched on his way back up for having a taillight out. But I backed out of it.

Q. What did you do to back out of it?

A. I texted Smack.

Q. Do you have that text?

A. No, it was erased. I checked with the phone company too, but I couldn't get it.

Q. What did it say?

A. "Not going—sorry bro."

Q. Why didn't you tell Smack in person?

A. Because he's scary.

Q. What do you mean?

A. I mean he's a scary dude. He gets wicked pissed off and it's scary.

Q. Is that why you were afraid?

A. Yes.

[§§7:132-7:139 Reserved]

V.   CULTIVATION

I like to think of marijuana cultivation cases as merely a case of the oppression of the local farmer. Unfortunately, judges and prosecutors don't share my same appreciation for the horticultural arts. Thankfully, in Maine, marijuana has been partially decriminalized. This is true in many states. Hopefully, this trend will continue, and marijuana cultivation charges will be a thing of the past.

§7:140   Analysis of Search Warrant Affidavit for Lack of Probable Cause

A proper analysis of the discovery means an analysis of the search warrant affidavit. Often we get tied up in looking at whether the warrant itself was followed and was sufficiently definite regarding the place to be searched, the time of search and so on. Sometimes we skip entirely the issue of the affidavit. Often an argument can be made that the warrant affidavit does not provide probable cause.

One thing I like to do at the outset is to see if I have, or a friend of mine in the business has, copies of other search warrants from the swearing officer. If you have viewed multiple affidavits from the same officer, you will note that most of them are written using a template. You can use this fact in your argument to suppress.

Really analyze the affidavit. Does it have indications of probable cause exclusive of hearsay? Often they do not. If they do have probable cause without needing hearsay, then you may have a good affidavit (i.e., did an undercover do a drug buy with your client?).

Many drug cases are built on snitches, however. And snitches don't like to be named in affidavits. So in the warrant affidavit, they are listed as confidential sources.

This gives you a narrow opening to try to work through. This opening was a lot wider before *Illinois v. Gates*, but it still exists.

In determining whether probable cause for a warrant exists, the magistrate applies the "totality of the circumstances" test adopted in *Illinois v. Gates,* 462 U.S. 213, 238, 103 S.Ct. 2317, 76 L.Ed.2d 527 (1983), which requires a "practical, common-sense decision whether, given all the circumstances set forth in the affidavit before him, including the 'veracity' and 'basis of knowledge' of persons supplying hearsay information, there is a fair probability that contraband or evidence of a crime will be found in a particular place."

Gates leaves some wiggle room, however. "Informants' tips doubtless come in many shapes and sizes from many different types of persons. … Rigid legal rules are ill-suited to an area of such diversity." *Gates*, 462 U.S. at 232. However, *Gates* was unequivocal that uncorroborated hearsay from a source whose credibility is itself unknown, standing alone, cannot support a finding of probable cause to issue a search warrant. *Id*. at 227.

Consider the case of a client of mine we'll call Tommy Farmer. Tommy has a felony conviction for previous drug activity, and lives in rural Maine. The local cops hate him, and are always looking to bust his chops for something or other. Over a period of years, Tommy stays clean and out of trouble.

A local yocal who claims to be friends with Tommy gets in trouble for something stupid. To lessen his own punishment, he starts telling law enforcement that Tommy is running a marijuana grow operation in his home. Another informant corroborates the information. The warrant affidavit, when stripped of its boilerplate language, has three relevant pages. They are as follows:

The facts and circumstances which lead your affiant to believe this are as follows:

1. On September 30, 2009, your affiant spoke with a confidential informant, said informant is herein referred to as 09-70. Your affiant would note that 09-70 is a completely separate and unrelated person than that of any other person providing information contained herein.

    Your affiant would note that 09-70 has provided your affiant with reliable information on drug dealers known to him/her in 2009. Your affiant would note that information provided by 09-70, which he/she has personal knowledge of, an/or that he/she obtained from associates of his/hers, has proven to be reliable and accurate. Your affiant would note that in 2009, with information primarily obtained from 09-70, which he/she obtained from an associate of his/hers, a search warrant was obtained for a suspected drug dealer/user. 09-70's information proved to be reliable and accurate, and said information was corroborated by the evidence seized and the suspect's own admissions.

    Your affiant would note that 09-70 has sold/used illicit drugs in the past, and 09-70 does personally know/associate with numerous known drug dealers/users. Further, 09-70 is a convicted felon.

    Your affiant would note that 09-70 is presently assisting your affiant in hopes that the District Attorney will take his/her cooperation into consideration regarding criminal charges that are presently pending against him/her.

2. Your affiant was advised by 09-70 that Tommy Farmer who lives in a farmhouse on Rural Road in Littleton reportedly presently has a large amount of marijuana plants drying at his residence.

    09-70 stated that Farmer and another male unknown to 09-70 reportedly recently harvested "a bunch" of marijuana plants. 09-70 stated that the marijuana plants are reportedly being dried on both floors of said barn.

    09-70 advised your affiant that in regards to the aforementioned information on Farmer, he/she received said information from an associate of his/hers who associates with Farmer and his reported male partner. According to 09-70, his/her associate advised him/her that they had seen said marijuana plants as referenced herein.

3. In regards to Farmer, your affiant is familiar with him, as well as his reported residence location. Your affiant would note that on May 22, 1997, your affiant had received information then, from an extremely reliable confidential informant (CI), regarding Farmer and his brother John, reportedly growing "all kinds" of marijuana plants, off of a road, near the herein described residence of Farmer. Your affiant was advised by the CI that a friend of his/hers had reportedly seen the marijuana plants personally. Your affiant would note that at some point in 1997, your affiant briefly flew over the reported grow areas, via a helicopter. Your affiant did not spot any marijuana plants. Your affiant would note that the exact area of said plants was not obtained by the CI, and your affiant did not thoroughly check the area around Farmer's residence so as not to tip them off. Further, the CI advised during the week of June 30, 1998, that the Farmer brothers were buying marijuana from drug dealers known to your affiant.

    On September 24, 1997, your affiant received an anonymous tip regarding marijuana plants being harvested behind 00 Rural Road a herein described residence. According to the information received, the caller's son was hunting behind the area of Farmer's residence and the son reportedly witnesses the Farmers and one of the marijuana suppliers of the Farmers' (per the info supplied by CI in 1998), "picking pot." Your affiant did not know the identity of the tipster.

4. On October 04, 2009, your affiant spoke with 09-07. 09-07 advised your affiant that Farmer still reportedly had the marijuana plants drying inside his barn, as well as marijuana plants drying in the attic area of his herein described residence. 09-70 stated that his/her associate, who had provided him/her with the prior information contained herein on Farmer had advised him/her that the marijuana plants were still being dried at this present time (October 04, 2009), at Farmer's herein described residence/barn. Your affiant would note that since September 30, 2009, the weather outside has been cool, with periods of rain. Due to this weather, if marijuana plants were being dried without the aid of heat/fans, it would take longer for said plants to dry for processing.

    09-70 advised your affiant that he/she personally knew Farmer as well as Farmer's brother, John. 09-70 stated that in past years, he/she has personally known that the Farmer's had involvement with marijuana, as he/she had used marijuana with them, as well as purchased small amounts from them. 09-70 has not personally had contact with the Farmer's lately, to include 2009.

5. In regards to Farmer, DOB/7/31/80 your affiant confirmed that Farmer does still reside at the residence in Littleton, as described by 09-70. Your affiant confirmed Farmer's address and date of birth, via the Maine Bureau of Motor Vehicles, which lists Farmer's address on his suspended driver's license as 00 Rural Road, Littleton. Your affiant also confirmed Farmer's address and date of birth via the Maine Sex Offender Registry, which also lists Farmer's address as 00 Rural Road, Littleton and Farmer's date of birth as 7/31/80. According to the registry, as of September 17, 2009, Farmer's address was confirmed as Farmer must register with the State, due to a prior felony sex crime conviction.

    Your affiant would note that Farmer's residence, per your affiant's own observation, is a white, two story single family dwelling (green metal roof/green trim), which has a long building and barn type building attached to it. Further, Farmer's residence is located at 00 Rural Road, and said residence is the first on the left hand side of the roadway, travelling east from the intersection of Rural Road and Local Street. Your affiant would note that Farmer's residence is located on the same side of the roadway, as described by 09-70.

    Your affiant would note that from September 30, 2009, through October 05, 2009, your affiant has driven by Farmer's residence once daily to see if any illicit activity could be detected. To date, your affiant has observed the same green/silver Ford truck parked in front of the barn area each day, with only one other vehicle being present, which was a white Ford car, on October 04, 2009. Your affiant did obtain the license plate number off of the Ford car, but your affiant has not been able to retrieve the license plate number off of the Ford truck. In regards to the Ford car, your affiant was unfamiliar with the registered owner of said motor vehicle.

    Your affiant would note that on October 02, 2009, Detective Sgt. Corroborator of the Somerset County Sheriff's Department walked past Farmer's residence (on the roadway), to see if he could smell the odor of marijuana. Detective Corroborator advised your affiant that he was unable to detect any marijuana odor, and further that there was a dog tied near the Ford truck in front of the barn, so he did not linger in front of said residence. Your affiant would note that the barn area is located approximately 120 feet from the roadway, so it is possible that if marijuana plants were present inside the barn as described herein, that the odor of said plants may not be detectable from the doorway.

6. Your affiant believes that Farmer, and others described herein are presently possessing marijuana/marijuana plants on their persons and/or—in/at the herein described residence/property/vehicles. Your affiant bases this conclusion on the information provided by 09-70 and others referred to herein.

    As noted herein, 09-70 was advised by his/her associate that as of October 04, 2009, Farmer still had marijuana plants drying inside his barn/attic area. Your affiant would note that 09-70 has obtained information from other associates of his/hers in 2009 which has proven to be reliable and accurate. Your affiant would also note that information has been obtained, as noted herein, regarding Farmer being involved with marijuana/marijuana plants in past years.

7. Your affiant has found it common for persons who are at drug dealers' residences and/or arrive at drug dealers' residences to possess illicit drugs on their person, and/or in their motor vehicles. Your affiant would note that if persons present at drug dealers' residences had just purchased illicit drugs from the drug dealer, then said persons would have said illicit drugs on their person and/or in their motor vehicle.

If you are not reading carefully, it is very easy to gloss over the utter lack of probable cause in the warrant affidavit. The probable cause is supposed to come from Confidential Source 09-70, but 09-70's information is stale at best. Likewise, 09-70 did not have direct information that Tommy Farmer was cultivating or drying marijuana. 09-70's information was based on his or her conversation with the anonymous informant whom the police did not speak to. As a result, while 09-70 may have been a historically reliable informant, 09-70's information is from an unknown source who may not be reliable.

§7:141   FORM 7-110 Memorandum on Defendant's Motion to Suppress—Defective Warrant Affidavit

My Memo on Defendant's Motion to Suppress in this case summarized the Warrant Affidavit as follows:

Here, when Officer Notenough's Affidavit is stripped of its boilerplate language, it contains facts that do not rise to the level of probable cause under the cases cited above. The facts amount to the following: (1) a confidential informant told Officer Notenough that the Defendant was drying marijuana in his barn and attic, (2) the confidential informant had not had any contact with the Defendant personally in 2009, (3) the confidential informant's information came from an anonymous informant who is unknown and is not named in the affidavit, (4) the reliability of the anonymous informant is not provided in the affidavit, (5) the basis of knowledge of the anonymous informant is not included in any way in the affidavit, (6) the confidential informant has provided reliable information in the past that he has received from other unknown individuals, but not the anonymous individual who gave information on the Defendant here, (7) Officer Notenough drove by the Defendant's house once a day from September 30, 2009 through October 5, 2009 to see if any elicit or illegal activity could be detected and none was detected, (8) Detective Sergeant Corroborator of the Somerset County Sheriff's Department walked past Mr. Farmer's residence to see if he could smell the odor of marijuana, and he could not, (9) on May 22, 1997, Officer Notenough received a tip that the Defendant was growing marijuana off of a road. Officer Notenough investigated the tip, flew above the suspected area via helicopter, and did not spot any marijuana plants. No charges were filed.

The information provided in the Warrant Affidavit in this case does not even make a close case for probable cause. At best, we have an anonymous informant, who is not known to be reliable, the basis of whose information is unknown, providing information to a confidential informant. The confidential informant is not a citizen informant, but is rather a confidential informant who is trying to get consideration for his or her criminal charges. The confidential informant had not had contact with the Defendant in the year 2009. As a result, all the information that we have is from the unknown and unreliable informant.

These warrant affidavits lacking probable cause are more common than you think. Defense counsel just often misses them. The phone may be ringing off the hook and you may be late for court already, but you need to read these warrants carefully and critically.

Warrant affidavits based on hearsay will almost always have circumstantial police corroboration to get over the hump of *Illinois v. Gates*. Sometimes, the attempts at corroboration, such as those here, actually fail to corroborate.

In Mr. Farmer's case, the police tried to bolster the credibility of 09-70's information. They claimed that there had been two anonymous tips regarding Tommy growing marijuana. Those tips, however, were from 1997 (this case took place in 2009-2010). Mr. Farmer was not charged as a result of those tips.

§7:142   Sample Cross-Examination of Cop at Suppression Hearing

In Tommy's case, the cops attempt to bolster hearsay was fruitless. They drove by the house, stopped and looked for evidence of a grow operation, and found nothing. When they find nothing in such a situation, or neglect to perform a basic investigatory function, throw it back in their faces at the motion to suppress hearing.[27]

Q. You drove by the house once a day between September 30, 2009 and October 5, 2009?
A. Yes.
Q. That's seven days straight that you went to the defendant's house?
A. Yes.
Q. You were trying to look for information of criminal activity?
A. Yes.
Q. You were doing this because you wanted to corroborate marijuana cultivation claims made by your informant?
A. We try to corroborate what any witness tells us.
Q. Getting corroboration yourself is important?
A. I believe so.
Q. Did you get out of your car on any of those trips and smell around for the odor of marijuana?
A. Yes.
Q. You've been trained what the smell of fresh marijuana is?
A. Yes.
Q. You were trained well, weren't you?
A. I was.

---

[27] Depending on your jurisdiction, you may or may not be entitled to a testimonial hearing if you are merely arguing probable cause. Some judges and some jurisdictions will limit your argument to the four corners of the warrant affidavit.

Q. And you were trained in the smell of burnt marijuana weren't you?
A. Yes.
Q. You've investigated marijuana grow houses before?
A. Yes.
Q. You can smell marijuana from the outside of a grow house sometimes can't you?
A. You can.
Q. It is common when you have a suspected grow house to try to smell for the odor of fresh marijuana or smoked marijuana?
A. Yes.
Q. You also wanted to see if there was any marijuana being grown in plain sight, but didn't see anything?
A. I did not.
Q. You didn't see gardens of any kind?
A. No.
Q. Did you see any bags of fertilizer?
A. No.
Q. Were the windows to the house or barn blacked out?
A. No.
Q. It is common in marijuana grow houses to see blacked out windows, isn't it?
A. I have seen them before.
Q. But you didn't see them here?
A. No.
Q. Often windows are blacked out because of the grow lights used to grow marijuana?
A. Yes.
Q. You didn't see any evidence of grow lights on Mr. Farmer's property?
A. No.
Q. Did you see any marijuana stalks on the property?
A. No.
Q. You didn't observe any illegal activity in the seven days you drove by his house?
A. No.
Q. You ran the registration on all the cars on my client's property?
A. Yes.
Q. And you didn't find anything corroborating what the confidential source told you?
A. I did not.
Q. There was nothing illegal observed?
A. No.
Q. There were no people coming and going that looked like customers?
A. There were not.

Happily, we won that motion to suppress and the case against our client was dismissed.

(This page intentionally left blank.)

CHAPTER 8

DRUNK DRIVING CASES

Drunk driving cases are among the most commonly charged criminal cases. As a result, they have become a somewhat specialized practice area, with specialists in drunk driving law spending their entire careers on this one type of crime. That is not a bad thing. There are plenty of intricacies with drunk driving cases and a constant flow of clients.

Drunk driving presents an interesting intersection of science and law. Those who truly specialize in drunk driving cases (unlike myself) become as proficient in the chemistry as a chemist. They understand toxicology like a toxicologist. They know this area backwards and forwards.

Since my practice does not specialize in drunk driving cases, I have approached them from a different perspective. I hope my strategies and experiences are helpful to you.

_____

(This page intentionally left blank.)

I.   ELEMENTS AND COMMON SCENARIOS

§8:01   The Elements

Depending on the jurisdiction, there are three primary elements to drunk driving. They are:
- Operating or driving a vehicle,
- While intoxicated by alcohol or under the influence of an impairing substance,
- On a public road or in a public area. (Some states do not require this element).

Drunk driving statutes have two definitions of impaired driving. Most states define a blood-alcohol level of .08 percent or higher as a per se offense for drivers over the age of 21 while operating a private vehicle. Lower limits exist for commercial drivers and those under the age of 21. If the driver has a blood-alcohol level in excess of the legal limit, then the driver is deemed guilty of a DUI regardless of the level of actual physical impairment.

A driver can be convicted of drunk driving with a blood alcohol concentration (BAC) under the legal limit. This is a performance based test. Evidence of a driver's impairment can be based on observable behavior such as erratic driving, field sobriety tests, and other factors. However, a blood-alcohol level below the legal limit, or the absence of a blood-alcohol test, typically makes it more difficult for the state to win a conviction.

§8:02   The Non-Criminal Drunk Driver

Many of the people I represent are criminals. No two ways around it. They are the traditional, cut every corner, find every angle, scam everyone they can, criminal. For these folks, when I see them and ask how things are going, they might say "I've got a few things I'm working on." When they say that, they don't mean they are working on painting a DaVinci reproduction. They are working on stealing a DaVinci.

Drunk driving defendants are very often not criminals, in my view at least. They may have committed a crime, but they are not ever looking to do it again. They are your average citizen. They had one too many and they got charged.

In many ways, representing these folks represents a lot of opportunity. They are usually scared. If they trust you, you shouldn't have client control issues. And if you manage to exceed expectations, they will refer all their friends your way because they will be so relieved to have survived the process.

§8:03   The Criminal Drunk Driver

The criminal drunk driver is the bad drunk. He or she has been charged with drunk driving multiple times. The criminal drunk driver also tends to have very high breath and blood tests.

I once represented a fellow who was out on bail for an assault on his girlfriend. I was working on the DV assault. It was clear that this guy was heartbroken, and had a bad alcohol problem. He also had a prior drunk driving conviction.

After the DV incident, he went on a bender. His girlfriend lived on the east end of Portland, near the Eastern Promenade, which looks out to the Atlantic. My guy, who couldn't stay away from her after drinking all day, started to circle around her house in his car. One time by, he passed out, and sideswiped six cars parked along the Eastern Promenade. The collision must have jolted him awake, and he continued circling the house. By the time he got back to the Eastern Promenade in his next circle, he passed out again, colliding with four more vehicles. He was a .44 by blood testing.

This gentleman is a criminal drunk driver. Identifying the criminal from the non-criminal drunk driver is significant. My guy with the .44 is pretty easy to identify. Sometimes you need to dig deeper. You need to understand the history of your client, recognizing that the client wants to look good for you. Tell the client that, to help him, you need to truly understand him, warts and all.

§8:04   Alcohol Counseling/Rehabilitation

While a first offense .11 will likely go to a licensed alcohol and drug counselor for a substance abuse evaluation, the hard core drinkers and those with multiple drunk driving convictions, even without a high test, need serious treatment. For my guy with the .44, it was 30 days inpatient and then a year in a good halfway house program with addiction resources (nowadays referred to as Sober Houses or Recovery Residences).

The initial substance abuse screening process is the first step. Stress the need with your client to be honest so the right treatment can be determined. It is important that the client know that this is a confidential process, and that we will only share information with the prosecutor if the client wants us to and if it will help.

That initial evaluation should help you judge the level of intervention needed. For those who need inpatient help, assist them in getting it. Most will only need good counseling. There is no "one size fits all," however.

[§§8:05-8:09 Reserved]

II.   CLIENT QUESTIONS AND MATERIALS

§8:10   The Initial Client Meeting

I have recommended elsewhere in this book that it is exceedingly important that attorneys spend significant time with their clients in their initial client meeting. I think it is important in all cases to get to know your client.

The drunk driving case sometimes requires more hand-holding than many other cases, however. In my practice, and probably in yours, the majority of the drunk driving cases are first offense cases. Among those first offense cases, the majority of our clients are also experiencing their first criminal charge.

As a result, even though we eat, sleep and breathe criminal defense every day, this is a completely new and scary experience for most drunk driving defendants. Chances are, if you have a robbery defendant, it's not his or her first rodeo. The robbery defendant knows what a motion to suppress is. The drunk driving defendant likely has no clue whatsoever. So you need to take the time out of your busy day and educate her.

Also be sure to establish reasonable expectations related to mandatory minimum fines, jail time, and other probable consequences. My father always taught me to lower expectations, then exceed them. It's good advice, but it is tricky. You don't want to scare the holy hell out of your client, but you also want to address realistic worries about the case. You want to set up a bad result/good result framework you can analyze like a report card throughout the case.

In nearly every criminal case, I like to set a list of priorities with my client. How does the client rank the priorities of a conviction over the priority over no jail time? Over license suspension issues?

Let's say you have a felony drunk driving case where jail time is a real option. I might want to try to come to a meeting of the minds with the client over our priorities in going forward. It might look like this: Priority 1, no felony. Priority 2, no jail. Priority 3, no conviction whatsoever. Priority 4, minimize license suspension consequences.

These discussions are very important, because they become part of getting to know your client. Perhaps one client already has a felony for something else, doesn't care about jail time, but really wants to keep his license because he is a truck driver. Knowing that, and shuffling his priorities, allows me to get creative with the prosecutor so that we can meet their needs of providing just punishment (if needed) and my client's need to protect his license.

My office uses a form that we ask the potential client to fill out when she first comes into the office. There may be information that you need that the client has, but doesn't think is relevant. I like to use the form as a jumping off point for our discussions as to how to handle the case.

§8:11   FORM 8-10 Intake Questions

OUI Intake Questions
1.   Date of Arrest   _____
2.   Time of Arrest   _____
3.   Town/Municipality where arrest Occurred: _____
4.   Court Date: _____
5.   Place of Court: _____
6.   Street or Location where you were stopped: _____
7.   Was there a breath test taken at the scene: _____
8.   If yes, what was the result:_____
9.   Was there a blood test taken: _____
10. If yes, what was the result:_____
11. Is this your first arrest for OUI/DUI/DWI Drunk Driving in your lifetime-anywhere?   _____

12. Please list all prior OUI/DUI/DWI/Drunk Driving arrests (even if dismissed) below, including year, city/state, and outcome (if known):

Year	City/State	Outcome of Case	Attorney
_____	_____	_____	_____
_____	_____	_____	_____
_____	_____	_____	_____

13. Are you currently on probation/parole for any OUI or criminal case: _____

14. Did you receive any other tickets/charges received with your present OUI charge: If yes, what for?

_____

_____

_____

15. Did the officer tell you why s/he stopped you? _____

16. If yes, why were you stopped?

_____

17. Was there an accident? _____

18. Was anyone injured? (Check all that apply)?

19. If yes, who was injured?

_____

20. Was anyone transported to the hospital? _____

21. Were you given field sobriety tests at the scene, hospital or police station? ___

22. Which tests were you given? (Check all that apply)
    - ☐ Portable Breath Test at scene
    - ☐ Eye Test (also known as Horizontal Gaze Nystagmus)
    - ☐ Walk the Line
    - ☐ Finger to Nose
    - ☐ Counting
    - ☐ Alphabet
    - ☐ Stand on one leg

    Other:

_____

_____

23. Did the police tell you that the tests were optional? (you could refuse)? _____

24. Is it possible that there were drugs/medications in your system? _____

25. Were you under any kind of doctors care on the date of your arrest? _____

26. Are there any witnesses who were with you before or during your driving that can testify for you?

_____

27. If yes, who? _____

_____

28. Do you have any prior injuries, or present disabilities, that might have affected your driving or testing that night/day? _____

29. Did the officer ask you if you had any injuries or disabilities that would affect your field sobriety tests?

_____

After the stop:

30. Did you tell the officer you had been drinking?

31. Did the officer ask you to rate your impairment on a scale of 1-10?

32. Do you remember what you were wearing for clothes? Shoes?

33. Do you remember what the weather was like?

[§§8:12-8:19 Reserved]

III.   STRATEGIES AND TACTICS

A. Preservation of Evidence

§8:20   Put Law Enforcement on Notice

In Chapter 2, I included my "Notice to Preserve Evidence to Law Enforcement" form (Form 2-10). This form should be supplemented in drunk driving cases, however.

It is important before discovery even begins to put the law enforcement agency on notice of their preservation duties. You should tailor your notice to your specific case situation, but preservation of such electronic evidence as cruiser cam recordings, interview room videos, and booking room videos are of crucial importance in many cases. Of course, you need to know your client before making the request. If your client tells you he was falling down during the field sobriety testing because he was so wasted, maybe you want to forget about providing the notice for that case.

§8:21   FORM 8-20 Notice to Preserve Electronic Evidence—Drunk Driving Cases

Date

Department
Address
Town, State Zip Code

     RE: State of Maine v. _____
          Docket No. CR-__-_____

Dear Court Officer,

     I represent _____ regarding an Operating Under the Influence arrest by your department on _____, _____. I am aware that certain items of evidence may be routinely disposed of prior to arraignment. To avoid any prejudice to my client I ask that you take reasonable steps to preserve any audiotapes, videotapes, call logs, officers' notes or other notes or other items of evidence in the possession of your department. With regard to radio and telephone call tapes and logs, I ask you to preserve them from the time of the first call relating to my client to the time of his release from custody. For general surveillance tapes such as those of booking areas, Intoxilyzer areas, etc., I ask that you preserve those that were taken while my client was present at the station.

     This is not a request that you provide me with these materials; I understand that I must go through the discovery process to obtain information. My goal is to preserve the items in the event they are needed in the defense of my client. By copy of this letter I am requesting that the District Attorney provide copies of all of the referenced materials to me as soon as possible.

     Thank you for your anticipated cooperation.

Respectfully submitted,

_____
Timothy E. Zerillo
Attorney for Defendant
ZERILLO LAW FIRM, LLC

TEZ/dar
cc: Client
_____ County District Attorney

[§§8:22-8:29 Reserved]

B. Qualifications of Arresting Officer and Breath Test Operator

§8:30   Don't Assume Qualifications

It is a mistake to assume the arresting officer or breath test operator is qualified to test your client. Field sobriety testing and breath testing require certifications. The cops often administer tests they have no right to administer. You can get these tests tossed based entirely on the officer's lack of qualification in some instances. And if you can't get them tossed, you can certainly do a lot of damage on cross-examination.

Usually, you can find out what the officer's certifications are by checking with your state's criminal justice academy. A simple letter should suffice.

§8:31   FORM 8-30 Letter Requesting Breath Machine Operator's Credentials

Officer Certification Records
Maine Criminal Justice Academy
15 Oak Grove Road
Vassalboro, Maine 04989

RE: State of Maine v.
Officer Intox, Portland Police Department
Certificate # 12345

Dear Sir or Madam:

I am writing to request that you kindly provide my office with proof that Officer Intox was certified to operate an Intoxilyzer 5000 on February 14, 2018. Please also provide proof that Officer Intox was qualified and deemed proficient to perform the HGN test on February 14, 2018. Also, please provide any other information relating to his training/certification relating to OUI investigation generally. I would also appreciate your telling me which version of the MCJA manual Officer Intox was trained with. I understand you receive significant requests for similar information and do sincerely appreciate your cooperating with my request. Obviously, I am requesting this material as I represent an individual charged with an OUI offense where Officer Intox was the Intoxilyzer operator.

Please bill this firm in the amount of $10.00 to cover the cost of this request. I appreciate your attention to this matter.

Respectfully submitted,

_____

Timothy E. Zerillo
Attorney for Defendant
ZERILLO LAW FIRM, LLC

§8:32   The Response

Your criminal justice academy should then provide in response to your request, a sheet similar to this:

05/19/2009 10:33   8778027   MCJA   PAGE 01/01

STATE OF MAINE
DEPARTMENT OF PUBLIC SAFETY
MAINE CRIMINAL JUSTICE ACADEMY
15 OAK GROVE ROAD
VASSALBORO, MAINE
04989

John Elias Baldacci
Governor

Anne H. Jordan
Commissioner

John B. Rogers
Director

Zerillo Law, LLC
Attorneys at Law
57 Exchange Street
Suite 103
P.O. Box 17721
Portland, ME 04112

RE: █████

Dear █████

We received your letter regarding the intoxilyzer certification on Officer ████████████ of the Portland Police Department. Officer █████ certifications are listed below.

Date of intoxilyzer certification	01/09/08 – 03/31/2011
SFST training	none
OUI/SFST refresher	01/21/08 and 01/05/09
SFST Proficiency	none shown in our records
Intoxilyzer manual	2005 version
DRE/OUI Investigation Refresher	2005

If I can be of further assistance please do not hesitate to call me at 877-8009 or e-mail james.a.lyman@maine.gov

Sincerely,

James Lyman
Training Coordinator

cc: Officer █████ Portland Police Department

PHONE (207) 877-8000   FAX (207) 877-8027   TTY 1-888-654-1244

Reading that sheet, if the Officer completed a Valentine's Day 2018 stop, he's got problems and our client's in good shape. His intoxilyzer certification had lapsed. Additionally, he's never received standardized field sobriety test (SFST) training or proficiency. Good news for anyone arrested by him.

You never know what you will find when you make these requests, so make them, and don't assume the officer who arrested your client was competent.

[§§8:33-8:39 Reserved]

C. The Arresting Officer's Story

§8:40   Talk to the Officer

Perhaps it is a reflection of my intellectual functioning, but I like the K.I.S.S. theory of legal preparation—*Keep it Simple, Stupid*. One very often overlooked, yet simple thing to do, is call the arresting officer on the phone and talk to him or her about the case. Talking to the cop can be especially helpful if your client behaved decently and has a good story.

Tell the cop your client's sob story. Her husband is an abusive son of a bitch. His wife is cheating on him. Pick a story from your client's life that may make the officer a little bit sympathetic.

I can't tell you how many cops I have talked out of going to bureau of motor vehicle hearings. If the cop no shows, my client keeps her license. While you may lose your ability to cross-examine the officer, your client's license is often so important to her that it is worth it if you can convince the cop to not show up.

I have talked cops into advocating for my client with the prosecutor's office. I even once had an arresting cop show up to testify at a sentencing for my client. My client was going through a divorce, had kids and a deadbeat abusive husband. The officer seemed sympathetic to her at the arrest, so I asked him to help with the District Attorney. It took an officer who was unusually sympathetic and the right circumstance, but it can happen.

Usually it won't work, but sometimes it will. At the least your client will see you as a hustler, and you can't knock the hustle.

§8:41   License Suspension Hearing

State laws on license suspension for pending drunk driving cases and for drunk driving convictions vary widely. As a result, I won't attempt to go into the intricacies of the bureau of motor vehicles hearing because of those variations.

If your jurisdiction suspends your client's license based on the charge alone, without any conviction to base the suspension on, you nearly always need to have a hearing before the DMV. In my jurisdiction, the officer will be provided, as long as you request the hearing within a certain period of time after the notice of suspension. In other jurisdictions you may need to subpoena the arresting officer. Getting the officer under oath and in a recording or transcript can be invaluable to your case, even if you don't have a prayer of getting the bureau of motor vehicles to restore your client's license. Since you have criminal charges pending, cross-examining the officer under oath and pinning him down as much as possible is important. Whenever you can get the cop to commit to specifics at the motor vehicle hearing do so, and then expose all the problems with his methodology at trial.

[§§8:42-8:49 Reserved]

D. Prior Convictions

§8:50   Strike Prior Convictions

Always consider the possibility of striking any prior convictions your client has in all second offense or higher cases. As you know, multiple drunk driving offenses means much higher punishments and usually mandatory minimums. Winning a motion to strike a prior drunk driving conviction can essentially win you your case.

The way we have had the most success attacking these is simply to find out if our client had counsel for the prior convictions. We have found that uncounseled pleas for first offense cases, where a fine is the only real punishment the client is aware of, are abundant.

Whenever possible, get the recording or transcript of the plea colloquy prior to filing your motion. Sometimes time does not allow this, and you will need to file your motion first. If you can get the recording or transcript, focus on the rights warnings given by the judge, which are often deficient.

In Maine, people arrested are brought before a judge if not already bailed within 48 hours of the arrest. A Lawyer of the Day is there for this group of citizens. Many enter pleas without the benefit of individual counsel. Many more enter pleas at their initial appearance without counsel, and, because they are not incarcerated, without access to the Lawyer of the Day. If they are looking for court appointed counsel, lawyers often are not assigned prior to the initial appearance. For first offense drunk driving cases below a .15, they are offered the mandatory minimum fine for a plea. Many take it. The fine is a lot less than the cost of a private lawyer.

The minimum requirement upon entry of a plea is that the defendant must be informed of the right of counsel, of all of the elements of the offense, and of the penalties that he faces when entering a plea of guilty. *Iowa v. Tovar*, 541 U.S. 77, 81 (U.S. 2004). When you review the record of the hearing, often the court informs the *pro se* defendant of his or her right to have a lawyer present only, not the maximum penalties and certainly not the collateral consequences for future charges. As a result, there is an opportunity to strike those convictions so they cannot be used in sentencing your client.

§8:51   FORM 8-40 Motion to Strike Prior Convictions

STATE OF MAINE   SUPERIOR COURT
CUMBERLAND, ss.   DOCKET NO. CR-14-1234

STATE OF MAINE,	)	
	)	
v.	)	MOTION TO STRIKE
	)	PRIOR CONVICTION
PETE PRIOR,	)	
	)	
Defendant	)	

Now comes the Defendant, Pete Prior, by and through Undersigned Counsel, Timothy E. Zerillo, and moves this Court to strike from the indictment or Complaint the allegation that DEFENDANT was convicted of "OPERATING UNDER THE INFLUENCE" on December 24, 2010 in the Portland District Court, Docket No. CR-10-4321 The grounds for this motion are that the alleged conviction was obtained without a valid waiver of counsel. A memorandum of law in support of this motion is set forth, below.

FACTS

The following facts are set forth on information and belief by counsel after reviewing the relevant tape recording at the Electronic Recording Division. A transcript has been ordered and will be submitted when it is obtained from the ERD.

On December 24, 2010, DEFENDANT appeared before Judge Soandso in the Portland District Court for a change of plea on a charge of Operating Under the Influence (OUI). Judge Soandso's plea colloquy did not inform DEFENDANT of the maximum penalty for OUI and did not inform him of the elements of the offense. A jail sentence of forty eight hours, a fine and license suspension were imposed.

At the time DEFENDANT entered a plea, he did not know the range of penalties he was facing, nor did he fully understand the elements of the offense of OUI.

DEFENDANT is now charged with felony OUI, upon this prior conviction. He moves to strike the allegation of that prior conviction, thus reducing this charge to one of OUI, Class D.

DISCUSSION OF LAW

A prior conviction may be used to enhance a current offense only if the prior conviction was constitutionally obtained. *State v. Cook*, 1998 Me. 40, ¶ 11; 708 A.2d 603, 606. A prior misdemeanor conviction obtained without counsel is generally available for enhancement where no jail sentence was imposed because there is no right to counsel in such a case. *Id.* A conviction for a charge in which there is a right to counsel that is obtained without a valid waiver of counsel, however, is tantamount to no conviction at all.

If the accused, however, is not represented by counsel and has not competently and intelligently waived his constitutionally right, the Sixth Amendment stands as a jurisdictional bar to a valid conviction and sentence depriving him of his life and his liberty…The judgment of conviction pronounced by a court without jurisdiction is void, and one imprisoned thereunder may obtain release by habeas corpus. *Johnson v. Zerbst*, 304 U.S. 458, 82 L. Ed.1461, 58 S. Ct. 1019 (1938).

While *habeas corpus* relief is available in some circumstances, a defendant who faces an enhanced sentence on the basis of such a conviction may collaterally attack the prior conviction within the case in which the state seeks the enhancement. *Custis v. United States*, 511 U.S. 485, 494 (U.S. 1994).

Where a jail sentence is imposed in the absence of counsel, a plea or conviction is unconstitutional unless a valid waiver of counsel and election to appear *pro se* appears on the record. *Cook*, 1998 Me. 40, ¶ 11. An accused may elect to proceed without counsel. This election requires that he be made aware of the dangers of self-representation. The record must reflect that he knows what he is doing and makes a choice with his/her eyes wide open. Where a voluntary, knowing and intelligent waiver does not appear on the record, the conviction is constitutionally invalid. *State v. Tomah*, 560 A.2d. 575 (Me. 1989).

Informing a defendant of the right to counsel and the other elements of a valid waiver consists of more than an *en masse* recitation of rights to an assembly of defendants prior to individual arraignments. *State v. Rowell*, 468 A.2d 1005, 1007 n.3 (Me. 1983). "The court must also take some "affirmative steps reasonably designed to make each defendant himself aware of his individual right[s]…." *State v. Holmes*, 2003 ME 42, ¶ 9, 818 A.2d 1054 (Me. 2003), quoting *Rowell*, 468 A.2d at 1007-08.

A waiver is "woefully inadequate" even where the defendant is individually informed of the right to counsel and that counsel will be appointed if the defendant is indigent. In order to be valid, a waiver must also reflect the defendant's understanding of the role of counsel and the consequences of proceeding *pro se*, coupled with a voluntary waiver of counsel. *Tomah*, 560 A.2d at 575-576. "[B]ecause it is a fundamental constitutional right, the right to representation by counsel requires that every reasonable presumption must be indulged against waiver. *State v. Watson*, 2006 ME 80, ¶ 15.

The minimum requirement upon entry of a plea is that the defendant must be informed of the right of counsel, of all of the elements of the offense, and of the penalties that he faces when entering a plea of guilty. *Iowa v. Tovar*, 541 U.S. 77, 81 (U.S. 2004). This inquiry by the court must appear on the record. *Cook*, 1998 Me. 40, ¶ 11. In this case the record shows DEFENDANT was only informed of the right to counsel. No inquiry was made regarding the elements or the maximum penalties at any time.

WHEREFORE the defendant respectfully requests that this court strike the prior conviction in Docket No. CR-10-4321 and preclude the State from arguing the fact of that conviction at sentencing. There is no evidence that Pete Prior was aware and knowingly waived his right to the same.

Dated this 14th day of November, 2014, at Portland, Maine.

Respectfully submitted,

_____

Timothy E. Zerillo
Attorney for Defendant
ZERILLO LAW FIRM, LLC

DRUNK
DRIVING CASES

STATE OF MAINE
CUMBERLAND, ss.

SUPERIOR COURT
DOCKET NO. CR-14-1234

STATE OF MAINE,   )
)
v.   )
)
PETE PRIOR,   )
)
Defendant   )

ORDER ON MOTION TO STRIKE PRIOR CONVICTION

Defendant's Motion to Strike Prior Conviction is hereby:

_____   GRANTED

_____   DENIED

Dated: _____

_____
Judge/Justice, Maine District Court

[§§8:52-8:59 Reserved]

E. Field Sobriety Testing

§8:60 The Standardized Tests

Field sobriety testing provides an ample opportunity for you to test your cross examination skills and to punch holes in the Government case. To do so, you need to understand the testing.

There are only three standardized tests, the Horizontal Gaze Nystagmus (HGN) test, the Walk and Turn test, and the One Leg Stand test. As a result of testing done by the National Highway Traffic Safety Administration in the 1970's, these test were determined to correlate well with impairment when they are used together and administered correctly. All other tests given by the officers are non-standardized tests. This means their reliability is in doubt, which needs to be pointed out to the jury.

§8:61 Horizontal Gaze Nystagmus (HGN)

Nystagmus is a slight jerking of the eye. Ingesting alcohol and certain other drugs causes Horizontal Gaze Nystagmus (HGN).

Proper administration of the HGN test, like all standardized tests, is crucial to its reliability. To perform the HGN test properly, the officer uses a stimulus, which the subject's eye is to follow. The stimulus needs to be small—the officer can't use a flashlight. A pen light, however, is sufficient. The officer is supposed to position the stimulus approximately 12 to 15 inches from the subject's nose slightly above eye level to begin. Starting with the left eye, the officer should then move the stimulus to bring the eye as far to the side as it can go and back.

The officer is to complete two passes with the stimulus on each eye. The officer is to observe if there is lack of smooth pursuit of the eye, nystagmus occurring prior to a 45 degree angle, and nystagmus at maximum deviation. It should take four seconds to get to the 45 degree angle. The officer is to look for as many as six clues while performing the HGN test.

Of course, there are a great many reasons why nystagmus may be present without intoxication. Some individuals have naturally occurring nystagmus. The case of *State of Maine v. Taylor*, 694 A.2d 907 (1997) indicates there are 38 other causes of nystagmus unrelated to alcohol.

PRACTICE TIP: *Find an optometrist*

Since a certain percentage of the population has nystagmus naturally, you need to develop a relation-ship with an optometrist. Whenever you get a case with a failed HGN test, you need to send the client to that optometrist and ask for a report to be sent to you. In many cases, you can knock out the HGN test this way.

Part of your job then, in discrediting the HGN findings against your client, is to determine other legitimate reasons why nystagmus would be present in your client other than drunk driving. Following are a few ideas:

Rotational nystagmus occurs when the person is spun around or rotated rapidly, causing the fluid in the inner ear to be disturbed. If you played the game as a kid where you put your head on one end of a baseball bat, put the other end on the ground and spun around, you would experience rotational nystagmus.

Post-rotational nystagmus is similar to rotational nystagmus. When the person stops rotating, the fluid in the inner ear remains disturbed for a period of time, and the eyes continue to jerk. So, if you did the spin with the baseball bat and then stood up, you would likely experience post-rotational nystagmus for a period.

Caloric nystagmus occurs when fluid motion in the canals of the vestibular system are excited by temperature extremes, like having hot water in one ear and cold in the other.

Optokinetic nystagmus is among the types of nystagmus based on neural activity. It occurs when the eyes fixate on an object that suddenly moves out of sight, or when the eyes watch sharply contrasting moving images. When an officer forgets to turn off his blue lights when completing the HGN testing, your client may have a defense that the nystagmus was not alcohol related. This is a very common occurrence that you can pick up in cruiser cam videos.

Pathologic nystagmus can occur in people with certain types of pathological disorders. They include brain tumors and other brain damage or some diseases of the inner ear. These are not terribly common, but keep them in mind.

§8:62   Divided Attention: Walk and Turn and One Leg Stand

The Walk and Turn and One Leg Stand tests are divided attention tests. The walk and turn requires nine heel to toe steps along a line, a pivot and a return of nine steps back. The one leg stand requires that the subject stand with one foot six inches off the ground and count to 30 by thousands. These tests are designed to test a person's ability to do two or more simple tasks at once. Like patting your head and rubbing your belly at the same time.

A reasonably dry, flat, hard surface is required to perform both tests according to the National Highway Safety Administration. The testing surface should always be attacked, and strategies for doing so in cross-examination are included in §8:167.

[§§8:63-8:69 Reserved]

F.   Breath Testing

1.   Basics

§8:70   Breath Machines Measure Breath Alcohol

No matter what type of breath test machine you encounter, the Datamaster, the Intoxilyzer or any other machine, you need to remember one thing: the machines are merely measuring breath alcohol and attempting to convert that into blood alcohol. Blood alcohol is an assumption of the machine.

§8:71   How Do I Read This Test Result?

So you get your discovery and in it is a printout showing your clients Intoxilyzer 5000EN breath test results. It looks like this:

DRUNK
DRIVING CASES

```
                S T A T E   O F   M A I N E
             Intoxilyzer - Alcohol Analyzer - ME Model 5000EN
         SN 68-010899              SANFORD PD              Date: 04/14/2011
                                  Copy 3 of 5
   SUBJECT ════════════════════════════════════════════════════════════════
   |   Name:      ████        ████      ●        ████              M    |
   |              Last        First     MI       DOB              Sex   |
   ARREST ═════════════════════════════════════════════════════════════════
   |  Officer: ALLEN                     Agency: SANFORD PD              |
   |    Date: 04/14/11                     Time: 21:55                  |
   |  Location:    MOUNT HOPE RD         SANFORD             YORK        |
   |                 Street                City             County       |
   ├─────────── TEST ═══════════════════════════════════════════════════┤
   |      Operator: CHAD M ALLEN              Cert. No: 05332            |
   |      Test Type: OUI              Start of wait period: 23:00        |
   |                                                                     |
   |         TEST           BrAC           TIME                          |
   |                                                                     |
   |      AIR BLANK         .000        23:16 EDT                        |
   |      INTERNAL 1        .100        23:16 EDT                        |
   |      INTERNAL 2        .196        23:16 EDT                        |
   |      INTERNAL 3        .295        23:16 EDT                        |
   |      AIR BLANK         .000        23:16 EDT                        |
   |      CAL. CHECK        .085        23:17 EDT                        |
   |      AIR BLANK         .000        23:17 EDT                        |
   |      SUBJECT TEST      .202        23:18 EDT                        |
   |        BREATH VOL.    1.580 LITERS                                  |
   |      AIR BLANK         .000        23:19 EDT                        |
   |      AIR BLANK         .000        23:20 EDT                        |
   |      SUBJECT TEST      .189        23:21 EDT                        |
   |        BREATH VOL.    1.643 LITERS                                  |
   |      AIR BLANK         .000        23:21 EDT                        |
```

TEST RESULT: 0.19 grams of Alcohol per 210L of breath.

CERTIFICATION

Signed: _____   Certified Operator.   3/28/11

Personally appeared before me the above named CHAD ALLEN   DHS Approval

and made oath that the statements contained in the foregoing certificate are true.

4/14/11   _____

Date   Notary Public

Rodney J. Storman
Notary Public, State of Maine
My Commission Expires August 2, 2014

SECRETARY OF STATE

The basic biographical data of the subject is included, as well as the breath test operator's information. Even though a certification number for the operator appears on the report, it isn't necessarily the operator's own number. Even if it is the operator's number, the operator's certification may not be current. See §8:30 for checking the operator's credentials.

Check the basics. I have seen these test results list the manufacturer of the machine in the spot where the police department name should go. A good ground for cross-examination for sure.

Perhaps you are baffled by what all these numbers mean. When you understand the numbers and their reference points, understanding breath testing itself is considerably easier.

In our test, you see six Air Blanks. An Air Blank simply purges the breath path and clears the sample chamber. This is done with the air of the room.

Next, you see three Internals. Internal tests are looking at the calibration of the machine within acceptable parameters. The internal standards are .100 for Internal 1, .200 for Internal 2 and .300 for Internal 3. These are all at a rate of plus or minus 5 percent. The internals are just a measuring stick. Light is run through a special filter. That filter is designed to absorb light that corresponds to the internal standards of .1 for internal 1, .2 for internal 2, and .3 for internal 3. An alcohol value within 5% of those amounts must be returned or the machine isn't working correctly.

In our example, Internal 1 is .100, which is right on the money. Internals 2 and 3 fall within the plus or minus 5 percent range. As a result, the internal tests for this machine for this test were acceptable.

You will also see Breath Volume recorded in the testing. A Breath Volume of 1.1 liters is necessary for the test to properly function. Additionally, if you have high Breath Volume of 7 or more liters, this will cause an error. Here, the subject's Breath Volume on each test is 1.58 liters and 1.643 liters, both within acceptable ranges.

Then, of course you see Subject Test. Those are the actual breath tests of your client, here measuring .202 and .189.

[§§8:72-8:79 Reserved]

2. Attacking Breath Tests

§8:80   The Observation Period

Always check your case for a violation of the wait or observation period. The observation period, usually 15 or 20 minutes, requires that the officer observe the subject to ensure that the subject puts nothing in the mouth and does not belch, regurgitate, or vomit. The purpose of the observation period is to ensure there is no mouth alcohol present during the testing.

Booking room videos are extremely helpful in this regard. Law enforcement has caught on to include in their forms that they observed your client for the full observation period, when the video often shows them either not looking at your client and playing Solitaire on the computer, or leaving the room. Also, if you time the wait period, they are sometimes short on time as well.

If we look in our example sheet, the observation period appears to have been followed. The wait period began at 23:00 and the first Air Blank was at 23:16. There was a 16 minute wait period, therefore, if keyed in properly by the officer, and assuming the officer actually observed the subject.

§8:81   The Blood Breath Partition Ratio

Breath testing equipment like the Intoxilyzer 5000EN and the Datamaster set the blood breath partition ratio at 2100:1. The ratio assumes that the concentration of alcohol in a person's blood is 2100 times the concentration of alcohol in the person's breath. This is an assumption based on averages. This also provides an opportunity for attack.

Actual blood breath partition ratios vary widely from the machine's 2100:1 ratio. Edward F. Fitzgerald noted in his book that Chemist Kurt M. Dubowski and others have found the normal range of our populations varies from 1100:1 to 3000:1. The effect of the true range on the assumption of the test can be profound. As Fitzgerald states: "All breath test devices, for example, will report a 0.10% for a subject who has a true BAC of 0.07% if he or she has a partition ratio of 1500:1 (instead of 2100:1), and conversely, a 0.10% for a subject who has a true 0.14%, if he or she has a partition ratio of 3000:1."

One of the factors that can affect the partition ratio is breath temperature. A higher breath temperature will increase evaporation and lower the partition ratio. The machine assumes the breath temperature to be 34 degrees

Celsius. The actual range of breath temperature is between 33.6 and 37 degrees Celsius. Actual breath temperature over the assumed breath temperature also produces increased false positives. A number of states have amended their drunk driving per se charge to define the offense in terms of grams of alcohol per 210 liters of breath. The amended definition may mean that partition ratio evidence is inadmissible at least to defend against a per se charge because it doesn't matter what the person's blood alcohol was, although it may still be admissible to defend against a charge of driving while impaired.

§8:82   Mouth Jewelry

This is a simple one, but don't forget to check for the removal of your client's mouth jewelry. If the officer is so enamored by your client's tongue ring that he forgot to have her remove it from her mouth, it will create error in the testing.

§8:83   GERD

Another attack can be made if your client has Gastro-Esophageal Reflux Disease (GERD). There, the breath detector is fooled into producing a false positive by the alcohol contained in stomach gas. According to some studies, nearly 10 percent of the adult population has GERD.[1]

The GERD defense is pretty easy to understand when boiled down. The alcohol in stomach gas has a much higher concentration of alcohol than a non-GERD breath. As a result, a small amount of reflux can create a significantly elevated result.

To get the GERD evidence in you need a diagnosis. If your client has a prior GERD diagnosis, get the his medical records and arrange, if possible, for his doctor to testify. If your client has upper GI complaints, however, and you suspect GERD, have him diagnosed.

§8:84   Machine Margin of Error

If you are dealing with the Intoxilyzer 5000EN or 8000, the machine margin of error is generally accepted to be ± .01. CMI, Inc., the manufacturer of the machine, claims the Intoxilyzer 5000EN to be accurate to a .005 margin for error. You need to see what your state's experts opinion is on this, but based on calibration checks, they will generally give you a ± .01 margin for error. Obviously this is only useful in the close case.

§8:85   Machine Calibration Issues and the State's Chemist

The ideal scenario is that you have your own chemist. Having your own expert in toxicology, physiology, breath and field sobriety testing can make a big difference. If your client is serious about his or her defense and has the money, this is the clear direction to take.

However, if your clients are like mine, they often are tapped out after they pay their legal fees. When I ask them for money for a chemist, they give me the stink eye. So in most cases where it is possible, I need to make the State Chemist my friend.

Dealing with State scientific-based witnesses is not as difficult as it seems. Beyond drunk driving work, the scientific experts for the Government who work in the crime labs tend to be very open to dealing with the defense in my experience. They work for the State, but they believe themselves to be neutral scientists in reality. Whether that is true or not is another story. But they will likely be open to talking with you certainly.

First, in breath testing cases you need to get into machine calibration issues with the appropriate State expert. You want to send whoever is named as an expert a letter requesting the testing and calibration of the instrument.

When you get the calibration records, you want to look for variations in the testing. Look for errors and repairs. Find out who repaired the machine. Find out how long before your client's test the last check was done. In short, do your homework and see if the machine was tested to be functioning properly or even tested at all.

---

[1] Dipero, et. al, Pharmacotherapy, 5th ed., McGraw Hill, 2002.

§8:86   FORM 8-50 Letter to State's Chemist Requesting Testing and Calibration Records of Breath Test Machine

Mr. Chemist
Health and Env. Testing Lab
12 State House Station
221 State Street
Augusta, ME 04333

      RE: State of Maine v. _____
            _____ Police Department
        Intoxilyzer 5000 Materials
        Serial Number _____

Dear Mr. Chemist:

     Thank you for your assistance with this case. I am requesting materials with respect to the Intoxilyzer 5000 Serial No. 123456789 downloads, weekly wet baths and other calibration materials from February 21, 2012 through the present date. I have enclosed a copy of my client's test results for your review.

                           Sincerely,
                           Timothy E. Zerillo
                           ZERILLO LAW FIRM, LLC

§8:87   Rising Alcohol Defense

     When you ingest alcohol, it doesn't immediately impact your brain. It takes time for alcohol to affect your brain. The alcohol is first absorbed through the stomach and small intestine. Once it hits the blood it makes its way to the brain. Once the absorption is complete, which varies by person and by other factors like food consumption, it begins to affect the brain.

     Once the alcohol is absorbed into the bloodstream, the liver eliminates it. The elimination rate also varies by person, but is between .15% and .20% per hour. Depending on the timing of your client's consumption, you may be able to argue that the client was still absorbing alcohol at the time of the stop. The client's blood alcohol was rising at the time of the test and was below the legal limit while he or she was driving.

§8:88   Affidavit of State Chemist

     You can often get the State Chemist to issue Affidavits to you to help with your bureau of motor vehicles hearing, or to help in plea bargaining your case with the D.A.'s Office. Below is an Affidavit (Form 8-60) signed by a State Chemist in a case with my office. It proved useful both at the bureau of motor vehicles hearing and in plea bargaining the case. You may be able to use this affidavit to support a rising alcohol defense. Obviously, if there was an error in the calibration of the machine, you want to mention that as well.

§8:89   FORM 8-60 Sample Affidavit of Chemist

AFFIDAVIT OF MR. CHEMIST
SECRETARY OF STATE HEARING

     I, Mr. Chemist, hereby swear under oath that the information set forth below in this affidavit is true and correct to the best of my knowledge, information and belief and that I make this oath under pains and penalty of perjury.

1)   My name is Mr. Chemist.
2)   I have a bachelor's degree in biochemistry and have extensive training and experience in the operation, maintenance and performance of the Intoxilyzer testing instruments.
3)   I have qualified numerous times in Maine Courts as the State's expert including in the fields of Intoxilyzer operation, maintenance and performance; breath alcohol testing by means of infrared testing generally;

and the mechanical and human factors that can affect the accuracy of infrared testing in general and the Intoxilyzer instruments in particular.

4) I have assisted in assembling the materials originally used in establishing the Intoxilyzer program in Maine, participated in the continued development and implementation of the Intoxilyzer program in Maine and participated in the development and some revisions of the Operation and Intoxilyzer Student Manual used by the Maine Criminal Justice Academy.

5) I am the chemist in charge of Intoxilyzer instruments used by the State of Maine for breath alcohol testing.

6) I approve, repair and inspect all Intoxilyzer instruments used in the State of Maine.

7) The Intoxilyzer 5000 EN Model is used by all police departments in the State of Maine. This instrument has a cumulative margin of error comprised of plus/minus .01 as the measurement tolerance of the instrument.

8) For a .08% BAC test result the range of error is plus or minus .01% for a test range of .07% to .09%.

9) Blood alcohol levels initially rise and then fall over time.

10) There is no way to tell from a single, two-sample intoxilyzer test result whether an individual's BAC is rising or falling at any point in time.

Mr. Chemist

[§§8:90-8:99 Reserved]

G.   BLOOD TESTING

1. Basics

Whole treatises have been written about blood testing in drunk driving cases, and I won't foolishly attempt to re-create them here. Rather, I want to give you a basic view of blood testing that you can apply if you run across one of the fairly rare blood test cases in your practice.

§8:100   What Is Blood?

It's pumping throughout veins every minute of every day. But what is blood really?

Blood is made up of cells, called corpuscles. We have red blood cells (also called erythrocytes), white blood cells (also called lymphocytes or phagocytes) and platelets (also called thrombocytes). Red blood cells have hemoglobin, which transports oxygen through the blood. White blood cells carry our immunity response agents.

Testing for alcohol in blood is generally done in one of two ways: through gas chromatography or through an enzymatic test.

§8:101   Gas Chromatography Basics

Gas chromatography (GC) testing generally involves the separation of solutes (or compounds). It is done with a gas chromatography system. The different sizes and characteristics of the molecules cause them to travel through a column at different speeds. The length of time it takes each molecule to exit the column is called the retention time.

A flame ionization detector is generally used to determine the retention time of each compound. Essentially, the solute is burned, during which time a signal is created. The size of the signal's peak can then be mapped, and compared to other known alcohol levels to determine the level of the sample.

§8:102   Enzymatic Testing Basics

To understand enzymatic testing, you need to understand the basic makeup of serum and plasma. Serum is the fluid that remains after a specimen is centrifuged (spun downward). It includes proteins in the blood not involved in the clotting process. Plasma contains the dissolved proteins, carbon dioxide, platelets, blood cells, mineral ions, hormones and glucose. Serum and plasma are essentially equivalent in their alcohol concentration.

Either serum or plasma can be combined with alcohol dehydrogenase to create acetaldehyde. This causes a chemical conversion to nicotinamide adenine dinucleotide (NADH). NADH is used to then measure alcohol concentration.

[§§8:103-8:109 Reserved]

2. Attacking Blood Tests

OK, if you are like me and you get a case with a blood test you say to yourself "Oh hell, this guy is done before we begin." Additionally, unless you have a biology or medical degree, the preceding sections may be Greek to you. What you really want are some ideas as to how to cross-examine a witness on blood testing. Here are a few arrows for your bow.

§8:110 Enzymatic Testing

Enzymatic testing most often occurs in a hospital setting when your client has been injured in a motor vehicle accident. If enzymatic testing was done, make sure it wasn't performed on whole blood. This is a rare error. Remember, enzymatic testing must be done on serum or plasma, not whole blood, which will result in false high readings.

Serum and plasma are equivalent in alcohol concentration. Serum and plasma also have a higher water concentration than whole blood. Since alcohol is attracted to water, serum and plasma have higher alcohol concentrations than whole blood.

Enzymatic blood tests, even though performed correctly on serum or plasma, yield results that are 16 to 25 percent higher than the alcohol concentration in whole blood. [See *Garriott's Medicolegal Aspects of Alcohol*, 5th ed., pg. 207.]

§8:111 Hemolysis

Hemolysis occurs when the red blood cell membranes are broken. When the red blood cells are broken, the hemoglobin is released in the sample. This can happen during the collection process. If hemolysis is present, the sample and test are compromised.

There are a variety of causes of hemolysis. They include specimen collection through evacuated tubes, improper collection via the syringe draw (such as drawing the syringe back too far), collection via peripheral IV catheters, mixing or shaking the specimen too forcefully, prolonged exposure to extreme heat or cold, and many more.[2]

§8:112 Fermentation

In Maine, we have some terrific apples. One of my favorite parts of autumn is getting fresh apple cider from Maine's great orchards.

If I leave my favorite apple cider out too long without drinking it, what will happen? It ferments and will contain alcohol. The sugar in the apple cider causes this fermentation.

Blood can ferment as well. Glucose (sugar) in the blood can cause fermentation and the production of alcohol in the sample being tested. When a device like a Gas Chromatography machine reads a fermented sample, it cannot tell when the alcohol in the sample was created.

Check for a lack of refrigeration in your sample. Even if your sample was refrigerated, fermentation can still occur. Check for periods of time when the sample may have not been refrigerated, but was later refrigerated. Perhaps it sat in an unrefrigerated evidence locker or a police cruiser for a while before it was transported to a lab.

Fermentation can be slowed, but never stopped, by the use of a preservative. If sodium fluoride was used, have an expert check the levels to make sure that the correct amount of preservative was used.

§8:113 Chain of Custody

Chain of custody arguments for blood samples can be used in drunk driving cases the same way you would in a drug case or any other case. Make sure to follow the chain of custody carefully, and attack any broken links in the chain.

---

[2] For some references on this, try the following: Burns ER, Yoshikawa N., Hemolysis in Serum Samples Drawn by Emergency Department Personnel Versus Laboratory Phlebotomists, Lab Med. 2002, 33:378-380; Procedures for the Handling and Processing of Blood Specimens; Approved Guideline 3rd ed. National Committee for Clinical Laboratory Standards, Wayne, PA: National Committee for Clinical Laboratory Standards; 2004. NCCLS Document H18-A3

§8:114   Qualification Issues

Check also to ensure that the blood drawer was qualified. Is the person a phlebotomist or merely a lab tech? Remember, the way the blood was drawn can significantly impact the quality of the sample. Consult your state's statutes or the requirements to draw blood in your jurisdiction. These statutes typically authorize doctors, nurses, and phlebotomists to draw blood.

[§§8:115-8:119 Reserved]

IV.   MOTIONS

A. Discovery

Our discovery motions start out as discovery requests sent to the District Attorney's Office. The type of request is entirely dependent on the type of testing done.

§8:120   Blood Testing

For blood testing, it is important that you get into discovery issues related to the way the blood was drawn and who drew it. The type of vial used is of equal importance. Likewise, the chain of custody, especially to create a fermentation defense, is essential.

Our practice in a blood case is to send the motion for discovery to the prosecutor requesting very detailed blood draw information. We then follow up with a Motion for Discovery related to the blood draw, and then Motions for Sanctions as appropriate. See §8:123 Form 6-70 Discovery Motion—Blood Draw. You will need to get orders on discovery and request sanctions if the discovery is not provided.

§8:121   Breath Testing

Breath testing gets a similar strategic approach. We want to file and have ordered breath testing discovery motions so that when they are inevitably not followed, we have a leg to stand on in our Motion for Sanctions. See §8:124 Form 6-80 Discovery Motion—Breath test.

§8:122   Expert's Report

As a part of our discovery motions packet, we also file a Motion for Preparation of Reports By Expert Witnesses. See §8:125 Form 6-90. Depending on your state's Rules of Criminal Procedure, the State may have no duty to furnish you with the expert's report, or require the expert produce a report at all, unless you request one.

§8:123   FORM 8-70 Discovery Motion—Blood Draw

STATE OF MAINE   _____DISTRICT COURT
CUMBERLAND, ss.   DIVISION OF _____
                                                  DOCKET NO.

STATE OF MAINE,   )
)
)   DEFENDANT'S MOTION FOR
v.   )   DISCOVERY WITH INCORPORATED
)   MEMORANDUM OF LAW
_____,   )
)
Defendant   )

Defendant, _____, by and through Undersigned Counsel, respectfully requests, pursuant to Rule 16 of the Maine Rules of Criminal Procedure, the following discovery, whether in the possession and control of the Office of the District Attorney or the _____Police Department. All requests for information, unless otherwise noted, shall pertain to the events and circumstances surrounding and subsequent to the arrest of the Defendant on or about _____.

This discovery request is deemed ongoing. If information that would have been furnished to the Defendant under this request comes within the prosecution's or the police's possession or control after this initial request has been satisfied, the attorney for the State shall promptly inform counsel for the Defendant.

1. Please provide the arresting officer's field notes pertaining to the incident that led to the Defendant's arrest in this case.

2. Please provide detailed protocol for doing blood alcohol analysis.

3. Please provide background details of _____, the person who drew blood and a copy of her current certification pursuant to Maine Rules 10-114A, Chapter 268.

4. Please provide information on the vacutainers used to sample Defendant's blood including the identification of fluoride, oxalate or other salts present in the tube.

5. Please describe how Defendant's blood sample was stored from _____ until it was analyzed on _____.

6. Please provide detailed chain of custody from the time that the blood was taken by _____ to the time it was analyzed in the laboratory including anyone who handled the sample and how it was stored and the security of that storage area.

7. Please supply detailed information on how Defendant's sample was analyzed including any dilutions, any transfer of blood into GC vials and volumes of material transferred and calibration of the syringe used to make the transfer.

8. If headspace analysis was carried out, please describe the procedure including all materials that were added to the blood, the lipid content of the blood, and the temperature of the sample when the headspace was sampled. Please provide information on calibration of the temperature on the autoinjector of the gas chromatograph.

9. Please supply detailed information on all standards used on _____ including the NIST standard and any other internally produced standards. Please provide as a minimum the date of purchase and the expiration date.

10. Please provide the maintenance manual for the dual column GC instrument to analyze Defendant's blood. Please provide information as to when the instrument was last serviced and whether it was done in a timely manner according to the manufacturer's recommendations. Please provide information on the columns used in the Defendant's blood analysis including diameters, packing, column length and when the columns were last changed. Please provide any information you have related to the baseline drift or calibration problems that you have had within the past year.

11. Please indicate if your laboratory is in compliance with Good Laboratory Practices regulations.

12. Please indicate if your laboratory is certified for alcohol and drug analysis by any other certifying body.

13. Please provide expiration dates for vacutainers used to sample the Defendant's blood and indicate where, when and from whom they were purchased.

14. If the sample was stored in a secure refrigerator, please provide the temperature log for that refrigerator.

15. Please provide radio transmission log and tape-recorded radio transmissions pertaining to, in any fashion, the circumstances surrounding the arrest in this case, including, but not limited to dispatch records, cruiser videos, and videos of the room where the blood was drawn.

16. Please provide copies of all OUI arrest reports made by the arresting officer between the dates of _____ to the present.

17. Please provide the name, address and qualifications of any expert(s) whom the State intends to call in any proceedings concerning this matter.

18. Please provide any and all statements, confessions, videotape recordings or admissions made by Defendant whether written or oral, subsequently reduced to writing or summarized in the officer's reports, copies or electronic storage thereof, within the possession, custody or control of the State, the existence of which is known or by the exercise of due diligence may become known to the attorneys for the State. This paragraph includes statements made to witnesses other than police officers of State agents at any time as well as the precise words attributed to Defendant which caused the State agents to conclude that Defendant unlawfully engaged in the acts alleged in the above-captioned petition. This also includes any

statement relevant to the offense charged, whether or not the State intends to introduce it in its direct or rebuttal case or any other portions of these proceedings.

19. Please provide the names and addresses of any and all persons who have knowledge pertaining to this case, or who have been interviewed by the State, or investigators or agents working in connection with this case.

20. Please provide the written statements, notes, reports, documents, writings or records of any person(s) provided in response to paragraph 13, and whether or not the State plans to call any such person as a witness at any hearing throughout these proceedings.

21. Please allow inspection by Defendant, his counsel or agents, of all physical evidence to be introduced by the State.

22. Please provide names and addresses of all witnesses that the State intends to call at any hearing throughout these proceedings.

23. Please provide any and all tape recordings, video tape recordings and statements made by witnesses to the alleged criminal conduct or witnesses that the State intends to elicit testimony from at any hearing throughout these proceedings.

24. Please provide the name, rank, position/location at all relevant times, and address of all State agents or other witnesses who participated in any way in the investigation of these matters.

25. Please provide such tangible objects which are in the possession, custody, or control of the State and which are material to the preparation of Defendant's defenses or intended for use by the State as evidence in chief at any hearing in the above-stated matters, and afford to Defendant access to inspect, photograph, copy, or have reasonable tests made with respect to each and every object.

26. Please provide any and all further reports of examinations and tests as numerated in Rule 16 of the Maine Rules of Criminal Procedure which are within the possession, custody, or control of the State, the existence of which is known or by the exercise of due diligence may become known to the attorney for the State and which are material to the preparation of the defense of this Defendant or intended for use by the State as evidence in chief at any hearing in these proceedings. *Brady v. Maryland*, 373 U.S. 83 (1963).

27. Please provide any and all material known to the State or which may become known or which through due diligence may be learned from the investigating officers or the witnesses or the persons having knowledge of this case which is exculpatory in nature or which might serve to mitigate punishment, including any evidence impeaching or contradicting potential testimony of State witnesses or instructions to State witnesses not to speak with or discuss the facts of this case with defense counsel. *Brady v. Maryland*, 372 U.S. 83 (1963); *United States v. Agurs*, 427 U.S. 97 (1976); *Giglio v. United States*, 405 U.S. 150 (1972); *Davis v. Alaska*, 415 U.S. 300, 39 L.Ed. 347, 94 S.Ct. 1105 (1973).

28. Please provide all criminal records of witnesses to be called by the State, both direct and rebuttal witnesses, at any hearing in these proceedings.

Counsel specifically reserves the right to make additional requests for material covered by *Brady v. Maryland* at the time this motion is argued, or at any such other time as the existence of such material shall become known to counsel for the Defendant and it is respectfully requested that the prosecution be aware that their duty under *Brady* is a continuing one.

Dated this _____ day of _____, at Portland, Maine.

                                                              Respectfully submitted,

                                                              _____
                                                              Timothy E. Zerillo
                                                              Attorney for Defendant
                                                              ZERILLO LAW FIRM, LLC

§8:124   FORM 8-80 Discovery Motion—Breath Test

STATE OF MAINE   UNIFIED CRIMINAL DOCKET
CUMBERLAND, ss.   DOCKET NO. CR-__-_____

STATE OF MAINE,   )
)
Plaintiff   )   DEFENDANT'S
)   MOTION FOR DISCOVERY
v.   )   WITH INCORPORATED
)   MEMORANDUM OF LAW
_____,   )
)
Defendant   )

Defendant, _____, by and through undersigned counsel, respectfully requests, pursuant to Rule 16 of the Maine Rules of Criminal Procedure, the following discovery, whether in the possession and control of the Office of the District Attorney or the Maine State Police. All requests for information, unless otherwise noted, shall pertain to the events and circumstances surrounding and subsequent to the arrest of the Defendant on or about _____, 20__.

This discovery request is deemed ongoing. If information, which would have been furnished to the Defendant under this request, comes within the prosecutions or the police's possession or control after this initial request has been satisfied, the attorney for the State shall promptly inform counsel for the Defendant.

1. The arresting officer's field notes.
2. Maintenance logs for the Intoxilyzer used for this arrest.
3. Intoxilyzer test report for all tests performed between _____, 20__ and _____, 20__ using the Intoxilyzer machine used for this arrest.
4. All certification documents for the Intoxilyzer used for this arrest.
5. Any and all police cruiser video depicting the Standard Field Sobriety Tests performed by and the subsequent arrest of the Defendant.
6. Audio and video recording of the Defendant performing the Intoxilyzer test that led to this arrest.
7. Records of any and all adjustments to the Intoxilyzer machine used for this arrest.
8. Operator's manual for the Intoxilyzer used for this arrest.
9. Radio transmission log and tape-recorded radio transmissions pertaining to, in any fashion, the circumstances surrounding the arrest in this case.
10. Copies of all OUI arrest reports made by the arresting officer between the dates of _____, 20__ to _____, 20__.
11. The name, address and qualifications of any expert(s) whom the State intends to call in any proceedings concerning this matter.
12. Any and all statements, confessions, videotape recordings or admissions made by Defendant whether written or oral, subsequently reduced to writing or summarized in the officer's reports, copies or electronic storage thereof, within the possession, custody or control of the State, the existence of which is known or by the exercise of due diligence may become known to the attorneys for the State. This paragraph includes statements made to witnesses other than police officers of State agents at any time as well as the precise words attributed to Defendant which caused the State agents to conclude that Defendant unlawfully engaged in the acts alleged in the above-captioned petition. This also includes any statement relevant to the offense charged, whether or not the State intends to introduce it in its direct or rebuttal case or any other portions of these proceedings.
13. The names and addresses of any and all persons who have knowledge pertaining to this case, or who have been interviewed by the State, or investigators or agents working in connection with this case.
14. The written statements, notes, reports, documents, writings or records of any person(s) provided in response to paragraph 13, and whether or not the State plans to call any such person as a witness at any hearing throughout these proceedings.
15. Inspection by Defendant, his counsel or agents, of all physical evidence to be introduced by the State.

16. Names and addresses of all witnesses that the State intends to call at any hearing throughout these proceedings.

17. Any and all tape recordings, video tape recordings and statements made by witnesses to the alleged criminal conduct or witnesses that the State intends to elicit testimony from at any hearing throughout these proceedings.

18. The name, rank, position/location at all relevant times, and address of all State agents or other witnesses who participated in any way in the investigation of these matters.

19. Such tangible objects which are in the possession, custody, or control of the State and which are material to the preparation of Defendant's defenses or intended for use by the State as evidence in chief at any hearing in the above-stated matters, and the affording to Defendant access to inspect, photograph, copy, or have reasonable tests made with respect to each and every object.

20. Any and all further reports of examinations and tests as numerated in Rule 16 of the Maine Rules of Criminal Procedure which are within the possession, custody, or control of the State, the existence of which is known or by the exercise of due diligence may become known to the attorney for the State and which are material to the preparation of the defense of this Defendant or intended for use by the State as evidence in chief at any hearing in these proceedings. *Brady v. Maryland*, 373 U.S. 83 (1963).

21. Any and all material known to the State or which may become known or which through due diligence may be learned from the investigating officers or the witnesses or the persons having knowledge of this case which is exculpatory in nature or which might serve to mitigate punishment, including any evidence impeaching or contradicting potential testimony of State witnesses or instructions to State witnesses not to speak with or discuss the facts of this case with defense counsel. *Brady v. Maryland*, 372 U.S. 83 (1963); *United States v. Agurs*, 427 U.S. 97 (1976); *Giglio v. United States*, 405 U.S. 150 (1972); *Davis v. Alaska*, 415 U.S. 300, 39 L.Ed. 347, 94 S.Ct. 1105 (1973).

22. All criminal records of witnesses to be called by the State, both direct and rebuttal witnesses, at any hearing in these proceedings.

23. Counsel specifically reserves the right to make additional requests for material covered by *Brady v. Maryland* at the time this motion is argued, or at any such other time as the existence of such material shall become known to counsel for the Defendant and it is respectfully requested that the prosecution be aware that their duty under *Brady* is a continuing one.

Dated this _____ day of _____, 20__ at Portland, Maine.

Respectfully submitted,

_____
Timothy E. Zerillo
Attorney for Defendant
ZERILLO LAW FIRM, LLC

§8:125　　FORM 8-90 Motion for Preparation of Reports By Expert Witnesses

STATE OF MAINE　　　　　　　　　　　_____ DISTRICT COURT
_____, ss.　　　　　　　　DOCKET NO. CR-__-_____

STATE OF MAINE,)	
)	
v.)	MOTION FOR PREPARATION OF
)	REPORTS OF EXPERT WITNESS
CLIENT,)	
Defendant)	

NOW COMES Defendant, _____, by and through Undersigned Counsel, and moves the Honorable Court, to require the State to have any expert whom it intends to call as a witness in any proceeding in this case prepare and provide Defendant a report stating the subject matter on which the expert is expected to testify, the substance of the facts to which the expert is expected to testify, and a summary of the expert's opinion and the grounds for each opinion.

Defendant requests that the State provide such reports no later than fourteen (14) day prior to the first date set for trial in this matter.

Dated this _____, day of _____, _____, Portland, Maine.

Respectfully submitted,

_____
Timothy E. Zerillo
Attorney for Defendant
ZERILLO LAW FIRM, LLC

[§§8:126-8:129 Reserved]

B. Motion to Suppress Blood Testing

§8:130　*Birchfield v. North Dakota*

In *Birchfield v. North Dakota*, 136 S. Ct. 2160 (U.S. 2016), the Supreme Court analyzed three consolidated cases that each raised issues related to the efficacy of a warrantless search for breath or blood in drunk driving cases. The Supreme Court drew a line between the search and seizure of breath evidence and the search and seizure of blood evidence.

North Dakota law made it a criminal offense for a motorist to refuse to submit to a chemical test of the person's blood, breath or urine upon arrest for driving under the influence. Two defendants (Birchfield and Beylund) challenged the North Dakota law. The third "B" in the triumvirate, Bernard, challenged a similar Minnesota law as it related to a breath test. A divided Minnesota court previously held that a warrantless breath test could be compelled as a search incident to an arrest. SCOTUS reversed and remanded *Birchfield,* affirmed *Beylund* and vacated and remanded *Bernard.*

The *Birchfield* opinion holds that the Fourth Amendment permits warrantless breath tests incident to a drunk driving arrest, but not warrantless blood tests. As a result, warrantless blood draws should be the subject of motions to suppress.

Birchfield notes that both the seizure of breath and blood are searches. *Id.* at 2174. Why then does a search and seizure of blood require a warrant? The distinction lies in the level of intrusiveness involved.

Birchfield holds that blood tests are considerably more intrusive than breath tests. In *Birchfield* the Court stated:

> Blood tests are a different matter. They "require piercing the skin" and extract a part of the subject's body … (blood draws are "a compelled physical intrusion beneath [the defendant's] skin and into his veins") … (blood draws are "significant bodily intrusions"). And while humans exhale air from their lungs many times per minute, humans do not continually shed blood. It is true, of course, that people voluntarily submit to the taking of blood samples as part of a physical examination, and the process involves little pain or risk. Nevertheless, for many, the process is not one they relish. It is significantly more intrusive than blowing into a tube. Perhaps that is why many States' implied consent laws, including Minnesota's, specifically prescribe that breath tests be administered in the usual drunk-driving case instead of blood tests or give motorists a measure of choice over which test to take.

> In addition, a blood test, unlike a breath test, places in the hands of law enforcement authorities a sample that can be preserved and from which it is possible to extract information beyond a simple BAC reading. Even if the law enforcement agency is precluded from testing the blood for any purpose other than to measure BAC, the potential remains and may result in anxiety for the person tested.

Birchfield v. North Dakota, 136 S. Ct. 2160, 2178 (U.S. 2016) *citations omitted.*

The distinction drawn by SCOTUS is logical. The degree of intrusion in a blood draw is significant. Moreover, blood tests often cause anxiety in the tested person. They further allow the government to hold a sample from which the government can extract more data than merely blood-alcohol content.

If the State chooses to argue that safety favors the intrusion, the State will find no shelter in *Birchfield*. The Court concluded that the government's interest in protecting highway safety was subsumed by personal privacy interests. While the balancing test may favor the government if the intrusion is a breath test, *Birchfield* holds that the government must give way to privacy if a blood draw is involved.

> **PRACTICE TIP:** *Your client may have allowed, but not legally consented to the blood test*
>
> In 2018, I had a motion to suppress hearing in a manslaughter case. The death resulted from a boating accident in which my client lost his identical twin brother. My client was the driver of the boat, and while making a turn, his twin fell out of the bow of the boat. His femoral artery was cut by the boat prop while he was in the water. He died later that day.
>
> When law enforcement arrived on the scene, they convinced my client that he needed to have his blood drawn. The government opposition to our *Birchfield* Motion to Suppress was consent. We were able to overcome their consent theory by setting the scene of the accident. There, my client's twin brother was grievously injured. He had been fished out of the water by my client and his friends. The tried desperately to stop the bleeding. This was, as you can imagine, a dramatic scene.
>
> Consent generally requires a knowing and voluntary waiver of rights. You may find facts, such as the ones in this case, that overwhelm the defendant's ability to consent. At your motion hearing, set that scene and establish that consent was not free and voluntary. Here, we were successful in our motion to suppress under *Birchfield*, and the State dismissed the manslaughter.

§8:131   *Missouri v. McNeely*

Exigent circumstances will not save the day if there is a warrantless blood seizure. In *Missouri v. McNeely*, Tyler McNeely was pulled over for speeding at 2:08 AM. *Missouri v. McNeely*, 133 S.Ct 1552, 1556, 185 L.Ed. 2d 696 (2013). The police officer who stopped Mr. McNeely observed that he had bloodshot eyes, slurred speech, smelled of alcohol and was unsteady on his feet. *Id.* McNeely acknowledged consuming "a couple of beers" to the officer.

McNeely refused a breath test, however. *Id.* at 1557. The arresting officer then transported him to a hospital for a blood draw. *Id.* The officer did not make an effort to obtain a search warrant. *Id.* at 1567.

At issue for the Court was whether or not the natural dissipation of alcohol in McNeely's blood presented an exigent circumstance. *McNeely* holds that the destruction of the evidence by the elimination of alcohol in the blood stream does not present a categorical exigency.

It is still possible under *McNeely* to establish exigency in special cases. However, those special cases establishing exigency should present the exception, not the rule. For example, *McNeely* points out that one officer can drive a suspect to a hospital while another officer gets a warrant. *Id.* at 1561. The Supreme Court holds that "In such a circumstance, there would be no plausible justification for an exception to the warrant requirement." *Id.* at 1561.

[§§8:132-8:139 Reserved]

C. Motions in Limine

§8:140   Highlighting the Officer's Inadequacies

Motions in limine, of course, are really only limited by your imagination. We often like to highlight the inadequacies of the officer for the judge prior to trial, and motions in limine can be a good way to do that. Consider a Motion in Limine to Exclude the Officer from Testifying Related to HGN Testing. See §8:131 Form 8-100.

This is sometimes a good move and sometimes a bad move depending on strategy. Sometimes the testing is so bad, I want to cross the officer. If you decide to strike HGN in your strategy however, a motion in limine to do so is provided below. The same goes for the other motion in limine that follows. It requests that the officer's testimony about your client's sobriety test performance be limited to the officer's observations. This is nice when you are trying to prevent the cop from saying the defendant failed a test.

Your motion in limine need not be a masterpiece of legal research. If you have a shot at punching a hole in the state's witness, do it.

§8:141   FORM 8-100 Motion in Limine to Exclude the Officer from Testifying Related to HGN Testing

STATE OF MAINE,	)	
	)	
Plaintiff	)	
	)	MOTION IN LIMINE TO
v.	)	EXCLUDE REFERENCE TO
	)	THE HORIZONTAL GAZE
JOHN DANIELS,	)	NYSTAGMUS TEST
	)	
Defendant	)	

Now comes the Defendant, John Daniels and respectfully requests that this honorable court exclude from trial any reference to the administration of the Horizontal Gaze Nystagmus (HGN) test.

The standard for the admissibility of the HGN test is well-established in Maine. *State v. Taylor*, 694 A.2d 907, (Me. 1997). The Law Court held that the HGN test should be admissible if a proper foundation is laid for its introduction in evidence. *Id.* at 911. A proper foundation shall consist of evidence that the officer or administrator of the HGN test is trained in the procedure and the test was properly administered. *Id.* at 912. The officer in *Taylor* was qualified as an expert witness pursuant to M.R.E. 702 and permitted to testify regarding the results of the HGN test because he was properly trained and found to have administered the test properly; however, the officer should not have been permitted to testify about the defendant's particular blood alcohol level. *Id.*

In the instant case Officer Ian Gotcha has not received and completed the requisite training as required by the Maine Criminal Justice Academy. Officer Gotcha has attended training on the administration of field sobriety tests, including the HGN test; however, he has not received course completion. As the Law Court has noted, proper training is an essential element of the admissibility of HGN testimony.

In addition, the officer in *Taylor* was permitted to testify as an expert witness relating to the HGN test. "Officer Green was qualified to testify as an expert on the HGN test. He was trained at a three-day course taught by instructors and has tested numerous subjects both in the field and in controlled situations. Thus, Officer Green is qualified by both his training and experience." *Id.*; see also M.R.E. 702. In this case, Mr. Daniels has requested that the State produce and designate any witnesses that the State intends to have testify as expert witnesses. M.R.Crim.P. 16(c). At no point has the State provided an expert report suggesting that Officer Gotcha is an expert witness in the area of HGN testing.

WHEREFORE the defendant respectfully requests that this court exclude a reference to Officer Gotcha's attempt to administer the HGN test in this case.

Respectfully submitted,

_____

Timothy E. Zerillo
Attorney for Defendant
ZERILLO LAW FIRM, LLC

§8:142   FORM 8-110 Motion in Limine to Limit Testimony to Performance of SFT's

STATE OF MAINE		SUPERIOR COURT
CUMBERLAND, SS		DOCKET NO.

STATE OF MAINE,	)	
	)	MOTION IN LIMINE TO LIMIT
Plaintiff	)	THE TESTIMONY OF OFFICER
	)	IAN GOTCHA REGARDING
v.	)	MR. DANIEL'S PERFORMANCE
	)	ON THE SFSTs
JOHN DANIELS,	)	
	)	
Defendant	)	

Now comes the Defendant and respectfully requests that the Officer Ian Gotcha's testimony regarding the Standard Field Sobriety Tests (SFSTs), be limited to the observations of Mr. Daniel's performance with no value-added descriptive language to characterize Mr. Daniel's performance of the SFSTs.

It is well-established that there are limitations to the admissibility of SFSTs as they relate to a subject's level of intoxication. *State v. Taylor*, 694 A.2d 907 (Me. 1997). A police officer trained and qualified to perform SFSTs may testify with respect to his or her observations of a subject's performance of these tests, if properly administered, to include the observation of nystagmus, and these observations are admissible as circumstantial evidence that the defendant was driving while intoxicated or under the influence. In so doing, however, the officer may not use added descriptive language to characterize the subject's performance of the SFSTs, such as saying that the subject " failed the test" or " exhibited" a certain number of " standardized clues" during the test. *United State v. Horn*, 185 F. Supp.2d 530, 533 (D.Md. 2002). To permit a police officer to testify about each of the SFSTs in detail, their claimed accuracy rates, the number of standardized clues applicable to each, the number of clues exhibited by the suspect, and then offer an opinion about whether he or she passed or failed, stopping just short of expressing an opinion as to specific BAC, invites the risk of allowing through the back door of circumstantial proof evidence that is not reliable enough to enter through the front door of direct proof of intoxication or impairment. *Id.* at 557 and 558.

WHEREFORE Officer Gotcha should be permitted to testify only regarding the observations of the SFSTs administered provided he is able to lay the proper foundation that he is adequately trained to administer the tests and that he did administer the test properly.

Dated this _____ day of _____, 20___, at Portland, Maine.

Respectfully submitted,

_____
Timothy E. Zerillo
Attorney for Defendant
ZERILLO LAW FIRM, LLC

[§§8:143-8:149 Reserved]

B. Sanctions and Dismissal

§8:150   When Should You File?

It's very likely that you can set up the District Attorney's Office for sanctions violations if you are properly requesting your discovery and getting discovery motions ordered. Things slip through the cracks of the system all the time, and when they do, it is up to you to point that out. See §8:142 Form 8-120 Motion for Sanctions/Motion to Dismiss for Failure to Preserve Evidence.

I have had newer lawyers ask me if they should hesitate to file sanctions motions because of some sort of stigma. My answer is always the same: if you have a legitimate sanctions argument you have a duty to file the sanctions motions. If the prosecutor is miffed, she will get over it. That said, I wouldn't file frivolous sanctions motions.

§8:151   Choosing an Appropriate Sanction to Request

Sometimes the hardest thing about a Motion for Sanctions is coming up with the sanction for your argument to the judge. Outright dismissal of the case is great, but the violation will need to be pretty severe to warrant it. Lesser sanctions can be very helpful, so consider alternative arguments related to the exclusion of certain evidence or witnesses, or the elimination of certain areas of testimony by State witnesses.

§8:152   FORM 8-120 Motion for Sanctions/Motion to Dismiss for Failure to Preserve Evidence

STATE OF MAINE,   )
)   DEFENDANT'S MOTION FOR
)   SANCTIONS AND TO DISMISS FOR
v.   )   FAILURE TO PRESERVE EVIDENCE
)
*********,   )
)
Defendant   )

NOW COMES, the Defendant, *********, by and through Undersigned Counsel, pursuant to M.R.Crim.P. 16(d) and requests that this Honorable Court dismiss the above-referenced matter and submits the following memorandum in support of his motion to dismiss:

FACTUAL SUMMARY

On December 20, 2012, ********* was arrested by Officer Troy Sloppy of the Topsham Police Department for Operating Under the Influence, Class D. Officer Sloppy began to follow Mr. ********* after he allegedly observed him stopping at a yellow light for approximately 20 seconds and swerving into the breakdown lane. Officer Sloppy stated that he detected the odor of intoxicants coming from the vehicle. Mr. ********* admitted to consuming one beer earlier that night. Mr. ********* did not have slurred speech nor he did he have bloodshot/glassy eyes, standard signs usually attributed to an individual impaired by alcohol. Officer Sloppy administered a battery of field sobriety tests (FSTs). It is important to note that the Maine Criminal Justice Academy's Record of Officer Sloppy's certification does not include proficiency in administering standard field sobriety testing (SFSTs). It is also important to note that Officer Sloppy's report only notes one administered standardized field sobriety test—walk and turn test (WAT). Officer Sloppy noted in his report that he observed two clues of impairment. Officer Sloppy then performed the finger-dexterity test (FDT) and finger-to-nose test (FNT). Neither tests are approved by the National Highway Transportation Safety Administrations nor is Counsel aware of any standardized clues associated with these two tests.

Ultimately, Mr. ********* was taken to the Topsham Police Department where he agreed to submit to an Intoxilyzer test. The result of the test was a blood alcohol content (BAC) of .14% BAC.

The guilt of Mr. ********* rests primarily on whether Mr. ********* can disprove that the breath test was valid and administered properly. Mr. ********* can meet this standard by presenting independent and unbiased evidence establishing that the Intoxilyzer test was not administered properly. The evidence that meets this standard and which was available to Mr. ********* was a video taken in the Intoxilyzer room of the Topsham Police Station. This video would show that the Intoxilyzer test was administered improperly, and it would refute Officer Sloppy's assertions that Mr. ********* was exhibiting signs of impairment.

Protection of evidence of this nature was requested by Counsel in a letter to the Topsham Police Department on January 29, 2013 and Counsel copied the Sagadahoc District Attorney's Office on said letter. *See Attached* **Exhibit 1**. Counsel sent a informal discovery request to the Sagadahoc District Attorney's Office on January 29, 2013 specifically requesting that the Intoxilyzer video, among other evidence, be provided to him. *See Attached* **Exhibit 2**. Counsel again requested this evidence in a Motion for Discovery filed on or about February 25, 2013, and copied to ADA Jonathan Dontcare in the Sagadahoc District Attorney's Office. Counsel also sent a follow up letter to Detective Mark Soandso specifically requesting that the Intoxilyzer video, among other evidence, be provided to him on March 7, 2013. *See Attached* **Exhibit 3**.

On March 25, 2013, ADA Dontcare informed Counsel that the Intoxilyzer video was not preserved and was overwritten. On March 26, 2013, Counsel received a letter from Lieutenant Boss of the Topsham Police Department indicating that Officer Sloppy did not request the Intoxilyzer video be preserved, as a result, it was recorded over. *See Attached* **Exhibit 4**.

ARGUMENT

A.   The State's Failure to Preserve Known Exculpatory Evidence Was in Violation of Mr. *******'s Fourteenth Amendment Due Process Rights.**

The State's failure to preserve this properly requested video that contained exculpatory evidence was is in violation of the Maine and United States Constitutions, pursuant to the Due Process Clause and the right to a fair trial. The Government is mandated to preserve and produce properly requested evidence that is exculpatory. The United States Supreme Court has held that "[t]he Due Process Clause of the Fourteenth Amendment, as interpreted in [*Brady v. Maryland* 373 U.S. 83 (1963)], makes the good or bad faith of the State irrelevant when the State fails to disclose to the defendant material exculpatory evidence." *Arizona v. Youngblood*, 488 U.S. 51, 57 (1988) (negligent failure of police to properly preserve evidence of assailant in a sexual assault case); see also *California v. Trombetta*, 467 U.S. 479 (1984). Under *Brady*, "the suppression by the prosecution of evidence favorable to an accused upon request violates due process where the evidence is material either to guilt or to punishment, irrespective of the good faith or bad faith of the prosecution." *Brady*, 373 U.S. at 87, 83 S.Ct. 1194. The duty to disclose applies even if the accused has made no request. *See United States v. Bagley*, 473 U.S. 667, 682, 105 S.Ct. 3375, 87 L.Ed.2d 481 (1985). The *Brady* rule also encompasses evidence "known only to police investigators and not to the prosecutor. *Kyles v. Whitley*, 514 U.S. 419, 438, 115 S.Ct. 1555,131,L.Ed.2d,490(1995). A "true *Brady* violation" has three components: "[t]he evidence at issue must be favorable to the accused, either because it is exculpatory, or because it is impeaching; that evidence must have been suppressed by the State, either willfully or inadvertently; and prejudice must have ensued." *Strickler v. Greene*, 527 U.S. 263, 281-82 (1999).

In this case, the Defendant properly requested the preservation of the Intoxilyzer video. The video has been inadvertently suppressed due to the arresting officer's failure to properly preserve the video. Thus, the State, through the Police Department was at minimum negligent with regard to the duly it owes defendants according to *Brady*.

B.   The State's Failure to Preserve Exculpatory Evidence Was in Violation of Maine Rule of Criminal Procedure Rule 16.

Alternatively, the State is required to preserve and produce evidence, "which [is] material to the preparation of the defense or which the attorney for the state intends to use as evidence in any proceeding or which [was] obtained or belonged to the defendant." M.R.Crim.P. 16(b)(2)(A).

The video at issue is vital to Mr. *********'s defense. The video was properly requested. The State is subject to sanctions for failure to obtain and preserve such evidence. M.R.Crim.P. 16(d). The State and the Topsham Police Department were provided notices by Counsel's office asking to preserve the Intoxilyzer room video on January 29, 2013. Almost two months later, Counsel was informed that the video no longer exists as a result of Officer Sloppy's negligence.

Other Jurists have found that "[it] has become clear that video recordings of arrests, booking and testing procedures have important evidentiary value in OUI cases. Authorities should be required to make all reasonable efforts to preserve this evidence." *See Attached* **Exhibit 5**[3]. Sanctions for failure to preserve evidence may result in the dismissal of the criminal action with prejudice or any other sanction deemed appropriate by this Court. M.R.Crim.P. 16(d). Mr. ********* avers that this case should be dismissed as the video evidence was properly requested and the State, through the Topsham Police Department, negligently failed to preserve the evidence. If the Court is not inclined to dismiss based on the above information, Counsel requests that the Intoxilyzer results be suppressed as a result of Officer Sloppy's failure to properly preserve the video.

C.   Conclusion

Based on the foregoing reasons, the Defendant requests that this Honorable Court dismiss this matter with prejudice. Dated this 27th day of March, 2013, in Portland, Maine.

Respectfully submitted,

_____

Timothy E. Zerillo
Attorney for Defendant
ZERILLO LAW FIRM, LLC

[§§8:153-8:159 Reserved]

---

[3] In *State v. Cole*, Justice Brennan denied the motion to dismiss but granted the suppression of the Intoxilyzer. In *Cole*, the Court found that the failure to preserve the Intoxilyzer room video was a result of a technical difficulty. In the present case, there was no technical difficulty. The failure to preserve the Intoxilyzer room video was the result of Officer Sloppy failing to notify the appropriate person to preserve the video. At the very least, this is clear negligence on Officer Sloppy's part for failing to properly preserve the Intoxilyzer room video.

V.   TRIAL

A. Opening Statement

§8:160   My Approach

Below is an opening statement in a post-accident drinking case. Your client's breath test hasn't given you much to work with. He was involved in an accident, and his defense is that he was drinking after the accident. While juries don't tend to love these, sometimes they can work, and sometimes it's all you have.

For tips on effective opening statements, see Ch. 2.

§8:161   Sample Opening Statement (Post Accident Case)

Good morning ladies and gentlemen of the jury, my name is Tim Zerillo, and I represent Yosoy Fiesta. Mr. Fiesta, as you might remember, lives in Gorham. He's 21 years old is currently finishing up his undergraduate degree in English at the University of Southern Maine. You heard the Clerk say the Defendant has said he is not guilty and put his case before his country which is you. And, it is true, Yosoy has placed his faith in you because, make no mistake about it, we are here today because the Government has charged Yosoy with a crime. They are, in fact, endeavoring to forever have you label him a criminal.

Your service here today is profoundly important to our system of justice, not only for Yosoy, but for all of those individuals charged by the Government with criminal offenses in this state.

Remember, your job right now is to presume Yosoy is innocent. That means that as you sit here, if you don't think Yosoy is innocent, well we've already got a problem. The State must prove its case beyond a reasonable doubt, before the presumption of innocence is removed. The State cannot and will not do so here.

My kids got me into the Harry Potter books and movies. Have you ever seen them? Well I like to think of this presumption of innocence like Harry's invisibility cloak. For those of you who have no idea what I'm talking about, Harry has an invisibility cloak that he can put over himself when he doesn't want to be seen. Even though you can see my client right now, you cannot see him as a criminal and be true to your oath. He is presumed innocent and he is covered by that cloak.

As the jury, you only get to rip that cloak off of him and call him a criminal, call him guilty of drunk driving, if you know beyond a reasonable doubt that he's guilty. Because the last thing you want to do is make that move if he's not guilty. That would be bad for you and bad for him.

Now the principal witness for the State, Trooper Sgt. Gotcha is an impressive officer. He's been around a long time. And he's no stranger to testifying in court. And, please, this is not TV: this case is not about whether Sgt. Gotcha is lying. Quite the contrary, it's simply about things being a little too routine. As you will hear, Sgt. Gotcha's problem is that he's been doing this sort of thing so long he doesn't ask all the pertinent questions, doesn't follow standardized procedures, doesn't write everything down, and, consequently, his investigation is deficient, and his memory of events is compromised. What this case is about then is the failure of the Government to prove that the Defendant engaged in criminal conduct, and is therefore deserving of the life-long label as a criminal.

One of the bizarre things about criminal trials is that you won't be instructed on the law you will have to apply in this case until the end of the case. I'll talk more about the law later on, but for now, it's important to keep two things in mind:

(1)   It is not against the law to drink and then to drive;

(2)   It is illegal to drive while impaired by alcohol or with a blood alcohol content of .08% or more.

Here, it seems my client Yosoy got into a fender bender. He was upset by this. He's a college student, without a lot of money, and he was upset about the damage to his car. It was a single car accident, no one else was involved.

As he waited for the tow truck, he began to drink. He wasn't going anywhere, he was stuck, and he had some beer in the car. He drank 2 cans of beer before the police showed up to question him.

Now remember, it is only illegal to drink in the car you are operating. He was not operating the car or attempting to operate it when he drank the beer. And combined with the other alcohol that day, he tested at a .12 for his breath test. .08 or more is the legal limit.

But that breath test is compromised. And we'll learn why. And you'll also learn that the State can't prove beyond a reasonable doubt what affect those two beers he drank after operation made on the test. The test doesn't differentiate whether the alcohol it tests for is before or after driving. And remember, you might not like it, but it is perfectly legal for someone to drive with a .07 blood alcohol content.

The law says I'm not permitted to tell you statements that happened outside of this courtroom that will not be testified to in this courtroom with one very important exception. Months ago Yosoy entered what's called a plea in this case. Without hesitation he denied the charge. He pled not guilty. Not guilty to the charge of drunk driving. You did not hear him say those words, but I can assure you it happened. And that denial is so important, that there's an exception to the law and I am permitted to tell you it happened. And it happened and is a matter of record in this case.

At the end of this case, you will not be able to tell beyond a reasonable doubt that Yosoy drove with .08 or more in blood alcohol content. Since you will not be able to tell by our standard of law—beyond a reasonable doubt—there will be only one verdict if you are true to the oath you took today: not guilty.

[§§8:162-8:169 Reserved]

B. Cross Examination of Arresting Officer

§8:170 Key Points

Nearly every drunk driving case I have has an intoxilyzer test, and nearly all those appear valid on their face. So everything we aim to do here is to distract from that test. We want to count the ways in which our client did not appear to be intoxicated in our cross.

This is basically a disconnect defense. In other words, the client acted completely sober, so how could the machine result possibly be correct?

Key points to make are:
- The client was driving normally.
- The client stopped normally and appeared normal inside the vehicle.
- He responded to the officer's commands, produced his license and registration, and had no trouble exiting the vehicle.
- He cooperated with the officer on the field sobriety tests.

With regard to field sobriety tests, you want to suggest that even sober people can have trouble with them. If the officer made mistakes in administering the tests, which they often do, you want to highlight each mistake, get the officer to admit the mistake, and get him or her to concede the tests must be administered correctly to have any evidentiary value.

PRACTICE TIP: *Essential manuals*
If you have a drunk driving practice, and are not using the National Highway Traffic and Safety Administration (hereafter "NHTSA") manual, you need to stop right now, and buy it. If you are not using your State's own Criminal Justice Academy Manuals, do the same thing; stop right now and go get a copy. These are absolutely invaluable tools in any cross of a police officer. These are the rules the cops need to live by in investigating drunk driving cases. They are often not followed, which creates fertile ground for cross.

For more tips on cross examining police officers, see Ch.2.

§8:171 Client's Driving

First, let's have the officer credit our client with properly operating the vehicle.

Q. Officer, we've gone through your training here today. One thing you are trained to notice is if there is evidence of impairment by the way a car is being driven?
A. Yes.
Q. You often are on patrol at night?
A. Yes.
Q. And at night especially, you are on the lookout for drunk drivers?

A. I'm on the lookout for anyone who may be breaking the law.

Q. OK, but looking for possible drunk drivers is near the top of your mind?

A. I guess.

Q. You were taught how to look for drunk drivers at the Academy?

A. Yes.

Q. It's another thing discussed in the NHTSA Manual?

A. Yes.

Q. The NHTSA elaborates on 20 clues you can use to detect drunk driving at night, isn't that true?

A. Yes.

Q. One of them is the car turning with an excessively wide radius?

A. Yes.

Q. You didn't observe that here?

A. No.

Q. Another is straddling the center lane?

A. Yes.

Q. You didn't observe that here?

A. No.

Q. Yet another is striking or nearly striking another object or car?

A. Yes.

Q. You didn't have that here?

A. No.

Q. Weaving?

A. Yes, weaving is one.

Q. But there was no weaving observed here?

A. Nope.

Q. Swerving?

A. Yes.

Q. There wasn't any swerving?

A. Not that I saw.

Q. Stopping in a lane for no apparent reason is one?

A. Yes.

Q. My client didn't do that, did he?

A. No.

Q. Braking erratically is another one in the NHTSA Manual, right?

A. Yes.

Q. My client didn't do that either, did he?

A. No.

Q. The NHTSA Manual has a few others, right?

A. Yes.

Q. None of those visual clues described in the NHTSA Manual did you observe my client doing?

A. No, sir.

Q. He showed no sign of impairment in the way he drove the car, did he?

A. No.

§8:172   The Stop

Now let's talk about how well our client did during the stop.

Q. You turned on your blue lights?

A. Yes.

Q. And you stopped my client's vehicle.

A. Yes.

Q. The NHTSA Manual also describes things you should look out for during the stopping sequence, doesn't it?

A. It does.

Q. It notes that various clues at the stop may reinforce that the driver is intoxicated?
A. Yes.
Q. These clues include an attempt to flee—was there any attempt to flee here?
A. No.
Q. They also include not responding to the stop—my client responded to you stopping him here?
A. Yes.
Q. They also include an abrupt swerve—did that happen here?
A. No.
Q. They also include a sudden stop—did that happen here?
A. No.
Q. They also include striking a curb or another object—did that happen here?
A. No.
Q. He did not show any sign of impairment in the way he stopped his car?
A. No.

Everything appears to be normal. Let's make it clear that nothing is out of the ordinary as the cop approaches the vehicle.

Q. You stopped your own vehicle behind my Client's car?
A. Yes.
Q. You took a look at his vehicle before you got out?
A. Briefly.
Q. You didn't notice anything out of the ordinary?
A. Not that I can think of.
Q. OK. Then you walked up to his car?
A. Yes.
Q. You could see him in the vehicle as you got closer?
A. Yes.
Q. He wasn't slumped over to the side?
A. No.
Q. He was sitting up?
A. Yes.
Q. His head wasn't down?
A. No.
Q. His head was up straight?
A. Yes.
Q. You didn't see any brake lights as you walked to his vehicle, did you?
A. I don't recall any.
Q. As you interacted with him, you later determined the vehicle was in park, right?
A. Yes.

§8:173   Inside the Vehicle

Let's now take a look inside the vehicle.

Q. When you approached his window, he already had the window down, didn't he?
A. Yes.
Q. When you spoke to him, he made eye contact with you?
A. Most of the time.
Q. Was his vehicle on or off when you started talking with him?
A. On.
Q. And you told him to turn the vehicle off?
A. Yes.
Q. He did that?

A.   Yes.
Q.   He didn't appear to have any difficulty doing that?
A.   Not that I noticed.
Q.   And you didn't reference any difficulties with that in your report, either?
A.   No.

§8:174   Producing License and Registration

Little details count, such as how the client did when producing his license and registration.

Q.   You asked my Client for his license and registration?
A.   Yes.
Q.   And he retrieved the registration from the glove box?
A.   Yes.
Q.   And you were watching him closely during this time for your own safety?
A.   Yes.
Q.   And he didn't have trouble getting into the glove box?
A.   Not really.
Q.   He didn't fall over?
A.   No.
Q.   He didn't miss the latch?
A.   No.
Q.   And inside the glove box was a small folder?
A.   Yes.
Q.   And there were multiple records in the folder?
A.   Yes.
Q.   And he was able to thumb through them and get the right document for you?
A.   Yes.
Q.   And his license was in his wallet?
A.   I think so.
Q.   And that was in his back pocket?
A.   I don't remember.
Q.   You remember that he gave you his license?
A.   Yes.
Q.   And it came from his wallet?
A.   Yes.
Q.   And you don't remember him having any problems getting his wallet?
A.   No.
Q.   And you don't remember any problems with him taking the license out of his wallet?
A.   No.
Q.   You don't remember him handing you a debit card by mistake?
A.   No.
Q.   He didn't show any signs of impairment in the way in which he retrieved his registration did he?
A.   I saw signs of impairment...
Q.   But not in the way he physically retrieved his registration, right?
A.   Not in the way he got it, no.
Q.   Same with the license?
A.   Yes.

§8:175   Exiting the Vehicle

Now, the client gets out of the vehicle. Again, make sure to credit the client with all that he did right as a way of attacking the Government's case.

Q. You asked my Client to get out of the vehicle?
A. Yes.
Q. He did it?
A. Yes.
Q. He didn't have any problem getting out?
A. He was a little slow to get out.
Q. Slow compared to what? Did you have a stopwatch on him?
A. No, I just thought he was slow to get out.
Q. Did you have to command him to get out twice?
A. No.
Q. Had you seen him get out of a car before that time?
A. No.
Q. So you don't know how quickly he normally gets out, right?
A. Right.
Q. You don't know if he has any physical problems?
A. No.
Q. When he got out of the vehicle, he didn't stumble?
A. No.
Q. He didn't lean on the vehicle for support?
A. No.
Q. He didn't lean on you for support?
A. No.

§8:176   Client's Cooperation on Field Sobriety Tests

The Field Sobriety Tests, if demolished with a proper cross-examination, can be effectively reduced to the junk science that they are in front of the jury. That requires, however, that you establish that, at a minimum, the officer made mistakes in the test administration or interpretation.

At the outset, I like the police officer to credit my client with behaving appropriately and cooperatively during the administration of the field sobriety testing.

Q. How many field sobriety tests did you ask Mr. Driver to do?
A. Well, there was the walk and turn, the one-leg stand, the horizontal gaze nystagmus test, the vertical gaze nystagmus test, the finger-to-nose test and the alphabet test.
Q. That was 6 tests?
A. Yes.
Q. Mr. Driver took all 6 of the tests?
A. Yes
Q. Mr. Driver was cooperative in taking the tests?
A. Yes.
Q. He did not refuse to take the tests?
A. No, he didn't.
Q. Would you agree he was pleasant to deal with?
A. I would say he was, yes.

§8:177   Testing Must Be Administered Correctly

Make sure you get the officer to agree that for the field sobriety testing to be reliable, that it must be done right.

Q. Officer, you stated earlier that you have been trained to detect and apprehend impaired drivers?
A. Yes.
Q. During your training you were issued a "standardized field sobriety procedure's officer's manual?"
A. Yes I was.
Q. The procedures in that manual have been adopted in Maine?

A.   Yes.
Q.   The manual indicates that when standardized tests are administered properly, they are reliable?
A.   Yes.
Q.   And you would agree then, that if the standardized tests aren't administered properly, they are not reliable?
A.   I don't know about all of the time. They may still be partially reliable depending on the test.
Q.   Do you believe that you can simply ignore the rules of the manual and get an accurate test?
A.   I'm not saying that.
Q.   You agree that those rules are there for a reason?
A.   Yes.
Q.   You agree that the testing should be standardized?
A.   I'm not sure what that means.
Q.   You agree that the testing should be done the same way be each officer administering tests so we get the best level of reliability from them?
A.   That would be ideal, yes.
Q.   You would agree with me then agree that if the testing is not standardized that it would not be reliable?
A.   Yes.

§8:178   Walk and Turn Test

Instructions

Now let's take a look at the walk and turn test. This is a pretty common field sobriety test that you may encounter. In crossing on this test, make sure to explain to the jury exactly what is involved. You want the jury saying, "Hey, I couldn't do that stone cold sober!"

Q.   You gave Mr. Driver the walk and turn test?
A.   Yes.
Q.   You told him to take 9 heel-to-toe steps down the line, turn around, and take 9 heel to toe steps back up the line?
A.   Yes.
Q.   You told him that when he turned to keep his front foot on the line and turn by taking a series of small steps with his other foot?
A.   Yes
Q.   That while he was walking to keep his arms at the side at all times and to count the steps out loud?
A.   Right.
Q.   And not to stop until the test is completed?
A.   Correct.

> ### PRACTICE TIP: *Exploit errors in test instructions*
> Make sure with all of these tests that the instructions are given clearly and correctly. The best way to do this is if you have audio from the stop or a cruiser cam recording. Often the instructions are given incorrectly, and you then have a fertile ground of cross examination. Other times the officer merely isn't clear or loud enough. More points for you on cross.

Condition of Roadway

Remember, the roadway in which these field sobriety tests are performed must be a reasonably dry, hard, level, non-slippery surface. If these conditions are not present, the validity of the test is compromised.

> ### PRACTICE TIP: *Establishing defects in the roadway*
> So, make sure to get over to the scene of the testing. In Maine, the roads are often bumpy and pitched. Take pictures. Take video. Measure the angles of pitch with a level and take photos and video of the level. It is entirely possible that the surface is far from appropriate for the testing the Government claims to be reliable.

Q.   Have you taken any time to go back to the location of the testing since Mr. Driver's test?

A.   Not that exact spot.

Q.   I'm showing you a photograph. Take a look at it. Is that a fair and accurate representation of how the location of the testing looked when Mr. Driver was tested?

A.   That is the spot. But it was at night, and this photograph is in the day.

Q.   And at night, you couldn't see those ruts in the roadway right?

A.   I don't remember them.

Q.   And you couldn't see that frost heave there, could you?

A.   I don't remember it.

Q.   The surface for field sobriety testing needs to be hard, right?

A.   Yes.

Q.   It needs to be non-slippery, right?

A.   Right.

Q.   It needs to be level?

A.   Yes.

Q.   You would agree that the area, as it appears in the picture, is not level.

A.   I think the roadside is level, but there are bumps in it in the picture.

Q.   Well, in fact the roadside is not level. Take a look at this photograph. I'm going to go through some measurements with you that show there is an 18 degree pitch off this breakdown lane toward the gully here. Does that surprise you?

A.   Not terribly.

Q.   I'm going to show you another photo I took here. Do you know what is pictured in this photo?

A.   The area of the testing I would assume, and a level?

Q.   Do you know how a level works?

A.   Yes.

Q.   How?

A.   If you are trying to find out if something is level, the bubble on the level should be in the center, between those lines there.

Q.   Right. And what does the level in the picture show?

A.   That the spot there is not level.

Q.   Does it even appear close to level?

A.   Not really.

Q   So, you would agree it's not flat entirely?

A.   Not entirely.

Q.   Your Honor, I'd like to admit these and publish them to the jury so that they can take a look at this roadway while I ask the Officer questions about it.

Test Administration

Now let's look at the testing itself.

Q.   The line that you asked Mr. Driver to walk, that is not an actual line is it?

A.   That's right.

Q.   It's not a line on the road.

A.   No.

Q.   It's not a line you drew?

A.   No.

Q.   It is an imaginary line?

A.   Yes.

Q.   Did you show Mr. Driver your imaginary line?

A.   I told him to walk a straight line out 9 heel to toe steps…

Q.   I understand that, but you didn't tell him what straight line to walk, right?

A.   I don't know what that means.

Q.   [Sometimes I'll take a ruler and draw for the jury]. There could be imaginary straight lines for him to walk, here, here and here, couldn't there be?

A. Yes, but I told him to walk in this direction.
Q. On your imaginary straight line?
A. Yes.
Q. And he wasn't able to stay entirely on the imaginary straight line that you saw?
A. No.
Q. But most of the time, he remained on your imaginary straight line, didn't he?
A. Most of the time.
Q. In fact, there are 8 standardized clues in the manual, correct?
A. Yes.
Q. I want to run through them with you. One is that the suspect cannot keep balance while listening to the instructions. You didn't observe that here, did you?
A. No.
Q. Two is that the suspect starts before the instructions are finished. You didn't observe that here, did you?
A. No.
Q. Three is that the suspect stops while walking in the test. You didn't observe that here, did you?
A. No.
Q. Four is that the suspect does not touch heel to toe. You did observe that here.
A. Yes.
Q. That was not for all of his steps though, correct?
A. No.
Q. He did properly touch heel to toe properly for most of his steps.
A. For most, yes.
Q. Five is that he steps off the imaginary line. You observed him step off your imaginary line twice.
A. He stepped off the line twice.
Q. Six is he uses arms to balance. You observed that here?
A. Yes.
Q. Seven is if he makes an improper turn. That is the turn with a series of small steps. He did that right?
A. He did.
Q. Eight is that he took an incorrect number of steps. He took the correct number of steps here?
A. Yes.
Q. Out of a possible eight clues, you observed only three, is that right?
A. Yes.

The Field Sobriety Tests, if demolished with a proper cross-examination, can be effectively reduced to the junk science that they are in front of the jury. That requires, however, that you establish that, at a minimum, the officer made mistakes in the test administration or interpretation.

§8:179   HGN Test

The horizontal gaze nystagmus test is the perfect opportunity to grab the jury with the junk science nature of field sobriety tests (in your view at least). Don't forget the obvious. Make sure your officer is qualified and certified to do the HGN test. You can usually get that information from your officer's police academy.

Below are two sample cross examinations. They assume the officers are certified. Both go through the correct procedures for administering the test and show that the officer does not known them and did not follow them.

Example 1:

Q. You gave Mr. Driver the horizontal gaze nystagmus test?
A. Yes.
Q. This is supposed to measure the smooth tracking of the eyeball when following a pen or flashlight?
A. Yes.
Q. You were trained in giving this test?
A. I was.
Q. You are trained to look for smooth pursuit of the object by the eyeball?

A. Yes.

Q. You were also trained to look for a jerking of the eyeball at a certain angle of onset?

A. Yes.

Q. The angle of onset is to determine at what angle with the nose the eye commences to jerk?

A. Yes.

Q. You were taught that when a person has a blood alcohol concentration of .10 or more, that the jerking will begin before the eyeball has moved 45 degrees to the side?

A. Yes.

Q. In applying the test, if you were wrong about where the 45 degree angle was compared to the eye, it could affect your conclusion?

A. Yes.

Q. You've never been tested for proficiency in estimating a 45 degree angle?

A. I don't know what you mean.

Q. You are estimating a 45 degree angle, right?

A. Based on my experience and training, yes.

Q. You don't measure the angle you use, do you?

A. No.

Q. Some people have naturally occurring nystagmus, don't they?

A. Some people do.

Q. You are familiar with optokinetic nystagmus?

A. Yes.

Q. Optokinetic nystagmus occurs when the eye watches an object that suddenly moves out of sight, or when there are sharply contrasted moving images?

A. Yes.

Q. Optokinetic nystagmus can occur when watching flashing lights?

A. Yes.

Q. Your blue lights were on during Mr. Driver's field sobriety testing, weren't they?

A. They were.

Q. Watching moving traffic at night can cause optokinetic nystagmus?

A. I believe so.

Q. These tests were performed on the side of a busy roadway, right?

A. Yes.

Q. You can't say for certain if the nystagmus you observed in Mr. Driver was not optokinetic nystagmus?

A. Not for certain.

Q. When you tested my client, you first looked for resting nystagmus, right?

A. Yes.

Q. And that is looking for the jerking of the eyes as someone looks straight ahead, right?

A. Yes.

Q. And you didn't observe resting nystagmus, did you?

A. No.

Q. You used a pen light to perform the testing?

A. Yes.

Q. In previous testimony, you said you held the pen light approximately 10 inches from my client's face in performing the HGN test, right?

A. Approximately.

Q. And the NHSTA Manual says you are to hold the stimulus, in this case the pen light, 12 to 15 inches away from the subject, correct?

A. Yes.

Q. You can make a person go cross-eyed if you hold the stimulus to close to them. Correct?

A. Yes.

Q. And you held it to close here, correct?

A. I held it approximately 10 inches…

Q. And if we take your approximation as true, the stimulus was too close to my Client, right?

A. Yes.

Q. And if the instructions in administering these tests aren't followed, the validity of the tests is compromised, right?
A. Yes.
Q. You started on your right side, meaning my client's left eye?
A. Yes.
Q. And you had my client follow the pen light out to 45 degree angle?
A. Yes.
Q. And we've already said that you don't measure that 45 degree angle, right?
A. No.
Q. So you are told to stop above the shoulder?
A. Yes.
Q. That's because if you go past the shoulder, you've gone too far.
A. Yes.
Q. That would be maximum deviation?
A. Yes.
Q. If you go to maximum deviation, everyone's eyes will bounce around won't they?
A. Yes.
Q. Even if they're stone cold sober.
A. Yes.
Q. When you performed this test on my client's left eye, how long did it take you to perform the pass?
A. I didn't time it.
Q. Can't you estimate it for us?
A. Approximately 3 seconds.
Q. And was it also 3 seconds to do the left eye, as well?
A. Approximately.
Q. You training manual says you are supposed to have a pace of 2 seconds out and 2 seconds back to center, for 4 seconds total each time. Do you remember that?
A. Yes.
Q. So your 3 seconds would have been faster than your training?
A. Yes.

Example 2:

Here is another way to approach an HGN cross. I love to hammer officers on HGN because they so often administer the test incorrectly.

Q. The only standardized test you gave to Mr. Driver was the HGN test
A. Yes
Q. And in that test you were looking for Nystagmus
A. Yes
Q. Which is basically an involuntary jerking of the eyes
A. Yes, that's basically it.

The following questions are open-ended. Open-ended questions should usually be avoided on cross. But here I expect the officer to mess up some of these answers.

Q. How many clues are there for the HGN?
A. I think there are four clues
Q. Four clues?
A. I believe so.
Q. I'm going to show you the NHTSA Manual. It says you are looking for six clues, right?
A. Yes.
Q. Four clues is wrong.
A. Yes.
Q. Ok, and when you test for nystagmus, you use a stimulus?

A. Yes.
Q. What was your stimulus?
A. My finger.
Q. And when you first move the stimulus, what do you check for?
A. Equal tracking.
Q. That's almost right—you are looking for equal tracking and equal pupil size, right?
A. Right.
Q. And did you score that?
A. I don't believe so.
Q. You aren't sure if you scored it?
A. I don't believe I did.
Q. You aren't supposed to score it, right?
A. I don't think so.
Q. They tell you not to score it in the NHSTA manual right?
A. Right.

HGN Clue #1—Lack of Smooth Pursuit

Q. What is the first clue you look for in HGN?
A. The lack of smooth pursuit.
Q. And how many passes do you perform for lack of smooth pursuit.
A. Two passes.
Q. When I say pass, I mean you start in the center, then move it out to your right, then back to center, then move it out to your left and back to center. That's one pass, right?
A. Yes.
Q. What pace did you use?
A. I didn't time it.
Q. Well, you do two passes, two seconds each eye out, two seconds back to center, for each eye, right?
A. I think so.
Q. You don't know the pace you are supposed to use?
A. I'm sure you're right.
Q. So that's 16 seconds total, right? Two passes, two seconds each eye out, two seconds back to center, for each eye, so 16 seconds in total?
A. Yes.
Q. How long did you do it in?
A. I don't know.
Q. Well, thankfully, we have the video. I'm going to give you this stopwatch, and when I play the video I want you to start the watch when you start the test and stop it when you end this portion of the test. Ok?
A. Ok.
(Playing video)
Q. How long did it take you to perform this portion of the test?
A. Ten seconds.
Q. Ten seconds. I was supposed to be 16 seconds, right?
A. Right.
Q. That was a mistake, right?
A. Yes.

HGN Clue #2—Distinct and Sustained Nystragmus of Maximum Deviation

Q. So lack of smooth pursuit is passes one and two—what are you checking for in passes three and four?
A. Distinct nystagmus at maximum deviation.
Q. OK. What pace did you use?
A. The same pace.
Q. The wrong pace then, right?

A. Right.
Q. To determine maximum deviation, you take the stimulus from center as far out as the eye will see, right?
A. Right
Q. How do you know when you are there?
A. I just go off the shoulder until where they would start to turn their head.
Q. It is supposed to be that you hold it until there is no white showing in the corner of the eye, right?
A. Right.
Q. You don't do that?
A. I think I do.
Q. But you don't check for it.
A. Not really.
Q. And you need to, for this test, hold the stimulus at maximum deviation for how long?
A. I don't remember.
Q. It is supposed to be a four second hold at a minimum.
A. Ok.
Q. Do you remember that now?
A. Yes.
Q. And the test shouldn't count if you don't do it properly.
A. I agree.
Q. People's eyes will bounce for a few seconds at maximum deviation.
A. Yes.
Q. That's why you hold it for at least four seconds.
A. Right.
Q. Did you hold each eye for at least four seconds here?
A. I don't know.

Go through each eye with stopwatch. This officer did it wrong every time. I had have say he did it wrong every time.

Q. There are a lot of mistakes here, right?
A. Right.
Q. So the test, it's not reliable, right?
A. Right.
Q. It shouldn't count, should it?
A. No, I don't think it should count.

§8:180 One Leg Stand Test

Q. You also gave Mr. Fiesta the one leg stand test?
A. Yes.
Q. You were trained in that test as well?
A. Yes.
Q. That test also requires reasonably dry, hard, level, and non-slippery surface, right?
A. Yes.
Q. Just like the walk and turn test?
A. Yes.
Q. And you've already agreed with me that the surface this area was performed on wasn't level?
A. Yes.
Q. It's also true that individuals with back, leg, or inner ear problems not suitable for the one leg stand test?
A. Yes.
Q. The one leg stand is a hard test?
A. I don't think so.
Q. The test is not to be given to people who are more than 50 lbs. overweight?
A. Yes.

Q. To people who are 60 years old or older?
A. Yes.
Q. To people who have inner ear problems?
A. Yes
Q. In fact its difficult for sober people, isn't it?
A. Not to me.
Q. I want you to look at the the second paragraph of page 54 of DWI Detection and Standardized Field Sobriety Testing.
A. Okay.
Q. That manual indicates the one leg stand test is difficult for sober people?
A. Yes.
Q. Did you ask my client if he had back, leg or inner ear problems?
A. I believe so.
Q. But you didn't note that in your report, did you?
A. I don't know. (Showing report) No, I didn't.
Q. And if it's not in your report, you can't be sure you asked my client if he had back, leg or inner ear problems?
A. Not sure, but I believe I did.
Q. When you are performing the one leg stand test, you are looking for 4 standard clues, right?
A. Yes.
Q. Those clues are if the person sways while balancing, uses arms for balance, hops, or puts his foot down.
A. Yes.
Q. Mr. Fiesta didn't sway while balancing, right?
A. No.
Q. He didn't hop?
A. No.
Q. He didn't put his foot down while balancing.
A. No.
Q. You did say he used his arms for balance.
A. He did.
Q. So you observed that he performed 3 out of the 4 tests correctly?
Q. Yes.

[§§8:181-8:189 Reserved]

C. Cross Examination of Government Expert on Breath Testing

§8:190   Key Points

With the variations on breath testing equipment, I am not discussing specific machines here, but rather, general ways you might frame an attack on the State's expert.

These cross-examination excerpts make the points that:

- The expert is not neutral, but rather part of the prosecution team
- (If partition ratios are admissible in your jurisdiction) Breath machine uses an average partition ratio, not the client's specific ratio, which may mean the machine overstated the client's results.
- (If you are mounting a GERD or similar defense) that alcohol in the stomach or mouth can overstate breath results.

§8:191   On the Government's Team

Let's be clear that the government expert is a part of the state's team.

Q. You're the State of Maine's expert?
A. Yes.
Q. You testify for the prosecution?
A. Yes.

Q. They called you to be here today?
A. Yes.
Q. You're a government employee?
A. Yes.

§8:192   Partition Ratios

Let's take a look at some cross on blood-breath partition ratios.

Q. Mr. Chemist the percentage of alcohol in expired lung air is not the same as the percentage of alcohol in the blood?
A. No. It's not.
Q. The manufacturers of the breathalyzer machine decided what percentage of alcohol in the expired lung air equaled the alcohol level in the blood?
A. Yes.
Q. The machine tests the alcohol level in an individual's breath?
A. Yes.
Q. And is trying to convert it to alcohol in the blood?
A. Not sure they are trying to convert it,
Q. There is a blood-to-breath ratio established with the breathalyzer machine?
A. Yes.
Q: The blood-to-breath ratio differs from person to person?
A. Yes.
Q. And the machine doesn't take into account the differences we all have with breath-to-blood ratios.
A. No.
Q. The blood-to-breath is fixed?
A. Yes.
Q. It's fixed at 2100 to 1?
A. Yes.
Q. The breathalyzer does not measure the individual's breath-to-blood ratio?
A. No.
Q. The breathalyzer that Mr. Fiesta blew into did not measure Mr. Fiesta's own blood-to-breath ratio?
A. No.
Q. It measured based on the machines fixed rate, right?
A. Yes.
Q. You have not studied Mr. Fiesta's blood-to-breath ratio?
A. No, I haven't.
Q. Individual differences in blood-to-breath ratio could dramatically change the breath testing result?
A. It would depend on the blood-to-breath ratio.
Q. If Mr. Fiesta's ratio is below the machine's ratio, then the actual blood alcohol content would be overstated by the test?
A. Yes.
Q. And we don't know what that is for Mr. Fiesta, right?
A. No, we only have averages.

§8:193   Mouth or Stomach Alcohol

Q. Mouth or stomach alcohol can also skew the results of the machine?
A. Yes.
Q. Blowing mouth alcohol into the machine contaminates the sample?
A. Yes.
Q. Mouth alcohol has a higher density than breath alcohol?
A. Yes.
Q. Stomach alcohol does too?
A. It does.

Q. Mouth alcohol is not blood alcohol?

A. It's not.

Q. Stomach alcohol is not blood alcohol is it?

A. No.

Q. In fact, Mr. Fiesta's blood was never tested directly for alcohol was it?

A. No.

Q. What is GERD, Mr. Chemist?

A. It is gastro esophageal reflux disease. Basically, food and drink from the stomach leak from the stomach into the esophagus.

Q. The esophagus is the tube that goes from the stomach to the mouth.

A. Yes.

Q. Many people suffer from GERD.

A. Yes.

Q. It's fairly common?

A. Fairly common. I'm not sure in percentages.

Q. I'm going to represent to you that there are studies indicating that approximately 10 percent of the adult population has GERD. Does that represent your knowledge in terms of percentages.

A. That sounds consistent.

Q. When someone has GERD, some of the symptoms are burping?

A. Yes.

Q. Belching?

A. Yes.

Q. Regurgitation?

A. Yes.

Q. And with burping, belching and regurgitation there can be contamination of the breath sample?

A. Yes.

[§§8:194-8:199 Reserved]

D. Closing Argument

§8:200   My The Approach

Let's examine a closing for our non-criminal drunk driving defendant, named Mr. Lafesta. He was driving down the road coming home from dinner with his wife when he was pulled over. He had a few too many glasses of wine, and "oops!" he's a .11.

§8:201   Sample Closing Argument

Here are the facts of this case boiled down: the validity of the field test has been compromised. The breath test has been contaminated. These facts represent reasonable doubt. These facts mean you let Mr. Lafesta go home. These facts mean Mr. Lafesta is not a criminal.

For you to determine whether the State has met its burden of proving this case beyond a reasonable doubt, you need to look at all the facts and circumstances. The State argues that you should merely accept the breath test of a .11 and enter a guilty verdict. The State thinks that you should accept very minor failures on field sobriety testing—testing that was not administered properly to begin with—and brand Mr. Lafesta a criminal for the rest of his life. We disagree.

The State is trying to build a bridge. It is a bridge between charging Mr. Lafesta and convicting Mr. Lafesta. For the State to succeed in what they want, they need each and every one of you to walk across that bridge.

But they're not asking you to actually look at the bridge or determine whether it is safe to walk across. They're asking you to ignore how rickety the bridge is when you step on it. They're asking you to ignore missing planks and holes in the bridge that you can fall through. They're asking for you to ignore all of those risks, and to blindly go forward and walk across that rickety old bridge. But your job as a jury is to look for those holes. Your job is to look for those danger zones. And it is my job to point them out to you.

You may have noticed many of them already. Mr. Lafesta was driving home with his wife after a nice dinner out at Fore Street. As he told the police, he had a couple of glasses of wine and a large meal.

The police officer pulled him over because he had a tail light out. You now know, having listened to the evidence, there are a number of ways in which police officers are supposed to detect drunk drivers on the road before pulling them over. In fact, there are twenty clues that the police officers manual says that the cops can use to detect drunk drivers at night. Not one of the 20 clues did Mr. Lafesta's driving exhibit. It was just random that he was pulled over with a tail light out.

Then there are clues in what we call the stopping sequence that is evidence that someone may be drunk while driving. And Mr. Lafesta didn't have any of those clues either. He didn't do anything in the stopping sequence or in his driving that would tell a police officer or anyone else that he was drunk while driving. And he was able to produce his license and registration, when requested. And turn off his vehicle. And get out of car without falling or stumbling. And talk to the officer. And communicate with the officer back and forth while having a conversation.

The officer says Mr. Lafesta's eyes were bloodshot. He said he smelled an odor of alcohol on his breath.

Well, Mr. Lafesta told the police officer he had a couple of glasses of wine. That would account for the odor of alcohol. By the way, that's legal. It is fine to drive after having drinks as long as you are not a .08 or higher. And as far as his bloodshot eyes, the stop occurred after 11:00 at night. Mr. Lafesta is a couple years older than I am, but not much. My eyes are bloodshot after 10:00 p.m.; I don't know about yours.

So the police officer does three tests on Mr. Lafesta. He does the HGN test, which is the horizontal gaze nystagmus test, the walk and turn test and the one leg stand test. If any of those tests is not performed in the correct circumstances, it can affect the result. It may mean that you need to throw the test out completely in your determination. It may mean that you decide that the test isn't entirely accurate. And these tests were done wrong. Plain wrong.

For the HGN test, at the very least the police officer held the stimulus my client was supposed to follow with his eyes 10 inches from his face. He admitted it. The people who created the test will tell you if you don't hold the stimulus up to 12-15 inches away from the person taking the test, you can make them go cross-eyed. That messes up the test. This means you shouldn't count it, because here it was too close to his face and the results of the test are skewed.

The one leg stand, and walk and turn test each need a reasonably dry and flat hard and level surface for the test to be performed correctly. I have shown you, and you have evidence that you can take with you in the jury room, that this surface was bumpy and sloped. The validity of both of those tests is in doubt because they were not done in the right conditions. When the tests are not performed correctly, you can't use them.

Aside from that, even with the wrong surface being used, Mr. Lafesta did pretty well! There are 8 possible clues the officer can observe at a walk and turn test. Even on this bumpy and sloped surface, Mr. Lafesta only had three. The vast majority he had right. And on the one leg test there were 4 possible clues, and Mr. Lafesta got all 4 right! I would submit to you that these field sobriety tests do not tell you much. In fact, what tells you more is how Mr. Lafesta was actually driving as observed by the officer before the stop. And his driving was good.

But then you say to me, "Tim, what about the .11 blood test?"

Well, first of all the .11 blood test is not a dramatically high test. Remember .08 is the legal limit. The chemist testified that there is a .01 variance in the test either + or −. On top of that the testing is skewed here because Mr. Lafesta has GERD.

You heard us talking about GERD. It's essentially when the stomach backs up into the esophagus. We all have food and drink that is in our stomach after eating. And the esophagus is just the tube that runs from your stomach to your mouth. Well, people with GERD have stomachs that periodically back up into their esophagus. And when those stomach contents back up into the esophagus you can have alcohol in the mouth. That mouth alcohol is a much higher concentration of alcohol than breath alcohol. In other words, when you have mouth alcohol from GERD, you can have a much higher test, a false high test. Here, we have a fairly low test anyway, of .11, with a .01 variance to begin with. And this GERD could have very well have caused the legal difference between legal driving at .07 and illegal driving at .08. The reality is the State has not proven beyond a reasonable doubt that Mr. Lafesta's blood alcohol content was above a .08.

So let's talk about that burden of proof that the State can't meet here. …

For tips on closing arguments and sample language for burden of proof and reasonable doubt arguments, see Ch. 2.

CHAPTER 9

FIREARMS OFFENSES: POSSESSION BY DISQUALIFIED PERSONS & OTHER FIREARMS CHARGES

Possession of firearms by disqualified persons is a growth industry. Prosecutions will continue to rise as domestic assault convictions rise, and as the definitions as to what constitutes domestic crimes continue to expand. Unlike other areas of the law discussed in this book, if you have a firearms case, there is a good chance you are in federal court. Federal firearms laws are broad. While the states have their own firearm statutes, my experience has been that the majority of firearm prosecutions are federal. This may be due to the fact that there are federal agencies, like the ATF, primarily devoted to gun prosecutions. We will be looking at federal firearm laws in this chapter.

FIREARMS OFFENSES:

FIREARMS OFFENSES:

I.   ELEMENTS AND COMMON SCENARIOS

§9:01   Summary of Elements of a Federal Firearms Possession Case

The defendant must be in possession or receipt of a firearm or ammunition. 18 U.S.C. §922(g).

Ask:
- Is there actual possession?
- Is there constructive possession?
- Is there sole or joint possession?

AND

The defendant must be in one of the following categories of disqualification:
- Felon (including persons under indictment on felony charges who received new firearms. See 18 U.S.C. §922(a), (g)(1). A felon is a person convicted in any court of a crime punishable by imprisonment for a term exceeding one year.
- Illegal drug user or addict. 18 U.S.C. §922(g)(3).
- Illegal alien or alien in the U.S. on a nonimmigrant visa. 18 U.S.C. §922(g)(5).
- A person subject to a domestic restraining order. The order must prohibit contact with an intimate partner, or child of the subject, and must have been issued only after a hearing of which the subject was notified and at which the subject had an opportunity to participate. The order must also find the subject poses a threat to the physical safety of the intimate partner or child or must prohibit the use, threatened use or attempted use of physical force. 18 U.S.C. §922(g)(8).
- A person with a prior conviction for domestic assault (including someone with a prior conviction for any assault or threatened use of a deadly weapon against a present or former spouse or partner or child or guardian of any such person). 18 U.S.C. §922(g)(9).
- A fugitive from justice. 18 U.S.C. §922(g)(2).
- A person who was dishonorably discharged from the military. 18 U.S.C. §922(g)(6).
- An individual who has been adjudicated as a mental defective or has been committed to any mental institution. 18 U.S.C. §922(g)(4). Watch out for what are commonly called "blue paper" institutionalizations. A blue paper, or a short involuntary stay in a psych ward, may not count as an "adjudication" that a person is a mental defective. *See for example United States v. Rehlander*, 666 F. 3d 45 (1st Cir. 2012).
- An individual who has renounced his or her United States citizenship. 18 U.S.C. §922(g)(7).

AND

The firearm or ammunition was transported across a state line or foreign borders at any time. 18 U.S.C. §922(g).
State firearm laws vary widely and the interstate commerce requirement does not matter. Some states only restrict felons. Other states, a growing number it seems, are also restricting those with domestic violence misdemeanors.

§9:02   Felon in Possession

Felon in possession cases are easy to spot. Perhaps your client needs a gun in his, ahem, occupation (drug dealer, etc.). Even though he knows he is prohibited, carrying a gun is a part of the job description.

There certainly are the occasional innocent possession cases. Perhaps a client was not warned that he couldn't possess. Or maybe he thought he could possess a rifle but not a handgun. While this type of *ignorant* possession is not a defense, truly *innocent* possession may be. Like the felon who doesn't know his spouse hides a gun under their bed. That said, most everyone now knows, even if they have not been warned by a defense lawyer, that a felony conviction restricts firearm rights.

§9:03   Domestic Violence

Less commonly known is that individuals convicted of misdemeanor domestic assault are just as disqualified from firearms possession as felons. Least well known is the firearms possession disqualification for individuals subject to "domestic violence restraining orders." It is hard for people to imagine that possession of a firearm while under a qualifying restraining order means they can be prosecuted for felonies in federal court.

§9:04   Domestic Violence for Law Enforcement and Military Clients

You may end up representing a cop or member of the military charged with a domestic assault or a felony. Those who possess guns in their occupations were not originally excluded from possession in their official capacities when the Gun Control Act was first enacted. This has been changed since.

The Gun Control Act was amended so that employees of government agencies convicted of misdemeanor crimes of domestic violence are not exempt from disabilities with respect to their receipt or possession of firearms or ammunition. This means that disqualified military members and police officers cannot possess firearms, even during the performance of their official duties. It also does not matter if the firearm or ammunition was purchased or is owned by the government. A misdemeanor domestic assault, in other words, can be career suicide.

[§§9:05-9:09 Reserved]

II.   STRATEGIES AND TACTICS

A. Has the Government Proven Defendant's Identity?

Sometimes, the most obvious points are the ones you need to train yourself to remember. We look at the facts of these cases so closely that we forget to see the forest for the trees. An easy element to miss in this process is identity.

§9:10   Domestic Violence Restraining Order

Imagine you are representing a client named Brutus Grant who is charged with possessing a firearm while as a prohibited person under 18 USC §922(g)(8).

The government has provided you with the restraining order that Brutus was subject to. The restraining order on its face identifies Brutus Grant as the defendant. It is clear that your client is also named Brutus Grant. He has admitted that to the cops.

Just because you have a Brutus Grant in a restraining order and a Brutus Grant in a criminal case doesn't make them one and the same. Is this Brutus the same Brutus who is subject to the restraining order?

The government, it seems to me, would need to call the plaintiff in the restraining order as a witness that Brutus is the person she had a restraining order against. The plaintiff would need to properly identify him as the one and the same Brutus in the restraining order. Sometimes, the government is not prepared for this.

If the government tries to prove identity at trial merely by admitting the restraining order, you may have an appeal issue. You should immediately raise a Confrontation Clause objection, noting that you can't cross-examine the restraining order on the issue of identity.

§9:11   Felony and Domestic Assault Convictions

This identity challenge, of course, works equally well with felony and domestic assault convictions. John Smith has a domestic assault conviction from 1999 for beating his wife. The government knows it has a John Smith as a defendant and assumes they are one and the same. This is a mistake that defense counsel should watch for (without telegraphing your intentions to the government).

Consider a Motion for Judgment of Acquittal in these situations (unless you have a judge who you think might let the Government re-open the evidence and correct the mistake). Let the Government put on its case and then move for Judgment of Acquittal on the ground that they have not proven identity. Or, as a matter of strategy, you may prefer to attack this issue of identity earlier. You could argue that the Government needs to provide a witness to identity related to the prior conviction. You can also fold in the Confrontation Clause arguments discussed above if you proceed in that fashion.

Federal Rule of Criminal Procedure 29 allows for entry of Judgment of Acquittal if the evidence submitted by the government is insufficient. This means that the evidence, viewed in the light most favorable to the government, does not establish the essential elements of the offense. *United States v. Villarreal*, 324 F.3d 319 (5th Cir. 2003). The court should grant a Rule 29 motion for judgment of acquittal if there is not enough evidence from which a reasonable jury could find guilt beyond a reasonable doubt. *United States v. Curtis*, 324 F.3d 501 (7th Cir. 2003).

[§§9:12-9:19 Reserved]

B. Was the Device a Firearm?

§9:20   What Is a Firearm?

Almost every firearm is based on the same simple concept. An explosion occurs behind a projectile to launch it down a barrel. While firearms come in all shapes and sizes, they all work off of that same basic construct. According to federal law, a "firearm" is:

(A) any weapon (including a starter gun) which will or is designed to or may readily be converted to expel a projectile by the action of an explosive; (B) the frame or receiver of any such weapon; (C) any firearm muffler or firearm silencer; or (D) any destructive device. Such term does not include an antique firearm.

18 USC §921(3).

§9:21   Antique Firearm Exception

What are antique firearms?

[A]ny firearm (including any firearm with a matchlock, flintlock, percussion cap, or similar type of ignition system) manufactured in or before 1898; or any replica of any firearm described in subparagraph (A) if such replica—is not designed or redesigned for using rimfire or conventional centerfire fixed ammunition, or uses rimfire or conventional centerfire fixed ammunition which is no longer manufactured in the United States and which is not readily available in the ordinary channels of commercial trade; or any muzzle loading rifle, muzzle loading shotgun, or muzzle loading pistol, which is designed to use black powder, or a black powder substitute, and which cannot use fixed ammunition. For purposes of this subparagraph, the term 'antique firearm' shall not include any weapon which incorporates a firearm frame or receiver, any firearm which is converted into a muzzle loading weapon, or any muzzle loading weapon, which can be readily converted to fire fixed ammunition by replacing the barrel, bolt, breechblock, or any combination thereof.

18 U.S.C. §921(a)(16).

> **PRACTICE TIP:** *Get an opinion about muzzle loaders*
>
> I commonly get questions about muzzle loaders. A muzzle loader may not be a firearm, but it will be considered a firearm by the ATF if it incorporates the frame or receiver of a firearm. If my client isn't sure if his muzzle loader qualifies as a firearm, I seek an advisory opinion from the ATF (assuming your client is not charged with anything). Be careful.

[§§9:22-9:29 Reserved]

C. Was the Defendant in Possession?

§9:30   Possession May Be Actual or Constructive

The government must establish beyond a reasonable doubt that the defendant possessed the firearm. Possession may be actual or constructive. *See United States v. Rogers*, 41 F. 3d 25 (1st Cir. 1999).

FIREARMS OFFENSES:

§9:31   Actual Possession

Actual possession is pretty easy to spot. A person with direct physical control of the firearm on or around his or her person is in actual possession of the firearm. *Rogers, supra.* Your client is out hunting with some buddies. The game warden wanders up to them while your client has his rifle in his hand. If your client is disqualified, your client is in actual possession and actual trouble.

§9:32   Constructive Possession

To establish constructive possession the government must prove that the defendant knew of the firearm and had control over it. Constructive possession is the subject of great debate, and often, liberal interpretation. There is sometimes room for the government to argue constructive possession if your client isn't caught with the gun in hand.

Consider the facts in *U.S. v. Mergerson,* 4 F.3d 337 (5th Cir 1993). Mergerson was convicted of count five of the indictment, which charged him with being a felon in possession of a firearm. *See* 18 U.S.C. §922(g)(1). On appeal, Mergerson claimed that the evidence was insufficient to prove one of the elements of §922--namely, that he was in possession of the firearm. The weapon, a handgun, was found between the mattress and boxsprings of the bed in a bedroom in the residence that Mergerson occupied. Mergerson stipulated that he had lived at the residence with his girlfriend and co-defendant, Sheila Guy, for approximately a month before his arrest. The evidence was essentially undisputed that Mergerson and Guy were cohabiting in the apartment and shared the bedroom in which the gun was found.

The government argued constructive possession. The argument was simple. Mergerson had access to the firearm, and, as a result, constructively possessed it. The 5th Circuit held:

> We have found constructive possession in such cases only when there was some evidence supporting at least a plausible inference that the defendant had knowledge of and access to the weapon or contraband.

Mergerson, supra.

The Sixth Circuit considered a constructive possession case in which the Defendant was driving a car with a gun under the seat. *United States v. Bailey*, 553 F.3d 940 (6th Cir. 2009). The Sixth Circuit found the fact that the defendant "was driving the car in which the police found the firearm is not enough to establish dominion over the premises and thereby dominion and control over the firearm." *Id.* To determine that a defendant has "constructive possession" over a firearm requires "additional circumstantial evidence beyond the defendant's having driven the car in which the firearm was found." *Id.*

The Sixth Circuit further noted that if it found constructive possession of a firearm every time there was a single occupant in a car, this would "institute an untenable strict-liability regime for constructive possession" under firearm statutes. *Id.* at 10. As a result, the Sixth Circuit reversed convictions in *Bailey* due to insufficient evidence of constructive possession.

> **PRACTICE TIP:** *Can others in the household own guns?*
>
> You might get questions by a disqualified client who wants to know if his or her significant other can possess firearms while they live together. If the guns are not the disqualified person's firearms, and they are kept in a gun safe that is locked always (a gun safe with a passcode combo, not a key – the disqualified individual arguably has access to the keys and therefore the guns), then I think it is possible. All that being said, you need to warn your clients in this type of situation that the police may not reasonably interpret the concept of constructive possession. While your clients may be following the letter of the law, they may have to go through hell to prove it.

§9:33   Knowing Possession

Violation of 18 USC §922 requires that the Government prove beyond a reasonable doubt that the defendant "knowingly" possessed the firearm. The Supreme Court has held that to establish a violation, the government must prove beyond a reasonable doubt not only that the defendant knowingly possessed the item, but also that the defendant knew "the item he possessed had the characteristics that brought it within the statutory definition of a firearm." *See Rogers v. United States*, 522 U.S. 252, 254-55 (1998); *Staples v. United States*, 511 U.S. 600, 619 (1994). Section 922 requires, therefore, that the government prove not only that the defendant purposefully possessed the firearm, but that he also knew that the alleged gun was, in fact, a firearm. *See United States v. Tomlinson*, 67 F.3d 508, 513 (4th Cir. 1995); *see United States v. Field*, 39 F.3d 15, 17 (1st Cir. 1994).

[§§9:34-9:39 Reserved]

D. Prior Domestic Assault Convictions

§9:40   Simple Assault Drop Down in Domestic Cases

It bears repeating, so I am going to say it twice in this chapter: a simple assault drop down from a domestic assault charge makes the defendant a prohibited person under the Gun Control Act. A United States Attorney merely needs to prove that the simple assault was on a domestic relation, even if the domestic assault charge was dismissed. *United States v. Hayes*, 555 U.S. 415, 129 S.Ct 1079 (2009).

What is frustrating about *Hayes*. in part, is that the defendant did not commit a domestic assault under West Virginia law. The Supreme Court found that the element of a domestic relationship in the predicate offense was unnecessary, however. The Court held:

> To obtain a conviction in a Section 922 (g)(9) prosecution, the Government must prove beyond a reasonable doubt that the victim of the predicate offense was the defendant's current or former spouse or was related to the defendant in another specified way.

Hayes, supra. This opens up a whole world of potential prohibited persons who may not have been convicted of domestic assault violations.

§9:41   Use of Force and Threatened Use of a Weapon in Misdemeanor Convictions

As state and federal statutes change, the definition of who is disqualified is always evolving. That said, with misdemeanor convictions, you need to consider whether your client's conviction is a misdemeanor crime of domestic violence under federal law. A misdemeanor crime of domestic violence under federal law requires as an element "the use or attempted use of physical force or the threatened use of a deadly weapon." 18 USC §922(g)(9)(A).

The typical domestic assault situation is easy to spot. If your client is convicted of hitting his wife, then you have a clear use of force. One can imagine a number of less than clear situations.

Imagine your client, Brutus, is out on bail for a domestic assault on his wife. He has a no contact order which he immediately violates. Brutus is love sick. He is charged with a bail violation for calling his wife and telling her he loves her. If Brutus pleads to a bail violation is he disqualified?

No, he's not disqualified. The contact on the bail violation is not a use or attempted use of force.

What if Brutus calls his wife while out on bail and tells her that she should remember his shotgun when she gets her subpoena to testify? If convicted of that bail violation, the conviction may qualify as threatened use of a deadly weapon, which could disqualify Brutus.

What if Brutus isn't charged with a domestic assault on his wife, but is rather charged with a domestic violence criminal threatening misdemeanor? Your state statute likely reads something like this:

> A person is guilty of criminal threatening if he intentionally or knowingly places another person in fear of imminent bodily injury, and the person against whom the threat is made is a domestic partner.

These are close cases. It's possible that a conviction for this conduct will not disqualify Brutus. It will likely depend on the facts, however.

You need to look beyond the conviction honestly in evaluating the client's risk. Specifically, you need to pay very close attention to the charging instrument and facts alleged in discovery. Does Brutus's threat imply an attempt to use force? Does the threat involve the threatened use of a deadly weapon? If so, it is disqualifying.

In Maine, we have a crime called Domestic Violence Terrorizing. It can be a misdemeanor or a felony if there are predicate priors. The law, in part, says:

FIREARMS OFFENSES:

[The Defendant] communicates to any person a threat to commit or to cause to be committed a crime of violence dangerous to human life, against the person to whom the communication is made or another, and the natural and probable consequence of such a threat, whether or not such consequence in fact occurs, is a reasonable fear that the crime will be committed. ...

This crime, while potentially dangerous, is probably not disqualifying if it is a misdemeanor. How do I come to that conclusion?

Here is the analysis in a nutshell: the statements made in Maine's terrorizing law must be "a crime of violence dangerous to human life." The feds disqualify a person if there's a "threatened use of a deadly weapon." If the Brutus says he's going to "kill" his wife, then this is a close call. He may have committed Terrorizing in Maine, but he didn't do it with a dangerous weapon or the use of force. If he says he's going to kill his wife with his shotgun, he's disqualified, in my view.

PRACTICE TIP: *Warn your clients repeatedly*

Part of the issue here is risk tolerance. Some clients don't care if their gun rights are removed. For others, it's a deal breaker. Additionally, any slight tweak of the federal law can change your analysis. Warn your clients at every turn. Warn them in person and in writing. If they want to roll the dice, you want to make sure they can never say you didn't tell them there could be problems.

PRACTICE TIP: *Read the Castleman decision*

The "New" Use of Force Requirement For Misdemeanor Domestic Assault Firearms Disqualification

In March 2014, the U.S. Supreme Court defined and expanded the use of force needed to make one a prohibited person based on a misdemeanor domestic assault in *United States v. Castleman*, 134 S. Ct. 1405 (2014).

The majority opinion, issued by Justice Sotomayor, held that a misdemeanor domestic violence offense of intentional or knowing assault in state court is a misdemeanor crime of domestic violence for disqualification purposes. Castleman was convicted in Tennessee state court of intentionally or knowingly causing bodily injury to the mother of his child. He was later charged by the feds for selling firearms on the black market. Castleman moved to dismiss the federal firearms charges, arguing that the Tennessee assault conviction was not disqualifying. He argued that the Tennessee statute did not have the essential element of the use of physical force. The District Court agreed and dismissed the case.

The Sixth Circuit, in a split decision, affirmed. The Sixth Circuit found that the degree of physical force required to be exerted in the underlying conviction was the same as that required for a violent felony under the Armed Career Criminal Act.

The logic in the Supreme Court's majority opinion distinguished the domestic assault situation from the violence in an ordinary assault situation. As Sotomayor and the majority concluded, the squeezing of someone's arm leaving a slight bruise would be hard to imagine as violent in many non-domestic assaults, but could represent an accumulation of several violent acts in a domestic situation. As a result, the majority found that Congress meant to include misdemeanor violations of state battery laws in its definition of those who are prohibited persons. In doing so, the majority rejected the Sixth Circuit's definition of violence contained in the violent felony definition of the Armed Career Criminal Act.

From there, Castleman was sunk quite easily. He had previously pleaded guilty in Tennessee to intentionally or knowingly causing bodily injury to the mother of his child, a person with whom he had a domestic relationship. As a result, the Supreme Court found that his knowing or intentional causation of bodily injury to the mother of his child necessarily involved the use of physical force.

Criminal defense practitioners will be wise to heed the *Castleman* warning. Pursuant to the *Castleman* decision, the use of force required for a disqualifying offense is likely to be very insignificant. Further, the majority opinion distinction between domestic assaults and non-domestic assaults, and the use of force required for each, will provide good fodder for the Government arguing close cases going forward.

FIREARMS OFFENSES:

§9:42　What Constitutes a Crime of Domestic Violence

Remember that to be disqualified the misdemeanor must be a crime of domestic violence. The question seems to be what constitutes a crime of domestic violence. This is determined in general by the state statutes from where the predicate conviction emerges. You are likely to find that these types of relationships are sufficient: crimes committed by a current or former spouse, parent, or guardian of the victim, by a person with whom the victim and the defendant share a child in common, by a person cohabitating with or has cohabitated with the victim as a spouse, parent or guardian, or by a person similarly situated to a spouse, parent or guardian of the victim. 18 U.S.C. §921 (a)(33).

§9:43　Old Domestic Violence Convictions and Retroactivity

Perhaps you have a situation where Brutus comes into your office, and he has a domestic assault misdemeanor conviction from 1974. Is he prohibited now based on this 1974 conviction?

The law prohibiting firearm possession for those with domestic violence convictions was effective September 30, 1996. 18 U.S.C. 922(g)(9). However, the prohibition applies to persons convicted of domestic violence misdemeanors at any time, even if the conviction occurred prior to the law's effective date. 18 U.S.C. Section 922 (g)(q). 27 C.F.R. 478 32 (Q)(9). Attempts to attack this retroactivity based on *ex post facto* arguments have not been successful.

So, Brutus, convicted in 1974, may not possess firearms. If a person was convicted of a misdemeanor crime of domestic violence at any time, he or she may not lawfully possess firearms or ammunition on or after September 30, 1996. 18 U.S.C. 922(g)(9).

What if the predicate conviction came from a statute that, at the time of the conviction, was not a domestic assault statute? Unfortunately, that doesn't matter.

Consider the Supreme Court case of *United States v. Hayes*, 555 U.S. 415, 129 S.Ct 1079 (2009). Hayes was convicted of a 1994 battery of his wife under an assault law in West Virginia. At the time of Hayes conviction, West Virginia did not have a domestic assault law on its books.

In 2004, there was another domestic violence 911 call at the Hayes residence. When the police responded, they found a shotgun in his home. Hayes was charged with a federal prohibited person possession of a firearm. He moved to dismiss, noting that the original West Virginia statute did not have as an element his domestic relationship to the victim of the assault.

The U.S. Supreme Court issued a tortured decision focusing on the syntax of the 1996 Gun Control Act. In sum, it concluded that the federal law prohibits the possession of firearms by anyone with a conviction for domestic assault, even if the domestic relationship is not an element of the offense. This means that the conviction need not disqualify the defendant on its face.

The government still must prove the domestic relationship. However, the predicate conviction does not need to have the domestic relationship as an element of its offense at the time of conviction. The government can cure the lack of domestic element by merely establishing a domestic relationship to meet the federal requirements at the time of the federal trial. As *Hayes* found:

> To obtain a conviction in a §922(g)(9) prosecution, the Government must prove beyond a reasonable doubt that the victim of the predicate offense was the defendant's current or former spouse or was related to the defendant in another specified way. But that relationship, while it must be established, need not be denominated an element of the predicate offense.

Hayes, supra.

The potential consequences of this reasoning, of course, boggle the mind. Be wary.

[§§9:44-9:49 Reserved]

E. Domestic Violence Restraining Orders

§9:50   Restraining Orders that Result in Disqualification

Restraining orders come up a lot in context of firearms possession by disqualified persons. Let's say your client is charged with a domestic assault. Very commonly, the police or domestic violence advocates suggest that restraining orders be placed on defendants who are already charged with domestic assault. While this may add insult to injury for the client, it also adds another layer to the analysis of firearm disqualification.

Under 18 USC §922(g)(8), your client is disqualified if he or she is subject to a court order that—

(A) was issued after a hearing of which your client received actual notice, and at which your client had an opportunity to participate;

(B) restrains your client from harassing, stalking, or threatening an intimate partner or child of the client or intimate partner, or engaging in other conduct that would place an intimate partner in reasonable fear of bodily injury to the partner or child; and

(C)(i) includes a finding that your client represents a credible threat to the physical safety of such intimate partner or child; or

(ii) by its terms explicitly prohibits the use, attempted use, or threatened use of physical force against such intimate partner or child that would reasonably be expected to cause bodily injury.

§9:51   Not a Lifetime Bar

Thankfully, restraining orders that prohibit possession do not impose the "death penalty" for gun owners. Unlike qualifying domestic and felony convictions, the federal prohibition on firearms subject to a qualifying restraining order is not lifetime prohibition. It exists only during time an individual is "subject to" the order.

§9:52   Restraining Orders That Don't Result in Firearms Possession Prohibition

Can a restraining order against your client not result in a federal firearms possession prohibition? I think it's possible, but you need to analyze it carefully. It is not enough to make sure the possession of firearms box on your standard court order is unchecked. The order cannot, in any way, imply that there is a finding that the defendant represents a credible threat to the physical safety of an intimate partner or child, or by its terms explicitly prohibits the use, attempted use, or threatened use of physical force against such intimate partner or child that would reasonably be expected to cause bodily injury. This would be a very bare bones order.

[§§§9:53-9:59 Reserved]

F. Client on Deferment

§9:60   Can Client Possess Firearms During Deferment Period

What if your client is on a condition of deferment of his charge? Many states have statutes that allow for a plea of guilty to a crime, but a delayed sentencing. That delay is a deferment period. During the deferment period, the defendant is to perform certain actions, and if they are completed successfully, the case is dismissed or a more favorable plea entered. Can the defendant possess firearms (if he is not otherwise disqualified) during the time of the deferment?

If you are in a jurisdiction where there is no precedent on this issue, there are two schools of thought to consider explained below. The issue is how a given court or circuit will view the admission made to get on the deferment to begin with.

§9:61   State Law Determines Time of Conviction

In one school of thought, we first consider which law applies to the question of when a conviction occurs. State law applies to determine the time of conviction. Therefore, if the state does not consider the person to be convicted, the person does not have the federal disability. 18 U.S.C. §921(a)(33).

In Maine, where I practice, a conviction occurs at the time of sentencing, rather than when a plea is entered. Here, the client can possess firearms during the deferment period because the client has not yet been sentenced.

Makes sense, right? But hold on. Here's another, perhaps more conservative view.

While a charge is pending under a deferment and there are conditions of probation or deferment, and the charge has not yet been dismissed, there are courts that count this as a conviction. *See e.g. U.S. v. Gispert*, 864 F.Supp. 1193 (S.D.Fla 1994) ("under Florida law when a defendant has pled guilty and the court has withheld adjudication of guilt, the plea of guilty constitutes a 'conviction' for the purposes of Title 18 U.S.C. §922(g)(1) only during the interval within which the adjudication remains withheld. However, once the defendant has successfully completed his probation, and the state court no longer has jurisdiction to adjudicate the defendant guilty, the plea of guilty cannot serve as a predicate 'conviction' under Title 18 U.S.C. §922(g)(1)).")

So, like in *Gispert*, a court could say that placing a defendant on deferment conditions constitutes a conviction during the period of time in which the deferment is ongoing. The view in *Gispert* is that the trial court still has the ability to punish, and during that period of time, the deferment is a conviction.

> **PRACTICE TIP: *Call the U.S. Attorney***
>
> Clients don't exactly love questions with no good answers. But if you take the time to explain your hesitation, then they can make an informed choice. I have called the U.S. Attorney for my district dealing with firearms cases and have simply asked her view on this, which I then share with my client. Of course, I always make sure the client knows that U.S. Attorney's change, and the next one may have a different take on this issue.

> **PRACTICE TIP: *Consider bail conditions***
>
> Even if your client is going to take a chance and possess during a deferment, don't forget to watch for bail conditions. They often restrict firearms use, and they may still be in effect during the deferment period, unless you modify them.

[§§9:62-9:69 Reserved]

G. Commerce Element

§9:70   Firearm Must Be In or Affecting Interstate Commerce

For federal firearms cases, the government must prove beyond a reasonable doubt that the firearm specified in the indictment was in or affecting interstate or foreign commerce. This means that the government must prove that at some time before the defendant's possession, the firearm had traveled in interstate or foreign commerce. This means the government must prove the gun crossed state lines or the United States border. The government does not need to prove that the defendant himself or herself caused it to cross state lines or a border, however.

This interstate commerce nexus is usually a dead letter. There is only a minimal interstate nexus required. In *Scarborough v. United States*, 431 U.S. 563 (1977), the Supreme Court held that the defendant was properly convicted of being a felon in possession of a firearm even though he had acquired the firearm before his conviction and it had not moved in interstate commerce since his felony conviction.

§9:71   Has the Weapon Ever Crossed State Lines

The interstate nexus may be a tough issue, but take a look at it anyway. Research whether there are other manufacturing plants for the firearm in your state. I practice in Maine. Smith and Wesson's headquarters for manufacturing is in Springfield, Massachusetts, but they have a manufacturing plant in Maine. If I have a Smith and Wesson gun case in Maine, I may argue that it cannot be established beyond a reasonable doubt that the gun moved interstate. Check for gun manufacturing plants in your state as well.

§9:72   Admissibility of Trace Reports

The government will generally use Trace Reports to get the interstate nexus information in. The defense should argue that the Trace Reports are inadmissible themselves. They are neither public nor business records under F.R.Evid. 803(8) or 803(6). *US v. Davis*, 571 F.2d 1354 (5th Cir. 1978).

The way the Government has historically gotten this information into evidence is through F.R.Evid. 703 during the testimony of the ATF agent. The agent, if qualified as an expert, is allowed under Rule 703 to rely on otherwise inadmissible evidence. That said, the Confrontation Clause opens up avenues of attack in attempting to admit this evidence. *See US v. Corey*, 207 F.3d 84 (1st Cir. 2000) (Chief Judge Torruella dissenting).

> In a criminal case a court's inquiry under Rule 703 must go beyond a finding that the hearsay relied on by an expert meets the standards of the Federal Rules of Evidence. If this Court is willing to allow a government agency to rely on its own internal manuals and post-indictment telephone calls to establish a basic element of a crime, simply by clothing the testifying agent with the unwarranted aura of "expert," then, in my opinion, the plain language of the Confrontation Clause has been emasculated beyond recognition.

Judge Torruella was clearly predicting the future of the next 10 years of U.S. Supreme Court precedent related to the Confrontation Clause. When you dovetail Judge Torruella's dissent with the Court's decision in *Melendez-Diaz v. Massachusetts*, 557 U.S. 305 (2009) you have yourself an argument.

At issue in *Melendez-Diaz* was whether a laboratory report, without live testimony from forensic experts, can be admitted in a narcotics case. In essence, it is an expansion of *Crawford v. Washington*, 541 U.S. 36 (2004), which revolutionized the practical application of the Confrontation Clause of the Sixth Amendment. In sum, *Crawford* held that earlier "testimonial" statements by a prosecution witness could not be admitted unless they were subject to cross-examination. What constitutes a "testimonial" statement has been dissected in numerous cases in *Crawford's* wake. *Melendez-Diaz* turned on whether the laboratory report is "testimonial."

Louis Melendez-Diaz was charged with trafficking crack cocaine. Crime laboratory reports were admitted as proof that the drugs seized were actually crack cocaine. The defense properly objected to the admission of those reports.

The majority opinion in *Melendez-Diaz*, authored by Justice Scalia, first found that the laboratory reports were "quite plainly affidavits." As a result, the majority determined that the statements were testimonial. Absent a showing that the witness was unavailable for trial and that the defendant had a prior opportunity to cross-examine him, the laboratory statements were inadmissible.

The Commonwealth of Massachusetts presented a variety of arguments that the reports were not testimonial. One argument was that the reports were merely scientific, and did not accuse the witness. This argument failed on the reasoning that the reports were being used to prove an element of the crime regardless of whether they were scientifically generated. Another failing argument by the Commonwealth was that the laboratory reports were like an official or business record.

Melendez-Diaz restricts a witness from testifying about lab reports created by another individual. In other words, a chemist testifying for the government cannot merely rely on the records of a testing chemist. The testing chemist must be produced. In gun cases, a similar Confrontation Clause argument can be made. The person who created the trace reports must be produced at trial or the Confrontation Clause is violated. Putting on an ATF agent to testify to trace reports he or she did not author is simply insufficient pursuant to *Melendez-Diaz*.

[§§9:73-9:79 Reserved]

III.   MOTION TO SUPPRESS REGARDING PROMISES OF LENIENCY

A. Overview

I have not included many motions to suppress in this book because they vary so much by case and jurisdiction. That said, I seem to find many promises of leniency to suspects by the police in gun cases. As a result, I wanted to include a Motion to Suppress from such a situation here. See §9:82 Form 9-10 Motion to Suppress Statements made after Promises of Leniency.

§9:80   Common Scenario

Mr. Grant's girlfriend calls the police one night claiming he assaulted her. His wife already has a restraining order on him. His girlfriend tells the police when they arrive that he has more than a dozen firearms kept in various places in the house.

The police ultimately pick him up and he's scared. The police tell Mr. Grant if he tells them where the guns are, they won't charge him with illegally possessing them. He tells them the guns are in his attic. The police search the attic and find nothing. Then he tells the police the guns are in a trunk of a car at his car mechanic's shop. They are ultimately recovered there. When the police don't find the guns right away, they feel like they have been burned and charge him with possession by a prohibited person.

§9:81   The Argument

The principal argument in the motion is that police trickery improperly caused Mr. Grant to waive his right to silence. In establishing waiver, the Government bears the burden of demonstrating "that the defendant knowingly and intelligently waived his privilege against self-incrimination and his right to retained or appointed counsel." *Burbine v. Moran*, 753 F.2d 178, 182-183 (1st Cir 1985) (*citing Miranda v. Arizona*, 384 U.S. 436, 175 (1966). "Moreover, any evidence that the accused was … tricked … into waiver will, of course, show that the defendant did not voluntarily waive his privilege." *Id.* at 183. In determining whether a person voluntarily and knowingly waived his or her right to counsel, the Government must show based on the preponderance of the evidence that:

The relinquishment of the right must have been voluntary in the sense that it was the product of a free and deliberate choice rather than intimidation, coercion, or deception; and

The waiver [also] must have been made with a full awareness of both the nature of the right being abandoned and the consequences of the decision to abandon it.

Moran v. Burbine, 475 U.S. 412, 421 (1986) (citation omitted).

The First Circuit has stated that some types of "trickery" can cause coercion. *U.S. v Byram*, 145 F.3d 405, 408 (1st Cir. 1998). Additionally in *Byram*, the Court stated "a false assurance might undercut the gist of a warning, raising questions whether *Miranda* [is] satisfied." *Id.* at 408.

The Government denied that they were bound by any promises to Mr. Grant. Additionally, the government's position was that even *if* Mr. Grant and the police had a contract, that Mr. Grant did not keep his side of the bargain. In its response to the motion, the government argued that Mr. Grant breached the contract when he did not promptly reveal the location of the weapons and therefore, the police were free to charge him.

§9:82   FORM 9-10 Motion to Suppress Statements Made after Promises of Leniency

UNITED STATES DISTRICT COURT
FOR THE DISTRICT OF MAINE

UNITED STATES OF AMERICA,   )
)
Plaintiff,   )
)
v.   )   Criminal No. 10-1234
)
Mr. Grant,   )
)
Defendant.   )

MOTION TO SUPPRESS AND DISMISS WITH MEMORANDUM OF LAW

The Defendant, Mr. Grant, by and through Undersigned Counsel, moves this Honorable Court to suppress all statements of the Defendant on the following grounds:

1. All statements made by the Defendant were in violation of *Miranda* rights.
2. All statements made by the Defendant were involuntary.
3. Due to the constitutional infirmities described herein, the statements of the Defendant, and the evidence seized as a result of the statements of the Defendant are fruit of the poisonous tree, and must be suppressed.

WHEREFORE, the Defendant moves that all statements of Defendant be suppressed and excluded as evidence, and that the search and the items found in the search be suppressed as fruit of the poisonous tree.

MEMORANDUM OF LAW

Counsel presents the following Memorandum of Law to the Court to attempt to expand on the suppression issues described above.

STATEMENT OF FACTS[1]

On February 15, 2010, South Portland law enforcement officers responded to a domestic violence assault call at the residence of Defendant's wife. Mr. Grant was the alleged assailant, and his wife the alleged victim. Neither Defendant nor his wife were present when the police arrived.

When the police arrived, they observed several guns in the residence. They followed up and the Defendant was interviewed in the South Portland Police Department.

The lead investigator in the case was Detective Webster, although others participated in the interrogation. The interrogation took place at the South Portland Police Station on February 15, 2010. The Defendant was read *Miranda*, and initially chose to answer questions. Mr. Grant attempted to cease questioning, however, and Detective Webster did not scrupulously honor the Defendant's attempt to cease questioning. When Detective Webster questioned Mr. Grant's story, the Defendant stated:

I guess this is where I have to have to stop and ask for a lawyer

(Interview at 21:34)

Rather then take the Defendant's demand to cease questioning and stop the interrogation, Detective Webster interrupted the Mr. Grant and stated "I was just looking for some honesty from you and I was not going to put the screws to you." (Interview at 21:35). Detective Webster continued to attempt to convince Mr. Grant to waive Miranda, and ultimately succeeded.

On its own, this police questioning is troubling. When it is coupled with promises of non-prosecution, it becomes even more disturbing.

Detective Webster cajoled Mr. Grant into talking again (after he tried to invoke *Miranda*), by promising that he would not be charged or prosecuted with possession of firearms by a prohibited person if Defendant told him where the firearms were. Detective Webster told the Defendant such falsities as: "If you tell me where the guns are, we will not charge you with being a prohibited person;" and "We will keep them here until the protection order stuff is done." (Interview beginning at 25:21).

On a dozen occasions throughout the interview, law enforcement officers told Mr. Grant that he would not be prosecuted if he informed them as to the location of his firearms and acknowledged that the firearms were his. They promised him that they would not take this promise back, stating: "This isn't television guy. We're not going to pull some BS because afterwards we need to explain everything." (Interview at 34:30) Another officer then

[1] The facts underlying this motion are derived from the Indictment, the reports of the officers, and the audio and video of the interview with Defendant and Law Enforcement Officers from the South Portland Police Department. This audio/video will be made available to the Court by the Defendant in advance of the hearing if the Court would like to review the interview in advance. When Counsel points out specific statements in the Memorandum from the interview, Counsel has cited the minute and seconds on the audio/video where the statement appears, for ease of use by the Court.

piped up as well and said: "I can't tell you one thing and go do another. That throws the whole case out and ruins my credibility." (Interview at 38:40)

Defendant ultimately complied. The promise of the officers was not kept, and Mr. Grant is charged before this Court.

ARGUMENT

I. LAW ENFORCEMENT VIOLATED *MIRANDA* NECESSITATING SUPPRESSION OF DEFENDANT'S STATEMENTS

A person who is in custody and subject to interrogation must be advised of the rights referred to in *Miranda v. Arizona*, 384 U.S. 436 (1966), in order for statements made during the interrogation to be admissible against him or her at trial. *State v. Bridges*, 829 A.2d 247, 254 (Me. 2003). "[A] *Miranda* warning is necessary only if a defendant is: (1) in custody; and (2) subject to interrogation." *State v. Higgins*, 796 A.2d 50, 54 (Me. 2002) (citation and quotation marks omitted).

A. Custodial Determination

Mr. Grant was in custody when he was being interview by law enforcement. He was handcuffed and taken to the police station. Custody exists for *Miranda* purposes when there is a "restraint on freedom of movement of the degree associated with a formal arrest." *State v. Holloway*, 760 A.2d 223, 228 (Me. 2000) (citation and quotation marks omitted). This test is an objective one, and the Maine Law Court has stated that in analyzing whether a defendant is in custody, a trial court may consider the following factors:

    (1) the locale where the defendant made the statements:

    (2) the party who initiated the contact;

    (3) the existence or non-existence of probable cause to arrest (to the extent communicated to the defendant);

    (4) subjective views, beliefs, or intent that the police manifested to the defendant to the extent that they would affect how a reasonable person in the defendant's position would perceive his or her freedom to leave;

    (5) Subjective views or beliefs that the defendant manifested to the police, to the extent the officer's response would affect how a reasonable person in the defendant's position would perceive his or her freedom to leave;

    (6) the focus of the investigation (as a reasonable person in the defendant's position would perceive it);

    (7) whether the suspect was questioned in familiar surroundings;

    (8) the number of law enforcement officers present;

    (9) the degree of physical restraint placed upon the suspect; and

    (10) the duration and character of the interrogation.

Id.

Mr. Grant was clearly in custody upon consideration of all the factors. He was involuntarily taken to the police station. He was handcuffed. He was not free to leave. Certainly, the custodial standard has been met.

B. Interrogation and Invocation of Miranda.

The interrogation should have ceased when Mr. Grant invoked his right to have counsel present during the interrogation. When a subject requests that an attorney be present during the interrogation, all questioning must cease until the lawyer is present. *Davis v. U.S.*, 512, 548 (1994). It is an objective inquiry in determining whether the suspect has invoked his right to counsel. *Id.* at 459. An objective inquiry "requires, at a minimum, some statement that can reasonably be construed to be an expression of a desire for the assistance of an attorney." *McNeil v. Wisconsin*, 501 U.S. 171, 178 (1991).

Court's in the State of Maine have recently indicated that the procedure after the invocation of the right to remain silent is crystal clear:

> Once warnings have been given, the subsequent procedure is clear. If the individual indicates in any manner,
> at any time prior to or during questioning, that he wishes to remain silent, *the interrogation must cease.*

State v. Grant, 939 A.2d 93, 104 (Me. 2008) (emphasis added) (citing *Miranda v. Arizona*, 384 U.S. 436, 473-86 S.Ct. 1602, 16 L. Ed.2d 694 (1996)). Any statement to law enforcement after Mr. Grant invoked *Miranda* must be suppressed because the prior invocation of his right to remain silent was not scrupulously honored. *See, Id.* (citing *Michigan v. Mosley,* 423, U.S. 96, 101-02, 96 S. Ct 321, 46 L.Ed.2d 313 (1975)).

The South Portland Police failed to stop the interrogation of Mr. Grant when he indicated he wanted to have an attorney present. Mr. Grant told Detective Webster "I guess this is where I have to stop and ask for a lawyer." (Interview at 21:34). Before Mr. Grant could say anything else, Detective Webster interrupted and stated "I was just looking for some honesty from you and I was not going to put the screws to you." (Interview 21:35). Following the standard set forth in *Davis* and *Mosley,* Mr. Grant's statement about wanting to stop and get an attorney should have been taken as an unequivocal demand to cease questioning.

The United States Supreme Court has made it absolutely clear that the interrogation must cease immediately when the individual indicates he wishes to stop the questioning and talk with an attorney. *Michigan v. Mosley,* 423, U.S. 96, 101-02, 96 S. Ct 321, 46 L.Ed.2d 313 (1975). Instead of ceasing the interview, the detective reformulated the questioning to persuade Mr. Grant to talk with him. He told Mr. Grant that "if you were going to be honest, I was going to just take the guns (and not charge you)." This trickery worked, and Mr. Grant began to talk. This lead to a confession and a consent to search for weapons. These fruits are all from the poison tree of the detective's failure to cease the interrogation at the time Mr. Grant requested an attorney. As a result, any statement made after the request to cease questioning must be suppressed.

II. LAW ENFORCEMENT VIOLATED *MIRANDA* BY TRICKING THE DEFENDANT INTO SPEAKING BY THE USE OF FALSE PROMISES OF LENIENCY

The South Portland Police Department tricked the Defendant into waiving his right to remain silent. In establishing waiver, the Government bears the burden of demonstrating "that the defendant knowingly and intelligently waived his privilege against self-incrimination and his right to retained or appointed counsel." *Burbine v. Moran,* 753 F.2d 178, 182-183 (1st Cir 1985) (*Cited Miranda v. Arizona,* 384 U.S. 436, 175 (1966). "Moreover, any evidence that the accused was … tricked … into waiver will, of course, show that the defendant did not voluntarily waive his privilege." *Id.* at 183. In determining whether a person voluntarily and knowingly waived his or her right to counsel, the Government must show based on the preponderance of the evidence that:

1. The relinquishment of the right must have been voluntary in the sense that it was the product of a free and deliberate choice rather than intimidation, coercion, or deception; and
2. The waiver [also] must have been made with a full awareness of both the nature of the right being abandoned and the consequences of the decision to abandon it.

Moran v. Burbine, 475 U.S. 412, 421 (1986) (citation omitted)

The South Portland Police Department intimated, coerced and deceived the Defendant by promising him that he would not be charged with a crime if the Defendant told the police where the guns were.

The First Circuit has stated that some types of "trickery" can cause coercion. *U.S. v Byram,* 145 F.3d 405, 408 (1st Cir. 1998). Additionally in *Byram,* the Court stated "a false assurance might undercut the gist of a warning, raising questions whether *Miranda* [is] satisfied." *Id.* at 408. In the present case, the Defendant, after invoking his right to counsel, was interrupted immediately by Detective Webster from the South Portland Police Department stating:

"I was just looking for some honesty and I was not going to put the screws to you … I don't want to put the screws to you. If you were going to be honest, I was just going to take the guns. I could tell you were not going to be honest."

(Interview at 21:34).

After the initial statement made above, Detective Webster continued to pressure the Defendant by stating:

"If you tell me where the guns are, we will not charge you with being a prohibited person. … We will keep them here until the protection order stuff is done. … When you have the right to have the guns back, we will give them to you."

(Interview at 25:21).

Once these initial promises were made to the Defendant, the Defendant than began discussing where the guns were.

The Detective knew the Defendant did not want to speak once he indicated he wanted an attorney; however, the Detective used intimidation by attacking the Defendant's credibility by calling him a liar and tricked the Defendant by using coercive and deceitful tactics, such as falsely promising the Defendant that he would not be charged if he spoke; therefore, the Government will be unable to show that the statements were free from intimidation, coercion or deceit.

The Government will not be able to prove that the Defendant was fully aware of giving up his right to remain silent and the consequences of that right. The Defendant had acknowledged the deal after he had told the police where the guns were by stating "you guys gave me a deal that all you had to do is give you the guns, it's a great deal." (Interview at 37:48). Shortly thereafter, an officer states "I can't tell you one thing and then go do another. That throws the whole case out and ruins my credibility." (Interview at 38:30). As the interview progressed, the Defendant stated "you've already given me a deal" and an officer replies "I have." (Interview at 49:50). Shortly thereafter, an officer states there is "no reason not to turn them in. I can't tell you that I am not going to charge you then go ahead and charge you." (Interview at 55:30). These statements would lead any person to believe that anything that was said was not going to be used against them, specifically, not going to be used against the Defendant in any potential firearm violation.

The Defendant was not fully aware of his right to remain silent and as a result did not understand the consequences that result from waiving that right. The officers repeatedly asked the Defendant to tell them where the guns were with the promise of not charging the Defendant. Even if the Officer did not have the authority to make such a promise, the Defendant believed that the promise was valid; resulting in confession related to the guns and consent to search. This is the specific situation *Miranda* was trying to protect against.

III. DEFENDANT'S STATEMENT WAS COERCED AND NOT VOLUNTARY

The facts outlined above also establish a cogent argument that the Defendant's confession and consent to search was involuntary. *U.S. v. Byram*, 145 F.3d 405 (1st. Cir. 1998) indicates that, while police trickery is not automatically coercion, it can be.[2] Here, the police trickery and coercion is enough to render Mr. Grant's confession and consent to search involuntary.

CONCLUSION

The police trickery in this case, coupled with a failure to acknowledge Mr. Grant's attempt to invoke *Miranda*, makes this a case where Defendant's statements should be suppressed. His consent to search, for example, is tainted by the fact that law enforcement promised him he would not be charged in order to gain that consent. The statements and the search are the fruit of the poisonous tree, and they must be suppressed as justice and the Constitution requires. *Wong Sun v. United States*, 371 U.S. 471, 484-88 (1963).

Dated this 9th day of June, 2010 in Portland, Maine.

Respectfully submitted,

_____

Timothy E. Zerillo
Attorney for Defendant
ZERILLO LAW FIRM, LLC

[§§9:83-9:89 Reserved]

---

[2]   In *Byram*, the issue was voluntariness only, and *Miranda* was not implicated. Here *Miranda* was read to the Defendant. In *Byram*, the First Circuit said: "Of course, a false assurance might undercut the gist of the warning, raising questions if *Miranda* had been satisfied..." *Byram supra* at 408.

B. Motion to Suppress Hearing: Testimony of Interrogating Officer

§9:90   Goals

Let's look at some testimony from the motion to suppress hearing on this issue. We will be reviewing the testimony of the lead detective in the case. I have to establish that the government made promises of leniency to my client that those promises should be binding. Additionally, we want to establish that the detective did not scrupulously honor our client's invocation of *Miranda*.

§9:91   Knowledge of Defendant's Background

Q. Prior to the incident we've been talking about, you had never previously met Mr. Grant?
A. Not to my knowledge, no.
Q. Prior to going into the interview, I assume that you ran his criminal record to see if he had a record of any sort?
A. I didn't.
Q. Did somebody from your police department run a record?
A. I would assume that Officer Unfriendly did because he's the one who told me that he was prohibited from having firearms due to a protection order.
Q. And there was no indication that he had any prior criminal record?
A. I didn't run his criminal history. I didn't know going into the interview, if that's what you're asking. The only thing I knew going in was that he was a prohibited person due to a protection order.
Q. You had no indication whether or not he had experience in dealing with law enforcement in the interview setting; is that fair to say?
A. I didn't know that at all.

§9:92   Knowledge of Interrogation Tactics

Q. You've done this for 23 years?
A. I've been a police officer for 23, yeah.
Q. And you've been trained in interview and interrogation techniques; is that correct?
A. I have.
Q. You know the law.
A. I'd like to think so, yes.
Q. And you know what you're doing in an interview; is that fair to say?
A. I'd like to think so.
Q. You have an advantage over the suspect in the interview room; isn't that fair to say?
A. Interviews to me are very basic; I ask questions and they answer them. I don't know if I would have an advantage.
Q. You don't employ any tactics in interviewing; you just ask questions?
A. I use my experience to my advantage.
Q. And that experience has taught you various tactics to use for a successful interview, hasn't it?
A. Sure, yes.
Q. And knowing those tactics gives you an advantage over someone especially who has no prior criminal experience in an interview; isn't that correct?
A. One could assume that.

§9:93   Admission That Defendant Was in Custody

Q. Officer Unfriendly was involved in the interview for parts of it, right?
A. He was there. I wouldn't say that he participated much while I was interviewing Mr. Grant, but he had some interaction.
Q. He spoke to Mr. Grant?
A. Yes.
Q. And Mr. Grant was in custody during the interview; there's no dispute about that, correct?
A. That's correct.

§9:94   Goals of the Interrogation

Q. The primary goal of the interview was to find the weapons?

A. That's correct.

Q. And to get a confession about possession of the weapons was the secondary goal?

A. My mindset at that point was not so much a confession, because in my mind we had already found several guns that I assume we could connect to him. So my goal was to get the guns. If he wanted to admit that they were his, we call that a bonus.

Q. It's always easier to prosecute somebody who confesses, in this case, to possession of the firearms, right?

A. Yes.

Q. Mr. Grant told you at some point that Mr. Junior owned some of the firearms; isn't that right? His wife's son owned some of the firearms.

A. I think he mentioned one of them, I think, yes.

Q. It's also helpful if you can get a consent to search; is that fair to say?

A. Yes.

Q. So that would have been helpful in this case and ultimately ended up being helpful, didn't it?

A. You mean as far as recovering the guns?

Q. Yes.

A. Yes.

Q. It helps if you can recover the weapons as well; isn't that correct?

A. It does help.

§9:95   The Deal Offered to the Defendant

Q. So the tactic you decided to employ with your experience was to tell Mr. Grant that you wouldn't charge him with possession of the weapons while being a prohibited person if he told you were the weapons were, right?

A. A tactic?

Q. Yes.

A. That would not be a tactic, because if I told him I was not going to charge him if he told me where the weapons were, I would not charge him, so a confession would do me no good.

Q. That assumes the you were going to be true to your word and not charge him if he told you were the guns were.

A. That's true.

§9:96   Miranda Warnings

Q. You read him *Miranda*?

A. I did.

Q. Okay. You agree with me that it's important to properly administer *Miranda*.

A. Yes.

Q. You would agree that it's important to honor *Miranda* if somebody invokes the right to silence?

A. Yes.

Q. Or the right to counsel?

A. Yes.

Q. You agree that these are important rights we're dealing with when we read and honor *Miranda*, right?

A. Very important.

Q. And you told him that he could have a lawyer during questioning present, right?

A. I did.

Q. You told him he could talk to a lawyer before questioning, right?

A. I did.

Q. You told him he had the right to stop answering at any time and all he had to do is tell you, right?

A. I did.

Q. You did not get a written *Miranda* waiver; isn't that right?

A. Correct, because I knew it was on tape.

Q. Just as important is reading *Miranda* properly—and you read it off of a card, right?

A. Yes.

Q. And that's to make sure that you get it right.

A. Correct.

Q. Just as important as reading *Miranda* properly is to make sure to listen for somebody to invoke his rights, correct?

A. Correct.

Q. And when a suspect ordinarily invokes a right to counsel or a right to remain silent, you automatically stop; isn't that right?

A. Yes.

Q. Because you want to make sure that you are honoring those rights; is that correct?

A. That is correct.

§9:97   Were Miranda Rights Violated?

Q. I'm going to play for you the portion where I believe Mr. Grant requests counsel, okay?

A. Okay.

(Video played.)

Q. I heard you say on direct examination that you talked over Mr. Grant. You said that, didn't you?

A. I did.

Q. There is a pause, and then silence and then he says "I guess this is where I have to stop and ask for a lawyer". Did you hear that as clearly as I did?

A. Listening to it right here I didn't hear him say "lawyer". I heard him say we got to stop, and while I'm speaking over him is when he's talking about a lawyer.

Q. So you heard him say "I guess this is where I'm going to have to stop," but didn't hear the "lawyer" part?

A. Correct.

Q. At that point you knew that he was asking for *Miranda* protection, didn't you?

A. No.

Q. You in fact told me a minute or two ago that when somebody asks to stop and invokes *Miranda* that you will stop the questioning; didn't you say that?

A. What he said was "I guess this is where I'm going to have to stop."

Q. Okay. You heard him say "stop".

A. I did.

Q. You took that to mean he wanted to stop questioning, right?

A. No, I did not.

Q. When somebody says to you I would like to stop something during an interview, what do you take that to mean, then?

A. He could have meant several things at that point. He could have meant that he wanted to stop answering that particular question, and then I kept talking and then the conversation just kept going.

Q. So for the purpose of this record, I want to make sure that I'm clear, you heard the portion where he said "I guess this is where I have to stop."

A. Correct.

Q. And you began to say I was just looking for some honesty from you and I wasn't going to put the screws to you or something along those lines.

A. Something, yes.

Q. You did not hear the portion where he said "and ask for a lawyer," correct?

A. I did not hear that.

Q. And you agreed with me earlier when I said it's important to listen for Miranda invocations; isn't that right?

A. That is correct, and if I had heard him say that, I would have stopped.

Q. You are often in these interviews dealing with people who are very distraught and crying, aren't you?

A. Yes.

Q. And you have to make sure to listen through those sobs for somebody trying to invoke their Miranda rights, don't you?

A. If I hear it. I did not hear it, sir.

Q. Well, you have to listen, though, don't you? That's the point, right?

A.   I do my best.

Q.   You don't have any hearing difficulties physically, do you?

A.   No, I don't.

Q.   You do not wear a hearing apparatus like a hearing aid?

A.   I do not. My hearing is quite good.

Q.   And he is not wearing a microphone of any sort on his shirt during this interview, is he?

A.   A microphone?

Q.   Yes, because I can hear him say "ask for a lawyer" on a tape, but you're saying you couldn't hear it sitting a few feet away from him. Is he wearing a microphone?

A.   Sir, I am a firm believer in the Fourth and Fifth Amendment. If I had heard him say that he wanted a lawyer I would have stopped. I did not hear him because I was speaking at the same time he was.

Q.   Sir, while that is heartening, that is not what I'm asking you. I am asking you, was he wearing a microphone?

A.   He was not wearing a microphone.

Q.   Thank you. And how far away from you -- were you seated from Mr. Grant at the time when he asked for a lawyer and to stop?

A.   Apparently about as far away as you and I are right now.

Q.   Which is what, 3 or 4 feet?

A.   A few feet, yes.

§9:98   Officer Reassured Defendant That Deal Was Genuine

Q.   When you said, I was just looking for some honesty from you and I was not going to put the screws to you, what you meant was you were not going to charge him, right, if he told you where the guns were?

A.   At that point?

Q.   Yes.

A.   I'm trying to think of at that point in—in the interview. I think I'd have to hear more of where I was coming from, if that makes sense.

Q.   Well, you used the term like "put the screws to you", right, that was your term?

A.   Yes.

Q.   Okay. That's a term that people use in everyday language, correct?

A.   Yes.

Q.   And when you're doing these interviews, another thing that I'm sure you've learned in your 23 years of experience, is that you speak the language that people speak when you're trying to talk to them, right?

A.   I have to speak many different levels, yes.

Q.   When you're talking to someone who is being interviewed and say his occupation is a mechanic, you speak in normal, everyday language; is that right?

A.   I wouldn't so much base it on their occupation. It's just a feel for the interview. Some people have a large vocabulary and some don't.

Q.   So in this particular interview you felt that you should speak in a normal, everyday language; is that fair to say?

A.   Yes.

Q.   Okay. I apologize to the Court for my use of profanity. At some point during this interview in fact you say you're not going to, quote, "trick fuck him," end quote, right?

A.   Correct.

Q.   You were trying to reassure him?

A.   Yes.

Q.   All right. So in any event, you didn't stop the questioning, correct?

A.   No, I didn't.

Q.   He didn't speak to a lawyer before continuing questioning, correct?

A.   No, he didn't.

Q.   You promised him at least a half dozen times during the course of this interview that you wouldn't charge him if he told you where the guns were, right?

A.   Correct.

Q.   You have no reason to believe that he didn't believe you; is that fair to say?

A.   I don't know if he believed me or not.

Q. Well, you went a long way to try to get him to believe you, right?

A. He had mentioned some problems he had with another police department, and I just told him I'm not them.

Q. The Gorham Police Department you're referencing related to return of firearms that they took for safekeeping; isn't that correct?

A. Yes.

Q. What I'm talking about now is you were trying to promise him -- is the promises you made not to charge him. That's what I'm talking about now at that point.

A. So the question is did I want him to believe me?

Q. Yes.

A. Yes, I did.

Q. And you did various things to try to assure him that you were trustworthy in that regard; isn't that right?

A. Yes, such as pointing at the camera.

Q. Let's look at that.

(Video played.)

Q. Okay, so you mentioned pointing at the camera, and that's in the clip we just observed, right, and heard?

A. Yes, sir.

Q. And you point at the camera to make him feel more comfortable that he can believe you, right?

A. I wanted him to believe me, yes.

Q. You're pointing out to him that this is on a recording and that there is -- that there's nothing for him to worry about, right?

A. Yes.

Q. You told him later that you wouldn't take back your promise not to charge him because your credibility would be ruined, correct?

A. As long as he was telling me the truth.

Q. I don't know that there is that caveat in that statement, Detective. You told him you wouldn't take back the promise not to charge him because your credibility would be ruined.

A. I believe the caveat goes back to our initial conversation. As long as he tells me where the guns are and he's honest, then he won't be charged.

Q. I understand that's your understanding, but the real question is Mr. Grant's understanding; would you agree with that?

A. Yes.

§9:99   Extent of Defendant's Cooperation in Locating Guns

Q. You mentioned that for approximately a half hour that Mr. Grant maintained that the handguns were in the attic of Glenda Girlfriend's residence.

A. Yes.

Q. In any event, he also told you that he would be happy to help officers look for the weapons as well, right?

A. Yes.

Q. He didn't just say the entire time I'm a hundred percent positive they're up in the attic, right?

A. He said several times they were in the attic.

Q. He said several times he believed they were in the attic and also offered to look for them if they couldn't be found there; is that fair to say?

A. When you say offer to look for them, at the residence?

Q. Yes.

A. He did offer to go to the residence, yes.

Q. You mentioned on direct that where you come from a deal's a deal and the deal with Mr. Grant was: You said tell me where the guns are and I will not charge you. Is that correct?

A. With possession of the guns.

Q. Yes, with possession of the guns.

A. Yes.

Q. The Government has argued in its filings that there was a contract between yourself and Mr. Grant that was broken by Mr. Grant when he didn't tell you where the weapons were; is that your point today?

A.   I guess my point is I made him a simple offer: Tell me where they are, and I will not charge you. And for a lengthy period of time he told me where they were. However, they weren't there.

Q.   And he ultimately did tell Officer Unfriendly where the weapons were, right?

A.   Yes.

Q.   In fact, you only found the weapons because he told Officer Unfriendly where they were, right?

A.   I would say that I found them quicker because this investigation was rather new. I am an investigator and I would have followed up on every lead I had, including his place of employment. Would I have found them in that vehicle? I don't know.

Q.   You had no immediate plans to follow up with his place of employment when you were talking to Officer Unfriendly on the phone from Mr. Grant's residence, did you?

A.   Wouldn't have been my first stop, but I'm not saying -- I'm just saying I may have ended up there.

Q.   When you were on the phone you talked about getting search warrants for his mother's house and for his storage unit, right?

A.   Correct.

Q.   Never getting search warrants for his work, right?

A.   On the phone, yes.

Q.   And it was your understanding that had he given you the information about where the weapons were that you would have been able to let him go and not charge him; is that right?

A.   With possession of the guns?

Q.   With the guns.

A.   Yes.

Q.   And you've done that before?

A.   I have done a lot of unorthodox things before, yes.

Q.   Would you consider this to be one of those unorthodox things?

A.   Yes.

§9:100   Defendant's Lack of Knowledge of Withdrawal of Deal

Q.   Were you animated on the phone with Officer Unfriendly when he was taking Mr. Grant to Cumberland County Jail?

A.   It could be described as animated.

Q.   So in that animated conversation you told Officer Unfriendly to tell Mr. Grant that the deal was off, right?

A.   Correct.

Q.   Did you know that Officer Unfriendly did not tell Mr. Grant that the deal was off?

A.   No.

Q.   You thought Mr. Grant knew that the deal was off when he told you or when he told Officer Unfriendly that the guns were in the trunk of the BMW, right?

A.   Yes, but I spoke to Mr. Grant as well when he was begging, and I kept saying too bad, too bad, you had your chance, and the best I can do is say you were cooperative.

Q.   But that was after he had already said where the guns were.

A.   Yes, yes, it would have been.

> **PRACTICE TIP: *Motion to Suppress has benefits even if denied***
>
> Unfortunately, this motion to suppress was denied. We lost both the Miranda argument and the promises of leniency argument. I still felt the Motion was valid and the process worthwhile. The obvious benefit is that a valid issue was preserved for appeal. Your client also will appreciate your fighting for him or her. You also get to know the officer and what the officer is like on the stand. Finally, you may learn helpful facts about your case. I generally feel like I know more about my case, win or lose, after a motion to suppress hearing.

[§§9:101-9:109 Reserved]

IV.   TRIAL

A. Opening Statement

§9:110   My Approach

Let's continue with Mr. Grant's case. Our Motion to Suppress is denied and he wants a trial. It's a tough case, for sure, because the police have recovered the guns, and Grant appeared to be deceptive when talking to the police. Let's look at how we might frame it in Opening.

In this opening, our goal is to establish a lack of knowledge that the firearms were in the attic. The prosecution has the guns and my client acting a little cagey with the police. I merely want to plant the seed here: No knowledge of the guns = not guilty.

§9:111   Sample Opening Statement

Your honor, Jury Foreperson, members of the jury, may it please the Court.

I am pleased and proud to represent Mr. Grant in this case. I am pleased and proud to represent Mr. Grant because the single greatest thing I get to do as a lawyer is to address you in open court in a trial. That is because jurors, like you, who listen carefully and who make hard decisions to apply the law of reasonable doubt, are the most important people in our court system. More on reasonable doubt later. For now, I want to tell you what this case really is about.

This case is about a bad relationship. We've all had them. Perhaps some of you have had relationships that go from bad to toxic. When they become toxic, they take on a whole life of their own.

We've all seen it. We've all had friends who feed off of unhealthy and toxic relationships. And we've all seen how that can turn completely rational people into completely irrational people.

Mr. Grant had one of those relationships with Glenda Girlfriend. According to her, in the middle of the night he punched her in the face. The evidence will show, however, that he did not punch her in the face, but he might have rolled over in the night and accidentally struck her. You might have had that happen; my wife does it to me all the time.

You are not here to decide if he struck her or not, but I bring it up because it angered her. Really angered her. And she asked her son to call the police.

Now, Glenda had been holding Mr. Grant's guns for him because he had a restraining order. She put them in the attic. After she got mad at him that night and he left, she took the guns out of the attic and spread them around the house for police to find.

Now why would someone do that? We believe the evidence will show that Glenda knew that Mr. Grant could not have firearms. She wanted to get him in trouble.

When the cop came, he didn't do anything with the guns. He did make a note of it in his report, though. And when they came back later, the guns were gone. They were later found in the trunk of a car at Mr. Grant's mechanic's shop.

If Mr. Grant doesn't know the firearms are in the attic, he's not guilty. If Mr. Grant doesn't know the firearms are in his car, he's not guilty. If Glenda Girlfriend set him up to get him in trouble, he's not guilty.

So why is he here then? He must have done something, right?

You have to remember and consider that Mr. Grant's arrest is not a sign of his guilt at all. The fact that Mr. Grant was arrested in this case does not indicate anything. The arrest is only a means to activate the system of justice so that 12 of his peers can come in here and listen to the evidence. You determine guilt or innocence—not the police officer and not the prosecutor—you.

As a result of that, the burden in any criminal case rests solely with the prosecutor at that table. In this case, the Government and that prosecutor have the entire burden of proving Mr. Grant's guilt. That burden never once shifts to this table. As a result, Mr. Grant does not have to do anything except sit at the table. He doesn't have to testify, his attorney doesn't have to cross-examine anyone, he doesn't have to present evidence – he doesn't have to do anything. And if he does nothing, the law says that you cannot view that as an admission of his guilt. The Judge will tell you so.

Why? Because the prosecutor has the opportunity to do all the advance investigation she wanted to do. She had every state government agency at her disposal and she had your tax dollars to burn in creating this prosecution. Now she has to show you the case and prove to you that she spent your money wisely.

In doing so, the elements of the charge against Mr. Grant must be proven. Each and every element of the charge must be proven beyond a reasonable doubt. Until that is done and all the evidence is in, Mr. Grant sits here innocent of the charge against him. He is innocent as he sits here now.

I was once riding up in the elevator with a woman going to jury duty in this very courthouse years ago. She was making friends with another prospective juror – they hadn't been picked yet. One of the women rolled her eyes about the idea of being picked to go on a criminal jury and the other one said: "Well, I figure they must have done something to deserve to be here."

If you have that in your heart and in your brain right now, you are violating your oath. I know you don't want to violate your oath because it is so important. But you cannot presume what reasons bring Mr. Grant here. You must only consider him to be innocent as he sits here today. That is as important a rule of law as we have in this country, and I ask you to apply it whether you like it, or agree with it, or not.

So, now that I'm done with that, let's talk about what the Government needs to prove in this case…

For general tips on opening statements and sample language about the presumption of innocence and burden of proof, see Chapter 2.

[§§9:112-9:119 Reserved]

B. Cross-Examination of ATF Agent

§9:120   Key Points

Let's look in on the cross of an ATF Agent in Mr. Grant's case. This cross examination is on the narrow issue of did the guns cross state lines. The Government in a federal case will provide an interstate nexus agent, usually from the ATF. This is usually a difficult area to exploit, but you can sometimes score some points. Here is a brief example.

§9:121   Sample Cross-Examination of ATF Agent

Q. On direct examination, you discussed the fact that several of these guns were Smith and Wesson handguns?
A. Yes, three of them were.
Q. Smith and Wesson is headquartered in Massachusetts?
A. Yes.
Q. But they also made weapons in Maine?
A. Yes.
Q. In Aroostook County?
A. Yes, in Houlton.
Q. Would you agree with me that it is difficult to tell whether the three weapons were manufactured in Maine or in Massachusetts.

A. Difficult in that it requires research.
Q. And you believe you can determine for a certainty that these guns were made in Massachusetts?
A. Yes.
Q. You spoke about markings on guns on direct, do you remember that?
A. Yes.
Q. Markings on a firearm do not necessarily reflect the place of manufacture, do they?
A. No.
Q. For example, a Smith and Wesson is marked, "Smith and Wesson of Springfield, Massachusetts," right?
A. Right.
Q. That marking doesn't mean that particular gun was manufactured in Massachusetts.
A. Not necessarily.
Q. You also spoke on direct about identification stamps. Do you remember that?
A. Yes.
Q. Identification stamps aren't necessarily a part of the original weapon.
A. I think they generally are.
Q. But guns are often cobbled together and an identification stamp on certain parts of the weapon may be from replacement or unoriginal parts.
A. That could be.
Q. These guns are old, right?
A. They are.
Q. You spoke to people at Smith and Wesson?
A. Yes.
Q. You didn't speak to anyone who was there at the time these guns were made?
A. No. They are too old.
Q. So the Smith and Wesson people tell you what has been told to them about where this gun was made?
A. What their research is.
Q. Can you tell for certain yourself how old these guns are?
A. Without research?
Q. Without research.
A. No, I can't.
Q. Without research, you can't tell if these guns were manufactured before 1898.
A. Not without research.
Q. Smith and Wesson was around in the 1800s weren't they?
A. Yes.
Q. There are also a lot of counterfeit firearms in circulation aren't there?
A. There are.
Q. There are a lot of replica firearms in circulation aren't there?
A. Yes, there are.

[§§9:122-9:129 Reserved]

C. Closing Argument

§9:130   My Approach

Now let's take a look at ways to approach a closing in Mr. Grant's case. This is the "hell hath no fury like a woman scorned" closing. I blame everything on Glenda Girlfriend as a means of casting doubt.

§9:131   Sample Closing Argument

Every time Mr. Grant's wife put a restraining order on him, he gave his guns to the police or to a friend for safekeeping. Every time. Why would this time be any different? It wouldn't be any different and it wasn't different.

When he was in Texas and his wife put a restraining order on him, he gave the guns to the police in Texas. When the restraining order was removed, he got them back.

When he was in Gorham and his wife put a restraining order on him, he gave the guns to the police in Gorham. When he was in Portland and his wife put a restraining order on him, he gave the guns to Mr. Friend.

You don't have to like him because he has all these restraining orders, that's fine. But the history we know is he's not trying to evade the police with his firearms.

What was different in this case? Nothing.

Glenda decided she was done with Texas and was moving back to Maine. At the same time Mr. Grant was served with another restraining order. He asked Glenda to take custody of the weapons and she agreed. He asked her to safekeep the weapons, and she agreed. And she did. She took them to Maine with her and stuck them up in the attic of her house where they sat until one fateful night.

Fast forward to the night in question. Mr. Grant and Glenda are a couple again, but their relationship is tumultuous at best. And when Glenda thinks he strikes her in the middle of the night, she is very angry. And she takes the weapons that he doesn't even know are in the attic, and leaves them where the police will find them.

Why? Because she's angry.

So he gets arrested. Why wouldn't he just give the police the weapons? He had done that before in Texas and Gorham. When the police asked for the weapons, he tried to comply and guessed at where they could be. He wasn't being evasive. He wasn't lying. He was wrong the first time because he was guessing at where the guns were because he didn't knowingly possess them.

The 2nd Amendment provides that US Citizens have a right to keep and bear arms. There are restrictions, however, for cases of people who have restraining orders against them. But the Government needs to prove quite a few things before they can convict Mr. Grant. Each and every time they try to take away Mr. Grant's 2nd Amendment rights, they are tested. The test here requires the Government prove their allegations beyond a reasonable doubt. Let's look at what needs to be proven and look at how the Government has failed to prove it beyond a reasonable doubt…

For tips on closing arguments and sample language for burden of proof and reasonable doubt arguments, see Chapter 2.

[§§9:132-9:139 Reserved]

FIREARMS
OFFENSES:

V.   SENTENCING

I have not included a lot of sentencing information in this book for the obvious reason that sentences vary from jurisdiction to jurisdiction, but since the vast majority of these cases are federal, let's run through a Federal Sentencing Guidelines analysis.

§9:140   Federal Sentencing Chart

Level 14 is the starting point for your Federal Sentencing Guideline calculations. The base offense level for firearm possession as a prohibited person is Level 14, 15-21 months.

Levels are added as described in the chart below.

Number of Firearms	Increase in Level
(A) 3-7	add 2 levels
(B) 8-24	add 4 levels
(C) 25-99	add 6 levels
(D) 100-199	add 8 levels
(E) 200 or more	add 10 levels

In short, the more weapons your client is caught with, the higher his or her base offense level.

§9:141   Upward Departure for Semiautomatic Firearm

Your client could also get an upward departure because the offense involved a semiautomatic firearm that is capable of accepting a large capacity magazine. A "semiautomatic firearm capable of accepting a large capacity magazine" means "a semiautomatic firearm that has the ability to fire many rounds without reloading because at the time of the offense (A) the firearm had attached to it a magazine or similar device that could accept more than 15 rounds of ammunition; or (B) a magazine or similar device that could accept more than 15 rounds of ammunition was in close proximity to the firearm. This definition does not include a semiautomatic firearm with an attached tubular device capable of operating only with .22 caliber rim fire ammunition." USSG §2K2.1, comment. (n.2).

§9:142   Example

Let's take the case of Brutus Grant, charged with Possession of Firearms by a prohibited person. He had 18 firearms, including an AK-47 with a detached 17 round banana clip.

Brutus has 18 firearms so he is level 14, plus 4 Levels for 8-24 firearms, for a Level 18. Brutus also gets an upward departure because of the AK-47 with the banana clip. This brings Brutus to a level 24. With a Criminal History Category I, the sentencing range is 51 to 63 months.

§9:143   Reduction for Acceptance of Responsibility

He may, however, get a reduction for acceptance of responsibility, if he admits to illegally possessing the firearms. Acceptance of responsibility is defined under the sentencing guidelines as follows:

§3E1.1. Acceptance of Responsibility

(a) If the defendant clearly demonstrates acceptance of responsibility for his offense, decrease the offense level by 2 levels.

(b) If the defendant qualifies for a decrease under subsection (a), the offense level determined prior to the operation of subsection (a) is level 16 or greater, and upon motion of the government stating that the defendant has assisted authorities in the investigation or prosecution of his own misconduct by timely notifying authorities of his intention to enter a plea of guilty, thereby permitting the government to avoid preparing for trial and permitting the government and the court to allocate their resources efficiently, decrease the offense level by 1 additional level.

The Commentary to the Guidelines defines truthfully admitting conduct as follows:

Truthfully admitting the conduct comprising the offense(s) of conviction, and truthfully admitting or not falsely denying any additional relevant conduct for which the defendant is accountable under §1B1.3 (Relevant Conduct). Note that a defendant is not required to volunteer, or affirmatively admit, relevant conduct beyond the offense of conviction in order to obtain a reduction under subsection (a). A defendant may remain silent in respect to relevant conduct beyond the offense of conviction without affecting his ability to obtain a reduction under this subsection. However, a defendant who falsely denies, or frivolously contests, relevant conduct that the court determines to be true has acted in a manner inconsistent with acceptance of responsibility. …

Acceptance of responsibility is a 2 point reduction for the defendant clearly demonstrating acceptance of responsibility for his offense. This would bring Brutus to Level 22, 41 to 51 months. An additional 1 point reduction for acceptance of responsibility is possible if the Government moves for it, which would bring Brutus to a level 21, 37-46 months. And there is your basic sentencing analysis for Brutus.

§9:144   Relevant Conduct

Remind your clients about the concept of relevant conduct in firearms sentencing. Note that, in determining the number of firearms, a court will consider "relevant conduct" under USSG §1B1.3. *See United States v. Brummett*, 355 F.3d 343 (5th Cir. 2003). Therefore, if there is proof by a preponderance of the evidence that Brutus possessed a firearm(s) other than the ones charged in the indictment, and such other firearms were possessed in the same course of conduct or as part of a common scheme or plan, such firearms will be considered by a court in applying this enhancement.

§9:145   Downward Adjustment for Collections

Possession of the semi-automatic weapon in Brutus case eliminates an argument regarding a collection. Make sure that you take a look at that when available, however.

(2) If the defendant, other than a defendant subject to subsection (a)(1), (a)(2), (a)(3), (a)(4), or (a)(5), possessed all ammunition and firearms solely for lawful sporting purposes or collection, and did not unlawfully discharge or otherwise unlawfully use such firearms or ammunition, decrease the offense level determined above to level 6.

USSG §2k2.1(b)(2)

Relevant surrounding circumstances for the departure include the number and type of firearms, the amount and type of ammunition, the location and circumstances of possession and actual use, the nature of the criminal history (i.e., prior convictions for offenses involving firearms), and the extent to which possession was restricted by local law. USSG §2K2.1, comment (n.6). Under the plain language of this provision, the mere fact that a defendant is a prohibited person does not foreclose application of this downward adjustment. A defendant bears the burden of proving his entitlement to this downward adjustment. The government does not carry the burden to disprove it. *United States v. Montano-Silva*, 15 F.3d 52 (5th Cir. 1994).

FIREARMS
OFFENSES:

§9:146   FORM 9-20 Federal Sentencing Memorandum—Possession of Firearm by Disqualified Person

IN THE UNITED STATES DISTRICT COURT
FOR THE DISTRICT OF MAINE

UNITED STATES OF AMERICA,	)	
	)	
Plaintiff,	)	
	)	Criminal No. 111111
v.	)	
	)	
	)	
BRUTUS GRANT,	)	
	)	
Defendant	)	

SENTENCING MEMORANDUM

We ask the court to consider sentencing Brutus Grant to a non-Guideline, or "variant" sentence of 12 months incarceration followed by 2 years of supervised release, based on application of the sentencing factors set out in 18 U.S.C. §3553(a) and in particular the nature and circumstances of the offense and the characteristics of the offender. *U.S. v. Martin*, 520 F.3d 87, 91 (1st Cir. 2008).

On October 28, 2010, Mr. Grant pleaded guilty to a one-count indictment charging him with possession of firearms by a person subject to a qualifying protection order (18 U.S.C. §922(g)(8)). He will be sentenced on February 16, 2011. Mr. Grant submits the following Sentencing Memorandum for the Court's consideration.

I. FACTUAL BACKGROUND

A.   Defendant's Personal Information

Mr. Grant is a 46-year-old man. At the time of his arrest, Mr. Grant resided in South Portland, Maine, with his wife, her two teen-aged sons, and one of his daughters. Mr. Grant is a lifelong resident of the Cumberland County area. His two daughters are teenagers, and his oldest is graduating from high school this June. His oldest daughter is emancipated and lives with her grandmother (Mr. Grant's mother).

B.   Defendant's Criminal History

Mr. Grant's criminal history is slight. He pleaded guilty to one charge of Violating a Protective Order in Somerset County Superior Court in Skowhegan, Maine, on November 5, 2009. The protective order, the same protective order underlying the instant case, prohibited Mr. Grant from having contact with his minor daughters. The Complaint in that matter alleged that Mr. Grant violated this protective order by having contact with one of his daughters. Prior to the entry of the order, initiated by Mr. Grant's ex-wife on behalf of the daughters, Mr. Grant had been the sole caretaker of his daughters for four years.

As a result of the contact, Mr. Grant pleaded guilty to Violation of a Protective Order, and received a $200 fine. Undersigned believes the plea was uncounseled. That is the total of his criminal convictions known to the Undersigned.

C.   Family Background

Mr. Grant is one of six siblings. He has a twin brother and four sisters, all living in Maine. Mr. Grant enjoys close relationships with all of his siblings, their significant others, and their children, his nieces and nephews.

Mr. Grant's father, with whom he was close and from whom he learned his trade of automobile repair, passed away in 1994. Mr. Grant's mother is 82. She visits her son weekly at the Cumberland County Jail.

Mr. Grant has two teenage daughters. Prior to the protective order mentioned above, Mr. Grant had primary residence of the girls and was their sole caretaker. The protective order mentioned above prohibits Mr. Grant from having contact with either of his minor daughters. His eldest daughter, however, applied for and was granted emancipation from the care of her mother in July 2010, so that she could visit Mr. Grant. She visits her father weekly at the Cumberland County Jail.

D.   Defendant's Employment History

Mr. Grant has had a very long and successful employment history. From approximately 1996 through 2009, Mr. Grant built from the ground up "Brutus's Auto." For a time, it was a highly successful mechanical repair shop. It began in South Portland, established itself on Riverside Street, and then ultimately expanded to Gorham. Brutus's grossed in excess of a million dollars a year for several fiscal years and grew rapidly. At its height, Brutus's had 23 employees.

Mr. Grant gave to various local charities through his business. He wanted his business to be connected to the community. In doing so, he received commendations from Camp Sunshine, the McDonald's House and the Seeds of Peace Camp, among others.

Unfortunately, Mr. Grant went through a very difficult divorce. As a result of the divorce, Mr. Grant was forced to sell the business to satisfy marital debts. This has left him without assets and with remaining business debts. The business still operates in Portland, however, with new owners.

In approximately 2009, Mr. Grant moved to Texas with his daughters, his current wife and her two sons. While in Texas, Mr. Grant worked at Cars-R-Us in McKinney, Texas. He worked primarily as a service writer.

When he returned to Maine, he worked at Maine Cars-R-Us as a service writer for a brief time. Mr. Grant has always been a very hard worker, and has a positive employment history.

E.   Defendant's Educational History

Mr. Grant graduated from Local High School. He earned an Associate Degree, and is 9 credits short of a Bachelor's Degree in Business Administration from the University of Southern Maine.

F.   Defendant's Substance Abuse History

Mr. Grant does not have a substance abuse history. While a prescription pill was found in his pants pocket during his arrest, the pills and the pants did not belong to him.

Mr. Grant submitted himself to two drug tests during his divorce, both of which came back negative. He also took a drug test prior to his employment at Cars-R-Us, which also came back negative.

Mr. Grant is a social drinker of alcohol. He may have four or so drinks a year.

G.   Conduct After His Arrest

Mr. Grant's post arrest conduct was appropriate. He was arrested without incident. Detective Fibber recovered most of the weapons and clips based on Mr. Grant's information.

Mr. Grant was arrested February 15, 2010, and will have been incarcerated 1 year when he comes up for sentencing before this Court. He has been a model detainee. He has been a positive influence in the Jail community and has a position of leadership within the Jail.

While in the Jail, Mr. Grant voluntarily availed himself of the 48 week Opportunity for Change Domestic Violence Education Program. A letter from Program Director/Instructor is attached as Exhibit 1. It indicates that Mr. Grant is close to finishing the 48 week program, and that "he is very quick to look at his behavior and how it impacts his family and others in his life." Id.

H.   Defendant Has Had a Very Positive Impact on His Family, Who Continue to Love and Support Him

Mr. Grant has a very loving and supportive Mother, siblings and daughters. His Mother has written a letter for the Court's consideration attached as Exhibit 2. Mr. Grant's Mother notes that Mr. Grant was a good father to his children, and a consistent and supportive force in their lives. Id.

FIREARMS OFFENSES:

Mr. Grant's oldest daughter has also written on Mr. Grant's behalf. Exhibit 3. She has stressed what a positive influence Mr. Grant has been in both her and her sister's life. Likewise, four sisters of Mr. Grant have issued glowing letters to this Court, discussing Mr. Grant's merits as both a father and a husband. Exhibits 4 through 7.

Due to the sometimes sensitive nature of these materials, including the names and addresses of the letter-writers, Counsel has filed these letters in hand with the Clerk's Office on the same date as the filing of this Sentencing Memorandum. Counsel has not argued from the specific facts of the letters in this Memorandum. That said, it is Counsel's belief that the testimony contained in those letters presents a compelling case for a variant sentence pursuant to §3553.

Also received today by Counsel is a victim impact statement from Mr. Grant's ex-wife. Counsel has not argued against that statement herein for two reasons. First, Counsel cannot argue against the same without including personal details to rebut the allegations that should not be in a public Sentencing Memorandum. Second, it seems that Mr. Grant's ex-wife's testimony is too remote to be relevant. Mr. Grant hasn't seen his ex-wife in approximately 5 years, and any non-hearsay testimony she would have should not bear on the issue before this Court for sentencing. She is not a victim of the conduct Mr. Grant is sentenced for here.

ARGUMENT

II. THE SENTENCING GUIDELINES 18 U.S.C. §3553(A) ARE ADVISORY, NOT MANDATORY, AND A SENTENCE BELOW THE GUIDELINE LEVEL SHOULD APPLY

The sentencing factors set out in 18 U.S.C. §3553(a), are:
(1) the nature and circumstances of the offense and the history and characteristics of the defendant;
(2) the need for the sentence imposed-
   (A) to reflect the seriousness of the offense, to promote respect for the law, and to provide just punishment for the offense;
   (B) to afford adequate deterrence to criminal conduct;
   (C) to protect the public from further crimes of the defendant; and
   (D) to provide the defendant with needed educational or vocational training, medical care, or other correctional treatment in the most effective manner;
(3) the kinds of sentence available;
(4) the kinds of sentence and the sentencing range established for-
   (A) the applicable category of offense committed by the applicable category of defendant as set forth in the guidelines-(i) issued by the Sentencing Commission pursuant to section 994(a)(1) of title 28, United States Code ...; and. ...
(5) any pertinent policy statement issued by the Sentencing Commission pursuant to section 994(a)(2) of title 28...;
(6) the need to avoid unwarranted sentence disparities among defendants with similar records who have been found guilty of similar conduct; and
(7) the need to provide restitution to any victims of the offense.

We urge the court to impose a sentence significantly below the current advisory guideline range based on the totality of the sentencing factors set out in 18 U.S.C. §3553(a), with particular reference to the nature and circumstances of the offense and the characteristics of the offender.

More specifically, it appears that throughout the majority of his 46 years on this earth, that Mr. Grant has been a fine employee, boss, father, son and brother. His criminal conviction is minimal, and is unfortunately not uncommon in the context of high conflict divorces as they currently occur in Maine.

Counsel has spent a great deal of time with Mr. Grant in preparing this case. Mr. Grant is shocked and amazed that convicted drug dealers and convicted violent felons are released with shorter sentences then the year he has already served. It is a difficult concept to grasp for someone who never spent a day in jail before this incident, and has now been incarcerated for a year.

While it is clear that there was tumult in his relationship with his ex-wife, that should not control over an otherwise law abiding life. Counsel hopes the Court will agree and impose a variant sentence of 12 months, with credit for time already served.

III. DEFENDANT CONTINUES HIS OBJECTION THAT THERE WAS NO MAGAZINE IN CLOSE PROXIMITY TO A SEMI AUTOMATIC FIREARM

Mr. Grant brought a duffel bag containing handguns to his workplace on or about February 15, 2010. Mr. Grant gave Detective Sven Fibber of the South Portland Police Department permission to retrieve the duffel bag. Detective Fibber did so, and gave the guns to the evidence technician. *See* Exhibit 8, Paragraph M, Affidavit of Detective Fibber. Detective Fibber: "…I never inventoried the guns at the scene. The guns were brought directly to E.T. Carlton who logged them in as evidence." Id.

Undersigned Counsel originally understood that the Government would seek to use the enhancement at sentencing in this matter for the possession of a semi-automatic firearm with a large capacity magazine in close proximity. Until recently, Counsel believed that the Government intended to argue that firearms seized in the residence at 55 Jefferson Avenue would be used for this purpose. Counsel intended to argue that because the magazines were not in close proximity to those weapons, that the enhancement did not apply.

On January 13, 2011, Counsel learned that the Glock seized in the duffel bag at Mr. Grant's workplace was the source of the enhancement argued by the Government. There was, in fact, a Glock seized in the duffel bag at Mr. Grant's workplace. The Glock 17 does come with a standard 17 round clip. Mr. Grant, from his memory, does not believe the Glock had a clip in it or in close proximity to it.

Counsel did not find information in the discovery to indicate that the clip was in the Glock or even in the duffel bag. Counsel sought clarification from AUSA Pros, who provided a picture of the clip and a report from ATF Agent Gunz, who confirmed that the magazine was a 17 round magazine that was not after market. This report was issued on January 21, 2011. Of course, Agent Gunz was not present for the seizure of the weapon or magazine, and he did not inventory the same.

Counsel is preserving the objection on this issue for the moment, however, because he is not aware that there is any evidence that the clip was in the Glock when seized, as represented by Probation Officer Super in Page 5, Paragraph 8 of the Revised PSIR.

Rather, it appears generally that there were several clips not in their weapons. In addition, many guns were without magazines altogether. Guns that were seized at 55 Jefferson Avenue, South Portland were combined with the guns that were seized at Mr. Grant's workplace (where the Glock was seized) when they were finally inventoried.

Consider, for example, the South Portland Police Department Evidence Report, attached as Defendant's Exhibit 9. This report lists the seizure of 22 firearms (Evidence Seq #2 through Evidence Seq #23). All the firearms are listed as seized from 55 Jefferson Avenue in South Portland. Id. The firearms are all logged in at 10 AM on February 15, 2010 because they were all inventoried at once. Id. The inventory does not describe whether or not the guns were seized with clips. Id.

The Commentary notes:

> A "semiautomatic firearm capable of accepting a large capacity magazine" means "a semiautomatic firearm that has the ability to fire many rounds without reloading because at the time of the offense (A) the firearm had attached to it a magazine or similar device that could accept more than 15 rounds of ammunition; or (B) a magazine **or similar device that could accept more than 15 rounds of ammunition was in close proximity to the firearm**. This definition does not include a semiautomatic firearm with an attached tubular device capable of operating only with .22 caliber rim fire ammunition." USSG §2K2.1, comment. (n.2).

The burden of proof on this issue rests with the Government. Additional clips were seized by the Government at the 55 Jefferson Avenue home. The clips were not always with the firearms. Since the Mr. Grant does not have evidence that the clip was found with the Glock, and because his own memory is that the clip was not with the gun, Counsel continues this objection of Mr. Grant's behalf.

Mr. Grant is not denying that he possessed the Glock. He accepts responsibility for possessing all the weapons. The issue is merely that whether there is insufficient evidence that the Glock was in close proximity to a high capacity magazine.

IV. DEFENDANT HAS GENUINELY ACCEPTED RESPONSIBILITY

The Probation Officer awarded Acceptance to the Mr. Grant. Amended PSR ¶20. The Government has reserved argument regarding the Acceptance of Responsibility by Mr. Grant.

FIREARMS
OFFENSES:

The Mr. Grant has pleaded guilty. He pleaded guilty in a timely fashion so as to allow the Government to not allocate resources toward a trial. In his interview with Probation and subsequent documents filed with Probation, Mr. Grant indicated that he knew it was wrong to not turn in his firearms, and that he illegally possessed those firearms. He acknowledges his sorrow that he broke the law. He has truthfully admitted the conduct for which he has pleaded guilty and the Probation Officer was correct in awarding him a three point reduction for acceptance.

V. THE FIREARMS AS A COLLECTION

Pursuant to §2K2.1(b)(2), a firearm collection may reduce the offense level to a level 6. Mr. Grant states that several of the guns, 4 of them from Mr. Grant's memory, were given to him by his father. Mr. Grant also indicates that at least one of the firearms is an antique, over 100 years old.

Further, Mr. Grant's fascination with guns is purely mechanical. He is someone with clearly a mechanical mind. He likes to take things apart and put them together. He likes to do the same with the guns and clean them.

Paragraph 8 of the Amended PSIR indicates that a number of weapons were seized from Mr. Grant in 2005. There was an ATF investigation into the firearms. Mr. Grant was not charged with any offenses.

The same weapons returned to Mr. Grant from 2005 were included in the 2010 arrest that brings us here. They were not illegally discharged, and were discharged infrequently when it was legal for Mr. Grant to discharge them. He considered them his collection, and as has been mentioned, several of the weapons were from his deceased father. Counsel requests this Court depart from Mr. Grant's sentence as a result of a collection departure pursuant to §2K2.1(b)(2).

WHEREFORE, Counsel requests this Court sentence the Mr. Grant according to the arguments contained in this Sentencing Memorandum.

Dated this _____ Day of _____, 20__ in Portland, Maine.

Respectfully submitted,

_____
Timothy E. Zerillo
Attorney for Defendant
ZERILLO LAW FIRM, LLC

See Ch. 2 on preparing a sentencing memorandum.

[§§9:147-159 Reserved]

VI.   OTHER FIREARMS OFFENSES

Possession of firearms by a disqualified person is far and away the most common gun prosecution you will run into. That said, there are plenty of other federal firearms offenses you need to watch out for.

§9:160   Gun Possession During a Drug Crime

Look out for mandatory minimum cases for possession of firearms during a drug crime. 18 U.S.C. §924(c) punishes firearm possession during a drug trafficking or violent crime. It provides mandatory minimum sentences that begin at five years and end at life imprisonment, or even death, if a death occurred with the use of the firearm in the drug offense. The mandatory minimum sentences increase depending upon the type of firearm used (sawed-off gun, silencer, etc.), whether more than one offense was committed, and whether gun was possessed, brandished, or discharged. A sentence imposed under 18 U.S.C. §924(c) must run consecutively to any other sentence charged in the same case. *See Deal v. United States*, 508 U.S. 129 (1993).

§9:161   The Armed Career Criminal Act

The Armed Career Criminal Act, 18 U.S.C. §924(e), imposes a mandatory minimum 15-year term of imprisonment for those convicted of unlawful possession of a firearm under 18 U.S.C. §922(g) who have three previous convictions for a violent felony or serious drug offense, or both, committed on occasions different from one another.

A defendant convicted under §922(g) normally faces a maximum term of 10 years imprisonment. Section 924(e)(1) increases this punishment range to a minimum of 15 years and a maximum of life, if a defendant has three prior convictions for violent felonies or serious drug offenses.

Violent felonies for the purposes of Section 924(e) are those that either (1) have an element of threat, attempt, or use of physical force against another person or (2) involve burglary, arson, extortion, or the like. Serious drug offenses are those punishable by imprisonment for 10 years or more. No pretrial notice is required to enhance a punishment under Section 924(e).

There has been a tremendous amount of litigation over who fits into the Armed Career Criminal Act. You might expect as much with the penalties imposed. The Supreme Court has held that a failure to report to prison is not a violent felony. *Chambers v. United States*, 129 S. Ct. 687 (2009). Likewise, a felony drunk driving conviction is not a violent felony. *Begay v. United States*, 128 S. Ct. 1581 (2008).

For a discussion on the categorical approach to determining what is a "violent felony," take a look at *Shepard v. United States*, 544 U.S. 13 (2005) and *Taylor v. United States*, 495 U.S. 575 (1990). For an examination as to the scope of a "serious drug offense," take a look at *United States v. Rodriquez*, 128 S. Ct. 1783 (2008).

§9:162   Firearms Transfer Offenses

There are a variety of offenses related to firearms transfers to be wary of as well. 18 U.S.C. §922(a)(6) makes it unlawful for any person in connection with the acquisition, or attempt to acquire, any firearm or ammunition from a licensed dealer to knowingly make any false oral or written statement intended or likely to deceive the dealer with respect to any fact material to the lawfulness of the sale under 18 U.S.C. §921. This offense is punishable by a statutory maximum term of up to 10 years.

Section 922(d) makes it unlawful for any person to sell or dispose of any firearm or ammunition to another person if he knows or has reason to believe that the buyer:

(1) Is under indictment or been convicted of a felony;

(2) Is a fugitive from justice;

(3) Abuses any controlled substance;

(4) Has been adjudicated as suffering from mental health issues;

(5) Is an (A) illegal alien or (B) an alien admitted under a non-immigrant visa;

(6) Has been dishonorably discharged from the Armed Forces;

(7) Has renounced his or her United States citizenship.

(8) Is subject to a restraining court order prohibiting harassing, stalking, or threatening an intimate partner or child; or

(9) Has been convicted of a misdemeanor crime of domestic violence.

This offense is punishable by a statutory maximum term of up to 10 years.

Section 924(a)(1)(A) makes it unlawful to knowingly make any false statement or representation with respect to the information provided in the transfer of the firearm. This is punishable by a statutory maximum term of up to five years.

FIREARMS
OFFENSES:

(This page intentionally left blank.)

CHAPTER 10

KIDNAPPING

In my experience, kidnapping cases are often overcharged, exaggerated versions of more minor criminal conduct. I usually don't get the type of case that the general public perceives as kidnapping—like a stranger who grabs a child off the street or a perpetrator who holds the victim for ransom. If you have one of those cases, it is likely making headlines locally, or even nationally, and the kidnapping charge might be the least of your troubles (those stories rarely end well). Those types of cases, while sensationalized, don't form the bulk of most criminal lawyers' kidnapping practice.

Rather, my kidnapping cases are often overcharged cases that come from one of two areas: 1) a parent in a child custody matter who flees with the children; or 2) an individual who, in the course of using self-help to resolve a disagreement or right a perceived wrong, restrains another individual or transports him or her from one place to another.

KIDNAPPING

I.   COMMON SCENARIOS

§10:01   Parental Kidnapping Cases

One very common scenario occurs when the defendant really puts the "kid" in kidnapping, and takes his or her child away from the other parent. These cases intermingle criminal actions with family actions. They often present the opportunity to raise abuse as a defense, however,

Consider this typical situation. Karla Knapper is charged with taking her child away from her husband and the child's father, Abe Usive. She took the child from Maine to Florida, where she lived for several months until she was caught. She admitted to the police that she secreted the child from Mr. Usive.

She met Abe Usive in a bar in California. They both have drinking problems. When they drink together, it is an explosive combination. Then they add meth to the equation. According to Karla, Abe often abuses her when he is drunk or high. She acknowledges she can be abusive as well when she's under the influence.

Eventually, Karla decided she could not expose her three year old daughter to the domestic violence dynamic of the household. She tried to get help from a public interest law organization, but they just told her to call the police. The police were no help. Ultimately, she decided to hit the road with her daughter. Of course, she was caught and charged with kidnapping.

PRACTICE TIP: *When there's no custody order in place*

Make sure to check your local rules when there is no child custody order in place. In a case where there is no custody order in place, you may have an argument that the taking of the child was not unlawful. This is very dependent on the jurisdiction involved, however. See §§10:30-10:32 for discussion of state parental kidnapping statutes.

---

§10:02   The Self-Help Situation

Another common situation for kidnapping charges occurs when the defendant confines or transports the alleged victim in an effort to correct a perceived injustice. For example, I once represented the patriarch of a family in the mountains of Maine who was charged with kidnapping after exacting a healthy dose of Yankee justice from his neighbor.

In this area of Maine, marijuana and guns are a way of life. The father of the clan, Gotsum Gunz, kept a fair amount of marijuana around the house. He wasn't selling it; he and his wife and son just liked to smoke it. Quite a lot of it, actually.

They had a next door neighbor named Snee Key. Mr. Key was regularly around the Gunz house and was friendly with them. One day, when the Gunz family was not home, Mr. Key let himself into their house. He found a pound of pot and took it.

Members of the Gunz family were less than pleased to discover that their stash was gone. Mr. Key, who was not a master thief, was clearly the culprit.

So Mr. Gunz approached Mr. Key. He had the pot, and had already smoked a lot of it with a friend. Mr. Gunz was furious. He pulled a revolver on Mr. Key and told him that Key was going to compensate him for the missing pot... or else.

Mr. Key apologized profusely, and said that he would withdraw money from his bank account if Mr. Gunz could give him a ride to the bank. Gunz complied with the request, Mr. Key withdrew funds from the ATM, and they went home.

Mr. Gunz was charged with kidnapping, among other things.

[§§10:03-10:09 Reserved]

II. FEDERAL AND STATE KIDNAPPING LAWS

A. Federal Laws

§10:10   The Federal Kidnapping Act

The Federal Kidnapping Act was created in response to the Lindbergh kidnapping. The son of the famous aviator Charles Lindberg was kidnapped from his home in New Jersey and held for ransom. At the time, there was no real mechanism for federal involvement in such a case. After the Lindberg child was found dead, the Federal Kidnapping Act, sometimes called the Lindberg Law, was enacted.

The Federal Kidnapping Act, codified at 18 U.S.C §1201, provides:

(a) Whoever unlawfully seizes, confines, inveigles, decoys, kidnaps, abducts, or carries away and holds for ransom or reward or otherwise any person, except in the case of a minor by the parent thereof, when—

(1) the person is willfully transported in interstate or foreign commerce, regardless of whether the person was alive when transported across a State boundary, or the offender travels in interstate or foreign commerce or uses the mail or any means, facility, or instrumentality of interstate or foreign commerce in committing or in furtherance of the commission of the offense;

(2) any such act against the person is done within the special maritime and territorial jurisdiction of the United States;

(3) any such act against the person is done within the special aircraft jurisdiction of the United States;

(4) the person is a foreign official, an internationally protected person, or an official guest as those terms are defined in section 1116(b) of this title; or

(5) the person is among those officers and employees described in section 1114 of this title and any such act against the person is done while the person is engaged in, or on account of, the performance of official duties

shall be punished by imprisonment for any term of years or for life and, if the death of any person results, shall be punished by death or life imprisonment. 18 U.S.C §1201(a).

A minimum sentence of 20 years imprisonment applies when the victim is a child under 18 and the perpetrator is over 18, unless the person taking the child is a parent, grandparent, sibling, aunt, uncle, or other individual with legal custody of the child. 18 U.S.C. §1201(g).

§10:11   Exclusion for Parents Who Kidnap Their Own Children

The Act specifically excludes kidnappings by parents of their own children. 18 U.S.C. §1201(a) ("Whoever … kidnaps … any person, *except in the case of a minor by the parent thereof* … shall be punished. …" [emphasis added]).

The intent to exclude family members dates back to the passage of the Federal Kidnapping Act. In 1932, during a House of Representatives debate, Chairman Dyer stated that "[t]here is not anybody who would want to send a parent to the penitentiary for taking possession of his or her own child, even though the order of the court was violated and it was a technical kidnapping." 75 Cong.Rec. 13, 296 (1932). The original wording of the Act required that the kidnapping be for "ransom or reward," because, in part, it was presumed that a parent would not kidnap a child for monetary reasons. *United States v. Boettcher*, 780 F.2d 435, 436 (4th Cir. 1985). The fingerprints of the Lindberg kidnapping, of course, were all over the Act.

Persons whose parental rights regarding the child have been terminated by a final court order are not considered to be parents. See 18 U.S.C. §1201(h). Does this mean there is no federal criminal action against parents whose rights have not been terminated for kidnapping their children in federal courts? Almost, but not quite.

KIDNAPPING

§10:12   International Parental Kidnapping Statute

To get dinged for parental kidnapping in federal court, a parent whose rights have not been terminated needs to have gone international. The International Parental Kidnapping statute, states:

(a) Whoever removes a child from the United States, or attempts to do so, or retains a child (who has been in the United States) outside the United States with intent to obstruct the lawful exercise of parental rights shall be fined under this title or imprisoned not more than 3 years, or both.

(b) As used in this section—

(1) the term "child" means a person who has not attained the age of 16 years; and

(2) the term "parental rights", with respect to a child, means the right to physical custody of the child—

(A) whether joint or sole (and includes visiting rights); and

(B) whether arising by operation of law, court order, or legally binding agreement of the parties.

18 U.S.C. §1204(a), (b).

§10:13   Affirmative Defenses to Violation of International Parental Kidnapping Statutes

There are at least three affirmative defenses to charges under the International Parental Kidnapping Statute. They are:

(1) The defendant acted within the provisions of a valid court order granting the defendant legal custody or visitation rights and that order was obtained pursuant to the Uniform Child Custody Jurisdiction Act or the Uniform Child Custody Jurisdiction and Enforcement Act and was in effect at the time of the offense;

(2) The defendant was fleeing an incidence or pattern of domestic violence; or

(3) The defendant had physical custody of the child pursuant to a court order granting legal custody or visitation rights and failed to return the child as a result of circumstances beyond the defendant's control, and the defendant notified or made reasonable attempts to notify the other parent or lawful custodian of the child of such circumstances within 24 hours after the visitation period had expired and returned the child as soon as possible.

18 U.S.C. §1204(c).

This effectively allows an affirmative defense in the Karla Knapper type of factual scenario discussed at §10:01. If Karla went to Italy instead of Florida, she could be charged in federal court. She would have the affirmative defense that she was fleeing a pattern of abuse, however.

Other than international cases, the feds don't criminalize parental kidnapping. The reason for this may be that all 50 states have parental kidnapping laws on the books.

§10:14   SORNA

The Sex Offender Registration and Notification Act (SORNA), 18 U.S.C. §2250(a), requires states to establish a registration scheme for monitoring convicted sex offenders. The states have the right to determine which crimes are sex offenses. SORNA places the offenses into three tiers with each tier having its own registration requirements depending on the seriousness of the offense and age of the victim. The kidnapping of a child, if not by the child's parent or guardian, can be a Tier III sex offense under SORNA. Thus, conviction of kidnapping a child, without any sexual contact whatsoever, can require your client to register as a sex offender.

[§§10:15-10:19 Reserved]

B. State Laws

1. General Kidnapping Statutes

§10:20　State Laws Vary Widely

State laws on kidnapping offenses are all over the map. Some states have a singular crime of kidnapping while others differentiate kidnapping by degrees. For example, the perpetrator's relationship with the victim, the degree of force used, and whether weapons were involved are common differentiating factors when determining the severity of the charge. Some states have separate parental kidnapping statutes, while others incorporate parental kidnapping into their general kidnapping statutory scheme.

§10:21　Model Penal Code

Under the Model Penal Code, a person is guilty of kidnapping if he or she unlawfully removes another person from his or her residence or business, or if he or she unlawfully confines another for a substantial period of time in a place of isolation, with any of the following purposes:

(a) to hold for ransom or reward, or as a shield or hostage; or

(b) to facilitate commission of any felony or flight thereafter; or

(c) to inflict bodily injury on or to terrorize the victim or another; or

(d) to interfere with the performance of any governmental or political function.

Model Penal Code, §212.1 (2001).

The Model Penal Code defines unlawful confinement as confinement accomplished by force, threat, deception, or, if the victim is under 14 or is incompetent, without the consent of the child's parent or guardian. Model Penal Code §212.1 (2001).

§10:22　Common Law Kidnapping

Common law kidnapping required two key elements. The features of these common law elements often show up in modern statutory kidnapping cases. Generally, kidnapping required asportation (which is the removal of a person from a place of security to one of increased danger) and detention.

Many modern statutes have dropped the asportation element, in part because it is a hard element to describe, and, therefore, hard to prove. States that have eliminated the asportation element rely on other circumstances of the charge to establish the danger of confinement.

In *Creek v. State*, 588 N.E.2d 1319 (Ind. App. 1992), a post-conviction review case, the question of whether you can kidnap a sleeping child was considered. There, the defendant demanded that his wife's friend bring his wife to see him. He threatened to kill the friend's sleeping son if she did not. The sleeping child was not moved nor aware of the danger. The Indiana Court found, perhaps in part because the facts of the case were so atrocious, that the kidnapping still occurred.

Further consider *People v. Taylor*, 184 A.D. 2d 218 (N.Y. App. Div. 1992). There, the victim was restrained in a vacant apartment and tortured after a robbery. The torturing, which was not essential to the robbery, but was cruel and ancillary, was sufficient to prove kidnapping.

[§§10:23-10:29 Reserved]

KIDNAPPING

2. State Parental Kidnapping Statutes

§10:30 Is a Custody Order Required?

All 50 states have a parental kidnapping analog to the traditional kidnapping statute. They have a variety of different names for this crime, like criminal restraint by a parent or custodial interference.

These criminal statutes vary significantly. Some require a court order awarding custody to someone other than the parent who took the child before the case can be charged. See, e.g., Utah Criminal Code, 76-5-103. While, in other states, the service of a pleading regarding child custody is sufficient. See, e.g., SC Code §16-17-495. Many still, require no court order as a precursor to the crime.

§10:31 Must the Child Be Removed from the State or Concealed?

Jurisdictions differ as to whether the child must be removed from the charging state to commit the crime. Most state statutes do not require the removal of the child from the jurisdiction as an element of the crime of custodial interference. There are exceptions. Maine requires that the parent remove the child from the state or hold the child within the state in a place the child is unlikely to be found. 17-A M.R.S.A. 303(5). See also the statutes in Mississippi, Miss. Code Ann. §97-3-51(2), North Carolina, N.C. Gen. St. §14-320-1, and North Dakota, N.D. Cent. Code §12.1-18-05.

§10:32 Defense of Imminent Harm

Finally, several state statutes provide protection for the parent in the form of a defense of imminent harm to the child. What needs to be established, of course, depends entirely on the level of protection included in the statute. At the very least, the imminent harm to the child defense is available in Arizona, Arkansas, California, D.C., Florida, Hawaii, Idaho, Illinois, Louisiana, Maryland, Michigan, Minnesota, Missouri, Nevada, New Hampshire, New Jersey, New York (if the child is removed from the state), Ohio, Pennsylvania, Rhode Island, Utah, Vermont, Washington, West Virginia, Wisconsin and Wyoming.

[§§10:33-10:39 Reserved]

III. STRATEGIES AND TACTICS

§10:40 Discovery through the Family Matter in Parental Kidnapping Cases

Parental kidnapping cases generally include a family matter component. In other words, a civil case involving the parents' rights to the child will often be pending at the same time as the kidnapping charges. The case could be brought by the child's other parent, the kidnapping defendant, or even by the state agency in charge of protecting children. The civil case often proceeds at the same time as the kidnapping case because the kidnapping parent could not be served with process while he or she was on the lam with the child or children.

These family matters provide both danger and opportunity. The danger, of course, lies in the testimony of your client in the family matter. Imagine that Karla Knapper, pending her kidnapping charge, is served with a custody petition related to her child, Dumplin. She has a very difficult choice. She will want to testify, but her testimony is dangerous.

Remind your client that the order of priorities needs to favor her liberty. This will be a hard pill to swallow. Also remind your client that she has a right to refuse to testify under the Fifth Amendment, even in the civil proceeding. However an assertion of the Fifth in a civil proceeding is not without consequences. The court in the civil case will be able to make an adverse inference against Karla in any matter in which she pleads the Fifth. *See Baxter v. Palmigiano,* 425 U.S. 308 (1976).

The opportunity for the accused's lawyer in these family cases is in the chance to attack crucial witnesses for the government. These government witnesses should be scrutinized in the discovery process of the civil case.

If you do family law work along with criminal defense work, the responsibility for examining these witnesses is yours. If there is separate family matter counsel, be sure to explain to them the areas of inquiry that may help in the criminal case. In either situation, make sure that the witnesses in the criminal case are put on the record in the civil case. This may involve the use of written discovery, depositions, and trial testimony.

It is often a bad move from the perspective of the child's other parent to bring these civil proceedings against the kidnapping parent, but they do it anyway. They are often misled by the authorities.

I once represented a woman whose son, a toddler, had been stabbed by a next door neighbor while he slept. The child's mother hired me because the Maine Department of Health and Human Services substantiated her for abuse (i.e., held her responsible for putting the child in jeopardy) as a result of the stabbing. Their idiotic reasoning was that the mother had been friendly with the neighbor who committed the stabbing. As a result, they found that she exposed the child to a dangerous condition. As you are probably not surprised to learn, we got that substantiation reversed with an apology.

A week later, I was in court to defend a restraining order in a different case. I saw my client in the stabbing case, and asked her what she was doing there. She said the police told her to bring a restraining order against the neighbor and criminal defendant.

A friend of mine, who was defending the criminal case against the neighbor, was licking his chops. The police gave my client bad advice. The criminal defendant was locked up and even if she was let out, bail conditions would prohibit her contact with my client and her son (who, by a miracle, survived). My client decided exposing herself to needless testimony didn't make sense, and she dropped the restraining order. I ruined the day for brother defense counsel on that one.

Most people won't get that advice. They will bring a restraining order, parental rights actions, divorce actions and more. Great! Make sure you have a sufficient fee and start intense discovery. Start the subpoena process. Get all the info you might not get in your criminal jurisdiction otherwise. And if you will not handle the family matter yourself, refer your client to someone good and coordinate your attack.

You may practice in a jurisdiction where you depose victims in criminal cases. I don't. If I get the opportunity in a family matter to file interrogatories, requests for admissions, requests for production of documents, and subpoena records, then follow that with a half day deposition of the alleged victim (parent or child), I'm happy.

§ 10:41   Abuse Defense in Parental Kidnapping Cases

Perhaps you are in a jurisdiction where some form of the imminent harm defense is statutorily authorized. In such a state, if that defense is available, be sure to use it. This means you can parade witnesses and wave evidence before the jury to establish imminent harm. This is a good way to cast a shadow over the state's parent "victim."

If you don't live in a jurisdiction where the imminent harm defense is permitted by statute, you will need to more deftly get the evidence in. If you can get the jury to hear that Karla Kidnapper did not take Dumplin because she wanted to circumvent the child custody process, but rather because Dumplin's dad was abusive, you will have a good case. Even if your jurisdiction does not recognize the defense, you may get an acquittal through jury nullification (if you can get that evidence before the jury).

§ 10:42   Consent Defenses in Non-Parental Kidnapping Cases

Explore consent defenses as well. They will likely not be available to you in the context of a parental kidnapping case because the law will remove the child's ability to consent. In other kidnapping cases, consent may be the defense you are left with.

The issue in many jurisdictions is whether the alleged victim was restrained unlawfully. That may mean that your client moved the alleged victim somewhere, from Point A to Point B (with or without the additional element of asportation (increased danger), depending on your jurisdiction), or your client substantially restricted the free movement of the alleged victim. In either case, the alleged victim's consent will generally be a defense.

If consent is your defense, your pre-trial investigation should focus on the ways in which consent was communicated to your client. These include both verbal and non-verbal assertions.

Obviously, the first order of business is to see if the alleged victim has re-thought his or her initial statement to the police. Assuming the alleged victim has not re-thought his or her initial statement and is sticking to the story as a kidnapping, how are you to prove consent? Do you need to put your client on the stand?

Not necessarily.

Consider the case of Mr. Snee Key and our client, Gotsum Gunz. Remember, Mr. Key snuck into Gotsum's house and stole his marijuana. When Mr. Key was found with the marijuana, he claimed that Mr. Gunz held him at gunpoint, took him to the bank, and forced him to withdraw some money to pay for it.

We approached Mr. Key with investigators on multiple occasions. Mr. Key would not relent from his initial story. He refused to say anything other than the fact that he was taken at gunpoint and ordered to drive to the ATM to withdraw money.

This testimony is obviously a problem. Mr. Key's story that he was taken at gunpoint and ordered to supply money to Mr. Gunz meets the definition of kidnapping. In this case, Mr. Gunz was not an attractive witness and was not someone I would suggest take the stand.

The approach I used was to really get into the nitty gritty of the car ride and the stops along the way. We learned from our client that they stopped for gas, they passed a police station, and Mr. Key went to the ATM in the lobby of a bank. We got surveillance videos from the gas station and the ATM. We produced still images from those videos. We reconstructed the car ride in a video-- all to show that Mr. Key had opportunity to escape or seek safe harbor if he really was kidnapped. This all went to our consent defense, which we were able to establish through the alleged victim, who really became our witness. See §§10:110-10:112 (cross-examination of Mr. Key).

[§§10:43-10:49 Reserved]

IV.   TRIAL

A. Parental Kidnapping Cases

1. Opening Statement

§10:50   My Approach

Let's now examine the way we might approach an opening in the Karla Kidnapper case. Effectively, I want to present a contrary point of view to the State's case: that parents should not resort to self-help in child custody disputes.

Instead, I am looking to not only explain Karla's plight, but also to start to plant the seed for the thinking that she was brave by fleeing.

For general tips on opening statements, see Ch. 2.

§10:51   Sample Opening Statement

They say you shouldn't judge a person until you've walked a mile in their shoes. In the Karla's case, you shouldn't judge her until you've not walked, but run, hundreds of miles in her shoes. Running away from a life of despair and danger. Running away from an abusive husband in order to protect her child. Running to a place safe.

Imagine it. Karla and Abe Usive have a tortured relationship. It is tumultuous and it is violent. And Karla has made plenty of mistakes along the way. But at some point along the line a maternal instinct kicked in.

Some of you have kids, and especially you mothers know. I was hiking in the White Mountains one time and we came across in the distance a black bear cub. My buddy who I was hiking with used to be an Outward Bound instructor, so he had a lot of wilderness experience. I wanted to get closer for a better look. It was only a cub after all. But my buddy reminded me that the Mama Black Bear was somewhere not far behind. She might not have eyes on that cub at that very moment, but if we were between her and the cub when she did, all hell would break loose.

Karla did not always have her eye on the ball. She was fine with drinking and drugging with Mr. Usive when they were single. And they would then get physical with each other. But when they had their child, at some point she had that moment of clarity. When she did, she knew what she had to do.

I am not suggesting she thought through the process very well. I am not saying she sought the right advice from the right people.

KIDNAPPING

But Karla has no law degree. Karla didn't have money for a lawyer. And Karla did not know what to do.

Rather than say she made the wrong choice, I want you to look at the guts it took. Look at the bravery. She had to secretly move out and hit the road with a young kid without any real resources. Unless you have been abused, you may not know the bravery it took, but I'm sure you can imagine it.

When you have lived with your abuser for years, you begin to believe the abuse is what you deserve. You believe it is all you were meant for. And the dirty little secret is that you get used to it.

It is like living in a pitch black room. You can't see anything. You live in the dark. You can't find a light switch and eventually, you get tired of looking for one. You just live with the dark.

Then suddenly, it is not just you in that dark room. It is your child. And you don't want them growing up in that complete and utter darkness. So you keep looking for a way to turn on a light. And if that means breaking through a wall to get to the sunlight, that's what you do.

When you finally hear the evidence in this case, you will conclude that Karla's actions were brave, not criminal.

[§§10:52-10:59 Reserved]

2. Cross Examination of Abusive Husband/Parent

§10:60   Key Points

Let's now take a look at the cross-examination of Abe Usive in the Karla Knapper case.

Remember that Karla and Mr. Usive had a hellish relationship. She claimed he abused her. When she wised up finally, she fled. When she was found in Florida, she was charged with parental kidnapping.

Points to make with this witness are:
- He's angry with the Karla, the defendant, wants to make her pay, and is not objective.
- He has cooperated with prosecutors, but refused to be interviewed by defense counsel.
- Their relationship was volatile; the police had come to their home several times.
- On one such occasion, she called 911 and reported he was beating her.
- She suffered injuries. Even though he denies causing them, jurors can draw their own conclusions from photos of the injuries and his improbable explanations.
- His parental rights to his daughter from a previous relationship were terminated by a court.
- At the termination hearing, the child's mother testified he had abused her.
- Karla, the defendant, was present and heard that testimony.
- When he and the defendant left the hearing, he was angry at the child's mother, and was yelling, screaming, and speeding.
- He threatened to kill the child's mother in the defendant's presence. Even though he denies the threat, jurors can draw their own conclusions from his admissions of his state of mind.
- In addition, Karla's state of mind is critical. The jury will hear Abe deny threatening the mother of his other child. However, if they do not believe Abe, then Karla has a really good reason to leave the relationship in a less traditional way to protect both herself and her daughter, Dumplin.

For tips on effective cross-examination, see Ch. 2.

§10:61   Establishing Bias Against the Defendant

Q. Mr. Usive, you love your daughter very much.
A. Of course.
Q. More than anything in the world.
A. Yes.
Q. She's your only child.

A. Yes.
Q. You would do anything to protect her
A. Yes.
Q. You'd run into a burning house to save her life.
A. Yes, I would.
Q. Because she's your child, you feel strongly about this trial.
A. Yes.
Q. You want to make sure you protect her interests.
A. I do.
Q. You tried to protect her interests in your testimony here today.
A. I told the truth in my testimony here today.
Q. OK, let's talk about that truth. You hate Karla don't you?
A. I'm not too thrilled with her at the moment.
Q. You are very angry with her?
A. I'm angry because she took my daughter from me.
Q. So you are angry with her.
A. Yes.
Q. You agree with me that you want to make her pay for what you think she did?
A. I want justice for what she did.
Q. But you would agree with me that you aren't objective about this case, are you?
A. I don't know what that means.
Q. You feel very strongly about this case, don't you?
A. Yes.
Q. And you've been working with the prosecutors, haven't you?
A. I don't know about working—
Q. You've given the prosecutor interviews haven't you?
A. Yes.
Q. And information?
A. Yes.
Q. And evidence?
A. Yes.
Q. When they call you, you call them back?
A. I do.
Q. And you talk to them.
A. Yes, I have.
Q. When I've called you, you haven't called me back, have you?
A. No.
Q. When my investigator called, you didn't call back, did you?
A. No.
Q. And that is because you are against Karla in this case, right?
A. I guess.

§10:62 Bringing Out Abuse of the Defendant

Now let's get into the nitty-gritty of what this guy is: an abuser the client needed to flee from with their child.

Q. You would agree with me that you've beaten Karla?
A. No, sir.
Q. You agree with me that you've hit her?
A. No.
Q. You would agree with me that you've threatened Karla?
A. Only that I would take her to Court.
Q. You would agree that your relationship with Karla was explosive?
A. I'd say it was heated at times.

Q. And by heated, you mean you would get physical with each other?

A. No, mostly yelling, mostly by her.

Q. Mostly yelling, huh? OK. You deny ever striking her?

A. Yes I do.

Q. Do you remember the police coming to the house when you lived in California?

A. Yes, several times.

Q. When the police came one time, do you remember Karla having a bruise on her forehead and a black eye?

A. I remember one time she had some marks on her, but she was drinking a lot and fell down a lot. She was also using a lot of meth. I didn't do that to her.

Q. You were using a lot of meth at that time too?

A. Yes.

Q. When you took meth, did it make you anxious?

A. Sometimes.

Q. Did it make it easy for you to lose your temper?

A. I wouldn't say that.

Q. But you remember a time when she had marks on her face and the police came?

A. Yes.

[SHOWING PHOTOGRAPH]

Q. Is that what she looked like on the day the police came to your door in California?

A. Yes.

Q. That right there looks like a large bruise on her forehead, do you agree?

A. That's what it looks like.

Q. And you didn't have anything to do with that?

A. Nope.

Q. How about that right there, looks like a black eye to me, is that what it looks like to you?

A. Yes.

Q. And you're telling the jury you had nothing to do with that?

A. That's right.

Q. Your explanation for these marks is that she fell down a lot?

A. I don't know how she got them.

Q. Did she fall down on your fist?

GOVERNMENT: Objection. Argumentative.

COURT: I agree. Jury is to ignore Counsel's last question.

Q. You don't remember a specific incident of her falling down and getting this black eye, do you?

A. No.

Q. You don't remember a specific incident of her falling down and getting this bump on her head, do you?

A. No.

DEFENSE: Move to admit Defendant's 23.

COURT: Objection?

GOVERNMENT: No objection your honor.

COURT: It's admitted.

DEFENDANT: Publish to the jury, your honor?

COURT: That's fine.

Q. The police came to your house the night of the photograph because Karla called 911?

A. Yes.

Q. Did you hear that call?

A. I was right there.

Q. And she told 911 that you were beating her?

A. Yes, but it wasn't true, and I wasn't even arrested.

Q. You weren't arrested because after she hung up with 911, you told her you would kill her if you got arrested that night, isn't that true?

A. No, no.

Q. Well, as you say, you weren't arrested that night, were you?

A. No, I wasn't.

§10:63   Termination of Parental Rights to Child of Prior Relationship

In this case, Mr. Usive had problems with another daughter and her mother. The daughter, Imin Truble, was taken away from Mr. Usive in a termination proceeding in California. What Mr. Usive told Karla Knapper about his treatment of Imin's mother is relevant to her belief that she needed to flee.

Q. You have another daughter too, don't you Mr. Usive?
A. Yes.
Q. That's Imin Truble?
A. Yes.
Q. How old is she now?
A. Uh, she must be 5 or 6.
Q. You're not sure how old she is?
A. Pretty sure she's 6.
Q. If I told you she was 7, would that surprise you?
A. No.
Q. It's been several years since you've seen her.
A. Yes.
Q. You and Imin's mother don't get along, do you?
A. Not really. I haven't talked to her for years though.
Q. You had termination hearings related to your parental rights of Imin?
A. Yes.
Q. Karla was at those hearings?
A. Yes.
Q. In fact, she was pregnant with Dumplin at that time?
A. Yes.
Q. Imin's mother and you were on opposite sides in Imin's termination hearings right?
A. I guess.
Q. She testified against you?
A. I don't know if I would say that.
Q. Well, didn't she say you were abusive to her?
A. She did, but it wasn't true.
Q. Was Karla in the courtroom when she said that?
A. She was there that day. I don't know if she was there at that time.

§10:64   Threats Against Prior Partner

Q. The day Imin's mother testified, you left the courthouse at the end of the day with Karla?
A. Yes.
Q. And you were driving?
A. I don't remember. Probably.
Q. And you were angry.
A. I was upset.
Q. You were very upset?
A. OK.
Q. And you were yelling?
A. I definitely raised my voice.
Q. Yelling?
A. I guess.
Q. Yelling about Imin's mother?
A. Yeah.
Q. You were swearing?
A. There was probably some of that.
Q. You told Karla that you would get revenge on Imin's mother.

A. No.

Q. You deny that?

A. Yes I do.

Q. You deny saying that you would kill Imin's mother?

A. Absolutely.

Q. You deny telling Karla that you would lure her to meet you on Route 78, kill her and dispose of the body?

A. Absolutely.

Q. OK, so Karla had no reason you are aware of to be scared of you?

A. No.

Q. Would you agree with me that you were aggressive in how you described your feelings toward Imin's mother?

A. I guess.

Q. Would you agree you were driving fast?

A. I don't know.

Q. You were yelling, you were swearing and you were upset, but you didn't threaten Imin's mother and you didn't speed.

A. I may have been speeding but I didn't threaten to kill Imin's mother.

Q. You have never threatened to kill Imin's mother?

A. No.

Q. Imin's mother claimed in her testimony that you beat her?

A. Yes.

Q. You did beat her, didn't you?

A. No.

Q. And you beat Karla, didn't you?

A. No way.

Q. You beat her while she was pregnant?

A. No.

Q. How about choking her, would you agree with me that you choked her during her pregnancy with Dumplin?

A. I did not.

Q. Did you push her ever?

A. I don't know, maybe I pushed her.

Q. You pushed her, but you never hit her or choked her?

A. I guess.

Q. And Imin's mother won that custody case didn't she?

GOVERNMENT: Objection.

DEFENDANT: I'll withdraw it.

[§§10:65-10:69 Reserved]

3. Direct Examination of Defendant

§10:70 Usually Best to Avoid, but May Be Necessary with Abuse Defense

Obviously, great care needs to be taken in any case in which the defendant decides to testify. It is a good practice to ask the court to inquire of a defendant whether she knows she does not have to testify before she takes the stand. If the court doesn't do it automatically, I request (outside the presence of the jury, of course) that the court do so. Actually, I often ask the court to discuss the Fifth Amendment with my client on the record whether the client is going to testify or not.

I haven't included a lot of defendant direct examinations in this book because my clients very often don't take the stand. In fact, I find that is normally the best practice. Often, if a client takes the stand, it is over my objection.

In the case of a defendant whose defense to kidnapping is abuse, you will often need client testimony. Abuse normally happens in secret. Often your client is the only witness. As a result, you may be thrust into a situation where your client's testimony is necessary to tell her story, especially since the abuse will likely be denied in cross.

§10:71   Key Points

Let's look at a direct of Karla Knapper. Points to make with this witness are:

- Her abusive husband and accuser told the defendant he lost his parental rights and had been accused of abusing the child.
- He blamed the mother of his older daughter for having his parental rights terminated.
- After the termination hearing, he was driving fast and yelling and swearing.
- He told her he'd rather kill the mother of his older daughter than let her get custody.
- He told her he was not going to return the child after his visitation and that he was going to kill her mother.
- He punched and choked her while she was pregnant, but she did not pursue charges.
- While they had broken up after their daughter's birth and she had moved to California with the child, he made no attempt to have contact with the child.
- The both used meth while together, but she has been clean for four years.
- They got back together and after a month he began physically abusing her again.
- When she returned to California for a visit, he called her often to accuse her of not being faithful to him.
- He threatened to take their daughter away from her.
- He threatened to kill her.

§10:72   Abusive Parent's Threats Against Prior Partner

Q. Karla, where did you meet Mr. Usive?

A In California when he was dating a friend of mine.

Q How long ago was that?

A 2003.

Q. Were you friends then?

A. At that time, we were just acquaintances.

Q. Did this change?

A. Yes

Q. To what?

A. A boyfriend-girlfriend thing.

Q. And you became romantically involved?

A. Yes.

Q. When was that?

A. We became romantically involved in 2004 after the birth of his first daughter with my friend.

Q. Do you know his first daughter's name?

A. Imin Truble.

Q. Did there come a time when you and Mr. Usive got married?

A. Yes.

Q. When was that?

A. 2006.

Q. And you became Imin's step mother?

A. Sort of

Q. What do you mean "sort of."

A. Well, she never lived with us and he didn't see her often.

Q. Do you know why that was?

A. Yes, well, what he told me.

Q. Which was?

A. He lost his parental rights because…

GOVERNMENT: Objection. Calls for hearsay.

DEFENSE: Not for the truth of the matter asserted. To show the effect on the listener consistent with her defense as to why she took the child.

COURT: Overruled. Ladies and gentlemen of the jury, this testimony is being offered to show the effect on Ms. Knapper when she heard the statement. It is not a statement offered to prove why or why not the child was taken by Mr. Usive.

Q. Thank you, your honor. Karla, what did he tell you about losing his parental rights to Imin?

A. He said that she had failure to thrive and that they accused him of abusing her but he denied that part.

Q. Had you had your own child by the time you heard this explanation?

A. No, but I was very pregnant. Third trimester I believe.

Q. And what was your reaction to hearing that Imin was taken away?

GOVERNMENT: Objection. Relevance.

DEFENSE: Goes to her state of mind as we establish the reasons she felt the need to flee with her child.

COURT: Overruled.

Q. What was your reaction to hearing that Imin was taken away from Mr. Usive?

A. It made me really nervous. But we were together, having a kid together, and I wanted to believe him that this was all made up.

Q. Did you support him then?

A. Yes. I was at every court hearing.

Q. What was Mr. Usive's relationship with Imin's mom like at the time?

A. During the hearings he blamed her. He thought she was the cause of his problems. She was trying to get the…

GOVERNMENT: Objection. Non-responsive.

COURT: Sustained.

Q. Were Imin's mom and Mr. Usive on the same side in the custody case over Imin?

A. No.

Q. Did you ever talk to Mr. Usive about Imin's mom during the custody hearing time period?

A. All the time.

Q. What type of things would he say?

GOVERNMENT: Objection. Calls for hearsay.

DEFENSE: Not for the truth of the matter asserted. Again, to show the effect on the listener. Additionally, with a little foundation this will be an exception to the hearsay rule as an excited utterance.

COURT: OK, lay the foundation.

Q. You were about to tell us something that Mr. Usive said to you about Imin's mom?

A. Yes.

Q. Do you remember the circumstances of the conversation you were about to talk to us about?

A. It was after a day of trial testimony by Imin's mom.

Q. And where did your conversation take place?

A. On the ride home.

Q. Who was driving?

A. Abe was.

Q. What, if anything, did you notice about his driving?

A. It was scary.

Q. What do you mean?

A. He was driving really fast. Swerving around. Being aggressive. Yelling and swearing.

Q. He was upset?

A. Very upset. Screaming and yelling.

Q. What did he say?

GOVERNMENT: Objection. Hearsay.

COURT: Overruled.

Q. What did he say?

A. That he'd rather go to jail and take care of Imin than her mom getting her.

Q. Did he say why he'd go to jail?

A. He said he'd rather kill Imin's mother then let her get Imin.

Q. Was that all he said about killing her?

A. No. He got very specific.

Q. In that same conversation in the car or a different conversation?

A. The same conversation.

Q. And was he still upset when he said what you are about to testify to?

A. Yes. It was at the same time.

Q. OK, what did he say he was going to do?

A. He told me that he was going to keep Imin from her when he was supposed to give her back after his visitation and that he was going to get Imin's mom to get into the truck with him by telling her that something was wrong with Imin, take her down to 78, and there is a trail that he was gonna' drive down and kill her and put her in the ground out there.

Q. What did you take "put he in the ground" to mean?

A. To kill her and bury her.

Q. How did that make you feel?

A. Really scared.

§10:73   Abusive Parent's History of Abusing Defendant

Q. Was Mr. Usive physically abusive to you at that point?

A. Not really, but he was becoming sporadic in the way he treated me. Yelling a lot, screaming a lot, punching walls. Not long after that though he started abusing me.

Q. How long after?

A. It was while I was still pregnant, so maybe a week or two after the driving thing I told you about.

Q. What happened?

A. We were fighting about another guy who had been paying some attention to me. Abe was really, really jealous of me. And he lost it and punched me three times in the face.

Q. What happened after he hit you?

A. I called the police. Or a neighbor did – I can't remember. But the police came, and I didn't press charges. But the police arrested him.

Q. What happened to that case?

A. I didn't cooperate and the prosecution dropped it.

Q. Why didn't you cooperate?

A. I was stupid. I was scared of him but also having a baby with him any week then. He earned all our money. I didn't have anything.

Q. Did he ever hit you again while you were pregnant?

A. No, but he choked me.

Q. When was that?

A. This was a few days before my due date.

Q. And what happened?

A. The cops came, but I didn't cooperate again.

Q. Okay. And there is some confusion about whether or not he was there when your daughter Dumplin was born.

A. He was at the hospital when I went for a checkup because I was two weeks overdue.

Q. Okay.

A. And when we went home to settle the insurance issues, because of his behavior at the previous appointment asking my mom "Does she really have to go in that far!"-- about the nurse checking my cervix--and I didn't feel like having his jealousy in my delivery room. So, I did not call him when I went into labor.

§10:74   Abusive Parent's Lack of Interest in Child

Q. Did you ultimately break up?

A. Yes.

Q. When?

A. After Dumplin was born.

Q. Did he stay in California?

A. No, he moved back to Maine.

Q. With Dumplin?

A. No, she stayed with me.

Q. Did you stay in California?

A. No, I moved back to Maine too.

Q. How long was it after Dumplin's birth that you moved back to Maine?

A. About a year.

Q. During that time, did Dumplin have any contact with Mr. Usive?

A. No. I had written him every occasion and sent pictures of Dumplin with whatever he had sent-- Oh. --and told him everything that she--I was teaching her, everything that we were doing, where we were going, who she was around.

Q. Did he have a phone number and address for you?

A. Yes, but he stayed away.

§10:75   Removing the Sting from Prosecutor's Anticipated Cross

> **PRACTICE TIP:** *Expose the warts before the prosecutor does*
>
> If your client is going to take the stand, you have to take the sting out of the prosecutor's cross. It's likely that your client has a lot of warts. If they can be exposed by the prosecutor, they should first be exposed by you, robbing the prosecutor of some drama.

Drug Use

Q. Did you and Mr. Usive have a healthy lifestyle when you were together?

A. Not in the least

Q. What was unhealthy?

A. Drugs.

Q. Who used them?

A. Both of us?

Q. What did you use?

A. Meth.

Q. And Mr. Usive?

A. Meth.

Q. You witnessed that?

A. Many, many times. We did it together.

Q. Do you still use it?

A. On November 1st, it will be four years since I've touched it.

Q. Why did you stop?

A. Because I found out I was pregnant. Okay. And so since then—I have not—that's it.

Q. Did Mr. Usive stop using during your pregnancy?

A. Ah, no. He slowed down, but he still did it.

Defendant Returned to Abuser

Q. Why did you move to Maine?

A. Abe and I got back together.

Q. Why?

A. I was stupid. And I wanted Dumplin to be with her father. And he told me he was different.

Q. Was he different?

A. No. At first it was OK.

Q. What do you mean?

A. We moved in to his grandparent's house with Dumplin, and he was working. I was staying at home with Dumplin. Everything was good for a couple of months. Then on Halloween of that year we had another fight.

Q. A physical fight?

A. Yes.

Q. So this is Halloween of what year?

A. Would have been 2008 or 2009.

Q. What happened?

A. We got into an argument because I asked him to hang up on the phone with his mom and stepdad so that he could help me get Dumplin ready for bed, and when I got upset, I took her to the bathroom, she went potty, and then on our way to her bedroom I realized I needed to brush her teeth. So, we made a U-turn, went to the bathroom, and when we went to the bathroom I closed the door behind me and began brushing her teeth, and he came and barged the door in. So, I slammed it shut, and then after I put Dumplin to bed and read her a book, I went to go into our bedroom, and he said that I wasn't allowed in there, that he had thrown my blankets and pillows out into the living room, and when I proceeded into there, he slammed me into the door frame. I was begging him to please let me out, and he didn't for a few minutes, and when he did, he threw me to the ground, and I immediately got up and went over by Dumplin's bedroom and called the police.

Q. And did the police respond?

A. They did.

Q. And was anybody arrested?

A. No. He was just asked to leave because they said that they couldn't prove who was the aggressor, if it was him or me.

Q. Did he leave?

A. Just for the night.

§10:76   Jealousy, Harassment, Threats—The Final Straw

Q. Were you having any jealousy problems like the ones in California?

A. All the time. But I went back for a visit to California, and it was worse.

Q. What happened?

A. He would call me constantly and ask me where I was, what I was doing, who I was sleeping with, and telling me that he was calling my friends to see where I was, checking in on me, and they were telling him that I was playing around sexually.

Q. I want to talk about the garage sale you had at the end of April.

A. Okay.

Q. You were selling some belongings.

A. Yes.

Q. Were you leaving your apartment?

A. Yes.

Q. Did you see Mr. Usive the day of the garage sale?

A. Yes. He came to the garage sale.

Q. What happened?

A. He came over to the driveway. He was yelling at me that he wants his half of the money that I was getting from the yard sale and that if I left that he was calling the police--or, no, he said that--not to leave because he had already called the police. Okay. Uh—And at that point I said, "Well, you're harassing me, and I'm calling the police." And he said, "Good."

Q. Did you call the police?

A. Yes.

Q. Why?

A. Because he was harassing me and he had threatened to take Dumplin away from me. He also threatened to take my life. I don't remember the specific words that he said. He also--at the moment, I can't remember what he said specifically but that he would take care of me and that I'd never see her again.

Q. Did the police take any action?

A. They came, but they just asked him to leave.

Q. What did you do?

A. I made up my mind. I needed to get out of there and hide. I needed to protect myself and I needed to protect Dumplin.

[§§10:77-10:89 Reserved]

4. Closing Argument

§10:90   My Approach

This closing is fun because we get to attack and point the finger at Abe Usive.

At this point of the case, what I am really fighting is the concept of self-help. I don't know if the jury believes my client 100 percent, but even if they believe 75 percent of what she says, it is enough to establish that she was escaping a difficult environment. So, in this closing, I want to continue the themes of an abused parent saving herself and her child, and I also want to address my concern that the jury may not want to acquit her because she took the law into her own hands.

§10:91   Sample Closing Argument

The government has handed you a piece of paper that they call an Indictment. On that piece of paper they charge Karla with kidnapping. But this is a really a case about self-defense. This is really a case about the defense of a child. And because that is what the case is really and truly about, I think you will find that a not guilty verdict is the only appropriate measure of justice here.

Long ago, a man went searching for the truth. He took everything he owned, and he sold it. And he searched the world high and low for the truth.

This search came at great personal sacrifice. His health suffered. He lost all his wealth. He was mentally fatigued. And his search went on for years and years without results.

Finally he found himself in a very remote corner of the world. He went into a small village, and did what he would normally do. He asked the locals if they had ever seen the truth. And the locals told him, "Yes, we know the truth. Up in those mountains, there is an old woman, and she is the truth. Go up and find her. She will be happy to talk to you."

So the man hiked up the humongous and dangerous mountain. It was a long difficult climb. At the top he found a small house. He knocked on the door and it was opened. There was a woman at the door who was the oldest woman he had ever seen. She was hideous looking and grotesque. She was so horrible to look at that he shuddered when he first saw her.

But he persisted. And he said, "I am sorry to bother you, but I have been searching for a long time for the truth. Are you the truth"?

And the old woman said to the man "Yes, I am the truth. Come in. Let me feed you."

And the man entered the house and he stayed with the old woman for a day. And she fed him and spoke to him and he felt reborn.

The following day, the man said to the old woman "Thank you for everything you've done for me. I have to leave now and tell the world about you."

The old woman looked at him and said "If you have to leave and tell the world about me, please tell them that I am young and fair."

The search for the truth is difficult. There will be mountains to climb. And when you find the truth, it is often ugly. And often, people don't believe the truth when it is ugly. Which means that they never find the truth.

The truth here is no less ugly. Mr. Usive abused Karla. He abused Karla in front of her child, and scared her. He scared her so much that she felt she was under the threat of death. She felt that threat in her bones. She felt that threat in her skin. She felt it in her entire body and it was real to her.

Like many women in abusive relationships, she came to understand very late that Mr. Usive was not going to change. You might sit in judgment of her. In fact, you do sit in judgment of her on the kidnapping charge. But you may also sit in judgment of her as a human being. That's natural.

You women especially might be sitting on this jury saying "I never would have let that happen to me. I never would put myself or my child in that situation."

You would be wise. You would be wiser than Karla. But the question is, if you did find yourself in that position, what would you do?

Karla spent years trying to justify Mr. Usive's actions. She took him back. She took him back after he punched her while she was pregnant. She took him back after he choked her while she was pregnant. You may say, that would be enough for me and I would never take him back. But that is not the issue.

I often tell my kids that wishing doesn't make it so. They'll say "Oh, I wish my homework was done." Well, wishing your homework was done doesn't make it happen. We know that as adults, don't we?

But adults still behave like children sometimes. And for whatever reason Karla behaved liked someone who was wishing to change a circumstance when she came back to Mr. Usive. When light finally dawned over Marblehead, Karla realized that Mr. Usive would never change. And Karla realized, or at least believed in her own heart, that Mr. Usive might someday abuse Dumplin.

That is the ugly truth that Karla realized. While it is easy for us to judge Karla, we all ignore the ugly truths about our situations from time-to-time. It is much easier for us in our lives to sometimes pretend the ugly truth doesn't exist. We don't need to eat better. We can get away with smoking. We don't need to lose an extra 20 pounds. We can skip our exercise today. But those justifications don't change the reality. And when adults, who sometimes behave like children, realize they have a problem facing the ugly truth, the question becomes what they do about it.

I don't dispute there were other ways to go about this. I won't dispute that Karla could have tried to work on some sort of civil process, but you need to recognize what she told you. She didn't have resources. She didn't know that she could get a restraining order. Even if she went and got a restraining order she didn't believe it would stick because Mr. Usive would lie about his abuse. And she believed she would end up dead. And she remembered what she heard Mr. Usive say about Imin Truble's mom. He said she would lure her away and kill her. Karla had those words tattooed on her memory. They came to her every time she thought of what she needed to do.

Karla knew what Mr. Usive was capable of, and she ran to protect Dumplin and herself.

I want you to imagine you have a child. Those of you who have children, I want you to imagine a time in their lives when they were at their most vulnerable, when they were infants.

Imagine you are taking your infant child for a walk. She is in a stroller. Suddenly, coming toward you is a large dog. It's growling and running at you. It looks extremely aggressive. It is charging you and your baby. You can't fight it, but you can run.

Do you run? Do you try to protect your child, or do you just hope it's a good puppy that wants to play?

Let's imagine the same scenario. But this time you know the dog. And it bit and severely hurt another child on the street. Do you run then?

I want to talk to you now about the elements of the offense and the burden of proof on the government in this case…

[See Ch. 2 for reasonable doubt arguments.]

My son, Anthony would kill me for telling you this story. He called me on the phone one day. He was about nine. And there was something that he was doing, I frankly don't remember what it was, but I remember this conversation.

I asked him if he needed help with whatever this task was. And he said "No Dad, I don't need you."

He didn't say "No, Dad. I know how to do this," or "No, Dad. I am all set." He said "No, Dad, I don't need you."

And I said to him "Anthony if you don't need me, should I still come home tonight?"

And he paused and there was silence on the phone. And then he answered "Yes, Dad, I want you to still come home."

That pause is the moment of reflection in the context of reasonable doubt. That's the pause of consideration. Anthony was taking that pause because he was giving real thought to my question.

When you consider this case, you need to take that same pause, and consider the facts against the standard of reasonable doubt. You need to consider the heavy burden of proof the government carries and how they haven't carried that burden here. Once you take that pause, I believe you will answer like Anthony did, and you will let Karla come home.

[§§10:92-10:99 Reserved]

B. The Self-Help Case

1. Opening Statement

§10:100 My Approach

Let's continue with the Gotsum Gunz case. See §10:02. How might we approach an opening in such a case? Like many cases, the Gotsum Gunz case is about making the victim look like the bad guy. Right off the bat, I am going to acknowledge that my client is a big marijuana smoker. I can't avoid it so I am going to address it up front.
  Then, this opening is about attacking Mr. Snee Key. I toss around some pejorative words in opening, calling Mr. Key a thief. The subtext is that even if there was a kidnapping, that he deserved it. At the same time, I look to point out the inconsistencies in his testimony.
  For tips on effective opening statements, see Ch. 2.

§10:101 Sample Opening Statement

This case is about whether you believe the word of a thief, plain and simple. Because Mr. Snee Key will tell you that he was taken at gunpoint and told to withdraw money to pay for some marijuana he stole from my client. We dispute that Mr. Key was forced to do anything. But there is one thing that is undisputed. What is undisputed is that Mr. Snee Key is a thief. And he will have to tell you that he is a thief in this case.

You may have forgotten me by now, but my name is Tim Zerillo. My client here is Mr. Gunz. I am very pleased and proud to represent him. And together with my colleagues there at this table we are going to do our best to represent him in this case. Because this is a very important time, in fact, it is a crucial time, in Mr. Gunz's life.

The evidence is going to show that Mr. Gunz and his family loved to smoke marijuana. Now I am aware that marijuana is illegal. I bet you are too, even though the laws on it have been rolled back quite a bit. But I am also aware and want to state to you, as I did in jury selection, that Mr. Gunz is not charged with a marijuana offense. He is charged with kidnapping. So whatever your feelings are on marijuana, good, bad, or indifferent, they should not bear on whether a kidnapping has occurred. In fact, you may want to evaluate this as you would any other theft. Something was stolen from Mr. Gunz, and that thing was marijuana. But the fact that it was marijuana has nothing to do with the case.

What is important is that Mr. Key stole the marijuana. That's important because one of the things that you must do as jurors in hearing the evidence and evaluating it is to determine the credibility of witnesses.

And you may consider, if you wish, if Mr. Key's credibility is in doubt. As you know, he will tell you he is a thief.

The second reason the theft is important is because of how it relates to the kidnapping charge. In essence, what is claimed is that Mr. Key, when he was caught red-handed, went to an ATM to withdraw money to pay for the marijuana that he smoked that was not his. And there is no dispute that Mr. Gunz drove him to the ATM. There is dispute as to whether Mr. Gunz drove him to the ATM under force.

If you find that Mr. Key voluntarily went to the ATM with Mr. Gunz, then a kidnapping has not occurred. On the contrary, if you find that Mr. Gunz forced Mr. Key at gunpoint to go to the ATM and withdraw money, than a kidnapping has occurred. The evidence, however, points to the fact that Mr. Key went voluntarily and not at gunpoint.

So, how will you know if Mr. Key is telling the truth? Evidence will be presented on this issue and you should take note of it.

First, there will be witnesses. Mr. Gunz's son and wife were present at the time that Mr. Key was caught with the stolen marijuana. And they will tell you that no gun was used by Mr. Gunz. That no threats were made. That Mr. Key knew he was caught red-handed, and he voluntarily offered to pay for the marijuana.

Second, the evidence will show that on the way to the ATM in Mr. Gunz's, car, they stopped for gas. This was at a self-serve gas station. And we have surveillance videos to show you from that station.

Now, surveillance videos are not usually high quality, and this one isn't any different. But it will show Mr. Gunz pumping gas outside of the car. It will show Mr. Key in the passenger seat of the car. At one point it seems like he is tuning the radio. You will not see Mr. Key flee from the car, or signal other drivers. In fact, it's quite busy at the gas station that day, and other drivers are coming and going. But you won't see Mr. Key flag anyone down. You won't see Mr. Key get out and run. And you won't see a gun.

Next they go to an ATM. And at the ATM Mr. Key withdraws money and we will show you a surveillance video of that ATM. Mr. Gunz does not even appear in the frame of the surveillance video. But there you have Mr. Key. He is at the ATM. He punches in his own pin number and he withdraws money.

This ATM is in the lobby of a bank. There will be no evidence that Mr. Key flags down a bank teller. There will be no evidence that Mr. Key runs. There will be no evidence that Mr. Key asks the bank security officer for help.

What is not evidence? The Indictment. The indictment is merely an accusation. It is made without the due process of the jury or a judge being present. It is merely a means to initiate the system of justice that brings you here today. It means nothing more.

Can you see my hand here as I hold it up? (holds up hand). You may say "Yes, Tim, I can see your hand."

But you can only see one side of my hand. And not until I turn my hand in this direction can you see both sides of my hands. The Indictment, the accusation, only sees one side of things. You get to see both sides of things, and you get to judge them on the basis of whether the Government has proven its case beyond a reasonable doubt.

[§§10:102-10:109 Reserved]

2. Cross-examination of Alleged Kidnapping Victim

§10:110 Key Points

Let's now turn to the cross-examination of Mr. Snee Key. Mr. Key, as you will recall, stole a pound of marijuana from his neighbor's house. He then turned around and charged the neighbors with kidnapping. We are arguing a consent defense.

Points to make with this witness are:
- He admits to stealing in the past from the defendant and others.
- He admits to stealing the marijuana from the defendant for which the defendant demanded payment.
- He has been convicted of theft.
- He had smoked a lot of marijuana and was high when he was allegedly held at gunpoint by the defendant.
- He claims the defendant forced him to withdraw money from the ATM by holding him at gunpoint and he was terrified.
- The defendant was parked on a busy street.
- The witness was not held at gunpoint when he walked to the defendant's car.
- He opened the door and got in himself.
- He didn't yell to his neighbors for help.
- He didn't try to flag down a passing car.
- While riding in the passenger seat in the car, he was not held at gunpoint.
- When they stopped for gas, the defendant left him in the car, but he made no effort to escape.
- He went to an ATM in the lobby of a bank to withdraw money. The defendant did not go in with him. While in the bank, he made no effort to escape or get help.

For tips on effective cross-examination, see Ch. 2.

§10:111 Extract Admission of Thefts and Prior Convictions

First, let's call a thief a thief.

Q. Mr. Key, you are a thief, aren't you?
A. I don't think I'd say that.
Q. OK, you steal things from people that aren't yours.
A. I have done that.
Q. Just like you stole from my Client.
A. Yes.
Q. And other people?
A. I guess.
Q. To steal something you need to be sneaky, right?
A. I don't know.
Q. You don't just walk into a house when the homeowners are home to steal things do you?
A. I don't.
Q. No, you wait until they aren't home, and then you sneak in.
A. I guess some people do.
Q. But not you?
A. I have, but that's not who I am.
Q. What you've done in the past is not who you are now?
A. No.
Q. Well, let's focus on your past then for a moment. You would agree with me in the past that you've been a sneak thief.
A. I snuck in and stole things from Mr. Gunz house.
Q. OK, and when you did that, you were sneaky about it.
A. I guess.
Q. And you've been sneaky like that a lot?

A. No.

Q. Are you the same Mr. Snee Key who was convicted of a Theft, Class D, in the Cumberland County Superior Court on June 8, 2009?

A. Yes.

Q. That wasn't for a break in at Mr. Gunz house, was it?

A. No.

Q. That was another theft you committed.

A. Yes.

§10:112 Framing Consent Defense

Let's now look at how we might frame the consent defense through this witness.

Q. Mr. Key, you just testified on direct that you were held at gunpoint?

A. Yes.

Q. This is during the time when Mr. Gunz found you with his stolen marijuana?

A. Yes, right after he found me.

Q. You had smoked a lot of that marijuana hadn't you?

A. Quite a bit.

Q. And you were really high?

A. Not really high, a little bit.

Q. A bit high?

A. Yes.

Q. You smoke marijuana a lot?

A. Not now.

Q. But during this time you did?

A. Yes.

Q. And you found that marijuana can make you paranoid, right?

A. Sometimes. It doesn't usually do that to me, but to some people.

Q. So you were a bit high when Mr. Gunz came to find you?

A. Yes.

Q. And you were scared?

A. Yeah.

Q. You must have been extremely scared?

A. I was.

Q. Were you terrified?

A. I was.

Q. You said on direct that you thought you were going to be killed, right?

A. I did.

Q. You claim he put a gun to your head and forced you to go withdraw money from the ATM.

A. He did.

Q. OK. So to get to the ATM you needed to take a car.

A. Yes.

Q. And the car was in the driveway in front of your house?

A. Yes.

Q. TO COURT: Permission to approach, your honor?

A. COURT: Go ahead.

Q. I'm showing you what I have marked as Defendant's 1. Do you recognize that photograph?

A. Yes, it's the front of my house.

Q. And that dirt driveway there is the driveway to your house?

A. Yes.

Q. And that is where Mr. Gunz car was parked when you went to the ATM that day?

A. Yes, over here.

Q. You are indicating that he parked in a portion of the driveway that is near the road.

A. Right.
Q. And that road is Route 25?
A. Right.
Q. That's a busy road.
A. Pretty busy.
Q. Thirty-five mile per hour speed zone past your house?
A. I guess.
Q. You don't know?
A. I don't drive.
Q. TO COURT: Publish Defendant's 1 to the jury, your honor?
A. COURT: Sure.
Q. OK. And it looks like there are houses right next to yours.
A. Yes.
Q. You walked from the backyard, down a walkway, and down a driveway to get into Gotsum's car?
A. Yes.
Q. You weren't at gunpoint then?
A. No.
Q. He didn't carry you to the car?
A. No.
Q. You walked on your own?
A. Yes.
Q. And you opened the car door yourself?
A. Yes.
Q. And you got in yourself?
A. Yes.
Q. You didn't yell to your neighbors for help?
A. I didn't know if anyone was home.
Q. You didn't yell to your neighbors for help?
A. No.
Q. You didn't flag down any of the cars passing on Route 35 for help?
A. No.
Q. And Gotsum's gun was not out at that time?
A. No.
Q. You rode in the passenger seat of the car.
A. Yes.
Q. And Mr. Gunz drove.
A. Yes.
Q. He didn't have a gun pointed at you during this time?
A. Not in the car, no.
Q. You made some stops along the way, right?
A. Yes.
Q. You stopped for gas.
A. Right.
Q. And Mr. Gunz pumped the gas, right?
A. Yes.
Q. And you were in the car alone.
A. Yes.
Q. Did Mr. Gunz bring his gun with him to pump gas?
A. I didn't see that.
Q. So the gun was in the car with you.
A. I don't know.
Q. Didn't you check?
A. No.
Q. You were terrified; didn't you want to escape?

A. I did, but I didn't know what to do.
Q. And there were other cars around, weren't there?
A. I don't remember.
Q. Showing you on the projector a series of photos, Defendant's 2A through 2E, already admitted, which are still photos of the surveillance video. (Go through photos and have him identify each time there was someone around who he could have asked for help).
Q. So then you went to the ATM.
A. Right.
Q. The ATM was in the lobby of a bank; it wasn't a drive up ATM, right?
A. Right.
Q. Mr. Gunz didn't bring a gun into the bank, did he?
A. No, he didn't go in.
Q. He didn't even go into the bank?
A. No.
Q. You went in yourself, right?
A. Right, but he told me to.
Q. And you were scared, so you followed what he said?
A. Yes.
Q. And you were in the bank with other people, right?
A. Yes.
Q. Bank tellers.
A. Yes.
Q. Bank managers.
A. Yes.
Q. And you know banks have alarms, right?
A. I guess.
Q. And you still didn't ask anyone to help you?
A. No.
Q. And you were terrified for your life?
A. Yes.

[§§10:113-10:119 Reserved]

3. Closing Argument

§10:120 My Approach

By the time we get to closing, I hope the jury agrees that Mr. Key is, in fact, a thief. Ultimately then, I want to the jury to have this mathematical formula in their heads: thief + liar = not guilty verdict.

§10:121 Sample Closing Argument

A thief is a liar. Plain and simple. The two character defects go hand in hand. A thief is a liar. We know Mr. Key is a thief. And he is a liar too.

(Writing on board in large words THIEF + LIAR)

Let's take a look at Mr. Key's claims. He goes into my client's house, steals his property, is caught, is made to pay for what he stole and then he complains about it to the police. This is incredible.

An effective lie usually has a grain of truth in it. An accomplished liar takes the truthful part of something and then adds or twists a fact. That way, you can corroborate part of the story and make yourself appear truthful when you aren't.

So, it is factual that Mr. Key stole the marijuana. But what he said happened after that, is part truth, part fiction.

In your deliberations, you need to ask yourself if Mr. Key's testimony makes sense. I submit to you that it does not.

He claims that he was scared when he was taken by my client to go withdraw the money. In fact, he says he was taken. He doesn't say he went voluntarily. He says he went at gunpoint.

But look at all of the chances he had to flee. He was outside walking on his own. Did he flag down a car? No. Did he run? No.

And then they get to the bank, and he walks in. Anyone who has ever seen a movie or TV show about a bank robbery knows banks have alarms. Does Key tell anyone that he has been kidnapped? No. Does he make any complaints at all? No. Does he call the police? No.

Unlike Mr. Key, we are not just making all of these facts up. We provided you an ATM photo showing Mr. Key withdrawing money from the ATM. Does he appear to be in distress? Do you see anyone holding a gun to his head? No.

Mr. Key is a man who got caught doing something. He was called on it by the person who caught him. He had to make a repayment for the thing he stole. And he didn't like it. That's why we are all here. That's why we are all spending this time together.

(Writing on board: THIEF + LIAR = NOT GUILTY)

Let's talk about what the state has to prove, and can't prove, beyond a reasonable doubt.

For tips on closing arguments and sample language for burden of proof and reasonable doubt arguments, see Ch. 2.

KIDNAPPING

CHAPTER 11

SEXUAL ASSAULTS AGAINST ADULTS

Sex crimes are such a big area of my practice, and have so many issues to deal with, I have tried to divide them in this book into several different areas. This Chapter focuses on sex crimes where adults are victims. In Chapter 12, we look at sex crimes where children are the victims, and then, in Chapter 13, we tackle child pornography.

SEXUAL ASSAULTS
AGAINST ADULTS

(This page intentionally left blank.)

I. COMMON ISSUES WITH SEXUAL ASSAULTS AGAINST ADULTS

While rape cases can cover a panoply of different situations and victim types, some issues are common to many of them.

A. Rape Shield Laws and Sex Offender Registration

§11:01 Rape Shield Laws

To properly prepare for trial in a sex case you need to understand your local rape shield law. Rape shield laws were enacted to protect victims of sex crimes during prosecution of the criminal case. With some exceptions, they prevent a defendant from introducing evidence of the victim's sexual behavior, history, or reputation. While they can be tricky, you often want to find a way around them that opens the door for rape shield-type evidence.

As you probably know, the old defense of: "Of course it wasn't rape, the victim's a whore! Look I have 150 witnesses…," will not fly. That said, there are usually openings in the rape shield law to introduce evidence of the victim's sexual behavior, history, or reputation. Rape shield laws allow evidence of the sexual history between the complainant and the defendant to rebut issues of consent. They also typically allow sexual history evidence to rebut claims related to your client being the source of injury or ejaculant. See, e.g., Fed. R. Evid. 412 (evidence of rape complainant's sexual history is inadmissible, except: (1) specific instances of complainant's sexual behavior when offered to prove that someone other than defendant was the source of semen, injury, or other physical evidence, (2) specific instances of complainant's sexual behavior with defendant when offered by defendant to prove consent or by prosecutor, or (3) when exclusion of the evidence would violate defendant's constitutional rights.)

Each of these situations can prove useful. For example, if your client is charged with raping a woman he met at a club, it is arguably admissible that she had sex at that club in the bathroom with another man earlier that evening. This evidence is not evidence that the alleged victim is promiscuous, but is rather evidence that your client was not the source of the semen she claimed came from him when she was examined the following day.

In short, know your rape shield laws, and find a workaround when you can.

§11:02 Sex Offender Registration

Sex offender registration requirements vary greatly from jurisdiction to jurisdiction and are the subject of much controversy. Each state is a little different, but the trend is, of course, to further punish behavior with more and more stringent registration requirements.

Here is the bottom line: consider that every sex case may have a sex offender registration component. That sounds simplistic, I know. Some cases may not be registerable. In Maine, for example, an unlawful sexual touching misdemeanor is not a registerable sex offense. I always tell people that what isn't registerable now, may be a registerable sex offense in the future. The trend is for more registration, not less.

Failure to warn your client of sex offender registration as a collateral consequence of a guilty or no contest plea is an omission that I believe (and hope) in future years will constitute ineffective assistance of counsel. In 2010, the U.S. Supreme Court handed down *Padilla v. Kentucky*, 130 S. Ct. 1473, 176 L.Ed.2d. 284 (2010), which found ineffective assistance of counsel when a defense lawyer did not warn a noncitizen client of the immigration consequences of a guilty plea. The ripple effect of *Padilla* on ineffective assistance claims is potentially fantastic.

Even before *Padilla*, some states found that the failure to warn defendants of sex offender registration requirements was ineffective assistance of counsel. New Mexico held that "In light of the harsh and virtually certain consequences under SORNA that flow from a plea of guilty or no contest to a sex offense, we follow *Paredez* and conclude that defense counsel has an affirmative duty to advise a defendant charged with a sex offense that a plea of guilty or no contest will almost certainly subject the defendant to the registration requirements of SORNA." *See State v. Edwards*, 141 N.M. 491, 499 (2007).

After *Padilla*, more courts are following suit. In 2011, the Michigan Court of Appeals in *People v. Fonville*, LC No. 2006-208493-FC found that the *Padilla* concept applied to sex offender registration requirements. *Fonville* held:

On the basis of *Padilla*, we recognize a significant parallel to be drawn from the Supreme Court's rationale in that case to the circumstances of this case. Similar to the risk of deportation, sex offender registration "as a consequence of a criminal conviction is, because of its close connection to the criminal process, …

difficult to classify as either a direct or a collateral consequence[,]" and that therefore "[t]he collateral versus direct distinction is … ill-suited to evaluat[e] a *Strickland* claim" concerning the sex-offender-registration requirement.

Bottom line, protect yourself and your client by warning about registration requirements.

[§§11:03-11:09 Reserved]

B. Investigating the Sexual Assault Case

§11:10   Launching Your Investigation

Don't rely on the police to spoon feed you discovery! You and your investigator must get out there and work the investigation.

Your investigation needs to start ASAP. I like to have a nearly immediate investigation meeting with the client right after I am retained. It is in that meeting that we discuss who needs to be interviewed, and in what order.

As always, having a good private investigator is essential. These people need to be fearless and efficient. It may take you some time to find the right person, but once you do, the investigator is worth her weight in gold.

The investigator should have good ideas as to how to investigate witnesses. The basics are social networking checks and inquiries as to lawsuit and restraining order abuse. The more complicated stuff involves pseudo-stings and surveillance. Be careful. You walk a fine line between legitimate investigation and a witness tampering or stalking charge. I can't tell you how often I have had to get my investigator out of trouble with the police. Sometimes, that is all in a day's work for a sexual crimes investigator.

Avoiding investigator problems has two components: First, make sure to hire good people. I have worked with good investigators and mediocre investigators. Get rid of the mediocre, lazy, uninspired investigators and get good quality people. They need to have an investigatory background (ex-detectives, federal agents, etc…) or have significant investigatory experience (as investigators, auditors, forensics people, etc…). Then, make sure your people know what tampering is and is not in your jurisdiction.

> **PRACTICE TIP:** *When the cops pressure you about victim tampering*
> Despite your best precautions, you will get the inevitable call from the police on occasion. The alleged victim often gets angry when investigated and then calls the police who try to lean on you. I politely tell them what the tampering statute is and to leave us alone. If they continue to threaten, I call the prosecutor and have him or her tell the cops to back off. If they don't, file a Motion to Dismiss and argue that they are chilling your right to prepare a defense.

§11:11   Interviewing the Alleged Victim

First things first, get to the alleged victim—as in, yesterday. By the time you get the case, you are already playing from behind. However, if you think that approaching the alleged victim first will cause other crucial witnesses to run and hide, then hold off.

Before going after the alleged victim, make sure you understand your State's ethics rules. This is an extremely touchy subject. To me, not making an attempt to interview the alleged victim is malpractice. You won't always find alleged victims willing to be interviewed, but the attempt, as long as it complies with your bar rules, should always be made.

Like all witness interviews, I like the alleged victim interview to be done by an investigator. First, a good investigator may be better at getting the information than an intimidating lawyer. The title "lawyer" will scare a lot of people off. Additionally, I don't want to make myself a potential witness by doing the interview myself. With an investigator, if the alleged victim makes a statement that he or she later denies at trial, I just call the investigator to the stand. If I did the interview myself, that gets sticky (because I obviously cannot be a witness and trial lawyer at the same time).

If the alleged victim isn't represented and your bar rules permit an interview, it should be off to the races. Unless the alleged victim tells your investigator to go away, the victim is fair game. The victim may be the lifeblood of your case.

Always talk to the alleged victim if you can. You never know what you will find when you peel back that onion, but I bet you it will smell. Even if you learn from the interview that the alleged victim is charming, intelligent, grounded and will make an excellent witness, that is valuable information, because it is information you need to think about when evaluating your chances at trial.

§11:12   Tone of Interview

If the alleged victim is willing to talk to your investigator, you should discuss with the investigator the tone of the conversation. Generally, the tone to use is soft and empathetic. People talk more if they feel they have a sympathetic ear.

On occasion, for example, when you feel the alleged victim is fabricating the story for a vindictive reason, you may wish your investigator to display a more aggressive tone. That tone may be that we are not going away and you need to deal with us. Steering clear of threatening language is a must, however.

§11:13   Get Details; Find Contradictions

Once you get the victim talking, you want her to recite the story in detail. Very often the police are doing the bare minimum. You want every little detail of the victim's interaction with your client. If your investigator gets into detail, you will learn things you never knew from discovery.

Most of my cases don't result in the alleged victim saying she made the whole thing up. I am looking for inconsistencies. That is why the interview requires detail. The investigator needs to get very small and minute. No small detail is unimportant. The more the investigator can get the alleged victim talking, the better off you are.

§11:14   Importance of Recording Interview

It is important that your investigator use a recording device. Your investigator also must be familiar with your state's rules on recording without two-party consent. In Maine, for example, only one party needs to consent to a phone recording. So, my investigators can record on the phone without telling the other party. They need to disclose the recording if they are recording a live interview in someone's home, however. Either way, your investigator must be familiar with your local rules and follow them.

On occasion, an alleged victim acknowledges a false complaint. I had one of these cases not long ago that underscores the need to record interviews.

Our client, a high school kid of 18, was at the end of his senior year in coastal Maine. He convinced a female senior classmate he had been pining over to take a drive with him after school. They drove down a dirt road, where she later told police that he pulled her into the back seat of the car and forcibly raped her.

This story smelled funny to me from the start. My client was dumb enough to brag about his conquest back at school. It was only after the bragging that the alleged victim made up the rape allegation. I wondered if the alleged victim had been embarrassed and the rape allegation then snowballed on her.

My investigator, Sheryl, had a real knack for dealing with female sex crime victims. We strategized dealing with this young lady, and we determined that Sheryl should take a gentle approach, which she did. Over a course of interviews, the alleged victim acknowledged that she never told our client "no," nor did she resist. This was completely contrary to the story she told the police, which was the basis of their claim that there was a sexual act by compulsion. In other words, there was no rape.

So, we drafted an affidavit. The alleged victim signed it with a few changes, and I went to the District Attorney's Office to pound the table and demand a dismissal.

The District Attorney had indicted my client by this time. He was deep into this case, therefore, and reluctant to dismiss it. We had litigated motions, and he had invested energy into this case. Prosecutors hate to waste the energy they expend in my experience.

So, after reviewing the alleged victim's affidavit, the District Attorney told me he wanted to talk to the alleged victim. I said okay, since I am powerless to stop him anyway.

The District Attorney and the lead detective re-interview the alleged victim. And she flip-flopped yet again! She very tearfully and convincingly told them that I made her sign the affidavit (with the investigator) and that we threatened her. The detective is now ready to arrest me!

What saved our bacon? The investigator recorded the alleged victim signing the affidavit. We played the recording for the District Attorney who shrugged his shoulders and the case was dismissed.

So, beat the bushes. But make sure to cover yourself when you do.

§ 11:15   Restraining Orders

Very often the sexual assault charge comes with a restraining order. For whatever reason, a foolish police officer or victim witness advocate has told the alleged victim to get a restraining order. The defendant looks at the restraining order as another problem to deal with. The skilled criminal defense practitioner looks at the restraining order as free discovery.

I would urge everyone involved in a sex assault defense practice (if you are not already doing so) to attend restraining order hearings on behalf of your client. Your client should plead the Fifth and not testify in almost all cases. That said, you should have a right to full cross-examination of the alleged victim. Make sure the hearing is recorded (many of them are not unless you request it) and make sure to fully cross-examine the alleged victim on all facts. Come prepared with case law related to your right to cross-examine in the event that you have a judge who sniffs out that this is merely a deposition for you, as opposed to a real defense of the restraining order. Getting the alleged victim under oath in these cases is a potential goldmine.

> **PRACTICE TIP:** *Have a colleague do the cross*
>
> Even better, if you are in a law firm with multiple attorneys or have a friend who will help, have that person cross-examine the alleged victim in the restraining order hearing. There are two benefits to this: 1) the alleged victim does not get used to your style of cross examination and 2) you get another set of eyes looking at the case that may look at it from a different and valuable angle.

You may have a case with a totally bizarre alleged victim. Perhaps the victim is crazy or motivated by money. Either way, the victim doesn't operate with the same set of rules we do.

I once represented a gentleman on a series of charges, let's call him Greg Gross. He had a sexual relationship with a woman we'll call Dawn Devourer. Greg and Dawn found each other somehow and began having sex. One night they had a threesome with another man they picked up at a bar they frequented.

Alas, sometimes those hot relationships burn out quickly, and Dawn charged Greg with rape and brought a restraining order against him. Unfortunately for Greg, it turned out that Dawn was never really into him, but rather was setting him up. So, here he was, charged with rape and barely making bail.

We used the restraining order as a discovery tool. Her claims were that Greg raped her repeatedly and on numerous occasions, and that he used money to control her. One of the dates on which she claimed to have been raped was the night of the threesome. So we put her on the stand at the restraining order hearing and pinned her down on dates and times of these forcible rapes. That would have been worthwhile enough on its own, but, as is described in the next section, we also found our mystery man.

§ 11:16   Video Surveillance

Video surveillance is often overwritten quickly. However, if you get a case quickly enough, and can preserve the evidence, you might just strike gold.

Imagine you represent a defendant who allegedly went out drinking with a date and sexually assaulted her outside a bar, in a busy area. I would want to get footage from any cameras showing her exiting the alleged assault. Is she running or walking calmly? How many people did she pass without calling for help? How many businesses?

> **PRACTICE TIP:** *Cameras are everywhere now*
>
> Look for business security cameras, of course. But also check traffic light cameras. Traffic lights are often equipped with cameras now to look for traffic violations.
>
> In Greg's case (§ 11:15), he had no idea who the other person was in their threesome, and Dawn wasn't talking to my investigator. So, I sent my investigator to the bar they met in to look for surveillance video. Just on dumb luck and shoe leather she found it (never underestimate the power of using shoe leather). The bartender identified the man in the video, and he knew that he lived in Auburn. My investigator found John Doe and subpoenaed him to testify at the restraining order hearing. Presto! The restraining order was dismissed (to clarify, we made sure to get in the alleged victim's testimony before dismissal).
>
> That still left the rape charge, however. I invited the District Attorney to meet with our mystery man at the restraining order hearing. Sensing that this case was a soap opera of epic proportions, he got the rape charge dumped as well.
>
> Crazy is not easily deterred, however.

§11:17   Phone Sting

Think like a DEA agent when approaching sexual assault cases. They generally record an inquiry about a drug buy with an informant and then proceed to the sale.

In some cases, you may be able to get incriminating information helpful to your client by having your client talk to the victim over the phone. Of course, you need to make sure you client is not violating bail conditions by talking to the victim. Don't use your client in a phone sting if it would violate his or her bail. If it would not violate bail, and there is some potentially useful information out there, consider working with your investigator to set up a phone sting.

In Greg and Dawn's case, despite the dismissal, Greg was not done with Dawn and she was not done with him either. She started having sex with a bouncer at a local bar to shake Greg down for some money. She found a sympathetic prosecutor to initiate charges on Greg in a different county. The bouncer she was having sex with threatened Greg within an inch of his life. Paying Dawn off started to sound really good to Greg. Paying her off was cheaper than my fees, after all.

We knew she wanted money, so we had Greg, with my investigator's assistance, make a series of recorded calls to Dawn. (Note that Greg did not have bail conditions prohibiting his contact with Dawn.)

> **PRACTICE TIP:** *Recording phone calls*
>
> If you haven't already figured it out, find out if your jurisdiction requires two- party consent to telephone recordings. I am very lucky that Maine does not. We have single party consent, and as long as the attorney or investigator is not recording for an unethical purpose, he or she can record over the phone. This is a staple investigative technique.

Here are samples of a longer conversation facilitated by my investigator and Greg with the alleged victim Dawn on the phone.

Greg	All right, just tell me what you want so we can take care of the situation. I mean obviously it's 10:00 at night. Nothing can be done right now, but tomorrow's a brand new day, right?
Dawn	Yeah.
Dawn	What do you think can resolve this?
Greg	You tell me. You're the one that's always in charge of these situations. You tell me.
Dawn	I'm not in charge of anything.
Greg	Yeah, okay.
Dawn	What's it worth to you?
Greg	Jesus Christ. To get you out of my life?
Dawn	Yup.
Greg	What's it worth to me to get you out of my life? Well, that's f**king wonderful.
Dawn	Yeah.
Greg	You tell me, Dawn. I mean what the f**k do you want me to say? F**king $2.00? What do you want me to say?
Dawn	Nothing. You tell me 'cause you're so good at doing that. Why don't you tell me? You had a figure yesterday. What happened to that?
Greg	Jesus Christ. Pretty bad. I got to pay my girlfriend, right?
Dawn	Whatever Greg. I'm going to end this conversation today, so—
Greg	You ended it a long time ago.
Dawn	Umm hmm.
Greg	So what do you want?

Dawn	I asked you—
Greg	—I mean you're already f**king—
Dawn	—you seem to be the one that keeps changing it.
Greg	Jesus Christ. I'm going to sleep well tonight, I tell ya. Unbelievable.
Dawn	Hello?
Greg	I'm right here. I'm just thinking of what you're—you're gonna say.
Dawn	If you want to think, call me back within 20—a half hour.
Greg	Just—just—what do you want from me? Just—what do you want—what do you expect me—what do you want from me? I need to know. What am I supposed to do? I mean you're trying to put me in jail for 15 f**king years. I mean give me a break.
Dawn	There's a reason for that. I'm going to see Meg (Deputy District Attorney) and I'm gonna go to the Cumberland County Sheriff's Department to see what they want me to do.
Greg	You're a wonderful lady. I—your kids must be proud.
Dawn	Don't insult me anymore. I'm not taking your insults any more. Don't make your comments, Greg. 'Cause you're really pushing me.
Greg	I had a swat team in front of my house. I don't think I could push you any much more.
Dawn	You're a rapist. Okay. That's why you had the swat team there.
Greg	Really. But the next day, you have sex with me right? 'Cause you—right? You think I'm gonna do something one day that—you blame something on me one day, but the next day, you have sex with me? Right? Are you there?
Dawn	I'm here.
Greg	Jesus. I don't want to f**king talk about this shit. What do you want? Just come on—tell me what you want so I can—so I know what the f**k to do.
Dawn	You come up with something. You're better at that than me.
Greg	What are you talking about? I'm better at that? You don't listen to anything I say.
Dawn	What do you want to do?
Greg	I want to f**king move on and f**king hopefully live my life. I mean and sell my house and move the f**k out of here in one piece.
Dawn	No shit. I know you're gonna do all that shit. I'm not talking about that.
Greg	You're not going to go peacefully; what's it going to take to get you away from me? Are you still there?
Dawn	Yeah, I'm here.
Greg	What do you want me to do? You tell me? I mean is—
Dawn	Three.
Greg	What?
Dawn	Three.
Greg	And that's not 300, is it?
Dawn	No.
Greg	I wish it was. That's cute.
Dawn	F**king forget it. If it's all right that easy, 4.
Greg	Shut up. It's not that easy. Jesus Christ.
Dawn	Greg.
Greg	All right. Fine. So three f**king thousand, that's what you told me?

Dawn	Four.
Greg	You said f**king three. Now it's four. It was two. Then it was five, now it's three, now it's four. And what do I get Dawn, for four thousand? Jesus Christ. What do I get?
Dawn	Your—I don't incriminate you.
Greg	Oh, my God. I've called every f**king police department there is.
Dawn	You don't think you can do anything without me, right?

This is only a small look into a real conversation with the "victim" in this case. Turned out, Dawn was exploiting many local men, and the information we received was used in future cases against her with Greg's permission. Criminal and civil defense lawyers have called me several times over the years related to Dawn and her claims against their clients.

The moral of this story is if you can record, do record. Had I told the prosecutor without this tape that my client claimed this was a sham complaint and that he was merely being extorted, she would have laughed at me. But the tape recording changed everything.

§11:18   Social Media

I won't dwell on social networking investigation, because I think most defense attorneys are well-aware of its potential benefits. Download any partying, drunk, drugged- up appearing pictures of the alleged victim that you can.

Sometimes the alleged victim will have a lot to say about his or her night out, how much she or he had to drink, what drugs she or he took, and so forth.

Now, to be sure, there are evidentiary limits to this at trial, but the information still may be useful. Before you ever get to trial it may help you win the plea bargaining battle with the prosecutor. You can say to the prosecutor "This is really who your alleged victim is," despite the story he or she has told.

At trial, however, you may still get a lot of this information into evidence. Imagine a date rape complaint cross:

Q. You said on direct that you had two beers while out that night?
A. Yes.
Q. Then after you left the bar you went home with my client?
A. Yes.
Q. And two beers doesn't get you drunk, right?
A. No, I wasn't drunk.
Q. You were stone cold sober (Note: let's say the prosecutor objects here—he's objecting to her sobriety? Not likely.)
A. I was sober.
Q. You're on Facebook, right?
A. Yes.
Q. Is that your page?
A. Yes.
Q. Didn't you say there on the day after that you were "wasted" the night before?
A. Yes.

I try to fit this type of impeachment into a prior inconsistent statement or as it relates to perception. In the above, if we get a relevance objection, her perception of the events she is describing is clearly relevant. Additionally, once boxed in, her Facebook post is a prior inconsistent statement.

§11:19   Preservation Requests for Social Media Evidence

Don't forget as well to use good ol' subpoena power to get social media records. Subpoenaing these records is not as difficult as you might think.

Facebook, for example, likes you to initially send a preservation request to the following address:

SEXUAL ASSAULTS
AGAINST ADULTS

Facebook
151 University Avenue
Palo Alto, CA 94301
Attn: Security Department
Fax Number (650) 644-3229

The preservation request does not need to be complicated. Something along thes lines of Form 11-10 (§11:20) is all they want.

§11:20   FORM 11-10 Social Media Preservation Request

STATE OF MAINE   DISTRICT COURT
CUMBERLAND, ss

_____
)
)
IN RE TONY SOPRANO JR.   )   NOTIFICATION OF PRESERVATION
)
)
_____   )

NOW COMES Tony Soprano Jr., by and through his Attorney, Timothy E. Zerillo and ZERILLO LAW FIRM, LLC, and orders preservation of the following information by Facebook:
1. Response date due: _____.
2. Full name of user(s): page name, Meadow Soprano.
3. Page creator: Meadow Soprano.
4. Networks: Newark, New Jersey
5. Period of activity: _____.
6. URL: www.facebook.com/meadowsoprano
7. Date of Birth: 1.1.1990
8. Known Email Addresses: meadow@sopranos.com

Please preserve all information about this page and all information related to the creation of this page. A subpoena for this information is forthcoming.

Dated this _____ day of _____ 20__ in Portland, Maine.

Respectfully submitted,

_____
Timothy E. Zerillo
ZERILLO LAW FIRM, LLC

Once you have preserved the records, you can subpoena them. All of these social networking sites appear to work on the same basic formula, so once you do a little digging, you will find the specifics.

§11:21   Cell Phone Records

Sometimes cell phone records can be useful. Maybe the alleged victim of the rape, who claimed to have been tortured by your client, called him 15 times the day after the rape. Or maybe you can create a timeline from the calls.

Regardless, if you need cell phone records, you can get them. Again, all you need is to do a little digging, and subpoena the correct carrier. Here is a sample AT&T Wireless Subpoena.

§11:22   FORM 11-20 Subpoena for Cell Phone Records

STATE OF MAINE		SUPERIOR COURT
CUMBERLAND, ss.		DOCKET NO:

STATE OF MAINE	)	
	)	
v.	)	**SUBPOENA**
	)	**(M.R.Crim.P.17)**
TONY SOPRANO JR.	)	
	)	

TO: **AT&T**
     National Compliance Group
     PO Box 24679
     West Palm Beach, FL 33416-4679
     Fax: 888-938-4715

You are hereby commanded to produce certain records detailed below in connection with the above-captioned matter on or before _____ at Zerillo Law Firm, LLC, 1250 Forest Avenue, Ste 3A, Portland, Maine 04103. **Production by email may be sent to tim@zerillolaw.com.**

You are commanded to produce cell phone records and a certification that the records are kept in the ordinary course of your business, including, but not limited to, call history as well as cell site/sector location at call origination and call termination, for the period _____ through _____, for the following phone number:

    (1)

**FAILURE TO COMPLY WITH THIS SUBPOENA
MAY SUBJECT YOU TO BEING HELD IN CONTEMPT OF COURT**

Dated this ____ day of _____, 20__.

                               _____
                                Timothy E. Zerillo
                                Attorney for Defendant
                                ZERILLO LAW FIRM, LLC

[§§11:23-11:29 Reserved]

II.   FORCIBLE RAPE

A.   Elements and Common Scenarios

§11:30   The Elements

    A forcible rape generally requires the sexual act itself, as defined in your jurisdiction, plus physical force or threats of violence or other compulsion. I use the word "forcible" here to distinguish these assaults from sexual assaults in which the victim is mentally or physically incapable of giving consent (e.g., the victim is a minor, drunk, drugged, or otherwise unconscious, or mentally incompetent).

§ 11:31   Forcible Rape by Stranger

Forcible rape cases may have a defendant who is a stranger or someone familiar to the victim. In a forcible rape stranger scenario, you usually are left with the "it wasn't me!" defense. This defense can work, as long as your client doesn't look like Charles Manson and he hasn't left DNA at the scene of the crime. Often these cases come down to an identity defense, and an attack on the victim's perception. For discussion of witness identification issues, see §§11:30, 11:41 and Chs. 5 and 7.

§ 11:32   Forcible Rape by Acquaintance

You can also have a forcible rape with someone the victim knows. Usually, your identification defense has gone out the window in this case because of the victim's familiarity with the defendant. While date rape can certainly be a forcible rape, the level of force in these types of cases generally exceeds the force used in the date rape scenario, discussed in detail later in this chapter.

§ 11:33   Common Scenario

Chris Getthepapers and Jonny Cupcakes are two botchagaloops who were up to no good. Chris is a 30 year old married man who is a full-time contractor and part-time hood. Jonny Cupcakes is a 22 year old part-time property manager and part-time boxer, who is single.

Like any good story gone wrong in Portland, Maine, Jonny and Chris are drinking out at a nearby watering hole on Commercial Street. It is almost noon, but hey, who's counting? They both decide they are horny and looking for action. It's a Wednesday at nearly noon—who isn't?

So they hop into Chris' truck and go trolling down Exchange Street. There, Jonny spots a woman he knows a little bit from around town. They pull over, ask her to get in. She declines. They roll off to another spot, but they scare the woman, and meanwhile, she calls the police. While this incident is not charged ultimately, it is certainly not helpful in negotiating.

Chris then gets a bright idea. He's been cheating on his wife with an 18 year old girl he met at the Dunkin' Donuts. She lives in Freeport. Why not take a trip north 20 minutes and see if she's up for some action?

The prosecutrix is named Mandy. Her report to the police goes something like this: She's gets off her shift at the Dunkin' Donuts and heads home to her house in Freeport. She lives there with her Mom, Dad, Sister and Brother. When she arrives, another friend of hers, Lucy, is there.

Shortly after Mandy arrives home, Chris shows up. He tells her to come with him. She is embarrassed because she slept with him previously and doesn't know what he wants. She is also embarrassed and nervous because he showed up unannounced at her home. He had never done that before. So she leaves with him in an effort to get him out of the house, and away from her friends and family.

They walk out to his truck, where another man is waiting. Chris tells her to get into the truck. Mandy is hesitant. She hems and haws about the fact that she just got home and shouldn't leave unannounced. Chris lifts her up into the truck.

They head toward Portland. She is scared, and still wearing her Dunkin' Donuts clothes. Chris is drunk and driving erratically. They stop for gas along the way. Jonny stays in the car with her while Chris pumps the gas.

They go to a small motel in South Portland. She takes a shower. After the shower, they try to get her to engage in sex. She claims she is restrained and raped by both men. They headbutt her to restrain her. She claims they force her to give them oral sex. She is penetrated vaginally. At least one man allegedly penetrates her anally.

When Chris and Jon are done, they drive her back to Freeport. At home, her family and friends want to know where she was. Her boyfriend even stopped by while she was gone and they didn't know what to tell him. Mandy discloses the rape the next day to her friend and the police are called.

The men, on the other hand, have the story you expect. She is a young lady who Chris had consensual sex with previously. She was up for a good time, and they were too. They claim there was no rape, just a consensual threesome.

This is a really dangerous case. You have a potentially innocent client who can be sent up for a long time if found guilty. If he gets clipped by the jury, a judge is going to land on him for forcibly taking a young woman from her home and raping her. Judges have daughters too.

These cases can be nightmares. Do the right thing and investigate thoroughly. Then make the decision on trial. In this case, with my client getting offers of no less than a decade in custody, he took his chances at trial, and won.

[§§11:34-11:39 Reserved]

B. Strategies and Tactics

1. Defendant Is a Stranger

§11:40   Cross Racial Identification

In the forcible stranger rape scenario, you may find that the alleged victim and perpetrator are not of the same race. Since the only one to identify the perpetrator is often the alleged victim, these are ideal times to use a cross-racial identification defense to the alleged victim's testimony.

Cross-racial identification is discussed in further detail in Ch 3 and Ch 5. The basic concept is that people tend to have more difficulty in identifying individuals of a different race. If the alleged victim and your client are of a different race and you have an identity case, consider employing an expert on this subject.

§11:41   Eyewitness Identity Problems

In addition to cross-racial identification problems, you've certainly by now heard of the problems with eyewitness identification in general. Thankfully, the law in this regard may finally be catching up with science. Eyewitness identification is discussed more thoroughly in Chs. 5 and 7, but suffice it to say that false identifications have sunken many people. Be prepared to research this area and employ experts whenever possible.

[§§11:42-11:49 Reserved]

2. All Cases

§11:50   Psychological Testing

You may want to have your client tested to obtain evidence that he does not fit the psychological profile of a sex offender. Sometimes there is no good defense reason to do forensic testing. Your guy has major problems, and all a test is going to do is confirm that. In such a case, move on to another strategy.

The Psycho-Sexual Evaluation is often used as a measure of potential sexual recidivism. It is similar to any other general psychological evaluation, although the Psycho-Sexual Evaluation focuses on sexual development, sexual attitudes, fantasies, and adjustment. Further, in the context of a criminal case, it employs collateral source data, such as discovery, in the assessment.

Several of the objective testing scales have fallen out of favor with my examiners over the last few years. Now, the examiners I use generally test using the Violent Risk Appraisal Guide, the Sex Offender Risk Appraisal Guide, the Child and Adolescent Taxor Scale and the Cormier-Lang Criminal History Scores for Violent and Non-Violent Offenses.

I don't know that I really believe that these tests are helpful. The reason I like the psychosexual assessment is that the objective testing is combined with clinical interviews, interviews with family and important client contacts as well as a review of discovery. This gives the evaluator greater insight into your client.

> **PRACTICE TIP:** *Know your prosecutor*
>
> You have to know your prosecutor first to determine if a psychosexual evaluation is worthwhile. If you don't know your prosecutor, ask a criminal defense lawyer who does. The same goes for the judge. Does the judge care about this testing? Does it matter to him or her at all?
>
> One prosecutor I know believes in the psychosexual evaluation if it is administered by one particular doctor. If I have a case with that D.A., I know that the testing may be meaningful if that doctor has done it.

§11:51   On Your Feet

Remember what I said about shoe leather. I think that in this electronic age (and I like computers as much as the next guy) we forget about face-to-face investigation techniques. If Jonny Cupcakes walks into my office after the rape, I can write a few memos, or I can get my rear end over to the motel where the alleged rape occurred. I want to see the room; I want to see the headboard; I want to photograph, measure, and deconstruct anything that could help my client.

> **PRACTICE TIP:** *Remember, you always need to get to "Why"*
> The question of why the victim would put herself or himself through this case is always the elephant in the room. During the investigation phase we need to be thinking of the reasons the alleged victim has to fabricate because the jury will ask the same question.

[§§11:52-11:59 Reserved]

C. Motions

§11:60   Motion to Sever Defendants

You may represent the most innocent of the group of defendants, and you might want to keep them joined to point the finger at the real bad guys. You might decide that you want to keep them all in your case because your client looks better by comparison. Or you might not want your baby-faced client dragged down by his Charles Manson-looking co-defendant.

To sever or not to sever, that is the question. That philosophical question is mooted if you can't sever, however.

The most common grounds of a Motion to Sever are found in *Bruton v. United States*, 391 U.S. 123, 88 S.Ct. 1620, 20 L.Ed.2d 476 (1968). The U.S. Supreme Court held that when a co-defendant's confession implicates a criminal defendant, and the co-defendant does not testify at trial, the admission of the confession violates the criminal defendant's rights under the 6th Amendment Confrontation Clause. Further, jury instructions that instruct the jury to disregard the co-defendant's confession in deciding the other criminal defendant's guilt are not adequate.

So, with the case of Jonny Cupcakes and Chris Getthepapers, we moved to sever. Why? Like many of these cases it comes down to feel. Jonny was a good looking, young kid. Chris was a slightly older married man and father, who at best was cheating on his wife and looked a little scary.

We moved to sever and lost. These things happen, and we preserved the issue for appeal. But there have been many other motions to sever I have won, and I have been very happy not to have a creepo friend of my client sitting on our side of the room.

§11:61   FORM 11-30 Motion to Sever Defendants

STATE OF MAINE	SUPERIOR COURT
CUMBERLAND, ss.	DOCKET NO. ***** **

STATE OF MAINE,)

Plaintiff)

v.)   **MOTION TO SEVER DEFENDANTS**

JONATHAN M. CUPCAKES,)

Defendant)

NOW COMES the Defendant, Jonathan Cupcakes, by and through undersigned counsel, and hereby moves this Honorable Court to sever his case from that of the case of *State v. Christopher T. Getthepapers*. In support of this Motion, the Defendant incorporates the following Memorandum of Law.

MEMORANDUM OF LAW

FACTUAL BACKGROUND

On April 4, 2002, the Defendant was indicted on two counts of gross sexual assault, Class A, and one count of criminal restraint, Class C. The undersigned attorneys entered their appearances in this case on February 14, 2002, well before the indictment was handed down.

On the date of the indictment, Megan Pros, the attorney for the State, filed a Notice of Joinder pursuant to M.R. Crim. P. 8(b), purportedly joining Defendants Jonathan Cupcakes and Chris Getthepapers. *See* Exhibit 1. **Undersigned counsel never received a copy of this Notice of Joinder.** *See* Affidavit of Thomas Hall, ¶ 2; Affidavit of Timothy E. Zerillo, ¶ 2; and Affidavit of Sheryl PI,¶ 4.

Mr. Cupcakes's case is a very important case. This office monitors very closely any correspondence or pleadings that are received related to Jonathan Cupcakes. No correspondence relating to the Notice of Joinder was received, nor was the Notice of Joinder itself received.[1]

When the deadline for filing the Notice of Joinder had lapsed and no notice was received, undersigned counsel began preparing for this case as a trial with a single Defendant. Obviously, preparation for a trial with a co-defendant is vastly different. This case is no exception.

On August 12, 2002, at a motion hearing on this matter, Attorney Pros commented to Attorney Hall that she had joined the cases. *See* Hall Affidavit, ¶ 3. Attorney Hall noted that she had not joined the cases, and that counsel had never received Notice of Joinder. *See* Hall Affidavit, ¶ 3.

The next day, undersigned counsel received the September jury trial list. The September list noted that the cases were joined. Exhibit 2, September jury trial list. Attorney Zerillo then went to the court to verify that there was a Notice of Joinder in the file, which there was. Zerillo Affidavit, ¶ 5. Again, undersigned counsel never received the Notice of Joinder, and had no knowledge of joinder until August 13, 2002.

ARGUMENT

I. MANDATORY NOTICES OF JOINDER WERE NOT PROVIDED TO THE DEFENDANTS

The Maine Rules of Criminal Procedure require that notice be provided to the parties when a written notice is filed. M.R. Crim. P. 8(b) and 49. Rule 49 states:

> Rule 49(a): **Service: When Required.** Written motions other than those which are heard ex parte, **written notices**, designations of the record or appeal and similar papers **shall be served upon each of the parties**.

Id. (emphasis added). Thus, notice is mandatory, perhaps particularly on occasions such as the instant matter. The filing of the Notice of Joinder immediately joins the proceedings, and is a *de facto* order issued by the prosecutor. Rule 8(b) requires that such a Notice be filed no later than 10 days post-indictment. This requirement is to enable defense counsel to timely file a Motion to Sever within the required 21 day motion filing deadline. *See* Rule 12(b)(3).

It is also worth noting that there is no reason why undersigned counsel should have been aware of such a joinder. This case was not listed as joined with Getthepapers's case on the June trial list; both cases were listed as separate cases. *See* Exhibit 3, June trial list.

Since the rendering of an indictment, this office has been preparing steadily for a trial on this matter. That preparation was premised on the idea that Getthepapers would not be sitting at counsel table with us. Having Chris Getthepapers as a co-defendant greatly changes how the defense would have prepared for trial over the past six months. Indeed, preparation to date has revolved around a theory of exclusion rather than inclusion of Defendant Getthepapers. Certainly, had Defendant Cupcakes received notice, counsel would have treated the co-defendant differently, rather than steadily steering a course away from Mr. Getthepapers. This decision may now cause Defendant Cupcakes unintended and unanticipated harm in that Mr. Getthepapers apparently considers Defendant Cupcakes part of the "conspiracy" to "get him." (*See, infra*).

As a result, if these cases are not severed now, given the Defendant's lack of notice and preparation for the trial without a co-defendant, the Defendant will be inexcusably prejudiced. These cases must be severed.

---

[1] Upon review of the file at the courthouse, Mr. Zerillo did **not** see a cover filing letter copying the Notice of Joinder to undersigned counsel. *See* Zerillo Affidavit, ¶ 5.

II. THERE ARE GOOD GROUNDS TO SEVER THE CASES HERE, ASIDE FROM THE PREJUDICE TO THE DEFENDANT BY THE STATE'S FAILURE TO NOTICE HIM OF JOINDER.

A. There is a Significant Question as to Getthepapers's Mental Capacity.

Normal procedure when a State's attorney files a Notice of Joinder is that the Defendant can file for relief from prejudicial joinder pursuant to M.R. Crim. P. 8(d). This gives the Court the power to order multiple simultaneous trials. *Id.*

If these cases remain joined, the Defendant will be significantly prejudiced. Getthepapers has recently gone through what can only be described as a psychotic episode. Allegedly, he recently held his wife hostage for several hours and raped her at knifepoint, all the while threatening to kill her and other members of his family. According to his wife, he has simply gone into a delusional state. *See generally*, Zerillo Affidavit, ¶¶ 8-9.

The day after Getthepapers was arrested for that alleged conduct, Getthepapers's wife, Linda, met with Attorney Zerillo. *Id.* She informed Attorney Zerillo that Getthepapers had suffered some type of psychotic paranoid break with reality. Part of that break with reality involved Cupcakes and Attorneys Hall and Zerillo. While he was holding his wife hostage, Getthepapers complained to her that she, Justice Arthur Brady, Cupcakes, Zerillo and Hall were all part of a conspiracy to jail him, and that they could all just make it "go away" if they chose to. *Id.* Getthepapers had previously made these statements directly to Attorneys Zerillo and Hall.

Attorney Goodguy has been appointed to represent Getthepapers in both his pending cases.[2] Attorney Goodguy would be remiss to not investigate Defendant Getthepapers's mental capacity. Upon information and belief, such an investigation will likely be initiated.

Should Defendant Getthepapers be determined incompetent, obviously the issue of severance is resolved. However, should Getthepapers not raise the competency issue, and proceed to trial, Defendant Cupcakes would be forced to proceed to a joint trial with an incompetent joint defendant. This may very well violate Cupcakes's due process rights. *See Medina v. California,* 505 U.S. 437 (1992).

> The Due Process Clause forbids the trial and conviction of persons incapable of defending themselves—persons lacking the capacity to understand the nature and object of the proceedings against them, to consult with counsel, and to assist in preparing their defense.

Id. at 457.

B. There is a *Bruton* Issue That Can Only be Resolved by Severing These Matters.

Defendant Getthepapers, during a taped telephone conversation from Cumberland County Jail, and in the presence of Freeport Police Officers, implicated both himself and Jon Cupcakes in the alleged conduct giving rise to the instant proceedings. Specifically, the taped conversation states:

> Linda: Who are the other witnesses?
> Chris: Well, they want to know who Jon is.
> Linda: Oh, you were with Cupcakes.
> ...
> Linda: Oh my God! Like he's going to testify to your innocence, right?
> Chris: Yeah, they're going to believe him, right.
> ...
> Linda: You're going up for rape charges.
> Chris: Right
> ...
> Chris: And you think I would make her do something against her will.
> Linda: Yes, the way you were last night—look at what you were doing to me!

Conversation between Chris Getthepapers and his wife, Linda, February 9, 2002. Exhibit 4.

---

[2] On information and belief, Attorney Goodguy supports Defendant Getthepapers in his request to sever these cases.

Chris Getthepapers's statements during a taped telephone conversation in front of Freeport Police Officers, implicate Jon Cupcakes as a witness/accomplice. Such an out of court statement by a non-testifying co-defendant violates Jon's Sixth Amendment rights. *Bruton v. United States*, 391 U.S. 123, 88 S. Ct. 1620, 20 L Ed. 2d 476 (1968).

C.   The Delay in Proceedings Also Mandates Severance

Competency questions concerning Getthepapers also lead to several practical issues requiring severance. The case is currently on the September 2002 trial list. While Cupcakes's Motion to Suppress has not yet been heard, it is anticipated that counsel will be ready to proceed no later than mid to late October 2002 in *State v. Cupcakes*.[3]

Defendant Getthepapers has continued to represent himself throughout the proceedings, and only within the last couple of weeks has Attorney Goodguy taken over Getthepapers's defense. Given the mental status of Getthepapers, and the lateness of Goodguy's appointment, Defendant Getthepapers will not be ready for trial until early 2003, at best. In all likelihood and depending on competency questions, it is not out of the realm of possibility that Getthepapers's case would not be heard until mid to late 2003.

The prejudice to Defendant Cupcakes is clear when viewed in that context, namely that his right to a speedy trial may be delayed for many months, perhaps until well after a year after the alleged criminal conduct occurred. Mr. Cupcakes wishes to be afforded the opportunity to face his accuser in a timely fashion. He has made significant personal and financial sacrifices over the past nine months in anticipation of his trial. Forcing him to endure the immeasurable delay that joinder with Getthepapers will cause is unconscionable, not to mention highly prejudicial given what is at stake here for MR. Cupcakes. This Court should err on the side of caution and sever these matters. Given the lack of notice of joinder and the prejudice Cupcakes now faces, severance is the only real way to ensure that he gets a fair trial.

CONCLUSION

WHEREFORE, for the above-cited argument and authority, the cases must be severed.

Dated this 10th day of September, 2002, at Portland, Maine.

Respectfully submitted,

_____

Timothy E. Zerillo
Attorney for Defendant
ZERILLO LAW FIRM, LLC

§ 11:62   Motion to Sever Joined Counts

You may run across a case in which the Government has joined Counts involving multiple victims. This creates obvious tactical worries. There may be reasons, I suppose, in some cases to keep them joined. That said, my general disposition is to make the Government try these cases one at a time if I can. They don't like that.

So how do you succeed in a motion to sever joined counts? The Government will always argue judicial economy. This can be a winning argument in a court flooded with pending cases. To get past the judicial economy argument, you need a big gun.

My greatest luck at severing counts has been on Fifth Amendment grounds. Consider it this way; your client may want to testify as to one count but not another. A joined trial does not permit that. The jury will automatically infer guilt on the non-testifying count. For support for this proposition, check out *Cross v. U.S.*, 335 F.2d 987 (D.C. Cir. 1964).

PRACTICE TIP: *Don't let the judge force an election*

When arguing one of these motions, you may get a judge who wants your client to decide whether he intends to testify as to one count, but not another. Beware of this tactic. The judge is obviously trying to gut

---

[3]   Counsel steadily saw the decline in the mental functioning of Getthepapers as time went on since his arrest. Counsel also knew that Getthepapers's growing psychosis had no effect on Cupcakes because the cases weren't joined. Had counsel known the cases were going to be joined in the future, we very well may have forgone our motions and tried this matter in June.

your argument. The answer, naturally, is that your client cannot and will not make a decision as to what he will testify to until he has heard the Government's case-in-chief. Forcing an election prior to that time would be a due process violation.

Another potential winning argument comes from the natural reaction of the jury in inferring criminal conduct because it involves multiple victims. Especially in sex offense cases, this can cause problems.

Imagine you have a client (like I had) who was accused of molesting a number of sleeping women. I represented him for quite some time, and can tell you with some authority, this seemed to be a habit of his.

In this particular case, he was charged with groping his mother-in-law and sister-in-law while they slept. The nature of the conduct alleged caused there to be different charges joined in the same indictment. We argued that the jury would prejudicially infer criminal conduct in Count 1 from Count 2 or *vice versa*. *United States v. Massa*, 740 F.2d 629 (8th Cir. 1984) (severance proper where jury could not be expected to compartmentalize evidence); *U.S. v. Lewis*, 787 F.2d 1318 (9th Cir.) (admissions of other crimes in one count prejudiced defendant on other joined count where evidence weak on second charge), *modified* 798 F.2d 1250, *cert. denied* 489 U.S. 1032 (1989). Our severance motion was granted on these grounds and on the Fifth Amendment grounds discussed above.

§11:63   FORM 11-40 Motion to Sever Joined Counts

STATE OF MAINE	SUPERIOR COURT
KENNEBEC, ss	DOCKET NO. CR-09-590

STATE OF MAINE,   )

v.   )   **DEFENDANT'S**
)   **MOTION TO SEVER**

Ned Turnover,   )   **JOINED COUNTS**

Defendant   )

NOW COMES the Defendant, Mr. Turnover, by and through Undersigned Counsel, and requests that this Court sever Counts 1 and 2 of the Complaint in this matter, pursuant to M.R.Crim.P 8(d). As grounds therefore, Defendant states as follows:

1. A Complaint was brought against Defendant alleging an Assault in Count 1, with the alleged victim being Victim 1, and an Unlawful Sexual Touching in Count 2, with the alleged victim being Victim 2. These allegations involve similar facts, that is, that the Defendant laid down with each of the alleged victims when they were sleeping and touched them in an unwanted way.

2. M.R.Evid. 404(b) precludes the introduction of prior (or subsequent) "crimes, wrongs or acts… to prove the character of a person in order to show that he acted in conformity therewith." Therefore, evidence of the alleged "crimes, wrongs or acts" in Counts 1 is not admissible as to Counts 2, and *vice versa*.

3. Counts 1 and 2 do not arise out of the same "act or transaction" do not involve the same person, and are not part of a common scheme or plan. *See* M.R.Crim.P. 8(a). In fact, the cases involve different alleged victims. Accordingly, they should not have been joined in the Complaint in the first place. *Id.*

4. The Defendant is prejudiced by the joinder of these cases, on several grounds. First, the Defendant may elect to testify as to one of the claims, but not as to the other. Severance should be granted on that cause alone. *Cross v. U.S.*, 335 F.2d 987 (D.C. Cir. 1964).

5. The Defendant also contends that the jury may infer criminal conduct in Counts 1 from Counts 2 or *vice versa*. *United States v. Massa*, 740 F.2d 629 (8th Cir. 1984) (severance proper where jury could not be expected to compartmentalize evidence); *U.S. v. Lewis*, 787 F.2d 1318 (9th Cir.) (admissions of other crimes in one count prejudiced defendant on other joined count where evidence weak on second charge), *modified* 798 F.2d 1250, *cert. denied* 489 U.S. 1032 (1989).

6. M.R. Crim. P. Rule 8(d) allows the Court to sever Counts 1 and 2 as relief from prejudicial joinder. A joined trial would create the danger that the jury would use evidence admissible as to either of the counts "to infer a criminal disposition" on the part of the Defendant as to the other counts. *See United States v. Foutz*, 540 F.2d 733, 736-38 (4th Cir. 1976); *United States v. Gregory*, 369 F.2d 185, 189 (D.C. Cir.

1966), cert. denied, 396 U.S. 865 (1969). A joined trial on all counts against the Defendant creates a grave danger that the evidence as to each separate count will "cumulat[e] in the jurors' minds." *Id.*; *see United States v. Halper*, 590 F.2d 422, 430 (2d Cir. 1978); *United States v. Gregory*, 369 F.2d at 189. For each of these reasons, severance of Counts 1 and 2 is essential under Me. R. Crim. P. 8(d).

WHEREFORE, Counsel requests this Court grant this Motion to Sever Count 1 from Count 2 for the foregoing reasons.

Dated this the 9th day of October, 2009 in Portland, Maine.

Respectfully submitted,

_____

Timothy E. Zerillo
Attorney for Defendant
ZERILLO LAW FIRM, LLC

[§§11:64-11:69 Reserved]

D. Trial

1. Opening Statement

§11:70   My Approach

So let's look at a segment of an Opening Statement in the prosecution of Case Jonny Cupcakes and Chris Getthepapers, with Mandy as the alleged victim. In nearly any violent crime case, especially a rape case, I am trying hard to just get the jury to listen to me in the opening. I want them to consider a point of view other than the one the prosecutor just drilled into their heads. Once I have gotten them to uncross their arms, wipe the scowl off their face and listen, we start to drop in some helpful facts.

For tips on effective opening statements, see Ch. 2.

§11:71   Sample Opening Statement Excerpt

… So now we have talked about reasonable doubt and we talked about the burden of proof. And I hope you feel comfortable at this time in understanding that the burden of proof never once shifts to Johnny Cupcakes, but that the burden of proof is always on the State to prove beyond a reasonable doubt that he forced Mandy to have sex with him.

Mandy will testify for you. You will get to hear exactly what she has to say. It's important when you hear from her that you wait until you hear all of her testimony. That you don't render a judgment until you hear everything that she has to say. That means that you don't listen to just one side of the examination. You shouldn't ignore what she says on cross-examination. And you shouldn't ignore what she says during direct examination. For you to get the full picture of what happened and to make a decision with the reasonable doubt standard, you have to hear everything she has to say. If you haven't heard both sides of the story, you haven't heard the whole story.

What we can guess that she is going to say what the prosecution has alluded to and talked about in their Opening. She is going to say that a man that she had previously had intercourse with, a married man, Chris, came to her house one day and he told her to get into his truck, and she did. She will say that when she got to the truck that there was another man there, who she did not know, who is Johnny. She will say that he drove to a motel in South Portland where they had sex over a several hour period. The lynch pin to this story is her claim that the sex was not consensual. That she was forced. If she's not forced, the defendants are not guilty.

Our second President, John Adams, once said that "facts are stubborn things," and the facts just don't fit. I believe you will hear evidence that on the way through the streets in South Portland they stopped for gas. While they stopped for gas, in an urban area, Mandy was left in the car with Johnny. Mandy was not bound. There will be no evidence that she was held by a weapon. The evidence will be, in fact, that she could have walked out of the truck at any given moment. But she didn't.

When they arrived at the motel, Mandy waited in the car as well. It was an urban environment—in an area in which Mandy could have walked across the street to the Dunkin' Donuts. She was, in fact, wearing her Dunkin' Donuts uniform. She could have walked into the motel and said to the person at the desk or any number of patrons that she was being held. But she didn't.

And yet again inside the motel room, there is evidence to suggest that Mandy had the opportunity on several occasions to leave through a window in the bathroom that was right there and open to her. But she didn't. The facts don't fit.

The question for you will be, is this sex with regret or rape? Because ultimately what you have here for evidence of rape is what Mandy tells you. And you might find the facts, like the ones I just described, poke holes in that box that's being held over my client's head. That is why you need to listen carefully and diligently to the evidence, and if you see a hole in the State's case, recognize it.

I'll highlight another fact that I expect you to hear. Mandy claims that the rapes were violent. She claims she was trying to fight these men off of her. She will testify that she was wearing fake fingernails and that she lost four or five of them in the context of scratching and clawing at the men.

Boy, that evidence sounds awful for these two men, doesn't it? But remember, don't render judgment until after you've heard all of the evidence.

For example, I expect Officer Badcall to testify. He's the lead officer in the case. Two days after this alleged rape he went to a jail where Chris was being held to interview him. And when he arrived he interviewed Chris, and I expect he will tell you that Chris did not deny there was sex, but that he told the officer that it was consensual. He also told him that he had consensual sex with Mandy other times.

But those are just words, right? Just like Mandy's statements are just words. Are there more than just words for you to look at?

Officer Badcall asked Chris in an interview two days later to remove his shirt. And the officer examined Chris's torso for scratches, and claw marks and abrasions. And there were none. There were none at all. I expect the officer to say his back appeared normal. Two days later it appeared normal. The facts don't fit.

So, I want you to listen carefully please, because it is very important. I understand you have other places to be. I understand you have busy lives. I understand many of you wish you weren't on this jury. But now that you are, I tell you that your job, your duty in this trial is to listen carefully and critically and compare the evidence you hear to the reasonable doubt standard.

When you listen, you need to look for inconsistencies. I am not trying to be one sided here. You need to look for inconsistencies with any witness that gives testimony.

But it is Mandy's words that have put us here, and you may choose to focus on her words in this trial. If you find that there are inconsistencies cropping up in statements about these alleged rapes, then you must be especially careful. If you find that Mandy told her story in several different ways, that alone may be a basis for you to find that the defendants are not guilty.

And by the way, remember that "not guilty" can mean two things. It can mean that someone is innocent, or can simply mean the case was not proven by the State beyond a reasonable doubt. You don't have to say whether you find someone to be innocent or whether you find the case simply to not be proven. They both fall within the term "not guilty." At the end of this case that is the verdict I will ask you to render.

[§§11:72-11:79 Reserved]

2. Cross-Examination of Key Witnesses

a. Cross-Examination of Alleged Victim's Friend

§11:80   First Complaint Doctrine

Let's take a look at Jonny and Chris' case. Remember, when the alleged victim Mandy came home after the alleged rape, her friend Lucy was there. Lucy testified at trial as the first complaint witness, i.e., the first person to whom the alleged victim confided the alleged rape. The first (or fresh) complaint doctrine allows the prosecutor to introduce testimony of a witness to whom the victim first reported the rape if the alleged victim takes the stand at trial and the complaint was made within a reasonable time after the alleged sexual misconduct. See Ch. 12 for further discussion.

Make sure you understand the rule in your jurisdiction so you can limit any first complaint testimony as much as possible. However, if the first complaint testimony is different than statements made by the alleged victim, you may want the testimony in so you can use it to attack the victim's credibility.

PRACTICE TIP: *First Complaint Motion in Limine*

First complaint motions may be fertile ground in your jurisdiction to limit the testimony of the first complaint witness to the bare fact that the complaint was made, and not the identity of the perpetrator. In some cases that makes sense, and in Ch. 12, a first complaint Motion in Limine is included.

Here, in the Cupcakes case, I didn't want to limit the first complaint evidence because there were so many inconsistencies between the first complaint testimony and the victim's statements that I wanted it all out on the table for the jury.

---

§11:81   Key Points

Key points to make with this witness are to:
- Establish a reason for the alleged victim to lie.
- Distinguish the way in which the alleged victim left the residence.
- Highlight inconsistent statements made by the alleged victim.

For tips on effective cross-examination, see Ch. 2.

§11:82   Witness Gave Statement to Help Alleged Victim

Q. Lucy, my name is Tim Zerillo and I represent Jonny Cupcakes. You said you have been friends with Mandy for 6 years?
A. Yes.
Q. You are good friends with her?
A. Yes.
Q. The morning after the incident you sat upstairs with Mandy and talked to her about what happened.
A. Yes.
Q. You talked to her about what happened the night before?
A. Yes.
Q. And you were upset with what she told you?
A. Yes.
Q. And like any good friend, you wanted to help her?
A. Yes.
Q. Because it was a tough time for her?
A. Yes.
Q. And you spoke to the police in order to help her?
A. Yes.
Q. You wanted to capture the men who had done this to her, right?
A. Yes.
Q. To help Mandy?
A. Yes.
Q. And that's what friends do, right?
A. Yes.
Q. They back each other up?
A. Yes.
Q. So you went to the police?
A. I didn't go to the police.
Q. Did you speak to Officer Badcall?
A. Yes.
Q. Okay, but it wasn't at the police station?
A. No.

Q. Where was it? At Mandy's house?
A. Yes.
Q. And Officer Badcall approached you about making a statement?
A. Yes.

§11:83　Witness Appreciated Need for Thorough, Accurate Statement

Q. And you spoke to him to help Mandy?
A. Yes.
Q. And you wrote out a statement for Officer Badcall?
A. Yes.
Q. You knew that statement was important?
A. Yes.
Q. You knew it needed to be accurate?
A. Yes.
Q. You knew it needed to be thorough?
A. Yes.
Q. And you wrote it to bring the men who had done this harm to your friend to justice, right?
A. Yes.
Q. And you signed that statement, right?
A. Yes.

§11:84　Facts Were Fresh in Witness's Mind

Q. And you wrote the statement the day after the alleged incident?
A. Yes.
Q. The morning after, actually.
A. Yes.
Q. And Mandy had told you her version of the events that same morning?
A. Yes.
Q. What Mandy told you was fresh in your mind at the time you wrote the statement?
A. Yes.
Q. We're now sitting in this courtroom 13 months after you wrote that statement?
A. Yes.
Q. You remembered the events better at the time that you wrote the statement than you do today?
A. Yes.

§11:85　Alleged Victim Willingly Accepted Ride

Let's set the scene of this alleged rape. It all starts when my client's co-Defendant, Chris Getthepapers went to Mandy's house. We need to paint the picture for the jury that this is not the forcible rape they imagine. This is done by showing how easily Mandy acquiesced to taking a ride with the Defendants.

Q. You had not met Chris prior to the time he walked into Mandy's house the day before?
A. No, I hadn't.
Q. Okay. But you knew who he was?
A. Yes.
Q. You had heard about him from Mandy?
A. Yes.
Q. You knew about Mandy's past relationship with him?
A. Yes.
Q. So, the day you first saw Chris in the kitchen with Mandy she told you who he was?
A. Yes.
Q. She said "That's Chris."

A. Yes.
Q. Mandy first met him at Dunkin' Donuts?
A. Yes.
Q. She worked at Dunkin' Donuts at the time?
A. Yes.
Q. And you were aware that Chris was involved sexually with Mandy.
PROSECUTOR: I am going object to the relevance of that from this witness.
COURT: You may answer the question yes or no.
A. No, not really.
Q. Not really? You knew they had a relationship that was more than friends, right?
A. Yes.
Q. And Chris and Mandy eventually ended their relationship?
A. Yes.
Q. This relationship broke up because—
PROSECUTOR: I am going to object, Your Honor, again it's hearsay.
MR. ZERILLO: Sidebar, Your Honor. (At sidebar) Mandy testified that she stopped seeing Chris because his wife
    started to catch on.
PROSECUTOR: I think what he should ask her is, "Did Mandy tell you why the relationship ended? Do you know
    why the relationship ended? Where did you get that information?"
MR. ZERILLO: It's the same thing, but its cross, so these open-ended questions suggested by the State aren't necessary.
COURT: Go ahead. You may ask the question.
Q. Mandy told you why her relationship with Chris ended, didn't she?
A. Yes.
Q. It was because Chris's wife was catching on?
A. Yes.
Q. And Mandy was afraid of getting caught?
A. Yes.
Q. The date of the alleged incident, Chris showed up at Mandy's house at 4:15 PM or so?
A. Yes.
Q. At the time, you were sitting upstairs.
A. Yes.
Q. You were just hanging out with Mandy's sister?
A. Yes.
Q. Mandy had just gotten home from her work at Dunkin' Donuts?
A. Yes.
Q. Mandy lives with her father?
A. Yes.
Q. And he was home at that time too, right?
A. Yes.
Q. Wendy, Mandy's other sister, came upstairs and said there was someone there to see Mandy?
A. Yes
Q. So you went downstairs with Mandy to see who it was?
A. Yes.
Q. Mandy didn't have any shoes on when she went downstairs?
A. No, she didn't.
Q. When she saw the person there was Chris, did she put shoes on?
A. Yes, she did.
Q. And that was so she could go outside with Chris, right?
A. Yes.
Q. And she went out the door that attaches to the kitchen?
A. Yes.
Q. Chris was behind her as she walked out the door?
A. Yes.
Q. Were you looking through the door?

A. No.
Q. Where were you looking?
A. In their house there's a living room and the kitchen, and they have a big, like, where a window would be, but there is no glass there, so you can see right through the living room and kitchen.
Q. And you could see Mandy walking with Chris.
A. Yes.
Q. And you said he was walking behind her with his hand on her back?
A. Yes.
Q. Sort of around her waist.
A. On her lower back, yeah, kind of around her waist.
Q. Okay. He wasn't shoving her out the house.
A. No.
Q. Pushing her?
A. No.
Q. Pulling her?
A. No.
Q. After Mandy and Chris went outside, you saw Chris help her into the truck, right?
A. Yes.
Q. I want to make this clear because it's important. You said on direct that he "put" Mandy in the truck. That's not true, is it?
A. I'm not sure.
Q. Okay. Well, let's just get it out there. Did he help her into the truck, as in, assist her in getting into the truck?
A. Like, I want to say "put," but that's not—yes, he helped her up into the truck.
Q. He assisted her?
PROSECUTOR: I think she can pick her word. I think she picked "put" and "help."
MR. ZERILLO: I think there is a difference I should be allowed to explore.
COURT: She may answer the question.
Q. Did he assist her in getting up into the truck?
A. Yes.
Q. He didn't push her into the truck?
A. Not as far as I could see.
Q. You didn't see him pick her up and place her into the truck?
A. No.
Q. Okay. And she sat between Chris and the other man?
A. Yes.
Q. And Mandy and Chris kissed in the truck?
A. That's what I thought I saw.
Q. That was your impression at the time?
A. Yes.
Q. When your memory was fresher than it is now?
A. Yes.

§11:86   Alleged Victim's Motive for Lying about Rape

Now we skip ahead to the next time this witness sees the alleged victim. It is obvious that you are looking for inconsistent statements made by the alleged victim. Less obvious, but equally important, is to try to explain to the jury why the alleged victim would lie.

Juries always wonder why the alleged victim of a sexual assault would go through the process of a criminal trial if she wasn't telling the truth. The reality is that there are innumerable reasons why people might lie to the police and to a jury ultimately. Here, we had the opportunity to explore through this witness a reason why the alleged victim may have lied.

Q. When Mandy arrived home that evening, you were still there?
A. Yes.

Q. And her two sisters were there?
A. Yes.
Q. And her brother was there?
A. Yes.
Q. And her father was there?
A. Yes.
Q. They were worried about her?
A. Yes.
Q. She didn't really say where she was going when she left?
A. No.
Q. And she came back two hours or so later?
A. Yes.
Q. Her boyfriend also came by while she was gone?
A. Yes.
Q. And he spoke to you?
A. Yes.
Q. And he asked about her?
A. Yes.
Q. And you told him Mandy took off with Chris and another man and they were kissing in the truck?
A. No, I didn't want him to get jealous.
Q. You were afraid you would get Mandy in trouble with her boyfriend?
A. Kind of.
Q. You'd seen that her boyfriend acted pretty possessive of her?
A. Yes.
Q. So, when Mandy arrived home, she learned that her sisters, brother and father were worried about her?
A. Yes.
Q. And she learned that her boyfriend had been there looking for her.
A. Yes.
Q. And they started asking her all sorts of questions.
A. Yes.
Q. And did she answer them?
A. Not really, she went upstairs and I followed her, and the next morning she told me about the rape.

§11:87 Alleged Victim's Inconsistent Statements

Now let's compare the statements made by Mandy to the police and later to the jury, to the statements she made to her friend the morning after.

Here, we'll just examine one inconsistency. The witness indicated that the defendants had both anal and vaginal intercourse with her. The alleged victim doesn't mention anal sex in her statements to the police.

The alleged victim and this witness were young adults when this happened. All humans are prone to exaggeration when telling an exciting story, and it is our job to find those exaggerations and point them out to the jury.

I didn't much care in this case who the jury believed was lying. Maybe the witness was lying and the alleged victim never mentioned anal sex to her. Maybe the alleged victim exaggerated and mentioned anal sex. Either way, someone is exaggerating.

The prosecution in this case compounded their problem. My speculation is that the prosecutor, knowing this inconsistency, suggested to this witness that when she said anal sex, she meant sex from behind. To me, this made the story even less believable.

Q. Mandy told you she had been raped by Chris and Jonny, right?
A. Yes.
Q. She said she was forcibly raped?
A. Yes.
Q. She said they had intercourse with her?
A. Yes.

Q. She said she had vaginal intercourse with Chris?

A. Yes.

Q. Did she say she had vaginal intercourse with Jonny?

A. I don't remember.

Q. She said she performed oral sex on them?

A. Yes.

Q. On both of them or only one?

A. I don't remember.

Q. Vaginal sex or vaginal intercourse is what you describe in your statement as "regular sexual intercourse," right?

A. Yes, sir.

Q. And Mandy had "regular sexual intercourse," meaning vaginal intercourse with Chris?

A. Yes.

Q. But Mandy also told you that they had anal sex with her, right?

A. No, she didn't.

Q. Okay. Now is it true that you wrote in your report that Mandy said that they had anal sex with her?

A. I don't remember if I wrote in my report "she said," but I know my report says that. I don't know if I wrote she said they had anal sex.

Q. Let me show you your report. (Permission to approach previously granted). You wrote "She told me that they had anal sex." Did I read that right?

A. Yes.

Q. And you wrote it, didn't you?

A. Yes.

Q. And the "she" in that statement was Mandy?

A. Yes.

Q. And the "they" in that statement was Chris and Jonny?

A. Yes.

Q. And that is what Mandy told you right?

A. What other people told me too.

Q. OK. So, you are confusing who told you what when?

A. Yes.

Q. But you said in your report that Chris and Jonny had "regular" sexual intercourse and "anal" sexual intercourse with her, right?

A. Yes, but I was confused then.

Q. You were confused. Let's talk about that confusion. On direct, you told the jury that you were confused about what anal sexual intercourse meant, right?

A. Yes.

Q. You testified that you thought it meant sex from behind?

A. Yes.

Q. You just graduated from high school, didn't you?

A. Yes.

Q. And you are going to school for nursing next year?

A. Yes.

Q. You've known you wanted to be a nurse for a while?

A. For a year or so.

Q. So in preparation for that, I'm sure you took some science courses?

A. Yes, I had to take science.

Q. And since you were going into nursing I'm guessing that you took a biology course, right?

A. Right.

Q. And since you are going into nursing, you probably got a good grade, right?

A. Right.

Q. And you probably also took an anatomy course, right?

A. Right.

Q. And you probably did well in that one too, right?

A. Yes.

Q. And in fact your anatomy grade for your last semester in school was a B+ wasn't it?
A. Yes.
Q. Good for you.
A. Thank you.
Q. And they talked about what the anus is in anatomy class, didn't they?
A. I think so … yes.
Q. Earlier you told us that when you said "regular" sexual intercourse that it meant vaginal sexual intercourse, right?
A. Yes.
Q. And you didn't describe vaginal sexual intercourse as "anal sex," right?
A. Right.
Q. And that was because you were distinguishing anal sex from vaginal sex?
A. I don't know.
Q. You were describing two different things?
A. Yes.
Q. So, clearly anal sexual intercourse must have meant to you sex involving the anus, correct?
A. Correct.
Q. You described this anal sex as occurring up against a wall.
A. I don't remember.
Q. Well, let me show you your statement again. It says "they had anal sex up against the wall." Did I read that right?
A. Yes.
Q. That's what you wrote for the police, right?
A. Yes.
Q. In fact, you wrote that both of these men had anal sexual intercourse with Mandy, right?
A. Yes.
Q. And that was based on what Mandy told you.
A. Yes.

[§§11:88-11:99 Reserved]

b. Cross-Examination of the Police Officer

§11:100 Key Points

Let's jump into the middle of the cross examination of Officer Badcall. Officer Badcall took the original report in Mandy's case. Remember this is a reported forcible rape situation, although the prosecutrix had previous consensual sex with one of the defendants. Let's take a look at a line of questioning from this trial where we do our homework and try to uncover more inconsistencies in the alleged victim's testimony through law enforcement.

Key points to make are to highlight inconsistencies between the victim's testimony and the evidence, as well as to show the police did not properly gather the evidence.

For more tips on cross examining police officers, see Ch.2

§11:101 Victim's Statements to Officer Suggest She Had Chance to Escape

Q. Officer Badcall, Mandy reported to you that she drove in Chris's truck from Freeport to South Portland?
A. Correct.
Q. She was between Chris and Jonny?
A. Yes.
Q. She reported she made a stop at the Mobil near the Maine Mall, right?
A. She remembers it being a gas station near the Maine Mall is what I remember.
Q. Okay. Do you know the area she was describing?
A. I believe I do.
Q. And is it close to the Maine Mall?
A. Yes it is.
Q. It's a busy area?

A. Yes.
Q. And she reported they stopped there?
A. Yes.
Q. And Chris went into the gas station?
A. Correct.
Q. And that left Mandy and Jonny in the truck alone?
A. Correct.
Q. Mandy didn't report to you that Jonny held her in the truck?
A. Uhm, no.
Q. She didn't report Jonny pulled a gun on her, did she?
A. No, she did not.
Q. Or a knife?
A. No.
Q. In fact, she didn't report being threatened by any weapons at any time, did she?
A. No, she did not.
Q. And she reported they went to the Cheapo Inn?
A. Correct.
Q. And they pulled up in the truck?
A. Yes.
Q. And Chris went inside to register?
A. Correct.
Q. And at that point Mandy and Jonny were in the truck alone, right?
A. Correct.
Q. And you interviewed the hotel owner, Mr. Bates?
A. Correct.
Q. And he told you he observed through the window of his office a man and a woman inside the truck?
A. Correct.
Q. And that he didn't see anything unusual?
A. Correct.
Q. And again, Mandy never reported being held by weapons when she was in the truck at the Cheapo Inn?
A. No, she did not.
Q. Inside the motel room, Mandy took a shower?
A. Yes. She told me she locked the door.
Q. She told you she was able to lock the door?
A. Yes.
Q. She didn't tell you the lock was not functioning?
A. No, she didn't.
Q. You didn't check the lock itself?
A. No.

§11:102 Missing Evidence

Remember, the alleged victim claimed she fought these men off. She lost fake fingernails in the process. I want to highlight the lack of thorough investigation of the scene by police through these fake fingernails.

Q. Mandy was wearing fake fingernails that day, wasn't she?
A. Yes.
Q. She told you she lost some fake fingernails, right?
A. Correct.
Q. She told you she lost them during the assault, right?
A. Correct.
Q. She said she lost them fighting off Jonny and Chris?
A. Yes.
Q. And she disposed of them at her house?

A. The remaining fingernails she had disposed of them at the house.
Q. And when you were at the house that Saturday morning did you go look for the fingernails?
A. When I had left the house I asked her sister to look for them.
Q. You asked Mandy's sister to do it?
A. Yes.
Q. Sir, you would agree with me that you are responsible for the evidence collection in those cases, aren't you?
A. Yes.
Q. Mandy's sister isn't responsible, is she?
A. No.
Q. And you never recovered those fingernails, did you?
A. No.
Q. That evidence is lost forever as far as we know.
A. Yes.

§11:103 Inconsistency Between Officer's Report and His Testimony

Q. When you met with Mandy at her house that Saturday morning after the alleged assault, you didn't notice any injuries to her did you?
A. I only noticed one.
Q. That was the injury to her forehead you discussed on direct?
A. Yes.
Q. That was a small bruise?
A. I thought it was a fairly large bruise.
Q. You filled out an arrest report in this case, didn't you?
A. Yes, I did.
Q. (Approaching witness, permission previously granted). I'm showing you now the arrest report of Chris. Did you fill this out?
A. Yes.
Q. You are listed as the arresting officer?
A. Yes.
Q. And the alleged victim in this arrest report is Mandy?
A. Yes.
Q. And there is a spot there on this arrest report form for injuries to the alleged victim?
A. Yes.
Q. And for Mandy, what did you report for injuries?
A. It says none.
Q. I'm going to show you this arrest report. This is the one you filled out for Jonny?
A. Yes.
Q. And again the victim you listed is Mandy.
A. Yes.
Q. And once again, you reported that Mandy had no injuries?
A. Yes.
Q. But you have now testified on direct examination that you observed a bump on Mandy's head?
A. Correct.
Q. You just missed that in your report then?
A. In the report system if you overlook a block, it defaults to none. I must have overlooked that block.
Q. You've already told me that it is important that your reports are accurate?
A. Yes.
Q. And thorough?
A. Yes.
Q. So, if we are to believe that you did observe a bump, we should also believe that your report is not accurate because it doesn't include that information?
A. Yes.
Q. And your report was not thorough?

A. I guess not.
Q. It had mistakes?
A. Yes.
Q. You take notes during interviews?
A. Yes.
Q. Then you take those notes and draft your report?
A. Yes.
Q. And you have the opportunity to draft a narrative?
A. Yes.
Q. That narrative can include whatever you want it to include?
A. Whatever I write.
Q. And you drafted a narrative here, right?
A. Right.
Q. And that narrative was taken from the notes you made that Saturday morning of the interview?
A. Yes.
Q. And you never noted in your narrative that Mindy had a bump on her head?
A. I did not.

§11:104 Defendant Had No Injuries

Whenever possible, make good on your promises made in opening to the jury. In the Opening here, I told the jury that two days later at the jail, Officer Badcall noted that Chris Getthepapers' back had no marks. On direct examination, the Officer testified it was five days later.

I need to get back to that ground and cover it, proving to the jury that what I told them was right. The jury will then gain trust in me. Sometimes, when I loop back to an opening theme like this, I will catch the jurors nodding along in agreement with me, as if to say, "You were right about this issue."

Of course, the opposite is also true. If you tell the jury you are going to do something in Opening and don't deliver, look out!

Q. After Mr. Getthepapers was arrested, you went to the Cumberland County Jail to interview him, didn't you?
A. Yes, I did.
Q. You told the jury on direct that your trip to the Jail was 5 days after the alleged incident.
A. That's what I remember.
Q. It was sooner than that though, right?
A. It could have been.
Q. You saw Chris at the Jail on February 10th, right?
A. I don't remember.
Q. (Approaching) Here's your report. It says you saw him February 10th, right?
A. That's right.
Q. The incident allegedly occurred February 8th, right?
A. Right.
Q. So, you saw Chris 2 days later?
A. Yes.
Q. And you had Chris remove his shirt during those incidents.
A. Yes, I did.
Q. And you checked the front and back of his torso for scratches, right?
A. Yes, I did.
Q. Or other abrasions?
A. Correct.
Q. Or bruises?
A. Yes.
Q. You were looking for wounds that Mandy might have inflicted in fighting back?
A. Correct.
Q. Because she reported to you that she fought back?

A. Yes.
Q. She reported she fought back hard?
A. Yes.
Q. She reported she lost 4 or 5 fingernails in fighting back?
A. Yes.
Q. Those are the fake fingernails you never recovered, right?
A. Yes.
Q. And did you examine Chris's front thoroughly?
A. Yes, I did.
Q. And did you examine his back thoroughly?
A. Yes, I did.
Q. And there were no scratches on him, were there?
A. There were none.
Q. There were no abrasions of any kind?
A. No.
Q. There were no bruises?
A. Nope.
Q. After you checked Chris for scratches, you had a conversation with him?
A. Yes.
Q. And he told you that Jonny and Mandy were going on a date?
A. That's what he said, yes.
Q. He told you they liked each other?
A. Yes.
Q. Did he also talk to you about the headboard?
A. Correct.
Q. He told you that the headboard had been loosely fitted to the wall?
A. That's what he told me, yes.
Q. Not ripped off the wall?
A. Correct.
Q. And he also told you he had prior consensual sex with Mandy, right?
A. Yes.
Q. And that this incident was a threesome that she consented to.
A. Yes.

§11:105 Officer's Investigation of Scene

Q. You went and visited the Cheapo Inn, didn't you?
A. Yes.
Q. It is in a populated area?
A. Yes.
Q. There is Dunkin Donuts right across the street?
A. Yes.
Q. There are lots of people around?
A. Yes.
Q. You went to the room to look for evidence?
A. Correct.
Q. You considered it a crime scene?
A. Yes.
Q. You examined the room very carefully?
A. Yes, I did.
Q. You were thorough in how you gathered evidence?
A. Correct.
Q. You viewed that as very important.
A. Yes.

Q. Properly preserving a crime scene is very important, isn't it?
A. Yes.
Q. You looked at the headboard, right?
A. Yes, I did.
Q. And you said on direct that the headboard had been ripped off the wall, is that right?
A. Correct.
Q. Mandy told you that she threw Jonny off of her and broke the headboard, right?
A. Yes.
Q. Did you look closely at the headboard?
A. Yes.
Q. You were trying to see if it was broken?
A. Yes.
Q. And it was not broken, was it?
A. No.
Q. And did you look closely to see how it was mounted to the wall?
A. Yes, I did.
Q. And it had been screwed to the wall?
A. Yes.
Q. (I have the actual headboard mounted into drywall that I am wheeling out and showing him at this time) This is the headboard you observed in the room, isn't it?
A. I don't know if that is the same one.
Q. Go ahead and get out of your seat and take a closer look. Is that it?
A. It sure looks like it.
Q. Looks the same to you?
A. Yes.
Q. I'm going to represent to you that this is the headboard that was in that room; does that surprise you?
A. No, it looks the same.
Q. From what you could see when you examined the wall, the headboard had been screwed into the wall?
A. Yes.
Q. Like I have it mounted here?
A. Yes. And there were plastic anchors.
Q. There were screws into anchors?
A. Yes.
Q. How many screws were there?
A. I can't recall. I think 3.
Q. I will represent to you that I have mounted this headboard with 3 screws and plastic anchors.
A. OK.
Q. Those screws weren't into studs, right?
A. No.
Q. They were just in the sheetrock, right?
A. Yes.
Q. Did you pick up the headboard?
A. Yes.
Q. It was pretty heavy, right?
A. Yes.
Q. You didn't do any stress testing on this headboard, did you?
A. No.
Q. You don't know how much pressure it would have taken to take this down?
A. No idea.
Q. It could be (now leaning on headboard prop and having it collapse with a thud) a small amount of pressure?
A. It could be.

PRACTICE TIP: *Make sure your demo works*

We all have been embarrassed in the courtroom. It is part of the job. We do something stupid, spill a water pitcher on the table, get chastised by the judge; it happens. So, it's okay to go red in the face and get embarrassed, but make sure your props work. If you are making a big point to close a cross, like my headboard above, that headboard better drop off the wall when I touch it with even a feather.

[§§11:106-11:109 Reserved]

c. Cross-Examination of Alleged Rape Victim

§11:110 Key Points

Now let's take a look at pieces of a cross-examination of the alleged victim Mandy. She's been left on the stand by the prosecutor crying and looking a mess. She's just testified that these men took her out of her house, drove her to Freeport against her will, and then forced her to have sex with them.

It is hard to know how tough to be with the alleged victim. It is even harder with the child witness (discussed in Chs. 2 and 12). Much of this is based on feel. Know your defenses and the points you are trying to score. If your defense requires an unrelenting cross, go for it. If more tact is needed, ease up a bit.

With the alleged victim here, the key was her inconsistencies. We needed to uncover every inconsistency we could and highlight her motive to fabricate. Key points to make are:

- The victim left her home with the defendants voluntarily
- She was embarrassed by her prior sexual relationship with one of the defendants and wanted to keep it secret.
- She had opportunities to escape while on the way to the scene of the alleged rape and at the scene, yet did not try.
- She changed her story about anal penetration.
- She was embarrassed when she returned home after the alleged rape and did not want her family, boyfriend, or friend to know about it.

For tips on effective cross-examination, see Ch. 2.

§11:111   Victim Left With Defendants Voluntarily

Q. Mandy I want to start by clearing up a couple things, okay?
A. OK.
Q. The day you have been talking about you had just gotten home from Dunkin Donuts, right?
A. Right.
Q. You arrived at your house in Freeport, and your Dad was there, your sisters were there, and your friend Lucy was there?
A. Yes.
Q. It wasn't long after you arrived that Chris came by.
A. No it was pretty quick.
Q. You hadn't even had a chance to say hello to your father yet, had you?
A. No.
Q. Your father knew what your shift was at Dunkin' Donuts that day, didn't he?
A. Yes.
Q. He was expecting you home, wasn't he?
A. Yes.
Q. Like most fathers, your father probably worries about you, doesn't he?
A. Yes.
Q. And you have a boyfriend named Max?
A. Yes.
Q. And Max was going to meet you at your house after your shift, wasn't he?
A. Well we hadn't set a time, but he was going to meet me after work.
Q. But Max had not arrived by the time you got home?

A. No.
Q. When Chris showed up he showed up unexpectedly?
A. Yes.
Q. He surprised you?
A. Yes.
Q. Your father didn't know you had a sexual relationship with Chris, did he?
A. No.
Q. And your sisters didn't know you had a sexual relationship with Chris, did they?
A. No.
Q. And I am guessing that Max didn't know that you had a sexual relationship with Chris previously?
A. No.
Q. So Chris arriving unexpectedly made you nervous, didn't it?
A. Yes.
Q. And you were still in your Dunkin' Donuts uniform when he arrived?
A. Yes.
Q. You were upstairs with Lucy when one of your sisters told you that someone was there for you?
A. Yes, I was.
Q. And you went downstairs and saw that it was Chris?
A. Yes.
Q. When you were upstairs, your shoes were off weren't they?
A. Yes, I took them off when I got home.
Q. When you saw it was Chris, you put your shoes on, didn't you?
A. Yes.
Q. Chris didn't tell you to put your shoes on, did he?
A. No.
Q. And you put your shoes on because you wanted to walk outside with him?
A. Yes, I wanted to get him out of the house.
Q. And you wanted to get him out of the house to avoid questions from your family and friends, right?
A. Yes.
Q. You were embarrassed by your previous sexual relationship with Chris?
A. Yes.

As you can see here what we are doing is not only establishing that Mandy left the house voluntarily, but we are also going to loop back to this in a very important point. She is embarrassed by her relationship with Chris and by the fact that she had sex with him. She wants no one else to know. She is going to become even more embarrassed when she arrives back a couple hours later after having sex with him and Johnny.

Q. So you went outside with Chris, and he asked you to take a ride with him?
A. He didn't ask. He told me to get in the truck.
Q. Are you trying to tell us that he commanded you to get in the truck?
A. He said "Get in the truck."
Q. And did you say no?
A. No.
Q. Did he shove you in the truck?
A. No.
Q. You stepped up into that truck yourself, didn't you?
A. Yes.
Q. You didn't call for help?
A. No.
Q. Chris' truck was parked next to the house wasn't it?
A. Yes.
Q. So you could have, quite easily, gotten away from him and the truck if you didn't want to go, right?
A. I was afraid he would follow me back in the house.
Q. Ok, so you got in the truck so that you wouldn't be embarrassed by having Chris around your family and friends?

A. I guess so.

Q. In fact, you really got into the truck because you were interested in being with Chris?

A. No.

Q. You kissed him when you got into the truck, didn't you?

A. No.

Note that this evidence is contradicted by Lucy's testimony on cross-examination. Inconsistencies within statements of a witness are great. Inconsistencies between the statements of witnesses who are supposed to be on the same side of things are even better.

§11:112 Victim Had Opportunities to Escape

Q. And when you were in the truck, my client, Johnny Cupcakes, introduced himself to you, didn't he?

A. Yes.

Q. You didn't see him holding or carrying any weapons?

A. No.

Q. No weapons of any kind?

A. No.

Q. And you didn't see Chris carrying any weapons, did you?

A. No.

Q. In fact, you didn't see any weapons at any time during this encounter, did you?

A. No.

Q. Are you telling us now that that these men forced you to come with them in the truck?

A. I don't know that I would say forced, but I didn't want to go.

Q. And you never told them that you didn't want to go, did you?

A. I told them I needed to be home, and that I just got off work ....

Q. But you never told them no, did you?

A. No.

Q. Did you have your cell phone with you?

A. Yes.

Q. Did you call anyone?

A. No.

Q. On the way down Route 295 South from Freeport to South Portland, you stopped for gas along the way, right?

A. Yes.

Q. And this was on a busy street, wasn't it?

A. Yes.

Q. There were lots of people around the gas station?

A. Yes.

Q. And Chris got out and pumped the gas?

A. Yes.

Q. And you and John stayed in the truck?

A. Yes.

Q. And Johnny didn't hold you there?

A. Yes.

Q. In fact you talked to him a bit?

A. Yes.

Q. He was pleasant to you?

A. Yes.

Q. You never attempted to flee the truck?

A. No.

Q. The truck wasn't locked was it?

A. I don't think so.

Q. You could have walked away from the truck couldn't you?

A. I don't know.

Q. Well you never attempted to flag down anyone for help did you?
A. No.
Q. And when you went to the Cheapo motel in South Portland, Chris pulled the truck right out in front of the motel, didn't he?
A. Yes.
Q. And you stayed in the truck with Johnny while he registered, right?
A. Yes.
Q. And you never attempted to get out of the truck at that point?
A. No.
Q. You never attempted to flee?
A. No.
Q. You never grabbed someone else at the motel who was walking by for help?
A. No.

§11:113   Inside the Motel Room

Now let's take a look at what happens inside the motel room. You want to be careful here because this can present the alleged victim's strongest point. It also presents a great crying opportunity on the stand for the alleged victim. Sometimes, it is best for the defense to work around the scene of the alleged rape, like I have done so far here. We questioned how things outside of the physical act of the rape discredit the victim's claims. But you can't ignore what happens in the room entirely.

Q. So you got inside the motel room?
A. Yes.
Q. And you were still in your Dunkin' Donuts uniform as we've said?
A. Yes.
Q. And you decided you were going to take a shower, right?
A. Yes.
Q. You worked a full shift that day?
A. Yes.
Q. Was it about 8 hours?
A. I think a little less than that.
Q. And so you wanted to take a shower to freshen up a bit?
A. I guess so.
Q. Chris didn't tell you to go take a shower, did he?
A. No.
Q. Johnny didn't tell you to go take a shower?
A. No.
Q. You took a shower, in fact, because you were planning on having sexual activity with these two men, isn't that true?
A. No. I was trying to think and get away from them.
Q. You were trying to get away from them?
A. Yes.
Q. Do you remember that bathroom?
A. Yes.
Q. There's a window in that bathroom, isn't there?
A. Yes.
Q. I am going to show you a picture (approaching witness). This is the window isn't it?
A. Yes.
Q. And that window leads right out onto the street, doesn't it?
A. Yes.
Q. That window is easily big enough for you to get through, isn't it?
A. I believe so.
Q. And across the street from this motel, is another Dunkin' Donuts, isn't there?

A. Yes.

Q. But you never went through that window, did you?

A. No.

Q. You weren't really trying to get away from these men, were you?

A. I didn't want to have sex with them.

Q. Might it be that you were just not sure you wanted to have sex with them?

A. No, I didn't want to have sex with them.

Q. And it was clear to you at least that Chris and John expected you to have sex with them, right?

A. Absolutely.

Q. That's why you were in the motel room to begin with, right?

A. Right.

Q. So they rented the motel room, and when you got there, you took a shower?

A. Yes.

Q. Now you told us on direct that when you emerged from the shower that they roughly forced you to engage in sex?

A. Yes.

Q. And that Johnny forced you to give him oral sex?

A. Yes.

Q. And that Chris had vaginal sex with you at the same time?

A. Yes.

Q. And you said that they had sex with you with their penises anally?

A. No.

Q. You didn't say that the men had anal sex with you?

A. No.

Q. Didn't you say to your friend Lucy that they had anal sex with you?

A. No, I never said that.

Q. Perhaps you exaggerated that to Lucy when you told her the story?

A. No I did not.

Q. So none of this story is an exaggeration?

A. No.

Q. And if Lucy told this jury that you told her that the men had anal sex with you, you would say that Lucy was incorrect?

A. Yes.

Q. Now is that due to the fact that the physical findings done and the sexual assault examination of you do not reflect that there as anal sexual activity?

A. I don't understand the question.

Q. On direct examination you discussed the sexual assault examination that you did, do you remember that?

A. Yes.

Q. And in that examination, the findings related to your anus were that there was no evidence of any trauma, do you remember that?

A. Yes.

Q. And your testimony today is that the men did not have anal sex with you, is that correct?

A. Yes.

Q. Now you said that the men had to restrain you to get you to perform sexual acts?

A. Yes.

Q. And you fought back from this?

A. Yes.

Q. You were violently opposed to having sex with these men?

A. Yes.

Q. Despite the fact that you had sex with Chris previously?

A. Yes.

Q. And you did not fight back at any other time during the trip down to the motel did you?

A. No.

Q. Despite the fact that you knew they were expecting sex, and that's why you were going to a motel, right?

A. Yes.

Q. So when you fought back, you gave it everything you had?

A. Yes, but they were too strong for me.
Q. You were wearing fake fingernails, weren't you?
A. Yes.
Q. And during this fighting back you lost four or five of those fingernails didn't you?
A. Yes.
Q. You scratched and gouged at Chris, didn't you?
A. Yes.
Q. You did as much damage as you could to him?
A. Yes.
Q. And Johnny too, right?
A. Yes.
Q. You would have expected to have seen evidence on the men of the marks you inflicted on them, wouldn't you?
A. I would expect so.
Q. You gouged them with your nails, didn't you?
A. Yes.
Q. You scratched at them didn't you?
A. Yes.
Q. You drew blood?
A. I don't really know.
Q. And you said that the headboard of the bed was knocked over when they threw you into it, didn't you?
A. I said that, yes.
Q. But you have no idea how the headboard was attached to the wall, did you?
A. No. I obviously didn't check that.
Q. It may not have been attached at all?
A. I don't know.

§ 11:114   Alleged Victim's Embarrassment on Returning Home

Now that we have established a host of problems with the victim's testimony, let's move our cross into bring out an answer to the "why" question. Remember, we always want to be telling the jury why she would fabricate.

Q. When you arrived home, it had been a couple hours since you left?
A. Yes
Q. You had left without anyone knowing where you going?
A. Yes.
Q. They were worried about you?
A. Yes.
Q. Your father wanted to know where you had been?
A. Yes.
Q. Your sister's wanted to know where you had been?
A. Yes
Q. Lucy wanted to know where you had been?
A. Yes.
Q. Lucy told you that Max had been there looking for you?
A. Yes.
Q. And she covered for you?
A. Yes.
Q. Were you embarrassed?
A. Yes.
Q. And your friends and family put pressure on you to tell them where you had been?
A. Yes.
Q. But you didn't tell them right away?
A. No.
Q. You waited until the next day?

A. Yes.
Q. And that's because the questions about where you had been were not going away were they?
A. They still wanted to know.
Q. And your boyfriend wanted to know?
A. Yes.
Q. You certainly didn't want to tell your boyfriend that you just had sex with two men?
A. No, I didn't want to tell him that I had been raped by two men.
Q. Ok. But you didn't tell your boyfriend you previously had sex with Chris?
A. No.
Q. And that's because you were embarrassed by it?
A. Yes.
Q. And you were embarrassed by this, weren't you?
A. Yes.

[§§11:115-11:119 Reserved]

3. Closing Argument

§11:120 My Approach

Let's highlight some closing points in the Mandy case. Here, we re-emphasize and highlight the theme of the case: sex that you later regret is not rape. To do this, we focus on the improbability of her story when combined with her inconsistencies. The goal is to keep the jury wondering if what we are saying is plausible. If it is, we should win.

For closing argument tips, see Ch. 2.

§11:121 Sample Closing Argument

What Mandy tells you that she didn't do is as important as what she claims happened. Look to the facts, ladies and gentlemen of the jury. Look to the facts. The facts don't lie, but people do.

The facts are that Mandy had already had sex with Chris. Chris was a married man, and that might make him a bad guy. I'm a married man, and I know my wife would think it would make me a bad guy if I did what Chris did. But we are not talking about bad guys versus good guys. We are talking about whether the sex that Mandy describes with Chris and Johnny was forced.

Fact number one, Mandy had arrived home from her shift at Dunkin' Donuts - she was wearing her Dunkin' Donuts uniform. She was surprised by Chris being there. But was she alarmed? No. Any number of people could have helped her. Did she cry out for help? No. She went along with him.

Fact number two, she voluntarily got in the truck with Chris and Johnny. She could not have been scared of them. She had a multitude of opportunities to escape and she got in because she wanted to.

And remember one important thing: She kissed Chris when she got in the truck. And Mandy denied that on the stand. But Lucy testified that she saw Mandy kiss Chris. Why is this so important? It's so important because it shows that Mandy was still into Chris, and it cuts against her testimony to you that she wasn't interested in Chris. It is also a lie. And if Mandy will lie to you about the small things, she will also lie to you about the big things.

Fact number three, if she was, in fact, afraid of Chris, she had innumerable opportunities to escape along the way. She wasn't held by a weapon, or by force or threat. They stopped on several occasions at the gas station and the motel. She could get out any time she wanted. She didn't, because she was going along for the ride.

I want you to remember something. Sex with regret is not rape. We see it all the time, don't we? You probably know people who have regretted something they had done sexually. Perhaps they had too many drinks and went home with someone they shouldn't have. Perhaps they went home with more than one person that they shouldn't have. Perhaps they got back together with an ex-boyfriend or girlfriend and they regretted it later on. Sex with regret is not rape.

And fact number four leads us toward the conclusion that this must have been sex with regret and not sex by force. Mandy knew they were going to the Cheapo Motel. And she knew what that meant. She told you. The men expected sex. If she didn't want to have sex with them, than she should have removed herself from that situation which she could have done very easily since she was not being held. She knew what was going to happen at the Cheapo Motel.

Women on this jury, I'm speaking to you directly. Would you have put yourself in this situation if you were not interested in having sex with these two men? I would submit to you that you would not.

Fact number five, the very description of the sexual act is in doubt. And I'm sorry I've been vivid in describing these sexual acts. I know it makes people uncomfortable and it makes me uncomfortable. But I have to do it, because I have to understand what happened here. And so do you. And what happened here doesn't add up.

Mandy tells us that she spent all of her energy and all of her strength in fighting these men off, that she gouged them, that she clawed them, that she may have drawn blood but wasn't sure. She did everything she could, and yet, two days later Chris had no scratches, no abrasions, bruises or marks of any kind that would reflect what Mandy claimed happened. The police officer told you himself.

That fact alone is grounds for you to find these men not guilty because it simply does not add up.

Sex with regret is not rape.

Fact number six, at the very least we know that Mandy, or Lucy, is wrong. Remember, according to Lucy, Mandy told her that the men had anal sex with her. And Lucy wrote that down on her statement to the police. She very clearly tried to back away from it, but couldn't because it's there in writing. Why was she trying to back away from it? Because these two witnesses have been prepped. Because these two witnesses have an interest in attempting to achieve the convictions of these two men because if they don't win, Mandy lied. And because, as Lucy agreed, friends back each other up.

That's the problem with a lie. It snowballs on you. You heard of this phrase no doubt: "What a tangled web we weave when first we practice to deceive." The web here has caught Mandy. And the quickest way out of it is to claim she was raped. The quickest way out of the web is to say that the men did not have anal sex with her, that Lucy was mistaken. Because if she does say they have anal sex with her, than that claim would be contradicted by the sexual assault examination.

Can you see how dangerous a game this is that they are playing? Sex with regret is not rape.

So let's say you agree with me. The question you may have is, why would Mandy do this then? Why would she put herself through this?

First of all, we need to recognize that there are any number of reasons people tell lies. Sometimes they are lies of convenience; sometimes they are lies of desperation. People tell lies for innumerable reasons. The fact that matters is they tell them.

But here is what may have happened. It's like a big lie snowball rolling down a hill. It gets bigger and bigger as it goes. Mandy got home and nobody knew where she was. Can she tell her father, her sisters, her friend and her boyfriend that she was having sex with two men? No! And when the questions don't go away the next day, she needs an answer.

Why Mandy would say there was a rape? I don't know. A good lie usually has some grain of truth. That's what makes it a challenge to disprove. Here the grain of truth is that there was sex. Mandy just needed to change it around a bit to make it rape. I don't think at the time that she lied that she knew how far it would go. I don't think she knew that she would be sitting on the stand in front of you one day. But that's the snowball part. You keep needing to cover that lie and you make it bigger. And you either need to tell everyone you were lying the whole time, or you just go with it. Mandy just went with it here.

Now let's talk some more about reasonable doubt ….

For tips on closing arguments and sample language for burden of proof and reasonable doubt arguments, see Ch. 2.

[§§11:122-11:129 Reserved]

II.   DATE RAPE AND SEXUAL ASSAULT

A. Elements and Common Scenario

§11:130 The Elements

Date rape is a type of rape in which the victim and perpetrator knew each other and had or had the potential for a romantic or sexual relationship. College campuses are a common setting for date rape cases. These cases frequently involve claims that the victim was plied with alcohol or drugged.

Date rape is often the ultimate he said/she said case.

§11:131 Common Scenario

Two college students, Jack and Jill, meet at a sorority/fraternity mixer go out for dinner. This is a first date. They are in a college town, nothing fancy. They grab a few drinks at dinner. They walk back across campus to the fraternity. They have a few more drinks and the Jill sleeps over at Jack's fraternity house.

The next morning, Jill walks back to the sorority. By the evening, she reports the first complaint of rape. She claims that she and Jack were making out at the fraternity house when she put the brakes on and Jack kept going. She claims forcible intercourse with a condom.

Jill also complains that she was being plied with alcohol both when out to dinner and at the fraternity house. Jack has a different story.

Jack says they had a nice meal. They had three drinks each at the restaurant. When they got back to the fraternity, they had a few drinks with the guys and then went to bed. He claims Jill was into his advances and they had consensual sex.

[§§11:132-11:139 Reserved]

B. Strategies and Tactics

Many of these cases come down to credibility. It is one thing to argue that Jill isn't believable; it's another to show it. So let's consider some ideas as to how to approach this case. These ideas don't represent an exclusive list, by the way. The ideas are only limited by your imagination and the rules of evidence.

§11:140 Social Networking Sites

This one is pretty obvious. Check all the social networking sites. Subpoena all private accounts. See §§11:18-11:20.

§11:141 Surveillance Cameras

Big brother is out there. That means that the eye in the sky is now watching us all like we are at a blackjack table in Vegas.

Here, Jack and Jill are on a college campus. There are cameras everywhere. Find out how to get a hold of those cameras. In Jack and Jill's case, I would canvas the campus or have an investigator do the canvassing. I would then file preservation requests with the Dean's Office or Campus Security, to be followed with subpoenas as necessary.

Ditto for the restaurant. Increasingly restaurants, bars and clubs have video surveillance. You might get lucky.

Am I looking for this surveillance for the purpose of proving that Jack didn't force himself on Jill later in the evening? No. I want it to poke holes in her story. If the restaurant video shows her ordering her own drinks, she's not being plied with alcohol. If the campus video shows her holding hands with Jack, kissing him, or making more aggressive moves on Jack on the way home, her intentions might be in question. Remember, this is about the credibility of Jill and her story.

PRACTICE TIP: *Don't sleep on video surveillance*

If you don't request surveillance video right off the bat, you will likely lose it. Right away, send a Letter to Preserve Surveillance Video (see §11:142 Form 11-50) so that it is not overwritten.

§11:142 FORM 11-50 Letter to Preserve Surveillance Video

March 2, 2015

Attn: Loss Prevention Officer
Joe Blow's Supermarket, Store #8230
1 Main Street
Rockland, ME 04841

RE: Preservation of Security Video

Dear Sir/Madam:

My office represents John Smith in a pending criminal matter in the Knox County Superior Court. I ask that you take reasonable steps to preserve any and all surveillance audio or video recordings **facing the cashier counters inside the store on January 24, 2014 between the hours of 4:00 p.m. and 5:00 p.m**. At this time I am not asking that you provide these tapes to me, but I will forward a Subpoena for them in the near future. Please contact me at the number below with any questions or forward this to the person who is able to accept service of a Subpoena on behalf of your store.

Thank you for your anticipated cooperation.

Respectfully submitted,

_____

Timothy E. Zerillo
Attorney for Defendant
ZERILLO LAW FIRM, LLC

TEZ/dar
cc: John Smith

§11:143 Video Recreations

I may lack the talent of Martin Scorsese, but the technological gaps between him and me are closing rapidly. It is easy and cheap for any idiot to shoot high definition video that can be easily edited to look professionally done.

Don't get me wrong. There are cheap ways and expensive ways to do video recreation. The expensive way is to hire a team, a real director, actors to play the alleged victim and the defendant, and a professional editor. Your local talent may depend on where you live. But you can always call a local TV station, ask who shoots their commercials and go from there.

Don't be afraid to do it on the cheap, however, because it can still look good. You can hire actors to play each party if you want. I think the easiest and most effective way to do this is to shoot it from the point of view of one of the parties. And if you don't want to do it all yourself, go to a film school and grab a college kid for a few hundred dollars to shoot or edit.

What good are video recreations? As we know a picture is worth a thousand words. So a video must be worth that much more. It is important to remember that you need to get this in front of the jury for it to have value. So, you want to present an accurate portrayal of the event that is slanted to your side of things.

It is undisputed that Jack and Jill were drinking. However, we want to focus on her ability to walk, talk and interact with people without difficulty. We want to focus on their kissing and Jill's willing participation. All of this is done to highlight the defense facts in a way that is not verbal.

In Jack and Jill's case, I would do a recreation in the restaurant. I would recreate the drinking. I would focus on the bill and credit card receipt if it reflects that Jill didn't drink as much as she let on. I would focus on the walk home. Where Jack and Jill stopped to kiss or engage in some friendly groping. I may videotape the fraternity house, focusing on who saw them, and the distances from room to room.

I especially like the idea of the walk home. Remember, Jill described a frightening rape. This can be used in cross. As she goes home across campus, you can show a video of every time she passed a campus police phone. Examine if she stopped anywhere. Who did she speak to? Did she get a coffee? Did she walk by Campus Security and still not say anything? We want the jury to think, "Wow, my reaction to the horrible rape she described would not be to go to Starbucks on the way home!"

In short, make your case come alive. Your jurors are used to watching TV shows, so give them one.

If you are looking to substantively admit a recreation video, then an appropriate foundation must be laid through one or multiple witnesses. It is hard to describe best how to do this in your jurisdiction since rules of evidence vary widely. However, if the foundation for all of the depictions in your video can be made, and the subject matter is relevant, you may be able to admit it.

I generally just use the video as demonstrative evidence and do not admit it substantively. So, let's say we are using the walk home video. I would probably use it in the cross of the alleged victim. Then I would pause the video and ask questions of the alleged victim as I went, like: "It looks like you might be passing Campus Security right there, is that right?"

§11:144 Measurements

You want to also have your investigator take measurements of the scene and photographs. You want to know who slept where. You need a headcount in the house that night. We also need to know how far the victim needed to flee to get to the nearest room and who was in it. How far did she need to go to get to the nearest phone? To the front door? How far away were the campus police?

These measurements can be used later in a variety of ways. I want to know who was in the next room because they may be witnesses that they did not hear a struggle. I want to know who was there who could have helped her. All of these facts are good fodder for cross and to support an argument that help or escape was available and if she were really threatened with rape, she would have availed herself of it.

Make sure your investigator not only takes the measurements meticulously, but also photographs them.

> **PRACTICE TIP:** *Don't forget noise levels*
>
> You can also measure noise levels. I have had cases where there is a claim of a violent rape with significant resistance in a house where many people stayed. I have had investigators measure noise levels with sound meters. They can station themselves in various locations within a house and measure the noise. If the walls are thin, you want to know it if no one else in the house heard anything that night.

§11:145 Witnesses

This one may be obvious but I will mention it anyway—get to all witnesses quickly. Everyone who saw the alleged victim in the fraternity that evening needs to be questioned and fast. The staff at the restaurant need to be questioned even faster, because they wait on a lot of people. Her sorority sisters also deserve a visit.

Thereafter, you need to hit the other witnesses. Old boyfriends/husbands are great. Does she like to get choked during sex and then regret it in the morning? Sometimes ex-boyfriends have lots to say. You may run into rape-shield law difficulties in admitting this substantively. You may be able to use it as impeachment evidence as described earlier in this chapter, however. See §11:01.

Get to anyone who hates her. Go back to her high school and see who will dish the dirt. I bet you will find something. I have had cases, for example, where we dig and find that the alleged victim's reputation was as a habitual liar. With that and a lot of follow up interviews, we were able to present evidence on the victim's reputation for untruthfulness.

§11:146 Victim's Records

Try as best as you can to get her school and work records. Sometimes you get push back on this, but your argument will be that it is related to your investigation of her. You will need to file discovery motions and perhaps subpoenas for this. Some of these records will be difficult to obtain, depending on your jurisdiction.

Look for her criminal record. That is obvious. Don't forget to search for restraining orders, however. They can be a great source of information. Check to see if she has filed any civil suits. Perhaps in the civil suits or restraining orders you find similar patterns of conduct. Perhaps she has complained of a rape multiple times. This does not mean that she wasn't raped, but it is a fact to be explored. Not everything you find will be admissible. You just want to get to know the victim.

§11:147 Clothing

If you happen to catch the case early, you will want to make sure your client gives you his clothing, unwashed. This is obviously something your P.I. can try to get a hold of from the alleged victim during the interview. Often the police will take the clothing if it supports the victim's story. A ripped tee shirt may go into evidence as indicative of a struggle. An intact tee shirt may not. So, try to get that evidence if you can.

§11:148 Polygraph

There are many types of cases in which a polygraph may be useful, but date rape is among the most significant, in my view. Date rape cases are often pure he said/she said cases. In a close charging case, the polygraph may be useful. I would likely have Jack take one and see how he does. Of course, never agree to a police polygraph. Private polygraphs only. For further discussion of polygraphs, see Ch. 2 and Ch. 12.

[§§11:149-11:159 Reserved]

C. Trial

1. Trial Themes

This can be creative stuff. Know the facts and then use your imagination. Remember, you need to explain the alleged victim's fabrication to the jury.

§11:160 S and M and Rape Fantasy

Human beings have sexual kinks that can vary from mild to wild. But to each his or her own. So arguing that someone is into rough sex or a rape fantasy may sound bizarre to one person and be the cat's meow to another.

Maybe Jill is into rough sex or being choked. Maybe she has a fantasy of being raped, but regrets it the morning after. Jill could be repressed and not in touch with those desires without "liquid courage."

§11:161 Failure to Inform Others Promptly

Always remember to attack the alleged victim with the failure to inform other people in her life promptly if it suits your needs. Jill is in a sorority, a sisterhood. Surely, she would have told a sister of the rape right away had it really happened. Or was it that she saw Jack later that week making out with Jenny and Jill got jealous?

§11:162 Failure to Report Crime Promptly

The same theme can be established related to a failure to report the alleged crime promptly. Establish all the opportunities she had to report the crime when she did not.

§11:163 Story Changes Over Time

Like any good tall tale, these stories sometimes grow over time. If you have a change in stories or statements, track it for the jury. Then, explain that Jill is an adult playing a child's game with Jack's life.

§11:164 Story Fabricated to Save Face

Reasons to fabricate a rape claim can be many. Guilt and shame can be powerful motives. The alleged victim may want to hide sexual activity from a boyfriend or girlfriend to preserve the relationship. It may be easier for the alleged victim to tell a parent she was forced into sexual activity rather than being a willing participant. The alleged victim may be seeking revenge against the defendant for some perceived wrong. Or she may simply be embarrassed to have her friends, roommates, or sorority sisters think she had sex with the defendant.

[§§11:165-11:169 Reserved]

2. Jury Selection

§11:170 Jury Questionnaires in Sexual Assault Cases

Sexual assault cases call for more sensitivity than the judge asking people to answer personal and sexual questions in front of the entire jury pool. Ask the court to give you permission for the pool to fill out a jury questionnaire in advance. You will often learn a lot.

§11:171 FORM 11-60 Sexual Assault Jury Questionnaire

STATE OF MAINE   SUPERIOR COURT
CUMBERLAND, SS.   CRIMINAL ACTION
                                   DOCKET NO. CR-12-1234

STATE OF MAINE   )
)
vs.   )
)   **JUROR QUESTIONNAIRE**
JACK   )
)
Defendant   )

Members of the Jury Panel:

This questionnaire asks a number of questions of a personal nature. The court regrets the inquiry on the private matters which this questionnaire addresses. This inquiry is necessary to assure that you can fulfill your duty to be objective and impartial jurors. One or more of the cases on which you may be asked to sit as jurors involve allegations of sexual abuse or sexual assault. In order to assure both the State and Jack a fair trial, the Court must determine if you have had any experiences or opinions that might affect your objectivity and impartiality in such cases. The questions are designed to address these concerns. They are presented in written form in lieu of the questions being asked orally in open court.

QUESTIONS:

1. Please state the following:
    Name: _____ Age: _____
    City of Residence: How long have you lived in Cumberland County? _____
      Place of birth:
2. Please state the following with respect to employment:
    Name of Employer: How long have you worked for your present employer? _____
3. Please state your marital status: . If married, name of spouse: _____ Number of children:
    Please state their ages and sexes: _____. Please state spouse's employer:_____ Type
    of work: _____ . How long has your spouse worked
    for current employer? City of spouse's birth:
4. Have you served in the Military Service?
    Yes No_____
    If yes, were you drafted ___ or enlisted ___
    What branch? Highest rank attained:
5. Have you or any member of your family been employed by a Local, State, or the Federal Government, other than the Military?
    Yes No_____
    If yes, what entity? What position:
6. Have you ever been a party to a civil suit?
    Yes No_____
    If yes, describe the type of case: _____
    _____
    _____

7. Have you ever been a witness in a civil suit?
    Yes No____
    If yes, describe:

8. Have you ever been the subject of a criminal investigation?
    Yes No____

9. Have you ever been formally accused of a crime (other than a traffic infraction)?
    Yes No____
    If yes, describe the type of case:

10. Have you ever been a witness or complainant in a criminal case?
    Yes No____
    If yes, describe the type of case:

11. Have you ever been involved in a political campaign?
    Yes No____
    If yes, which ones?

12. Do you know any other member of this panel?
    Yes No____

13. Do you have any physical problem that could interfere with your jury service?
    Yes No____
    If yes, explain:

14. Is there any reason why you cannot serve as a juror?
    Yes No____

15. Have you ever been a victim of sexual abuse or sexual assault?
    Yes No____

16. Do you have a close relative or friend who has been a victim of sexual abuse or sexual assault?
    Yes No____

17. Have you or a close relative or friend ever been subjected to a charge of sexual abuse or sexual assault
    or been investigated for sexual abuse or sexual assault?
    Yes No____

18. Have you and other family members ever been separated from one another due in whole or in part to
    sexual abuse or sexual assault or claims of sexual abuse or sexual assault?
    Yes No____

19. Have you had any experiences in life that would make it difficult or impossible for you to consider evi-
    dence in a case of alleged sexual abuse or sexual assault objectively and impartially?
    Yes No____

20. Is there any reason why you could not consider evidence in a case of alleged sexual abuse or sexual assault
    objectively or impartially?
    Yes No____

21. What is your spouse's educational background?

22. Are you a member of or otherwise involved in any charitable, religious, political or civic organizations?
    Yes No____
    If yes, please describe the organization and the nature of your involvement: _____

    _____

23. Please indicate and identify your main source of news:
    Newspaper (names)
    Radio (names)
    Television Station (name)
    Websites (names or addresses)

24. Please list your favorite tv shows ; movies: ; magazines: .

25. The evidence and testimony in this case may contain detailed descriptions of alleged sexual acts, including
    intercourse and oral sex, mouth to penis and mouth to vagina. Would being exposed to such evidence and
    testimony affect your ability to be fair and impartial?
    Yes No____

26. The evidence and testimony in this case contains allegations of a sexual act performed without the marital bond.
    Would being exposed to such evidence and testimony of premarital sex affect your ability to be fair and impartial?

Yes No_____

27. The evidence and testimony in this case contains allegations of a sexual act performed with the use of a condom. Would being exposed to such evidence and testimony affect your ability to be fair and impartial?

28. Would you prefer not to sit as a juror on a case involving an alleged sexual assault?
Yes No_____

29. Would you be satisfied, if you were the defendant in this case, to have your case judged by someone in the same frame of mind as your frame of mind?
Yes No_____

30. This case involves allegations of what is popularly known as "acquaintance rape" or "date rape." Do you hold any opinions with respect to "acquaintance rape" or "date rape" that would affect your ability to impartially decide this case?
Yes No_____

31. The defense in this case is consent. Would you be able to fairly and impartially consider the defense of consent in this case?
Yes No_____

32. Is there anything in your life experience that you think could affect your ability to be fair and impartial in this case?
Yes No_____
If yes, please explain:

33. Have you ever served as a juror in a case before:
Yes No_____
If yes, please describe the case.

_____
_____ .

Did you deliberate and reach a verdict?
Yes No_____

34. How did you feel about your jury experience?

35. Is there anything else you think the Court should know about your ability to fairly and impartially judge thus type of case? If Yes, please describe below:

_____
_____
_____
_____

The answers to the above questions are true to the best of my knowledge and belief.

Dated: _____

Name _____
Juror No. _____

§11:172 FORM 11-70 Sexual Assault Voir Dire

STATE OF MAINE
CUMBERLAND, SS.

SUPERIOR COURT
CRIMINAL ACTION
DOCKET NO. CR-12-1234

STATE OF MAINE   )
)
VS.   )
)
)   **JACK'S REQUESTED VOIR DIRE**
JACK,   )
)
Defendant   )

Pre-trial Publicity/Media Issues

1. Have you discussed this case with anyone else?
2. Have you seen or read recent articles on sexual abuse, rape, or date or acquaintance rape, so-called?
3. Has anything that you have either watched, heard, read or discussed about sexual correctness, sexual abuse, rape, or date or acquaintance rape affected your attitude toward [Defendant] or this trial?
4. Have you either formed or expressed an opinion as to the guilt or innocence of [Defendant] at this time?
5. Has any other person in your presence expressed an opinion as to the guilt or innocence of [Defendant] in this case?

Burden of Proof and Indictment

6. As [Defendant] sits here, do you understand that he is presumed innocent now and throughout the trial?
7. Do you understand [Defendant] entered a plea of not guilty, which clothes him in a mantel of innocence?
8. Do you have any difficulty presuming [Defendant] innocent now?
9. Do you understand that the government is required by law to prove the [Defendant] guilty beyond a reasonable doubt?
10. If the government fails to meet the burden, do you understand that you must find [Defendant] not guilty? Would any of you have any difficulty in doing so?
11. Do you understand that [Defendant] has no burden to prove his innocence?
12. Do you understand that [Defendant] does not have to testify or call witnesses at trial, and nothing can be inferred from his not testifying or calling witnesses on his behalf?
13. Do you understand that the indictment is merely a piece of paper which notifies [Defendant] that he is being charged with a crime?
14. An indictment is only an accusation. Do you understand that it is the physical means by which a defendant is brought to trial; its sole purpose is to notify an individual of the charges?
15. Do you understand that an indictment is not evidence that the offense charged was committed and may not be considered as evidence by you in your deliberations?

Bias, Prejudice and Weight of Testimony

16. Do you think that you would give more weight to the testimony of government officers or employees?
17. Have you ever had an unpleasant experience with law enforcement?
18. Do you feel that you possess bias or prejudice with respect to the present case in view of your experience as a victim or being close to a victim of a crime?
19. Have you ever belonged to a group or organization that is involved with social issues, treatment or prevention of sexual abuse or assault or rape?
20. Have you had any experience or done any work with a program or agency concerned with sexual abuse?
21. Have you ever belonged to a group or organization that is involved with social issues, treatment or prevention of rape?
22. The evidence and testimony in this case will contain detailed descriptions of sexual acts. Would being exposed to such evidence and testimony affect your ability to be fair and impartial?
23. This case involves allegations of a sexual act that occurred without the bond of marriage. Do you hold any opinions with respect to premarital sexual acts that would affect your ability to impartially decide this case?
24. Evidence may be presented in this case concerning both male and female oral sex—mouth to penis and mouth to vagina. Do you hold any opinions concerning both male and female oral sex that would affect your ability to impartially decide this case?
25. There will be evidence in this case that [Defendant] used a condom during intercourse. Do you hold any opinions concerning the use of birth control that would affect your ability to impartially decide this case?
26. The defense in this case is consent. Would you be able to fairly and impartially consider the defense of consent in this case?
27. Would you prefer not to sit as a juror on a case involving an alleged sexual assault?
28. Do you live in Lewiston, frequent that area or have any involvement in that community? If yes, will your familiarity or involvement with that area interfere with your ability to fairly and impartially judge this case on the basis of the evidence alone?

29. Is there anything in your life experience which you think the Court should know about that could affect your ability to be fair and impartial in this case?

Dated at Portland, Maine, this ____ day of _____, _____.

Respectfully submitted,

_____
Timothy E. Zerillo
Attorney for Defendant
ZERILLO LAW FIRM, LLC

[§§11:173-11:179 Reserved]

3. Cross-Examination of Alleged Victim to Date Rape

§11:180 Key Points

The key to this cross is to plant that seed of doubt about Jill's story of how the rape occurred. You want to show that her story is not supported by the details of the situation. She was wearing skinny jeans, yet she claims Jack held her down and took off those jeans while putting on a condom like he's Harry Houdini. That facts are that she drinks like a fish, but claimed Jack got her drunk. These types of facts are each little seeds of doubt that you want to bloom in the minds of the jury.

Points to make with this cross are:
- Jill has been disciplined by her sorority and could face further discipline for being drunk and staying out all night.
- She has a history of drinking too much.
- She knew Jack, found him attractive, and looked forward to their date.
- During the encounter she was drunk; she allowed kissing; her testimony about the force used is inconsistent with physical evidence (clothes not torn, skinny jeans difficult for Jack to remove while holding her down and putting on a condom).
- She slept in his room after the alleged attack, rather than fleeing.
- After the event, she walked back to her sorority and did not call authorities.
- Because she returned to her sorority after being out all night, she was the subject of rumors and gossip.

For tips on effective cross-examination, see Ch. 2.

§11:181 Alleged Victim's Disciplinary History

In the Jack and Jill case, they are both in college. So, they have rules they need to live by. One of the sets of rules for Jill relates to her sorority house. We want to establish that she is not following these rules, she has already been disciplined, and that additional discipline would have more consequences for her.

Q. And you are fairly new to the sorority as a sister?
A. I finished pledging the Spring Semester of last year.
Q. So the Fall Semester was your first as a sister.
A. Yes.
Q. And this incident happened on October 4, 2012, right?
A. Yes.
Q. You were at the start of the Fall Semester?
A. Yes.
Q. You lived at the sorority house?
A. Yes.
Q. Thirty-one other women lived there with you?
A. At that time, yes.

Q. And there are codes of conduct associated with your sorority?
A. Yes there are.
Q. And there are punishments if those codes of conduct are broken?
A. Yes.
Q. The Code of Conduct for Delta Delta Delta requires that you "model personal and professional attitudes and behaviors that are consistent with fraternal values and beliefs, and challenge students to model attitudes and behaviors that are consistent with them as well."
A. Yes.
Q. And one of the personal beliefs of Delta Delta Delta is to encourage "morality in all things, including our behaviors with other students."
A. Yes.
Q. There is a disciplinary committee at the sorority?
A. Yes.
Q. And offenses are graded and then punished by their grade?
A. Yes.
Q. Multiple offenses can get you in more trouble.
A. Yes.
Q. In September, you were written up for a noise violation?
A. Yes.
Q. And it was indicated that you were drunk and disorderly during curfew hours?
A. Yes.
Q. And you were ultimately issued a warning?
A. Yes.

§ 11:182 How Defendant and Alleged Victim Met

Now, let's make Jack the attractive, young man that he is. This is a date after all. Jill wants to go out with him. She was looking forward to it. Jack didn't ply her with alcohol and take advantage of her. Jill likes to drink, and in fact met Jack while drinking.

Q. You met Jack the week before the incident at a mixer between your sorority and his fraternity?
A. Yes.
Q. You had never met Jack before?
A. No.
Q. You were drinking that evening?
A. Yes.
Q. It was margarita night?
A. Yes.
Q. That's what you were having?
A. Yes.
Q. You approached him, didn't you?
A. Well, he was with a friend of mine.
Q. After having 2 margaritas?
A. Yes.
Q. You are 5 foot 2 inches tall?
A. Yes.
Q. You weigh 105 pounds?
A. Yes.
Q. Were you drunk when you approached him that night?
A. No.
Q. And he freshened your margarita for you?
A. Yes.
Q. Three times that night?
A. I think so.

Q. By the end of the night you were drunk?
A. Just buzzed.
Q. And you hung out with him for several hours that night?
A. Yes.
Q. And he asked you out?
A. Yes.
Q. And you said yes?
A. Yes.
Q. And you were excited about it?
A. I guess.
Q. You found him attractive?
A. Yes.

§11:183 At the Scene of Alleged Rape

Let's skip ahead to back at the fraternity. By now you have established that Jill had three drinks at the restaurant. Jack and Jill walked back across campus and held hands for a time. They went to the fraternity where they were seen by several people. They had three more beers and socialized. Then he went back to show her his room.

Now, let's get into the mechanisms of the alleged attack. The point we want to make is that the victim consented to some level of sexual contact. The sexual contact she allegedly didn't consent to involves a story that doesn't add up. On top of that, her reaction to the alleged attack is questionable.

Q. So you went to Jack's room?
A. Yes.
Q. No one else was in the room.
A. No.
Q. But there were a lot of people in the hallway and common area?
A. Yes.
Q. And the door to Jack's room was open?
A. I think so.
Q. Well, you could hear other people?
A. Yes.
Q. Were you drunk?
A. No, just buzzed.
Q. Just buzzed again?
A. Yes.
Q. You began kissing Jack.
A. He began kissing me.
Q. But you didn't object?
A. Not to kissing, no.
Q. And you were sitting on his bed?
A. Yes.
Q. And he took off your shirt?
A. Yes, and I told him no.
Q. But your shirt did come off.
A. Yes.
Q. And you resisted that?
A. Yes, I told him no.
Q. So he ripped the shirt off of you.
A. Pretty much.
Q. (Approaching) Is this the shirt?
A. Yes
Q. The shirt isn't ripped, is it?
A. No.

Q. Are any of those buttons ripped off?
A. No
Q. And did he also rip off your bra?
A. Yes.
Q. Did it rip your bra?
A. No.
Q. Did you let him take off your jeans?
A. No.
Q. But he got them off you anyway?
A. Yes.
Q. He held you down and was able to pull them off?
A. Yes.
Q. And you had sex?
A. He raped me.
Q. And he wore a condom?
A. Yes.
Q. He put that on?
A. Yes, he did.
Q. And did he take off your panties?
A. No, he pushed them to the side.
Q. And you were fighting all this time?
A. Yes.
Q. If you could have run out that door you would have?
A. Yes.
Q. But you didn't run out that door?
A. I couldn't because he was holding me down.
Q. He was able to hold you down and get your blouse off?
A. Yes.
Q. He was able to hold you down and get your bra off?
A. Yes.
Q. Without ripping it?
A. I guess …
Q. Hold you down and get your jeans off?
A. Yes.
Q. Those are skinny jeans by the way, aren't they?
A. Yes.
Q. He was able to hold you down and take his own clothes off?
A. Yes.
Q. And he held you down and put the condom on?
A. He was wearing a condom.
Q. He held you down with one hand and opened a condom with the other and put it on his penis?
A. I don't know how he did it, but he did.
Q. After the sex was over you fled?
A. No.
Q. He held you down all night?
A. No, I fell asleep.
Q. And you left in the morning?
A. Yes.

§11:184 The Walk of Shame

Q. You left the fraternity house at approximately 9 AM the following day.
A. Yes.
Q. Did you still feel buzzed?

A. No.

Q. Did you have a good memory of the night before or was it foggy?

A. I had a good memory.

Q. When you went to sleep you had just been held down and raped, right?

A. Yes.

Q. So when you woke and remembered that, you ran out of that room and called the police, right?

A. No.

Q. You called 911 right?

A. No.

Q. You went to campus police?

A. No.

Q. You stopped at an emergency phone on campus?

A. No.

Q. You went back to the sorority?

A. Right.

Q. And this was right during breakfast time?

A. Yes, some people were eating breakfast.

Q. And when you walked in they took notice?

A. Yes.

Q. You got teased?

A. Yes.

Q. And the rumors started to spread?

A. What do you mean?

Q. Rumors that you had sex with Jack on your first date?

A. I guess.

Q. That concerned you, didn't it?

A. Not really, because I was raped.

Q. Okay. Sisters in the fraternity can be quite judgmental?

A. I guess.

Q. They can be gossipy?

A. Sometimes.

Q. And there was a lot of gossip about you.

A. I would say yes.

Q. When you told the sisters that you had been raped, they really cared for you?

A. Yes.

Q. They gave you a lot of sympathy?

A. Yes.

Q. The police did as well.

A. Yes, they were great.

(This page intentionally left blank.)

CHAPTER 12

SEXUAL ASSAULTS AGAINST CHILDREN

In this chapter I hope to provide some insight into the ugliness and opportunity inherent in handling a child sexual assault case. I base the motions and trial materials in this chapter on a case I tried several years ago. I am using this case because it was far from easy for the defense. It also raises issues common to the more difficult child sex cases from the defense perspective.

(This page intentionally left blank.)

I.   INTRODUCTION

§12:01   Representing Accused Child Sex Offenders

"And what did you say to your Dad?"

The child looks up at the prosecutor—this blonde little girl with her hair in pigtails, wearing a pretty yellow dress. She is 10 years old.

At the start of her direct-examination she had been upright. She spoke in a clear voice. She kept her voice up. She looked the prosecutor in the eye.

Now her body has slumped. She appears tired. Verbally beaten. Re-victimized from telling a courtroom full of strangers the horrors of sexual abuse perpetrated on her by her father.

"I told him I didn't want to play games with him anymore. I told him he hurt me when he had sex with me. I felt sick. I told him I wanted him to stop having sex with me."

"Did he stop?"

The girl looks up, tears in her eyes and running down her face. "Not until I told on him and the police took him away."

Your witness.

"You Monster!"

Are you a monster? I sure don't feel like one. But I do defend people accused of sex crimes against children. The sexual abuse of children is a monstrous, horrific act. Does that make a sex crime defender a monster, though?

Ironically, I am writing these words on my way down to Disney World, on a trip with my own children, my wife, my father, and other family including two young nephews of mine. I hate the idea of anyone harming them in any way, and a sexual assault is among the worst of ways.

So how do I reconcile this? The fact that we have such a visceral disgust for sexual acts against children is the same reason they are so dangerous. They can cause an over-reaction. They cause us to fly off the handle.

If you think an investigator, or a counselor, or even a sexual assault examiner is not susceptible to that rage and disgust, you are wrong. So, if Susie says that Daddy touched her when giving her a bath, Mommy is going to react in an extreme way, which can cause a whole host of other people to act in an extreme way.

It is our very disgust about these types of cases that sets them up to ensnare the innocent. Representing people accused of these crimes does not make you a monster. It makes you someone doing a very important job that you won't always like.

§12:02   Sex Offender Registration

I won't say much about sex offender registration here because it is very state specific. It is the modern-day scarlet letter, and it has a real detrimental effect on those who are being publicly shamed long after they have done their time.

My only point is to warn your clients thoroughly and tell clients you can't predict future registration requirements. These registration acts are trending in the direction of being more onerous, not less. I tell people in cases in which there is a 10-year registration, that some legislators may want it to be lifetime registration eventually. I say that non-registerable offenses may be registrable later.

§12:03   Scenario

Our prosecutrix is named Tammy. She is 11 years old at the time of trial. She has an older, teenage sister, named Tabitha. Her mother is named Tracey.

Tammy, Tabitha and Tracey live together in an apartment in a rural section of Southern Maine. Also living there is Tracey's husband, John, and their son Jaime, who is three years old.

Tammy, for most of her life, had visits with her father, Bob, every other weekend. Bob and Tracey went through an ugly divorce. They have brought each other back to court on post-judgment divorce motions on a yearly basis ever since. Usually they fight over child support.

Tracey and Tabitha have been at odds since Tabitha got to middle school. Now in high school, Tabitha is uncontrollable. Tabitha's father is not really in the picture, and she sneaks off to her boyfriend's house every chance she gets.

Tammy acts up as well, and Tracey cannot stand the pressure of Tabitha and Tammy both running amuck.

Bob, who has no other children, lives with his girlfriend Sally, and her teenage daughter, Nancy. Bob gets a call out of the blue one evening from Tracey, who tells Bob and Sally to come get Tammy because she can't handle her any more. Bob and Sally head right over. They pick up Tammy and take her home to live with them.

This involves a change in schools for Tammy, and Bob and Sally spend a significant amount of time getting her enrolled. She has trouble acclimating to her new home and school, and often expresses a desire to go home and live with her mother.

Bob and Sally have their problems too, and at times Bob has to move out of Sally's house, with Tammy in tow, to stay at his father Lionel's place. Usually, Bob and Sally patch things up, and he moves back in with Tammy.

One day, approximately one year into this situation, Tammy is talking to her uncle Sean, who is a year younger than she (strange, but true). She discloses in this conversation that Bob, her father, touches her sexually. Tammy's grandmother overhears this conversation, and calls Tracey, who, as you would expect, goes berserk.

The police are called and interviews are arranged. At the police station, Detective Lippy interviews Tammy two times. Tracey, her mother, is present each time.

Tammy discloses that her father began sexually abusing her within weeks of her moving in with him. The touching began when she was nine and continued after she turned ten. The sexual abuse started with touching. He would touch her "privates" when they watched TV and movies. Then it graduated to him having her touch him "until the white stuff came out." He then taught her how to perform oral sex on him and he did the same to her.

Just before she was ten, she claimed that he penetrated her with his penis. This happened multiple times. Tammy said he would ejaculate on her. She also claimed that he had anal sex with her.

Tammy further disclosed that Bob goaded her into allowing him to penetrate her deeper vaginally. She said he disclosed his sexual contact with an ex-stepdaughter Tammy's age. Tammy told Detective Lippy that "He said he could fit it all the way inside the other girl."

Detective Lippy scheduled an interview with Bob, who looked shocked at the allegations, and denied all inappropriate sexual touching. Detective Lippy cut Bob loose, and Bob then had a bit of a breakdown, causing Sally to call the police to check on his safety.

Tammy was sent for a forensic examination. Dr. Howard saw Tammy and found that she had a deep notch in her hymen at 6 o'clock. Dr. Howard opined that the physical findings were consistent with the sexual abuse history recounted by Tammy.

All witnesses are available to testify, including, of course, Tammy. Best of luck.

[§§12:04-12:09 Reserved]

II.   COMBATING JUNK SCIENCE AND BS SEXUAL "FINDINGS"

§12:10   Injuries to the Hymen

All child sex cases are difficult. When you have a little girl with a tear in her hymen and complaints about your client, they are doubly difficult. What most lawyers do in such a case can be boiled down to three basic reactions: 1) plead and plead fast, 2) ignore the problem, or 3) rely on straddle injuries to explain the hymenal trauma.

Forget about straddle injuries. You might throw them into cross as a little smoke, but most experts are aware of them and are ready to hand you your hat if that is all you have. And don't ignore a problem that will be very significant to the jury. The jury's mindset is simple: little girl complains of abuse, combined with physical findings of hymenal trauma, equals a five minute guilty verdict.

So, what do you do? First, let's find out if you even have a problem. To do that, we need to understand the hymen. The easiest way is to look at a clock.

The clock is how the area of the notch or place of transection in the hymen is identified. The clock represents the hymen with the child lying on her back. Twelve o'clock is toward the front of the body and 6 o'clock is toward the back. Between 3 o'clock and 9 o'clock is the *inferior* or *posterior* (toward the back) portion of the hymen. Between 9 o'clock and 3 o'clock is the *anterior* (toward the front) portion of the hymen.

Now, please note that I am a long way from earning my medical degree and I have no formal medical training. What I will try to teach you here comes from many hours of studying medical texts, talking and examining experts and talking to other lawyers with insight into this topic. My hope is this provides you with a basic framework of understanding.

§12:11   Why Is the Location Significant?

When we are talking about injury to a hymen we need to understand the terms "transection" and "notch". A transection is a complete perforation of the hymen membrane that goes all the way through the membrane.

A notch is an insult to the hymen membrane that does not completely perforate the membrane. There are different grades of notches that we will discuss more below. When you are trying to determine if an insult to the hymen is from a sexual act, you determine the location and nature of the injury. Here, we discuss location.

Notches in the anterior portion of the hymen provide an automatic defense—a penis or digit does not tend to enter on that side of the hymen. Posterior/inferior notches and transections are to be watched closely. They are associated with sexual penetration.

So, you get a bad case. Your client is accused of having sex with a 9 year old girl. Let's also say there is a notch in the hymen. First, determine if the notch is inferior/posterior. Remember, inferior/posterior aspect of the hymen is from 3 to 9 on the clock. In our scenario the notch is at 6 o'clock. So we have an inferior/posterior notch, which means we have trouble.

§12:12   Why is the Type of Injury Important?

If you have an inferior/posterior notch, next check the notch depth. As we have said, a "deep notch" is half or greater the depth of the membrane. A superficial notch is less than half the depth of the membrane.

Why is this significant? It is significant because a superficial notch is not diagnostic for sexual abuse. The presence of superficial notches are not diagnostically useful as evidence of prior penetrating trauma. For evidence of a prior penetrating trauma there should be evidence of a deep notch or a transection. There is medical support to be found for this proposition in the literature. A good place to start is Lahoti, "Evaluating the Child for Sexual Abuse," *Am Fam Physician*, 2001 Mar1; 63(5): 883-893.

The presence of a superficial notch then raises obvious cross-examination issues. You should be able to get the expert to acknowledge that there is no medical evidence that a superficial notch means that there was a prior penetrating trauma. You can also lead the expert through the various other ways in which superficial notches can occur, including natural causes and other, non-sexual trauma.

If you have an inferior transection, you have trouble. A transection simply means that the hymen membrane has been completely perforated. Again, find the location of the transection. If it is anterior, you may be safe. If you have an inferior/posterior transection, look out. This is diagnostic for sexual trauma. You will need to come up with a reason for an inferior transection that makes some sense, like an alternative suspect theory. Additionally, depending on the age of the child, she may have inserted an object causing the transection or engaged in a sexual act with someone else.

§12:13   Debunking Commonly Raised Signs of Abuse

I don't have formal training in medicine, anatomy, or biology. I make up for my ignorance by reading, however. So, when you don't have the time to go to medical school, start reading. I like to search medical journals. Many are online to which you can get a subscription and sometimes a 24-hour pass. If you don't want to deal with that, find a medical school and get into its library.

So, the child goes to the doctor with complaints that her father had sexual intercourse with her. There are commonly thought of signs of abuse that you may see in the medical reports. What you want to do is research the common signs of abuse, and compare them to the results of real life studies. Some signs commonly believed to be dispositive of abuse are:

- Redness.
- Labial adhesions.
- Midline scars.
- Enhanced vascularity.
- Bumps/Tags.

- Urinary tract infections.
- Enlargement of the clitoris.
- Increased hymenal opening.

§12:14   Useful Studies

Consider, for example, a study published in the *Journal of Pediatrics* that involved 79 normal, prepubertal girls. There, the hymen had increased vascularity 37 percent of the time. The posterior fourchette (the area of where the labia minora meet posteriorly) had increased vascularity 15 percent of the time. Gardiner, "Descriptive Study of Central Variation in Healthy, Non-Abused, Premenarchal Girls," February 1992, Volume 120, Issue 2, Pages 251-757, *Journal of Pediatrics*.

Take a look also at a study of 192 pre-pubertal girls with a history of penetration against 200 age and race matched girls with no history of penetration. Berenson, "A Case-Control Study of Anatomic Charges Resulting From Sexual Abuse," *Am.J.Ob.Gyn.*, 2000 Apr; 182(4):820-831. Both groups had equal incidence of labial adhesions. *Id*. The hymens of each group had equal incidence of bumps, tags, intravaginal ridges, superficial notches, and external ridges. *Id*.

Another interesting study involved 147 non-abused premenarchal girls (77% of whom were Hispanic). Heger, "Appearance of the Genitalia in Girls Selected for Nonabuse: Review of Hymenal Morphology and Nonspecific Findings," *J. Peds. Adolesc. Gyn.*, 2002 Feb; 15(1): 27-35. Those girls had the following potentially relevant findings:

- Intravaginal ridges.....94%
- Hymenal tags.....3%
- Hymenal bumps.....34%
- Erythema.....49%
- Isolated/increased vascularity.....37%
- Labial adhesions.....16%
- Partial posterior hymenal notch.....18%

Id.

There are some brilliant studies by brilliant scientists who are debunking the junk science myths of these very dangerous allegations. I have yet to scratch the surface here. If you can compare the real science to the junk science in your case, you can turn the government expert from God into someone who is just guessing.

PRACTICE TIP: *Time to get reading!*

Some of my favorite studies in this area are as follows:

1. Adams, "Guidelines for Medical Care of Children Who May Have Been Sexually Abused," *Journal of Pediatric and Adolescent Gynecology*, 2007.
2. Berenson, "A Case-control Study of Anatomic Changes Resulting from Sexual Abuse," *American Journal of Obstetrics and Gynecology*, April 2000
3. Berenson, "A Longitudinal Study of Hymen Development from 3 to 9 Years of Age," *Journal of Pediatrics*, May 2002.
4. Heger, "Appearance of the Genitalia in Girls Selected for Nonabuse: Review of Hymenal Morphology and Nonspecific Findings," *Journal of Pediatric and Adolescent Gynecology*, February 2002.
5. Lahoti, "Evaluating the Child for Sexual Abuse," *American Family Physician*, March 1, 2001.
6. McCann, The Appearance of Acute, Healing, and Healed Anogenital Trauma, Child Abuse Negl., 1998 Jun; 22(6): 605-15.
7. Myhre, "A Longitudinal Study of the Anogenital Development in Girls from 6-12 Years of Age," *Journal of Pediatric and Adolescent Gynecology*, April 2008.
8. Reece, Lea & Febiger, *Child Abuse: Medical Diagnosis and Management*, 1994.
9. Slaughter, "Patterns of Genital Injury in Female Sexual Assault Victims," *American Journal of Obstetrics and Gynecology*, March 1997.
10. Swerdin, "Cutaneous Signs of Child Abuse," *J. Am. Acad. Dermalol*, 2007 Sep; 57(3): 371-372.

§12:15   The Anus

I focus in this chapter on the sexual abuse of girls because it is the most common case I see. Occasionally, I get a case involving the alleged sexual abuse of a boy or a girl involving an allegation of anal penetration. I have heard in my cases that the following are believed to be signs of abuse of the anus:

*   Redness/Hyperpigmentation.
*   Skin tags.
*   Fissures.
*   Dilation (immediate/>1 cm).
*   Winking.
*   Rectal prolapse.

Junk science abounds in these cases. Consider anal winking. The anal wink is the contraction of the sphincter upon stroking of the skin around the anus. It was developed by Dr. Bruce Woodling as proof that a child had been sodomized. His testimony was made famous in the McMartin Preschool case. There were seven defendants in that case and 321 counts of child abuse against them involving 48 children. Ultimately, there were no convictions, but one defendant, Ray Buckley, was held for five years without bail as a result of Dr. Woodling's testimony.

Again, any findings by the medical examiner should be compared to studies by real scientists. Consider the study by McCann, "Perianal Findings in Pre-pubertal Children Selected for Non-Abuse," *Child Abuse Negl*, 1989, 13(2) 179-93 which found the presence of the following in non-abused children:

*   Erythema.....41%
*   Pigmentation.....30%
*   Skin tags.....11%
*   Anal dilation.....49%
*   Winking.....62%

Like the hymen, findings related to the anus provide real problems and possibilities of junk medicine. If you have an examination after an acute injury, findings to be wary of include spasming, fresh tears, and the presence of sperm. If the examination is not shortly following an acute injury, you should be concerned about findings of greater than two centimeters in dilation, scars and venereal disease.

§12:16   The "My Child Was Acting Strangely and Was Therefore Abused Argument"

I keep a ridiculous brochure in my office by the Department of Health and Human Services in Maine. I picked it up at a courthouse one day. It is called "Sexual Behaviors in Your PreSchool Child." Among those "abnormal" sexual behaviors are listed developing an unusual interest in sex, wanting to withdraw, spending time preoccupied with his/her body, masturbating and exposing himself or herself to others.

You often hear these types of complaints as the initiation of an investigation against a dad or step-dad. Perhaps mom and dad are divorced or separated, and have a shared custodial situation. When mom gets her daughter back from dad's house, she notices her wanting to be alone and catches her masturbating. She takes her to a therapist. The therapist says this is unusual; she must have been abused. And then the government comes marching in.

Again this is junk science. See Friedrich "Normative Sexual Behavior in Children: A Contemporary Sample," *Pediatrics,* April 1998, Vol. 101, Issue 4, among other studies. Masturbation, interest in the opposite sex, touching of genitals at home, the showing of genitals to adults, among many other behaviors, are all within the realm of normal experience. So attack the "my kid was molested because she was behaving sexually" argument with science.

§12:17   Defense Experts

I go back and forth on the issue of hiring defense experts. I know very good practitioners who hire them all of the time. This is completely fine and sometimes make sense.

However, I have a tendency to hire medical experts for the primary purpose of helping me prepare for cross-examination. I find that the defense medical experts can sometimes be wishy-washy about giving an opinion that the government expert is wrong by the time you get to trial. Instead, they are good at giving alternative explanations to sexual contact. That is useful, but I can do that on cross.

I am not saying I would never use a defense medical expert, but I think it depends on the expert and the case. So, I hire the expert to consult on the case first. After a review of the discovery and the gathering of other materials, I find out if our expert has a contrary opinion to the government expert. If the expert does have a contrary opinion, I want to find out why it is contrary and whether the contrary opinion is supportable (as opposed to the defense expert just showing off for me, or expressing a dislike for the government expert). If the contrary opinion is strong and supportable, I may call the defense expert as a witness. If it is not, I use the expert to help me develop cross-examination strategies.

§ 12:18   Polygraphs

I have used polygraphs with success in many cases in recent years. I can think of four of my cases in one year that were not been charged as a result of a polygraph examination.

I likely don't need to tell you this, but I will anyway: do not submit your client to a police polygraph at the outset. The polygraph examiner I use fails my clients approximately 80 percent of the time. Every one of those clients swore up and down to me that they were innocent, but they failed the polygraph regardless. Whether those failures represent a failure of the polygraph system or if they were lying to me, I don't know. Regardless, I don't want them to fail a police polygraph.

The vast majority of situations in which I use the polygraph are pre-charge. My client comes to see me because he or she was called by a detective or heard that a child has made a claim of sexual assault against him or her. The client has not been charged. The client denies the accusation. I suggest a private polygraph examination.

If the client fails the private polygraph, no one knows but you, the client, and the polygrapher. If your client fails badly, it may help the client come to grips with the fact that he or she has a problem.

> **PRACTICE TIP:** *Have the client give your office the funds to hire the polygraph examiner*
> If the lawyer hires the polygraph examiner, the results are likely covered by privilege. If the client does the hiring, they may not be.

> **PRACTICE TIP:** *Advise client to wait before telling family about poly*
> I strongly urge clients not to tell their loved ones that they are even taking the polygraph. Those loved ones may use it as a litmus test of guilt or innocence. I tell the clients they can tell their loved ones that they took the poly once they pass it.

If the client passes, have your polygraph examiner write a report. Share that report with the prosecutor and urge him or her strongly not to charge an innocent person.

The prosecutor may want a police polygraph done. This happens if your polygraph examiner is not well-known, not well-respected or if you have a generally skeptical prosecutor. I always ask my polygraph examiner if he feels confident in the test. If the answer is yes, and if my client consents, I am usually in favor of a police polygraph re-test.

Only once in my career has the police re-test not resulted in a dismissal. This case drove me crazy and I feel compelled to tell you about it.

My client, Jason L., had been in custody for over three years when I met him. He was convicted at trial of gross sexual assault on his pre-pubertal daughter. His conviction had recently been reversed in the appellate court when I met him. Jason was serving a 20-year sentence and facing re-trial.

Jason proclaimed his innocence to me at the outset. I asked if he wanted to take a polygraph and he agreed. To my surprise, he passed.

I asked the prosecutor to dismiss the case and she flat-out refused. Flabbergasted, I asked if she would reconsider after a police polygraph. After all, an innocent man sat in prison for three years on her case. She reluctantly agreed.

Jason passed the police polygraph with a very high score, indicating a low likelihood that he was being deceptive. Gleeful, I asked the prosecutor to dismiss. She once again refused.

In my view, this prosecutor was so invested in this case that she could not let it go. She could not concede that Jason was not a child rapist of his own daughter.

I'm sure I don't need to tell you how frustrating this was. We had been strung out for months. I have never seen it work this way before or since.

However, even with an intractable prosecutor, we still benefited from the polygraph. Our client had been previously held on $50,000 cash bail, which he simply could not raise. We used the positive polygraph examination to get him out on bail. See §12:18 Form 12-10 for my Motion to Amend Bail. The court released Jason over the state's strong objections. While the court would not explicitly say on the record that Jason was released because of the polygraph results, the Justice did indicate that the fact that he passed two polygraph examinations was a significant factor in his decision.

With Jason out on bail after nearly four years in jail (at that point), some of the pressure was off. Of course, now, we needed to win the trial. I tried to get the polygraph results admitted into evidence. I filed a motion in limine on the issue, which can be found at §12:19 Form 12-20. It was never heard, because at jury selection the prosecutor dismissed the case.

I understand polygraphs aren't perfect. However, even when they aren't perfect, a good polygraph can still be helpful.

§12:19   FORM 12-10 Defendant's Motion to Amend Bail Based on Polygraph Results

STATE OF MAINE   UNIFIED CRIMINAL DOCKET
CUMBERLAND, SS   DOCKET NO. ****

STATE OF MAINE   )
)   DEFENDANT'S
v.   )   MOTION TO AMEND BAIL
)   (STATE'S POSITION UNKNOWN)
JASON L,   )
)
Defendant   )

NOW COMES the Defendant, Jason L., by and through Undersigned Counsel, and Moves to Amend Bail as follows:

1. Defendant was convicted in this Court of multiple sex offense counts. On March 27, 2014, the Defendant's convictions were reversed and the case remanded to this Court.
2. On April 14, 2014, bail for Defendant was set, requiring $50,000.00 cash. Defendant cannot meet that bail and has been held in the Cumberland County Jail.
3. Counsel was hired in this matter thereafter. The Defendant submitted to a polygraph examination administered by Mister Polygrapher in October 2014. Defendant indicated that he did not engage in the charged conduct. The polygraph results were that the Defendant was truthful. *See generally*, *Affidavit of Mister Polygrapher* attached as *Exhibit 1*.
4. Counsel informed the District Attorney's Office of the same and strenuously requested the case against Defendant be dismissed. The State refused. Counsel requested the State perform their own polygraph examination of Defendant with their own polygraph examiner, Detective Police Polygrapher of the Portland Police Department. The State agreed to the same.
5. On April 2, 2015, Defendant submitted himself to a polygraph examination administered by Detective Police Polygrapher. Defendant indicated that he did not engage in the charged conduct. The polygraph results were that the Defendant was truthful.
6. Once again, the Undersigned asked the District Attorney's Office to dismiss the case against the Defendant. They refused.
7. Maine Pretrial Services screened the Defendant for supervision on bail. Barbara L, of Maine Pretrial Services, has accepted the Defendant into their program as of May 22, 2015. Ms. L is waiting for an amendment of bail to draft the Maine Pretrial Services Contract.
8. An innocent man has spent nearly 4 years in custody. To let his continued incarceration go on a moment longer is a travesty.
9. Defendant seeks amendment of his bail as follows: eliminate the requirement of a $50,000 cash bail in favor of $500 cash bail and a Maine Pretrial Services Contract.
10. The State objects to this Motion.

MEMORANDUM OF LAW

Amendment of bail is permitted in this instance on a showing of changed circumstances or upon the discovery of new and significant information. 15 M.R.S.A. s.1026(3)(C). The relevant statute says:

> Upon motion by the attorney for the State or the defendant and after notice and upon a showing of **changed circumstances or** upon the **discovery of new and significant information**, the court may amend the bail order to relieve the defendant of any condition of release, modify the conditions imposed or impose further conditions authorized by this subsection as the court determines to reasonably ensure the appearance of the defendant at the time and place required, that the defendant will refrain from any new criminal conduct, the integrity of the judicial process and the safety of others in the community.

Id.

These standards are met based upon changed circumstances and two new facts that have been discovered since bail was last set: 1) that Defendant has now passed two polygraph examinations and 2) that Maine Pretrial Services has agreed to supervise him.

FACTUAL BACKGROUND

Jason was born in Augusta, Maine. He was raised in Gardiner, Maine and graduated from Gardiner High School in 1991. He did not present any behavioral problems in school, graduated on time and played on the school hockey team. He has two semesters of college studying graphic design.

In 1995, at the age of 22, he enlisted in the U.S. Army. He remained on active duty in the Army until 1999. Thereafter, he joined the Inactive Ready Reserves for a four-year period. He rejoined the Army in the Reserves in September of 2005. He served in Iraq from September 2005 through November 2006.

He has been married three times. His marriage to his ex-wife Cathy produced three children, including the alleged victim in this matter. This marriage was tumultuous at best. While Counsel does not intend to recite the details of the marital events, suffice it to say that there is significant animosity on all sides.

Counsel is unaware of any prior incidents of criminal charges against Defendant.

Jason has availed himself of various programs while incarcerated. Most significant of which is the *Opportunity for Change* program. *Exhibit 2* is a May 26th letter from the Director and Instructor of *Opportunity for Change*, indicating that the Defendant completed the program long ago, but still voluntarily continues to attend it. *Exhibit 2.* Mary and Brian C. write that Jason "continues to be the most attentive of all the inmates I have encountered in my many years of doing this work in the jail system." *Exhibit 2.*

I. THE POLYGRAPH EVIDENCE IS SUFFICIENT EVIDENCE OF CHANGED CIRCUMSTANCES OR NEW AND SIGNIFICANT INFORMATION TO WARRANT AMENDMENT

A.　The Polygraph Results

The *Affidavit of Mister Polygrapher*, attached as *Exhibit 1*, establishes that Defendant has taken two polygraph examinations and passed them both. The first examination, administered by Mister Polygrapher, produced a result of a +3 score. *Exhibit 1* at 17. The probability of Defendant being deceptive using the Empirical Scoring System is a chance of less than 7 in 100. *Id.* at 18. Using an algorithm in the Objective Scoring System, Version 3, the likelihood of Defendant being deceptive was 1.9%. *Id.* at 19.

On April 2, 2015, Detective Police Polygrapher of the Portland Police Department tested the Defendant. *Id.* at 19. The District Attorney's Office approved of this testing. Detective Police Polygrapher scored Defendant's score as +12. *Id.* at 32. The likelihood that Defendant is being deceptive is a chance of four out of 1,000. *Id.* at 33.

Jason's truthful answers to both polygraphs included outright denials of his sexually abusing his daughter. *Id.* at 16; 31. Considering all the data, there is a less than 2% chance that the Defendant is not being truthful when he denies sexually abusing his daughter. *Id.* at 34.

B.   The Polygraph Results Should be Considered at the Bail Stage

Bail determinations do not hinge on the admissibility of evidence. Every day this Court considers evidence at bail hearings that would not be admissible at trial. The use of police reports at the bail stage is probably the most common example of this. While a police report is inadmissible at trial, it is frequently relied upon at bail hearings by the Court. Judges often read from them on the bench before setting bail.

There is nothing wrong with this practice, of course. In fact, it is not only by practice, but is also by Rule. The Maine Rules of Evidence state:

> **(b) Rules inapplicable.** These rules--except for those governing privilege—do not apply to the following…
> …**(8)** Bail proceedings…

M.R.Evid. 101(B)(8).

As a result, the Maine Rules of Evidence do not bind this Court at the bail stage. This Court should consider the two successful polygraph examinations, without ruling on their trial admissibility, when setting bail.

II. MAINE PRETRIAL SERVICES

Barbara L. has indicated to the Undersigned that Maine Pretrial Services will supervise Defendant. He has been screened to reside at the home of a friend in Carrabassett Valley. A local supervisor in Farmington will supervise him. Rides have been arranged for Defendant to get to and from Court.

III. THE APPLICATION OF THESE NEW FACTS TO THE BAIL STANDARDS MERIT REDUCTION IN BAIL FOR JASON

Defendant requests this Court amend bail to release him on $500 cash bail with a Maine Pre-Trial Contract. This is an appropriate bail under the circumstances.

The standards for a modification are that Jason's release "reasonably ensure" the appearance of the Defendant, that the Defendant will refrain from new criminal conduct and that the bail will not affect the integrity of the judicial process or the safety of others in the community. 15 M.R.S.A. s. 1026(3)(C).

A.   Reasonably Ensuring His Appearance

Defendant has no history of failure to appear, nor any history of criminality. He is a man in his 40's. He has served a distinguished military career.

Further, he is not trying to parlay his appeal victory and polygraph results into some sort of deal, even though he could. He has asserted his innocence from the moment of his first questioning in this case. He asserts his actual innocence today. He looks forward to appearing in Court again. He will not run away.

Even if he was the type to run away, which he clearly is not, he would not get far. He has no financial resources whatsoever.

B.   Refraining From New Criminal Conduct

Counsel is not aware of Jason having been charged with any crime other than the ones at bar. He will take the conditions of his release seriously. *Exhibit 2* indicates that he has engaged in significant and important treatment while in custody. These factors should sufficiently ensure the Court that he can be released with appropriate conditions.

C.   The Integrity of the Judicial Process

This Court should ensure that bail does not impact the integrity of the judicial process. 15 M.R.S.A. s.1026(3)(C). Jason's bail will not injure judicial integrity. To the contrary, the integrity of the judicial process will be offended if Jason is not released. To allow a man to sit in jail when he has established proof of his innocence at any level favors his release on conditions.

D.   Safety of Others

Conditions can certainly be fashioned to ensure the safety of others, just as they are in every sex offense involving a minor. These include no direct or indirect contact with females under the age of 16 (aside from incidental public contact or when supervised by the child's parent or guardian). Additionally, there should be no direct or indirect contact with the alleged victim.

CONCLUSION

When this Court sets pre-conviction bail on a Gross Sexual Assault charge, it almost always knows less about matters in mitigation to the defendant than it knows here. We are once again at the pre-conviction bail stage. While this Court does not need to believe the polygraph examination results to any level of certainty, they present more evidence of Jason's innocence than this Court ordinarily encounters in a bail determination for a sex offense. If any gross sexual assault case deserves bail, this one is it.

Bailing Jason would not create some *per se* rule making polygraphs relevant in bail determinations. Each case deserves individual scrutiny. In this case, however, where there are two polygraph results, one administered by the State's polygraph examiner, along with a Maine Pretrial Services Contract, release is appropriate.

Jason has spent nearly 4 years in custody in this case. He deserves to breathe fresh air again and to be released pending trial.

WHEREFORE, Counsel respectfully requests this Court grant this Motion to Amend Bail.

Dated this 29th day of May 2015, at Portland, Maine.

Respectfully submitted,

_____

Timothy E. Zerillo
Attorney for Defendant
ZERILLO LAW FIRM, LLC

§12:20   FORM 12-20 Motion in Limine Requesting Admission of Polygraph Testing

STATE OF MAINE   UNIFIED CRIMINAL DOCKET
CUMBERLAND, ss.   DOCKET NO. ******

STATE OF MAINE	)	
	)	DEFENDANT'S
v.	)	MOTION *IN LIMINE* REQUESTING
	)	ADMISSION OF POLYGRAPH
JASON L.,	)	TESTING WITH MEMORANDUM
	)	OF LAW
Defendant	)	

NOW COMES the Defendant, JASON L., by and through Undersigned Counsel, and moves *in limine* to admit evidence related to his polygraph testing as follows:

1. Defendant was previously convicted in this Court of multiple sex offense counts. On March 27, 2014, the Defendant's convictions were reversed and the case remanded to this Court.

2. The Defendant submitted to a polygraph examination administered by Mister Polygrapher in October 2014. Defendant indicated that he did not engage in the charged conduct. The polygraph results were that the Defendant was truthful. *See generally, Affidavit of Mister Polygrapher* attached as *Exhibit 1*.

3. Counsel informed the District Attorney's Office of the same and strenuously requested the case against Defendant be dismissed. The State refused. Counsel requested the State perform their own polygraph examination of Defendant with their own polygraph examiner, Detective Police Polygrapher, of the Portland Police Department. The State agreed to the same.

4. On April 2, 2015, Defendant submitted himself to a polygraph examination administered by Detective Police Polygrapher. Defendant indicated that he did not engage in the charged conduct. The polygraph results were that the Defendant was truthful.

5. Once again, the Undersigned asked the District Attorney's Office to dismiss the case against the Defendant. They refused. Undersigned filed a Motion to Amend Bail which was granted. Defendant is currently on a Maine Pretrial contract. The State continues to refuse to dismiss this matter and the Defendant will try this case yet again.

6. Counsel brings this Motion to request a testimonial hearing related to the admission of the polygraph results described above. Thereafter, the Undersigned hopes the Court will grant this Motion and allow the admission of the polygraph results at trial.

MEMORANDUM OF LAW

I. FACTUAL AND PROCEDURAL BACKGROUND

Defendant's daughter accused him of sexual abuse, covering a time period in which she was approximately five to eight years old. She alleged a history of vaginal penetration. She was examined by Spurwink. There was no history of prior penetrating trauma found. The examination was not completed until the alleged victim was approximately 16 years old.

The Defendant denied to the police and to anyone who would listen that he was guilty of this offense. In his first trial, there was a mistrial. In his second trial, he was convicted. The Law Court reversed the conviction. *State v. L.*, (cite).

Since the remand from the Law Court, the Defendant has taken two polygraph examinations and passed them both *Affidavit of Mister Polygrapher*, attached as *Exhibit 1*, The first examination, administered by Mister Polygrapher, produced a result of a +3 score. *Exhibit 1* at 17. The probability of Defendant being deceptive using the Empirical Scoring System is a chance of less than 7 in 100. *Id.* at 18. Using an algorithm in the Objective Scoring System, Version 3, the likelihood of Defendant being deceptive was 1.9%. *Id.* at 19.

On April 2, 2015, Detective Police Polygrapher of the Portland Police Department tested the Defendant. *Id.* at 19. The District Attorney's Office approved of this testing and attended a portion of the testing. Detective Police Polygrapher scored Defendant's score as +12. *Id.* at 32. The likelihood that Defendant is being deceptive is a chance of four out of 1,000. *Id.* at 33.

Mr. L.'s truthful answers to both polygraphs included outright denials of claims that he sexually abused his daughter. *Id.* at 16; 31. Considering all the data, there is a less than 2% chance that the Defendant is not being truthful when he denies sexually abusing his daughter. *Id.* at 34.

II. STANDARDS FOR THE ADMISSION OF EXPERT TESTIMONY IN MAINE DO NOT REQUIRE GENERAL ACCEPTANCE IN THE SCIENTIFIC COMMUNITY, BUT RATHER REQUIRE MERELY AN INDICIA OF RELIABILITY

Maine's standard for the admission of expert testimony is more relaxed than the *Daubert* or *Frye* standard from other jurisdictions. The standard in Maine is explained in *State v. Williams*, 388 A.2d 500 (Me., 1978) in which the Law Court held:

The controlling criteria regarding the admissibility of expert testimony, so long as the proffered expert is qualified and probative value is not substantially outweighed by the factors mentioned in Rule 403, are whether in the sound judgment of the presiding Justice the testimony to be given is relevant and will assist the trier of fact to understand the evidence or to determine a fact in issue.

Id. at 504.

The *Williams* Court went on to explain:

'General scientific acceptance' is a proper condition for taking judicial notice of scientific acts, but not a criterion for the admissibility of scientific evidence. Any relevant conclusions which are supported by a qualified expert witness should be received unless there are other reasons for exclusion. Particularly, probative value may be overborne by the familiar dangers of prejudicing or misleading the jury, and undue consumption of time.

Id. at 503.

Williams remains good law in Maine. In 2009, the Law Court explained;

The genesis of the test for determining whether expert testimony is admissible was our decision in *State v. Williams,* 388 A.2d 500 (Me.1978). We held that the "proponent of expert testimony must establish that (1) the testimony is relevant pursuant to M.R. Evid. 401, and (2) it will assist the trier of fact in understanding the evidence or determining a fact in issue." Before engaging in this two-prong inquiry, the trial court must make a preliminary finding that the testimony meets a threshold level of reliability. "[W]here expert testimony rests on newly ascertained, or applied, scientific principles, a trial court may consider whether the scientific matters involved in the proffered testimony have been generally accepted or conform to a generally accepted explanatory theory in determining whether the threshold level of reliability has been met." Nevertheless, a finding of general acceptance is not required. *Id.*

State v. Bickart, 963 A.2d 183 (Me. 2009) *citations omitted.*

Bickart involved the admission of palm print data in a sexual assault trial. The evidence there was novel, and had not gained the status of general scientific acceptance. Applying *Williams,* the Law Court allowed the admission of the palm print testimony, explaining:

Instead, the question is whether the court is satisfied "that the proffered evidence is sufficiently reliable to be held relevant." ...the factors that may be considered to make this threshold determination include:

(1) whether any studies tendered in support of the testimony are based on facts similar to those at issue; (2) whether the hypothesis of the testimony has been subject to peer review; (3) whether an expert's conclusion has been tailored to the facts of the case; (4) whether any other experts attest to the reliability of the testimony; (5) the nature of the expert's qualifications; and (6), if a causal relationship is asserted, whether there is a scientific basis for determining that such a relationship exists.

Id. at 187-188.

III. THE ADMISSION OF POLYGRAPH EVIDENCE IS APPROPRIATE FOR THE LIMITED PURPOSE OF CORROBORATING THE DEFENDANT'S TESTIMONY.

The Law Court has traditionally not permitted evidence of polygraph testing into evidence. In *State v. Mower*, the Court had concerns about the scientific development of the polygraph. 314 A. 2d 840 (Me. 1974). In *State v. Jones*, the Law Court did not permit defense counsel to argue that defendant's willingness to take a lie detector test indicated innocence of the crime. 580 A. 2d 161 (Me. 1990). However, in a more recent decision, the Court did allow the State to use Defendant's statements during, before and after a polygraph examination. *State v. Lavoie,* 1 A. 3d 408, 2010 ME 76 (Me. 2010). The Law Court has indicated that polygraph tests are valuable tools in the investigation of crime, for example, in developing leads. *State v. Mower*, 314 A.2d 840, 841 (Me. 1974) *emphasis omitted.*

In Federal Courts, where the *Daubert* decision governs expert witness admissibility, the judge acts as a gatekeeper in admitting or excluding polygraph results. If the *Daubert* standard is met (which is a harder standard for admission than *State v. Williams,* discussed above), the polygraph evidence may be admitted.

The United States District Court Middle District of Florida recently ordered a polygraph examination admissible at trial. *Exhibit 2, United States of America v. Jesus Hernando Angulo Mosquera* order. The Court there found that the polygraph evidence satisfied the three prongs for expert testimony under Federal Rule Evidence 702. The purposes of the Order there are effectively the purposes for which the Defendant seeks polygraph admission here: as corroborative of testimony by Defendant, should he choose to testify at trial.

Defendant has consistently and repeatedly denied sexually touching his daughter. He denied the same in both polygraph exams. The evidence that Defendant took two polygraph exams where he denied sexually touching his daughter should be admitted to corroborate his prior statements and expected testimony.

The fact that he passed the polygraph examinations should be equally admissible. Undoubtedly, the error rates of polygraph examinations are fair game on cross-examination. The arguments related to the error rates go to the weight of the evidence, not its admissibility.

The error rates of the polygraph examination are in the 10 percent range generally (a 90 percent rate of accuracy). This Court allows testimony on a variety of topics at such a rate of error. Field sobriety tests in Operating Under the Influence cases come to mind. There, the error rates of field sobriety tests compared to measured blood alcohol are in the range of 90 percent accuracy.[1]

In virtually every drunk driving case in this court, those field sobriety tests are admitted without question. It is up to defense counsel to cross-examine the police officer related to those tests and their error rates. Here, it is no different.

Finally, to the extent that this Court has concerns that this evidence will go to the ultimate issue, that fear can be ameliorated with a jury instruction. This Court can simply issue an instruction that the jury is not permitted to consider the polygraph as usurping their role as the finder of fact, but rather that the evidence is corroborative of the Defendant's previous statements.

WHEREFORE, Defendant requests that this Court:
1. Hold a testimonial hearing pursuant to M.R.Evid. 104 to hear evidence to decide whether the above mentioned evidence is admissible and to make a record of the same for the purpose of appellate review if needed;
2. Grant this Motion *in Limine*.

Dated this _____ day of August, 2015, at Portland, Maine.

Respectfully submitted,

_____

Timothy E. Zerillo
Attorney for Defendant
ZERILLO LAW FIRM, LLC

§12:21   Interviewing Child Victims

A ripe area for attack is often found in the child forensic interview. I don't know if I have ever seen an interview done entirely correctly.

The gold standard for an appropriate and effective forensic interview is the National Institute for Child Health and Human Development (NICHD) Protocol. This Protocol, if properly employed, which it never seems to be, is designed to elicit an accurate and comprehensive child interview.

The reason for the development of the NICHD Protocol is the constant slew of horrible child interviews that are routinely administered. However, the fact that the authorities routinely screw this up provides an opportunity for you to attack.

As a starting point, find the paper by Lamb, et al. called "Structured Forensic Interview Protocols Improve the Quality and Informativeness of Interviews with Children: A Review of Research Using the NICHD Investigative Interview Protocol," *Child Abuse and Neglect*, 2007; 31(11-12): 1201-1231. Therein, some of the author's of the NICHD Protocol express their shock and dismay in explaining that, despite police training, investigators still do their interviews incorrectly. The NICHD protocol is itself explained in the paper and is attached to it. This presents a great starting point for evaluating the forensic interview in your case.

[§§12:22-12:29 Reserved]

---

[1]   Statistical Evaluation of Standardized Field Sobriety Tests, *J Forensic Sci,* May 2005, Vol. 50, No. 3. ("The data show that the officer's accuracy in estimating whether a person's BAC is over or under 0.08% depends on the MBAC (measured blood alcohol). If MBAC is lower than 0.04, the officer is generally 80% or more accurate at predicting a subject's category (above or below 0.08% MBAC) in the sample studied. If the MBAC is greater than 0.09%, then the officer is about 90% or more accurate at predicting the subject's category. However, if the MBAC is around 0.08%, specifically, between 0.06 and 0.08, the SFSTs are only about 30–60% accurate in correctly predicting whether a subject's MBAC is ≥0.08% or <0.08%.")

III.   STRATEGIES AND TACTICS

§ 12:30   Using Restraining Orders and Family Matters to Your Advantage

I have touted the benefits of using restraining orders to your advantage elsewhere in this book, and I will not repeat them here. See Ch. 3. That said, many alleged victims continue to make the mistake of bringing restraining orders in their cases. I got a call from a woman in a long custody dispute. She had charges pending for sexual assault and wanted me to unravel a child custody case that had not gone her way. Her ex-husband claimed she molested one of her sons and sought a restraining order barring her from seeing him. The woman was represented by a different attorney at the restraining order hearing. Her lawyer worked out a deal where they dropped the restraining order and they entered a family matter order giving the ex-husband custody. This lawyer probably thought she was doing a great job. After the custody order was entered, my client was charged with the sexual assault.

To my mind she has just made my case more difficult. I tell my clients to prioritize, and here the priority of jail and a criminal record is much bigger than having a restraining order issued against you. Instead, I tell people that we need to bring in everyone and have a real three ring circus in the restraining order hearing. I need to get the alleged victim on the stand. I need the cop on the stand. I need dad on the stand. Let's put them all under oath and have the judge tearing his hair out.

And in the end we will probably lose on the restraining order. But we will have testimony. And, with sex abuse charges pending, that is more valuable than just about anything.

§ 12:31   The Child of Divorce and Separation

At least anecdotally I can tell you that it is very common to see sex abuse claims in the case of parental separation and custody battles. Consider parental alienation syndrome and whether the child is being used as a lever in a custody battle. Even if you don't have anything that extreme, just consider if the child is attention-seeking as a result of a recent separation. There are a great many scenarios to explore. Perhaps the child is angry at your client because your client doesn't see the child as often. Maybe your client seems different now. Perhaps the child feels pressure to choose sides in a divorce. Or it could be that the child doesn't like a new boyfriend, girlfriend or sibling that is now around. There is a lot to consider.

§ 12:32   Competence of Child Victim and Taint Hearings

If the alleged victim is a young child, you may need to bring a child competence motion to prevent the child from testifying. Obviously, the child's ability to tell the truth is always an issue. Even if you have a borderline child competence case, the motion should be brought. Even if the child is not disqualified, you will have the benefit of getting testimony from the child.

Taint hearings may also be needed to determine influence on the child's testimony, if they are allowed in your jurisdiction. This motion is designed to determine the "taint" on the child's testimony and to restrict the testimonial taint that may come from the influence of parents, investigators, or others.

§ 12:33   FORM 12-30 Motion for Hearing on Competency of Child Witness

STATE OF MAINE   _____COURT

_____, ss.   DOCKET NO.: _____

_____   )
)
Plaintiff   )
)   MOTION FOR HEARING
v.   )   ON COMPETENCY
)   OF _____
_____   )
)
Defendant   )

NOW COMES the Defendant, by and through Undersigned Counsel, _____, and moves this Honorable Court to hold a hearing to determine the competency of _____ to testify at trial in the above-captioned matter. In support hereof, the Defendant further states:

1. On _____, 20__, Defendant was indicted on one count of Gross Sexual Assault (Class A) with one count of Unlawful Sexual Contact (Class B).
2. The State's case relies on the testimony of a ___-year-old child: _____, born _____.
3. The Indictment alleges that the alleged criminal acts occurred on or about _____. The minor child would have just turned _____ years old at that time.
4. Approximately two years later, the Child's Mother, _____, alleges her daughter described sexual acts with the Defendant.[2]
5. Twenty-four (24) days after _____ made the allegations to Law Enforcement, the child was interviewed by the State's Expert, _____, regarding the alleged sexual abuse. The police never performed their own forensic interview with the child.
6. Counsel has serious concerns with the child's competency in this case. In particular, as argued in Defendant's Motion for a Taint Hearing, Counsel has serious concerns that the child lacks any reasonable ability to perceive the matter as a result of the child's manipulation and suggestive investigative techniques employed in this case.
7. Though Defendant's Motion for a Taint Hearing focuses on Rule 602 of the Maine Rules of Evidence, many of the facts described in that Motion are applicable in determining whether the child witness is competent to testify. Some of the facts that should be considered in determining the competency of the child include, but not limited to:
    a. Interviewer bias (includes child's Mother and Father);
    b. Repeated interrogations by child's mother;
    c. Lack of control by outside influences;
    d. Failure to test child's resistance to suggestion; and
    e. Failure to probe outlandish statement.
8. A child witness cannot be competent to testify if the child's memories have been tainted to reflect an alternative reality. The discovery in this case suggests the child's memories have been tainted.
9. Counsel respectfully requests a pre-trial hearing be granted to determine whether the child is competent to testify at trial pursuant to M.R. Evid. 601(b).

MEMORANDUM OF LAW

A child witness's susceptibility to manipulation, cues and fantasy are a serious concern in sexual abuse cases. Rule 601(b) and Rule 602 of the Maine Rules of Evidence provide some protection to the Defense in assuring the child witness is competent to testify and testifies to their personal knowledge of events. Counsel won't reiterate his argument for a pre-trial hearing on taint pursuant to Rule 602 here, but incorporates it into this Motion.

Rule 601(b) of the Maine Rules of Evidence provides in pertinent part:

A person is disqualified to be a witness if the court finds that (1) the proposed witness is incapable of communicating concerning the matter so as to be understood by the judge and jury either directly or through interpretation by one who can understand the proposed witness, (2) the proposed witness is incapable of understanding the duty of a witness to tell the truth, (3) the proposed witness lacked any reasonable ability to perceive the matter or (4) the proposed witness lacks any reasonable ability to remember the matter.

M.R. Evid. 601(b). The Maine Supreme Judicial Court, sitting as the Law Court, has held that "a child of any age is competent to be a witness unless disqualified under Rule 601(b)." *State v. Hussey*, 521 A.2d 278, 280 (Me. 1987). A child must have "sufficient capacity to understand, in some measure, the obligation of an oath." *Id.* (citation omitted). The requirement that a child witness understand the duty to tell the truth may be satisfied if the child manifests an understanding that it is wrong to falsify and that he or she may be punished for not telling the truth. *Id.* (citation omitted).

---

[2] Based on information and belief, Counsel believes the Department of Health and Human Services spoke with the child in _____. At that time, the child denied any sexual abuse by the Defendant. Counsel has submitted a Motion for Access to DHHS with this Motion to confirm the same.

A trial court may rule on witness competency by holding a pretrial hearing or by listening to and evaluating a witness's trial testimony. See *State v. Roman*, 622 A.2d 96, 100 (Me. 1993).

In the present case, Counsel has serious concerns that the child's memory has been manipulated due his/her parent's coercive investigative techniques, bias, and poor interrogation techniques by the State's expert. Counsel has serious concerns that the Defendant cannot obtain a fair trial without examining these concerns at a pre-trial hearing.

As the Honorable Kermit V. Lipez pointed out "this phenomenon of memory falsification, whether it be the result of poor investigative techniques or fantasy, creates the danger that child's testimony will be unreliable because that testimony no longer reflects the personal knowledge of the child. If that is the case, traditional cross-examination in the presence of a jury may be ineffective at exposing the unreliability." V. Kermit Lipez, *The Child Witness in Sexual Abuse Cases in Maine: Presentation, Impeachment, and Controversy*, 42 Maine L. Rev. 284, 347. If the child's testimony is unreliable because the testimony no longer reflects the child's personal knowledge, logically, the child lacks any reasonable ability to perceive the matter and lacks any reasonable ability to remember the matter.

WHEREFORE, the Defendant moves this Honorable Court to hold a hearing as soon as possible to determine the competency of _____ to testify at trial in the above-captioned matter. Should the Court require additional information before ruling on this Motion, Counsel requests a hearing on this Motion.

Dated at Portland, Maine, this _____th day of _____, 20____.

Respectfully submitted,

_____

Timothy E. Zerillo
Attorney for Defendant
ZERILLO LAW FIRM, LLC

§12:34   FORM 12-40 Motion to Conduct a Taint Hearing

STATE OF MAINE   _____COURT

_____, ss.   DOCKET NO.: _____

_____	)	
	)	
Plaintiff	)	
	)	MOTION TO CONDUCT
v.	)	A TAINT HEARING
	)	
_____	)	
	)	
Defendant	)	

NOW COMES the Defendant, _____, by and through Undersigned Counsel _____, Esq., who respectfully makes this motion to conduct a *taint* hearing.

1. Defendant _____ ("Defendant") seeks to conduct a Taint hearing of and concerning the State's proposed witness, _____.
2. This hearing is needed to ascertain whether the proposed witness is competent by Rule 602 of the Maine Rules of Evidence, to testify from personal knowledge.[3]
3. Proposed witness _____ (hereafter, "child") was interviewed by her Mother, State's Expert Witness, _____, and has also been treating with and evaluated by other possible expert witnesses. There is reasonable concern that the child's memory of events has been tainted by the interviews and/or treatment such that the child is not competent to testify pursuant to M.R. Evid. 602.
4. These reasonable concerns come from Counsel's review of the discovery that has been provided to Counsel and Counsel's investigation of this case.

---

[3] Maine Rules of Evidence 602 states "[a] witness may not testify to a matter unless evidence is introduced sufficient to support a finding that the witness has personal knowledge of the matter. Evidence to prove personal knowledge may, but need not, consist of the testimony."

5. First, based on information and belief, Counsel believes that at the Department of Health and Human Services in 2011 (hereafter, "DHHS"), the child denied any sexual abuse by the Defendant. Counsel has filed a Motion for Access to DHHS records with this Motion to confirm the same.

6. This motion is made pursuant to Maine Rules of Evidence 104, 401, 403, 602 and 703, on the grounds that should the Court determine that the child has been tainted by the process of treatment such that the child is not likely to testify from personal knowledge, any testimony proffered by this witness will be irrelevant, a waste valuable court time and unduly prejudicial. In *State v. Pinkham*, the Law Court stated "a child's ability to perceive, remember and communicate an accurate account of events may be weighed by a presiding justice in deciding whether the probative value of the testimony is substantially outweighed by the danger of unfair prejudice, confusion of the issues or misleading the jury or by considerations of undue delay, waste of time or needless presentation of cumulative evidence. 411 A.2d 1021, 1023 (Me. 1980). These factors are embraced in Rule 403 of the Maine Rules of Evidence. The Honorable Kermit V. Lipez has noted that: "the qualification indicates discomfort with the narrow competency standard set forth in Rule 601 and retention indirectly of the broader competency standard set forth in the case law prior to the adoption of Rule 601." *The Child Witness in Sexual Abuse Cases in Maine: Presentation, Impeachment, and Controversy*, 42 Maine L. Rev. 284, 352. A taint hearing would eliminate the narrow discomfort that the Honorable Kermit V. Lipez describes.

7. This is not a motion for Competency pursuant to Rule 601 of the Maine Rules of Evidence. Counsel has filed a separate motion regarding Rule 601 along with this Motion. However, many of the issues outlined in this Motion may align with Rule 601 as well. See Kermit V. Lipez, *The Child Witness in Sexual Abuse Cases in Maine: Presentation, Impeachment, and Controversy*, 42 Maine L. Rev. 284, 343-252.

8. Like confessions and identification, the inculpatory capacity of statements indicating the occurrence of injury and anticipated testimony about these occurrences requires that special care be taken to ensure their reliability. An understanding of whether the questioning, interviews, interrogation or counseling of the child witnesses was unduly suggestive requires a highly nuanced inquiry into the totality of the circumstances surrounding verbal interactions between the child and adults. *See New Jersey v. Margaret Kelly Michaels*, 642 A2d 1372, 1377 (1994).

9. Defendant asks this court to determine from this hearing that the child witnesses' statements were founded upon "unreliable perceptions, or memory caused by improper investigative procedures," and any proffered testimony reflecting those accusations would lead to an unfair trial.

10. A pre-trial taint hearing is required to assess the competency of the child witnesses to make statements reliably based upon personal knowledge

11. This must be accomplished before any hearing into whether the child witnesses' statements were developed with sufficient indicia of trustworthiness to be admitted in this matter. .

WHEREFORE, Defendant respectfully requests that this honorable Court conduct a Taint Hearing to determine whether the proffered child witness is reasonably capable of testifying from personal knowledge. Should the Court require additional information before ruling on this Motion, Counsel requests a hearing on this Motion.

Dated at Portland, Maine, this _____th day of _____, 20__.

Respectfully submitted,

_____

Timothy E. Zerillo
Attorney for Defendant
ZERILLO LAW FIRM, LLC

§12:35   Alibi and Opportunity/Access to Child

Sometimes we get so tied up in the fact that a child is making an allegation that we forget the small stuff. If you have solid dates on which the sexual assault occurred, try to come up with an alibi.

If the child was home with dad that day, were other people around? When did they take vacations? When was your client gone for work? You may be able to develop a timeline that creates reasonable doubt.

§12:36   Child Is Inconsistent

This is the most common way to attack these cases. Rare are the situations in which you will pound the table and call the child a liar during cross. There is usually too much sympathy for the child to get away with that. Instead, make up ground by tracking the child's inconsistencies as you review discovery. Later in this chapter, we will use this strategy in our case example. See §§12:90, 12:130-12:133, 12:160, 12:161.

§12:37   Child's Timeline Makes No Sense

In evaluating the child's consistency, make a timeline of the child's version of events. Often this will lead to more inconsistencies. Pile these inconsistencies on top of each other and map them for the jury. See §12:160.

§12:38   Child's Failure to Tell Anyone about Assault

Remember also to use the strategy of failing to inform others of abuse if some time went by between the alleged abuse and the report. This tactic is less persuasive to juries than it used to be in my view, because it is well accepted that victims of sexual abuse often keep it a secret. But you should not ignore this line. It is not just a failure to promptly inform relatives by the way. Perhaps the child has a good relationship with a teacher, a daycare provider or a coach. You may point out that the child would have confided in one of them had something actually occurred.

§12:39   Character Evidence that the Defendant Is a Good Parent

When you have a parent or step-parent defendant, consider using character evidence to help rebut the charges. A defendant in a criminal prosecution may offer evidence that he or she has a pertinent character trait, and if the evidence is admitted, the prosecutor may offer evidence to rebut it. See Fed. R. Evid. 404(a)(2)(a).

A character trait is pertinent "if the existence or non-existence of the trait would be involved in the commission or non-commission of a particular crime charged . . . or [it would affect] the likelihood that the accused would engage in such contact." *State of Maine v. Naylor*, 602 A.2d 187, 189 (Me. 1992). There, the character trait of being a good father was found to be a pertinent trait of character to the charge of sexual abuse of a daughter. *Id.* at 189. *Naylor* states that "sexually abusing one's child is so alien to the inclination of a loving and responsible parent that an excellent father would be less likely to commit such a traumatic crime." *Id* at 189. There may be similar cases in your jurisdiction, or you can use *Naylor* as persuasive authority to try this tactic where you practice.

[§§12:40-12:49 Reserved]

IV.   INVESTIGATION AND DISCOVERY

A.   Witnesses and Potential Witnesses to Interview

§12:50   Government Experts

Interview government experts before trial if the prosecution will allow you to do so. The point is to find out their opinions and then research real science to contradict them at trial. Some experts will get into extended discussion with you. If so, document these discussions as best you can. You want to nail down the expert's opinion before trial if possible. Please also make sure to request a written report of your expert if one is not already provided. You can then study that report and be prepared to launch an attack on any junk science misstatements.

§12:51   FORM 12-50 Sample Letter to Government Expert

I like to send the government expert a letter along with the studies I will cite at trial.

First, if the expert agrees they are authoritative, I can read sections of them at trial without evidentiary concerns. Further, if the expert does not agree they are authoritative, I can prepare to hammer the expert as not considering the science in his or her opinion.

Dr. Lawrence Howard
The Child Abuse Program
Portland, ME 04103

    Re: *State of Maine v. Bob*

Dear Dr. Howard,

    Enclosed please find the following publications regarding sexual abuse examinations of children:

1. Lahoti, "Evaluating the Child for Sexual Abuse," *American Family Physician*, March 1, 2001.
2. Adams, "Guidelines for Medical Care of Children Who May Have Been Sexually Abused," *Journal Pediatric and Adolescent Gynecology*, 2007.
3. Heger, "Appearance of the Genitalia in Girls Selected for Nonabuse: Review of Hymenal Morphology and Nonspecific Findings," *Journal of Pediatric and Adolescent Gynecology*, February 2002.
4. Myhre, "A Longitudinal Study of the Anogenital Development in Girls from 6-12 Years of Age," *Journal of Pediatric and Adolescent Gynecology*, April 2008.
5. Slaughter, "Patterns of Genital Injury in Female Sexual Assault Victims," *American Journal of Obstetrics and Gynecology*, March 1997.
6. Reece, Lea & Febiger, *Child Abuse: Medical Diagnosis and Management*, 1994.

    It is my intention to discuss these with you during your examination in the above-captioned case. Please contact me immediately if you do not find any of these materials to be a reliable authority under M.R.Evid. 803(18).

    Kindly also send me a copy of your CV and any publications you have authored at your earliest convenience.

                                 Respectfully submitted,

                                 _____

                                 Timothy E. Zerillo
                                 Attorney for Defendant
                                 ZERILLO LAW FIRM, LLC

§12:52   Speak to the Child to Uncover Inconsistencies

    Whenever possible, talk to the child victim. It certainly is not always possible, but if you can do it (with a recording device rolling), or if your investigator can talk to the child, it will likely be worth it.

    How you approach the child victim largely depends on her age. I would not approach a child younger than high school age without a custodian's consent. With older, high school aged children, I might send my investigator to their school campus or their after-work job.

    The idea, of course, is just to get their mouths moving. If you get them talking, they will likely produce inconsistent statements. And if they don't, that is also valuable information because you might have confirmed that your case is junk. Either way, what you need is insight.

§12:53   Speak to the Child's Parents to Explore Settlement Options

    Maybe you can't get to the child without going through the parents first. There are plenty of reasons to talk to the parents anyway. Just don't expect them to be pleasant.

    You may want to talk to these parents just to find out if there is a way to resolve this outside of criminal court. Long restraining orders and a civil judgment may be in order. This is sensitive, I know, and you can't have your negotiations smack of a payoff of some kind. Throwing a bag of money on the table at the start of a meeting will offend most people.

    On the other hand, if your client is of reasonable means, and such a discussion can be sensitively interjected, it is worth trying. By the way, I am not even discussing a millionaire client here. Anyone with a house to mortgage or a 401(k) to tap may favor a settlement to jail.

    Further, it may be favorable to the victim and her family. Many want the court to bury your client under the jail, but many others just want accountability. Financially devastating the client may be accountability to some people.

This is why you shouldn't limit your thought process on this to millionaires. If you have a client with modest assets, a settlement can be more attractive to the victim's family, because they are punishing the perpetrator. In one case I was able to resolve, I brought in a bankruptcy lawyer to analyze my client's financial situation and then break it down for a victim's family and their lawyer. It became clear that he would offer nearly everything he had, and they accepted that.

If the family is without a lawyer, this strategy can be even more alluring. The pitch can be made that it makes no sense to give a lawyer one-third, especially when you are voluntarily disclosing all assets to them.

Remember, this civil resolution may very well not bind the government in your jurisdiction. In Maine, we can do an accord and satisfaction as to misdemeanors, but not felonies. You need to find a way to secure your client with more than a civil release. How to do this is a very state-specific inquiry.

Obviously, even if a civil suit is not an option, you or your investigator will do well to convince the parents to give you access to the child. As I mentioned previously, it is important to interview that child victim.

One investigator I use is very good at this. She approaches the parents and effectively says that the interview is their opportunity to keep the case out of court. If I know from the child's mouth that he or she is a strong witness, then perhaps it makes me plead my guy out. Some parents respond to this sales pitch.

Of course, many families will tell you to bug off and call the police. We respect those wishes, but I must say I like to warn them a bit if they aren't responding. I don't threaten anyone. I don't pound the table or point my finger. I just want to let them know a little bit of what they are in for.

I might say, "Before I go, I just want to mention that I am here because I hope we don't have to try this case. I truly hope we don't. There is this thing in the Constitution called the Confrontation Clause. And it means I get to fully cross-examine Tammy in open court. And it means that you don't get to be up there with her. The prosecutor can't stop me and neither can the judge. It is one of my least favorite things to do. But if there is no other alternative, I'll have to. But if you can think of another way to solve this, please let me know."

Always leave them with the idea that they can come back to you.

§12:54   Speak to the Child's Friends, Daycare Providers, Teachers, Coaches

Sometimes we miss the most obvious people to talk to. We can fall into the trap of assuming that everyone in the child's life will automatically believe the child. That simply isn't true. You will hit a brick wall most of the time, but do your due diligence. Speak to the child's friends, coaches, daycare providers, teachers, etc…All it takes is one friendly witness to break a case.

[§§12:55-12:59 Reserved]

B. Documents/Evidence to Gather

§12:60   Divorce, Paternity and Restraining Order Pleadings and Judgments

Make sure to gather all judgments and pleadings between mom and dad in other cases. What people write in complaints and motions is amazing. You may be able to, just through pleadings in other cases, establish the animosity between mom and dad.

§12:61   Photos, Videos, Cards, and Drawings

Another obvious area often missed is photographic and video evidence. I always ask my clients to gather all videos and all photos from the time of the alleged abuse. This evidence can be gold. If you have a picture of the daughter hugging dad from the same weekend she was allegedly sexually assaulted and withdrawn, you may have a dichotomy the jury has trouble reconciling.

Cards and pictures drawn by the alleged victim to your client can again create an inconsistency that the jury will struggle with. I will often simply introduce them through the child in cross. If the child drew a picture of her and her dad building a snowman and having fun during the same period of time as the abuse, admit it through the child.

§12:62 School Records

They prove nothing, but obtaining school records of a child who is academically achieving won't hurt your case in the least. Again, you need to paint a picture that the jury will not understand. If the child gets straight A's in school, point it out to them. How can the child, who is getting straight A's, is an All-Star soccer player, and has healthy relationships in all other respects have been abused by her father? See §12:63 Form 12-16 Motion for Discovery of Child's School Records.

§12:63 FORM 12-60 Motion for Discovery of Child's School Records

STATE OF MAINE _____ COURT
_____, ss. DOCKET NO.: _____

_____)
)
Plaintiff)   DEFENDANT'S SECOND MOTION
)   *IN LIMINE* FOR PRIVILEGED
)   OR PROTECTED INFORMATION
v.)   MR.U. Crim.P. 17(d) WITH
)   MEMORANDUM OF LAW
_____)
)
Defendant)

NOW COMES the Defendant, _____, by and through his attorney, _____, and in accordance with Rule 17(d) the Maine Rules of Unified Criminal Procedure, hereby requests the following:
1. Defendant has been tried twice on charges of Gross Sexual Assault. The Defendant's first trial resulted in a mistrial. His second trial resulted in a conviction, then a reversal and remand from the Law Court.
2. The alleged victim is Defendant's daughter.
3. The Defendant seeks, through a subpoena, copies of the alleged victim's school records.

MEMORANDUM OF LAW

I. THE PRELIMINARY RULE 17(D) RUBRIC

In general, the discovery of confidential records, if material, is required. *Cf. State v. Greene*, 512 A.2d 330, 332 (Me. 1986). The court should not quash "…the production of documentary evidence on the ground that those materials may not be admissible at trial." *Id.*, citing *State v. Willoughby*, 507 A.2d 1060, 1067 n.6 (Me. 1986) (discussing M.R.Crim.P. 17(d)).

The Maine Rules of Unified Criminal Procedure provide the mechanism for the disclosure of the records sought here. There, if the party seeking the subpoena knows that the records may be privileged or confidential, the movant files a Motion *in Limine*. The Motion *in Limine* must contain:

> …a statement setting forth (1) the particular documents sought by the subpoena with a reasonable degree of specificity of the information contained therein; (2) the efforts made by the moving party in procuring the information contained in the requested documents by other means; (3) that the moving party cannot properly prepare for trial without such production of the documents; and (4) that the requested information is likely to be admissible at trial. The motion *in limine* shall be accompanied by a copy of the yet unserved subpoena.

M.R.U. Crim. P. 17(d).

A.   The Information Sought

Here, the Defendant seeks all school records from the alleged victim's school attendance at the _____ School in _____, _____ Middle School in _____ and _____ High School in _____.

B.   Other Means

Absent a court order compelling them, the records are confidential and will not be released. There are no other means of obtaining the records sought.

C.   Counsel Cannot Adequately Prepare for Trial Without the Records

Last week, Counsel was given access to funds by MCILS to consult with experts. After consulting with experts yesterday, September 1, it is clear that the records sought are needed for continuing consultation with experts and discussions of trial strategy. Likewise, the evidence sought may provide statements regarding the offense as well as admissible reputation evidence.

It is the Defendant's contention that the alleged victim made false allegations of sexual contact by the Defendant. It is necessary to review the alleged victim's student records to establish her level of functioning in the school environment, which directly relates to her claims and her credibility. Moreover, a lack of reporting by the alleged victim would be relevant. Also, the school records may show behavior that is contraindicative of someone who is a victim of intra-family molestation.

D.   The Records Are Likely To Be Admissible At Trial

It is extremely likely that the records on their own, or aspects of the records, will be admissible at trial. By all indications, this is a child who did well in school. Counsel imagines that the child's records will support a highly-functioning child during the time period of the alleged abuse. These records may be admissible as a basis for an expert's opinion, or may just be used in cross-examination.

In addition, reputation evidence may be present in the records which may also be admissible. Further, a lack of reporting of abuse may be admissible. Finally, the alleged victim's record in the school environment may relate to her credibility.

II. THE STEPS AFTER THE MINIMUM THRESHOLD IS MET

The four steps described above are sufficient to meet the "minimum threshold" of information needed to proceed. M.R.U. Crim.P. 17(d). That threshold having been met, this Court should next direct the clerk to set the matter for hearing. *Id.* The hearing notice must:

> ...state the date and time of the hearing and direct the subpoenaed individual or entity from whom the documentary evidence is sought to submit the documentary evidence subject to the subpoena for in camera review by the court or to adequately explain in writing any reasons for a failure to submit the documentary evidence for in camera review.

Id.

Once the notice is issued, the Undersigned will serve the subpoena, the motion, and the notice on the keeper of records for _____ High School[4]. Enclosed please find subpoena to _____ High School which has not been served.

Dated this ___ day of _____, 20___, at Portland, Maine.

Respectfully submitted,

_____

Timothy E. Zerillo
Attorney for Defendant
ZERILLO LAW FIRM, LLC

---

[4]   Counsel's office has been informed that the records follow the student when they leave a school district. The _____ School Districts have informed us that the alleged victim's records from the _____ School and _____ Middle School will be contained in the _____ High School records.

§ 12:64   Social Networking Sites

I won't belabor this point of social networking research because it has been discussed at length in Ch. 11. Suffice it to say, kids are on social networking sites as much or more than adults, so scour the internet for their online interactions.

§ 12:65   Seize the Child's Computer and Phone and Have Them Analyzed

If your client has access to the child's computer or phone, have it analyzed by an expert. As you know, virtually nothing you ever do on a computer is erased. As a result, the child's interactions online can be mapped from that computer or phone, and may give you greater insight into what is really going on.

Obviously, you don't want your client stealing the child's phone or computer. However, if they are owned by the client, he or she should be able to have them analyzed. If you are not so lucky, you can try to get them through discovery. However, establishing your need for the items for more than a fishing expedition may be difficult depending on the facts of your case.

§ 12:66   Health and Human Services Records

Sometimes the local child protection agency has intervened in the lives of the family. Even if the intervention relates to a sibling of the alleged victim, you need to get the records. Human Services organizations must keep detailed notes of their investigations. If there is turmoil in the house where the alleged victim lived, you want to understand that turmoil.

Most states have confidentiality statutes that restrict your access to these records. That said, your state will also have a procedure to get the records by court order.

Your procedure may be more clearly defined than the one in Maine, or maybe it is not. What I do is add some language to my discovery motion, like this:

> Counsel likewise requests that this Court Order release all Department of Health and Human Services (hereafter "DHHS") records regarding the alleged victim, Jane Doe. On information and belief, Jane Doe has been the subject of a DHHS case. Counsel believes the prior DHHS case may have involved allegations related to alleged sexual assaults by persons other than the Defendant. This information is potentially exculpatory and is appropriate for production under *Brady*, supra, and *Kyles*, supra. Counsel has drafted an Order on Defendant's Motion to Produce DHHS Records that protects this sensitive information while still allowing the Defendant to review the material for exculpatory evidence.

Appended to your Motion should be an Order. See § 12:67 Form 12-70. The idea is to give the court the ability to protect confidential Health and Human Services Records, but provide you the discovery you deserve.

§ 12:67   FORM 12-70 Order on Defendant's Motion to Produce Department of Health and Human Services Records

STATE OF MAINE   SUPERIOR COURT
CUMBERLAND, ss.   DOCKET NO. CR-11-1234

STATE OF MAINE,	)	
	)	
	)	ORDER ON DEFENDANT'S
v.	)	MOTION TO PRODUCE
	)	DEPARTMENT OF HEALTH
JOHN DOE	)	AND HUMAN SERVICES RECORDS
	)	
Defendant	)	

This matter comes before the Court on Defendant's Motion to Produce Department of Health and Human Services (hereafter "Department") records relating to Jane Doe. The Court is mindful of the need to weigh the confidentiality of those records against the necessity for the Defendant to have access for preparation and trial of Defendant's case. With those issues in mind, the Court makes the following Order:

The Department shall deliver all records regarding Jane Doe to this Court within thirty (30) days. To assist the Court in its in camera review of the file, a Department representative may identify those portions of the records which the Department believes are not relevant to the proceeding or are of a particularly sensitive and confidential nature that they should not be released.

If the Department has not marked any documents for preliminary in camera inspection by the Court, the Defendant's attorney and the prosecuting attorney's office shall be permitted to review the entire file subject to all of the restrictions within this Order. If the Department has specifically identified particular documents for preliminary in camera review, the Defendant's attorney and the prosecuting attorney's office shall be permitted to review those portions of the file that the Court has not excluded based on its preliminary in camera review. The records are to remain in the Superior Court Clerk's Office in and of the County of Cumberland at all times. No duplicates or copies are to be made of any of the records and no information contained in those records is to be disclosed to the Defendant or any other party except by further Order of Court.

In the event that either the prosecuting attorney or defense counsel desires to receive copies of any of the records reviewed by them, to discuss the contents of the records with anyone, or to make use of the contents of the records for any purpose, he or she shall list the documents or information sought to be released and present request for release to the Court. The Court will then review the records and make a further order as to whether those records may be copied and released to the requesting party, or whether information in the records may be released to any party or any other person. These documents are subject to any motions *in limine* brought by the opposing party. A copy of the request for release shall be provided to counsel for the Department reasonably in advance of any hearing or conference on the request.

In the event that documents or information are provided to either party, both parties should be mindful that the records remain confidential and may be used only for the purposes of prosecuting or defending the present criminal action. Counsel shall take such steps as may be necessary to preserve the confidentiality of those records while they are in their office files, and shall not further disseminate the information without Court order.

Dated:_____   _____
                                                          Justice, Superior Court

§12:68   Medical Records

The child's medical records may also prove important depending on your facts. If the child has significant sexual trauma that the child's pediatrician never caught during the well-child visits, you may have a colorable case to breach medical privilege and get those records. See §12:69 Form 12-80 Motion for Discovery of Medical Records.

§12:69   FORM 12-80 Motion for Discovery of Medical Records

STATE OF MAINE   _____COURT
_____, ss.   DOCKET NO.: _____

_____   )
)
)   DEFENDANT'S MOTION
Plaintiff   )   *IN LIMINE* FOR PRIVILEGED
)   OR PROTECTED INFORMATION
v.   )   MR.U. Crim.P. 17(d) WITH
)   MEMORANDUM OF LAW
_____   )
)
Defendant   )

NOW COMES the Defendant, _____, by and through his attorney, _____, and in accordance with Rule 17(d) the Maine Rules of Unified Criminal Procedure, hereby requests the following:

1. Defendant has been tried twice on charges of Gross Sexual Assault. The Defendant's first trial resulted in a mistrial. His second trial resulted a conviction, then a reversal and remand from the Law Court.

2. The alleged victim is Defendant's daughter.
3. The Defendant seeks, through a subpoena, copies of all medical records from the alleged victim's pediatrician.
4. This critical evidence is relevant to the absence of physical evidence of abuse on examination, as testified to by _____ of _____. The examination by Nurse Practitioner _____ came 9 or 10 years after the alleged abuse. Ms. _____ is expected to testify that injuries from the alleged abuse could have healed by the time she conducted her examination of the alleged victim. As a result, records of medical examinations of the alleged victim during the time period of the reported abuse are essential. Additionally, reports made by the alleged victim in the records sought may be highly relevant to show behavior contraindicative of someone who is a victim of intra-family sexual abuse.

MEMORANDUM OF LAW

I. THE PRELIMINARY RULE 17(D) RUBRIC

In general, the discovery of medical records, if material, is required. *Cf. State v. Greene*, 512 A.2d 330, 332 (Me. 1986). The rules does not allow the court to quash "…the production of documentary evidence on the ground that those materials may not be admissible at trial." *Id.*, citing *State v. Willoughby*, 507 A.2d 1060, 1067 n.6 (Me. 1986) (discussing M.R.Crim.P. 17(d)).

The Maine Rules of Unified Criminal Procedure provide the mechanism for the disclosure of the records sought here. There, if the party seeking the subpoena knows that the records may be privileged or confidential, the movant files a Motion *in Limine*. The Motion *in Limine* must contain:

…a statement setting forth (1) the particular documents sought by the subpoena with a reasonable degree of specificity of the information contained therein; (2) the efforts made by the moving party in procuring the information contained in the requested documents by other means; (3) that the moving party cannot properly prepare for trial without such production of the documents; and (4) that the requested information is likely to be admissible at trial. The motion *in limine* shall be accompanied by a copy of the yet unserved subpoena.

M.R.U. Crim. P. 17(d).

A. The Information Sought

Here, the Defendant seeks information regarding the medical records of the alleged victim held by Dr. _____, _____ Pediatrics, _____ Drive, _____, ME 04__. Dr. _____ is a Pediatrician, who was the alleged victim's doctor when she was a child and during the time of the alleged abuse.

B. Other Means

Absent a court order compelling them, medical records are privileged. Here, the records sought are maintained by a medical provider and no other copies are known to the Undersigned. There are no other means of obtaining the records sought.

C. Counsel Cannot Adequately Prepare for Trial Without the Records

At the last trial in this matter, the State presented Nurse Practitioner _____ as a witness. She testified that she performed an exam on the alleged victim 9 or 10 years *after* the alleged abuse occurred. The alleged abuse included allegations of vaginal and anal penetration by Defendant.

_____ testified that there were no physical findings on examination 9 or 10 years after the alleged abuse. She also testified that injuries that could have been present in the past and healed over time.

Dr. _____ saw the alleged victim for physicals at least annually during the period of time in which the abuse occurred and thereafter. Her records are necessary to determine whether there were any unusual physical findings on examination, to determine whether the findings were normal during this period of time, to determine if there were complaints made by the alleged victim and to determine the scope of the medical examination.

D. The Records Are Likely To Be Admissible At Trial

The Nurse Practitioner will indicate that the absence of physical findings of sexual abuse does not rule out the fact that the abuse may have occurred. This is, of course, a common theme of the State's case where there are allegations of abuse, but no corroborative physical findings.

Here, Counsel understands that the alleged victim was examined nearly contemporaneously to the alleged abuse. It is impossible to imagine a situation where such evidence would not be admissible, especially given the expected testimony of _____.

Additionally, the records, if disclosed, will be shared with a defense pediatric expert. Those records will likely be relied upon in forming the opinions of that defense expert, which may be equally admissible at trial.

Finally, reports made by the alleged victim in the records sought may be highly relevant to show that her behavior is contrary someone who is a victim of sexual abuse by her Father. In addition, the alleged victim's own statement to her pediatrician may be relevant.

II. THE STEPS AFTER THE MINIMUM THRESHOLD IS MET

The four steps described above are sufficient to meet the "minimum threshold" of information needed to proceed. M.R.U. Crim.P. 17(d). That threshold having been met, this Court should next direct the clerk to set the matter for hearing. *Id*. The hearing notice must:

> …state the date and time of the hearing and direct the subpoenaed individual or entity from whom the documentary evidence is sought to submit the documentary evidence subject to the subpoena for in camera review by the court or to adequately explain in writing any reasons for a failure to submit the documentary evidence for in camera review.

Id.

Once the notice is issued, the Undersigned will serve the subpoena, the motion, and the notice on Dr. _____. Enclosed please find a subpoena to Dr. _____ which has not been served.

Dated this ____ day of _____, 20____, at Portland, Maine.

Respectfully submitted,

_____
Timothy E. Zerillo
Attorney for Defendant
ZERILLO LAW FIRM, LLC

[§§12:70-12:79 Reserved]

V.   MOTION IN LIMINE TO PRECLUDE EVIDENCE

§12:80   In General

I am a little torn on motions *in limine*. In some cases, I have felt that alerting the Government to issues of evidence admissibility has helped prepare them. That said, motions *in limine* are a useful tool that you may wish to employ depending on the situation.

Below is my first Motion *in Limine* in Bob's case, which I brought to control some of the expected hearsay in the case. See §12:XX for the scenario. In it I moved to limit or exclude:

- First complaint testimony by both the child victim and the child to whom she made the first complaint.
- Any mention at trial of the defendant's alleged prior sexual encounters with a minor and statements allegedly made by the defendant to the victim about the sexual encounters. The prior sexual encounters with a minor was crucial evidence to keep out. The alleged victim explained to the police that the defendant bragged of his sexual exploits with the minor during his sexual contact with the alleged victim. However, the defendant was never charged in this other case.
- Any mention of protection from abuse orders (in other words, domestic violence restraining orders) in which Bob was the defendant.
- Any mention of the defendant's prior misdemeanor conviction for furnishing a place for minors to consume alcohol.
- The defense medical expert's testimony concerning the victim's credibility.

These should give you some ideas for your own cases. These are very fact-intensive cases, so your motions are only limited by your creativity.

§ 12:81   Limiting First Complaint Testimony

First complaint testimony can get tricky. The rules may vary from place to place, but it is important to understand the rule in your jurisdiction and limit any first complaint testimony as much as possible.

The first (or fresh) complaint doctrine allows the prosecutor to introduce testimony of a witness to whom the victim first reported the sex crime if the alleged victim takes the stand at trial and the complaint was made within a reasonable time after the alleged sexual misconduct. First complaint statements are made in the State's case-in-chief to show that the victim reported a rape or sexual misconduct to a third party. *State v. Calor*, 585 A.2d 1385, 1387 (Me. 1991); *see State v. True*, 438 A.2d 460, 464 (Me. 1981). The purpose of first complaint testimony is "to forestall the natural assumption that in the absence of a complaint, nothing . . . had occurred." *True*, 438 A.2d at 464.

Since the first complaint doctrine is so narrow, move *in limine* to limit first complaint testimony at trial. You don't want witnesses, especially child witnesses, running off at the mouth. You want to limit their testimony to the bare fact that the complaint was made. The testimony should not concern the details of the alleged sexual misconduct.

The Massachusetts Supreme Judicial Court has specifically limited the first complaint witness to the single "person who was first told of the assault." *Commonwealth v. King*, 445 Mass. 217, 243 (2005). *King* holds that "[p]ermitting a single first complaint witness to testify will accomplish the primary goal of the [first complaint] doctrine, which is to refute any false inference that silence is evidence of a lack of credibility on the part of rape complainants." *Id.*

Further, "[i]t is the alleged victim's first complaint, the point at which the accusation first surfaced, that is the most pertinent to the jury's understanding of what motivated the victim to come forward and is the most useful in assessing the victim's credibility." *Id.* Allowing only the first person told of the assault to testify, no matter when the complaint was made, reduces any prejudice to the victim that may arise if the witness does not complain promptly. *Id.* at 242.

One caveat is to consider what the alleged victim said as the complaint. Sometimes as defense lawyers we immediately look to exclude bad evidence at trial without first considering it. If the first complaint testimony is different than several other statements made by the alleged victim, you may want all the hearsay in as a matter of strategy.

§ 12:82   FORM 12-90 Motion in Limine to Limit First
Complaint Evidence and Preclude Other Evidence

STATE OF MAINE	SUPERIOR COURT
CUMBERLAND, ss	DOCKET NO. CR-11-1234

STATE OF MAINE	)	
	)	
v.	)	DEFENDANT'S MOTION
	)	*IN LIMINE* AND
	)	MEMORANDUM OF LAW
BOB	)	
	)	
Defendant	)	

NOW COMES Defendant, Bob, by and through Undersigned Counsel, and hereby makes his Motion *In Limine* and attached Memorandum of Law as follows:

1.   Motion to Limit Scope of First Complaint Testimony.

Counsel requests the Court order that the State's first complaint testimony be limited to only the bare facts of the alleged victim's complaint. This testimony should not include any details of the alleged events or the identity of the alleged perpetrator.

The extrajudicial statements of the alleged victim are admissible as a "first complaint" in the State's case-in-chief to show that the victim had reported a rape or sexual misconduct complaint to a third party if the alleged victim takes the stand at trial and the complaint was made within a reasonable time after the alleged sexual misconduct. *State v. Calor*, 585 A.2d 1385, 1387 (Me. 1991); *see State v. True*, *438 A.2d 460*, 464 (Me. 1981). The statements are admissible "to forestall the natural assumption that in the absence of a complaint, nothing . . . had occurred." *True,* 438 A.2d at 464. To be admissible as a "first complaint," the victim's statements may not contain details of the complaint, such as the identity of the perpetrator, but are limited to evidence that the complaint was of rape or sexual conduct, and evidence of the time and place of the incident. *Id.* at 464-5. The witness' testimony should be carefully limited to ensure it does not include inadmissible evidence. *See Calor,* 585 A.2d at 1387 (the court carefully limited first complaint testimony to ensure it did not include identification of the accused or the victim's description of events.). "[T]he court should exercise careful control of the testimony by allowing counsel to lead the witness with specific questions, or by cautioning the witness prior to the testimony" to avoid the admission of inadmissible evidence that will impermissibly strengthen the alleged victim's accusations. *State v. Naylor,* 602 A.2d 187, 189 (Me. 1992). This is especially important in cases such as this, where the credibility of the alleged victim is crucial and any inadmissible corroboration of her testimony will result in undue prejudice to the accused. *Id.*

"The bare *fact* that a complaint has been made is admissible." *True,* 438 A.2d at 464. However its admissibility is limited to "the purpose of corroborating the victim's testimony . . . not as proof that the crime was in fact committed." *Id.* To ensure the jury does not impermissibly consider the testimony as substantive evidence of the crime, the Defendant requests that a limiting instruction be given to the jury as the testimony is admitted and again during the Judge's final instructions to the jury.

2.   Motion to Limit First Complaint Evidence to Sean.

Counsel requests that the first complaint evidence be limited to testimony by Sean, the first person Tammy reported the alleged assaults to. Maine's first complaint doctrine, outlined above, allows testimony that would otherwise be excluded as hearsay to be admitted if it meets certain criteria. Traditionally, that evidence is admissible as testimony by the first person the witness told of the alleged abuse. *See Naylor,* 602 at 188, ("[T]he State elicited testimony from the victim's mother concerning the first time the victim brought the accusations to her attention."), *State v. Joel H.,* 755 A.2d 520, 526 (2000) ("Over a hearsay objection, the victim's father testified that the victim had reported the sexual abuse to him on January 6, [the day the abuse had occurred].")*, Calor,* 585 A.2d at 1387 (Defendant's supervisor testified that the victim told him about his sexual relationship with an adult male when the supervisor questioned the victim after suspicions about the relationship arose.).

The Massachusetts Supreme Judicial Court has specifically limited the first complaint witness to the single "person who was first told of the assault." *Commonwealth v. King,* 445 Mass. 217, 243 (2005) It stated that "[p]ermitting a single first complaint witness to testify will accomplish the primary goal of the [first complaint] doctrine, which is to refute any false inference that silence is evidence of a lack of credibility on the part of rape complainants." *Id.* Further, "[i]t is the alleged victim's first complaint, the point at which the accusation first surfaced, that is the most pertinent to the jury's understanding of what motivated the victim to come forward and is the most useful in assessing the victim's credibility." *Id.* Allowing only the first person told of the assault to testify, no matter when the complaint was made, reduces any prejudice to the victim that may arise if the witness does not complain promptly. *Id.* at 242.

In this case, the first person to whom Tammy made the accusations about the Defendant was Sean. It is Sean's testimony regarding those allegations that would be most useful to the jury's assessing Tammy's credibility. Therefore, any first complaint evidence should be limited to that gleaned from the testimony of Sean. Additionally, Counsel requests that a limiting instruction be given at the time Sean testifies and again in the Judge's charge to the jury that his testimony cannot be considered as substantive evidence that the crime occurred, but only as evidence that a complaint was made.

3.   Motion to Exclude Hearsay Statements by Tammy, Alleged Victim, Made to Law Enforcement, DHHS, Spurwink Personnel, Hospital Staff, and Relatives of Alleged Victim Other Than the First Complaint Witness.

Counsel moves this Court to exclude as hearsay any out of court statements made by Tammy to Law Enforcement, DHHS, Spurwink Personnel, Hospital Staff, and her relatives, other than the first complaint witness, Sean. In addition to limiting who may be called as a first complaint witness, defense counsel requests that the number of first complaint witnesses be limited. In Massachusetts, "[l]aw enforcement officials, as well as investigatory, medical, or social work professionals, may testify to the complaint only where they are in fact the first to have heard of the assault, and not where they have been told of the alleged crime after previous complaints or after an official report."

Id. at 243. Limiting the number of witnesses who can testify as to what the alleged victim told them of the assault is done to eliminate the prejudicial "piling on" of first complaint witnesses. *Id.* at 245 (*See also Commonwealth v. Trowbridge*, 419 Mass. 750, 761 (1995) ("The repetition of fresh complaint testimony creates a risk that the jury will use the details of the fresh complaints as substantive evidence that the crime actually occurred.")).

The Maine Supreme Court recognizes that prejudice to the Defendant occurs if inadmissible corroboration of the alleged victim's testimony is admitted and it instructed the courts to carefully limit evidence that might have the impermissible effect. *See Naylor,* 602 A.2d at 189; *Calor,* 585 A.2d at 1387. The admission of inadmissible hearsay evidence that constitutes obvious error affecting substantial rights will warrant the overturning of a conviction. *True,* 438 A.2d at 467. In *State v. Phillipo*, a case similar to this, which turned on the credibility of the child victim and her brother, the Law Court held that "testimony [impermissibly] admitted as prior consistent statements of the children was so repetitive and detailed, it is not highly probable that the error did not affect the jury's verdict" and vacated the Defendant's conviction. 623 A.2d 1265, 1268 (Me. 1993).

As none of the above individuals are the first complaint witness, their testimony must fit another hearsay exception to be admissible, such as excited utterance or a prior consistent statement. They do not. Statements made by Tammy to Law Enforcement, DHHS, and her relatives, other than the first complaint witness, Sean, do not fit any hearsay exception.

Statements made by Tammy to Spurwink personnel and Hospital Staff may be admissible under M.R.Evid. 803(4) as Statements for Purposes of Medical Diagnosis or Treatment if they carefully are limited to exclude the identity of the accused and the scene of the alleged assault. *True,* 438 A.2d at 467 (that it was intercourse that caused the prosecutrix to see the doctor and the time and place of the intercourse were admissible under the 803(4) hearsay exception, but identity of alleged rapist and scene of alleged rape were not). To avoid the impermissible admission of repetitive and detailed corroboration of Tammy's testimony, testimony by any medical providers should be carefully limited to the type of sexual activity and the number of occurrences of sexual activity. Likewise, Tammy's statements to Law Enforcement, DHHS, and her relatives, other than the first complaint witness should be excluded.

4. Motion to Exclude Prior Uncharged Bad Act Evidence Regarding Alleged Victim Named Jane.

At the Defendant's arraignment and bail hearing the State referred to an unsubstantiated allegation of sexual abuse against the Defendant made by Jane Doe in 2004. Further, the discovery indicates that the Defendant allegedly told the alleged victim that he could "fit it all the way inside" Jane Doe. Counsel requests the Court exclude from the trial any mention of alleged prior acts involving Ms. Doe as inadmissible if used to show the character of the Defendant or that the Defendant acted in conformity therewith per M.R.Evid. 404(b).

The Adviser's Note to Rule 404(b) indicates there are exceptions to M.R.Evid. 404(b), which make evidence of prior bad acts admissible if those acts are relevant to an issue other than the Defendant's acting in conformity with the behavior, including motive, opportunity, intent, preparation, plan, knowledge, identity, or absence of mistake. *State v. DeMass*, 743 A.2d 233, 236, 2000 ME 4 (*quoting State v. Works*, 537 A.2d 221, 222 (Me. 1998)). The issues of motive, intent, preparation, plan knowledge, identity, and presence or absence of mistake will not be raised by the defense and would not be rebutted by Ms. Doe's unsubstantiated allegations. Although the Defendant states that he did not have the opportunity to commit the alleged abuse, evidence of Jane Doe's allegations would not serve to counter that defense.

If the State does wish to enter 404(b) evidence for one of the acceptable purposes, it "must articulate with particularity the purpose and its relationship to a disputed issue in the case." *Id.* (*citing* Field & Murray, *Maine Evidence* § 404.4 at 129 (4th ed. 1997)). "General assertions that the evidence has some usefulness with respect to a laundry list of permissible purposes does not satisfy this requirement." *Id.*

Additionally, Counsel objects to any reference to the allegations by Jane Doe because any probative value it might have is substantially outweighed by the danger of unfair prejudice. M.R.Evid. 403. The Maine Supreme Court, in *State v. Goodrich*, held that

> "[e]vidence suggesting that the defendant had been involved with another girl similar to the offense for which he was on trial was extremely prejudicial: (1) because of the inevitable pressure on lay jurors to believe that if the defendant did it before he probably did so this time, and (2) because if the jury believed that the defendant had not been punished for a prior offense, that may well have impelled them to convict him, even if they had a reasonable doubt as to his guilt in the case before them."

432 A.2d 413, 471-18 (Me. 1981) (*quoting State v. Roy*, Me., 385 A.2d 795, 798 (1978) and *State v. Gaudette*, Me., 431 A.2d 31, 34 (1981) *internal quotations omitted*). In Goodrich's trial, the prosecutor asked the victim's mother,

Virginia, whether her prior statements that she "made it all up" referred to the incident with the victim. *Id.* at 415. Virginia replied "With the other girl;" the defendant objected and moved for a mistrial. *Id.* The Court agreed with Goodrich's assertion that Virginia's answer "informed the jury that the defendant may have been involved in unlawful sexual activity with someone other than the prosecutrix, [which] unfairly prejudice[d] the jury against him." *Id.* at 417. Any mention of Jane Doe during this trial should not be tolerated because of its extremely prejudicial nature.

This is the type of testimony that a curative instruction cannot cure. As *Goodrich* indicates, this type of statement is so prejudicial that it may compel the jury to convict the Defendant if they believe the Defendant was not punished for the prior act with Jane Doe. The Defendant asks that the Court not only exclude this evidence, but also to instruct the State to caution their witnesses against testifying about the same.

5. Motion to Exclude Prior Uncharged Bad Act Evidence Including Any Mention of PFA's Against the Defendant.

Counsel moves this Court to exclude from trial any mention of any Protection From Abuse Orders in which Bob is the Defendant. As detailed above, although evidence of other crimes, wrongs or acts is admissible for a few limited purposes, the Protection From Abuse Orders do not fit any of the enumerated functions. M.R.Evid. 404(b). In *State v. Palmer*, the first complaint witness testified that she and the victim were "in court to obtain a restraining order [against Palmer] when the victim disclosed the abuse to her." 624 A.2d 469, 470 (Me. 1993). "Based on the trial court's admission of [this] unfairly prejudicial evidence barred by M.R.Evid. 404(b)," the Law Court vacated Palmer's convictions. *Id.* at 471. Evidence of Protection From Abuse Orders is, by its nature, unfairly prejudicial, so no evidence of them should be admitted here.

Additionally, these Orders are not relevant to the case at hand and should be excluded. M.R.Evid. 402. Even if the Protection From Abuse Orders are found to be relevant, any probative value they might have is outweighed by their extremely prejudicial nature. M.R.Evid. 403.

6. Motion to Exclude Evidence Regarding Defendant's Conviction for Furnishing a Place for Minors to Consume Liquor.

Further, Counsel moves this Court to exclude from trial any mention of Defendant's being convicted of the misdemeanor of Furnishing a Place for Minors to Consume Liquor in 2001. This is not a felony conviction, nor does it involve a crime of dishonesty or false statement, and must be excluded under M.R.Evid. 609.

7. Motion to Exclude Dr. Howard's Testimony Concerning the Credibility of the Victim.

Dr. Howard examined the child and issued a report where he found the alleged victim's disclosures to be credible. Counsel requests the Court exclude Dr. Howard from testifying that the child appeared credible or that she presented with the hallmarks of a child who had been sexually abused.

Counsel acknowledges that Dr. Howard may be allowed to testify that the notch found in the alleged victim's hymen is consistent with penetration under *State v. Roman*, 622 A.2d 96 (Me. 1993). Any testimony that the child appeared credible in her disclosures or presented as a rape victim should be excluded, however. First, it is outside the scope of this witness' knowledge to give opinions related to the alleged victim's credibility. Dr. Howard is a medical doctor, not a mental health professional. Even if he was a mental health professional, for his testimony regarding the credibility of the alleged victim to be relevant and helpful, it would need to be based upon a scientifically reliable predictor of truthfulness. *State v. Woodburn*, 559 A.2d 343, 346 (Me. 1989); *State v. Black*, 537 A.2d 1154, 1157 (Me. 1988). Third, admission of such evidence would be unfairly prejudicial under M.R.Evid. 403. Essentially, it would amount to improperly bolstering the alleged victim's credibility.

Dated this 11th day of August, 2008, at Portland, Maine.

Respectfully submitted,

_____

Timothy E. Zerillo
Attorney for Defendant
ZERILLO LAW FIRM, LLC

[§§12:83-12:89 Reserved]

SEXUAL ASSAULTS
AGAINST CHILDREN

VI.   TRIAL

A. Trial Strategy

§12:90   Raising Reasonable Doubt

So, to get our jury to find reasonable doubt, we need them to question Tammy's claims. In order to do that, we need to:

1. Raise doubt about her truthfulness.
2. Provide a plausible alternative explanation/reason for her allegations.
3. Provide a plausible alternative explanation for the injury to her hymen.

§12:91   About Tammy's Truthfulness

In order to raise reasonable doubt about Tammy's truthfulness, I stressed the following at trial:

- The inconsistency of Tammy's story. Every time she tells it, it changes.
- Bob's lack of access to Tammy. He was virtually never alone with her during the times she claims sexual contact occurred.
- The normalcy of Tammy's life with Bob. He came to get her immediately after her mother ditched her. He enrolled her in school and sports, attended her sporting activities, behaved appropriately and modestly around her.
- Tammy's history of lying.

§12:92   Explaining the "Why" of her Allegations

We always need to work toward the "why" in a child sexual assault trial. Why would the child make up such an atrocious story? Why would he or she subject themselves to cross-examination by the mean defense attorney? Why would they put themselves through that?

You will lose your trial unless you can provide the jury with an answer to the "why" question. Here are some alternative explanations for Tammy's allegations that we tried to develop at trial:

- To get attention/sympathy/love from her mother and others. Her mom's attention had been divided between a problem older sister and a new baby brother, leaving Tammy the forgotten child. She had a clingy, needy personality. She seems to have a need to stir up drama: she calls DHS on mom; tattles and pits her friends against each other; runs away; has a phony suicide attempt and so forth.
- To please her mother who wanted custody returned to her. Mom impulsively decided to send Tammy to live with dad and then wanted her back. Mom had a financial motive to seek custody because she had to pay child support to dad from her disability income. Mom and Tammy secretly plotted for a change of custody with Tammy reporting on how she was punished by dad and mom recording it to give to her custody lawyer.
- To return to live with her mother, sister, and brother. She lived most of her life in her mom's home. She missed her sister, brother, and friends. Her dad was nearly a stranger to her, and dad's girlfriend, Sally, and daughter, Nancy, were total strangers. She didn't get along well with Sally and dad was a strict disciplinarian.
- Because she was made at her dad. Tammy was mad at her dad for disciplining her, going out to eat without her, and returning her to mom.

§12:93   Explaining her Injury

We also need to explain the hymen injury. We do this by developing alternative theories for the injury. Some plausible alternative explanations for Tammy's injury are:

- Tammy did it to herself while attempting to insert a tampon.
- It was caused by someone else molesting her.
- It has some unknown cause other than sexual activity.

[§§12:94-12:99 Reserved]

B. Jury Selection

§12:100 Jurors to Seek

I wish I could tell you I had an image of an ideal juror in this type of case. Of course, I don't. Child molestation is so horrific that any right-thinking juror is not going to want to sit on your case. He or she would much rather be a juror in a murder case or a boring contract dispute.

So really then, all we are looking for are people who are open-minded. I know that sounds trite, but I don't care about the fact that jurors are disgusted by the allegation. I expect that. However, finding people who can get past that disgust and still fairly judge the facts is the trick.

It will likely not surprise you that I am concerned about Bob's case. We have a willing, pre-teen alleged victim, with physical evidence of an injury to her hymen. My client does not look like a choir boy. Rather, he looks pretty rough around the edges, even after we clean him up. This is not an easy case.

§12:101 Use of Jury Questionnaire

Since I don't get the benefit of individual voir dire in Maine, the jury questionnaire in sensitive cases is very important. People just aren't excited about raising their hands in a group of people they don't know to say they have been molested. As a result, I use a jury questionnaire, and then ask the court for some sidebar jury questioning.

Some judges are better than others. I did a case in which the Magistrate Judge allowed sidebar questioning of the venire, but would not allow me to speak directly to them. This created an awkward situation where we were all standing around a microphone and I had to ask the judge, with the juror standing there, what I would like the judge to ask the juror. Totally ridiculous. If your jurisdiction is similar, come up with some lines of questioning for the judge in advance.

§12:102 Sample Voir Dire Questions

- If a grade-school girl testifies, would you be more likely to believe what she says because she is a child?
- Do you believe that all children know the difference between imagination, or dreams, and real life?
- Do you find it hard to believe that a child would make up a story, for whatever reason—for fun, to get attention, out of fear, or to protect someone?
- Do you have feelings or beliefs that would make it difficult for you to hear a case where the alleged victim is a child?
- The evidence and testimony in this case will contain detailed descriptions of sexual acts. Would being exposed to such evidence and testimony affect your ability to be fair and impartial if the sexual acts involved a child?
- Would you prefer not to sit as a juror on a case involving an alleged sexual assault of a child?
- Does anyone have a child who is close to 10 years old, the age of the complainant in this case?
- Does anyone have any difficulty with the fact that child witnesses will testify in this case and be the subject of direct and cross examination?
- Do you feel that just because a child testifies about a sexual assault that it must necessarily be true?

§12:103 FORM 12-100 Jury Questionnaire—Child Sexual Assault

STATE OF MAINE   SUPERIOR COURT
CUMBERLAND, SS.   CRIMINAL ACTION
                                                       DOCKET NO. CR-07-1490

STATE OF MAINE   )
)
vs.   )
)   JUROR QUESTIONNAIRE
BOB,   )
)
Defendant   )

Members of the Jury Panel:

This is a questionnaire which asks a number of questions of a personal nature. The court regrets the inquiry on the private matters which this questionnaire addresses. This inquiry is necessary to assure that you can fulfill your duty to be objective and impartial jurors. One or more of the cases on which you may be asked to sit as jurors involve allegations of sexual abuse or sexual assault. In order to assure both the State and Bob a fair trial, the court must determine if you have had any experiences or opinions that might affect your objectivity and impartiality in such cases. The questions are designed to address these concerns. They are presented in written form in lieu of the questions being asked orally in open court.

QUESTIONS:

1. Please state the following:
Name:_____
Age: _____
City of Residence: _____
How long have you lived in Cumberland County? _____
Place of birth: _____

2. **EMPLOYMENT**
Please state the following with respect to employment:
Name of Employer:_____
How long have you worked for your present employer? _____
_____.

3. **FAMILY**
Please state your marital status:_____.
If married, name of spouse: _____.
Number of children: _____
Please state their ages and sexes:
_____.
Please state spouse's employer: _____.
Type of work: _____.
How long has your spouse worked for current employer? _____.
City of spouse's birth: _____.

4. **MILITARY**
Have you served in the Military Service?   Yes _____ No _____
If yes, were you drafted or enlisted _____.
What branch? _____.
Highest rank attained: _____.

5. **GOVERNMENT EMPLOYEE**
Have you or any member of your family been employed by a Local, State, or the Federal Government, other than the Military? Yes _____ No _____
If yes, what entity? _____.
What position: _____.

6. **CIVIL COURT EXPERIENCE**
Have you ever been a party to a civil suit? Yes _____ No _____
If yes, describe the case: _____.
Have you ever been a witness in a civil suit? Yes _____ No _____
If yes, describe the type of case and testimony: _____.

7. **CRIMINAL EXPERIENCE**
Have you ever been the subject of a criminal investigation?   Yes _____ No _____
Have you ever been formally accused of a crime? Yes _____ No _____
If yes, describe the type of case: _____
_____
_____

Have you ever been a victim in a criminal in a criminal case? Yes _____ No _____
If yes, describe the type of case: _____
_____
_____

Have you ever been a witness in a criminal in a criminal case? Yes _____ No _____
If yes, describe the type of case: _____
_____
_____

8. **JUROR SERVICE ISSUES**
Do you know any other member of this panel? Yes No _____
If yes, who? _____
Do you have any physical problem that could interfere with your jury service?   Yes _____ No _____
If yes, explain: _____
_____
_____

Is there any reason why you cannot serve as a juror? Yes No _____

9. **SEXUAL CRIMES EXPERIENCE**
Have you ever been a victim of sexual abuse or sexual assault?   Yes_____ No _____
Do you have a close relative or friend who has been a victim of sexual abuse or sexual assault?
Yes _____ No _____
Have you or a close relative or friend ever been subjected to a charge of sexual abuse or sexual assault or been investigated for sexual abuse or sexual assault?   Yes No _____
Have you and other family members ever been separated from one another due in whole or in part to sexual abuse or sexual assault or claims of sexual abuse or sexual assault?   Yes _____ No _____
Have you had any experiences in life that would make it difficult or impossible for you to consider evidence in a case of alleged sexual abuse or sexual assault objectively and impartially?   Yes _____ No _____
Is there any reason why you could not consider evidence in a case of alleged sexual abuse or sexual assault objectively or impartially? Yes _____ No _____
Have you ever belonged to, worked for or had any experience with a group, program, agency or organization that is involved with social issues, prevention and treatment of sexual assault?   Yes _____ No_____
If yes, please describe the organization and the nature of your involvement:
_____
_____
_____

The evidence and testimony in this case may contain detailed descriptions of alleged sexual acts, including intercourse. Would being exposed to such evidence and testimony affect your ability to be fair and impartial?
Yes_____ No _____
The evidence and testimony in this case contains allegations of a sexual act performed with a child by the child's parent. Would being exposed to such evidence and testimony of sex assault on a child affect your ability to be fair and impartial?
Yes_____ No _____
Would you prefer not to sit as a juror on a case involving an alleged sexual assault? Yes _____ No _____

10. MISCELLANEOUS

Would you be satisfied, if you were the defendant in this case, to have your case judged by someone in the same frame of mind as your frame of mind? Yes_____ No_____

Is there anything in your life experience which you think could affect your ability to be fair and impartial in this case? Yes_____ No_____

If yes, please explain: _____

_____

_____

_____

Have you ever served as a juror in a case before?   Yes ___ No ___

If yes, please use the following chart to describe the type of jury service:

_____ Court   ___state   ___state federal

_____ Jury   ___state trial   ___grand

_____ Case   ___state criminal   ___state civil

Did you deliberate and reach a verdict? Yes _____ No _____

How did you feel about your jury experience? _____

_____

_____

_____

Do you hold personal feelings about the subject of child sexual assault that the Court and parties should know in considering you as a juror? Yes _____ No _____

If yes, please explain: _____

_____

_____

The answers to the above questions are true to the best of my knowledge and belief.

Dated: _____

Name _____

Juror No. _____

[§§12:104-12:109 Reserved]

C. Opening Statement

§12:110 My Approach

As you can imagine, after the State's opening totally prejudices the jury against both my client and me, my primary goal is just to have the jurors open up their minds a bit. I want them to actually listen to my cross-examinations, not ignore them entirely.

For general tips on opening statements and sample language about the presumption of innocence and burden of proof, see Ch.2.

§12:111 Opening Statement Excerpt—Urging Jurors to Keep an Open Mind

Tammy is a very troubled girl, but that is not because Bob sexually assaulted her.

When a child accuses someone of a crime, it is like launching a missile. When that child says her father sexually abused her, it is a nuclear bomb. Anyone who hears it gets upset. They get repulsed. They feel a disgusted feeling in the pit of their stomachs.

This disgust is normal. It is human. You can't help it. I think of it as a fog. That fog clouds your brain with anger and your stomach with a sick feeling.

If you were watching it on a television show or hearing about it on the news it would be OK to stay in that fog. But you cannot stay that way here. Because you took an oath. That oath was to, without passion or prejudice, decide this case.

Now, I am no student of body language. But when I got up here, there were a great many of you with daggers in your eyes for me. Many of you with your arms crossed. That's OK. You were in the fog. You had just heard the prosecution's Opening Statement and she told you all sorts of heinous things she is trying to prove against my client. If you weren't in that fog, I would have been surprised.

But now you know how to recognize it. You know that you need to keep your mind open to obey your oath. And when you feel that fog of hatred and disgust coming next time, you can tell yourself, "I am going to wait until I hear what else is going to be said about this before I make up my mind."

By the way, that same fog extends to the police. They get a call that a little girl is coming in to tell them that her dad was sexual with her. They get angry, they get disgusted. Sometimes the police are so angry that they want to do anything they can to put the defendant away. So they don't follow the guidelines they need to follow. They don't investigate. They just rush to judgment. They take whatever that child says for granted. They act like advocates for the child instead of neutral investigators.

You do not have that luxury if you are obeying your oath. You are not a child advocate. You are a juror who swore to uphold the law. You can go home and hug every child you love after this case, but while you are on this jury, your job is to apply the law of reasonable doubt to the facts that come out in the evidence. That is it and that is all.

I want you to consider something else as well. These cases that make you feel nauseous based on the allegation alone are the most dangerous types of cases. Blind outrage can lead to injustice. You have to look through that fog before you can see the ugly truth. There is no one in the world who can do that in this case but you. And we are counting on you to do it.

Now let's talk about the evidence I expect you to hear

[§§12:112-12:119 Reserved]

D. Witness Examinations

§12:120 The Witnesses

Below are the following witness examinations from Bob's trial. See §12:03 for the scenario.
Prosecution's Witnesses:
- Tammy, alleged victim (direct, cross, redirect, and recross examinations). See §§12:130-12:133.
- Prosecution's expert (cross examination). See §12:140.
- Sally, the defendant's former girlfriend (cross examination). See §12:141.
- Officer Lippy, investigating detective (cross examination). See §12:142.
- Tracy, mother of alleged victim (cross examination). See §12:143.

Defense Witnesses:
- Bob, the defendant (direct examination). See §12:150.
- Victim's day care provider (direct examination). See §12:151.
- Victim's aunt (direct examination). See §12:152.

[§§12:121-12:129 Reserved]

1. Alleged Victim

§12:130 Prosecution's Direct Examination of Child Victim

I include here the direct and cross examination of Tammy, our child victim, warts and all. I include it especially for those who have never tried this type of case before. I am not a fly-by-the-seat-of-your-pants type of person. If there is a way to research how to do something, I will do it before walking blindly into a situation. The availability of full transcripts of a child sexual assault victim cross is limited. I hope this gives both the novice and seasoned practitioner at least one good idea as to how to approach this horrific task.

Introductory Questions and School History

During 5th grade, Tammy attended three different schools:
- She began at Generic Primary.
- Moved to City Elementary.
- Moved again to Suburb Elementary.
- Returned to Generic Primary.

In the same year Tammy lived in Standish, Gray, and multiple locations in Westbrook.

Q. Good morning Tammy.
A. Good morning.
Q. How old are you Tammy?
A. Eleven.
Q. And when's your birthday?
A. April 1, 2000.
Q. Okay. And I am going to ask you a silly question probably but have you ever been married?
A. No.
Q. Okay. What grade are you going to go into this year?
A. Sixth.
Q. Sixth grade. What school will you go to?
A. I'm not sure yet.
Q. Why aren't you sure?
A. Right now I am living in a group home and I am going to be moving soon.
Q. Okay. So if you move back in with Mom where are you going to school?
A. Generic Middle School.
Q. And what grade will you be going into?
A. Sixth.
Q. Sixth grade all right. Now we have met before today, right?
A. Uhm-hum.
Q. So we have talked a little bit about what I expect you to talk about today?
A. Yeah.
Q. One of the things that we talked about was you have gone to a lot of different schools right?
A. Yes.
Q. Okay. But from grades first through well, kindergarten actually through fourth grade?
A. Yeah.
Q. You went to one school?
A. Yes.
Q. What school was that?
A. Generic Primary School.
Q. Okay and then fifth grade is when you start jumping around in different schools right?
A. Yeah.
Q. All right. Where did you start school in fifth grade?
A. Uhm, I started at Generic Primary School.

Q. And how long did you go to Generic Primary School?
A. Maybe, I'm not sure, but maybe a few months.
Q. Okay or maybe even a few weeks?
A. Yeah.
Q. Okay. And then you went to another school right?
A. Yes.
Q. And what school was that?
A. Uhm, I went to a school in Portland, I can't remember the name.
Q. Would that have been City Elementary?
A. Yeah.
Q. Okay and do you remember how long you went to City Elementary?
A. Maybe a week or two.
Q. Okay. And then you went to another school right?
A. Yes.
Q. What school was that school?
A. Uhm, Suburb Elementary.
Q. Okay. And when did you stop going to the Suburb Elementary?
A. Uhm, like in the Spring.
Q. And do you remember about what time, what was happening around that time that you stopped going to Suburb Elementary?
A. Uhm, I don't understand.
Q. Did you move?
A. Yeah.
Q. About the time you stopped going to Suburb Elementary?
A. Yeah.
Q. And why did you stop going to Suburb Elementary?
A. 'Cuz I didn't want to live with my Dad anymore.
Q. So you moved in with who?
A. My Mom.
Q. All right. So around about the time that you moved from your Dad's to your Mom's is when you stopped going to Suburb Elementary?
A. Yeah.
Q. Did you go back to school at that point to finish out the year?
A. Yes.
Q. You did. Where did you go to school?
A. Generic Primary School.
Q. All right. Now you went to a lot of different schools and you moved a lot during your fifth grade year right?
A. Yeah.

History of Living and Sleeping Arrangements

During 5th grade Tammy lived in five different locations:
- With her mother, sister, brother, and step-father in Standish.
- With her father and father's girlfriend Sally in Gray.
- With her father, Sally, and Sally's daughter Nancy in Westbrook.
- With her father and grandfather in the grandfather's trailer which she moved into and out of several times.
- In a group home.

Q. Let's go back through where you lived okay. The summer before fifth grade where were you living?
A. Uhm, with my Mom.
Q. Okay and what town was that in?
A. Standish.
Q. Okay. And who lived in the house with you in Standish?
A. Uhm, my Mom, me, my older sister, my baby brother and my stepfather.

Q. What's your stepfather's name?
A. John.
Q. Okay and we established that you didn't stay there right?
A. Yes.
Q. When did you move out of your Mom's house?
A. Sometime during the summer I think.
Q. And where did you move?
A. To Gray.
Q. Who lived at the place in Gray where you lived?
A. Sally, my Dad, me.
Q. Okay and do you know whose house that was?
A. Sally's brother.
Q. What kind of a house was that?
A. It was big and it had a garage and a tree house in the back and that's kind of like all it was.
Q. Okay. Now you didn't stay there that whole year right?
A. No.
Q. Where was the next place that you lived?
A. Westbrook.
Q. When did you move to Westbrook do you remember?
A. Like October-ish.
Q. Was it before or after Thanksgiving?
A. Before.
Q. And when you moved to Westbrook where did you move? To Country Road?
A. Yeah.
Q. And who lived in that house with you?
A. The same people-- my Dad, me and Sally and Nancy.
Q. Nancy didn't live there right off the bat did she?
A. No she moved in like oh maybe a month or week or two after.
Q. And then well, let me go back to the house in Gray did you have your own room?
A. Uhm-hum.
Q. And where was everybody's bedroom in that house?
A. Uhm, everybody's bedroom was on the second floor.
Q. Okay. You had your own room?
A. Uhm-hum.
Q. And where did Sally sleep?
A. In my Dad's room next room over.
Q. And then when you moved to the place on 302 did everybody have their own room there too?
A. Yeah.
Q. You had your own room?
A. Uhm-hum.
Q. And where did Sally sleep?
A. In my Dad's room.
Q. And then when Nancy moved in where did she sleep?
A. In my old room.
Q. And when she was in your old room where did you end up sleeping?
A. In the computer room.
Q. And what did you sleep on in the computer room?
A. A futon.
Q. Okay. Somewhere around the spring you moved out with your Dad right?
A. Yes.
Q. Where did you guys go?
A. To my Grandfather's house in the trailer park.
Q. How many times did you move in with your Grandfather?
A. Maybe two or three.

Q. And was it for a long time or short time?

A. Short time.

Q. And when you stay at your Grandfather's where did you sleep?

A. In my Dad's room. It's like it's the room after the living room.

Q. Okay and who slept in that room with you if anybody?

A. My Dad.

Q. Did you have your own bed?

A. I had an air mattress on the floor.

Q. What about Dad where did he sleep?

A. He slept on like the top bed like in the end of the room.

Q. Okay and was there a door on that room?

A. Yes.

Q. What about Sally and your Dad's room at Country Road was there a door there?

A. Yes.

Q. And what about the house in Gray was there a door to Sally and your Dad's room there?

A. Uhm, I'm not sure.

Q. Now you said somewhere around May you moved back in with your Mom?

A. Yeah.

Q. And your Mom at the time was with John and your brother and sister right?

A. Uhm-hum.

Q. Okay. But you didn't stay with your Mom, right?

A. No.

Q. Okay. You ended up going someplace. Where did you go?

A. Spring Harbor Hospital.

Q. What town is Spring Harbor in?

A. Westbrook.

Q. Why did you go to Spring Harbor?

A. Because I had a lot of trauma going on and I had a lot of anxiety attacks.

Q. And what did they do for you at Spring Harbor?

A. They put me on some medication and they taught me how to use some coping skills and talk when I was upset.

Q. Okay. And so you didn't stay at Spring Harbor right?

A. No.

Q. Where did you go from Spring Harbor?

A. Bridge Crossing.

Q. Tell everybody about what Bridge Crossing is?

A. It's a group home where twelve different kids live and you are not there forever, just until you find a family or until you are able to feel safe and like be successful in your life and not have issues with your family.

Q. Okay. What do you do at Bridge Crossing?

A. We play games; we go on bike rides; we go on trips. Like Tuesday we are going to go to watch a Sea Dogs game.

Q. Cool.

A. And we do all kinds of fun activities and we do summer school and we do regular school there.

Q. So this past year you have been going to school at Bridge Crossing?

A. I have been going to Maine School.

Q. Maine School?

A. Yeah, because I'm a public schooler now.

Q. Oh, so you did like an extra year somewhere between fifth and sixth grade?

A. Yeah.

Q. Okay. Let's talk about what subjects you like?

MR. ZERILLO. Objection. Relevance.

COURT: I'll allow.

A. I like math, reading and science.

Q. And you were telling me about a project that you did that you were really proud of?

MR. ZERILLO. Objection. Relevance.

COURT: I'll allow it.

A. Yeah, I made this volcano and my baby brother loves little foot so I put all the little foot characters on it and we exploded them after.

Q. What is little foot for people who don't know?

A. He is a long neck dragon, I mean dinosaur and he's like his parents died and he's living with his grandparents.

Q. And Jamie's your little brother?

A. Yes.

Q. How old is Jamie?

A. Turning three in August.

Q. And he really liked the exploding part?

MR. ZERILLO. Objection. Relevance.

COURT: I'll allow it, but move it along.

A. Yeah.

Discipline While Living with Defendant

Q. Now let's talk a little bit about when you were living with your Dad and Sally. Did you ever get into trouble?

A. Yeah.

Q. What sort of things would you get into trouble for?

A. Like if I went to my friends and I didn't ask to go or if I lied about something.

Q. What sort of things would you lie about?

A. Uhm, like not doing my homework or like telling something I shouldn't tell like, like I don't know like something.

Q. Okay. And how did they punish you?

A. Just they would send me to my room.

Q. Okay. Were you are ever spanked?

A. Sometimes.

Q. And who would usually discipline you?

A. My Dad.

Q. Did Sally ever discipline you too?

A. No, only once.

Q. And if you were sent to your room, how long were you sent to your room for?

A. Maybe a day or two.

Q. The whole day or two?

A. (Nods head affirmatively.)

Q. Somebody bring you food?

A. Yeah, sometimes or sometimes I would go out and get my food.

Q. Okay. Now were you punished a lot for doing those sorts of things?

A. No, just maybe once a week or like once a month.

Child's First Complaint about Alleged Assaults

Q. Okay and, Tammy, you know why you are here in court today, right?

A. Yeah.

Q. Why are you here?

A. 'Cuz my Dad did something he shouldn't have.

Q. Do you see your Dad here in the courtroom today?

A. Yes.

Q. Would you point to him and tell everybody what he is wearing?

A. He is wearing a blue tie and a white shirt and black jacket (indicating).

Q. Now who was the first person that you told about why you are here today?

A. My Uncle.

Q. What's your Uncle's name?

A. Sean.

Q. How old is Sean?

A. He is turning eleven in December.

Q.   So you are older than Sean, right?

A.   Yes.

Q.   Okay. Now why did you tell Sean?

A.   Uhm 'cuz I feel like I can trust him and he, he's like a brother to me, and he's like, like I can trust other people but I just trust him a lot.

Q.   Okay. Do you remember what you were doing when you told Sean?

A.   We were watching this—we were riding bikes and playing on the trampoline.

Q.   Okay and how did it all come about, how did you get to talking about this?

A.   Uhm, well, I really don't know. I just felt like I wanted to tell him 'cuz I know he wouldn't tell anybody and I had to get it off my chest 'cuz it made me feel really sad.

Q.   What did you tell Sean?

A.   That my Dad was being inappropriate with me and having sex with me.

Q.   Are those the words you used, or did you use other words for Sean?

A.   Like I used, like I said he was being inappropriate and he was touching me in a bad way.

Q.   Okay. Tammy, I want to talk about body parts with you, okay, do you want a sip of water right now?

A.   (Nods head affirmatively.)

Q.   Okay. If I told you—let me ask you this what's this called?

A.   Your arm.

Q.   What's this?

A.   Your hand.

Q.   These are the easy ones, right, what's this called?

A.   Your head.

Q.   All right. What do you the call the part of your body that a girl goes pee from?

A.   Uhm, her private.

Q.   Is that the only word you use for it?

A.   (Nods head affirmatively.)

Q.   What about the part of the body that a boy goes pee from?

A.   His private.

Q.   Okay. And what do you call this part of somebody?

A.   His butt.

Q.   His butt, okay, and you would say that's your butt too, right?

A.   (Nods head affirmatively.)

Q.   I know it's a little bit embarrassing what we are going to talk about, okay, but it's good that you are able to talk with me about it, okay. You said you told Sean?

A.   Ohm-hum.

Q.   And who was the next person who found out about all this?

A.   My grandmother.

Q.   What do you call her?

A.   Mamie.

Q.   Mamie, okay, from the time you told Sean until Mamie found out do you remember how many days had gone by?

A.   Hum-uhm (negative).

Q.   Was it the same day you told Sean that Mamie found out?

A.   No, it was like maybe two weeks or so.

Q.   Okay and when that happened what were you doing when she found out?

A.   We were pulling into Wendy's.

Q.   Who was in the car?

A.   Me, my uncle Sean and my Mamie.

Q.   Mamie was driving?

A.   Yeah.

Q.   I hope so. Okay. And where were you in the car?

A.   I was in the back seat.

Q.   And where was Sean?

A.   In the front seat.

Q.   He was in the front seat okay. How did it all come out that she ended up finding out about this?

A. Well, my uncle, we were watching TV and like few minutes before we went to Wendy's and we saw this commercial about drugs and my Uncle was like, well, doesn't your Dad do drugs?

MR. ZERILLO: Objection sidebar.

(A sidebar conference was held.)

THE COURT: Members of the jury, two things, first is that you should disregard entirely the witness's last answer and whatever Sean may or may not have said while they were watching TV on the occasion in question is not evidence and should not be considered by you in any way in connection with this, the charges that are involved here. I am looking at the clock as well and what we are going to do we started late but I think it's a good time to take the mid morning break at this point so we will break for 15 minutes.

PRACTICE TIP: *First complaint evidence*

In this case I made a conscious decision not to overly limit the first complaint evidence. I felt that the family dynamic here was what pushed Tammy into fabricating these stories, so there was a certain amount of first complaint evidence and hearsay I wanted in. That is not the way in all cases however. For a discussion of first complaint testimony, see §12:81. For a motion in limine to limit first complaint testimony, see §12:82 Form 12-90. Remember, in many jurisdictions first complaint evidence is extremely limited, as it should be, and you may have a reason to keep anything that strays from first complaint evidence away from the jury.

THE COURT: Ms. Pros.

BY MS. PROS:

Q. Thank you. Tammy, remember where we left off we were talking about you going out in the car with Mamie and Sean?

A. Yeah.

Q. And you had a conversation with Sean before leaving the house, right?

A. Yeap

Q. And based on that conversation is what made you want to tell?

A. Yeah.

Q. Okay. I'm sorry; it's what made you talk about it with Sean in the car?

A. Yeah.

Q. Okay. So what did happen in the car?

A. Uhm, well, once we ordered our food from Wendy's we went straight back to my Mom's house because that's where we were at the time, and then we told, my grandmother told my Mom and my Mom --

Q. Let me stop you right there, okay, when you told Mamie where were you?

A. Wendy's.

Q. You were in Wendy's in the parking lot?

A. Yeah.

Q. Were you guys still in the car?

A. Yes.

Q. And were you doing anything when you were telling her?

A. No, I was crying.

Q. You were okay. How did that it make you feel when you told her?

A. Ohm, made me feel like better, but like felt like it was off my chest, but like I was scared.

Q. What were you scared about?

A. I didn't want my Dad to find out that I told.

Q. Why didn't you want your Dad to find out?

A. Because he told me if I told that he would hurt me.

Q. And what was Mamie's reaction?

A. Ohm.

Q. Not what she said but what did she do?

A. She just said she was like surprised.

MR. ZERILLO: Objection.

BY MS. PROS:

Q. I think she can comment on that Your Honor.

THE COURT: Yeah, I will overrule if that's, without what she said her demeanor.

BY MS. PROS: .

Q. And so I think you said then you drove back to your Mom's house?

A. Ohm-hum.

Q. Where was that house? What town was that in?

A. Standish.

Q. Do you remember what time of day this was?

A. Ohm, like dinnertime.

Q. 'Cuz you said you had just eaten at Wendy's, right?

A. Yeah.

Q. Did you guys actually eat at Wendy's?

A. We went through the drive through.

Q. And do you remember if you told before or after you went through the drive through?

A. Before.

Q. Before, okay, so you head back to Standish your Mom's house?

A. Uhm-hum.

Q. And was your Mom home?

A. Yes.

Q. What did Mamie do?

A. She went upstairs and told my Mom.

Q. You weren't there when she told your Mom, right?

A. No, I was down in the car.

Q. You still sat in the car?

A. Yeah.

Q. And after she disappeared into the house, did anybody come out of the house?

A. No.

Q. Did you go in the house?

A. Well, my Mom came back down to get me, put me in the van and take me to the hospital.

Q. Did you talk with your Mom though before she put you in the van?

A. No.

Q. No. Okay. On the drive in the van to the hospital did you talk with your Mom?

A. Yeah, just like—

Q. Did you tell her the same thing that you had told Mamie?

A. Yeah, I told her what, what I have told, what I told my Mamie.

Q. Okay. So now you have told Sean and you have told Mamie, now you told Mom, right?

A. Yeah.

At the Hospital

Q. Where did you guys go when you went into the van?

A. We went to the hospital.

Q. What hospital did you go to?

A. Maine Med.

Q. Did you go into the emergency room?

A. Yeah.

Q. Okay. What happened when you got to the emergency room?

A. Ohm, they just checked my privates to make sure nothing was wrong.

Q. Okay. So did you have to get undressed for that?

A. Yes.

Q. How long were you in the hospital?

A. Maybe not even an hour cuz they said they didn't check.

Q. No, don't tell me what anybody said, but you were there for about an hour or so?

A. Yeah.

At the Police Station

Q. And then did you go home after the hospital?
A. Uhm, no, we went to the police station in Westbrook.
Q. Okay, and do you remember about how long you were at the police department?
A. Like an hour maybe, an hour or two.
Q. Did you talk to a police officer there?
A. Yeah.
Q. Did you tell him what you are telling us now?
A. Yeah.
Q. Was it this police officer (indicating)?
A. (Nods head affirmatively.)
Q. Or did you talk to him that night or did you talk to him on a different night?
A. Uhm, I think I talked to you that day.
Q. Did you also talk to another police officer too?
A. Yeah.
Q. And after you went to the police department did you go home then?
A. Yeah.
Q. Do you remember what day of the week this was?
A. No.
Q. And if I say that it was June 3rd does that mean anything to you?
A. I know it was in June, but I can't remember the date.

Examination by Prosecution's Medical Expert

Q. A couple days later did you go see another doctor?
A. Uhm-hum.
Q. Do you what that doctor's name was?
A. No.
Q. Do you know the name of the place that you went to?
A. Uhm, not sure.
Q. Did a doctor examine you at that place?
A. Yeah.
Q. Was this a little bit more than the exam that you have at the hospital?
A. Yeah.
Q. How long were you there at that place?
A. Uhm, around an hour probably.
Q. And I know it was a long time ago?
A. Yeah.
Q. And did you have to get undressed there too?
A. (Nods head affirmatively.)

Child's Description of Alleged Assaults

Q. So I want to talk to you a little bit about what you told all these different people, okay, and some of it's going to be a little embarrassing maybe, okay, but it's good that you are able to talk about it. Now you said you told Sean that your Dad had done something to you that was inappropriate?
A. Uhm-hum.
Q. And something that was sexual, right?
MR. ZERILLO: Objection.
COURT: Sustained.
Q. What did he do that you thought was inappropriate?
A. He was touching my privates and putting his privates in mine.
Q. Now did this happen once or twice or more than that?

A. More than that.

Q. Do you know where was the first time that he put his privates in your privates?

A. In Westbrook.

Q. It was in Westbrook, okay. Now when he did things to you where did they usually happen?

A. In his bedroom.

Q. In his bedroom, was that the only place that this ever happened?

A. Well, once it was in the living room, mostly it was always in his room.

Q. When it happened in the living room what house was that at?

A. Westbrook.

Q. Now what time in the day would these things happen?

A. After school.

Q. And what about when you were staying with your Grandfather; what time of day would it happen?

A. Uhm, I don't know.

Q. Daytime or nighttime?

A. Nighttime.

Q. Nighttime, okay. Now when it happened during the daytime, who was home?

A. Nancy.

Q. Nancy was home?

A. (Nods head affirmatively.)

Q. And where would she have been in the house?

A. In her room.

Q. Did she have a door on her bedroom?

A. Yeah.

Q. Would the door have been open or shut?

A. Shut and she always had her music on.

Q. Could you tell us a little bit about Nancy?

A. Well, she was really nice to me. She treated me like her sister, and when she got her car and she got her permit me and Sally and her were driving some places sometimes and she was really nice to me. Sometimes she like acted awkward, but—

Q. Is she a shy person, or is she an outgoing person?

A. She is shy.

Q. She is shy?

A. Yeah.

Q. Did she like to go out with friends and stuff?

A. Not often.

Q. Did she stay in her room a lot?

A. Uhm-hum.

Q. And so you said Nancy would be home during the afternoons when this would happen?

A. Uhm-hum.

Q. Where was Sally?

A. At work.

Q. What time did Sally get home from work?

A. Like 6ish.

Q. Okay. And does she own her own business?

A. Yes.

Q. Now you would be going to school on these days too, right?

A. Yes.

Q. What time could you get out of school?

A. Uhm, three.

Q. And how would you get home?

A. Uhm, sometimes I went to my Aunt Athena's and my Dad would pick me up, or sometimes I took the bus to the house.

Q. And Aunt Athena is that Dad's sister?

A. Dad's brother's.

Q. Wife?
A. Yeah.
Q. And what did Aunt Athena do?
A. Babysat.
Q. So she had a daycare, didn't she?
A. Yeah.
Q. Okay. So sometimes you would go over her house?
A. Yeah.
Q. And then Dad would pick you up there?
A. Yeah.
Q. And sometimes you would go straight home by yourself?
A. Yeah.
Q. Did Dad ever pick you up at school?
A. Yeah, sometimes.
Q. During that year that you lived with Dad what was he doing for work?
A. He worked for a delivery service.
Q. What did he do for them?
A. He would like deliver pool tables and like furniture sometimes.
Q. Can everybody hear her? No, okay. You have to kind of keep your voice up a little bit, okay, so Dad was a delivery driver?
A. Yeah.
Q. What sort of hours did he work?
A. Uhm, like early in the morning to like in the afternoon.
Q. Did it kind of depend—
A. Yes.
Q. —on what he was doing that day what time he would get home?
A. Yeah.
Q. So sometimes what would be the earliest he would get home from working?
A. Uhm, 2:45.
Q. Okay, and what would be a late night for him?
A. Uhm, like 5:30.
Q. So would you have been at home alone sometimes?
A. Uhm, 'cuz Nancy would be there, but she would always be there but like once or twice I was home alone.
Q. And were you ever home alone with Dad?
A. Yeah.
Q. Did that happen often, or was that a really rare occurrence?
A. Really rare.
Q. It was rare?
A. Yeah, before Nancy moved in we would be there alone, but when she moved in she was always there.
Q. Would she come out of her room though?
A. Just to get breakfast, lunch and dinner sometimes or to watch TV.
Q. So were you and Dad alone for a while in the house?
A. Yes.
Q. Now, Tammy, when bad things would happen how did, how did it start?
A. Uhm.
Q. Well, let me talk about the first time that something happened that made you feel uncomfortable, okay, where were you living?
A. Uhm, in Westbrook.
Q. In Westbrook or was it in Gray?
A. No, in Gray I mean.
Q. In Gray?
A. Yeah.
Q. What happened, how did it start?
A. Well, he just was talking to me about it and then --

Q. Well, let me ask you this you told me about a car trip?

A. Yeah.

Q. Okay. Tell me about this car ride.

A. Well, he took me on this dirt road where nobody would go and like there was just all kinds of trees and stuff, and then he just showed me stuff that was inappropriate.

Q. Okay, and I hate to do this to you but you are going to have to talk a little bit more than just generally, okay.

A. All right.

Q. He showed you something, what did he show you in the car?

A. Well, he got out of the car and pulled down his pants and showed me stuff that came out of his privates.

Q. And how did it end up coming out of his privates?

A. Just rub his hands on his privates.

Q. What did it look like the stuff that came out?

A. It was whitish.

Q. Okay. What did Dad do after he did that?

A. Uhm, nothing, he just got in the car and drove us home.

Q. Okay. Did he say anything to you?

A. No.

Q. No, okay. And the next time that something happened were you still living in Gray?

A. Yeah.

Q. What did he ask you to do?

A. To just pop pimples on his back.

Q. And how did he bring this up?

A. Just lay down on the couch and take his shirt off.

Q. Okay, and he would ask you to pop the pimples on his back?

A. (Nods head affirmatively.)

Q. Did he have pimples on his back?

A. (Nods head affirmatively.)

Q. What did you do when he said that to you?

A. I just said fine. If I said no I didn't know what he would do so I just always said yes.

Q. Okay, and after you did that or did you do it then?

A. (Nods head affirmatively.)

Q. After you did it what happened?

A. I don't know.

Q. Did he ask you to do something?

A. Sometimes.

Q. When you were living in Gray what did he ask you to do?

A. Uhm, to touch his privates sometimes.

Q. Okay, and what did you touch his privates with?

A. My hands and sometimes my mouth.

Q. Did he do the same to you?

A. (Nods head affirmatively.)

Q. He touched your privates with his hands?

MR. ZERILLO: Objection, leading

COURT: Overruled.

A. Uhm-hum.

Q. And with his mouth?

MR. ZERILLO: Objection, leading.

COURT: Overruled.

A. (Nods head affirmatively.)

Q. How many times did that happen when you lived in Gray?

A. Like once or twice.

Q. Was it once or was it more than once?

A. Like twice or three times.

Q. Okay. Where would this happen when he would do these things to you?

A.   In his room.

Q.   How did it make you feel?

A.   Scared and like uncomfortable.

Q.   Did he say anything to you when he was doing this or when you were doing that?

A.   No, he just like told me if I told anybody then he would be in big trouble and I wouldn't be able to see him anymore.

Q.   All right. Now when he did these things to you did you look at his privates?

A.   (Nods head affirmatively.)

Q.   Were they doing anything, were his privates doing anything?

A.   Just like, he said they, he could make them dance and he moved them up and down.

Q.   Now you said white stuff came out of his privates at sometimes, right?

A.   Uhm-hum.

Q.   What did he do with the white stuff?

A.   He put it in a paper towel and then he threw it away.

Q.   Okay. And did he do anything after he was finished usually?

A.   Well, he told me take a shower and sometimes he told me take a shower and he would get in the shower with me.

Q.   And did you both wash up then in the shower?

A.   (Nods head affirmatively.)

Q.   What about laundry?

A.   Uhm, well, once it got on the bed and he went and did the laundry and washed them.

Q.   Okay, so that was in Gray. Did he ever put his privates in your privates when you lived in Gray?

A.   Hum-uhm (negative).

Q.   Let's talk about this. Did you guys ever watch movies together, you and your Dad?

A.   (Nods head affirmatively.)

Q.   Did you watch normal movies?

A.   Hum-uhm (negative).

Q.   What kind of movies did you watch with Dad?

A.   Like people having sex.

Q.   Where in the house would you watch the movies?

A.   In his room.

Q.   Did you see where he got the movies from?

A.   In his drawer.

Q.   Where was the drawer?

A.   Uhm, like where his TV was.

Q.   On a dresser?

A.   Yeah.

Q.   Was it an end table or side table?

A.   On his dresser.

Q.   And you said the movies were about people having sex?

A.   Yeah.

Q.   Were there different movies you ended up watching?

A.   Yeah.

Q.   About how many different movies?

A.   Like maybe half a drawer or drawer full.

Q.   How long would you watch the movies?

A.   We would just watch some parts of them.

Q.   Okay, and what was he doing when he was watching the movies?

A.   Touching himself and touching me sometimes.

Q.   Did you have your pants on or your pants off?

A.   Pants off.

Q.   What about Dad?

A.   He had his pants off. Can I have a drink of water?

Q.   Sure. If you need a break you just tell me you want a little break, okay. And so you said he would touch himself?

Q.   Did he do this a lot?

A.   (Nods head affirmatively.)

Q. Did he do this when you lived not only in Gray but in the other place as well?

A. (Nods head affirmatively.)

Q. Now when you lived in Gray you said that Dad touched you did you say?

A. (Witness nods head affirmatively).

Q. Where did he touch you?

A. On my private.

Q. Was it on top of your clothes or under your clothes?

A. Under my clothes.

Q. Okay. And what did he touch you with?

A. His fingers and sometimes his mouth.

Q. His fingers and his mouth, okay. What did he do with his fingers?

A. Stuck em in my private.

Q. Did he do that to you when you lived in Westbrook on the Country Road too?

A. (Nods head affirmatively.)

Q. What about at your Grandfather's house?

A. (Witness shakes head negatively).

Q. He didn't do that there. What about let's see what did he do when he put his fingers into you, I mean did he keep his hands still or did he move it around?

A. He moved it around.

Q. How did that feel?

A. It hurt.

Q. And what did he say when he was doing it?

A. He just asked me if it felt good or not.

Q. What did you tell him?

A. I just said yes, I didn't know why I just did.

Q. How many times did he put his fingers into you, do you remember when you lived in Gray?

A. Like once.

Q. What about how many times did he put his mouth on you?

A. Once, the same day that he stuck his fingers in me.

Q. Okay, all right. Now we talked a little bit about your move to Westbrook, right?

A. (Nods head affirmatively.)

Q. Before Thanksgiving you said somewhere around October?

A. (Nods head affirmatively.)

Q. And you moved in with Sally?

A. Uhm-hum.

Q. Do you like Sally?

A. (Nods head affirmatively.)

Q. Got along really well with Sally?

A. Yeah, she was like a second mother to me.

Q. Did you confide in her at all?

A. Uh?

Q. Did you talk to her about personal stuff?

A. Yeah.

Q. Now did Dad do things to you that made you uncomfortable when you lived on Country Road?

A. Uhm-hum.

Q. What if anything did he do with his finger to you on the Country Road?

A. He stuck 'em in my private.

Q. And did he do the same sort of thing that he did in Gray?

A. Uhm-hum.

Q. And the times that he would do that to you there how many times do you think he did it to you when you lived in Westbrook at that address?

A. Like every other day maybe.

Q. All right. Is that all he did to you when you lived on the Country Road?

A. No.

Q. What other things did he do to you?

A. He would like touch his privates and just that stuff.

Q. Did he do anything between your privates and his privates?

A. He stuck his privates in my privates sometimes.

Q. How many times did he do that?

A. Once a week.

Q. How did it feel?

A. It hurt really bad.

Q. Did you tell him that?

A. (Nods head affirmatively.)

Q. What did he say?

MR. ZERILLO: Sidebar.

(A sidebar conference was held.) Note: You may recall that the alleged victim said that her Father bragged about his ability to have sex with another little girl, telling her he could "fit it all the way in" the other girl. I moved *in limine* to strike this statement. The ruling was reserved. I was concerned that the witness may blurt that out during this questioning so I asked for a sidebar. My objection was sustained on this issue.

THE COURT: Members of the jury what we will do is we are going to take, it's a little earlier than we thought but having a look at all the timing we are going to take the lunch break now…

BY MS. PROS:

Q. Tammy, I think where we left off we were talking a little bit about when your Dad put his privates in your privates, right?

A. (Nods head affirmatively.)

Q. And also when he put his fingers in your privates?

A. Yeah.

Q. I think you told me that it hurt?

A. Yes.

Q. Did one way hurt more than the other way?

A. When he put his privates it hurt more.

Q. Did Dad tell you something about a sack?

A. (Nods head affirmatively.)

Q. What did he say about that?

A. He said it's like a cherry and if something hits it that it will pop and blood will just come out for a few minutes.

Q. And he said that to you when?

A. When we were living in Westbrook.

Q. Okay. Did he tell it to you when he was doing these things to you?

A. (Nods head affirmatively.)

Q. Okay. Do you recall whether or not you did bleed?

A. I did not.

Q. You didn't bleed?

A. (Witness nods head affirmatively)

Q. Yes or no was your Dad able to put his privates all the way into your privates?

A. No.

Q. All right. Now we already discussed you moving into your Grandfather's trailer a couple times, right?

A. (Nods head affirmatively.)

Q. That was in the spring of 2007?

A. Yeah.

Q. What did your Dad do to you there if anything that made you feel uncomfortable?

A. Uhm, he would do the same thing, it happened like once or twice there.

Q. And when you say the same thing what did he do to you?

A. He just stuck his hands in my private and his private in my private.

Q. Okay. Did he put his mouth on your privates there too?

A. (Nods head affirmatively.)

Q. Okay. Would he usually do all three things at one time?

A. Sometimes.

Q. Sometimes but not every time?

A. (Nods head affirmatively.)

Q. And—

THE COURT: The witness is fairly soft spoken and I haven't seen people raising their hands. If people are having trouble hearing her then raise your hand and I will ask people to repeat or speak up and I am going to ask the witness if she would too just speak up a little.

BY MS. PROS:

Q. And I am not sure if I actually asked you this already but the movies that you would watch with your Dad what did they show in the movies?

A. Uhm, show people having sex.

Q. Okay. Boys and boys or boys and girls or boys and—

A. Boys and girls.

Q. Boys and girls, okay, and one final question you said sometimes white stuff would come out of Dad's private?

A. Yeah.

Q. Where would the white stuff go when it would come out?

A. What do you mean?

Q. Would it go on the floor, on the bed, on him?

A. Sometimes like once he put it on me.

Q. What did he do when he put it on you?

A. He just rubbed it on my body.

Q. Where on your body did he rub it?

A. On my chest and on my legs.

Q. How did that feel?

A. It made me feel uncomfortable.

Q. And then did you clean up afterwards?

A. (Nods head affirmatively.)

Q. Tammy, I don't think I have any other questions right now but I think Mr. Zerillo has a few for you okay.

A. Okay.

    I can tell you having read this transcript now several times that what doesn't come through is the emotional impact of what this girl was saying. She cried virtually the entire time. She was soft-spoken. She was dressed as you would expect a little girl to dress. She was diminutive in size. She was extremely pitiable. So as I am walking up to the microphone to cross her, the jury is looking at me as though I am Satan incarnate.

    With a child witness like this, I am rarely if ever looking to pound the table. Yell at the cops, yell at the experts, but don't attack the child witness. That does not mean you kowtow to her either. It is a fine line. I have seen horrible cross-examinations done of children that don't set the right balance. You need to be firm, but pleasant. For more tips on cross-examining children, see Ch. 2.

    Here, I am starting out with some facts as to Tammy's home life before she moved in with Dad. It is a troubled home, to be sure.

§12:131   Defense Cross-Examination of Child Victim

Family Situation When Living with Mother

    Initially, I want to establish some rapport with the child. I begin with the basics-- who she lived with before she lived with her Dad. This is important to establishing the instability in Tammy's life.

Q. Hi Tammy. My name's Tim.

A. Hi.

Q. I'm your Dad's lawyer. I want to talk to you a little bit about the time before you moved into your Dad's house, okay?

A. Uh-huh.

Q. Now you were living in Standish?

A.   Yeap.

Q.   And was that in a house or an apartment?

A.   An apartment.

Q.   And you were living there with your sister Tabitha?

A.   Yes.

Q.   And how old was Tabitha then?

A.   Uh, 15.

Q.   Okay. Did she go to high school?

A.   Yes.

Q.   And you had another person who lived there?

A.   Yes.

Q.   And who's that?

A.   Jamie.

Q.   And Jamie is your Mom and Step-Dad's child?

A.   Yes.

Q.   And your Step-Dad is John ?

A.   Yes.

Q.   And he lived there too?

A.   Yes.

Q.   And your Mom lived there obviously?

A.   Yes.

Q.   And you had a couple cats?

A.   Yes.

Q.   Did you have your dog Buddy at that point?

A.   Yes.

Q.   Did you like Buddy a lot?

A.   Yes.

Q.   And you had two cats?

A.   Yes.

Q.   You liked them too, right?

A.   Yes.

Q.   You did. Before you moved in with your Dad were you having a lot of fights with your Mom?

A.   Uhm, not often.

Q.   No. But did you have fights with your Mom on the day that you moved in with your Dad?

A.   Uhm, yes.

Q.   Did Tabitha and your Mom have a lot of fights?

A.   Yes.

Q.   And did you get involved in the fights, get sort of caught in the middle of the fights with Tabitha and your Mom?

A.   Sometimes.

Q.   And was there lots of yelling?

A.   (Nods head affirmatively.)

Q.   Yes?

A.   Yes.

Q.   This nice lady is taking down everything you say so sometimes I will ask you to say yes if you nod at me if the answer is yes, OK?

A.   All right.

Q.   Okay. So before you moved in with your Dad you went to Generic Primary School?

A.   Yes.

Q.   And how were your grades in school at Generic Primary School?

A.   Good.

Q.   Good. Did you get A's and B's or Cs and B's?

A.   C's and B's.

Q.   C's and B's mostly?

A.   Yeah.

Q. And before you moved in with your Dad you still saw him every once in a while, right?
A. Yes, every other weekend.
Q. And is that the way it was for most of your life until this time, every other weekend?
A. Yes.
Q. And that was contact that you enjoyed with your Dad?
A. Uhm, sometimes we spent time together but most of the time I was just over with my friends 'cuz he was working.
Q. Yeah. He works a lot?
A. Yeah.
Q. Did you know Sally before you moved in with --
A. Uhm, no.
Q. So the first time you met Sally was the day that you moved into the house in Gray, right?
A. Yes.

Moving in with Defendant

Q. So I want to talk about the day that you moved in with your Dad, okay, and there was a big fight that day, right?
A. Yes.
Q. Between your Mom and Tabitha?
A. (Nods head affirmatively).
Q. Yes?
A. Yes.
Q. And were you involved in that fight?
A. Uhm, I don't recall being in it.
Q. You don't recall, okay. Was there a lot of yelling?
A. Uhm, a little bit.
Q. And was your Mom yelling?
A. A little bit.
Q. How about Tabitha?
A. Yes.

Here we are with this tumultuous home environment, and the nine year old is allowed to make decisions to leave. We always want to be getting to the "why." Why would this child lie about something so horrible? Here, we want to set it up so that it is clear that she leaves in the midst of chaos, but she is leaving a lot behind that she wants to get back to later.

Q. Okay. And did you hear your Mom call up your Dad?
A. Uhm, yes.
Q. When she called up your Dad, she sounded pretty angry?
A. (Nods head affirmatively.)
Q. Yes?
A. Yes.
Q. And did she say for him to come get you?
A. Yes.
Q. And did you know that you were going to be leaving your home on that day?
A. I asked to leave.
Q. You did?
A. 'Cuz I didn't want to hear the fighting.
Q. You didn't want to hear the fighting between Tabitha and Mom?
A. Yes.
Q. And was Step-Dad involved in this?
A. Uhm, yes.
Q. And in the fighting?
A. Yeah.
Q. And you didn't want to be involved in fighting with Step-Dad either?

A. Yeah.

Q. Okay. So you asked to leave and your Mom called your Dad?

A. Uhm-hum.

Q. Yes?

A. Yes.

Q. And you—how long before your Dad got there?

A. Uhm, maybe half-an-hour.

Q. Now what's the longest time that you had ever spent with your Dad before that?

A. Uhm.

Q. Sort of an open question. Let me ask you something else, did you ever spend like a week in a row with your father before that?

A. No.

Q. How long did it take your Dad to get there from your Mom's call?

A. Half-an-hour maybe.

Q. Did you have time to pack?

A. Yes.

Q. You did. Did you take your cats with you?

A. No.

Q. How about your dog Buddy?

A. No.

Q. And obviously your brother and sister stayed behind?

A. Yes.

Q. You must have had a lot of friends in Standish too, right?

A. Yes.

Q. Was it, was it difficult for you to leave?

A. Uhm, kind of.

Q. You didn't, you didn't want to leave because you didn't love your Mom?

A. No.

Q. You love your Mom a lot?

A. Yes.

Q. It was just too much fighting?

A. Yes.

Q. I have to discuss some hard questions just like Attorney Pros did.

A. Okay.

Q. Okay. I want to talk about prior to you moving in with your Dad.

A. Yeap.

Q. Did anyone ever touch you in a sexually inappropriate way as you said prior to the time that you moved in with your Dad?

A. No.

Q. Did anyone ever touch you with their finger in a sexually inappropriate way?

A. No.

Q. With their mouth in a sexually inappropriate way?

A. No.

Q. Okay. So you remember the day you moved in with your Dad?

A. Yes.

Q. Do you have a good memory of it as you sit here today?

A. Uhm, it's okay.

Q. It's not 100% clear, your memory?

A. Not 100%.

Q. The day you moved was the first time you met Sally?

A. Yes.

Q. And Nancy wasn't in Gray, was she?

A. No.

Q. She didn't move in until you lived in Westbrook?

A. Yes.
Q. So it was just you and your Dad and Sally then in Gray?
A. Yes.

Defendant's Lack of Opportunity

Where you can, establish lack of opportunity. Just because a child lives with the defendant does not mean the defendant had opportunity to engage in the acts claimed. I am peppering in lack of opportunity defenses throughout this cross.

Q. And you had your own room in Gray, right?
A. Yeap.
Q. Now this is when your Dad was working a lot of long hours, right?
A. Uhm-hum.
Q. Yes?
A. Yes.
Q. And Sally wasn't working at the time, was she?
A. No, I don't believe so.
Q. So when you first moved to Gray, Sally was taking you around by car quite a bit?
A. Yes.
Q. She was—were you staying home with Sally alone?
A. Uhm, sometimes.
Q. Okay, and when your Dad went to work, he went to work pretty early in the morning?
A. Yes.
Q. Before you got up lots of times?
A. Yes.
Q. And he would come home around suppertime?
A. Yes.
Q. And during that period of time when Dad was at work, Sally was around?
A. Yes.
Q. Now you also went to school obviously?
A. Yes.
Q. And in the summertime you went to daycare?
A. Yes.
Q. And that day care was with Athena?
A. Yes.
Q. And Sally was the one usually to pick you up from daycare, right?
A. Sometimes.
Q. Did you go to daycare when you were living in Gray?
A. No.
Q. Okay. So I have sort of moved this on to Westbrook. I'm sorry about that.
A. Yes.
Q. So sometimes you were picked up by Sally?
A. Yeah.
Q. In Westbrook, and at that point Sally was back to work?
A. Yes.
Q. And sometimes were you picked up by your Grandpa?
A. Yes, sometimes.
Q. Do you call him Grandpa or Grandfather?
A. Grampy.
Q. Grampy and that's Lowell?
A. Yes.
Q. And he picked you up too?
A. Sometimes.

Q. Sometimes. And how about your aunt?
A. Uhm, she did once in while, not a lot.
Q. Did you say she did once in a while?
A. Yeah.
Q. And that's Sherry?
A. Yes.
Q. Okay. But when you lived in Gray, Sally picked you up almost all the time, is that right?
A. Yes.
Q. And was your Dad keeping the same work schedule when you moved to Westbrook as he did in Gray?
A. Uhm.
Q. Was he still leaving early in the morning when you lived in Westbrook?
A. Yes.
Q. Coming home late at night?
A. Uhm, not often, he would come home a little bit early.
Q. A little bit early?
A. Yeah like maybe 3ish.
Q. Okay, and that was unusual though, right?
A. Yeah.

Positive and Normal Aspects of Life with Defendant

Point out positive things that the child can't deny about the time with your defendant. Did the child take up a new sport or instrument? Learn origami? There are two reasons for this. First, you need to take the jury away from the emotional place where the sexual assaults allegedly took place. Second, you want to present a dichotomy that the jurors cannot account for. You want them saying, how could this person, who taught her to play the violin, have been sexually assaulting her? And why did this child flourish if he or she was being abused?

Q. And you went to school in Gray for a little bit, right?
A. Yeap.
Q. And you also went to school in Westbrook?
A. Yes.
Q. Now did your grades get better from the time you started living with your Dad?
A. Uhm, yes.
Q. You went from like C's and B's to A's and B's, right?
A. Yes.
Q. Very good. And you began playing sports for the first time, too, didn't you?
A. Yes.
Q. You played soccer, right?
A. Right.
Q. You don't play that anymore?
A. No.
Q. Didn't you win the Most Improved Player award for soccer?
A. Yes.
Q. Congratulations, that's great.
A. Thanks.
Q. Now did your Dad go to your games?
A. Yep.
Q. And practices?
A. Sometimes.
Q. OK. I think generally is it fair to say that you liked living with Dad?
A. Yeah.

Here I am attempting to point out that she had a normal life with her Dad and his family. Again, push everything toward normalcy if possible. Don't only focus your cross on the alleged sexual acts.

Q. And during the time that you were in Gray did you ever just sort of hang out with your Dad and watch TV?
A. Sometimes.
Q. In Westbrook too?
A. Yes.
Q. Did Dad and Sally go out a lot?
A. Uhm, sometimes.
Q. Yeah. When they did they left you with a sitter?
A. Uhm, Nancy sometimes.
Q. So that would have been when you were in Westbrook?
A. Yes.
Q. And Nancy would babysit you a little bit?
A. Yeah.
Q. You said Nancy is shy I think you said?
A. Yeah.
Q. Does that mean she keeps to herself?
A. Yeah.
Q. Does she stay home a lot?
A. Yes.
Q. So when you were home in Westbrook, Nancy was almost always home, is that right?
A. Yes.
Q. Was there ever a time when you were home at Westbrook and she wasn't there that you can remember?
A. Yeah, sometimes.
Q. But not very often?
A. No.
Q. So you didn't avoid your Dad when you were living in Westbrook, is that fair to say?
A. Yeah.
Q. You hung out with him you said, right?
A. Yeah.
Q. And you hung out with him and his family too, right?
A. Yeah.
Q. You hung out with him and Aunt Sherry?
A. Yeah.
Q. And Sherry's friend Lola?
A. Yeap.
Q. And at Grandpa's?
A. Yeah.

Former Girlfriend's Bias against Defendant

Sally became a real issue in the case. The Defendant's live-in girlfriend was on the Defendant's side until they broke up, and then her allegiance shifted. I point this out briefly here because it becomes an issue in the trial and I want to continue a theme of Sally's bias.

Q. I think you said that you liked Sally?
A. Yeah.
Q. Did you like Sally the whole time you were there?
A. Uhm, sometimes, but we get along now.
Q. Now you still see Sally, don't you?
A. Yes.
Q. After you moved out with your Dad you went back to live with your Mom initially?
A. Yes.
Q. Did you ever see Sally over at your house?
A. Uhm, we went and visited her sometimes.
Q. You and your Mom went and visited Sally?

A. Yeah.

Q. And where was she living?

A. In Westbrook over by her friend Jen.

Q. So is it fair to say that you sort of like Sally more now that you have moved out?

A. Yes.

Q. At the time that you were living with your Dad, you got into a lot of fights with Sally, isn't that right?

A. Yeah, sometimes.

What Went Wrong at Defendant's Home

Now we start to transition into what went wrong at Dad's house. We need to continue our theme of getting to the "why."

Q. Did you try to run away at one point?

A. Yes.

Q. You tried to run away from your Dad's house?

A. Yes.

Q. And you were punished?

A. Yes.

Q. You didn't like that, did you?

A. No.

Q. Were you trying to run away to your Mom's house?

A. I don't know.

Q. At one point you started talking to your Mom a lot on the phone when you lived with your Dad too, right?

A. Yes.

Q. Did you do that like a secret?

A. Yeah, sometimes.

Q. When you started talking to your Mom in secret had you decided that you wanted to move out of Dad's house?

A. Yes.

Q. And did you talk to your Mom about how you would move out of the house?

A. Yes.

Q. And did you start to talk about ways that you could move out of the house?

A. Uhm, kind of.

Q. Is that around the time that you tried to run away?

A. Uhm, no, it was like I started talking to her after I tried to run away cuz he left me home and went out to eat because I was grounded.

Q. So he went out to eat with Sally?

A. And Nancy.

Q. And Nancy. Was it a celebration?

A. I don't know. They just wanted to go out to eat I guess.

Q. And you were alone?

A. Yes.

Q. And you were upset by that?

A. Yes.

Q. And that's when you tried to run away?

A. Yes.

Q. Is that when you were, one of the times that you were punished?

A. Yes.

Q. I think you said when you were speaking to the other lawyer that you were punished for not doing homework or telling something you shouldn't have told something like that, right?

A. Yes.

Q. You were punished for lying about things?

A. Yes.

Q. And how often were you punished about that?

A. Uhm, once every two weeks maybe.
Q. Now I think you said that you were sent to your room for a really long time when you were punished, right?
A. Two or three days.
Q. Two or three days?
A. Yes.

So I stumbled upon an exaggeration here in my view. Keep her going with it, and turn the exaggeration into a lie. You will be arguing later that if she lies about the little things, she will lie about the big things too.

Q. Wow, 2 or 3 days in your room is a long time isn't it?
A. Yes.
Q. Now I wrote down in my notes and I might be wrong about this because sometimes my notes aren't right that you said that you were punished for one or two days when this attorney spoke to you, do you remember that?
A. No, I said like two or three days.
Q. You said two or three days, so for two or three days you would be put in your room?
A. Yes.
Q. And you weren't allowed to come out?
A. Only to get my breakfast sometimes.
Q. But they didn't let you out for lunch.
A. No.
Q. Or dinner?
A. Maybe for dinner, sometimes for dinner.
Q. Did you miss school because you were in your room for two or three days?
A. No.
Q. Were those all the reasons that you were disciplined while you lived there?
A. Yes.
Q. You were disciplined for trying to run away, right?
A. Yes.
Q. You forgot about that one the first time, right?
A. Yeah.
Q. We should add that to the list?
A. Yeah.
Q. Okay. How about a sidebar, sorry, Your Honor.
(A sidebar conference was held)
THE COURT: Ladies and gentlemen, we are going to break briefly at this point and I am going to try and hope that that is five to ten minutes but we are going to excuse you for at least that long. Remember that all the existing instructions remain in effect and thank you very much.
BY MR. ZERILLO:
Q. When we stopped before we were talking about reasons you had been punished at your Dad's house.
A. Yes.
Q. And I think we said you had been punished for lying, right?
A. Yes.
Q. And for not doing homework?
A. Yes.
Q. Were you punished for anything else that you remember?
A. Running away.
Q. For running away, thank you, that was the third one we added, right?
A. Yes.
Q. Anything other than lying, not doing homework and running away?
A. Uhm, no.
Q. Were you ever punished for taking money that didn't belong to you?
A. No.
Q. Were you ever punished for threatening to kill yourself?
A. Uhm, I don't remember.

Q. You don't remember if you were punished for that?
A. (Nods head affirmatively.)
Q. Did you say you do not remember?
A. I did not remember.
Q. Do you remember ever saying that to anybody?
A. Yes.
Q. To who?
A. Uhm, I don't remember to who but I know that I told somebody that.
Q. Was that when you were in Westbrook?
A. Yes.
Q. Did these punishments create a lot of arguments?
A. Sometimes.
Q. Did you talk to your Mom about that when you were having phone calls with her?
A. Yeah, sometimes.
Q. Punishments make you angry?
A. Kind of.
Q. You didn't like them?
A. No.
Q. In fact you said that your Dad spanked you?
A. Yes.
Q. And that was in addition to him making you go to your room for long periods of time, right?
A. Yes.
Q. Would he spank you and then make you go to your room for two or three days?
A. Yes.
Q. He would do both?
A. (Nods head affirmatively.)
Q. Yes?
A. Yes.
Q. And how many times did he spank you in the time you lived in Westbrook?
A. Like once or twice.
Q. Do you remember both of those times well as you sit here now?
A. I remember one of them well,
Q. So it could have been maybe it was just one time?
A. Yeah.
Q. And in that time he spanked you on your butt?
A. Yes.
Q. And was that during the time when you threatened to run away?
A. No.
Q. No, it wasn't?
A. (Witness shakes head negatively).
Q. That was a different punishment?
A. Yes.
Q. And did you complain to your Mom on the phone about that spanking?
A. Yes.
Q. And you told her that you didn't like it?
A. Yes.
Q. Told her it hurt?
A. Yes.
Q. Did you tell her about anything else?
A. No.
Q. That you didn't like?
A. No.
Q. How did you get along with Nancy?
A. Fine.

Q. Okay, and how old is she?
A. Uhm, I don't know.
Q. Is she grown up?
A. Yeah.
Q. A young grownup?
A. Like 20.
Q. Teenager?
A. 20 maybe.

Mother's Secret Plan to Regain Custody

Now, this is interesting. If Mom pushed Tammy to help re-establish custody of her, it gets to the "why" issue. So I want to develop this line for future argument.

Q. Okay. And did you tell her things?
A. Uhm, I told her once that my Mom was writing down what I told her to tell her lawyer.
Q. That your Mom was writing down what you told her on the phone?
A. Yeah.
Q. To tell her lawyer?
A. Yes.
Q. That was a secret right?
A. Yes.
Q. You told Nancy that?
A. Yeah, and I told her that I wanted to move out so she told Sally and Sally told my Dad.
Q. Okay. Is that how you came to move out?
A. Yes.
Q. Didn't your Dad find out that you were having conversations with your Mom secretly?
A. Yes.
Q. And did he call up your Mom?
A. Yes.
Q. And do you have a speaker phone, you know what a speaker phone is?
A. Yes.
Q. Did he have a speaker phone at his house?
A. Uhm, I'm not sure.
Q. Do you remember him calling up your Mom?
A. Yes.
Q. Were you able to hear her on speaker phone?
A. No.
Q. So you only—did you hear what your Dad's side of the conversation was then?
A. Uhm, what do you mean?
Q. In other words, you couldn't hear what your Mom was saying?
A. No.
Q. But could you hear what your Dad was saying?
A. Yes.
Q. Did your Dad sound angry?
A. He was frustrated.
Q. Yeah. He appeared to be frustrated to you?
A. Yes.
Q. Did he tell you he was frustrated?
A. I could just see it in his face how he was frustrated.
Q. And that was—did you know what that frustration was about?
A. Me not telling that I wanted to move out.
Q. He was, to you he appeared to be frustrated that you were keeping that secret?
A. Yes.

Q. Did you have conversations with or did you talk to your Aunt Sherry a lot when you lived with your Dad in Westbrook?
A. Sometimes.

Tampon as Explanation for Hymen Injury

The tampon portion of the cross coming up is to help me with the expert later See §12:XX. I don't know until I ask if Tammy will admit or deny the attempted tampon insertion. Even if she denies it, as she does here, I will raise it with Sally and Aunt Sherry.

Q. I want to talk to you about tampons. Do you know what a tampon is?
A. Yes.
Q. When you lived with your Dad did you ever try to insert a tampon?
A. No.
Q. Never once?
A. (Witness shakes head negatively).
Q. No?
A. No.
Q. Sally didn't see you do that?
A. No.
Q. Did you ever talk to anybody about doing that?
A. No.
Q. Didn't talk to Aunt Sherry about doing it?
A. No.
Q. Didn't talk to Lola about doing it?
A. No.

More Details of Alleged Assaults; Inconsistencies; Lack of Opportunity

Q. Okay. So let's go back to Gray and talk about the dirt road that you talked about, okay?
A. Yes.
Q. Did that happen during the time that you lived in Gray?
A. Yes.
Q. Did you—you spoke to Detective Lippy about this case?
A. Yes.
Q. He's that gentleman sitting right there?
A. Yes.
Q. Did you talk to him about that incident on the dirt road?
A. Uhm, not sure.
Q. You don't remember?
A. No.
Q. Do you remember your conversation with Detective Lippy?
A. Not really.
Q. No. You have any memory of talking to him at all?
A. I just remember there was a girl there.
Q. And do you remember him asking you questions about your Dad?
A. Yes.
Q. But you don't remember if you told about the dirt road?
A. Yes.
Q. So if I understood your testimony before you said that your Dad didn't put his privates into your privates when you lived in Gray, right?
A. No.
Q. He did not?
A. He did not.
Q. Thank you. He didn't put his privates in your privates until you lived in Westbrook, right?

A. Yes.
Q. Okay. So you said he had inappropriate behavior and that's why I am using that, okay.
A. Yes.
Q. That inappropriate behavior that was in Gray was him touching you with his fingers?
A. Yes.
Q. And that happened one time, right?
A. Uhm, in Gray, yes, once.
Q. One time he used his fingers in an inappropriate way?
A. Yes.
Q. And that was the same one time that he used his mouth?
A. Yes.
Q. But there was no—have you ever heard the term intercourse?
A. No.
Q. Okay. There was none of him putting his privates in your privates when you were in Gray?
A. No.
Q. And you're sure of that, right?
A. Yes.

The confusion here was to eliminate some counts of the indictment, which we were able to do with this clarification. Of course, it was a 25 count indictment, so it was a small consolation.

But as you will notice here in the upcoming cross, the alleged victim is all over the road. The jury looked cross-eyed when the cross was over.

Q. So when you went to Westbrook, the first time that he put his privates in your privates was at the Bridgton Road apartment, is that right?
A. Yes.
Q. And that was before you went to move in with grandpa, right?
A. Yes.
Q. I'm sorry, that's not what you call him. What do you call him?
A. Grandpa.
Q. Before you moved in with him that didn't happen, correct?
A. Yes.
Q. And you said that you got in the shower—
A. Yes.
Q. —with Dad, and how often did that happen?
A. Like once.
Q. And that was during the time period that Nancy was home a lot, right?
A. Yes.
Q. So she would have been home a lot or she would have been home during the first time that he put his privates into your private?
A. Yes.
Q. And you said that that first time took place where?
A. In his bedroom.
Q. Okay. And you have to go out into the hallway from his bedroom to get to the shower, right?
A. Yes.
Q. And you went from that hallway into the shower with him?
A. Yes.
Q. And Nancy was home during that time?
A. Yes.
Q. And did that—did you take a shower with him one time you said or more than once?
A. Once.
Q. And only in Westbrook, right?
A. Yes.
Q. And not at Grandpa's house?

A. No.

Q. And this was during the period of time that Sally was working then, huh?

A. Yes.

Q. Did you tell anyone else that your Dad had put his privates in your privates when you lived in Gray?

A. No.

Q. You didn't tell Detective Lippy your Dad put his privates in your privates when you lived in Gray?

A. No, I told I thought you meant like when I was living in Gray.

Q. I'm sorry. I probably asked you a bad question. After you left your Dad's house?

A. Yes, I did tell him.

Q. And you told Detective Lippy that your Dad put his privates in your privates in Gray, right?

A. Yeah.

Q. But that wasn't true?

A. No, it was true.

Q. He did put his privates in your privates in Gray?

A. Yes.

Q. And so now you are saying that he did?

A. He did, and I told Mrs. Pros, I think I told Mrs. Pros that.

Q. Okay. So before I asked you if that had happened in Gray. Do you remember me talking about that?

A. Yes.

Q. And we said there was the incident on the dirt road, right?

A. Yes.

Q. And we also said that there was a time where he used his finger and his mouth at the same time, right?

A. Yes.

Q. And I asked you if he put his privates in your privates in Gray and you said that he didn't, right?

A. Uhm, I didn't know what you said.

Q. Okay. So just to be clear now you are saying that he did put his privates in your privates in Gray?

A. Yes, he did.

Q. He did. And how many times did that happen?

A. Once.

Q. One time. Did you tell Detective Lippy, this man, that it happened three times?

A. No.

Q. You didn't tell him that. So if Detective Lippy says that you told him it happened three times you would disagree with that?

A. Yes.

Q. You would say you never said that.

A. I never said that.

Q. And if that is in his report, his report is wrong.

A. I never said that.

Q. So I've got to go back to Gray now, okay, so the time when he put his privates in your privates in Gray where did that take place?

A. In his bedroom

Q. Okay. Did you tell Detective Lippy that it took place in the bathroom?

A. No.

Q. You didn't tell him that?

A. Uhm, not sure.

Q. Was that the time that he said that there was the cherry that you talked about?

A. He said that in Westbrook.

Q. Okay. So he had already put his privates in your privates before he said that there was a cherry?

A. Yes.

Q. He didn't mention the cherry and the blood the first time he put his privates in your privates?

A. No.

Q. What was the house like on Bridgton Road in Westbrook?

A. It was like three apartments, and there was Sally and he had his room, I had my room, then next room down the hallway.

Q. And that was who was in Westbrook, you and Sally and Nancy and your Dad?

A. Yes.

Q. And your Dad you already said was still working a lot?

A. Yes.

Q. And where did—I think you said that the inappropriate sexual activity happened once a week when you were in Westbrook?

A. Yes.

Q. Now how many weeks did you live there roughly?

A. Uhm, I don't know.

Q. Did you live there a few months?

A. Yeah.

Q. Are you sure it happened once a week?

A. Like more than once a week, like, like sometimes when he picked me up from school before softball.

Q. But still it would take place in the house in Westbrook?

A. Yes.

Q. And was he picking you up at school before softball a lot?

A. Uhm, sometimes.

Q. And you played softball in Westbrook?

A. Yes.

Q. Did you have a position?

A. Outfield.

Q. You like playing softball?

A. Yes.

Q. And your Dad took you?

A. Yes.

Q. Did he participate in softball practices or the games?

A. Yes.

Q. You didn't have any problems going with him to softball, right?

A. No.

Q. You are probably a pretty good player?

A. Yes.

Q. Really? Good. Okay, so it happened maybe more than once a week then when you were in Westbrook?

A. Yes.

Q. And would it always happen in his bedroom?

A. It happened once in the living room.

Q. Okay. And was Nancy home that time too?

A. No.

Q. Was Sally home?

A. No.

Q. But most of the time Sally and Nancy were home?

A. Uhm, yes, not Sally, most of the time Nancy was.

Q. Because Sally was working at that point?

A. Yes.

Q. Is it fair to say that you didn't have any sexually inappropriate behavior or activity with your father until the time Sally started working again?

A. Uhm, yeah, except for in Gray that two times or one time.

Q. But had Sally started working at that point?

A. Uhm, yes, actually she had.

Q. So I think you said that you moved into Grampa Lowell's house two or three times during this period?

A. Yes.

Q. Is that right?

A. Yes.

Q. You sure you didn't just move in there once?

A. I'm sure.

Q. How many times do you know, two or three?
A. Two probably.
Q. Two probably?
A. Yeah.
Q. Now that's a trailer though, right?
A. Yes.
Q. Is it a pretty small place?
A. Yeah.
Q. Your Dad put his privates in your privates in your bedroom in the trailer?
A. Uhm, once or twice in the trailer but mostly it was, that was in Westbrook.
Q. Okay. Let's talk about the trailer now, so I think you said before that it happened once in the trailer, am I right about that?
A. Uhm, yeah.
Q. And that's what you believed it was one time in the trailer?
A. Yeah.
Q. And that happened in the bedroom you were staying in?
A. Yes.
Q. Now right off of the bedroom you were staying in there is a living room, right?
A. Yes.
Q. And was your Grandfather out in the living room a lot watching TV?
A. Well, it was always at nighttime. It happened at nighttime when he did it, so he was sleeping.
Q. Didn't your Grandpa stay up late watching TV?
A. Sometimes.
Q. How many days did you stay there, do you remember?
A. Maybe a week, not even.
Q. And you think it happened one time probably?
A. Yeah.
Q. Now Ms. Pros asked you if the door closed in that bedroom?
A. Yes.
Q. Do you remember that?
A. Yes.
Q. Wasn't the doorknob broken on that bedroom?
A. No.
Q. The door closed all the way?
A. Yes.
Q. Did it lock?
A. No.
Q. So it closed but didn't lock?
A. Yes.
Q. And during the time that you had this inappropriate sexual activity with your Father at the trailer, your Grandfather was there, correct?
A. Yes.
Q. And this is during the time that your Grandfather used to pick you up at school sometimes?
A. Yes.
Q. And you would go to Athena 's day care?
A. Yes.
Q. When you went to the—do you remember going to Maine Medical Center?
A. Yes.
Q. And you met with a couple doctors there?
A. Yes.
Q. And did they ask you how often your father put his privates into your privates?
A. Yes.
Q. And did you tell them six or seven times?
A. Like, like sometimes he would do it I don't remember how many times I said it, how many times I said.

Q. Okay. And you spoke to Dr. Howard?
A. Yes.
Q. Dr. Howard also did an exam of you?
A. Yes.
Q. And did you tell him that your father put his privates anywhere other than your privates?
A. In my mouth.
Q. Did you tell him that he put it in your butt?
A. Yes, actually I did.
Q. And was that true?
A. Yes.
Q. And when did that happen when he put it in your butt?
A. Uhm, in Westbrook.
Q. On Country Road or at your --
A. Yes, Country Road.
Q. Yes. And that happened one time?
A. Ohm, yes.
Q. And was Nancy home at that time?
A. Uhm, yes.

I have had several cases involving allegations of anal sex. It seems to be an add-on to the complaint some-times. If it is, and there are no medical findings, bring it up with the child, and highlight it in the cross of the expert. Here, it is hard to imagine the victim being anally penetrated with someone else in the house not hearing or noticing anything.

Q. Do you make up stories sometimes?
A. No, I used to, but I don't anymore.
Q. When did you stop making up stories?
A. Uhm, like maybe a month before I moved back with my Mom.
Q. And why did you stop making up stories a month before you moved back with your Mom?
A. 'Cuz I knew if people thought I was still lying then nobody would believe me.
Q. So when you used to make up stories they were sometimes about things that didn't happen?
A. Yeah.
Q. Did you make up the stories more when you were upset or when you were happy?
A. Sometimes when I was upset.
Q. You tried really hard to get along with Sally, right?
A. Yes.
Q. In fact you called her Mom, didn't you?
A. Yes.
Q. But ultimately you wanted to get out of there, right?
A. Yes.
Q. You used to write her cards, right?
A. Yeah.
Q. And when you got into trouble you would write her an apology card, right?
A. Yes.
Q. Okay.
MS. PROS: Your Honor, can the witness have a tissue?
THE COURT: I'm sorry.
MS. PROS: Can she have a tissue please. Thank you.
BY MR. ZERILLO:
Q. Did you ever stay over at Sally's house without your Dad?
A. Uhm, when do you mean?
Q. Before you—well, at any time.
A. Uhm, I don't think so.
Q. But you don't remember?

A. Yeah.

Q. I am going to talk a little bit about the Country Road house in Westbrook. Your Dad's and Sally's room was across from the kitchen?

A. Yes.

Q. And so to get out of their room you had to walk through the kitchen?

A. Yes.

Q. And then to get from their room to the bathroom where the shower was you needed to walk through the kitchen and then the living room?

A. Uhm, like right at the doorway of the living room.

Q. And the living room was next to Nancy's room, right?

A. Yes.

Q. I think you said that you watched, I don't remember how you described it, did you watch, you said you watched a dirty movie with your Dad?

A. Yeah.

Q. Or a movie with people doing things with their privates?

A. Yes.

Q. Had you ever watched a movie like that before then?

A. No.

Q. You never did?

A. No.

Q. I think you said that you didn't remember your interview with Detective Lippy very well today, right?

A. No.

Q. But you remember you did meet with him?

A. Yes.

Q. And your Mom was there with you?

A. Yes.

Q. You held her hand?

A. Yes.

Q. And when your Mom appeared to be upset you gave her a hug?

A. I think so.

Q. Squeezed her hand when she appeared to be upset?

A. I think so.

Q. Your Mom was encouraging to you in talking about this?

A. Yes.

Q. She encouraged you to talk to Detective Lippy?

A. Yes.

Q. Detective Lippy encouraged you to talk to him?

A. Yes.

Q. He told you he believed you?

A. Yes.

Q. You felt good about that?

A. Yes.

Q. Are you living in Bridgton now?

A. Yes.

Q. And you like it there okay?

A. Yeah.

Q. But you still want to get back and live with your Mom?

A. Yes.

Q. After you came back to live with your Mom out of your Dad's house you and your Mom spent a lot of time together, didn't you?

A. Yes.

Q. You got really close to her?

A. Yes.

Q. And you want to move back in there now?

A. Yes.
Q. You are still trying to get back to your Mom?
A. Yes.
MR. ZERILLO: Nothing further. Thank you.

§ 12:132 Prosecution's Redirect Examination of Child Victim

Q. Just a couple questions for you, Tammy, okay?
A. Okay.
Q. You said Mom's encouraged you throughout the course of what's been happening, right?
A. Yes.
Q. And you are very close to your Mom now?
A. Yes.
Q. Did anybody including your Mom ever tell you what to say?
A. No.
Q. And these events they happened quite a while ago now, uh?
MR. ZERILLO: Objection, leading.
COURT: Overruled.
A. Yes.
Q. A year and a half, two years ago almost, right?
A. Yes.
Q. Is it fair to say that everything was more fresh in your memory at the time it happened than it is today?
MR. ZERILLO: Objection, leading.
COURT: Overruled.
A. Yes.
Q. Why, don't you tell the jury what time did you get up this morning?
A. Like six.
MR. ZERILLO: Objection, relevance.
THE COURT: I'll overrule it, allow her to explain her today's situation.
BY MS. PROS:
Q. What time did you get up today?
A. Like 6:45ish.
Q. Is that earlier than when you usually get up?
A. Yes.
Q. Are you tired today?
A. Yes.
Q. All right. Let's see, since you moved out from Dad and Sally's --
how many times do you think you have seen Sally?
A. Uhm, once maybe.
Q. Once, okay. Are Mom and Sally friends? I mean do they see each other as far as you know?
A. Yes.
Q. A lot?
A. Uhm, she is okay with her, she doesn't mind her.
Q. But do they do things together as far as you know?
A. Uhm, no, the first time that we saw her was in Westbrook.
Q. When was that, do you remember?
A. I can't remember, maybe a few months after I left Dad's house.
Q. Okay. Remember when you moved out of your Mom's house and into Dad's house?
A. Yes.
Q. Did you have the conversation with your Mom about moving back and forth?
A. Uhm, not sure.
Q. Did Mom tell you something about whether or not you could actually move back and forth between the two houses?
A. Uhm, I don't know.
Q. Okay. Who is more strict, who disciplined you more Dad and Sally or Mom?

A.   Uhm, Sally doesn't discipline me a lot, she only disciplined me once. Mom doesn't discipline me anymore, uhm, so—

Q.   When you were living with your Mom versus when you were living with Dad who—where would you get punished or disciplined more often?

A.   Uhm, they were like equal.

Q.   Okay. So when you were punished by Mom how would Mom punish you?

A.   Uhm, just go to my room for maybe an hour.

Q.   Did Mom spank your butt?

A.   No.

Q.   So you basically got timeouts?

A.   Yeah.

Q.   Is that what she called them timeouts?

A.   Yeah.

Q.   Now you talked to Sally about a lot of personal things, right?

A.   Yeah.

Q.   Did you talk to Sally about your period?

A.   Uhm, once.

Q.   Okay. Did Sally let you look at a sanitary pad, a sanitary napkin?

A.   Uh?

Q.   Do you remember her looking at—you wearing a sanitary pad to try it out once?

A.   Once.

Q.   Once?

A.   Yeah.

Q.   How did that come about?

A.   Well, well, 'cuz I had bladder problems right now, so they thought I started my period, but I didn't, it was bladder problems.

Q.   So, but you have never used a tampon, is that right?

A.   No.

Q.   Going back to when Dad would do things to you that you didn't like.

A.   Yeah.

Q.   You talked about he did basically three different things to you, right?

A.   Yes.

Q.   Would he do all three things every single time?

A.   Uhm, no.

Q.   So he would do some things sometimes, sometimes he would do everything?

A.   Yes.

Q.   And you said you would sometimes make up stories?

A.   Yes.

Q.   What would you make up stories about?

A.   Uhm, like I don't know, like silly stuff like.

Q.   Give me one example of silly stuff that you would make up a story about.

A.   Like I would say like somebody was something and they weren't or something like that.

Q.   Would you make up stories about something for instance Tabitha did to you or what Jamie did to you?

A.   No.

Q.   No. Thank you very much.

§12:133   Defense's Recross Examination of Child Victim

Q.   Hi, again.

A.   Hi.

Q.   I know you're tired.

A.   (Nods head affirmatively.)

Q.   You are not so tired that you can't remember to tell the truth, right?

A.   Yeah.

Q. If I asked if your name is Tammy Jones what would you say?
A. No.
Q. Okay, because that's not true, right?
A. No.
Q. And you told the truth when I was asking you questions?
A. Yes.
Q. Your Mom and Sally are friendly now I think is that what you said?
A. Yes.
Q. You guys have all been hanging out in the hallway out here together?
A. Yes.
Q. I think I saw her showing you some pictures on her phone.
A. Yeah.
Q. You were also asked on the last time there about whether your Mom ever spanked you?
A. Yeah.
Q. And your Mom never—
A. No.
Q. —physically punished you?
A. Uhm, once she hit me in the face.
Q. And that happened one time?
A. Yeah, she's never ever spanked me after that.
Q. Just that one time she hit you in the face?
A. Yeah.
Q. Nothing further. Thank you.
MS. PROS: I have no other questions, Your Honor

[§§12:134-12:139 Reserved]

2. Cross-Examination of Other Prosecution Witnesses

§ 12:140 Cross-Examination of Prosecution Medical Expert

Another reason I used this case as an example is because it shows a cross-examination of a difficult expert witness—an expert whose credentials are unchallengeable and who has handled every type of defense lawyer known to humanity.

Research is the key. You will never know more than the expert. But perhaps you can find little chinks in the armor along the way. Once you do, understand everything you can about those weaknesses.

What I did do, I think, is distinguish myself with this expert as someone he needed to deal with. He was giving me grudging respect at the end. And the jury knew it. There is no doubt in my mind that they did.

This case is a horrible defense case, as you now see. I have a crying eleven year old who said her dad raped her. That alone may be enough for a conviction. On top of it, though, I have this learned expert who has examined her. He has confirmed for the jury in a detailed direct examination that a physical examination of her hymen revealed evidence that was consistent with the sexual abuse her father allegedly perpetrated on her. Specifically, she has a deep notch in her hymen.

The State's direct of the medical expert was typical. The child describes a sexual assault. That was confirmed by the inferior deep notch. The State's medical expert testified that this was consistent with a prior penetrating sexual trauma and the history the victim offered. Now we need to plant seeds of doubt through our cross.

All I want at the end of cross is for the jury to think that the case is not as clear as it was at the end of the expert's direct, when the case appeared to be a slam dunk for the government.

Bias: Doctor Testifies Primarily for State

Q. Good morning, doctor.
A. Good morning.
Q. How long did you say you have been licensed in Maine?

A. Since 1981.

Q. Now I think you gave us a number of times a year you have been testifying lately, but can you estimate how many criminal trials you have testified in in Maine?

A. You know, I would probably say five or so a year since 1986, so you are talking 20 years, perhaps a hundred.

Q. How many of those approximate a hundred cases have you testified for the state?

A. Most.

Q. And how about in DHS cases, you testify for the state there as well?

A. I testify for whoever calls me, and I have testified for the state and in DHS cases, and I would say most of the time I have testified in child protective hearings it has been for the state, yes.

Q. And I think I heard you say that you do testify out of the State of Maine as well?

A. Yes.

Q. And you are available for hire to testify for the defense out of the State of Maine?

A. I'm available for hire as you say to testify for anybody that asks me to review a case for them.

Q. But that tends to happen more outside the State of Maine, is that true?

A. Yes, I have been asked to help work with defense attorneys in the state. I have done that. Most of the cases where I have worked with defense attorneys in the state have not gone to trial because if I offer a finding that disagrees with other medical experts then often it doesn't end up in trial.

Q. So have you ever testified for a citizen of the State of Maine against the state?

A. Yes.

Q. How many times have you done that?

A. I couldn't tell you.

Q. Well, of the approximate hundred cases that you have testified in since 1986 can you estimate?

A. So you are asking me in terms of a citizen, are you talking criminal or child protective?

Q. Let me narrow it down. Let's just talk about a criminal case right now.

A. Okay, okay.

Q. In the State of Maine of the approximate hundred cases in which you have testified, in how many have you testified for a citizen?

A. Probably a couple.

Q. Two or three?

A. Two or three.

Q. And how about in the child protective custody context, how many have you testified for the parents instead of DHS?

A. Again probably very few, less than ten I would say.

Q. You have testified in Ms. Pros' cases before?

A. Yes.

Q. You consulted with her prior to your examination here today?

A. Yes

Authoritative Medical Texts

> **PRACTICE TIP:**
> Send your expert texts you want him or her to rely on as authoritative, then use them in cross-examination. Here, this expert was very slippery, in that he would recognize nothing as authoritative. This was not his first rodeo.

Q. I provided you a number of medical texts before this trial, correct?

A. Yes

Q. Did you review those texts?

A. I reviewed them. I did not read them in detail.

Q. Okay. Did you review the text "Evaluating the Child for Sexual Abuse" from the American Family Physician March 1st, 2001?

A. Why don't you show me that one?

Q. Sure

A. Yes, I did review this.

Q. And did you find that text to be authoritative?

A. No, and I will tell you categorically that I don't find any text authoritative. I find statements within text to be authoritative but not text to be authoritative.

Q. Okay. So I don't think I will need to show you this one. You reviewed some chapters in "Child Abuse Medical Diagnosis and Management" which is a 1994 book?

A. Yes. I have contributed to that book.

Q. So I assume you find that to be authoritative?

A. As I said, you know, we can have this conversation about every article, but I will tell you I do not find any particular text authoritative.

Q. You find your own text or your own writing on that book to be authoritative, is that fair to say?

A. From 1994, probably not anymore.

Note: I moved on here because I was a little tripped up by this professional expert's trick, that no text is authoritative, only statements within them being authoritative. Most experts are not that slippery. However, I will go back to that as I continue to cross.

Importance of Taking Careful Medical History

Q. You have to be especially careful in these types of cases when you are doing your examination, don't you?

A. I have to be especially careful in every examination I do.

Q. In cases where there is a child custody component you have to be especially careful, is that fair to say?

A. I am careful, I am the same degree of careful in every evaluation I do.

Q. I understand you are careful but statistically there is a difference between unsubstantiated sexual abuse claims in the context of child custody cases versus in the context of not child custody cases, isn't there?

A. You know, that's been debated in the literature over the last 20 years or so. There are certainly authors who would say that's not true. There are authors who would say it is true. I think where we have to be very careful in our evaluations is when we do definitive investigative interviews of children, not in physical examination. We exert the same amount of care in the physical examination in every case.

Q. So, in other words, taking the history, not that it's not important in other cases, but it's even more important in the child custody context?

A. Well, that can be exactly right if there is a significant component of child custody particularly with very young children like three, four, five-year-olds then we are much more careful in how we interpret the history when that child custody component exists. I can tell you that that becomes less significant when we are talking about older children because they tend to be clearer in their statements when for example a four-year-old saying daddy touched my peepee doesn't quite have the same weight as a ten-year-old saying daddy put his penis in my peepee.

Q. That depends on the developmental age of the child, correct?

A. Sure.

Q. And the emotional state of the child potentially?

A. Right.

Q. And you also have to be careful when you are taking history about who you are taking history in front of correct?

A. Yes.

Q. Such as the parent who has custody or might want custody, right?

A. I kind of missed your point there. You said in front of. You mean who I am taking the history from or who is present in the room when I am taking the history.

Q. Let's talk about both, actually they are both important, aren't they?

A. Well, it's always important to categorize who is giving me the history. It's also important to categorize who is in the room when I take that history, yeah.

Q. Thank you for clarifying that.

A. Sure.

Interview of Tammy and her Mother

Q. So you took an interview from Tammy's mom first?

A. Yes, and that was without Tammy present.

Q. Okay, and then did the examination with her mother present?

A. Yes.

Q. And then you had her mother leave the room?

A. Yes.

Q. Okay. So Tammy didn't give you any history until the time that her mom had left the room?

A. Yes.

Q. Did you record that historical interview with Tammy?

A. You mean on some kind of media?

Q. Yes.

A. No, I did not.

Q. Do you ordinarily do that?

A. I do not record my medical interviews. We sometimes record our forensic evidentiary interviews where the interview is intended to stand on its own. Particularly when requested by attorneys or law enforcement or DHS, we will video record those interviews, but for the medical interviews which tend to be fairly brief and focused, we do not audio or videotape those interviews.

Q. How long was the interview with Tammy itself?

A. Five minutes. It was by no means intended to be a definitive forensic interview.

Q. Okay.

A. Yeah.

Q. Thank you. Now when you are taking that history from Tammy it's very important not to ask the child leading questions, correct?

A. Yes.

Q. And you did that here?

A. Yes.

Q. It's important to maintain a neutral tone?

A. Yes.

Q. Since history is so important, would a history of other past sexual abuse be important to you?

A. Yes.

Q. And if the patient was not an accurate historian would that be important to you?

A. Yes, it could be absolutely.

Q. Did Tammy's mom give you any history of any prior sexual abuse of Tammy?

A. She did not.

Q. And Tammy did not?

A. She did not.

These questions establish that Tammy did not complain of a history of prior sexual abuse. If we develop later that she was molested by another person, that fact was undisclosed to the doctor.

Examination of Child Victim

Q. Now I think I heard you on direct say that you only examined her in the frog leg position?

A. Yes.

Q. I may be mistaken but I know the frog leg position has another term. What else is the frog leg position called?

A. Supine recumbent.

Q. Didn't you also examine her in the prone recumbent position?

A. Oh, let me look at my report.

Q. Please do, Page 3, third paragraph down.

A. My apologies, I entirely missed that. I actually examined her in all three positions.

Q. And there is the knee chest position?

A. Yes.

Q. And which one is that?

A. That's, well, the third one on my list prone knee chest position, yeah.

Q. And what is the prone?

A. Supine recumbent is laying flat on the back. Prone recumbent laying flat on her stomach. Knee chest is laying on her stomach with her legs tucked up under her stomach.

SEXUAL ASSAULTS AGAINST CHILDREN

Q. Okay. Now different positions that you examine the child in changes the dimension of the hymen?
A. I'm not sure I could say that.

I think it is interesting that Tammy is not anxious during this highly intense physical exam. I wondered if Tammy liked the attention. I wondered if a female child who was horribly sexually abused by her father would be so relaxed when intrusively examined by a male physician.

Q. Okay. You said that I think the Assistant District Attorney asked you to rank Tammy's level of anxiety.
A. Yes.
Q. And you said she was one out of five?
A. Yes.
Q. And I assume that the one is the side of being minimally anxious?
A. Yes.
Q. Okay. She didn't appear nervous to you, is that fair to say?
A. That's right, by appearances, that's right.
Q. Now you said that the hymen is a thin membrane?
A. In prepubertal girls, yes.
Q. And that's where we are here, correct?
A. Yes.
Q. Because it hasn't gotten to the point yet where it started to thicken as you have described as you start to go through the menstruation process, correct?
A. That's correct.
Q. Would you agree with me that it's also a delicate membrane?
A. Fairly delicate. I mean it is, you know, a little resistant to trauma. You can touch the hymen and it won't, you know, tear, but putting something through it of sufficient size can certainly lead to an injury to the hymenal tissue.
Q. And there are a variety of different structures of hymens in children, correct?
A. Shapes, yes.
Q. They can be completely across the vaginal vault?
A. That would be an imperfect hymen, very unusual, but certainly something that can happen.
Q. It can be absent from birth?
A. It can be absent?
Q. Yes.
A. No, that's not true.
Q. That's not true?
A. No.
Q. You have described Tammy's hymen as U-shaped?
A. Yes.
Q. Isn't that, that's also sometimes called a crescentric hymen?
A. Crescentic, that's correct.
Q. That U shaped hymen means that there is no tissue generally between eleven o'clock and one o'clock, correct?
A. Generally that's what that means, that's right.
Q. And is that what you saw here in Tammy's hymen?
A. Yes.
Q. Just so I can be clear, can you all see this? (Note: I'm drawing during the examination on a board.) So in a U-shaped hymen such as Tammy's there is no tissue from here from here to here?
A. That's right, as opposed to say an annular hymen where there would be tissue going all the way around the top.
Q. Okay, thank you. And that's not indicative of any trauma in itself?
A. No, not at all, that's probably the most common normal variant.
Q. Now you had never seen Tammy before as a patient prior to this examination, correct?
A. That's right.
Q. So obviously you had never seen her hymen before this examination?
A. That's correct.
Q. You couldn't compare what you were seeing for that notch to something else you had seen in her hymen previously, is that fair to say?

A. That's fair.

Q. There is a blood supply that goes to the hymen as well obviously?

A. Yes, it's like the mucous membrane inside the mouth.

Q. And there is no evidence of vaginal discharge here?

A. Not, not when I saw her, no.

Q. No evidence of bleeding?

A. No.

Q. Did you photograph the notch in Tammy's hymen?

A. I did.

Q. You did?

A. Yeah.

Q. Do you have those photographs?

A. No.

Q. And what became of those photographs?

A. They are in our office.

Q. Sidebar please.

(Note: a sidebar conference was held in which I asked for a mistrial for a discovery violation, for failure to produce the photographs, which was denied).

BY MR. ZERILLO:

Q. So you photo document the injuries?

A. Yes.

Q. With a 35 millimeter slide or digital?

A. Video camera.

Q. And you video tape?

A. Yes, it's in the report.

Q. You say in your report that video colposcopy was used?

A. Right.

Q. Now that's not with the colposcope though?

A. That's right.

Q. When you say video colposcopy, you mean with the video camera?

A. Yes.

Q. Okay. Did you take handwritten notes in your examination?

A. I did.

Q. Do you have those notes?

A. No. In my chart I have notes of the physical examination and the child history, yes.

Q. Do you retain that chart after you have your report typed?

A. Yes.

Q. So you have that as well?

A. Yes.

Q. You did write a report here?

A. Yes.

Q. And that report is accurate, correct?

A. Yes.

Q. And thorough?

A. I hope so.

Q. But you aren't sure it is thorough.

A. I believe it is.

Q. Okay. You knew your report could be used in legal proceedings, is that fair to say?

A. Yes.

Injury to Hymen and Possible Causes

Q. So were you able to measure the size of the notch that you found?

A. I wouldn't measure the size of the notch. What's important about the finding is how deep it goes, whether it's close to or completely transected the hymen, not how deep it is from top to bottom.

Q. So you don't measure the thickness of the hymen, in other words, when you are doing your evaluation?

A. No.

Q. The notch in the hymen that you found, it was fully healed?

A. Yes.

Q. It was at least weeks old, correct?

A. Yes.

Q. And could have been many months old?

A. Or older.

Q. Could have been years old?

A. Could have been.

Q. You can't say with any certainty?

A. That's right, I can't.

Q. It could predate 2006 in fact?

A. It could.

Q. Some—I heard you talk about straddle injuries and some injuries can't cause the type of notch that you see here, correct?

A. That's right.

Q. Like bike riding you said?

A. That's right.

Q. But some types of sex play can cause that type of notch, correct?

A. Not without penetration, no. I'm not quite sure what you mean by sex play. Perhaps you can be more precise.

Q. A finger inserted into the vagina could rupture the hymen or cause a notch?

A. With penetration.

Q. Yeah, but it doesn't take a lot of penetration, is that fair to say?

A. Well, big enough finger doesn't have to be a lot of penetration.

Q. I mean can you, a couple of inches, is that correct?

A. Penetration of a couple of inches, yes.

Q. And when you say the notch didn't transect the hymen, which is a term of art obviously, you mean that it didn't go all the way through?

A. All the way through to the base, that's right.

Q. So if I understand you, you alluded to superficial notches and deep notches. I just want to try to get an explanation of them. A superficial notch is less than or equal to half the thickness of the hymen membrane?

A. Yes.

Q. And a deep notch is more than half the thickness of the membrane?

A. Right.

Q. And a notch that extends to the vestibule is a transection?

A. Exactly.

Q. It's difficult sometimes to determine whether a notch is a superficial notch or a deep notch, isn't it?

A. It can be, particularly for inexperienced examiners, yes.

Q. And there is a lot of, rather than going through it all, there is a significant amount of literature on how it can be difficult to distinguish between a superficial notch and a deep notch, isn't there?

A. Yes, yes.

Q. Does your video documentation allow you to create still images?

A. That is possible, yes.

Q. Are the stills ever done in grayscale with the millimeter ruler?

A. Only bruises. Typically I will use a forensic ruler for bruises but not for genital-rectal examination. The numbers in the genital-rectal area, you know, how wide the hymenal opening is, how thick the hymen is, are so variable that we have long since stopped measuring that.

Q. The notch here is at six o'clock?

A. Yes.

Q. And that's the posterior side of the hymen?

A. Towards the rectum, that's right.

Q. It's also sometimes called the inferior portion of the hymen?

A. Yes.

Q. And if there was a superficial notch meaning less than half the thickness of the membrane that would not be indicative of prior penetrating trauma, isn't that correct?

A. Well, it could be. The problem is I wouldn't be able to tell whether it was a normal variant or the result of prior trauma, so the fact is that it can easily be a normal variant to be a superficial notch meaning normal. It can also be the result of prior trauma, but I wouldn't be able to tell the difference.

Q. And that's standard in the field, correct, superficial notches are not indicative necessarily of prior penetrating trauma?

A. They are not diagnostically useful.

Q. Now there have been studies that indicate that superficial notches are not significantly more common on girls alleging non-abuse compared to girls alleging they were penetrated, correct?

A. Well, exactly right, I mean the fact is they are common in everybody.

Q. Right. There have been studies in fact of adolescent girls who have had deep notches posteriorly who have denied intercourse, isn't that correct?

A. You would have to show me that. Yes, I think I see the 29 the adolescent study is probably what you are referring to. I helped to write this paper, yeah, Joyce Adams, right, 2004.

Q. I was asking you if you are aware of any studies finding no statistically significant difference in the frequency of deep notches in the appearance of the hymen in adolescent girls admitting to consensual sexual intercourse compared to girls who denied consensual sexual intercourse?

A. Sure, yes, yes, that's correct, that's what that study said, study of the appearance of the hymen in adolescent girls admitting consensual intercourse compared to girls who denied such contact there was not a statistically significant difference in the frequency of deep notches in posterior rim of the hymen, that's correct.

Q. That's a mouthful.

A. It is and it's probably true. I mean I would agree that that's what that study showed.

Q. You said that insertion of a tampon could cause a notch?

A. Hypothetically it could cause a tear in the hymen.

Q. It could in fact cause a deep notch, isn't that right?

A. It can cause a tear in the hymen that could result in a deep notch, yes.

Q. And I assume then that masturbation involving penetration can also cause a deep notch?

A. Well, now again hypothetically the answer would be yes, but in practicality that's not how girls masturbate to the point where they cause trauma.

Q. You are making a generality there, fair to say?

A. That's right, I am not saying, you know, hundred percent of the time, right.

Q. Now you said that you have never seen any literature where there was a tampon inserted and a notch in the hymen, isn't that right?

A. Oh, no, I didn't say that. I said I have never seen any literature that documented that tampons caused this injury, these findings.

Q. Have you seen any studies that discuss insertion, reported insertion of a tampon and then a notch or transection in the hymen?

A. I can't say I am aware of that.

Q. I gave you this study titled the Longitudinal Study of the Anogenital Development in Girls from Six to Twelve Years of Age? Do you remember seeing this?

A. I did, yes.

Q. Now in that study there was a girl who was classified to have probably a deep notch and transection in her hymen and this girl reported a painful insertion of a tampon, isn't that correct?

A. Yes.

Q. And a transection in the hymen is beyond a deep notch, when it's gone all the way through?

A. That's correct, that's correct, so I guess that is one case reported in the literature and as I said, it is certainly hypothetically possible that, you know, unusual, painful, difficult traumatic penetration with a tampon could produce that kind of trauma. I agree that's probably, probably accurate.

Q. Are you aware of any studies indicating that the appearance of notches posteriorly should not be considered diagnostic for sexual abuse?
A. I would not consider this finding diagnostic for sexual abuse. I would consider it consistent with the history being offered me.
Q. But I am asking, okay, and I appreciate that. Your findings are not diagnostic for sexual abuse?
A. No.
Q. I am also asking if you have seen any studies that say that the presence of notches at all posteriorly should not be considered indicative of sexual abuse?
A. I wouldn't disagree with that statement. I'm not sure if you are referring to Joyce Adams' work or somebody else's, but I wouldn't disagree with that a notch, a deep notch as opposed to a transection is not independently diagnostic of penetrating trauma. It is simply consistent with the prior history if that history is being offered, and for example the article that you showed me earlier I think accurately says that after the history one should take great care in interpreting this finding.
Q. And you just alluded to something there that I wanted to try to flesh out—there is a big difference in a finding with a complete transection than a deep notch?
A. Absolutely.

Examination of Anus

Q. Tammy told you that she had also had anal sexual intercourse with her father, correct?
A. Yes.
Q. Now did you examine her anus?
A. Yes.
Q. And that was normal, correct?
A. Yes.
Q. Did you video document that?
A. Yes.
Q. There was nothing about the appearance of the anus that concerned you?
A. That's correct.

I could have gone further here and asked the "wouldn't you expect to see anal trauma with such an allegation?" question. I know this expert though. He will worm around it, so I let that sit to argue it to the jury without his explanation.

Loss of Video Tape of Examination

I am fast-forwarding here a bit. The video tape of the examination was erased. My motions to dismiss were still, inexplicably, denied, but I was allowed a little more cross. Thankfully, I was prepared for this eventuality, and had researched him thoroughly. I was ready for him. This section of cross shows how, in a miserable case with everything against you, you can sometimes find diamonds if you keep digging.

Q. Dr. Howard, you're an expert in photo documentation of injuries, is that correct?
A. Yes.
Q. In fact you lecture on the subject?
A. Yes.
Q. You were lecturing in Mississippi I believe in April of this year, weren't you?
A. I think so, yes.
Q. I asked you earlier about a videotape, correct?
A. Yes.
Q. And that was the videotape of your examination of Tammy, correct?
A. Yes.
Q. And you told me that this videotape was at your office, correct?
A. You asked me if that exam had been videoed, yes.
Q. I asked you if you had it with you?

A. And I said no.
Q. And you stated it was at the office, right?
A. I may have said that.
Q. Okay. The videotape in fact has been erased, isn't that correct?
A. That is my suspicion.
Q. And it's your suspicion because you can't find the videotape, right?
A. That's correct.
Q. You agree that it's important for you to keep evidence that you gather in your examinations around, correct?
A. Yes.
Q. You would also agree with me that it's difficult for other experts to check your work if you don't have any videotape or photographic evidence, correct?
A. Yes.
Q. We talked before how sometimes you work for defense lawyers out-of-state?
A. Yes.
Q. If a defense lawyer called you up and said I have a report saying there is a deep notch at six o'clock, I have no photos, no video, no drawings, no measurements, you would probably say there is not a lot I can do for you, wouldn't you?
A. That's exactly what I would say.
Q. In fact you wrote an article or coauthored an article for the United States Department of Justice on photo documentation and the investigation of child abuse, didn't you?
A. I did.
Q. And in that article you indicated that accurate courtroom evidence can be hindered by the following, "ineffective camera equipment and film," right?
A. Okay, yeah, it's been a long time since I have looked at that. That's pretty old. I believe you when you are saying that.
Q. Well, you don't have to believe me, I will just show you, and I don't have it memorized, I will just have to stand here, okay?
A. Right.
Q. It says that ineffective camera assistance can hinder accurate courtroom evidence?
A. Camera equipment, yes.
Q. Insufficient methods of photographing the victim or the victim's injuries can too?
A. Yes.
Q. Misinformation regarding the photographs of the case?
A. Yes.
Q. Mislabeling the child abuse information including photographs?
A. Yes.
Q. And all of those things can hinder accurate courtroom evidence, correct?
A. Yes.
Q. And you would agree with me also that erasing the videotape could hinder accurate courtroom evidence, true, right?
A. Yes.

§12:141 Cross-Examination of Turncoat Ex-Girlfriend

On occasion, your defendant's confidants will betray him and turn government witness. With Bob's ex-girlfriend here, Sally, that is precisely what happened. Of course, with such a witness, we want her to make portions of our case for us, like it or not.

Bias against Defendant and Friendship with Child Victim's Mother

Sally now hates our client. She used to be on our client's team, but she has since then switched allegiances. She testified for our client at his bail hearing. The transcript is not available, but Sally doesn't know that. So I immediately remind her of her bail hearing testimony to try to control her.

Q. Thank you, Your Honor. You testified for Bob at his bail hearing, correct?
A. Correct.
Q. After that you ended your relationship with him at some point?

A. Correct.

Q. You don't like Bob, is that fair to say?

A. I would say that I don't care for Bob liking –

Q. You don't care for Bob, how's that?

A. That's correct.

Q. At the time that you were going out with him you didn't care for Tracey, right?

A. I never particularly knew her in any other fashion than what I got from Bob.

Q. So did you or did you not care for Tracey when you were going out with Bob?

A. I didn't have a feeling one way or the other for her because I didn't know her.

Q. You socialize with Tracey now?

A. No, I do not.

Q. She hasn't been over to your house?

A. No. She and her daughter came over one time unexpectedly, stayed for approximately five minutes and then left.

Q. And do you talk to her on the phone?

A. I have talked to her maybe three times on the phone regarding court dates here.

Q. And you meet her for court dates, don't you?

A. I don't meet her specifically. She's here when I get here.

Q. You've come to Bob's other court dates leading up to this trial?

A. I have.

Q. And when you're there you speak to Tracey?

A. I speak to Tracey and Bob's ex-wife, yes.

Relationship with Defendant before Child Comes to Live with Them

Q. How long had you been living with Bob at the time that Tammy came to live with the two of you?

A. Uhm, approximately two months.

Q. And you moved in pretty fast?

A. Very fast.

Q. I think you—so it was still a pretty new relationship when Tammy came to live with you, is that right?

A. That would be correct.

Q. And you were living at your brother's house in Gray?

A. Not at, not originally.

Q. The time Tammy came to live with you, you were living at your brother's house in Gray?

A. Correct.

Q. And Bob had visits with Tammy before Tammy came to live with you?

A. Uhm, yes.

Q. But I think you said you met Tammy once before she came to live with you, is that right?

A. No, I didn't say that.

Q. So you hadn't met her at all before you—

A. I had met her, yes.

Q. How many times had you met her before she came to live with you?

A. She had come for a weekend, then she came I think the week or maybe two weeks after that for a week, and then she was every other weekend.

Q. So she came for a whole week at one point prior to the move-in, is that right?

A. Correct.

Q. Your stepdaughter Nancy did not live with you in Gray?

A. Correct.

Q. And you had moved into the Gray house shortly before Tammy came to live with you?

A. Approximately a month.

Child Comes to Live with Defendant and Witness

Q. You had a speaker phone at the house in Gray?

A. Correct.

Q. Was that your speaker phone or your brother's?

A. My brother's.

Q. Do you have a speakerphone yourself?

A. On my cell phone I do.

Q. Okay, not on your home phone?

A. I did not own a home phone at the time or now

Q. You got a call at some point though from Tracey on that speaker phone in Gray?

A. Bob did, yes.

Q. Okay, but did you hear her voice on speaker phone?

A. I did on her second call.

Q. And on that second call she sounded very upset?

A. Uhm-hum, yes, she did.

Q. She said something like, "you've got to come get your fucking daughter right now?"

A. I believe it was to that extract, extreme.

Q. And she said Tammy is out of control?

MS. PROS: Objection, Your Honor, this is hearsay.

BY MR. ZERILLO:

Q. This is regarding what she testified to and it's an excited utterance.

THE COURT: I will overrule.

BY MR. ZERILLO:

Q. She said Tammy—

THE COURT: You may answer.

BY MR. ZERILLO:

Q. I'm sorry. She said Tammy is out of control?

A. She said that Tammy was out of control, correct.

Q. She said, I can't take this anymore?

A. She I believe said you need to come get your daughter. She's out of control if my memory serves me correctly.

Q. You don't remember her saying I can't take this anymore?

A. She may have. Tracey gets very excited. She may have.

Q. Okay. So you went to Standish?

A. Correct.

Q. And you saw Tracey?

A. Yes, I did.

Q. She appeared very upset to you?

A. Yes, she did.

Q. And you saw Tabitha?

A. I saw Tabitha from a bathroom window.

Q. You saw Tammy?

A. I did.

Q. She appeared to be upset?

A. She was. Tammy was upset, but she was also angry.

Q. Okay, and the police were there?

A. Not at that time, no.

Q. But they came at some point during that trip, right?

A. They were just arriving when we left.

Q. Okay. Now Tracey was yelling during part of the time that you were there in Standish, right?

A. Correct.

Q. She said something along the lines of "You fucking called DHS on me once, you are not doing it again." Do you remember that?

A. I'm hesitating because it was part of the conversation I was away, so—

MS. PROS: Objection, Your Honor, as to what Tracey said.

THE COURT: Well, what somebody said as opposed to factual testimony I will allow it for what was—as evidence of what was said, not of whether anything actually happened, but what was said, except that only what she can, she personally heard. She can't testify to what someone else told her was said.

BY MR. ZERILLO:

Q. Thank you, Your Honor. So did you hear her say "You fucking called DHS on me once you are not doing it again!"?
A. I believe I did hear her say that to Tammy.
Q. Did you hear her say to Tammy "I have had it with you. You are going with your fucking father right fucking now!"
A. I do believe she said that.
Q. So you took Tammy that night or that afternoon?
A. It was evening, yes.
Q. Okay. This is probably a pretty significant change to your new household with Bob, is that fair to say?
A. That's very fair.
Q. Tammy had her own room?
A. Correct.
Q. You and Bob shared a room?
A. Correct.

Defendant's and Witness's Work Schedules

Q. Now Bob was working a lot at that time, right?
A. Bob was, yes, he had just started his new job.
Q. Okay, because before that he had been at Shapely Tree, correct?
A. For two weeks that I knew him, yes.
Q. Okay, and then he switched to Maine Delivery?
A. Correct.
Q. Okay, and that new job had some pretty long work hours, right?
A. There were times when it would be long. There were times when it would be short. It depended on the loads that they had to deliver.
Q. He wasn't able to take time off of work however because he had just started this new job at the time Tammy moved in, right?
A. I don't know. I just automatically offered it. I don't believe, I can't remember if he asked his employer or if we just agreed I would do it.
Q. Do you remember testifying previously that it was impossible for him to take time off of work at that time?
A. Financially for us it was impossible.
Q. So you agree it was impossible for him to take time off of work at that time when Tammy first moved in with you?
A. For us financially it was, correct.
Q. Okay.
A. If his employer would have allowed him I don't know.
Q. Okay, yeah, I am not asking.
A. Yeah, okay.
Q. And you own a driving school?
A. That's correct.
Q. I'm a little confused by what I heard you testify to on direct related to your work status there. Did you say you were working part-time when Tammy first moved in with you?
A. No. I own the company, and my work schedule is what I make it. I can lighten my load or heavy my load as my personal life would allow.
Q. Okay. So did you stop working altogether during this time when Tammy first came to live with you in Gray?
A. I did for I think three, maybe four days I did stop working, and then I started part-time. When she was in school, I worked her school hours.
Q. Okay. Now are you telling me today that you did work at the driving school during the period of time that you lived in Gray with Tammy and Bob?
A. Yes.
Q. Do you remember being shown an affidavit from Detective Lippy at the last hearing you testified in this case?
A. No, I do not.
Q. Do you remember saying that it was impossible that Bob had any sexual contact with Tammy because you were around all the time and not working?

A. That might have been misconstrued in that I was saying. I was working when Tammy was in school, why would I stay home and do nothing if she is in school? I was saying that I was the one that brought her to school, and I picked her up from school.

Q. Okay. So if you had said previously it's impossible because I was not working at the driving school at that time?

A. I was probably referring to the three to four days that I took off because she came with no clothes and she basically didn't have anything so I took time to go help her get clothes.

Q. Okay. Bob's work schedule for Maine Delivery had him leaving very early in the morning, correct?

A. Correct.

Q. He always needed to be to work by six a.m. is that fair to say?

A. That's not fair to say, he had to be to work by 7, 6 if they needed him.

Q. And was it usually 6 or 7?

A. It was usually 6 but that was because he wanted the extra time but it wasn't his normal hours.

Q. And it could be earlier than 6?

A. I don't recall it ever being, it may have, but I do not recall it.

Q. Your testimony today is that he could be to work by 7?

A. My testimony is a lot of times he was to work by 6 but his normal hours started at 7.

Q. You previously testified he has to be to work at 6 a.m., correct, yes?

A. I guess, yeah.

Q. Do you want me to show you?

A. Yeah.

Q. Is that correct?

A. That his day normally started at 6, yes.

Q. Okay, and sometimes it started earlier than that, right?

A. I think very rarely if he had to go way up north it might have started earlier than six.

Q. He went way up north on a certain day of the week, right?

A. Not every week.

Q. Most weeks?

A. No. He went south to Massachusetts but to north, northern Maine I think he only had that maybe two times that week.

Q. And south to Massachusetts on Tuesdays I think?

A. I can't remember the exact day but I do know there was a day.

Q. A set day a week?

A. Yes.

Q. And you have seen him get home, you know, as late as ten at night, is that fair to say?

A. I think he got home from work late like that maybe two times in the time that I knew him. It wasn't a common thing to be out that late.

Witness's Relationship with Child

Q. Okay. Fair to say that you became a mother figure for Tammy?

A. Very fair to say.

Q. You were involved with her school?

A. Yes, I was.

Q. Spoke to her teachers?

A. Yes, I did.

Work and School Schedules in Westbrook

Q. Okay. So your brother needed the house so you moved into the apartment in Westbrook, right?

A. No, my brother asked us to leave the house and we moved to Westbrook, yes.

Q. Okay. You moved to Westbrook?

A. Uhm-hum.

Q. Yes?

A. Yes.

Q. Into a three bedroom apartment?

A. Correct.

Q. And your daughter moved in?

A. Yes.

Q. She was not working, correct?

A. Correct.

Q. She had her own bedroom, right?

A. She did, uhm-hum.

Q. Bob and you had a bedroom?

A. Uhm-hum.

Q. Yes?

A. That's correct.

Q. And Tammy had a bedroom as well?

A. Correct.

Q. And Bob's work schedule at that time when you moved to Westbrook didn't change, did it?

A. No.

Q. Still to work usually by six a.m.?

A. Uhm-hum.

Q. Yes?

A. Correct.

Q. And back between three p.m. and ten p.m., let's say that's the range?

A. I was—if l had to put a range on it l would say between two and five average.

Q. Tammy's in school at that time, am I correct?

A. Correct.

Q. And before I leave the subject of his schedule, you used to get up in the morning and help him get ready for work, right?

A. It depended on how well we were getting along.

Q. Okay. This was a pretty frequent occurrence for you to get up in the morning and help him get ready for work?

A. No, towards, no.

Q. Did that ever happen?

A. Yes, it did happen, but it wasn't an every time occurrence because he—no, it wasn't an every time occurrence. I would frequently get up but I wouldn't get up and help him get ready for work. He's a big boy. He can do it himself.

Q. Did you say at the last hearing—

A. Uh-huh.

Q. —actually Bob and I get up together because he has to be to work at six, but I get up?

A. Correct.

Q. At the last hearing you didn't say every once in a while did you?

A. No. You asked me if I helped him get ready for work.

Q. "I make him coffee, I make him his lunch and out the door he goes."Didn't you say that?

A. Uhm-hum.

Q. Yes?

A. That's correct.

Q. Tammy was getting to school on the bus in Westbrook?

A. That's correct.

Q. Did you get her to the bus usually?

A. I would if my schedule allowed. If my schedule didn't allow then Nancy did, and there was a couple times she got herself on the bus.

Q. Okay, but Bob wasn't the one to get her on the bus?

A. Not as a rule.

Q. And after school she would go to daycare, right?

A. Yes.

Q. And day care ends at five p.m.?

A. Correct.

Q. And then usually you would pick her up?

A. Usually I would towards the end of our time with Tammy it started to be more and more that Bob was picking her up because I was teaching class.

Q. You were working more at that point?

A. And I was teaching class so I couldn't even with a student come get her.

Q. And would her aunts sometimes pick her up, do you know?

A. Not that I know of.

Q. How about her Grandfather?

A. He did pick her up. I think there was a couple times we tried to get him to go get her, couple times he could, couples times he couldn't. It wasn't consistent. I think he tried to if his schedule would allow.

Move to Grandfather's Trailer

Q. Okay. Tammy and Bob moved into Grandpa's house at one point, right?

A. Correct.

Q. That was in April of 2007?

A. And I think they also went in March.

Q. You remember two times they moved out?

A. I know two times that they went over there.

Q. Okay. Two times they went over for a visit or literally moved out?

A. One, one time in April Bob literally moved all of his things out. In March they left to go over there, and they didn't move their stuff out, they stayed there a couple days.

Q. And that's a mobile home he lives in?

A. Correct.

Q. And you have been there?

A. I have.

Q. Have you had the opportunity to carry on conversations in that mobile home with people?

A. Uhmhum, yes, I have.

Q. You previously testified that the walls in that residence are very thin, isn't that correct?

A. That's correct.

Q. And you previously testified that Grandpa is somebody who doesn't go out very often in your experience, right?

A. Correct.

Concerns about Child's Behavior

Q. Okay. Did you ever have Tammy stay over at your house without Bob being present?

A. One time.

Q. In April of 2007?

A. Yes.

Q. And she stayed overnight?

A. Correct.

Q. And Bob was not there?

A. Correct.

Q. Did you witness Tammy express any sexual behavior towards you during that sleepover?

A. Yes, I did.

Q. And what was that sexual behavior?

A. We were sleeping in the bed together. She wanted to sleep in the bed with me because she wanted to be close and snuggle. We were watching Chitty Chitty Bang Bang, and while we were laying there she said, I wish you was my Mom, and I was hugging her and telling her that, you know, she's special, she has two Moms, and then she goes, yeah, but then I could be, then when I was a baby I could have been sucking on your boobie.

Q. You were concerned about that?

A. Yes, I was.

Q. And you tried to diffuse that situation?

A. I asked her where that came from. I asked her—I told her that that was inappropriate behavior, and she says, I know, but I would just love to be that close to you, and then I addressed it with Bob when I saw him to why would she talk like that.

I asked these questions because I think they show that Tammy made strange remarks bordering on sexual comments, in order to be close to a mother figure. This goes to the "why" question, supporting that she would fabricate this story to move back with her own Mom.

Q. You and Bob were having troubles that in a way related to Tammy with your own relationship, is that fair to say?
A. Part of our troubles was Tammy's behavior, yes.
Q. There were instances where Tammy got upset because you and Bob went out to dinner for example?
A. Uhm-hum.
Q. Yes?
A. Yes.
Q. And you saw her express being upset with Bob for going out to dinner with you?
A. Yes, because she wanted to go.
Q. And before—Tammy left in May of 07, is that right?
A. May 17 or 18 of 07.
Q. And was that prompted by a call to Tracey?
A. Yes.
Q. And was Tracey on speaker phone for that call?
A. Yes.
Q. And did she sound upset when she was talking to you?
A. She sounded concerned but not upset. She –
Q. Was Tracey confronted about, about logging phone calls with Tammy?
A. Yes.
Q. She denied that?
A. She did not. What I believe she said because she was on speaker phone was, Tammy, I'm not doing that. I'm just keeping track of what you're saying, or something, I think it was something to that effect. There was something that she was keeping. I don't know if it was on her phone because Tammy told us it was on her phone, but Tracey said something else to that effect they were aware of it. They were aware of what Tammy was saying.
Q. Okay. And Tracey came and got Tammy?
A. Yes, yes, she did.

Defendant's Modest Behavior around Child

Q. Would you describe Bob as having been very modest in his dress around Tammy?
A. I would have to say over all if he was in the bedroom in just his underwear and she would happen to walk in he would try to cover himself up, yes.
Q. So if he was wearing his boxer shorts and she walked into the bedroom he would go put on a pair of sweatpants for example?
A. Correct.
Q. And he would lock doors, the bathrooms that you observed when he was using the bathroom?
A. I don't know if that bathroom had a lock.
Q. Which one, in Westbrook or Gray?
A. Yeah, in Westbrook I don't think that door had a lock.
Q. So if somebody was showering in that bathroom anybody could walk in?
A. Yeah, and I'll tell you why because he walked in on Nancy one time, and she was in there because there was no lock. It was a big mistake, but --
Q. Walked in, there was like a shriek or something?
A. Whoops and out, so I don't believe there was a lock on that door.
Q. Okay, thank you. So you'd agree with me that he was, he was pretty modest around Tammy when it came to his dress, is that fair to say?
A. Uhm, yeah, between Tammy and my daughter Nancy, yes.

Normalcy of Child's Activities

Q. During this period of time, I don't know if I asked you this, let me skip back to Gray, Tammy did well in school at Gray?

A. She did fair.

Q. She did well in school in Westbrook?

A. She did better in Westbrook but didn't particularly care for it, but she did do better in Westbrook.

Q. And she engaged in soccer and softball?

A. Yes.

Q. And Bob would take her to softball games or practices, right?

A. Yes.

Q. And they had social activities together that you observed?

A. Uhm-hum.

Q. Yes?

A. Yes.

Q. In fact you were engaged in social activity with them too?

A. I would, sometimes they would go to the game because they would have practice before the game, the two of them would go get a bite to eat and go to the game, and then I would show up after I finished work.

Q. Yeah, and you would see them playing out in the yard when the weather was okay, right?

A. I did in Gray. We didn't so much in Westbrook.

Q. Okay, Gray's fine. You were shocked by the allegations, is that fair to say?

A. I was.

Child's Attempted Tampon Use

Q. Did Tammy have a discussion with you about using a tampon?

A. Yes, she did.

Q. Did you ever catch her trying to insert a tampon?

A. I caught her. She had it in the bathroom. My daughter, my birth daughter, had been up, and she had started her period, and so I went to the store and I bought her pads and Tampax, and Tammy had one, and she was asking about how to use it because her sister Tabitha uses them apparently, and so I was telling her how they are used, and I told her that she should not insert them inside of herself because she could hurt herself, she is too young, and I had her put a pad on. I let her walk around the house for about half hour with a pad on so she could see how that felt.

Q. Did you ever observe her attempting to insert a tampon?

A. I didn't observe her attempting to do it.

Q. Okay. Did she ever tell you that she attempted to do it later?

A. I am trying to think. I know that it was an inquisitive thing, with her with her sister, so I didn't observe her do it. If it happened it might have been something she mentioned to me that she might have tried. I don't know.

Q. Do you mention, do you remember, do you have an active memory now of her mentioning to you that she tried to insert a tampon?

A. No, I do not.

Q. You're just not sure one way or the other, is that fair to say?

A. That's fair to say.

Child's Lying and Other Troubling Behavior

Q. Were you there when Tammy expressed suicidal ideation when you lived in Westbrook?

A. No, I wasn't there.

Q. Were you there for the issues of her attempting to run away or talking about running away?

A. I was there for the conversations about it, yes. I was there for the conversations about the suicide, but I wasn't there when the act was happening.

Q. Okay. So Tammy got in trouble for telling stories and lying, correct?

A. Uhm-hum.

Q. Yes?
A. Yes.
Q. Okay. Did she get in trouble for taking money?
A. Well, at first she did, and then after we, Bob and I sat down and talked to her we found out that the money that she had found, I think it was $3, and it was all wet, and she said it was her money. We couldn't really decide where actually this all came about, and so for us we decided that for us to say she took it was really not—we couldn't prove one way or the other how she got the money.
Q. There was an incident with money however?
A. Once, $3.
Q. All right. Was there who did most of the punishing, you or Bob?
A. He did.
Q. Okay, and, you know, was the child ever sent to her room for two or three days at a time?
A. Straight?
Q. Yeah.
A. Not straight.
Q. Okay. That would be—
A. That would be pretty cruel.
Q. That would be excessive?
A. Yeah.
Q. And did you see Bob frequently spanking her?
A. He didn't frequently spank her, but he did spank her.
Q. Once, right?
A. Uhm, once in Westbrook in the kitchen he laid her over his knee and then once in the living room and then I think it was twice.
Q. Okay.
A. That I saw.
Q. You're not sure about the twice but you think so?
A. I believe it was twice, once in the kitchen and then there was another incident in the living room. Both times he laid her over his knee.
Q. Let's talk about the stories that you talked about Tammy making up on direct. Sometimes they involved kids' stuff, is that fair to say?
A. That's fair to say.
Q. Sometimes they in your view got beyond kids' stuff, is that right?
A. That's correct.
Q. In fact there were stories that were made up about your relationship with Bob, right?
A. That's correct.
Q. There were stories that Tammy made up about your sexual relationship with Bob, right?
A. There were stories that she knew about our sexual relationship, yes.
Q. How did she know about your sexual relationship?
A. We don't know.
Q. So there is a, there is a time for example in this bail hearing transcript that I can find if we need where you talk about her making up a story about, about you and Bob's sexual relationship, do you remember that?
A. (Nods head affirmatively.)
Q. Yes?
A. Yes, I do.
Q. So some of the stories were more adult than kids' stuff, is that fair to say in your view?
A. Oh, definitely.

It is certainly true that a child's unusual discussion of sexual matters at a young age cuts both ways. Jurors could infer that the sexual knowledge came from the Defendant. However, in a case where there appears to be a sexual injury of some type, and we are raising other possibilities of abuse, it is worth getting into Tammy's proclivity to tell tall tales.

Q. Tammy's was a very clingy child?

A. Yes.
Q. She was clingy to Bob?
A. Yes.
Q. She was clingy to you?
A. Yes.
Q. When she was clingy to Bob you never saw her expressing fear of Bob?
A. No.

§12:142 Cross-Examination of Detective

Now let's see what Detective Lippy has to say. In short, Detective Lippy worked up the case. He took the complaint, interviewed the Defendant and then sent the case to the prosecutor to charge. So, we have two sets of statements to attack with Detective Lippy, the alleged victim's statements and the Defendant's statements.

In this cross-examination my goals are to:
- Cast doubt on thoroughness of investigation and competence of detective.
- Raise issue of a tainted interview with the victim.
- Get in testimony about what victim told him to lay groundwork for pointing out inconsistencies.
- Confirm that the Defendant steadfastly maintained his innocence both when interviewed and when interrogated more aggressively.

See Ch. 2 for general tips on cross-examining police officers.

Training

Q. So you were a detective at the time that you took on the Tammy case?
A. Yes.
Q. And you are no longer a detective?
A. I'm not.
Q. You're a sergeant?
A. I am.
Q. And you supervise patrol officers?
A. I do.
Q. You went through some extensive training in becoming a police officer, correct?
A. I went to the police academy, yes.
Q. Okay, the Maine Police Academy?
A. Maine Criminal Justice Academy, yes.
Q. Correct. And you review texts like the Maine Law Enforcement Officer's Manual?
A. From time to time, yes.
Q. And this text, actually the Maine Law Enforcement Officers Manual is a publication sponsored by the Maine Criminal Justice Academy, right?
A. Yes, it is.
Q. And part of your training do you have any specific training related to dealing with children who have allegedly been victims of sexual abuse?
A. Yes, I have been through a number of different training schools, things like that.

Accuracy of Report

Q. The training regarding generally being a police officer involves in part dealing with accurately writing police reports, is that fair to say?
A. That's fair to say.
Q. It's important that your police reports are accurate?
A. Yes.
Q. It's important that they are thorough, correct?
A. Yes.
Q. And you wrote reports in this case, didn't you?

A. I did.

Q. And those reports here were accurate and thorough?

A. To the best of my ability.

Proper Procedures for Interviewing Child Victims

Q. You also need to be careful when you are interviewing a child because of your status as an authority figure, is that fair to say?

A. Yes.

Q. Now before you interviewed Tammy you spoke to a DHHS worker I think, right?

A. Yes.

Q. And you spoke to Tracey who is Tammy's Mom, right?

A. I spoke to her briefly, yes.

Q. You speak to her about the case itself?

A. Yes.

Q. So she was sort of briefing you about the case before you spoke to Tammy?

A. I had asked her some questions. I don't know if she was briefing me.

Q. She was giving you some information, is that correct?

A. Yes, because she had just come from Dr. Howard's.

Q. Okay. And you questioned her as you said in Tracey's presence?

A. Questioned?

Q. Tammy.

A. I interviewed her in Tracey's presence, yes.

Q. Okay, I will say interview too. Was there any time during the interview of Tammy that Tracey was not present in the room?

A. I took Tammy and walked her out to the bathroom for a few minutes.

Q. But you weren't interviewing her at that time?

A. No, small talk.

Q. I assume that you have learned that it's very important that a child only be questioned in these types of cases by a properly trained person, isn't that right?

A. If you know, in theory, you know, that's a good practice, but reality around this state there aren't a whole lot of—some police departments have, you know, the chief is also the dog catcher, so if there is a case that person has to take it whether they are trained or not.

Q. But you have been trained in this?

A. Yes.

Q. And you agree that it's the best practice to have a properly trained person interview a child, right?

A. It is a good practice.

Q. It's also important that the investigative interview be done with an open mind, correct?

A. Yes.

Q. You have to complete this interview with the child with the assumption that there could be multiple explanations for what's being alleged, isn't that right?

A. I think going into it you have an open mind, but once you start hearing what is said and gauging the person you can draw opinions based on that, conclusions.

Q. But you should, throughout the interview at least until you heard everything, be engaging in the interview with that open mind, right?

A. Try and keep an open mind.

Q. You have to also be very careful about rewarding children in these interviews with too much attention, isn't that right?

A. I guess. It all depends. I mean every interview is different and every kid's different, and, you know, the age has a lot to do with it. It all depends you don't want to shower someone with rewards because they are giving you, you know, certain answers, I'll agree with that.

Q. And attention can be a reward to some kids, isn't that true?

A. To some kids.

Q. There are—and you've also learned I'm sure that there are a whole number of reasons why children can tell you things that may or may not be accurate in these interviews, is that correct?
A. Yes.
Q. Do you belong to the American Professional Society on the Abuse of Children?
A. No.
Q. Are you familiar with this handbook on child maltreatment?
A. Never seen it before.
Q. It's true that though you said there can be a variety of different explanations for why a child might say something, isn't that right?
A. Yes.
Q. One of the explanations might be a child distortion from a traumatic memory?
A. Perhaps, if the book says it.
Q. Maybe a child's account might be affected by suggestions, is that fair to say?
A. Could be.
Q. You have to be concerned about that, right?
A. Yes.
Q. The interviews should also take place in a neutral setting if at all possible, right?
A. I, I, I don't know.
Q. Doesn't the Maine law enforcement officers manual suggest that the interviews take place at the child's home?
A. I don't know what it suggests.
Q. Before I approach you here, isn't it true that the law enforcement officers manual does say that a busy police station may be an unwise place to interview a child?
A. I don't know what it says. If it says that I can see where a busy police station people in and out and distractions could be a problem.
A. There is probably some guidelines there, yeah.
Q. Do you want to take a look at them before I start asking you questions about?
A. If you would like to, sure.
Q. Do you remember the items in this list from your training?
A. Some of them. I mean I haven't looked at that chapter probably a long time, but some of those things were in the trainings.
Q. And did you do all—did you complete all the items on this list as far as you can tell?
A. I don't go down a checklist. I kind of play it by ear as we go.
Q. Okay. So you don't really follow this, that chapter in this book by the letter, is that fair to say?
A. I don't follow a chapter of any book by the letter. I basically it's a guideline, there are some useful things on any book, tips, but basically, I go by experience, what's worked for me, what the situation is presented.

Lack of Interviews with Other Witnesses

Q. Did you—one of the things that's important for you to do is to interview other adult witnesses, right?
A. Yes.
Q. And did you interview Tammy's Grandfather?
A. No.
Q. Did you interview Nancy?
A. No.
Q. Athena?
A. No.
Q. Did you interview Tammy's teachers?
A. No.

Lack of Crime Scene Investigation

Q. There is a whole section in this book about crime scene investigation in cases involving children, isn't there?
A. There could be.

Q. Let me show it to you again. I am not asking you read it. I am just asking you if there is a section in the book about it?

A. There is a section labeled crime scene search.

Q. Okay. Do you agree with me that it's important to follow up on any leads that you get in your interview, correct?

A. Yes.

Q. You for example got a lead that Tammy had been shown pornography by Bob, right?

A. Yes.

Q. And did you go to Bob's house to look for that pornography?

A. No.

More on Proper Procedures for Interviewing Children

Q. All right. Let's talk about interviewing kids some more. You also don't want to display or show any shock or discomfort when you are interviewing the child about these types of allegations, right?

A. Try not to.

Q. Because you don't want to allow the child to pick up any clues from you, correct?

A. Try not to.

Q. Are you unable to follow these guidelines Sergeant?

A. I try to.

Q. But you don't always succeed.

A. No interview is perfect.

Q. And you want to avoid leading questions?

A. When you can.

Q. That's something you want to avoid if at all possible, right?

A. Try.

Q. You are also supposed to establish sort of the details of the day as you look into when a certain assault took place, isn't that right?

A. If you can.

Q. And is that something you did here?

A. Tried to.

Q. Were you able to do that or were you unable to do that?

A. To the best of my ability.

Q. Okay. So did you attempt to establish details of the day for the last episode she recounted to you?

A. The best one that I was able to find really a date was the allegation at Grandpa's trailer on or about March 11th.

Q. And that one you were able to reconstruct the day?

A. Uhm, I don't mean not the full day but just basically when, when they had moved in there and what activity took place there. We didn't talk from, you know, waking up to going to bed.

Q. Okay. But you didn't interview Grandpa, correct?

A. No.

Interview of Alleged Victim

Q. When you started off talking to Tammy she was reluctant to speak to you?

A. Not reluctant to speak to me but reluctant to discuss the details of the alleged abuse.

Q. She wasn't volunteering any information that her father had assaulted her, is that fair to say?

A. No, it's just more that she was uncomfortable I think talking to me because I'm about the same age as her Dad and, you know, to interview an 11-year-old by a man, you know, so there was a little disconnect there, had to try and build rapport.

Q. You are guessing about that level of discomfort?

A. That was my feeling.

Q. That's your feeling, though she didn't tell you that, did she?

A. No, she didn't tell me.

Q. And you don't know, do you?

A. No.

Q. So let's stop guessing. My question was she wasn't in there volunteering information until you had to prod her a little bit, is that fair to say?

A. I don't know if prod is the right word, but, yes, I had to elicit some information from her.

Q. And you say, "You know, did your Dad do something to you that you didn't like?" right?

A. I believe I said that.

Q. In fact you said that to her at least three times before she gave you any information about sexual assault, isn't that right?

A. I don't know if it was three times. I said it a few times.

Q. A few times at least?

A. Sure.

Q. And before that when you were saying, "Did your Dad ever do anything with you that you didn't like she'd say something like" and she answered "Well, they went out to dinner without me" right?

A. Yeah, there was an incident that we discussed.

Q. And during that time you said that Tracey didn't interfere in this interview?

A. I wouldn't call it, I mean, yes, she did not interfere.

Q. But she was, she was a presence there, is that fair to say?

A. She was in the room.

Q. She was in the room but not only that, she was holding Tammy's hand, right?

A. Yes.

Q. Would you agree with me she was encouraging Tammy?

A. Uhm, she was encouraging her to use her own words and talk to me.

Q. She was encouraging her to disclose it all, wasn't she?

A. Uhm, disclose it all, what I remember is that she was, whenever Tammy would look up to her mother when I asked her a question she would just say you need to say in your own words.

Q. You don't remember her saying stuff like "You're a big girl, you're a big strong girl"?

A. I don't remember those words.

Q. You don't remember?

A. It's possible, but I don't remember that.

Q. You remember her mother praising her when she did finally disclose?

A. Uhm, I think she encouraged her throughout the interview in different times.

Q. And you encouraged Tammy too?

A. Yes.

Q. You told Tammy "I believe you?"

A. I did tell her I believed her.

Q. You said "We won't tell anybody about what you say," didn't you?

A. I don't know if it came out like that, but it was more—

Q. You promised her that you weren't going to tell people what she was saying to you, right?

A. That's not the way it came out. It's more like I am not going to advertise this to the world, that type of thing.

Q. You knew people were going to know about this?

A. Absolutely.

Q. You were saying that to try to get her to disclose the alleged abuse to you, is that fair to say?

A. I was trying to set her mind at ease so she would open up.

Q. And at some point and at other points in the interview she said I don't want to disclose abuse to you, right?

A. I don't recall her saying I don't want to do it.

Q. Do you remember her mother saying "you have to tell these things?"

A. I think she said that, I'm not exactly sure the wording, but, yes, she was telling her she needed to tell the police, tell me what happened.

Interview and Interrogation of Defendant

Q. Okay. You interviewed Bob twice and we saw those interviews, right?

A. Yes.

Q. There aren't any other interviews of Bob, right, just those two times?

A. Not with me, just two times.

Q. Right. And both times Bob—well, take them one-by-one. First Bob was on the road in Massachusetts and you called him?

A. Yes.

Q. And he came in?

A. He did.

Q. He came in relatively promptly I think you would agree with me, right?

A. When he got out of work, yes.

Q. And you were using certain investigative or interview techniques I think is what you described in direct examination with him, right?

A. Yes.

Q. I mean in the first interview technique to some extent you were sort of trying to get on his side, is that fair to say?

A. I was trying to keep the door open and just --

Q. You were saying you don't judge these things, right?

A. Yes.

Q. Offering him up other explanations for, you know, what might have happened, right?

A. Explanations, I'm not sure, I mean possibilities.

Q. Okay, possibilities, that's a good word, and the idea of opening up those possibilities is to try to ultimately get him to confess to you, right?

A. Actually I wasn't looking for that on the first day because it was early on, and I hadn't had a lot of information, but I was trying to feel him out.

Q. Okay. And so one of the ways you do that is sort of befriend him a little bit, is that fair?

A. Build a rapport with him so he will talk with me.

Q. Okay. And as we saw he denied, denied any sexual contact with Tammy, right?

A. He did.

Q. I mean at one point I see him on that tape, and I don't know if the jury could hear it, I'm sure you remember it, where his head is in his hands and he is sort of muttering something under his breath, you remember that?

A. Yes.

Q. And he was saying why "Tammy, why?" wasn't he?

A. He was.

Q. He said that over and over again throughout that interview, didn't he?

A. He said it three times.

Q. Okay. So the second time, and before I go to the second time, I think on the first tape you said, and I think this is probably accurate, you said, you know, this must be a blur to you, Bob, or something like that, right?

A. Yes.

Q. And that's common for people brought into that situation in your experience, right?

A. Uhm, I would think so if that was an allegation.

Q. Yeah. I'm sorry.

A. Posed to me I would feel probably the same way.

Q. Yeah, I think any of us would. So the second time you interviewed him you had spoken to Tammy at that point?

A. Yes.

Q. And Bob noted in that I think that Tammy wasn't getting along well with Sally?

A. During the first interview?

Q. No, I am on two.

A. No, we didn't talk about Sally the second time. First one we did talk about the relationship. He said that he thought they had a good relationship, but she wasn't getting along with his girlfriend Sally.

Q. Okay, thank you. The second one did he talk about her—one of these two he talked about her trying to run away, right?

A. That was the first interview. We didn't get that far on the second.

Q. All right. The second interview is when you really are trying to get the confession out of him, right?

A. Yes.

Q. And in this interview as we heard that interview becomes sort of antagonistic, right?

A. Yes.

Q. And it's designed to be that way, isn't it?

A. Well, it didn't go the way it was really designed because for obvious reasons I mean he wouldn't separate from Sally. I wanted to talk to him alone, and I did want to interrogate him at that point instead of just interviewing him.

Q. Yes, but the plan, okay, and I understand it didn't go as designed, and there was no confession, so that's another reason why it didn't go as designed, right?

A. There was no confession, you're right.

Q. Okay, so you—I guess what I was getting at though is the second one is sort of a harder charging interrogation, right?

A. It was an interrogation.

Q. Yes, okay, and you told him he sexually abused his daughter, right?

A. I did.

Q. And he denied it every time you said that?

A. He denied doing it.

Q. Yeah, and you argued with him and said, "Yes, you did! Yes, you did!" and he denied it, right?

A. Yes.

Q. No matter what you tried to do to him, befriending him or interrogating him, he always denied sexually assaulting his daughter, correct?

A. He did say those words.

Q. You used your best efforts and all of your experience to get a confession?

A. I did the best I could given the scenario.

Q. And that was really the primary end of your investigation, isn't that correct?

A. Just about.

Search of Defendant's Residence

Q. There was no—I asked you before if you ever, if you ended up and went and searched Bob's residence, and I think you said no, right?

A. No, that's correct.

Q. Have you ever since then searched Bob's residence?

A. Uhm, yes.

Q. When was that?

A. I did a couple bail checks when he was out on bail. He had a condition of random search.

Q. And you did those personally?

A. Yes.

Q. And did you find anything, did you find any porn?

A. No.

Q. And I think I asked you this before, and I don't want to belabor this, but you didn't interview Tammy's teachers, right?

A. That's correct.

Inconsistencies in Victim's Story

Q. Okay. So you heard Tammy's testimony at trial?

A. I did.

Q. You heard her testify that there was no time in Gray where her father put his privates in her privates, and then later say that one time in Gray he put his privates in her privates, you heard that, right?

A. I did hear, I heard her say no at first and then say one or two times, and then I acquiesce to one time, right.

Q. And she told you it happened three times in Gray?

A. Yeah, in June of 07 she told me three times in Gray.

Q. And I don't mean three times including digital and mouth, literally she told you there were three times in Gray where her father put his privates in her privates, correct?

A. That's what she said in June of 07.

Q. You also heard Tammy say that in Westbrook it happened once a week that there was some sort of sexual activity, do you remember that at trial?

A. At trial, yes.

Q. She didn't tell you that in her interview, right?

A. She told me, if you want me to say how many, she didn't say that, not those exact words.

Q. Okay. Tammy said at trial that her father put his privates in her butt, did you hear her say that?

A. I did.

Q. She didn't tell you that either, did she?

A. No, she didn't tell me that.

§12:143 Cross-Examination of Child's Mother

In sex cases with child victims, you usually end up with all sorts of other "nothing" witnesses to deal with-- biased witnesses who don't have much to say. Here is a cross of Tammy's Mother, and how I tried to shade her testimony toward our view of the case.

Instability of Mother's Relationships

Q. So Bill Black is Tabitha's Dad?
A. Yeah.
Q. Bob is obviously Tammy's Dad?
A. Correct.
Q. And John is your current husband?
A. He is.
Q. And that's Jamie's Dad?
A. Yeap.
Q. But I think you said that you're in the process of a divorce?
A. I am going through a divorce now, yes.

Child's Prior History of Alleged Sexual Abuse

Q. Before Tammy went to live with Bob, did she ever tell you that she had been sexually abused by anyone else?
A. Not that she was sexually abused, no.
Q. Did she ever tell you that she was involved in some sort of sexual activity before she went to live with Bob?
A. Not hardly. There was an incident when she was about two-years-old I think. She was in the process of potty training, and she said that someone had touched her, but it was an eleven-year-old boy and when he pulled up her pullup or whatever she was wearing.
Q. And that was when Tammy was two-years-old?
A. Yes, she was very young.
Q. And you are certain it was two?
A. Well, I had completely forgotten about it, but, yeah, I can't even remember the name of the person that did it.
Q. Did you tell Bob about that?
A. No, I didn't as far as I know.
Q. And did you go to the police regarding that?
A. No, I didn't.
Q. Do you remember the year of this?
A. If she was like two-years-old then it would have been in '99.

Mother's Concerns about Child Attention-Seeking Behavior and Truthfulness

Q. You said that Tammy has no personal boundaries, is that right?
A. She doesn't respect personal space; sometimes you have to remind her.
Q. And I think you said that she likes to be around adults a lot?
A. She does.
Q. Would you characterize her as attention-seeking, is that fair to say?
A. She likes attention I think.
Q. You said she didn't want to be away from people?
A. Tammy aims to please. She likes to be with people.
Q. And was that true before the time that she went to live with Bob?
A. Yes, that's true today.
Q. You had a talk with Tammy about being truthful before she went to the ER, right?
A. Yes, I did.
Q. You had some concerns about her being truthful?
A. I think with any allegations of sexual abuse any parent should make sure that their child is telling the truth.

Q. So you didn't have any specific concerns related to Tammy being truthful?

A. I believe my daughter until she gives me a reason not to.

Q. Did you have a talk with Detective Lippy of the Westbrook Police Department about that?

A. I really don't remember a whole lot of the conversation that I had with him.

Q. Do you remember saying that you were concerned about the truthfulness of Tammy's allegations?

A. I said I hoped she was lying. I'm sorry, but I would rather have her tell that lie than have it ever be true.

Q. So you don't remember saying that you were concerned that she would tell the truth about this to Lippy?

A. No, I don't remember that.

Q. Did Tammy during this period of time have a tendency to make up stories that weren't true?

A. Not any more than any other kid would.

Q. So you don't recall that part of the conversation regarding Tammy's truthfulness with Detective Lippy, is that right?

A. No.

Q. And you went to the doctor with Tammy?

A. Correct.

Q. Do you remember taking her to Maine Medical Center?

A. Yes.

Q. And there were several doctors there, is that right?

A. I remember two I think, two or three.

Q. Were you there when Tammy talked to them about intercourse happening with her Dad?

A. Yes, I was in there.

Q. And she told them at that point that it happened 6 or 7 times, is that right?

A. Something like that, yeah.

Upheaval at Home and Mother's Strained Relationship with Daughters

Q. You said your house at the time that Tammy went to live with her Dad was hectic I think was the word you used?

A. Yeah.

Q. Most of the problems dealt with Tabitha?

A. That's correct.

Q. Tabitha was not obeying house rules?

A. Yes.

Q. She was having boys coming into the house when they weren't supposed to be there?

A. She did once.

Q. Was Tammy there at that time?

A. No, she was living with us but she wasn't there.

Q. Was that the day that you ended up having Tammy go live with her Dad?

A. No.

Q. Tammy used to sort of get in between you and Tabitha when you were having an argument?

A. Yeah.

Q. Those arguments were physically violent?

A. I wouldn't say they were violent. I was well within my rights as a parent.

Q. What do you mean by that?

A. To restrain my daughter.

Q. Did you physically discipline her during these periods of time?

A. I physically restrained her during some of these periods of time and that's what her sister did not like.

Q. Did you physically discipline meaning spank during these periods of time?

A. I might have spanked her once, but spankings didn't do a whole lot with a 15-year-old.

Q. Right. How about hitting other than spanking, did you get involved in any of that during periods?

A. No, it was more I would say a wrestling match than –

Q. Prior to that did you physically discipline Tammy?

A. On occasion.

Q. That ever involve slapping her?

A. Yes.

Q. In the face?

A. Once.

Q. When Tammy came to live with Bob, you were at a point where you just could not deal with Tammy anymore, is that fair to say?

A. It wasn't that I couldn't deal with Tammy. It was that I needed a break so I could get things under control with Tabitha.

Q. The day that she went to live with Bob you were very upset, is that fair to say?

A. Sure, I was.

Q. Would you say that the situation had sort of gotten out of control on that date?

A. Absolutely.

Q. And you called up Bob, right?

A. I did.

Q. And you said something like you got to get your fucking daughter right now, right?

A. Something like that, get over here, yeah.

Q. And you were yelling?

A. I was probably yelling at Tabitha, yes.

Q. And when Bob arrived Sally was with him, yes?

A. Correct.

Q. And were things still out of control at that point?

A. I wouldn't say they were completely under control, but things had kind of turned a little bit. It was more revolving around what was going to be going on with Tammy than so much with Tabitha.

Q. Now was it Tammy's choice to leave the house at this point?

A. She said "I want to go see my dad" or "I want to call my Dad." I said, fine, we will call your Dad.

Q. And at that point you said come get her?

A. Yeah, I told him he needed to come over.

Q. And by the time he got over there were you yelling at Tammy?

A. I might have been.

Q. Did you tell him that he had to take this fucking little bitch, did you tell him that?

A. No, I don't believe I did.

Q. Did you say that Tammy wasn't going to treat you this way?

A. I probably did say that.

Q. Tammy have a chance to pack?

A. She and Sally packed some stuff. Like I said, it wasn't a big bag. It wasn't meant to be a long period thing.

Q. And Tabitha stayed there with you, right?

A. She did, and I got in touch with some services for her.

Change of Custody

Q. And then Bob went into court and arranged change of custody?

A. In January.

Q. And he became the primary parent?

A. That's correct.

Q. And along with that there came a change in child support?

A. Correct.

Q. He was paying you child support before, correct?

A. Correct.

Q. Then you began paying him child support?

A. Correct.

Q. Prior to the time that Tammy came back to live with you, you began having phone calls with her?

A. I would talk to her, sure.

Q. Did you tell her that you were logging the calls?

A. No.

Q. You didn't tell her that your attorney told you to log the calls for your custody case?

A. No. I put some information into my phone.

Q. June 3rd was the day that you took her to the Maine Med ER, right?

A. Correct.

Q. And June 4th you filed a motion to modify child support, didn't you?
A. I did I think, yeah.
Q. That was a motion for the court to stop you paying child support to Bob, right?
A. Yeah.
Q. At that time were you out on disability?
A. No.
Q. What is your disability?
A. I have physical and mental disabilities. I'm disabled through Social Security.

Child's Return to Mother's Home

Q. So again I want to set the time. I am not trying to be confusing but the day that Bob called and asked you to pick Tammy back up, you remember that day?
A. May 18, yes, I do.
Q. And I thought you said at one point during your direct examination that you were sleeping when he called, is that right?
A. No.
Q. You didn't say that?
A. No, I didn't. I was in the bathtub when he called.
Q. And Bob told you that Tammy had been threatening to run away?
A. Yes.
Q. Did Bob also tell you that Tammy had threatened to kill herself?
A. No, I found that out when I showed up there.
Q. And Bob told you?
A. He told me that my daughter tried to commit suicide by putting a bag over her head.
Q. That was that same day you went to pick her up?
A. That's when he told me. I don't know when it actually happened.
Q. You say you told Bob about the incident with the older boy when Tammy was younger?
A. Yes, I did.

[§§12:144-12:149 Reserved]

3. Direct Examination of Defense Witnesses

§12:150 Direct Examination of Defendant

God, do I hate putting defendants on the stand. But no matter how often you warn them, sometimes you can't keep them off, in these types of cases especially. So, while I avoid it as much as I can, I find that sometimes Defendants accused of raping their own kids who proclaim themselves to be innocent will insist on saying it to the jury, despite my warnings.

When the Defendant insists on testifying, as Bob did here, you may have to put him or her on. I don't like to do it, and I warn my clients against testifying, but sometimes they insist.

To prepare, I like to have someone in my firm prepare a brief cross, acting like the prosecutor. The client needs to know that staying pleasant with the prosecutor, but firm in denial of the criminal conduct, is the key.

Bob is a monster if you believe the allegations. So our direct needs to be about humanizing our client.

MR. ZERILLO: The defendant has elected to testify, Your Honor.
THE COURT: Fair enough.

Personal and Employment History

Q. Bob, where did you grow up?
A. In Limington.
Q. The whole time in Limington?

A.   No, I moved to Portland and then to Westbrook.

Q.   And where did you go to high school?

A.   Deering High School.

Q.   You have family in the area?

A.   Yes.

Q.   And tell me a little bit about your employment history, where have you worked?

A.   I have had a few jobs, most recently would be Generic Tree.

Q.   How long were you there?

A.   Between six and eight years.

Current Employment and Work Schedule

Q.   And where do you work now?

A.   At Maine Delivery.

Q.   And what do you do for Maine Delivery?

A.   I am a truck driver. I deliver furniture, appliances.

Q.   How many hours a week do you ordinarily work for Maine Delivery?

A.   Between 55 and 65.

Q.   55 to 65?

A.   Yes.

Q.   Now what's your, what's your work schedule for Maine Delivery usually?

A.   Monday through Saturday.

Q.   Do you usually work Saturdays?

A.   Yeah, occasionally I will have one off, but most of the time every Saturday.

Q.   So a Saturday off is a rarity?

A.   Very rare.

Q.   And do you have a set schedule? Well, where do you deliver to?

A.   All over the State of Maine, Massachusetts and Vermont.

Q.   And do you have set days where you go to Massachusetts?

A.   Tuesdays.

Q.   And do you have set days when you go to Vermont?

A.   No, they are not a set day. We try to shoot for long distance deliveries done on Thursdays.

Q.   And do you have any long distance deliveries in the state within the State of Maine?

A.   Yes.

Q.   And where do you go?

A.   Presque Isle, Van Buren.

Q.   Do you have a set day where you go a long distance delivery in the State of Maine?

A.   Once again I try to do all long distance on Thursdays depending on the customer.

Q.   So long distance could be Vermont or northern Maine but it would all be on Thursday usually?

A.   Yes, yes.

Q.   When do you normally get out of work?

A.   Normally five o'clock, four o'clock.

Q.   What's the earliest you usually get out of work?

A.   Four.

Q.   You heard some testimony that you get out as early I think as 2:45, is that right?

A.   Very rarely will I ever get out that early.

Q.   What's a normal time for you to get out of work?

A.   Five o'clock, six o'clock.

Q.   And when do you go into work?

A.   Tuesdays I have to be there at five because we go long distance. Thursdays I have to be there at five because we go long distance.

Q.   And where do you mean by there?

A.   Maine Delivery.

Q.   Where is that?

A. In Portland.

Q. So not far from where you live?

A. No.

Q. So Tuesdays and Thursdays you have to be there by when?

A. Five.

Q. A.m.?

A. A.m.

Q. And on those Tuesdays and Thursdays when do you get back usually?

A. Most of the time six or later. When I go to Presque Isle, it's six hours up six hours back and I have deliveries in between going up there and coming back.

Q. So Monday, Wednesday and Friday and Saturday you have to be in by when?

A. Six o'clock unless, unless we have that rare occasion where a customer, long distance customer needs a delivery done.

Q. Six a.m. obviously?

A. Six a.m.

Q. And you heard Sally testify about being there at seven?

A. Correct.

Q. Is that true?

A. That's incorrect.

Q. By six a.m.?

A. I have to be there by six.

Relationship with Daughter While She Was in Mother's Custody

Q. Before Tammy came to move with you, move in with you how often would you see her?

A. Every other weekend, school vacations, once in a while maybe I would get her for a few days in the summer when she wasn't at school, but most of the time Tracey made me stick to the schedule.

Q. And what's the longest you have ever gone before she moved in, what was the longest stretch you ever had with her?

A. A week.

Q. And was that frequent?

A. School vacations once in a great while when she was at school.

Q. And how long have you had the type of schedule with Tammy?

A. Since she was born.

Q. Since she was a baby?

A. Yeah.

Q. Can everyone hear him? And prior to the time you moved in, she moved in with you what would you, how would you characterize your relationship with Tammy?

A. Great.

Q. Typical father daughter?

A. Yes, definitely.

Q. Did you—when you had those visits with Tammy did anyone accompany Tammy on those visits?

A. No.

Q. How about her older sister come with her?

A. At the beginning I had both the children Tabitha and Tammy.

Q. You are not Tabitha's father though?

A. No.

Concerns with Daughter's Living Situation with Mother

Q. You had concerns with—well, did you have any concerns with Tammy's living situation before she moved in with you?

A. A lot.

Q. What did those concerns involve?

A. Her well-being.

Q. How so?

A. Uhm, the fights they would have, the phone calls I would get from Tracey, from DHS, the phone calls I get from Tammy and even on occasion from Tabitha.

Daughter's Move from Mother's to Defendant Father's Home

Q. At the end of 2006 do you recall receiving a telephone call from Tracey?

A. Yes.

Q. Do you remember that day?

A. I do.

Q. What was said in that phone conversation? There was a lot said. She basically told me I had to "come get the fucking little bitch." She wasn't going to be doing this stuff to me no more. She wasn't going to be calling DHS.

Q. I want to stop you there. You just said "get the fucking little bitch," are those your words?

A. Those are her words.

Q. Whose?

A. Tracey's.

Q. And what did you say about DHS?

A. That Tammy would threaten to call DHS and Tracey had basically said to Tammy that she wasn't going to be calling DHS on Tracey anymore.

Q. Tracey was telling you this in this phone call?

A. Yes.

Q. And what did Tracey's voice sound like to you, was it subdued, excited?

A. She was very angry.

Q. And what did you do?

A. I dropped everything I was doing and drove right up there.

Q. From where?

A. From Westbrook, I mean from, yeah, Gray.

Q. Gray?

A. Yeah.

Q. Now how long had you been living in Gray at that point?

A. Not very long, just about a few months maybe.

Q. Who were you living with?

A. Sally.

Q. At Sally's brother's?

A. Originally started at Sally's apartment, and then we moved to Sally's brother's because he moved out of the country and needed somebody to watch his house.

Q. Okay. So at the time that you got the phone call you just described where were you living?

A. In Gray at Sally's brother's.

Q. Okay. And you said you did what?

A. I dropped everything and went right up there.

Q. And what did you see when you got there, and where is where, Standish?

A. Standish.

Q. What did you see when you arrived in Standish?

A. I saw Tabitha and Tracey, Tammy having an extremely loud argument, some physical confrontation between Tracey and Tabitha. Tammy was yelling and stuff like that for Mommy to stop and Tabitha to stop, she doesn't like confrontation like that.

Q. And who was, who was there at that time when you arrived at the house in Standish?

A. Tabitha, Tracey, Tammy, I do believe John was there and the baby Jamie.

Q. Okay. Were the police there?

A. They arrived shortly thereafter. It was just a couple of minutes.

Q. And during this altercation what was, what did you hear Tracey say?

A. She was basically screaming at Tabitha to stop screaming and hollering and fighting, and I can't remember exactly I know it was.

Q. There was a lot of screaming?

A. A lot.

Q. So what did you do with Tammy?

A. The situation had stopped, and Tracey and Tammy come out onto the deck with me and Sally, and that's when we had started the original conversation of what was going on, what we were going to do.

Q. Okay, and what did you end up doing?

A. Uhm, the police had showed up while we were having that conversation, and then the police officer and I had suggested we take Tammy out of there, and Tracey had also suggested we take Tammy out of there.

Q. And so you did?

A. And I did.

Q. And did you pack a bag for her?

A. I didn't pack the bag. Sally went in and got the—she went to the dirty clothes and got a little bit of clothes.

Relationship with Girlfriend and Sexual Practices

Q. Your relationship with Sally then was still?

A. New.

Q. New. And how long did you say you had been living with her at that point?

A. I'd say maybe a month or two maybe if that.

Q. Since that time you have broken up?

A. Yes.

Q. Since Tammy moved out?

A. Yes.

Q. While we are talking about Sally I'll ask you embarrassing questions about Sally shaving her private area. Did you request that she shave her private area?

A. Never.

Q. Did she shave her private area?

A. Yes.

Q. All the time?

A. Not all the time.

Q. Was that something that you demanded?

A. No.

Q. How about her description of the two of you having anal sex, is that something that occurred?

A. We tried. It didn't work. It was too painful.

Q. Okay. Not for you?

A. Not for me.

Q. And how many times did you try?

A. Once or twice.

Q. And is that something that you demanded she do?

A. No, not at all.

Q. Who brought up the idea of engaging in anal sex if you remember?

A. It was her idea. We were trying to figure out a way to spruce up our sex life because it wasn't going so well.

Q. Okay. And that was an idea that who brought up?

A. Sally.

Sally had indicated on direct that Bob frequently insisted on having anal sex with her.

Layout of House in Gray

Q. Okay. All right, Well, let's talk about the house in Gray. Actually could I ask you to stand up and draw the interior if you could, and you don't have to be an artist to do this, okay.

A. It's a two story farmhouse.

Q. Okay. Why don't you show, draw me the living area.

A. The living area.

Q. Draw me the first floor and second floor.

A. Right, when you walk through the door you enter kitchen here and then here on this side is a little computer room. If you walk, it was pretty much only these two rooms, when you walk through the door for the first floor and you would walk to your left over here there would be a living room here on your right coming out of the living room there is like not even a very big hallway, then there is a breezeway here that goes out to Route 202. There that hallway you would come into another like a little kids play room here, and then there was a set of stairs that went up to the second floor.

Q. Okay, and you have drawn the kitchen into the computer room without a wall, is there a wall there?

A. Yeah, there is a little bit of a wall right here.

Q. Is it pretty much open in the downstairs or is it all wall?

A. No, it's all sectioned off except for these two rooms here.

Q. Okay.

A. This is the living room then there is a wall here with a door opening into the breezeway.

Q. Okay. Why don't you draw me the sleeping space then which I assume is the second floor.

A. Correct.

Q. Keep it on the same page, go ahead.

A. Like I said you have to go up the stairs, as soon as you got up the stairs you pretty much had to take a left was a bedroom here and a bedroom here.

Q. Okay. Now did you occupy one of those bedrooms to sleep in?

A. This is my bedroom.

Q. And who stayed in there with you?

A. Sally stayed in here with me.

Q. And what is this separation between the two rooms, a hallway?

A. I'm sorry, I didn't mean to put it. This is just a wall right here.

Q. Okay, and who stayed in this bedroom?

A. This was Tammy's room here.

Q. So they shared a wall?

A. Yes, they were side by side.

Absence of Time Alone with Daughter

Q. Okay. You can sit back down for a moment. When Tammy came to live with you was it during the school year?

A. Yes.

Q. And were you keeping that same schedule for Maine Delivery getting there by six?

A. I had to.

Q. And who would pick up Tammy after school when you were living in Gray?

A. Sally would pick Tammy up from Standish.

Q. Okay. Now what about when she went—so the entire time that she continued in school in Standish who picked her up that whole time?

A. When we were living in Gray, Sally.

Q. When you were living in Gray, but Tammy still went to school in Standish?

A. Correct.

Q. Sally picked her up?

A. Correct.

Q. All the time?

A. All the time.

Q. Who—now did she eventually go into Gray schools?

A. Yes.

Q. And who would do the pickups and drop-offs then?

A. Sally would do the pickups and drop-offs then.

Q. In Gray did you ever do pickups or drop-offs?

A. Never at school, just the first day I took her to school.

Q. That was a drop-off?

A. That was a drop-off.

Q. Did you ever—why did you do it that day?

A.   It was her first day at school. It was a special thing. I wanted to get pictures.

Q.   Okay. So did she ever take the bus in Gray?

A.   Uhm, she never took it to school, but she would take it to her grandparents, to her step-grandparents, Sally's parents.

Q.   Do you remember ever picking her up at school while during the time that you lived in Gray?

A.   Never.

Q.   And how long did you live in Gray from when Tammy came to live with you?

A.   It wasn't very long. It was couple of months.

Q.   A few months?

A.   Yeah, it wasn't very long at all.

Q.   And you moved in for a little while then with who?

A.   When I left Gray we went to my sisters in Westbrook.

Q.   Okay. Before we go there, sorry for skipping around, were there times when you were in Gray that you were alone with Tammy?

A.   No, because Sally wasn't really working. It was still really fresh. We were still trying to feel the whole thing out. Sally really liked that she had another kid in the house, so she really spent a lot of time. She took Tammy shopping because she didn't have many clothes. She didn't have any toys. She didn't have nothing.

Q.   So the whole time that you were in Gray I mean you, for example, just described taking her to school, were you alone then?

A.   Uh, no, I don't think I was.

Q.   You think Sally was with you?

A.   I do. Sally was there taking pictures because I have pictures of me and Tammy together at the school.

Q.   So you don't believe there was a time when you were in Gray where you were alone with your daughter?

A.   No, not at all.

Normalcy of Father-Daughter Relationship

Q.   During the times that you were in Gray what types of things would you and Tammy and/or Sally do together?

A.   Oh, we would do all kinds of things. Her brother had left a couple of dogs for us to take care of. We would go for walks through the path through the back of the woods. We would play in the fort that we had all built out back. We would go rides in my jeep, go four wheeling in the new jeep. We would go everything, everything we can imagine and think of.

Q.   Was she enrolled in—well, that wouldn't have been softball season, right?

A.   It hadn't started yet.

Q.   So did you keep up on Tammy's grades during the time before she came to live with you?

A.   Oh, yes.

Q.   What type of grades would she get, was she getting say the year before she came to live with you?

A.   C's and D's, C's and B's, it would vary each quarter.

Q.   And what type of grades did she get after she came to live with you?

A.   The first quarter of school she got B's and I do believe it was straight B's. The next two quarters she was straight A's.

Q.   And is that in Westbrook then?

A.   In Westbrook and she made honor roll twice.

Q.   You heard the allegations made by Tammy at this trial about being in Gray, right?

A.   Yes.

Q.   Now did that make you feel when you heard those?

MS. PROS: Objection.

THE COURT: Emotions are not an issue, so I sustain.

BY MR. ZERILLO:

Denial of Sexual Activity with Daughter in Gray

Q.   Did you engage in any of the sexual activity—

A.   Absolutely not.

Q.   Let me just finish—that Tammy described in Gray?

A. Absolutely not.

Q. Did you engage in intercourse with her?

A. Absolutely not, absolutely not.

Q. Did you engage in any sort of oral sex with her?

A. Absolutely not.

Q. Did you engage in any sort of digital finger sex?

A. No, absolutely not.

Q. Did you—you heard Tammy talk about the story with the dirt road?

A. Yes.

Q. Did you ever take Tammy down a dirt road?

A. We have gone for walks with the dogs. I have never driven down a dirt road with her.

Q. Did you ever masturbate in front of Tammy?

A. Never, absolutely not.

Discipline of Daughter

Q. Was Tammy disciplined when you lived in Gray?

A. Yeah, yeah, she was disciplined.

Q. Was she ever sent to her room?

A. Yeah.

Q. Was she sent to her room for two or three days at a time?

A. No, no.

Q. Okay. What about spanking did you ever spank her?

A. Once.

Q. One time in Gray or one time during?

A. One time in Westbrook.

Q. Okay. Did you spank her at all in Gray?

A. Never.

Q. And when you spanked her in Westbrook it was a spank where?

A. On her bottom.

Q. Was Sally there for that?

A. Yes.

Move to Sister's Home

Q. Okay. So you moved in with your sister for a week or so?

A. Yeah.

Q. And why was that?

A. Me and Sally were having some differences.

Q. Is that the first time you moved out?

A. Yes.

Q. And you took Tammy with you?

A. Yes.

Q. And how did it go when you were at your sisters?

A. It was fine.

Q. Have you even, after you moved out of there did you have times to socialize with them when Tammy lived with you?

A. Oh, yes.

Q. With Tammy as well?

A. Yes.

Layout of Apartment in Westbrook

Q. And then where did you move?

A. To Westbrook.

Q. Okay. And what is that structure, what type of building is that?

A. It's three apartments, one on the bottom, one up front, one on the top and one out back.

Q. Okay. Stand up again for me. Do this one in green. Why don't you draw the layout of that place for me.

A. The whole place or our apartment?

Q. Your unit.

A. Okay, we come in the driveway here, and there is another driveway that loops here. This is where we always entered through this door here. When you enter you enter into a kitchen. If you go into the kitchen and take an immediate right you'll have a living room right here with a small bathroom right here.

Q. Okay. Let's start to label this stuff because I will forget. Put a K for the kitchen.

A. Kitchen, living room, bathroom.

Q. Okay, keep going.

A. If you're standing into the kitchen there is a bedroom here, and this is mine and Sally's bedroom. When you go through the kitchen down through the living room there is another door right here and that was Nancy's bedroom.

Q. Put an N there for Nancy.

A. Then there is a door between these two that lead out this way to the front exit.

Q. Okay. And—

A. Which is coming out of the living room.

Q. There is a bathroom, right?

A. Oh, I'm sorry, yeah, this is the bathroom. Tammy's room is right here, will be Tammy's room, and then there is a door just the other side of her door.

Q. Okay. So to go from your and Sally's room into the bathroom how would you have to travel?

A. Through the kitchen, into the living room and then into the bathroom.

Q. And Nancy's room abutted the living room?

A. Correct.

Q. Was there, was a door there?

A. There is a door there.

Q. Okay, you can take your seat again. Was Nancy's door always closed as it's been characterized?

A. Not always, not always.

Q. Was it closed a lot?

A. Uh, during the day, no, when she was sleeping, yes.

Q. Was she home a lot?

A. All the time.

Q. Were you involved in enrolling Tammy in the Westbrook schools?

A. Between me and my sister, yes.

Q. Were you in contact with the school?

A. Yes.

Q. With her teachers?

A. Yes.

Q. And we already know she was in day care during this time, right?

A. Shortly thereafter, yes.

Q. And how would Tammy get to school in Westbrook?

A. Uhm, Sally would take her most of the time. My father has once or twice I do believe.

Q. How about you, do you take her?

A. I was always gone to work.

Q. How about pickups at day care?

A. I have a few times picked her up.

Q. And you shared that duty?

A. It was mostly everybody else. I did it if I got out of work early, yes, so I didn't inconvenience anybody else.

Q. When did day care close, do you remember?

A. I do believe it was five.

Q. So days that you got out before that?

A. Yes.

Q. And what would you do after you picked her up at day care?

A. Uhm, we would go play softball. We would go over and visit my father. She really liked going over to the trailer park because that's where all of her friends are. She only had one friend on the Route 302, and it was way down the street, so I didn't let her go there by herself.

Denial of Sexual Activity with Daughter at Gray and Westbook

Q. You heard your daughter testify that you had sexual contact with her?
A. Yes.
Q. Did you do that?
A. Absolutely not.
Q. You heard her say that you had digital finger sex with her at the Westbrook address, did you?
A. Absolutely not.
Q. Oral sex?
A. Absolutely not.
Q. I can't recall now whether she said you showed her pornography in Gray or in Westbrook, but you heard her testify to that, right?
A. Yes.
Q. Did you ever show her pornography?
A. Absolutely not, no.
Q. Have you ever watched pornography with your daughter?
A. No, absolutely not.
Q. You ever expose yourself to her?
A. No.
Q. Did you ever have anal sexual intercourse with your daughter?
A. No.

Discipline of Daughter

Q. Let's talk about punishments. Did you need to dole out any punishments of your daughter in Westbrook?
A. Yes.
Q. What for?
A. Lying, stealing, running away.
Q. Actually running away or threatening?
A. Trying.
Q. What do you mean by trying?
A. She opened her window and tried to run away.
Q. Out of where?
A. Out of her bedroom window, she was going to go down to her friend's house on 302 I later found out.
Q. Did you, did you talk to her about that?
A. Yes.
Q. You punished her?
A. She was punished at first, that's why she tried to run away because she was mad that I punished her.
Q. Why did you punish her at first?
A. Because she lied about stealing money.
Q. Was she in contact with her mother during this time as far as you know?
A. Yes, any time she wanted to.

Layout of Grandfather's Trailer

Q. All right. I am going to have you draw one more time and this time I want you to draw, we only have two colors, you can pick whichever one you want, I would like you to draw the inside of your father's trailer.
A. Living room, there's an island that separates the living room from the kitchen here. Here's the kitchen, then this is the island.
Q. Put a K please.
A. If you go right from the living room there is a hallway right down here. This was my room just a few feet down the hallway there is a little laundry nook right there.
Q. Where is your Dad's room?
A. My Dad's room is right here.

Q. Now from your Dad's room can you see down into the living room?
A. Oh, yes.
Q. Put a D for your Dad on there, and from the living room can you see into your bedroom?
A. Not all of it, but you can see into half my bedroom basically. You can't see this back wall here and here.
Q. All right, that's good, go ahead and sit.
A. Bathroom there too.
Q. Okay, draw the bathroom.
A. Bathroom is right here where the laundry nook is.
Q. Okay, thanks. Now during the time that Tammy lived with you, how many times did you move in with your Dad?
A. Once.
Q. Your Dad, once?
A. Once.

Denial of Sexual Activity with Daughter at Grandfather's Trailer

Q. Did you engage in any sort of sexual activity with your daughter at your father's house?
A. Absolutely not.
Q. Not sexual intercourse?
A. There was no sexual intercourse.
Q. Sexual touching?
A. Nothing.
Q. Oral sex?
A. Nothing.
Q. Do—your father testified that he tends to stay up I think between 10:00 in the evening and midnight before he goes to bed, do you remember that?
A. Yeah.
Q. Is that true?
A. Very true.
Q. And did you go to bed before him?
A. We would stay up sometimes together. Tammy would go to bed. We would stay up and watch a movie.
Q. You got to get up pretty early?
A. Sometimes I would go to bed early, yes.
Q. And where—there's a trundle bed in the—
A. Yes.
Q. And where would Tammy sleep?
A. She would sleep this way on the floor on an air mattress.
Q. Air mattress?
A. Yes.
Q. There are only two bedrooms in that trailer?
A. Only two bedrooms. I wanted to leave her in the living room, but my father and I like to stay up so--

Return to Mother's Home

Q. Okay. So eventually Tammy came back to live with her mother?
A. Eventually, yes.
Q. And how did that come about?
A. I come home from work. Sally and Nancy and Tammy were in the kitchen, and they said they needed to have a talk with me, so I basically said, okay, you know, let's talk, let's do this. Tammy once again had tried to run away.
Q. This was a second time?
A. Yes.
Q. Okay.
A. Nancy had told me some stories of Tammy trying to kill herself.
Q. Did you talk to Tammy about that?
A. I immediately confronted Tammy about it.

Q. I'm sorry, go ahead.

A. She told me that she laid a plastic bag on her pillow and laid there.

Q. What did you do?

A. Started to cry a little bit, but I was a little frustrated because I had been doing everything I could.

Q. So was there a time after that that you were in contact with Tracey?

A. Immediately after that it was still going on it was really fresh.

Q. And you called her?

A. Yeah, I put her right on the speaker phone. Tabitha, I mean Tammy was there. Sally was there, and Nancy was there, and I was there. I talked.

Q. Were you upset?

A. Very.

Q. And did you confront Tracey about anything?

A. I asked Tracey if it had ever happened before, and she had made a mention of a—

MS. PROS: Objection.

THE COURT: Yeah, I think, sustained.

BY MR. ZERILLO:

Q. That's not where I was going so that's okay with me, Judge. What happened after—short circuit this, okay, what happened after this phone call?

A. Uhm, Tracey said she couldn't come get her right away, that I do believe she was in the tub. It was 45 minutes to an hour. Things had calmed down. Tracey showed up. We talked for a couple minutes outside without Tammy, and then Tammy came out into the little breezeway there and we had talked for a couple of minutes, hugged and kissed her and said I love you and she went with her mother.

Police Interview, Interrogation, and Arrest

Q. Now let me fast forward to you being called by Detective Sean Lippy, you remember that day?

A. I do.

Q. How long after this time, was it this time that Tammy left, weeks, months, years?

A. Month maybe, two.

Q. You're not sure about that though?

A. I'm not a hundred percent sure.

Q. Okay, all right. In any event—

A. I am not paying attention to that stuff.

Q. Okay. You got called by him and asked to come in?

A. Yes.

Q. And where were you when you got called?

A. Massachusetts coming back, Massachusetts.

Q. On a load?

A. Yes, I was picking up furniture.

Q. Okay. So you did what once you got back into Maine?

A. Off loaded my truck and went straight to see Detective Lippy.

Q. And what did you think you were going there for?

A. Child support papers.

Q. Okay.

A. As usual.

Q. You thought you were going to get served with something?

A. I did.

Q. Child support, okay. Now you spoke to Detective Lippy who I guess is now Sergeant Lippy, correct?

A. I believe so, yes.

Q. We saw the tape. (Note: The videotape interview was shown to the jury during Detective Libby's direct-examination).

A. Yes.

Q. Did you trust Detective Lippy when you began talking to him?

A. No.

Q. How would you describe your feeling in the interview?

A. I was anxious to see what it was all about. I had a lot of anxiety. That's pretty much how I felt.

Q. And did you tell, did you state whether or not you were guilty or innocent of these things?

A. Oh, I told him several times I was not guilty.

Q. All right. And talk to you a little bit about body language when you are in there. During much of that tape as I see it you are sort of looking down at the table, do you remember that?

A. (Nods head affirmatively.)

Q. Yes?

A. Yes.

Q. Did you have something in your hands?

A. Most of the time, yes.

Q. What was it?

A. Picture of Tammy.

Q. Were you looking at that picture?

A. Most of the time, yes.

Q. I heard you say during that interview why "Tammy, why?" several times, do you remember this?

A. Yes.

Q. Why were you saying that?

A. I can't figure out to this day why. What have I done that's so severe?

Q. And Sergeant Lippy cut you loose from that interview, right?

A. Yes.

Q. What did you do?

A. I went to my father's house.

Q. Okay. How were you feeling at that time?

A. Very confused, very frustrated because I have worked so hard to try to make her life better.

Q. Were you scared?

A. Oh, yeah.

Q. Did you place a call to Sally?

A. I do believe I did, yes.

Q. Okay. So and did you ever say that you would never see her again?

A. No.

Q. What did you say to her?

A. I told her I didn't want her involved in what was going on.

Q. Why was that?

A. It's gross. It's not something you would want anybody involved with.

Q. So Sally testified that she met up with you at your father's house?

A. No, she did not.

Q. What were you feeling at that time?

MS. PROS: Objection.

THE COURT: Overruled.

BY MR. ZERILLO:

Q. What were you feeling at that time?

A. Angry, sad, confused, all the above, I just, my brain was going 500 miles-an-hour.

Q. Now did you tear up photographs of your daughter after that?

A. Never, never.

Q. Do you have photographs of your daughter now?

A. Most definitely.

Q. Okay, and the next day you received a phone call Detective Lippy?

A. Yes.

Q. And because of that phone call you ended up going back to the police station?

A. Yes.

Q. Was Sergeant Lippy's tone the same with you that next day?

A. No, it was different.

Q. And what was the difference?

A. It was much more aggressive.

Q.   What were you—how did you feel about that?

A.   Confused, I guess.

Q.   Were you emotional about it?

A.   Very.

Q.   Were you angry?

A.   Yes.

Q.   And he accused you more than once?

A.   Several times, yes.

Q.   And every time he asked you if you did it what did you say?

A.   I denied it. I'm not guilty. I'm not guilty.

Q.   At one point after asking you many times you said something like prove it, is that right?

A.   Yes.

Q.   What did you mean by that?

A.   I was starting to get angry. I was frustrated. I couldn't answer the questions. I myself I felt it was the end of the conversation, and he needed to do what he needed to do, so I just told him prove it.

Q.   Were you trying to challenge his authority in any way?

A.   No.

Q.   At that point were you arrested?

A.   Yes.

Q.   And you were forced down into the chair?

A.   Correct.

Alternative Explanations for Hymen Injury

Q.   Okay. Let's talk about the prior sexual contact with Tammy and the boy that's been talked about, okay. Do you remember a time when Tracey called you to talk about Tammy had been touched or something like that?

A.   Yes.

Q.   And how old was Tammy at the time if you know?

A.   She was between four and five. I cannot pinpoint it, but I know she was between four and five.

Q.   And did you ask, did you ask Tracey if she had contacted the authorities?

A.   Yeah.

Q.   Did Tracey tell you that she witnessed or caught this going on?

A.   Said she saw it going on. She caught the two in the act.

Q.   And what did she say she observed if you remember?

A.   I don't remember exactly what she said she observed.

Q.   Something that was less than intercourse, however if you don't remember you don't remember?

A.   I don't remember exactly. I am trying to think back. I don't remember exactly. When she said it I was, wow, I didn't know what to do. I asked if she got ahold of the authorities, stuff like that. I did ask who. She wouldn't tell me.

Q.   I spoke to Sally about whether she caught Tammy trying to insert a tampon, you heard that, right?

A.   Yes.

Q.   And I think she said that she could not recollect?

A.   Uhm-hum.

Q.   Yes?

A.   Yes.

Q.   Do you remember having a conversation with Sally about that?

A.   Yes.

Q.   And what did she tell you about that?

A.   She told me she observed Tammy with an open tampon trying to insert it.

Q.   In what room in the house?

A.   I do believe it was Nancy's room.

Q.   So this must have been in Westbrook?

A.   Yes.

Q.   Did you ask her to have a conversation with Tammy after that?

A.   She had told me she had already had a conversation with Tammy.

Daughter's Personality

Q. Okay. Tracey characterized Tammy as a child who doesn't want to be alone, you heard that, right?

A. She doesn't want to be alone, yes.

Q. You would agree with that?

A. Yes.

Q. You would characterize her in the same way?

A. Yes.

Q. You would characterize her as clingy?

A. Very.

Q. Bob, do you have any idea why she is making these allegations?

A. I don't know why. I don't know if she is mad at me for having her move back home, putting her in an unstable environment, I don't know.

Denial of Sexual Activity

Q. Did you do what she alleged that you did sexually?

A. Absolutely not.

Q. Did you do any of the things that she alleged?

A. No, absolutely not.

Q. Have you ever behaved in a sexually inappropriate way with your daughter?

A. Absolutely not, never.

Q. Nothing further. Thank you.

§ 12:151 Direct Examination of Day Care Provider

Included here are a series of short direct examinations trying to prove that the home was normal.

Q. Good afternoon.

A. Hello.

Q. Do you know Bob?

A. Of course I know Bob, yes.

Q. How do you know him?

A. I took care of his child in my child care facility after school care.

Q. Okay. And so then you know Tammy?

A. Yes, she went to my daycare when she lived with Bob.

Q. And Tammy is not currently at your day care, correct?

A. Correct.

Q. And was that 2007?

A. Uhm, no, I think 2006.

Q. Was it during a time when she was living with her father or living with Tracey?

A. No, living with her father. She had just went with her father actually she was happy, that's what she kept saying every day to me.

Q. Okay. And how long did you say she was in the daycare with you?

A. Four months.

Q. And you have other children in the day care?

A. Yes, I have had a daycare for eight years.

Q. How many children are in the daycare?

A. Twelve.

Q. You are a licensed day care?

A. Yes, I'm licensed.

Q. And you observed Tammy being picked up and dropped off from your daycare?

A. Yes.

Q. Who would ordinarily drop her off?

A. Well, no, not dropped off, excuse me, it was after school care the bus would drop them off.

Q. Okay. And who would pick her up ordinarily?

A. Bob or Sally and occasionally her Grandfather, Bob's father, or once in a while Bob's sister.

Q. Okay. And did you have chances to see Tammy's demeanor when her father would come to pick her up?

A. Of course.

Q. Can you describe the demeanor when her father would come?

A. She was very very happy, and actually I can say 99 percent of the time she ran to him and hugged him. She would hang off him because she is, you know, a tall girl. She would see Dad, or she would see him pull in the driveway and she often asked to call to him.

Q. There was a sense of excitement though?

A. Of course, yeah.

Q. Did you have any difficulty with her and the other children in your day care?

A. I did. Oftentimes when a new child joins the day care there is a group of kids and then the new one will come in there is some transition period, but with Tammy what happened was the kids were getting along fine, and then Tammy joined us, and she would manipulate some other children. She would say one thing that wasn't right, wasn't correct about a child and make another child tattletale. It was like common childhood tattletaling but more manipulative. She would try to bring herself out of it, and it would be focused on the other children like say child A would say, oh, child B said da, da, da, da, and really it was her in the background saying it. That's what I would find out after I, you know.

Q. Investigate?

A. Investigate the whole situation, you know.

Q. This was happening regularly?

A. Yeah. Actually one time I had to talk to Bob about it. I said, I don't know what's going on but…

Q. Would you characterize Tammy as a clingy child?

A. Yes, very affectionate, very clingy. Actually there were several times where she didn't want to go play with the other children she wanted to stay inside, I have small children, play with the little ones.

Q. Did she appear to you to be clingy to Bob when you observed her?

A. Oh, yeah.

§12:152 Direct-Examination of Aunt

In this case, there was another Aunt we used to establish that the household was normal, and also to continue to raise the tampon issue.

Q. Good afternoon.

A. Hi.

Q. You know this gentleman over to my left here?

A. I do.

Q. And who is that?

A. He's my brother Bob.

Q. Okay. Now where do you live, ma'am?

A. I live in Westbrook, Maine.

Q. What do you do you for a living?

A. I'm a Registered Nurse.

Q. And who lives in Westbrook with you?

A. My partner.

Q. And did you live there in 2006?

A. Yes.

Q. And 2007 as well?

A. Correct.

Q. Was there a time period where Bob and Tammy came to live with you?

A. Yes.

Q. And how long was that?

A. How long?

Q. First when did it take place?

A. You know, I can't remember dates. I know they stayed with me for a week or so. It was just prior to them moving into Westbrook.

Q. And where had they been before that?

A. Gray.

Q. And was Tammy there for that year or so when they lived with you?

A. Yes.

Q. And they came to live with you because?

A. Uhm, Bob and Sally were having some problems, and they come to stay with us.

Q. Okay, and this is right as they were leaving Gray you said?

A. Yes.

Q. Did you have the opportunity to observe Tammy with her Dad during that period of time?

A. Yeah, yes, I did.

Q. And did you know Tammy prior to her moving in with Bob?

A. I did.

Q. How often did you see her prior to her moving in with Bob?

A. Uhm, we stayed in touch with Tracey so we could see the kids so we would see them four or five, six times a year.

Q. So you knew her as she was growing up, is that fair to say?

A. Yeah.

Q. Now were there any personality differences that you noticed with Tammy at the time that she came to live with you from the Tammy you knew before?

A. I did. Tammy's never been all that outgoing, and when she was with Bob she seemed to be very much more outgoing, and she's done much better in school and was excited about getting into things. She actually joined the softball team and, you know, was doing things that a normal kid does.

Q. Does Bob have an experience that you know of playing baseball or softball?

A. Oh, yeah, well, the whole family plays baseball or softball, yeah, it's a big thing with us.

Q. So would you say he was encouraging her?

A. Oh, absolutely.

Q. So during that week or so did you observe, did you observe them doing things like playing softball?

A. Well, they didn't play softball, but we were interacting as a family does as far as getting her enrolled in school and being with her, you know, every day I know I was with her every day that week, and Bob would go to work, then when he would come home we would all eat together and be together.

Q. You haven't been here for the trial but Tammy has been described many times in this trial as clingy, would you agree with that?

A. Yes.

Q. Would you agree with her being clingy to Bob from what you observed?

A. Yes.

Q. Was that from what you observed did that clinginess appear to be in a perfectly appropriate way?

A. She was just clingy with Bob just as she was with the rest of us, you know, when you sat and watched TV she liked to sit in your lap versus sitting by herself. She was just really an affectionate child.

Q. And you would observe her being affectionate with her father that way?

A. Yes.

Q. And not in any way that gave you any concern?

A. No.

Q. Was there anything that you observed during the time that they were living with you that gave you any concern?

A. Not at all.

Q. How about disciplining Tammy was that an issue during the time they stayed with you?

A. Uhm, for myself?

Q. Yes.

A. Uhm, well, no, there was a time when, you know, she would interact with the other kids and kind of, you know, do her kid stuff or tattletaling, that type of thing that I would need to tell you you need to stop your lying or telling on the other kids, and she would kind of pit them together and try to get the other kids in trouble.

Q. Let me ask you this did you still stay in contact with them even when they weren't living with you?

A. Yes.

Q. With Bob?

A. I have always tried to stay in contact with the kids.

Q. And they moved out of your place to what town?

A. To Westbrook, apartment in Westbrook.

Q. So you were in the same town?

A. Yes.

Q. And did you socialize with Tammy and Bob after they moved out?

A. Yeah, we helped out with getting her to school and picking her up and going to a couple of her softball games and things like that, yeah.

Q. Do you remember having a conversation with Tammy about a tampon?

A. Yes.

Q. What was that conversation?

A. Well, from what I gather her sister had just started having her periods, and she was, and I guess she was using tampons, and she was just really curious about them, and I'm sure she has probably seen them in my house, and she wanted to try them, and I explained to her give it time, you'll be, you know, you will have your chance, but that it wasn't good for her to try that sort of thing now. When she had her, got her period that we would talk about it again then.

Q. Okay. Did Bob ever refer Tammy to you to deal with any feminine issues?

A. Yes, he didn't like dealing with those, the female issues is what he calls. He gets all kind of red faced and stumbling on it.

Q. Okay. Do you know whether or not Tammy's grades improved at the time that she moved to Westbrook?

A. Yeah, I actually had a lot to do with her schooling. They knew me at the school to be picking her up, and I would help get her registered and things when she would come to our house for a visit or after school we would sit down with her homework and stuff like that and she greatly improved and greatly improved with the kids just that way.

Q. So let me talk to you about a couple of things that you observed or maybe you did with Tammy and Bob and maybe Tammy, did you guys ever go out to eat together with Tammy and Bob?

A. Yes.

Q. And did there appear to be appropriate father daughter interaction there?

A. Yes.

Q. Did you ever watch movies together?

A. Oh, yes.

Q. And the same thing, appropriate father daughter interaction?

A. Absolutely.

Q. Did you ever go to ball games or anything?

A. Yeah, Tammy's.

Q. Tammy's ball game?

A. Tammy's ball games.

Q. Everything seemed appropriate from your point of view?

A. Everything did.

Q. Nothing further. Thank you.

[§§12:153-12:159 Reserved]

E. Closing Argument

§12:160 Inconsistencies Chart

Closing strong is important. Again you have to answer the question as to why the child would lie. One way to point it out in a complicated factual story is in the use of a chart. Sometimes I will create a chart like this to project for the jury. Since we all learn differently and some of us learn visually, it is important to do something like this to help the jury learn.

INCONSISTENCIES IN TAMMY'S TESTIMONY

Subject	Version 1	Version 2	Version 3	Version 4	Version 5
When Did you First have intercourse	Statement: in Westbrook	Told police it happened in Gray			
Trip down dirt road in Gray	Told no one until August 2008				
Did he ever have intercourse with you in Gray	Tells her mother intercourse 7 times in Gray	Tells police three times during interview	August 2008 tells the DA it never happened in Gray	In trial, she tells me it never happened in Gray—I asked her 2x—I asked if she was sure of that—she said yes	Later in trial she told me it happened once in Gray But she denies at trial telling the police that it happened 3x
Did he have digital or oral sex with you at your Grandfather's house	No.	Yes he put hands on my private and mouth at Grandfather's trailer.			
How many times Westbrook intercourse	1x per week in statement	More than once a wk at trial			
Grandpa's house/trailer intercourse	Happened once, statement	Happened once or twice, second statement	Trial—"Do you think it happened one time?" "probably—yeah."		
In Her Anus	Didn't mention anything of it to police or anyone	Mentioned to Dr. Howard—normal physical exam	At trial said there was anal sex		

§12:161 Sample Closing Argument

Here is an approach to Closing that I took in this case. My theme at closing is simple. If this child is going to lie about the little things she will lie about the big things. So, I want to focus on the point where believability is stretched to an unbelievable point.

For tips on closing arguments and sample language for burden of proof and reasonable doubt arguments, see Ch. 2.

The wilder the story that you hear, the more reasonable doubt you have.

And this is a pretty wild story. It is a story of Tammy at 9 years old coming to live with her Father. She says he has vaginal sex with her. Anal sex with her. With his own daughter. That is as wild a story as it gets.

We want to believe kids. But we need to look critically at a wild story.

Those of you who have kids have heard some variation of a tall tale from them. If you don't have kids, perhaps you have heard these tall tales from kids you know.

Imagine your kid comes up to you at 9 years old. He says. "Billy up the street is mean to me." OK, you can see that.

He follows that up with "Billy hit me." You believe that. Kids get into fights.

How about this one: "Billy's parents yelled at me." Now you are getting a bit concerned. You wonder if you need to go investigate.

Your kid says next "They have guns over there and they told me they were going to shoot me."

At some point, depending on your level of gullibility, you may be starting to wonder whether this is a tall tale.

Then your kid says "They also have a dungeon in their basement where they keep their pet dragon, and by the way, the parents are vampires and Billy is Frankenstein."

Now, even the most gullible among us have abandoned ship, and are wondering if our own kid is playing at something or has a screw loose.

Remember though: the story started out as a believable story—"Billy's mean to me." Somewhere along the way it became fantasy. But where did it become fantasy? And if the end is fantasy, can you believe the beginning?

You cannot believe any part of an unbelievable story when you sit on a criminal jury. If Tammy will lie about the small things, she will lie about the big things. And any of those lies are reasonable doubt.

It is believable that Tammy is a troubled girl. She was abandoned by her mother—abused by her mother—and forced to leave her family because of tremendous chaos. She was forced to live with her father and she wanted to go home. But then at some point it slips into lying or fantasy.

There are a lot of inconsistencies in what Tammy told you. Maybe they are lies, maybe they are fantasy. Either way, they are reasonable doubt. Let's take a look…

Post-Script

So, there is the impossible child sex case, warts and all. For those of you who are interested, the jury hung.

CHAPTER 13

CHILD PORNOGRAPHY

FROM THE ORDINARY

The once noble and talented lawyer cuts off his ankle monitoring bracelet in the dead of night, and leaves rural Rome, Maine. He is a federal fugitive. The First Circuit has only just partially overturned his appeal, and he is heading back to federal prison as a result. He doesn't like the sound of that idea.

Like a scene out of the TV show *Breaking Bad*, he is ultimately caught by the U.S. marshals in New Mexico. Once the top drug prosecutor in Maine, he has been accused and convicted of child porn offenses. He will spend years in federal prison.

The story of James Cameron (the former Maine lawyer, not the famed director) is unusual only because he was a former drug prosecutor. Otherwise, it is more common than I would hope.

Child pornography defense is the wild, wild, west for the criminal defendant. It is an untamed and raw environment without any gold in them there hills. It is a new frontier in which your client can get more time for a child porn case than for a cold-blooded murder.

Forget firearms ballistics, computers are the weapon. Computer forensics are your fingerprints and DNA analysis. Crimes aren't committed in single shots, but in single keystrokes.

The click of a mouse is often more dangerous than pulling a trigger. I recently had a child porn sentencing in federal court for a 32 year-old man. He had no criminal history, and was a part-time medical student at the time of the offense. His Federal Sentencing Guideline calculation was between 720 months and 720 months. He broke the scale. It was a *de facto* life sentence.

In this Chapter I attempt to deal with this complicated and risky area of the law.

TO THE BIZARRE

As I am writing this Chapter, I am one day away from sentencing in one of my federal child porn cases. The Assistant United States Attorney called me within moments of my writing this. She tells me that the FBI has just made her aware of videos that we need to see. Through an unusual set of circumstances (including the first AUSA going out on maternity leave) she just learned of these videos. They concern my client's previously undisclosed sexual cannibalism fetish.

What?

Now, I'm no prude. I feel like I have heard and seen a lot. Sometimes too much. But sexual cannibalism is a new one to me.

Apparently, some people have a fantasy about having sex and then cooking and eating their partner. My client apparently stages this fantasy. Elaborately. Even worse, he uses photographs of his now adult daughter from when she was a child and does a voiceover where he has sex with her, cooks her and eats her.

This is a bad sentencing fact. The daughter was, ironically, planned as my star sentencing witness.

Long story short, these cases can be just plain gross. Everyone reacts differently to this stuff. Allow yourself to be human. You aren't a robot. The Department of Justice offers mental health counseling and therapy to their people who deal with the difficult subject matter inherent in these cases. Process and emotionally deal with the ugliness of what you are seeing. Then shrug it off and get down to business.

(This page intentionally left blank.)

I. ELEMENTS AND COMMON SCENARIOS

§13:01   Child Pornography Defined

Congress has defined child pornography as any visual depiction of sexually explicit conduct, where—

A. The production of the visual depiction involves the use of a minor (person under the age of 18) engaging in sexually explicit conduct;

B. The visual depiction is a digital image, computer image, or computer-generated image that is, or is indistinguishable from, that of a minor engaging in sexually explicit conduct; or

C. The visual depiction has been created, adapted, or modified to appear that an identifiable minor is engaging in sexually explicit conduct.

18 U.S.C. §2256(8).

A visual depiction includes any photograph, film, video, picture, or computer or computer-generated image or picture, whether made or produced by electronic, mechanical, or other means. 18 U.S.C. §2256(8).

An identifiable minor is a person—

• Who was a minor at the time the visual depiction was created, adapted, or modified; or

• Whose image as a minor was used in creating, adapting, or modifying the visual depiction; and

• Who is recognizable as an actual person by the person's face, likeness, or other distinguishing characteristic, such as a unique birthmark or other recognizable feature.

18 U.S.C. §2256(9).

Proof of the identity of the identifiable minor is not required. 18 U.S.C. §2256(9).

For purposes of §2256(A) and (C), sexually explicit conduct includes actual or simulated: 1) sexual contact; 2) beastiality; 3) masturbation; 4) sadistic or masochistic abuse; or 5) the lascivious exhibition of the genitals or pubic area of a child. 18 U.S.C. §2256(2)(A).

For purposes of §2256(B), sexually explicit conduct includes actual or simulated: 1) graphic sexual contact; 2) graphic or simulated bestiality, masturbation; or sadistic or masochistic abuse; or 3) graphic or simulated lascivious exhibition of the genitals or pubic area of any person.

Additionally, in federal court there must be a Commerce Clause hook, meaning that federal jurisdiction requires that the offense occurred in interstate or foreign commerce. This is usually satisfied by the fact a computer or computer equipment that was used that was manufactured in a different state or country or that the images were transmitted across state lines.

State statutes often mirror the federal law, without the Commerce Clause requirement.

§13:02   Elements of Possession

Possession of a visual depiction of a minor engaging in sexually explicit conduct is illegal, as are sufficiently sexually suggestive nude images of children. To prove a possession charge, most statutes require the government prove that the defendant knowingly possessed at the least one image of child pornography. See, e.g., 18 U.S.C. §2252(a)(4)(B). Possession usually includes both active possession (meaning physical control) and constructive possession (the power to exercise physical control). Knowledge means an act that was done voluntarily and intentionally and not by mistake or accident.

§13:03   Elements of Production and Distribution (i.e., Sexual Exploitation of a Child)

Child pornography production is charged federally as sexual exploitation of a child. 18 U.S.C. 2251(a). This requires the government prove beyond a reasonable doubt that:

1. The alleged victim was a minor;

2. That the minor was employed, used, persuaded or coerced to take part in sexually explicit conduct;

3. That the depictions crossed into interstate or foreign commerce, or that the person producing the image had reason to know that the depictions would impact interstate or foreign commerce.

For a distribution offense, the defendant must knowingly mail, transport or ship the child pornography by using interstate or foreign commerce. In the peer-to-peer network context, this can be very troubling. Many peer-to-peer networks automatically share anything you downloaded. So a possession case can become a distribution case quite easily. Of course, you may have defenses as to "knowing" possession if the distribution was automatic.

§13:04   Possession Only Scenario

A potential client, Parker, walks into your office one day. He is scared as hell. Parker is a retired executive whose kids are grown and have moved away. He lives with his wife of 43 years.

What has unnerved Parker is the knock on his door by the police the afternoon before. They asked to look at his computers. They said something about a Limewire transaction. He didn't know what to do and he didn't want to look guilty in front of his wife, so he gave up his computers. He signed a consent to search form.

You ask—already fearing the answer—what he has to worry about. "30,000 or so pictures of child pornography," he tells you.

Oh, that's all.

§13:05   Production and Distribution Scenario

Randy is bright and stupid at the same time. He is 32 years old with no criminal history.

He can be brilliant and he can be foolish. In his times of brilliance, he works on nuclear submarines and attends medical school. In times of stupidity, he hacks the Facebook account of a woman who jilted him in high school and threatens to torture her with the release of nude photos he finds. Predictably, the woman reports him. When the police arrive at his home, he makes a second stupid move and consents to the release of his computers. Then, after causing this mess, he hires a lawyer. Isn't that always the way. …

On one laptop, which belonged to his wife, but to which he had access, are 314 images of child pornography. They are mostly commercial child pornography, the type already identified by the National Center for Missing and Exploited Children (discussed in more detail in §13:34). There are some images not identified, including three images, which later come to be known as the Minor A images. The Minor A images show a close up of a toddler-aged child's vagina. In one instance, what appears to be a male finger spreads the child's labia.

The computer where the child pornography was found had been wiped. Unfortunately for Randy, it wasn't wiped well enough. Someone using that computer used a Yahoo! Messenger Photo Sharing Program. That program created a hidden subdirectory of images. This is where the child pornography images were seized.

Law enforcement, especially a local detective, suspects that the Minor A images are of Randy's toddler daughter. Randy's wife at the time, Amanda, says it is her child in the images. She says that the finger appears to be Randy's. She identifies the blanket the child appears to be lying on.

The images of Minor A were uploaded through the Yahoo! system. The federal case adds production and distribution to the ordinary possession charge. The production and distribution charges are based on the Minor A images. The Government alleges that the defendant shared the images on a Russian website where hardcore child pornography viewers share their images.

[§§13:06-13:09 Reserved]

II.   INVESTIGATION AND DISCOVERY

§13:10   How Did They Come To Knock On My Client's Door and Why Does It Matter?

I imagine that many of you wonder how law enforcement came to knock on your client's door in the first place. When I started working on these cases, I knew nothing about how law enforcement would come to target my client. I continue to learn about this topic through litigation. See §13:11 Form 13-10 Memorandum in Support of Motion for Discovery of Database 1 Data.

We have to understand the basics of how they came to target our clients for at least two reasons. First, this information may be important at trial. Second, while I have consistently said that this book is not about suppression, there are interesting suppression issues hidden in these riddles.

The basic scenario in the cases I see involves the use of peer-to-peer (hereafter "P2P") networks. These networks can be extremely complicated. I will attempt to explain the elemental functioning of them.

PRACTICE TIP: *Do not let technology scare you*

You cannot be scared off by the complexity of the technological issues in these cases. I do not have a computer science background. Heck, I have a Bachelor's Degree in English. This hardly qualifies me as a techie.

However, you need to dig into these cases to understand them. What I will explain to you in the next few paragraphs took me a lot of time in litigation to learn.

The P2P network is effectively a collective. Users can join the network. When doing so, they are generally assigned a Globally Unique Identifier (hereafter "GUID") which is sometimes also called a Client Hash. This GUID is assigned when the user signs up for the P2P network. The user probably does not know that he has been assigned a GUID.

Image files and video files are assigned hash values. Again, the user of the file does not know the hash value. However, the hash value remains the same regardless of where the file is transferred.

There are a variety of different types of hash values. There are Sha1 hash values, MD4, MD5, etc… Each uses a different alpha-numeric series. All you really need to know about these files at the moment is that the hash value is assigned to the photo or video and remains the same no matter where the photo or video goes.

I am writing this section on an airplane traveling at 35,975 feet on my way to JFK Airport in New York. Imagine that my wife snaps a picture on her phone of herself and my kids. She sends it to my phone and I get it when I land. If I then text it to my father in Maine, the hash value remains the same. It is the same value when the image is created at 35,975 feet; it is the same when it is viewed on the tarmac at JFK; and it is the same in Maine when my father receives it.[1]

The Government has designed software to take advantage of the hash value system. There appear to be a variety of different programs in use by the Government. I will describe how the system works in cases in which I have litigated discovery and suppression issues. I have attempted to gain access to test this software, but have been unsuccessful so far. The Government carefully protects these secrets.

The law enforcement software I am most familiar with is Database One or Operation Roundup (collectively referred to here as "DB1"). DB1 seems to monitor P2P networks. Whether the monitoring is automated or not is a matter of current debate in the litigation I am involved in.

Either way, DB1 (or law enforcement officers using DB1) follows various P2P networks, like Ares, Limewire, Frostwire, eMule, and so forth. When monitoring these networks, DB1 looks for hash values of files of interest. These files have been identified by the National Center for Missing and Exploited Children (hereafter "NCMEC") as child pornography in most cases (more on NCMEC in § 13:34). I am not certain if DB1 has its own catalogue of child pornography images by hash value, but I suspect it does.

I was able to log on to the web portal for DB1 in the course of litigating one of my cases. The government attempted to satisfy my discovery requests by showing me the system. Once the higher-ups in the Attorney General's Office learned that I was allowed that access, it was quickly taken away.

DB1 identifies which GUIDs are of interest to a particular jurisdiction by IP address. Since the IP addresses are specific to a particular state, this allows law enforcement of any agency to focus on their particular geographic area.

Nearly universally, P2P networks have defaults when you sign-up that allow files you downloaded to be available for sharing with your peers. So, if I download the U2 album the *Joshua Tree* on eMule, unless I have changed the standard settings, that album is always available from my GUID to share with my peers. It generally doesn't matter if I change the location of the album on my computer and move it to a different folder.

P2P networks usually operate with swarm technology. This means that for faster downloading, I did not download the *Joshua Tree* album from just one peer. I downloaded it from many peers. I got bits of the file from the swarm until I had the complete album. This is also generally automated.

Law enforcement sees these exchanges of contraband in DB1. So, a Maine Computer Crimes officer can log in to DB1 in Maine, and by IP address, identify all the exchanges (uploading and downloading) of potential contraband. The officer can match the GUID to the IP address to see if they are always the same (presumably the same person on the same computer network). This is the information used to gather their search warrants. That is

---

[1] Now, I don't want to make it sound like hash values are infallible. Of course, they are not. The Government likes to say they are like digital fingerprints, and that may be an apt analogy, especially if you consider the failures of fingerprint technology. This is too big a topic to cover here, however. That said, keep in mind that there may be grounds to contest the infallibility of a hash value depending on the facts of your case.

how they end up at your client's door. If U2 albums were contraband, they could see that I downloaded the *Joshua Tree* album. Then, every time another peer downloaded the album and I automatically shared a piece of my U2 album in the swarm, DB1 would capture that as well.

§13:11   FORM 13-10 Memorandum in Support of Motion for Discovery of Database 1 Data

STATE OF MAINE	SUPERIOR COURT
CUMBERLAND, ss	DOCKET NO. 1234

STATE OF MAINE   )
)   DEFENDANT'S BENCH
)   MEMORANDUM IN SUPPORT
v.   )   OF HIS MOTION FOR
)   DISCOVERY
MM   )
)

NOW COMES the Defendant, MM, and submits this Memorandum to aid in this Court's decision on his Motion for Discovery as it relates to the request for Database 1 information.

ARGUMENT

I.   **The Discovery of Database 1 Data; Including the Testing of That Data, Is Mandated, Material and Relevant Under State of Maine and United States Constitutional Standards**

In his *Motion for Discovery and Expert Witness Production*, Mr. M requests, among other things:

Defendant requests all material related to the law enforcement program referenced in discovery as "Database One." On information and belief, the Database One program is a program maintained by the State Police of various states, and is used by the State of Maine to investigate child pornography and/or peer-to-peer networks. Defendant requests law enforcement's complete file on Database One, including but not limited to all manuals and protocol documents related to the operation of Database One and the law enforcement protocols and instructions in using the same. Counsel further requests all law enforcement memoranda or documentation related to instructions to law enforcement officers in their use of Database One and instructions or memoranda to law enforcement officers regarding drafting search warrants related to Database One searches. Defendant requests access to Database One by the Undersigned Counsel's expert for testing of its operation.

The State has indicated that it opposes this Motion.

The Supreme Court of the United States has held that the prosecution has a due process obligation under the Federal Constitution to disclose material evidence favorable to a criminal defendant. *Brady v. Maryland*, 373 U.S. 83 (1963). Favorable evidence is quite broad. Favorable evidence can include anything reasonably positive to the defense. In *United States v. Bagley*, 473 U.S. 667 (1985), the Supreme Court held that regardless of the request, general or specific, favorable evidence is material, and constitutional error results from its suppression by the Government, "if there is a reasonable probability that, had the evidence been disclosed to the defense, the result of the proceeding would have been different." *Id.* at 682.

The United States Supreme Court has continued in its case law to re-emphasize the importance of Government disclosure to the Defense:

In *Brady*, this Court held that the suppression by the prosecution of evidence favorable to an accused upon request violates due process where the evidence is material to guilt or to punishment, irrespective of the good faith or bad faith of the prosecution. We have since held that the duty to disclose such evidence is applicable even though there has been no request by the accused, and that the duty encompasses impeachment evidence as well as exculpatory evidence. Such evidence is material if there is a reasonable probability that, had the evidence been disclosed to the defense, the result of the proceeding would have been different. Moreover, the rule encompasses evidence known only to police investigators and not to the prosecutor. In order to comply with *Brady*, therefore, the individual prosecutor has a duty to learn of any favorable evidence known to others acting on the government's behalf in [a] case, including the police.

Strickler v. Greene, 527 U.S. 263, 280-81 (1999) (*citations and quotation marks omitted*).

The protections of *Brady* stem from the requirement of due process and the right to a fair trial. *Bagley* at 675. A showing of materiality under *Bagley* does not require proof by the defendant that disclosure of the evidence would result in the defendant's acquittal. *Kyles v. Whitley*, 514 U.S. 419 (1995). All that is required is a "reasonable probability" that the information is necessary in order for the defendant to receive a fair trial, meaning a trial that results in a verdict worthy of confidence. *Id.* at 434.

Bagley requires that the undisclosed evidence be material when determining whether an error has occurred. In other words, if favorable evidence is not disclosed, the Defendant does not need to show that disclosure of the evidence would have resulted in an acquittal. Under *Kyles*, the issue is only whether there was a "verdict worthy of confidence." *Id.* at 434-435. This confidence is not necessarily related to the ultimate outcome, although it can be. *Id.* Materiality of the evidence is primarily related to the process and underlying fairness of the proceedings. *Id.*

A defendant's rights under *Brady* apply equally to the pretrial stage as they do in the trial stage. *See Gaither v. United States,* 759 A.2d 662 (D.C. 2000), *mandate recalled and opinion amended by,* 816 A.2d 791 (D.C. 2003) (remanding for an evidentiary hearing, to determine if *Brady* information had been withheld regarding suggestive procedures used in the identification process). In *United States v. Gamez-Orduno*, 235 F.3d 453, 461 (9th Cir. 2000), it was a violation of *Brady* when the Government failed to disclose a report that would have demonstrated that defendants had Fourth Amendment standing to challenge a search. The Ninth Circuit noted that "[t]he suppression of material evidence helpful to the accused, whether at trial or on a motion to suppress, violates due process if there is a reasonable probability that, had the evidence been disclosed, the result of the proceeding would have been different." *Id.* at 461.

In *Smith v. Black*, 904 F.2d 950, 965-66 (5th Cir. 1990), the nondisclosure of *Brady* information related to eyewitness identification may have affected the fact-finder's findings at the suppression hearing. The Fifth Circuit found that "timing is critical to proper *Brady* disclosure, and objections may be made under *Brady* to the state's failure to disclose material evidence prior to a suppression hearing." *Id.* at 965, *citing cases omitted*; *see also Nuckols v. Gibson*, 233 F.3d 1261, 1266-67 (10th Cir. 2000) (*Brady* violation when Government failed to disclose allegations of theft and sleeping on the job by the police officer whose testimony was needed concerning the admissibility of a confession).

Although they are subservient to the Constitution as interpreted through *Brady* and progeny, the Maine Rules of Criminal Procedure equally allow for discovery of the Database 1 data. The Rules hold that "a defendant may make a written request[2] to have the State provide any other books, papers, documents, electronically stored information, photographs (including motion pictures and videotapes), or copies or portions thereof, **or tangible objects**, or **access to buildings or places**, that are material and relevant to the preparation of the defense." M.R.Crim.P. 16(c)(1).

The hallmark of the Maine Rule and the *Brady* rules are the same, therefore: materiality. Maine adds a requirement that constitutional precedent does not: relevance. In either event, both standards are met here.

Defendant believes Database 1 is specialized law enforcement software used in peer-to-peer network searches.[3] The Massachusetts and Pennsylvania State Police run the database. Law enforcement searches various peer-to-peer websites using the Database 1 software and collects data on downloads of images and videos that law enforcement believes to be child pornography. It is unknown whether Database 1 searches for any data other than child pornography. Law Enforcement determines if the images are child pornography by searching the image hash values[4] and comparing them to the hash values of known child pornography. When there are downloads or uploads of known sexually explicit materials by hash value, Database 1 records the internet protocol ("IP") address of the file sharer. Database 1 sends a list of Maine IP addresses to Maine Computer Crimes. Every few weeks, Maine Computer Crimes reviews the Maine IP address list generated by Database 1, and compares it to known hash values of child pornography. This forms the basis for Computer Crimes search warrants, like the one here.

---

[2] Defendant has made written requests for Database 1 discovery.

[3] The information regarding the operation of Database 1 comes from a telephone conversation between the Undersigned and Trooper L of the Maine State Police Computer Crimes Unit on October 22, 2014.

[4] Images have a series of numbers and values associated with them that are generally known as a hash value, although there are several different types of hash values.

In *Defendant's Third Motion to Suppress and Dismiss*, he argues for suppression of the warrantless seizure of data related to Database 1 searches. *See Defendant's Third Motion to Suppress and Dismiss*, paragraphs 12-13. Defendant will argue that the culling and dissemination of private subscriber information without a warrant fails to comply with the requirements of the Fourth Amendment. On information and belief, this issue has never been squarely presented to the Maine Supreme Court.

Relevant to this inquiry is how Database 1 operates. Counsel cannot find cases related to it or internet information. It is shrouded in secrecy. Its actual functioning has not been tested to Counsel's knowledge. Just as a defendant must be given the opportunity to independently test the State's evidence in any other type of case, so should this Defendant be permitted to test the Operation of Database 1 and review literature on its operation.

The relevance of a variety of facts, such as the discovery of what tools are available to the Government in searching peer-to-peer networks that are not otherwise available to the public, are relevant to the Motion to Suppress argument, and cannot be discovered in any other fashion.

One argument in retort to *Defendant's Third Motion to Suppress and Dismiss* will be that the search does not implicate a reasonable expectation of privacy as it is in plain view. Certainly, this Court does not need to resolve that issue at this juncture. However, it is the precise nature of that argument that makes this Discovery Motion material and relevant.

Under the plain view exception to the warrant requirement, the police may seize an object in plain view if 1) the officers are lawfully in the position from which they view the object; 2) the object's incriminating character is immediately apparent; and 3) the officers have a lawful right of access to the object. *Horton v. California*, 496 U.S. 128, 130 (1990) ("We conclude that even though inadvertence is a characteristic of most legitimate 'plain-view' seizures, it is not a necessary condition."). There is, of course, nothing inadvertent about the warrantless seizure here. Determining the functionality of Database 1 is clearly relevant to the plain view argument that will likely be made by the State.

In addition, the Database 1 information is relevant to trial issues and cross-examination of law enforcement and/or the State's proposed forensics experts. There are a myriad of issues that are ripe for cross-examination regarding this technology. If Counsel is not given access to the discovery sought, he will be limited in his ability to effectively cross-examine. Additionally, a failure to provide this information will hamper Mr. M's ability to present a defense case.

By way of example, Counsel is not aware that any of the images observed by the Database 1 software as being shared by Mr. M's associated IP address were ever discovered on Mr. M's computer. As a result, the files that brought law enforcement to Mr. M's home, as far as Counsel can tell, were never found on Mr. M's computer. The Defendant needs access to the data sought to develop defense theories as to how this could have happened. Mr. M's defense team should be permitted to develop these theories through the Database 1 literature and by testing of the functionality of the software.

On information and belief, Database 1 is a system that operates beyond the ordinary functionality of any other user who uses eMule. As a result, the Government is purposefully intruding into the digital world with a specialized tool. The Defendant must be able to have access to that specialized tool to research and discover how it functions. To deny him that right is to deny him Due Process.

CONCLUSION

For the reasons stated above, this Court should grant Defendant's Motion for Discovery as it relates to Database 1. The remainder of the discovery requests in the Motion at bar, along with further argument regarding the Database 1 discovery, will be made at the May 22, 2015 hearing before this Court.

Dated this the 18th day of May, 2015, in Portland, Maine.

Respectfully submitted,

_____
Timothy E. Zerillo
Attorney for Defendant
ZERILLO LAW FIRM, LLC

§13:12   Suppression Arguments for Evidence Collected Using DB1 and Similar Software

Understanding how the Government identified your client and collected evidence against him has a variety of uses. There are motions for discovery that can be attempted where you try to get access to software programs like DB1. See §13:11 Form 13-10. I have included a Bench Memorandum on a Motion to Suppress in which I argue that the use of DB1 is akin to a warrantless search. See §13:13 Form 13-20.

This argument is derived from the Supreme Court decision in *Kyllo v. United States*, 533 U.S. 27, 121 S.Ct. 2038 (2001). There, the Government set-up surveillance across the street from a residence, and used a thermal imager to detect infrared radiation emanating from the house. This thermal imager was not looking at private or intimate details inside the home. Rather, it was measuring heat coming off the exterior walls of the house. The technology in issue there, a thermal imager, was not in general public use (although, presumably anyone could buy one). The Supreme Court held:

> Where, as here the Government uses a device that is not in general public use, to explore details of the home that would have been previously unknowable without physical intrusion, the surveillance is a "search," and is presumptively unreasonable without a warrant.

Id. at 40.

Likewise, the Government uses specialized tools not in general public use when it uses DB1. For a private citizen to develop such a tool would require extensive software development experience, time and money. Like in *Kyllo*, where it was unlikely that a private citizen would have a thermal imaging device, the use of the specialized tool DB1 is a search.

I understand that these are difficult arguments. They will be met with skepticism by the courts. However, it is important that we push warrantless search arguments, especially as government surveillance of its citizens expands.

Likewise, look for *Franks* issues. A search warrant is invalid when it is obtained by use of a deliberately misleading affidavit. *Franks v. Delaware*, 438 U.S. 154, 98 S. Ct. 2674, 57 L. Ed. 2d 667 (1978). *Franks* holds that if the affiant deliberately, or with reckless disregard for the truth, makes false statements that are necessary to establish probable cause, the search warrant must be voided and the fruits of the search suppressed to the same extent as if probable cause were lacking on the face of the affidavit.

If you have a search warrant, you are ordinarily going to be stuck arguing that the four corners of the warrant affidavit itself do not establish probable cause. However, if you can develop a *Franks* argument, you may find some interesting information at suppression.

I have noticed that the search warrant affidavits in child pornography cases are filled with *Franks* issues. Child pornography warrants are particularly dangerous because the judge or magistrate may have very little knowledge or understanding of how the child pornography investigation works. The judge may have no information as to the functionality of the technology explained in §13:10. So, you will sometimes find a deceptive warrant, or a warrant that is misleading, once you understand how the technology works. See §13:14 Form 13-30 Memorandum in Support of Request for Franks Hearing.

Finally, understanding the functionality of the software helps you if you end up at trial. Understanding that the P2P software automates sharing may have a particular utility for you depending on the facts. For example, did your client download a bulk search for teen porn, end up with child pornography and then delete it, only to have the P2P software continue to make it available for sharing? Was the government actually able to recover the files observed on DB1 or were they never found? This may lend credence to a theory that there was a remote malicious user.

There are too many ways that you can use this information to document here. However, I hope this primer was helpful as you dig into the technology in your next case.

§13:13   FORM 13-20 Memorandum in Support of Defendant's Motion to Suppress

STATE OF MAINE	SUPERIOR COURT
CUMBERLAND, ss	DOCKET NO. CR-1234

STATE OF MAINE   )
)
)   **DEFENDANT'S BENCH**
v.   )   **MEMORANDUM IN SUPPORT**
)   **OF DEFENDANT'S THIRD**
)   **MOTION TO SUPPRESS**
MM   )
)
)

NOW COMES the Defendant, MM, and submits this Memorandum to aid in this Court's decision on his Motion to Suppress. Please note, not all of the suppression issues presented by the Defendant are described in this Memorandum. Rather, Counsel highlights issues related to *Miranda*, warrantless search, and general warrant defects.

ARGUMENT

The Fourth Amendment of the United States Constitution guards against unreasonable searches and seizures: "The right of the people to be secure in their persons, houses, papers, and effects, against unreasonable searches and seizures, shall not be violated, and no Warrants shall issue, but upon probable cause, supported by Oath or affirmation, and particularly describing the place to be searched, and the persons or things to be seized. The Fourth Amendment applies to the States by virtue of the Fourteenth Amendment of the Federal Constitution. *New Jersey v. T.L.O.*, 469 U.S. 325, 334, 105 S.Ct. 733, 738, 83 L.Ed.2d 720 (1985). Likewise, the Maine Constitution's search and seizure provision is co-extensive with the Federal Constitution.

I. LAW ENFORCEMENT VIOLATED *MIRANDA* NECESSITATING SUPPRESSION OF DEFENDANT'S STATEMENTS

A person who is in custody and subject to interrogation must be advised of the rights referred to in *Miranda v. Arizona*, 384 U.S. 436 (1966), in order for statements made during the interrogation to be admissible against him or her at trial. *State v. Bridges,* 829 A.2d 247, 254 (Me. 2003). "[A] *Miranda* warning is necessary only if a defendant is: (1) in custody; and (2) subject to interrogation." *State v. Higgins,* 796 A.2d 50, 54 (Me. 2002) (citation and quotation marks omitted). Quite simply, if there is custody and interrogation, there must be *Miranda*.

A.   Custodial Determination

Mr. M was in custody when he was interviewed by law enforcement. Custody exists for *Miranda* purposes when there is a "restraint on freedom of movement of the degree associated with a formal arrest." *State v. Holloway*, 760 A.2d 223, 228 (Me. 2000) (citation and quotation marks omitted). This test is an objective one. Of course, custody does not require actual arrest to implicate *Miranda*. The question for the Court is whether the facts would demonstrate as a matter of law that a reasonable person would have felt he or she was at liberty to terminate the interrogation and leave. *State v. Lowe*, 2013 ME 92 (Oct. 2013). This will likely be the linchpin of the Court's analysis.

In *Lowe*, the Law Court re-stated the factors this Court should consider in determining if custody exists for *Miranda* purposes. These factors are:

    (1) the locale where the defendant made the statements;

    (2) the party who initiated the contact;

    (3) the existence or non-existence of probable cause to arrest (to the extent communicated to the defendant);

    (4) subjective views, beliefs, or intent that the police manifested to the defendant, to the extent they would affect how a reasonable person in the defendant's position would perceive his or her freedom to leave;

(5) subjective views or beliefs that the defendant manifested to the police, to the extent the officer's response would affect how a reasonable person in the defendant's position would perceive his or her freedom to leave;
(6) the focus of the investigation (as a reasonable person in the defendant's position would perceive it);
(7) whether the suspect was questioned in familiar surroundings;
(8) the number of law enforcement officers present;
(9) the degree of physical restraint placed upon the suspect;
(10) the duration and character of the interrogation.

Id.

The interrogation audio, which has been provided to the court as *Joint Exhibit 1*, suggest that a reasonable person would not feel free to leave or terminate the interrogation on those facts.

At the outset, Mr. M questioned his need for an attorney.

MM: Do I need to talk to an attorney about something?
Detective Bosco: That's a choice that you have to make I can't make any of those decisions for you.

Joint Exhibit 1, Audio 1 File 6:27-6:30

Despite the fact that the interrogation occurred in his home, there can be no doubt that Mr. M's movements were restricted. He was not permitted to get dressed. He was separated from his Wife and Son.

MM: Can I get some clothes on?
Detective Bosco: Yeah, sure. I gotta go with you if you're goin'.
MM: Oh.
Detective Bosco: Anywhere you go, I'm comin' with you.

Joint Exhibit 1, Audio File 1, 7:42

When the Defendant was separated from his Wife, the pressure on him to give statements was amplified. Detective Bosco emphasized this point, indicating that the police would not "go away" until they were satisfied.

Detective Bosco: And I think it makes your life a lot easier in the long run. Umm.
MM: And you want?
Detective Bosco: We are here to tell you, **we're not just going to go away without finding our answers.** So, it's, I think it behooves you to help us.
MM: Yeah.
Detective Bosco: And to try to figure out why this is happening.

Joint Exhibit 1, Audio File 1, 11:10-11:23

Mistakenly, Detective Bosco blurred the line between his right to search, and the Defendant's right to decline to make statements to him. Detective Bosco made it appear to Mr. M that he was obliged to speak with him based on his authority to conduct the search.

Detective Bosco: Well, I have a search warrant, so you don't really have a choice of me being here or not.
MM: Well, I understand that, but I'm not giving you a hard time.

Joint Exhibit, Audio File 1, 21:04-21:11

Detective Bosco continued to attempt to lure Mr. M into making statements, while at the same time reiterating that "We're not going away with no answers."

Detective Bosco: This is, this is, this a big deal, and you know, we're not going to go away with no answers, and he's being ummm very deceptive in his answers.

MM: I don't even, I don't even know.

Detective Bosco: And he's going around, rather than being honest and I understand that.

Joint Exhibit 1, Audio File 1, 24:41-24:57

Much of the dialogue between Detective Bosco and the Defendant occurred in front of H M with MM listening. Even when MM asked for an Attorney, Detective Bosco continued to engage him. On at least five different times between 27:30 and 38:47 on *Joint Exhibit 1, Audio File 1*, Bosco continued to engage Mr. M in conversation after Mr. M told him he could not speak to him any further because he wanted an attorney.

Detective Bosco continued to cajole the Defendant. He reiterated that if Mr. M made a statement, that he would get the police out of his house faster.

MM: I guess I'm just wondering what's the point of talking to me about it without an attorney present before you talk to me about….

Detective Bosco: That's why I'm not, I guess, yeah.

MM: You told me before that you wanted me to cooperate.

Detective Bosco: I'd, yeah.

MM: It goes a lot easier, is that what you're suggesting? Uhh….

Detective Bosco: It makes things easier.

MM: Easier for you, I guess.

Detective Bosco: For you too, it gets us in and out of your house a lot quicker.

H M: It seems like you've already made up your mind.

Joint Exhibit 1, Audio File 1, 32:15-33:26

Mr. M correctly asked an excellent question in the middle of the interview. Detective Bosco indicated he needed to read Mr. M his *Miranda* rights if he wanted to ask him questions. Mr. M correctly asked why he was not read *Miranda* at the outset?

Detective Bosco: If you want to talk to me, or ask me questions, I'm going to have to read you your *Miranda* rights and at which time you could either waive them or not, but….

MM: *Miranda* rights?

Detective Bosco: Yup.

H M: Your right to remain silent, you have the right to an attorney.

MM: Oh, ok.

Detective Bosco: I won't be able to answer any questions. I won't be able to discuss anything with you.

MM: You didn't do that in the beginning.

Detective Bosco: No, I didn't have to.

MM: Why would you have to now?

Joint Exhibit 1, Audio File 1, 37:46-38:12

The tone of the interrogation was clearly aggressive at times. The police repeatedly told the Defendant that they would tear apart his house if he did not give them the information they wanted (in case of following exchange, the location of a laptop).

Detective Armstrong: I'm going to say this, **I can tear this house apart, ok?** I don't want to do that, ok? I'm personally losing my patience alright so if you want me to do that to try to find it, because no one says it's probably at my office. It's either at your office or somewhere within this premise, be it car, whatever. So just give it to me so I don't have to go tear everything.

MM: It might be in my car, I've said that, and you're not letting me leave the house.

Detective Armstrong: No, you didn't. You just said, it's probably in my office, so, like I said, the search warrant can allow us to go into ceiling, into sides, into walls, whatever, but I ask you nicely, **just tell me where it is so I don't have to destroy your house.** I just don't want to do that.
MM: Honestly, I would need to see if it's in my car.

Joint Exhibit 1, Audio File 1, 42:10-42:53

Once again, Mr. M was left with the impression that he was in custody and his freedom of movement was substantially restricted.

MM: I take it I can't go to the bathroom?
Detective Bosco: Yeah, just let me go in and make sure there's no guns, bombs or bazookas in there and you can go to the bathroom.

Joint Exhibit 1, Audio File 1, 53:36-53:45

Mr. M was in custody throughout the course of this search and interrogation. The State will attempt to avoid suppression by arguing that the restriction on Mr. M's movements were to preserve the scene and for officer safety. As Justice John O'Neil, Jr. has pointed out, however, that does not relieve the State of its *Miranda* obligation:

By commanding the Defendant to "have a seat" multiple times, the officer transformed the encounter into one of custodial interrogation that required *Miranda* warnings. The officer was entitled to exercise that degree of restraint, both to protect himself as well as the integrity of the scene. However, to interrogate the Defendant at that point required *Miranda*.

State v. Nathaniel Ohman, York County Superior Court, CR-14-754.

B. Interrogation

There can be no doubt that this was an interrogation. Counsel will not brief this issue further as a result.

C. The Invocation of Miranda Was Not Scrupulously Honored

Additionally, the interrogation should have ceased when Mr. M invoked his right to have counsel present during the interrogation. When a subject requests that an attorney be present during an interrogation, all questioning must cease until the lawyer is present. *Davis v. U.S.*, 512, 548 (1994). It is an objective inquiry in determining whether the suspect has invoked his right to counsel. *Id.* at 459. An objective inquiry "requires, at a minimum, some statement that can reasonably be construed to be an expression of a desire for the assistance of an attorney." *McNeil v. Wisconsin*, 501 U.S. 171, 178 (1991).

Courts in the State of Maine have indicated that the procedure after the invocation of the right to remain silent is crystal clear:

Once warnings have been given, the subsequent procedure is clear. If the individual indicates in any manner, at any time prior to or during questioning, that he wishes to remain silent, *the interrogation must cease.*

State v. Grant, 939 A.2d 93, 104 (Me. 2008) (emphasis added) (citing *Miranda v. Arizona,* 384 U.S. 436, 473-86 S.Ct. 1602, 16 L. Ed.2d 694 (1996)). Any statement to law enforcement after Mr. M requested counsel must be suppressed because the prior invocation of his right to remain silent was not scrupulously honored. *See, Id.* (citing *Michigan v. Mosley,* 423, U.S. 96, 101-02, 96 S. Ct 321, 46 L.Ed.2d 313 (1975)).

The United States Supreme Court has made it absolutely clear that the interrogation must cease immediately when the individual indicates he wishes to stop the questioning and talk with an attorney. *Michigan v. Mosley,* 423, U.S. 96, 101-02, 96 S. Ct 321, 46 L.Ed.2d 313 (1975). As a result, any statement made after the request to cease questioning must be suppressed.

II. THE WARRANTLESS SEARCH OF DEFENDANT'S COMPUTER REQUIRES SUPPRESSION

The story of how law enforcement came to Mr. M's door has its roots in a warrantless search. That warrantless search came from a law enforcement tool, Database 1 (hereafter "DB1"). DB1 searches peer-to-peer software, in this case, eMule, and searches for hash values of images that it believes to be child pornography. The internet protocol (hereafter "IP") addresses associated with those images are transmitted to the Maine State Police Computer Crimes Unit (hereafter "Computer Crimes"). Thereafter, Computer Crimes prepares search warrants and does interrogations of with suspects.

At its initiation, however, the search by DB1 of the eMule account maintained by MM is a warrantless search. Mr. M has standing to contest the search and an expectation of privacy in his computer data.

> Individuals need an ISP address in order to access the Internet. However, when users surf the Web from the privacy of their homes, they have reason to expect that their actions are confidential. Many are unaware that a numerical IP address can be captured by the websites they visit. More sophisticated users understand that that unique string of numbers, standing alone, reveals little if anything to the outside world. Only an Internet service provider can translate an IP address into a user's name … In the world of the Internet, the nature of the technology requires individuals to obtain an IP address to access the Web. Users make disclosures to ISPs for the limited goal of using that technology and not to promote the release of personal information to others. Under our precedents, users are entitled to expect confidentiality under these circumstances.

State v. Reid, 945 A.2d 26, 33 (N.J. 2008).

In *Kyllo v. United States*, 533 U.S. 27, 121 S.Ct. 2038 (2001), the Government set-up surveillance across the street from a residence, and used a thermal imager to detect infrared radiation emanating from the house. This thermal imager was not looking at private or intimate details inside the home. Rather, it was measuring heat coming off the exterior walls of the house. The technology in issue there, a thermal imager, was not in the general public use (although, presumably anyone could buy one). The Supreme Court held:

> Where, as here the Government uses a device that is not in general public use, to explore details of the home that would have been previously unknowable without physical intrusion, the surveillance is a "search," and is presumptively unreasonable without a warrant.

Id. at 40.

Likewise, the warrantless search here uses specialized tools not in general public use. Those tools allow DB1 to do several things that the public cannot do on the eMule peer-to-peer network.[5] DB1 can:
1. Allow law enforcement to initiate a single source download.
2. Allow law enforcement to initiate fake file sharing. Fake file sharing appears to have been used in this case based on the law enforcement log type descriptions. This is denied by law enforcement officer Glenn Lang, however, in his Affidavit.
3. Use a file hash system that allows law enforcement to coordinate with the National Center for Missing and Exploited Children.
4. Allow law enforcement to save records on the eDonkey server.
5. Allow law enforcement to engage in geographic matching.

DB1 allows law enforcement to use a specialized tool not readily available to the general public. For a private citizen to develop such a tool would require extensive software development experience, time and money. Even so, it is doubtful that the functionality of the law enforcement software could be duplicated by a private citizen.

Where such information has been obtained in the absence of a valid search warrant, the resultant search and seizure are fruit of the poisonous tree and suppression is the only remedy. *Wong Sun v. United States*, 371 U.S. 471 (1963).

---

[5] As has been previously briefed, eMule is the peer-to-peer network at issue here.

III. THE WARRANT LACKED PARTICULARITY,
WAS OVERBROAD AND AUTHORIZED A SEARCH FOR LEGAL CONTENT

"The Fourth Amendment commands that a warrant issue not only upon probable cause supported by oath or affirmation, but also 'particularly describing the place to be searched, and the persons or things to be seized.'" *Berger v. State of N.Y.*, 388 U.S. 41, 55 (1967). "The requirement that warrants shall particularly describe the things to be seized makes general searches under them impossible and prevents the seizure of one thing under a warrant describing another. As to what is to be taken, nothing is left to the discretion of the officer executing the warrant." *Marron v. U.S.*, 275 U.S. 192, 196 (1927).

Despite this constitutional admonishment, the warrant here relies principally upon the discretion of the officer executing the warrant. The first items to be seized are "images of child pornography in any form." The warrant, however, fails to contain a definition of pornography. Further, the possession of child pornography is not a punishable criminal offense within Maine Statutes.

"Child pornography," in its common parlance, is "pornography using a child or children as the subject.[6]" "Pornography" means "obscene writings, drawings, photographs, or the like, especially those having little or no artistic merit.[7]" Therefore, the term "child pornography," as used in the warrant, authorizes a search for legal materials, including writings.

Underlying this is the actual language of the warrant, which allows the seizure of "images of child pornography **in any form**." The Warrant authorizes the search of legal materials, which it then says can be seized in any form. This underscores to the searching law enforcement officer (who is not supposed to be in a position to guess as to what he can seize) that he can seize anything he views as child pornography.

The Maine Statute for possession of sexually explicit material requires that the material depict a minor engaged in "sexually explicit conduct." 17-A MRSA s.284(1). The definition of "sexually explicit conduct" is:

    A. A sexual act;

    B. Bestiality;

    C. Masturbation;

    D. Sadomasochistic abuse for the purpose of sexual stimulation;

    E. Lewd exhibition of the genitals, anus or pubic area of a person. An exhibition is considered lewd if the exhibition is designed for the purpose of eliciting or attempting to elicit a sexual response in the intended viewer; or

    F. Conduct that creates the appearance of the acts in paragraphs A to D and also exhibits any uncovered or covered portions of the genitals, anus or pubic area.

17-A MRSA s.281(4).

To be certain then, the warrant here authorized the seizure of potentially legal material when it authorized the search and seizure of Mr. M's computers. Instead, the warrant should have authorized the seizure of sexually explicit materials, as defined above.

"A warrant unconstitutional for its lack of particularity authorizes a search in terms so ambiguous as to allow the executing officers to pick and choose among an individual's possessions to find which items to seize. This will result in the general 'rummaging' banned by the fourth amendment." *U.S. v. Wecht*, 619 F. Supp. 2d 213, 232 (W.D. Pa. 2009). This directive should be especially well-heeded in cases involving potentially protected material. Officers in other cases have demonstrated an inability to discern between lawful pictures of nude minors, and sexually explicit material punishable under Maine law. "Like obscenity statutes, laws directed at the dissemination of child pornography run the risk of suppressing protected expression by allowing the hand of the censor to become unduly heavy." *New York v. Ferber*, 458 U.S. 747, 756 (1982). As the United States Supreme Court held:

Where the materials sought to be seized may be protected by the First Amendment, the requirements of the Fourth Amendment must be applied with scrupulous exactitude. … Where presumptively protected

---

[6] child pornography. (n.d.). *Dictionary.com Unabridged*. Retrieved February 19, 2015, from Dictionary.com website: http://dictionary. reference.com/browse/child pornography

[7] pornography. (n.d.). *Dictionary.com Unabridged*. Retrieved February 19, 2015, from Dictionary.com website: http://dictionary.reference. com/browse/pornography

materials are sought to be seized, the warrant requirement should be administered to leave as little as possible to the discretion or whim of the officer in the field.

Zurcher v. Stanford Daily, 436 U.S. 547, 563 (1978) (Internal citations and quotations omitted).

The warrant for Mr. M's home provides no guidance to the executing officers as to what would constitute the crimes of possession or dissemination of sexually explicit materials, except that the materials may be legal "child pornography."

The danger, as already exhibited in Mr. M's case, is that images which do not meet the statutory definition of child pornography will be impermissibly seized. "Procedures which sweep so broadly and with so little discrimination are obviously deficient in techniques required by the Due Process Clause of the Fourteenth Amendment to prevent the erosion of the constitutional guarantees." *Marcus v. Search Warrant*, 367 U.S. 717, 733 (1961).

In any event, we cannot forgive the requirements of the Fourth Amendment in the name of law enforcement. This is no formality that we require today but a fundamental rule that has long been recognized as basic to the privacy of every home in America. While (t)he requirements of the Fourth Amendment are not inflexible, or obtusely unyielding to the legitimate needs of law enforcement ... it is not asking too much that officers be required to comply with the basic command of the Fourth Amendment before the innermost secrets of one's home or office are invaded.

Berger v. State of N.Y., 388 U.S. 41, 62-63 (1967).

The failure to define what constitutes child pornography under Maine law is a fatal defect and one that necessitates suppression. "The uniformly applied rule is that a search conducted pursuant to a warrant that fails to conform to the particularity requirement of the Fourth Amendment is unconstitutional." *Massachusetts v. Sheppard*, 468 U.S. 981, 988 n.5 (1984).

WHEREFORE, Undersigned Counsel respectfully requests that the Court grant his Motion to Suppress.

Dated this the 11th day of January, 2016, in Portland, Maine.

Respectfully submitted,

_____

Timothy E. Zerillo
Attorney for Defendant
ZERILLO LAW FIRM, LLC

§13:14   FORM 13-30 Memorandum in Support of Request for Franks Hearing

STATE OF MAINE	SUPERIOR COURT
CUMBERLAND, ss	DOCKET NO. 1234

STATE OF MAINE   )
)
)
)   **DEFENDANT'S BENCH**
v.   )   **MEMORANDUM IN SUPPORT**
)   **OF HIS REQUEST FOR A *FRANKS***
)   **HEARING**
)
MM   )
)

NOW COMES the Defendant, MM, and submits this Memorandum to aid in this Court's decision on his request for a *Franks* hearing. Appended to this Memo, and incorporated by reference herein, is the *Affidavit of BB* and attachments.

The Defendant is merely asking for a *Franks* hearing at this point. The Defendant has developed clear facts that support the many material defects in Detective Bosco's warrant affidavit. These false facts and omission of material facts necessitate a *Franks* hearing if justice is to be served.

ARGUMENT

A search warrant is invalid when it is obtained by use of a deliberately misleading affidavit. *Franks v. Delaware*, 438 U.S. 154, 98 S. Ct. 2674, 57 L. Ed. 2d 667 (1978). *Franks* holds that if the affiant deliberately, or with reckless disregard for the truth, makes false statements which are necessary to establish probable cause, the search warrant must be voided and the fruits of the search suppressed to the same extent as if probable cause was lacking on the face of the affidavit. *State v. Rand*, 430 A.2d 808, 821 (Me. 1981).

Material omissions in the warrant affidavit may also furnish the basis for a *Franks* challenge. The omission must be intentional or reckless, and the redacted information must be sufficient to vitiate probable cause. *See United States v. Tanguay*, 787 F.3d 44 (1st Cir. 2015). A literally true affidavit is sufficient to generate a *Franks* challenge[8]" ... if it deliberately omitted material facts which, when included, would defeat the probable cause showing and thus render false the original 'literally true' affidavit." *United States v. Tate,* 524 F.3d 449, 456–57 (4th Cir. 2008). Similarly, "[a] police affiant has a duty to disclose facts in his possession bearing on an informant's unreliability as well as facts bearing on reliability." *Commonwealth v. Jones*, 1992 WL 455407 (Pa.Com.Pl. 1992) (*Franks* hearing needed when police affidavit failed to disclose informant's criminal record). *See also State v. Lefkowitz*, 618 F.2d 1313 (9th Cir. 1980) (defendants permitted to challenge affidavits in hearing when material facts were omitted); *Peters v. State*, 213 Ga.App. 488 (1994) (*Franks* challenge was sufficient when the informant's reliability was based on information he provided for a seizure of his own marijuana).

Further, an officer may have an independent duty to perform a further investigation before presenting the warrant affidavit. The First Circuit recently explained this in *Tanguay, supra*. There, an informant gave law enforcement information that another individual possessed child pornography. *Id*. at 47. The police did an investigation and requested a warrant. *Id*. The investigating officer was aware that there may have been more to investigate concerning the informant's reliability, but chose not to investigate further. *Id*. at 48. The First Circuit held:

> To sum up, our holding is that the district court erred in ruling as a matter of law that an affiant never has a duty to make further inquiry before presenting a warrant application to a magistrate. Because the court below, erroneously relying on its categorical disavowal of any duty of further inquiry, did not pose any of the further questions that had to be asked, we must regard its order denying the appellant's motion to suppress as without force pending the completion of the further proceedings described below.

> ...All that is required to trigger an officer's duty of further inquiry is **her knowledge of an obvious and unexplored reason to doubt the truthfulness of the allegations**.

Id. at 53 (emphasis added).

Extra sensitivity must be applied to warrants in the context of child pornography searches. The judges who review these warrants are at a real disadvantage when analyzing probable cause. Judges are skilled at applying legal analysis to facts. They can easily analyze whether an informant has supplied enough reliable probable cause in a drug case. When it is a police computer software program that provides the probable cause, however, the judge may be forced to accept the conclusory statements of the affiant, without any true ability to weigh these assertions. It is likely that the reviewing Judge will just assume that what the officer is saying is accurate due to the highly technical nature of the information.

Here, Detective Bosco recklessly or intentionally hid the appropriate probable cause analysis from the reviewing judge. State's Suppression *Exhibit 1*, is Detective Bosco's emule[9] history spreadsheet. This spreadsheet is Bosco's own creation. Detective Bosco unequivocally knew that he could not confirm that there was any illegal contraband possessed by the target. He knew that if the target did not have the sexually explicit materials, that no crime was committed. He knew that he could easily have confirmed the presence of the contraband with a single source download. Detective Bosco clearly had a duty to investigate further, which he plainly ignored.

---

[8] The Affidavit here is not literally true in its entirety and is false or misleading in many respects. See Affidavit and Report of Benjamin Birney. However, even if the court considers this a literally true Affidavit, the omitted facts are sufficient for a *Franks* hearing.

[9] The emule history spreadsheet (State's Suppression Exhibit 1) describes the files of interest, as determined by Detective Jason B at the time he drafted the warrant affidavit. This spreadsheet is clearly inaccurate compared to the warrant affidavit (for example, on June 24, 2013, B describes 11 files of interest, yet there were only three different files of interest on June 24, because four of the files contained duplicate entries). Most significant, of course, is that the police could not confirm that the Defendant actually possessed any of the files upon which they based their warrant affidavit.

We are only at the preliminary stage of our request for a *Franks* hearing. If we had a *Franks* hearing, the Defendant would bear the burden of a *Franks* challenge by a preponderance of the evidence. *State v. Hamel*, 634 A.2d 1272, 1275 (Me. 1993). However, "[t]o require a defendant to come forward with a preponderance of evidence in his favor *prior* to the hearing is not warranted." *Id*. Counsel would argue that the Defendant's standard to get a *Franks* hearing is akin to a probable cause standard.

At a bare minimum, the following points should have been added to Detective Bosco's affidavit:

1. That he was unable to confirm that the target had any of the sexually explicit materials in issue;
2. That he made attempts to verify that the target possessed sexually explicit materials, and he was unable to verify the same;
3. That Database One allows law enforcement to perform a single source download. This would establish whether or not the target computer possessed the complete file (meaning a file that could actually be used and contained sexually explicit materials). This was not attempted here.

Had these facts been included[10], a prudent reviewing judge would not have found probable cause.

WHEREFORE, Undersigned Counsel respectfully requests that the Court grant his request for a *Franks* hearing.

Dated this the 10th day of December, 2015, in Portland, Maine.

Respectfully submitted,

_____

Timothy E. Zerillo
Attorney for Defendant
ZERILLO LAW FIRM, LLC

§13:15   Alibi Evidence

Sometimes you will catch a case in which your client denies any involvement with child porn. Consider developing alibi evidence early on.

In a case I am working on now, our client's IP address was observed by law enforcement to share child pornography *via* eMule. We caught the case early and looked to develop alibi evidence right off the bat. We didn't have the computer forensics or discovery yet. We knew, however, that law enforcement had been tracking the client's recent movements, so we tried to gather information that might contradict their evidence. The types of things we looked for were:

- Purchase receipts.
- Credit card information.
- Retail store video surveillance footage.
- EZ pass toll receipts.
- Personal and business calendars.
- Employment billing and time records.
- Traffic light surveillance videos.
- Witness affidavits.
- Family photos.
- Phone and email data.

With the right tools and the time to do it, you can assemble a nice alibi case in some instances. You will probably want to hire an investigator to track down leads, serve subpoenas, and so forth. From this information, you can assemble an alibi timeline. Then, when your computer forensics expert is doing his or her review, have your expert match up your data to the alleged times when illicit activity occurred. If the government claims that your client downloaded child pornography from eMule at the same time surveillance video shows him at Home Depot, that may be compelling to the jury. All it takes is one good date in question to supply a reasonable doubt argument.

_____

[10] There are a great number of other troubling facts relevant to the Defendant's Request for a *Franks* hearing, which are discussed in the Affidavit and Report of BB.

§13:16   View the Government's Evidence Yourself

I know it is no fun, but you need to do your due diligence and review the images yourself. Generally, they will be made available to you on a government computer, but they must be made available to you. In most cases, I review the evidence at either a police station or the prosecutor's office. My expert reviews the information separate from me, generally at a law enforcement facility.

In federal court cases, the government must keep the evidence. 18 U.S.C. §3509(m). The statute requires that "any property or material that constitutes child pornography shall remain in the care, custody, and control of either the Government or the court." 18 U.S.C. §3509(m)(1). Since the court doesn't want it, the government keeps it. The government is required to make the evidence "reasonably available to the defendant." 18 U.S.C. §3509(m)(2)(A).

When viewing the evidence you are generally looking for two things. First, is it child pornography as defined in the charging statute or code? Or are the images or videos merely artistic and not criminal? Second, you want to determine the ages of the child. Contraband containing depictions of children under 12 often presents an enhancement.

Even if the images do not present absolute defenses, they may be mitigating. Are the images a mixture of teen and pre-teen nudes, or do they depict the torture of infants? Mitigating factors should be argued if the child pornography depicted is among the least offensive type of such offensive material. On the other hand, aggravating factors must be understood and be prepared for. If the material is among the nastiest stuff you have ever seen, you must know that and prepare for it.

> **PRACTICE TIP:** *Don't take possession of the contraband*
>
> Be careful with state court cases in which the court or the district attorney wants to give you or your expert the contraband directly under to some sort of protective order or rule. These state laws may contradict the federal law. The last thing you need is you or your expert getting arrested. I suggest that you let the prosecutor keep the contraband and you review it at a government facility.

§13:17   Get Your Own Expert

You need an expert for your case. That person may or may not be able to testify, but, at the very least, you need an expert to consult with.

The expert will need to forensically examine the hard drive of the computer on which the images were found. The expert is needed to answer questions like this (and more):

- Was there file sharing? (This is relevant because of possible enhancements for distribution of child pornography).
- Is there proof of who downloaded the child pornography files? (You will want to establish that someone else downloaded the files if possible.)
- Is there proof of who viewed the child pornography contraband? (Determine if the government can establish who viewed the files. If they cannot, your alternative suspect theory may take flight.)
- Where were the files stored? (Were the files purposely stored in an area hidden from view? This creates two competing theories, first, that your client hid them and collected them or, second, that a malicious user hid them from your client.)
- Were they renamed? (This goes to an issue of whether your client was exhibiting collecting behavior, which is often indicative of an intense interest.)
- Were they in allocated or unallocated space? (Allocated space means they were saved to a location on the hard drive. Unallocated space may mean that the files were accessed at one time, but never saved or were deleted. This may prove to be important evidence as to whether your defendant is a serious collector of child porn, or someone who views it occasionally, regrets it and then deletes it).
- When were the images last opened? (You sometimes will have a case where your guy hadn't accessed the files for a while. Perhaps it was a dark period of his life. If so, the last accessed dates of the contraband may be helpful to you).
- Does the computer have viruses, Trojan horses or malware? (Of course, this is the most common attack on these cases. A full malware analysis by most experts is extensive. Trying to find a malicious user is difficult. The police forensics expert will usually provide a malware report as a starting point. If you find evidence of malicious activity, of course, it can be very helpful to establishing reasonable doubt.)
- Is there relevant information about any user accounts on the computers? (Here, I am trying to understand the ways in which other users accessed the computer.)

- Is there relevant information about email, chat logs, internet history and other data to help the case? (This may be a way to gather alibi and alternative suspect information. For example, imagine that your client's wife sends an email to her friend within minutes of contraband being downloaded.)

These ideas are merely the tip of the iceberg. Collaborate with your experts and you may come up with novel defenses, or at least some help in forming ideas to cross the government expert.

For your expert to meaningfully review the evidence, you will need to have the court enter a protective order. See §13:18 Form 13-40. This is not usually a big deal, but you need to get this Protective Order in place or your expert is arguably violating the law.

§13:18   FORM 13-40 Stipulated Protective Order

UNITED STATES DISTRICT COURT
DISTRICT OF MAINE

UNITED STATES OF AMERICA	)	
	)	
v.	)	Criminal No. 1234
	)	
RANDY	)	

STIPULATED PROTECTIVE ORDER

WHEREAS, on or about _____, 20__, Amanda gave consent to law enforcement for the search of the Sony Vaio Laptop computer (hereinafter "Computer Evidence") she shared with the Defendant, Randy;

WHEREAS, The United States Department of Justice, Child Exploitation and Obscenity Section has custody of the original Sony Vaio Laptop computer office and has produced mirror image copies of the hard drive and has provided these mirror image copies to the United States Secret Service;

WHEREAS, Defendant, through his undersigned counsel, has retained Ur Xpert to provide expert testimony should this matter proceed to a trial;

WHEREAS, Defendant's counsel has requested that Ur Xpert be permitted to conduct a forensic examination of the mirror imaged copies of Computer Evidence;

WHEREAS, Title 18, United States Code, Section 3509(m) provides:

    (m) Prohibition on reproduction of child pornography

(1) In any criminal proceeding, any property or material that constitutes child pornography (as defined by section 2256 of this title) shall remain in the care, custody, and control of either the Government or the court.

(2)(A) Notwithstanding Rule 16 of the Federal Rules of Criminal Procedure, a court shall deny, in any criminal proceeding, any request by the defendant to copy, photograph, duplicate, or otherwise reproduce any property or material that constitutes child pornography (as defined by section 2256 of this title), so long as the Government makes the property or material reasonably available to the defendant.

(B) For the purposes of subparagraph (A), property or material shall be deemed to be reasonably available to the defendant if the Government provides ample opportunity for inspection, viewing, and examination at a Government facility of the property or material by the defendant, his or her attorney, and any individual the defendant may seek to qualify to furnish expert testimony at trial.

To permit Defendant's counsel and computer forensic examiner to examine the Seized Computer Evidence in a manner that complies with Title 18, United States Code, Section 3509(m),

IT IS HEREBY STIPULATED AND AGREED by and among the United States, Defendant's counsel, and the Defendant's computer forensic examiner, Ur Xpert, (together "the parties"), that:

1. The United States may provide Defendant's counsel and Ur Xpert with an opportunity to inspect, view and examine the Computer Evidence;

2. The United States will make the Computer Evidence available for inspection, viewing and examination at the offices of United States Secret Service, New York, New York).

3. Ur Xpert will be permitted to use his own equipment to inspect, view and examine the Computer Evidence, subject to the requirements of Title 18, United States Code, Section 3509(m) and the provisions of this order. No equipment may be connected to the Internet or otherwise enabled to permit the transmission of any data outside of the USSS OFFICE.

4. Ur Xpert and Defendant's counsel shall not copy, photograph, duplicate, or otherwise reproduce any property or material that constitutes child pornography (as defined by section 2256 of title 18) or any images of children.

5. Ur Xpert and Defendant's counsel shall not remove any property or material that constitutes child pornography (as defined by section 2256 of title 18) or that depicts children from the USSS OFFICE.

6. Prior to each instance in which he departs the USSS OFFICE after conducting the aforementioned forensic examination of the Computer Evidence, Ur Xpert shall certify that he has not copied, photographed, duplicated or otherwise reproduced any material that constitutes child pornography (as defined by section 2256 of title 18) or depicts children onto any piece of equipment, item or material that he will remove from the USSS OFFICE.

7. Ur Xpert may remove from the USSS OFFICE facility materials or work product that he creates during his forensic examination that do not contain material that constitutes child pornography (as defined by section 2256 of title 18) or depicts children.

8. Ur Xpert and Defendant's counsel shall be permitted to inspect, view and examine the Computer Evidence solely for use in the defense of this case and for no other purpose whatsoever without prior approval of the Court. Any work product that Ur Xpert or defense counsel generates from their inspection, review and examination of the Computer Evidence shall be used only in the defense of this case and for no other purpose whatsoever without prior approval of the Court.

9. The provisions of this Stipulated Protective Order shall continue to be binding pending further order of this Court.

Respectfully submitted,
Ms. Pros
United States Attorney

By:

_____   _____
Timothy Zerillo, Esquire   Ms. Pros
Attorney for Defendant   Assistant United States Attorney

_____
Ur Xpert

Dated: _____, 20__

AND NOW this _____ day of _____, 20__, the foregoing Stipulated Protective Order is hereby accepted and entered by this Court.

_____
Honorable Judge
United States Magistrate Judge

§ 13:19   Pointing the Finger

Don't forget to develop finger-pointing evidence, if it is available on your facts. Perhaps the computer was on an unsecured, unpassword-protected network, yet the cops looked at your client because he registered the IP address. Maybe others had access to the computer? On occasion, you will find the opportunity to point the finger at someone else.

[§§13:20-13:29 Reserved]

III.   STRATEGIES AND TACTICS

§13:30   Innocent Possession

Consider whether your client may have innocently or unknowingly possessed the contraband child pornography. Generally speaking, an act is done "knowingly" if the act was done voluntarily and intentionally and not because of mistake or accident. If your client was not aware of the images, maybe he could not have knowingly possessed the images.

Images found in the computer's cache only may provide a defense. The computer cache is a file system that saves images in the computer's memory that were recently used for quick access. The user may not know that the images were saved in the cache. Those cache images may also have never been accessed by a user because they may have been on a portion of a web page that the viewer never opened.

Consider *United States v. Moreland*, in which the defendant, his father, and his wife all had access to the computers on which the images were found. 665 F.3d 137, 140 (5th Cir. 2011). Moreland was prosecuted for possession of 112 images of child pornography found in the unallocated space of two home computers. *Id.* at 144. The Court in *Moreland* found that the evidence was insufficient to establish that the defendant had the requisite knowledge and ability to access images in the computer cache and to exercise dominion or control over them. *Id.* Several Circuits considering this issue have come to the same conclusion. *See e.g. United States v. Kuchinski*, 469 F.3d 853, 863 (9th Cir. 2006); *United States v. Miller*, 527 F.3d 54, 67 (3d Cir. 2008); *United States v. Dobbs*, 629 F.3d 1199, 1209 (10th Cir. 2011); *United States v. Romm*, 455 F.3d 990 (9th Cir. 2006); *United States v. Flyer*, 633 F.3d 911 (9th Cir. 2011).

It is fairly common to have a bulk download of pornography that includes some child pornography. In such a case, the defendant may have been seeking non-contraband pornography, but got some anyway in the download. This is very common in the peer-to-peer file sharing context. Often these files don't have names that indicate that they are child pornography. If the user opens the file, discovers it is child pornography, and deletes it, the file may still be in the computer cache. Either way, you have an argument that the contraband was not knowingly possessed.

What if the images were found in the slack space of the computer? The unallocated space or slack space is created when blocks or clusters of memory are requested by the computer system. The leftover space is where data can be stored when file sizes don't match the size of the blocks or clusters they are stored in. The argument could be made that your client was not the person who put the images in the slack space of the computer, and therefore was not in knowing possession on the date of indictment. In other words, your client's failure to actually allocate a location for the contraband on his computer may lead to an argument that he lacked *mens rea*.

> **PRACTICE TIP:** *Receipt can be worse than possession*
>
> States are now closing down this argument much like the feds have. Federal statutes punish receipt of child pornography as well as possession. Ironically, a first offense possession case has no mandatory minimum, but a receipt conviction can carry a five year statutory minimum. This can create a Hobson's choice for the defendant.
>
> I have a situation now where the government has not yet found my client's contraband. However, they have hash values of child pornography he allegedly downloaded on his P2P network. They may now charge him with receipt, which could lead to a potentially worse result than mere possession.

§13:31   Morphed Images

Consider whether or not you can score some points with the jury in close cases by showing them how easy it is to morph and distort ordinary images. Get yourself some photoshop or similar software, find some innocent images, and change them. If you can't do it and don't have the energy to photoshop, find a young person to teach you. For a few hundred dollars and some time you can show a jury how anyone can change virtually any image. You can use this in multitudes of different ways in trial.

Be careful in choosing how to morph the images, however. Lawyer and technology expert Dean Boland morphed images of children's heads onto the bodies of adults performing sex acts. He displayed the images while testifying as an expert in child pornography cases. His testimony came to the attention of the FBI, which seized files on his computer. Ultimately he entered a pretrial diversion agreement in which he admitted violating 18 U.S.C. §2252A(a)(5)(B) by knowingly possessing a "visual depiction [that] has been created, adapted, or modified to appear that an identifiable minor is engaging in sexually explicit conduct."

When the children's parents found out, they sued under the civil-remedy provisions of two federal child-pornography statutes. Boland was forced to pay a $300,000 judgment which was upheld by the Sixth Circuit. *Doe v. Boland*, 698 F.3d 877 (6th Cir. 2012).

As the Sixth Circuit acknowledged,

He could have shown the difficulty of distinguishing real pornography from virtual images by transforming the face of an adult onto another, or inserting a child's image into an innocent scene. If he felt compelled to make his point with pornography, he could have used images of adults or virtual children. *Id.*

§13:32   Client Treatment and Analysis—Get Thee To The Doctor!

I know I sound like a broken record, but getting your client treatment privately is a good idea in child porn cases as well as in many other types of criminal matters. If you have a possession only case, it is important to try to provide the court evidence that your client's is not having sexual contact with children and can be treated. The best way to establish that the defendant is not committing contact offenses is by a lack of history of complaints and charges, psychiatric testing and sometimes with the use of a polygraph exam.

> **PRACTICE TIP:** *Be familiar with the mandatory reporter laws for your jurisdiction*
>
> While your client needs treatment, we don't want to walk him or her into a worse situation if the client discloses something reportable during the treatment process. Usually this issue can be strategized with your client and the treating provider in advance, but it should always be considered.

§13:33   Alternative Suspects

Even if you have a lousy case otherwise, you may have an alternative suspects defense. There are at least two obvious ones.

The first is to point the finger at others with direct access to the computer or device. Roommates, spouses, children, and parents are often thrown right under the bus.

The second is the idea of a malicious user who is accessing and storing information on your client's computer like a child pornography storage bin. After all, if you are a CP collector you don't want to keep that stuff on your own computer.

Jurors understand the possibilities of remote access more and more. They have heard of things like malware and Trojan horses. They understand someone may be able to "hack" into your computer and control it. This theory can be developed through your expert's malware analysis. If you cannot develop this argument forensically you may still be able to raise it through cross of the government forensics expert. You can attack their methodology and the sufficiency of their malware analysis as well.

§13:34   NCMEC Child Identification Reports

If you do child pornography cases you will get used to receiving National Center for Missing and Exploited Children (NCMEC) "Child Identification Reports through the discovery process." These NCMEC Reports give you catalogued data on certain images allegedly possessed by your client. The Reports will go something like this:

NCMEC Request #:	12345
Series:	Helen
Agency:	National Crime Squad (U.K.)
Investigator:	Tom Thomas
Preferred Method of Contact:	tom@ukgenericpoliceoffice.com
Case #:	54321
Files found:	11A.jpg, 22B.jpg, 33B.jpg

Of course, the receipt of a NCMEC Report does not mean that the file contains an image of a child. It merely means that a child has allegedly been identified as the subject of an image. This information is used to date the images (and therefore the age of the child) and to establish that the image is of an actual child. An NCMEC report can be problematic for the defense because it can help identify the age of the child and provide contact information for the local investigator who handled that child exploitation crime. If the age of the child depicted is an issue in your case, whether the child is available to testify about his or her age when the images were acquired would be significant.

§13:35 Tanner Scale

Sometimes the individuals pictured in the images at issue are not clearly children. Sometimes they are clearly minors, but it is not clear that the child depicted is under 12. (There are usually sentence enhancements if the child depicted is under 12.) The government will often present a medical witness who will talk about the Tanner scale of the person in the image. The Tanner scale measures breast development in females, genitalia development in males and pubic hair development for both males and females. For each of these categories there are 5 Tanner stages, from which the medical professional will try to give an opinion as to age.

Tanner scale testimony has been subject to significant criticism. In fact, James Tanner, for whom the scale is named, has indicated that the scale should be used very carefully in child pornography cases, as it was not developed for that purpose. Rosenbloom AL, Tanner, JM (1998). "Misuse of Tanner Puberty Stages to Estimate Chronologic Age". *Pediatrics* 102 (6): 1494. Dr. Tanner has indicated that the scale is not appropriate for estimating chronological age.

If the government is presenting Tanner scale evidence, there are a number of ways to attack it. You can certainly present your own expert. This is probably the best practice. However, if that is impracticable, you can cross the government expert with the argument that the expert is using the Tanner scale for a different purpose than it was derived.

§13:36 IP Address

When dealing with CP cases, you will often hear about IP addresses. "IP" is short for "Internet Protocol" address. Like a street address labels your home, the IP address labels your computer. Every computer that accesses the Internet has a unique IP address. Often, the government will introduce evidence that CP was downloaded to an IP address associated with your client's computer.

The vast majority of computer users do not own their IP addresses. Rather they are leased from Internet Service Providers (ISPs). Basically, internet registrars assign blocks of IP addresses to ISPs who assign them to the computers of their customers. The IP address is often dynamic, which means it is subject to change. So, proof of the same may be of limited use.

A computer's IP address can change if:
- The lease term has expired.
- The ISP makes certain changes to its network or to the router responsible for the address.
- The ISP has a network failure.
- The computer user changes ISP providers.
- The computer moves to a different location.
- The computer is a laptop that connects to the Internet from different WiFi networks.
- The IP address is dynamic. In other words, it is periodically recycled by the provider.

You may argue that if the government cannot establish that the IP address belongs to your client, that they cannot establish that it was his computer downloading or uploading contraband. This may raise both suppression issues (i.e., did the government have probable cause to search if they didn't establish the IP address to which the images were downloaded or from which they were uploaded was the defendant's IP address at the time) and trial issues (related to the thoroughness of the police investigation, for example).

§13:37 Computer Experts

Very often I do not call a defense computer expert at trial. I use them during the case as often as my client can afford it. In the unfortunate experience of most of my clients, the experts agree with the government forensics folks. So, I often use them to help me with cross examination ideas for trial.

Of course, a computer expert can be used at trial and some occasions call for it. In an alibi case, for example, a computer expert can be used to confirm alibi details. Or, the government expert may have made mistakes in their investigation.

While it is not essential to call your expert at trial, it is certainly prudent to have an expert to consult with on the case.

§13:38　Jury Waiver

Child porn defense may be one of the few areas where it is legitimate to waive a jury trial. Child porn is so despised, you will want to discuss the issue of a bench trial with your client.

This is not to say that judges will like child pornography cases more than a jury. However, if you have technical defenses, you and your client may decide a bench trial is the way to go.

[§§13:39-13:49 Reserved]

IV.　PRETRIAL MOTIONS

§13:50　Motion in Limine to Limit Jury's Viewing of Images

If you have a jury trial with more than a few images, consider a motion to limit the images of child pornography the jury will see. See §13:51 Form 13-50 Motion in Limine to Restrict or Limit the Showing of Child Pornography to the Jury. Publishing of images to the jury will prejudice and inflame the jury. The court should engage in a balancing of unfair prejudice against the relevance of the images. *Old Chief v. United States*, 519 U.S. 172 (1997). If the images are cumulative, you may have an argument that the balancing test favors exclusion. This is even more significant if you are stipulating to the admission of the images. Of course, some attorneys will never agree to admit the images. In many of my cases, however, there are thousands of images, all of which are clearly child porn. I don't want to make my trial about those images, so I often stipulate and try to get an agreement from the government to my proposed limitation.

You may argue for outright restriction of the images. By that, I want to exclude all the images under the theory that no jury could ever not be prejudiced by them. I have never won on that issue, but the court's fallback position often is to significantly reduce the images the jury sees. Even if they are admitted, you may just want to limit the publication of the images. In the Eleventh Circuit, for example, the publication of 5 out of 4,650 images was not prejudicial or cumulative. *United States v. Alfaro-Moncado*, 607 F.3d 720, 734 (11th Cir 2010).

PRACTICE TIP: *A contrary view*

There is a contrary point of view to the idea of hiding the child pornography images from the jury. The question is if the images are coming into evidence anyway, are they made somehow special or sacred when they are quickly shown to the jury, then put in a special envelope and given to the clerk? Or, should they be shown multiple times to the jury to inoculate them from the shock value of the images. I think it depends on the nature of the images and the facts of your case. We should not lose sight of the fact that when we treat the images differently than other evidence, we make them special or important in the eyes of the jury.

---

§13:51　FORM 13-50 Motion in Limine to Restrict or Limit the Showing of Child Pornography to the Jury

UNITED STATES DISTRICT COURT
FOR THE DISTRICT OF MAINE

UNITED STATES OF AMERICA,　)
　　　　　　　　　　　　　　)
　Plaintiff,　　　　　　　　　)
　　　　　　　　　　　　　　)
　v.　　　　　　　　　　　　)　　　　　Criminal No. 12345
　　　　　　　　　　　　　　)
RANDY,　　　　　　　　　　)
Defendant.　　　　　　　　　)

DEFENDANT'S MOTION *IN LIMINE* TO RESTRICT OR LIMIT THE SHOWING OF CHILD PORNOGRAPHY TO THE JURY

NOW COMES Randy, by and through Undersigned Counsel, Zerillo Law Firm, LLC, and moves *in limine* for the exclusion and limitation of the below described evidence and testimony that will be offered by the Government at trial. The Defendant respectfully requests that the Court hear oral argument before disposing of this motion.

I. THE JURY SHOULD NOT BE SHOWN THE CHILD PORNOGRAPHY, OR, IN THE ALTERNATIVE, A VERY LIMITED NUMBER OF IMAGES SHOULD BE SHOWN TO OVERCOME THE PREJUDICIAL AND CUMULATIVE NATURE OF THE EVIDENCE

The Defendant has agreed to enter into a stipulation with the Government that the images, other than those of Minor A, contain visual depictions of minors engaging in sexually explicit conduct under 18 U.S.C. §2256, and that the visual depictions were transported in interstate commerce *via* a computer.[11] As a result of this stipulation, Mr. Randy argues that the contraband images should not be shown to the jury.

It is no longer relevant to show the jury the images after the stipulation. Additionally, the publishing of the stipulated images to the jury will prejudice and inflame the jury. Unfair prejudice will result in the case of an evidentiary issue that is not in dispute. F.R.Evid. 403. This Court must engage in a balancing of unfair prejudice against the relevance of the stipulated images. *Old Chief v. United States*, 519 U.S. 172 (1997).

If this Court declines to outright restrict the images from publication to the jury, Mr. Randy requests this Court significantly limit the images shown to the jurors. In the Eleventh Circuit, for example, the publication of 5 out of 4,650 images was not prejudicial or cumulative. *United States v. Alfaro-Moncado*, 607 F.3d 720, 734 (11th Cir 2010).

There are 314 images in this case. If this Court will not restrict the publication of the images to the jury outright, Counsel asks that the Government only be allowed to submit 1 image to the jury for publication.

CONCLUSION

WHEREFORE, the Defendant requests this Court grant his Third Motion *in Limine*.

Respectfully submitted,

_____

Timothy E. Zerillo
Attorney for Defendant
ZERILLO LAW FIRM, LLC

§13:52   Motion to Limit Testimony of Defense Computer Expert

Be wary of computer experts or agents who will try to stretch their expertise at trial. You should be concerned, for example, that a case agent will try to provide information as to the characteristics of child pornographers, the terminology of child pornography seekers and distributors, including the ways in which child pornography is searched for and obtained, and the words or terms used for the same. They will also try to testify to the forensic significance of their findings, how their findings relate to knowing possession of child pornography, the way in which certain child pornography websites operate and the culture and customs of the members of various child pornography websites concerning the trade or distribution of child pornography.

These case agents are merely law enforcement officers. Sometimes, they have independent computer forensics background; often they do not. However, they are often vested with enormous latitude in their testimony. For example, the case agent will try often to turn himself or herself into a child pornography profiler. That is the last thing you need. Use F.R.Evid. 702 to limit this testimony in advance of trial. See §13:53 Form 13-60 Motion in Limine to Limit Testimony of Government Computer Forensics Experts.

---

[11] This Motion does not include the 4 images of the so-called "Minor A," which are not subject to stipulation.

§ 13:53   FORM 13-60 Motion in Limine to Limit Testimony of Government Computer Forensics Experts

UNITED STATES DISTRICT COURT
FOR THE DISTRICT OF MAINE

UNITED STATES OF AMERICA,	)	
	)	
Plaintiff,	)	
	)	
v.	)	Criminal No. 12345
	)	
RANDY,	)	
Defendant.	)	

DEFENDANT'S MOTION *IN LIMINE* TO LIMIT THE TESTIMONY OF GOVERNMENT COMPUTER FORENSICS EXPERTS

NOW COMES Randy, by and through Undersigned Counsel, Zerillo Law Firm, LLC, and moves *in limine* for the exclusion and limitation of the below described evidence and testimony that will be offered by the Government at trial. The Defendant respectfully requests that the Court hear oral argument before disposing of this motion.

II.   LAW ENFORCEMENT PERSONNEL SHOULD NOT BE PERMITTED TO TESTIFY AS COMPUTER FORENSICS EXPERTS AND THEIR TESTIMONY SHOULD BE LIMITED

As of the drafting of this Motion, the Government has designated three experts, Secret Service Special Agent 1, Ms. 2 from the Department of Justice, and Mr. Cop, of the Maine Computer Crimes Task Force. Counsel requests this Court significantly limit the potential testimony of all three of these law enforcement witnesses (hereafter collectively referred to as "proposed experts").

The use of law enforcement experts provides a variety of concerns that can be limited by this court. The jury in this matter will hear about highly technical electronic evidence that they likely know little or nothing about. If the proposed expert's testimony is not limited, the jury will blindly accept their conclusions. This is impermissible. *United States v. Raymond*, 2010 WL 1254664 (D. Me. Apr. 2, 2010) (Hornby, J.) (citing *Gen. Elec. v. Joiner*, 522 U.S. 136, 146 (1997)).

The concern of the defense is that unless this Court sets parameters for the proposed expert's' testimony, it may roam into dangerous areas. The Undersigned is concerned, for example, that the proposed experts may attempt to provide opinion related to the following: 1) characteristics of child pornographers, 2) the general nomenclature of child pornography seekers and distributors, including the ways in which child pornography is searched for and obtained, and the words or terms used for the same, 3) the forensic significance of their findings in this matter, 4) testimony related to their findings as they relate to knowing possession of child pornography, 5) the way in which certain child pornography websites operate and the culture and customs of the members of various child pornography websites concerning the trade or distribution of child pornography.

Without a check on this testimony, the proposed expert moves from merely an examiner, to the anointed position of child pornography profiler. The jury will not be able to distinguish their normal function, which is to run the forensic software, from testimony they may give regarding the online habits and profiles of child pornographers.

F.R.Evid. 702 limits the expert testimony as coming from a qualified witness whose testimony is based on reliable factors that will assist the trier of fact in understanding the evidence or determining a fact in issue. None of the proposed experts are qualified to give the opinions expressed above. Likewise, those unqualified opinions would not serve the jury in completing its task. Further, the jury will merely accept those opinions as fact if they are mixed with the findings of the actual forensic evaluation. Finally, the admission of this testimony fails on the grounds of relevance and prejudice to the Defendant. F.R.Evid. 401 and 403.

The Defendant seeks an order that limits the proposed expert's testimony as follows:

1. Testimony related to their qualifications;
2. Testimony related to the bare facts of the forensic examination: an explanation of what, where, when and how they found the alleged child pornography;

3. Testimony related to computer technology concepts that explain the use of forensic software and the ways in which the computer at issue allegedly stored the contraband;
4. Testimony related to any testing they have done themselves personally.

The Defendant seeks an Order that the proposed experts are restricted from testifying related to:
1. The characteristics of child pornographers;
2. The general nomenclature used by child pornography seekers and distributors, including the ways in which child pornography is searched for and obtained, and the words or terms used for the same;
3. The forensic significance of their findings in this matter;
4. Testimony related to their findings as they relate to knowing possession of child pornography; and
5. The way in which certain websites operate and the culture and customs of the members of various child pornography websites concerning the trade or distribution of child pornography.

CONCLUSION

WHEREFORE, the Defendant requests this Court grant his Forth Motion *in Limine*.

Respectfully submitted,

_____

Timothy E. Zerillo
Attorney for Defendant
ZERILLO LAW FIRM, LLC

[§§13:54-13:59 Reserved]

V.   TRIAL

A. Opening Statement

§13:60   My Approach

Here, we will look at Randy's case. He is charged with production, distribution and possession of child pornography. See §13:05 for a summary of the facts. It is a very difficult case. While much of the computer has been wiped, there are still 314 images of child pornography, and 3 images that the prosecution claims he created and distributed of his daughter. The prosecution believes that he used a fairly ominous handle—Shadow—when distributing these images and downloading other child porn.

In this opening my goal is to:
*   Express appreciation to the jurors for their inconvenience.
*   Point out that the computer on which the images were found did not belong to Randy and was not password protected, so others had access.
*   Suggest the government's forensic reconstruction of Randy's computer is flawed.
*   Raise doubt about whether Randy knowingly possessed images in the hidden Yahoo messenger directory.
*   Raise doubt that the Minor A images were of Randy's daughter and were uploaded by him.
*   Educate the jury on the meaning of the presumption of innocence, burden of proof, and beyond a reasonable doubt.

§13:61   Sample Opening Statement

Your Honor, jury foreperson, members of the jury, may it please the Court, my name is Tim Zerillo and I'm pleased and proud to represent Randy here today.

Randy has been waiting quite some time to get this case in front of you and he is grateful to have the case in front of you. You know the greatest thing that I get to do as a lawyer is to address people like you. For you, I recognize jury duty is an inconvenience. For some of you, it's a major inconvenience. I heard what you had to say just yesterday at sidebar. I know you all have things going on and I get that. But you've been selected and you've been qualified because of the answers that you gave yesterday. I don't want to just assume that this is fun and games for you. I know it's an inconvenience and I appreciate you listening.

This is way beyond inconvenience for my client. What we are dealing with here is a man's life. So, while this is a big inconvenience for you, my client will ask you to put that aside, as his future weighs in the balance of your decision.

One of the things that you're going to be looking at here is the forensic reconstruction of Randy's computer, and by the way, although I might refer to it as Randy's computer, it's really Amanda's computer. It was a gift to her. The evidence will show that Randy had access to it. In fact, the computer did not even contain a password, so anyone who had physical access to it could have flipped it open and used it.

This case is about the forensic reconstruction of Amanda's computer and whether or not it fits the facts. I don't know if you've ever gotten a gift that you wanted to give back. This happens to my kids all the time. It just doesn't work or your child already has it. First, you have to struggle to get the thing opened. Then when they don't want it, you try to put the pieces back into the packaging to return it. I can never get it to get back in there the way it came out. Similarly, the Government can't fit the technology pieces together to establish proof of Randy's guilt beyond a reasonable doubt. They are trying to force everything into a neat package, but it just didn't fit. Like a square peg in a round hole.

I'm not going to get into a long recitation of the facts of this case right now. You're going to hear them with your own ears and then we're going to talk about them some more at closing, but I do want to address some of the things that the Assistant U.S. Attorney has just said.

First of all, there are two groups of images that we really are concerned with, or at least that's how I categorize them, in two groups. They are found in the Yahoo Messenger photo sharing directory.

So, if we use Yahoo Messenger and I take a picture of the jury and I send it to you and you decide to save it, maybe you call it "jury" and you save it on your hard drive. You put it there. You named it. But it would also be in a place you didn't put it, with a name you didn't give it. It would be in a hidden directory you don't even know about, and that's the Yahoo Messenger photo sharing directory. You're all going to hear a lot of information about Yahoo Messenger. What is important is it works in a way that, in some cases, even if the picture is not saved on the hard drive and renamed, it will be saved in this hidden folder.

So, the first group of images the prosecutor discussed is found in a hidden directory. And this may cause you to ponder whether Randy knowingly possessed the images that were hidden from him by Amanda's computer.

We're going to talk about what "knowingly" means later because it's a very specific term, and the Judge is going to talk to you about it and he will give you detailed instructions on that later. For now it's just something to put a post-it note on to flag it to go back to.

Now, for the second group of pictures, the Minor A photographs. The Minor A photographs are the photographs that the Government is alleging that my client took of his daughter. They are also alleging that he distributed them. So for the Minor A photographs, one of the things that you're going to be looking for is this: whether the Government has evidence beyond a reasonable doubt that those photos were uploaded or downloaded by Randy.

The Government will contend that the photos were uploaded by Randy to be shared on the World Wide Web, but the question for you will be: were they uploaded or downloaded? I will ask you to ponder if Randy only downloaded the images, why would he have downloaded images that the Government says he created? That wouldn't make much sense.

These charges are horrible. Make no mistake. But they are merely accusations. The Judge has told you that already. He's told you quite correctly that an indictment is merely an accusation and you'll have to remember that Randy being accused here is not any evidence at all of his guilt. The indictment is merely a way to activate the system of justice so that we can come before the 14 of you and you can ultimately decide the facts beyond a reasonable doubt. That means that you determine guilt or innocence, not the prosecutor, not myself, not Special Agent Frank.

Now, as a result, the burden in this or any other criminal case rests solely at the Government's table. There are very subtle clues that reflect this in the course of a criminal trial, like the fact that the Government went first in its Opening Statement, like the fact that the Government will have the last word in this case. These all reflect the burden that this table bears entirely. The burden in this trial never once shifts to the table where I will sit with Randy. It does not shift for one minute, for one second, to our table. That means Randy does not need to do anything altering the course of this trial. He doesn't have to have me give an opening statement. You'll notice that the Judge said if I choose to give an opening statement, I could and I've chosen to, but I didn't have to. And Randy doesn't have to do anything other than sit there. He doesn't have to testify, he doesn't have to bring in witnesses, he doesn't have to do anything and the law says that you cannot hold that against him.

I'll add one more thing to that thought. The law says you don't hold against him the number of witnesses or lack thereof that he brings. The same goes for the number of exhibits. This is not a contest as to who can put in the most exhibits or who can call the most witnesses. That does not matter at all.

I often wonder at the beginning of a trial—maybe, I would guess, most of you have never been on a jury before. So, I picture you with a newspaper and cup of coffee this morning saying "hmmm, I'm on a jury today, I wonder what I'm going to have to do?" And you might say to yourself "Well, I guess what I'm going to have to do is I'm going to have to keep an open mind. That sounds fair and that's what I'm going to do."

I would submit to you that that's a nice notion, but it's not true. It's not true because it doesn't go far enough.

You can't just have an open mind. You must realize right now as you sit here that my client is innocent. That is what the law says. As you sit here, in all of your minds, you need to know and believe that my client is innocent. So an open mind is not enough now. You need to believe him to be innocent.

The state court at Cumberland County, perhaps you've been there, it's across the street. Several years ago I was riding up the elevator going to a criminal jury selection, much like the one you went through yesterday, and there were prospective jurors coming up as I got in the elevator. They were sort of rolling their eyes about having to be on a criminal jury and one of them said to the other one "Well, I figure they've done something wrong to be here today."

I just want to caution you because it's so important—if you have that in your heart and in your mind right now, then you are not applying the correct rule of law. You must apply the rule of law that my client is currently innocent. And be truthful with yourself right now, before you hear any evidence. Because if you have been looking at this the wrong way, you can still correct that thought process, and look at it the right way.

The judge said that the evidence in a trial comes in like a jigsaw puzzle. It comes in a bit at a time and you are looking for a picture to take shape. I think that's an accurate analogy, but I would add one thing to that analogy. One of your jobs as jurors is to look for missing pieces of that jigsaw puzzle, because those missing pieces are reasonable doubt.

You're going to hear all sorts of—and you've already started to—you're going to hear all sorts of horrible accusations about Randy. They're going to say horrible things that they accuse him of or that he was doing on his wife's computer. They're going to accuse him of horrible things related to his own daughter. The Government, as you know, is going to show you some images of child pornography.

It's okay to feel badly about that. You're going to see it and you're going to—we are all humans, you'll all have different reactions to it. Some of you may be angry; some of you may feel sick to your stomach. There may be a variety of feelings that you'll have and that's fine on one condition. That one condition is that you put your emotional reaction aside when it's time to judge these facts and that do it in a businesslike way and apply the law. That involves, a lot of times, making tough choices.

The tough choices I'm going to ask you to make at the end of the case is to say "I didn't like what I saw, but the Government has not proven its case beyond a reasonable doubt."

For general tips on opening statements and sample language about the presumption of innocence and burden of proof, see Ch. 2.

[§§13:62-13:69 Reserved]

B. Cross-Examination of Key Witnesses

1. Cross-examination of Detective

§13:70 Key Points

Child porn cases are emotionally charged affairs. These emotions can affect the investigator just as they can the parties involved. Here, I cross Detective Amy, the primary detective in Randy's child porn production, distribution and possession case.

Here, the primary detective was not a computer forensics investigator. Rather, she got assigned to the case to investigate whether some of the child pornography images were of Minor A, who was alleged to be Randy's daughter. Since Randy's daughter was a small child, she did not have any testimony to offer herself. Additionally, the child's face was not visible in the images. Instead, the image depicted the legs and vagina of a small, female child, with an adult hand spreading the vaginal lips. The child appeared to be laying on a baby blanket.

The child's mother testified that Minor A was her daughter, and that she was pictured sitting on a blanket given to her by her Aunt as a baby shower gift.

What I attempted to do with the detective was cross her on bias. This was an emotional case. On our theory, the detective crossed the line from logical and dispassionate officer to advocate for the child's mother. I attempted here to establish the detective's bias as a method for undermining her credibility.

For more tips on cross examining police officers, see Ch.2

§13:71 Background and Training

Q. You've been a detective for, I think you said, 28 years; is that right?
A. I've been a police officer with Sanford for 28 years.
Q. A detective for how long?
A. Since 1988, so about 23, about 23 years.
Q. 23 years as a detective in Sanford?
A. Yes.
Q. And before you became a detective, you went through a lot of police officer training; is that right?
A. Yes.
Q. Part of what you were trained in was how to write police reports; isn't that right?
A. Correct.
Q. And you would agree with me that it's important that police reports are accurate?
A. Yes.
Q. And thorough?
A. Yes.
Q. And you issued reports in this case?
A. Yes, I did.
Q. And you believed those reports to be accurate?

A. Yes.
Q. And thorough?
A. Yes.
Q. You received additional training in writing police reports once you became a detective; didn't you?
A. Yes.
Q. And you also received training as a detective in investigations; right?
A. Correct.
Q. And investigation skills?
A. Yes.
Q. And techniques?
A. Yes.

§13:72   Work on the Case

Q. And you took every step you could think of to investigate this case; didn't you?
A. Yes.
Q. You wanted the investigation to be thorough?
A. Correct.
Q. You executed multiple search warrants in this case; right?
A. Yes.
Q. You took evidence?
A. Yes.
Q. You took photographs of Randy's hands that were just shown; right?
A. Right.
Q. You seized computers?
A. Right.
Q. You had them analyzed?
A. Yes.

§13:73   Box In Questions to Set the Stage for Bias

Let's box the Detective in for later use. We want to establish here that the detective agrees that it is a function of her job to be fair. We want her to agree that she should not abuse her power by locking someone up without cause. We will use this later to our advantage.

Q. It's also very important as a detective that you get the facts of the case right; isn't that correct?
A. Yes.
Q. You need to look at all the angles; isn't that right?
A. Yes.
Q. And you need to consider other possible suspects sometimes when you're investigating a crime; isn't that right?
A. Yes.
Q. You also need to examine the evidence in an unbiased fashion; right?
A. Yes.
Q. And you need to draw independent conclusions from that evidence; right?
A. Right.
Q. Even though sometimes people might be saying things that are different to you than your conclusions; right?
A. Yes.
Q. It's important to be unbiased as you view the evidence; is that right?
A. Yes.
Q. And you need to be fair in how you treat people; right?
A. Yes.
Q. Did you take an oath, detective?
A. Yes, I did.
Q. And that oath was you would be fair in viewing the evidence; wasn't it?

A. Yes.

Q. And it's dangerous if you have a detective investigating a crime who is not fair in viewing the evidence; would you agree with that?

A. Yes.

Q. It's wrong to lock somebody up in jail unnecessarily; would you agree with that?

A. I agree with that.

Q. It's wrong not to give someone due process of law as a detective; would you agree with that?

A. Yes, I do.

Q. And it's dangerous for a detective to be biased against a particular person because it can impact the way they view the evidence; isn't that right?

A. Yes, that is right.

§13:74   Establishing Bias Against Defendant

This was a Federal case, but there were also State charges pending. I convinced the State court to give me all correspondence between the detective and Amanda, which included emails between them. I used those emails to craft this cross-examination.

Q. Would you agree with me that you grew to have a relationship with Amanda that's different than you have with most witnesses in the cases you investigate?

A. No.

Q. You don't agree that your relationship with Amanda is different than your normal relationship with other witnesses?

A. No. If I have a big case, a lot of times I communicate a lot with the witnesses.

Q. Okay. So you normally give them advice about child custody matters?

A. No, I don't.

Q. But you did here?

A. I did.

Q. Do you normally give them advice about when the father of their child should talk to or see their child; do you normally do that?

A. I do not normally do that.

Q. But you did here?

A. Yes.

Q. Do you normally write letters to judges in the context of child custody cases advocating on behalf of a witness in a case?

A. No.

Q. So, your relationship with Amanda was different, wasn't it?

A. I don't know I would say that.

Q. And you told Amanda here you were going to work hard so you could get Randy; right?

A. To get what?

Q. To get Randy; right?

A. I'm going to work hard to get whoever is responsible for the case.

Q. Do you believe you were unemotional about this case?

A. It is an emotional case.

Q. So you were emotional?

A. There were times during the case that were emotional.

Now that we've established that she was emotional about the case, how far would she go to advocate for Amanda and lock up Randy?

Q. When you were getting ready to have him arrested in this case, you planned to have that arrest coincide with the Thanksgiving holiday; didn't you?

A. No.

Q. You had an arrest warrant for him in November of 2010; didn't you?

A. Yes.

Q. And you actually waited an extra day to execute the warrant; didn't you?

A. We waited until we knew he would be out of the house.

Q. You waited the extra day with the hopes that he would be locked up over the long holiday weekend; isn't that correct?

A. No. We waited the extra day because of safety considerations.

Q. You were communicating with Amanda at this time; weren't you?

A. Yes.

Q. Via e-mail primarily?

A. Yes, a lot of e-mails.

Q. I'm going to show you what's been marked for identification as Defendant's Exhibit 5. Isn't it true that this is an e-mail from you to Amanda and you told her: "We're going to wait until tomorrow to do the arrest and hopefully he will spend the weekend in jail" didn't you write that?

A. Yes, I did write that.

Q. So you agree with me that you were hoping that he would spend the weekend in jail if you waited to execute this arrest warrant; right?

A. Well, the reason that we were waiting to execute the warrant—

Q. Yes or no, you were hoping he would spend the weekend in jail, ma'am?

A. Yes.

Q. And you knew the courts were going to be closed for the Thanksgiving holiday; right?

A. Yes.

Q. And the Friday following the Thanksgiving holiday; right?

A. No, I didn't know about the Friday following.

Q. You didn't know that?

A. No.

Q. And you wanted him to spend the weekend in jail; right?

A. Yes.

Q. And you didn't want him to have access to the setting of bail; right?

A. I believe he could have been bailed.

Q. He couldn't get in front of a judge though; right?

A. I—

Q. You don't know?

A. That I don't know.

Q. And you trusted Amanda with this secret about the arrest warrant; right?

A. Yes.

Q. And that arrest warrant was sealed by the court until it was executed; wasn't it?

A. I don't believe it was sealed, no.

Q. The arrest warrant was published in open court before it was executed?

A. I don't believe it was sealed. I don't—

Q. You told Amanda to keep it a secret anyway; right?

A. I did tell her, yeah, not to tell Randy.

§13:75   Casting Doubt on Identification of Randy's Finger in Photo

In this case, Amanda identified the adult finger spreading the child's labia in the Minor A photos as Randy's finger. I want to cast doubt on that identification to cast doubt on production. To do so, I focus on the government's methodology for generating the photos, which I discovered during a Motion to Suppress.

Q. Okay. I'm going to show you three photographs. First one has been admitted as Government's Exhibit 18A; do you recognize that photograph?

A. Yes.

Q. The second one has been admitted as Government's Exhibit 18B; do you recognize that photograph?

A. Yes.

Q. And third has been admitted in Government's Exhibit 18C; do you recognize that photograph?

A. Yes.

Q. So for reference, we have been calling those three photographs the Minor A photographs.

A. Okay. I wasn't aware of that.

Q. No, that's fine. Related to those Minor A photographs, do you agree with me that in the course of your investigation that you became concerned that you would not be able to identify who the child in those photographs was?

A. Yes.

Q. And that was because you didn't observe any identifying markings on the child; right?

A. Correct.

Q. You agree with me that you revealed confidential information to Amanda?

A. It's possible that I did, yes.

Q. You agree with me that you shared things with Amanda that you shouldn't have?

A. I think I probably did throughout some of the investigation because we were e-mailing back and forth.

Q. You would also agree with me, I believe, that you were desperate to prove that Randy produced images of child pornography; right?

A. Well, I did say that in an interview.

Q. You said that you were desperate to show that he made his own photos; right?

A. I did say that in an interview.

Q. And you meant it when you said it, didn't you?

A. Yes.

Q. Now, not including the Minor A photographs, there were 314 images of child pornography seized; is that right?

A. Yes.

Q. And 200 of those images were identified through the NCMEC; is that correct?

A. Yes.

Q. So there were 114 images, not including Minor A, that were unidentified images?

A. Correct.

Q. And those three images were the ones that you were desperate to prove that Randy had created?

A. Yes. Three of those images were out of this 114, yes.

Q. And you leaned on Amanda to help with that identification?

A. I don't know if I leaned on her. I don't understand.

Q. You used her to help to identify those images?

A. Yes, I did have to show her the images.

Q. You knew she was vulnerable?

A. Yes.

Q. You knew she'd have an emotional reaction?

A. I—yes.

Q. You expected it?

A. I expected if she recognized anything that she would have an emotional reaction, yes.

Q. And did you—to try to get an identification of the finger and the one image in which a finger appears, did you isolate the finger and just show her that finger?

A. No, I showed her the full picture.

Q. You photographed Randy's hands?

A. My supervisor did, yes.

Q. 17 photos were taken?

A. I believe so.

Q. They were taken from a variety of different angles?

A. Yes.

Q. Taken from a variety of different poses?

A. Yes.

Q. They were measured?

A. Yes, they were measured.

Q. Close-up pictures of the hands were taken?

A. Yes.

Q. And you took those pictures of Randy's hand to try to match them to the finger that appeared in the photograph of Minor A in which a finger appears; correct?

A. The finger and then the hand.

Q. Well—

A. Or the fingers.

Q. Showing you what's been admitted as Government's Exhibit 18A, I see a finger in the middle of that picture; is that what you see?

A. Yes.

Q. Do you see another finger?

A. No.

Q. So you took the pictures of Randy's hands to try to match them to that finger in that photograph 18A; right?

A. Yes.

Q. And then you or someone associated with your office sent those photographs, those 17 photographs of Randy's hands, down to a forensic consultant; didn't you?

A. We sent the photographs that you have in your hand along with, I think, some of the photographs. I don't believe we sent them all.

Q. Okay. You sent the best ones?

A. Yes.

Q. And you sent them down to try to get that person to make a match between the hands or the finger in Government's Exhibit 18A that I just showed you and the pictures you took; right?

A. Yes.

Q. And that person was somebody you thought was qualified to make a match?

A. Yes.

Q. And that person was unable to make a comparison between the hands in the photograph of Minor A and the photos of Randy's hand that your office took; right?

A. Yes, because of the quality—

THE COURT: The answer is yes.

A. Yes.

MR. ZERILLO: Thank you. Move to strike the remaining answer other than that answer "yes."

THE COURT: The answer to the question was yes. The jury will disregard any remaining answer.

Q. To clarify, the expert you sent the photos to was unable to make a comparison between the hands in the photograph of Minor A and the pictures of Randy's hands your office took, right?

A. Yes.

Q. And you sent these photos to this consultant, I'm calling him, after the time that Amanda had come in and made the identification in your office; right?

A. I believe so.

§13:76   Casting Doubt on Identification of Background in Photo

The same goes for the background of the Minor A images, which was a baby blanket. Amanda identified it as her daughter's blanket to further bolster her identification of the child in the Minor A photographs as her daughter. This baby blanket was a real problem for us at trial. Amanda's Aunt made it and gave it to Amanda at a baby shower. The Aunt testified at trial and identified the blanket. The blanket appeared to be a quilt, but on further investigation, I learned it was actually a pattern imprinted on the fabric. So my goal here is to establish that the individual squares are just a single sheet of fabric that could have been sold thousands of times all over the world.

Q. You also analyzed the blanket as it appears in the Minor A photos; right?

A. Yes.

Q. And you did everything you could to establish that the blanket in the Minor A photo was the same as the blanket that Amanda's aunt had given her?

A. Everything I could, yes.

Q. You spoke to Amanda's aunt?

A. Yes.

Q. That's Jane?

A. Yes.

Q. You asked her about where she got the pattern for the blanket; right?

A. The material, yes.

Q. And she told you she got it at Marden's?

A. Marden's, yes.

Q. And did you call Marden's to see if they had that material?

A. No.

Q. Did you do any sort of investigation into whether or not material with that pattern was sold elsewhere in Maine?

A. No.

Q. Elsewhere in the United States?

A. I assumed that it's been sold all over the United States.

Q. And maybe the world?

A. Yes.

Q. Do you know where it was from, where the material was from?

A. I don't.

Q. You don't know what country it was manufactured in?

A. No, I don't.

Q. You took custody of what you thought was the blanket itself?

A. Yes.

Q. Amanda gave it to you?

A. Yes. When I first saw the blanket, I thought it was an individual square—

Q. Okay, I'm going to ask you about that, but you wanted to try to match them; right?

A. Yes.

Q. From looking at Minor A photos, you thought there were individual squares on the blanket; right?

A. Correct.

Q. Meaning that it looked like each square had been sewn or quilted by hand, right?

A. Yes.

Q. And your thought was these were individual squares like a quilt?

A. Like a quilt, yes.

Q. And, in fact, the blanket you received from Amanda is not made up of individual squares? *

A. Correct.

Q. This is from one sheet of fabric, so to speak?

A. Correct.

Q. And you were hoping that if these were individual squares, that would help you compare the blanket?

A. Yes.

Q. And in part, the reason you were hoping for that was because of the way the squares could then be arranged in different patterns; right?

A. Correct.

Q. And you concluded eventually that it was possible that it was the same blanket, but that it was possible it wasn't the same blanket as in the Minor A photos; right?

A. Correct.

[§§13:77-13:89 Reserved]

2. Cross-Examination of Forensic Law Enforcement Officer

§13:90   My Approach

Now let's look at a cross-examination of a computer forensic law enforcement officer. These are the guys with training in computer crimes, and often no other real computer experience, who are called on to tie everything together for the factfinder. Here is a cross of Secret Service Special Agent Franks from Randy's case.

I've included a cross examination of the forensic law enforcement officer in a case where I did not have an expert testifying at trial. I did not have an expert because the several experts I hired all agreed with this law enforcement officer's conclusions. You may be stuck in a position like we were in this case where you need to soldier on and make your best effort at a good cross examination.

When I am stuck in that position, as I was here, I simply attack the methodology. This requires thought and research, but can nearly always be done.

Here, I attempt to attack Agent Franks methodology in an effort to muddy the waters.

For tips on cross-examining experts, see Ch. 2.

§13:91   Anonymity of Internet

We begin by looking at his examination of an internet relay chat program. An internet relay chat is simply a program designed to allow a group chat among a group of users. Generally, the chats also feature the ability for users to privately message each other. Here, the prosecution claimed that Randy was on certain chats, offering to trade images of his daughter for other child pornography.

The point here in part is to establish how anonymous and open the internet can be. Anyone can claim to be anyone else, as long as that user name is available. Here, the forensic investigator discovered a screen name for various chat rooms that they said Randy was accessing to trade child pornography. That screen name was "Shadow."

Q.   Good afternoon. You talked about investigating or examining an Internet relay chat program; correct?
A.   Correct.
Q.   And that was the mIRC program; right?
A.   Yes.
Q.   And you found that the mIRC program was used to access various chat rooms; right?
A.   Correct.
Q.   And you've discussed some of those chat rooms with the jury today, yes?
A.   Yes.
Q.   And you examined the log files of those chats; right?
A.   Yes.
Q.   And you found that all of the chat logs were for the same day in March of 2009; correct?
A.   Correct.
Q.   And that's March 4th of 2009; isn't that right?
A.   Correct.
Q.   You didn't find any chat logs from before March 4th of 2009?
A.   I did not.
Q.   You didn't find any chat logs from after March 4th of 2009?
A.   I did not.
Q.   Your computer forensic examination does not tell you who logged in to the mIRC on March 4, 2009; right?
A.   That's correct.
Q.   And whoever that was, based on what you were able to find, they never logged in again; is that right?
A.   As far as we can tell.
Q.   And when you create a user account for the mIRC, you can put any user name you want into that program; isn't that right?
A.   Correct.
Q.   And the user name could be a nickname, for example?
A.   Yes.
Q.   And if you want to put somebody else's name into the mIRC, you could?
A.   Yes.
Q.   And the same goes, I suppose, for the Imagesrc.ru website; correct?
A.   Correct.
Q.   That's the Russian website you were talking about?
A.   Correct.
Q.   And so when somebody creates a user account for that website, they can put anything they want in as a user name; correct?
A.   Correct.
Q.   And the website doesn't do any verification for the user who creates a user name on the Imagesrc.ru website?
A.   Not that I know of.
Q.   And then anyone can post to Imagesrc.ru if they create an account; right?
A.   They have to create their credentials, but they would post under the—whatever name they created, yes.
Q.   They can post under something other than their true name?
A.   Yes.
Q.   Related to the Yahoo accounts, anyone can setup a Yahoo e-mail account name without verification, that's true too; isn't it?

A. Yes.
Q. So I could setup the name AgentFrank@Yahoo.com and Yahoo wouldn't verify that I am, in fact, Agent Frank; correct?
A. That's correct.

§13:92 Education and Experience

Don't assume these guys have computer science degrees. Usually, their forensic experience is just from a course by their agency.

Q. You say you have a college degree, I believe, Special Agent Frank; is that right?
A. Yes.
Q. And I didn't hear you say what that degree was in.
A. Criminal justice.
Q. You don't have a computer science degree; is that right?
A. No, I don't.
Q. All the computer forensics training you have was done through the Secret Service, right?
A. That's correct.
Q. You haven't done any forensic computer work not through the Secret Service, right?
A. That's right.

§13:93 CP Free Devices Owned by Defendant

Make sure to mention devices your client had on which no child porn was found.

Q. So I just want to be clear, there were no images of child pornography found on the Randy's iPhone; is that right?
A. I didn't examine the iPhone, but I'm familiar with it and nothing was found.
Q. There were no images of child pornography found on the desktop or tower computer; isn't that correct?
A. There were no images of child pornography.
Q. And the only images were found on the Sony Vaio laptop; isn't that right?
A. Yes.
Q. I mean images of child pornography; is that correct?
A. That's correct.
Q. So the images that had been put into exhibits so far that the Assistant U.S. Attorney showed you, those all came from the Sony Vaio laptop; correct?
A. Correct.

§13:94 Alternative Suspects

Here, because Randy has a difficult case, I want to open up any potential questions I can for the jury. Jurors are often skeptical of computers. They are skeptical of people accessing computers maliciously. So, whenever possible, I try to interject this alternative theory that someone else used the device as their child porn storage bin.

Q. Now, Randy's house had a wireless home Internet network; is that right?
A. I'm not sure.
Q. You don't know whether their network was secured or unsecured?
A. I don't know.
Q. If there is an unsecured network, if they were operating on an unsecured network, that means that anyone can access that network who is within proximity of it; is that correct?
A. They could have accessed the network, correct.
Q. And I assume then that you're not aware whether or not Randy's home network had a firewall?
A. I don't know.
Q. What is a firewall?
A. A firewall can be set up to block access or to monitor people that are connecting over a network.

Q. And you don't know whether there was a firewall installed there?
A. No, I don't know.
Q. Do you know whether or not there was a password on that Sony Vaio laptop computer?
A. I don't know.
Q. Now, I think I heard you say towards the end of the direct-examination that you did not find viruses on the Sony Vaio laptop; is that right?
A. No. The prosecutor asked me if there was antivirus installed. He didn't ask me if there were viruses on it.
Q. Okay. So were there any viruses on the laptop?
A. It's not something that we routinely look for so I can't say.
Q. So you don't know if there were viruses?
A. No.
Q. You don't know if there were Trojan Horses?
A. No.
Q. What is a Trojan Horse?
A. A Trojan Horse is a type of virus that generally allows a user, a malicious user, to get access to a system. So if I were a hacker or network intruder, I would setup Trojan Horses and ship them out in a variety of fashions, either via email or social networking sites in hopes that somebody selects the file and downloads it and installs it on their system and then that virus allows me, the malicious user, to have access to that particular system.
Q. Legitimate software exist in the market today that allow you to access your system remotely; isn't that correct?
A. Yes. They are called remote administrators.
Q. And there are also Trojan Horses that can allow malicious users, as you say, to access computers maliciously; right?
A. Yes.
Q. And Trojan Horse programs, like the legitimate programs, can upload and download file directories?
A. Yes.
Q. It gives essentially—some of those programs, some of those Trojan Horse programs can give that malicious user remote access to that computer; isn't that right?
A. Yes.
Q. And so with that correct mechanism, with that mechanism we're talking about of the Trojan Horse, that person, that malicious user, can control the computer without the actual computer owner knowing it; is that right?
A. Yes.
Q. And those Trojan Horse files are hidden; right?
A. Generally, yes.
Q. They are designed to be secretive; correct?
A. Some of them are, some of them aren't.
Q. But most of them are designed to be secretive?
A. Yes.
Q. Malicious users don't like to draw attention to themselves.
A. No.

§13:95 Image Sharing Within Yahoo Messenger

Many CP cases are forensically less complicated than this one. I use this case, however, to illustrate how it can be useful to find out how this stuff works. Here, we are dealing with this Agent's claims, from his testing, that he can determine when an image was shared within the Yahoo Messenger system. The agent testified on direct that his testing of the Yahoo Messenger system allowed him to determine when a file had been shared over the system. Therefore, he claimed to be able to establish that Randy had distributed the Minor A images through Yahoo Messenger.

Q. You've talked about the Yahoo Messenger photo sharing system; correct?
A. Yes.
Q. And you did tests on that system to discover how it operates; correct?
A. Yes.
Q. The Yahoo Messenger photo sharing directory on the Sony Vaio laptop, Randy did not create that directory; correct?
A. That is correct.

Q. That's because the photo sharing directory is created automatically; is that right?

A. It's created by user interaction so those directories wouldn't be created if a user, an end user, didn't perform some function. In this instance, an end user would upload or, you know, tell a software that I want to share a particular file or distribute a file and then on the back end, if it wants to receive a file, that user would also have to indicate to the software that it wants—that the user wants to receive it. When the files are being shared, the user would access an area that they are aware that there is images—

Q. What I'm asking you is if the photo sharing directory is created automatically; is that correct?

A. It's created by the software, yes.

Q. It does not require user intervention to create the photo sharing directory?

A. Well, it does require the user to tell the software that the user wants to, you know, distribute or receive images.

Q. Okay. So let's say that I sign up for Yahoo Messenger photo sharing, that directory is automatically created; isn't that right?

A. If the Yahoo Messenger directory is created?

Q. Yes.

A. I'm not sure when the photo sharing directory gets created.

Q. You don't understand how that process works?

A. No.

Q. And the directory doesn't contain the name Shadow anywhere in the directory; does it?

A. No.

Q. So that Yahoo photo sharing directory doesn't contain information related to a specific Yahoo account?

A. No.

Q. And the Yahoo file names and folder names in that photo sharing directory are randomly generated; is that right?

A. It appears random to me. I'm sure it means something to somebody, yes.

Q. Okay, but as far as you can tell, it appears random?

A. Yes.

Q. And those are generated independent of any account name; is that right?

A. Correct.

Q. So you tested Yahoo Messenger?

A. Yes.

Q. And you were testing specifically the photo sharing aspect of Yahoo Messenger?

A. Yes.

Q. And as you said, when somebody uses Yahoo Messenger, they can use it to send or receive photos; right?

A. Yes.

Q. If the person is receiving photos, they get an invitation to receive the photos; is that right?

A. Yes.

Q. If the invitation is accepted, then the photos are downloaded to the receiving computer; right?

A. Yes.

Q. The user of the receiving computer does not know what those photos are when they accept the sharing invitation; isn't that correct?

A. Correct.

Q. The receiving computer doesn't display the photos before the invitation is accepted; right?

A. Correct.

Q. So if I wanted to share pictures with you, I could send an invitation to you and you wouldn't be able to view the contents of the pictures until you accepted the invitation and downloaded the photos; isn't that right?

A. Correct.

Q. And then after you accept that invitation and download the photos, then you'd see those photos for the first time at that point; right?

A. Just a point of clarification, the images appear in Yahoo Messenger and they're technically on your system, the underscore m file is on your system, but to say they are downloaded, the user has an opportunity to view them within Yahoo Messenger and then if that user wants to save them, which is how I define downloading, then they would be stored and there the user tells those images to be stored.

Q. What about for the purpose of somebody sending photos by invitation. When you accept the invitation, that's when the photos are seen for the first time; isn't it?

A. Yes.

Q. And then when they're seen and downloaded, they're automatically saved in the photo sharing directory; isn't that correct?

A. Yes.

§ 13:96   Hidden Yahoo Directory

Now I want to weave in the fact that the Yahoo! directory is hidden by the system itself.

Q. And that Yahoo photo sharing directory that those files are automatically saved in is a hidden directory; isn't that right?

A. Correct.

Q. It's not visible to the computer user?

A. Generally no.

Q. In fact, it's hidden by the Windows operating system; isn't it?

A. Yes.

Q. So if you accept a photo in Yahoo photo sharing, you don't know what it is until you get it and then the program saves it whether you want it or not; is that correct?

A. Correct.

Q. And it saves it in a place that you as the user of the computer cannot see; right?

A. Generally, yes.

Q. So if you're browsing through your hard drive looking at files, you do not see those photos at all; isn't that true?

A. It would be very difficult for the user to find them.

Q. And it would, in fact, require that the user set his or her computer to show hidden files and folders; correct?

A. Correct.

Q. And can you tell if Amanda's Sony Vaio laptop, was set to show hidden files and folders?

A. Not that I'm aware of.

Q. When you start up the computer, when Yahoo Messenger is installed, Yahoo Messenger starts up automatically by default; right?

A. Yes.

Q. And when Yahoo Messenger starts up, it logs into the messaging services by default as well; isn't that true?

A. I'm not sure about the default settings.

Q. Because you—you weren't able to discover what the default settings were; correct?

A. Yes, because the program was uninstalled, a lot of those settings were missing.

Q. Okay, but you know the default settings of Yahoo Messenger?

A. I don't remember.

Q. And so when those photos are shared, as we said they're shared in a hidden area of the system or saved in a hidden area of the system; correct?

A. Correct.

Q. And most users would not be aware of the fact that those files have been created; correct?

A. Correct.

Q. And you were not even aware that the files were being created until you did some testing; correct?

A. Correct.

Q. Regarding the pictures that I've been referring to as Minor A, do you know what I mean when I say that?

A. Yes, I do.

Q. Just to clarify what I'm talking about in the Minor A photographs, I'm talking about the images admitted as 18A, B and C; do you understand that? Government's Exhibit 18A, B and C.

A. Yes, I understand.

Q. From your examination, you can't tell who was using that Sony Vaio laptop computer at the time those images were shared; is that right?

A. The only information we found was the circumstantial information about the syncing of the iPod or the iPhone, excuse me, in the computer within an hour, roughly an hour, but anything closer than that, no.

Q. So what you know is that the computer was on at the time they were shared and Yahoo Messenger was running; right?

A. Yes.

Q. Anyone with access to that computer could have sent or received messages using Yahoo Messenger; right?

A. Correct.

Q. And those pictures of Minor A were not located on the hard drive anywhere else other than in the Yahoo photo sharing folder?

A. That's correct.

Q. The photos of Minor A could have come from a thumb drive; isn't that right?

A. And then shared, if that's what you're saying.

Q. Yes.

A. They could have come from an external device and then shared, yes.

Q. That would be true for any of the images shared using Yahoo Messenger; right?

A. Yes.

§13:97   Other Evidence

Now I want to know if he found any other evidence related to the images other than his bogus testing.

Link Files

Q. Do you know what a link file is?

A. Yes.

Q. It's a shortcut that's created when a file is opened for viewing; is that right?

A. Correct.

Q. And those link files are created automatically; is that correct?

A. Yes.

Q. And if a file was opened by a user on the computer, on a certain computer, there would be a link file that would tell you it was opened; is that correct?

A. Yes.

Q. Did you look at the link files on the hard drive of the Sony Vaio laptop?

A. Yes.

Q. And when you examined the link files on the Sony Vaio laptop, did you find any evidence that any of the files shared using Yahoo Messenger were ever opened on the hard drive of the computer?

A. Because I don't know the original file names of the files that were shared, it's very difficult to determine what the file may have been.

Q. So the answer to that question is no.

A. No.

Metadata

Here, the Minor A images were allegedly produced by my client. As a result, you would expect to see metadata. Metadata or EXIF data is data embedded in the image itself. Since there was no metadata of the Minor A images, I want to point that out to the jury.

Q. So in your September 25, 2011, report, you discussed looking at the images of Minor A; right?

A. Yes.

Q. And one of the things you were looking for was metadata regarding the images of Minor A; isn't that right?

A. Yes.

Q. Now, metadata in regard to pictures is information that's contained inside the image itself; isn't that right?

A. Yes.

Q. It can provide the date the image was taken; right?

A. Yes.

Q. The time the image was taken?

A. Yes.

Q. The camera or the phone that took the image?

A. Yes.

Q. The brand of camera that took the image?

A. Sometimes, yes.

Q. The dates and times that the image was saved to a computer?

A. Some of them have the date and time. That wouldn't be in the metadata. That was the date and time that was created on whenever device took that image.

Q. And that image data is also called EXIF data; is that right?

A. Yes.

Q. And there were no markers on the images of Minor A that have been admitted to this jury indicating the source of those images; isn't that right?

A. That's correct.

Q. There was no metadata or EXIF data for the images of Minor A whatsoever; was there?

A. That's correct.

Q. And so there is no date or time when the images of Minor A were taken in the photographs?

A. Correct.

Q. There is no information about the camera used to take those images?

A. Correct.

§13:98   Back to Yahoo Messenger Testing

Now I'm looping back to his testing, which I argue is flawed. As you will see, he uses the wrong version of the software when testing it, creating an opportunity for attack.

Q. Okay. So you did your testing of Yahoo Messenger; right?

A. Yes.

Q. And you've created a virtual computer system to test the way Windows Vista Business and Yahoo Messenger interrelated; isn't that right?

A. Yes.

Q. And Windows Vista Business is the operating system that was found on Randy's computer?

A. I believe he was using Windows Vista Business.

Q. Did you use Windows Vista Business?

A. I didn't use Windows Vista Business. I used Home.

Q. Why didn't you use Windows Vista Business when you were—

A. Because I didn't have a license for Business.

Q. You could have purchased a license for Business; couldn't you?

A. I could have, but there's no disparity between the two. In my opinion, it is negligible. Business has some enhanced features, but the background of the operating system functions the same.

Q. And your opinion is not based on any testing related to any differences between the way Yahoo Messenger operates with Windows Vista Business or with Windows Vista Home; is that correct?

A. That's correct.

Q. Alright. So you found that if the photos—and what you did test, you found that if the photos are shared then we have this unique file structure that we talked about already; right?

A. Correct.

Q. And that doesn't require, as we said, anything other than the user of that computer share photos; right?

A. Correct.

Q. And your knowledge as to the dynamics of this photo sharing are based on this test; right?

A. Correct.

Q. So you would agree with me if your testing is in some way flawed, that the results could be inaccurate; right?

A. Yes.

Q. And if your testing was incomplete, the results could be inaccurate; right?

A. Yes.

Q. You tested a variety of different versions of Yahoo Messenger; isn't that right?

A. Yes.

Q. You originally tested Version 2152; is that right?

A. I thought I did, yes.

Q. You reported that incorrectly?

A. Yes.

Q. You actually tested Version 2160; isn't that right?

A. Correct.

Q. Now, Version 2152 and Version 2160 gave you different results; didn't they?

A. Yes, they did.

Q. But you also tested Version 2018; didn't you?

A. Yes, I did.

Q. And did that give you different results from Version 2152?

A. It did, yes.

Q. And did it give you different results than Version 2160?

A. It was much more consistent with 2160. I wouldn't be able to tell you if there were any differences. I don't remember differences between 2018 and 2160.

Q. What version was installed on the Sony Vaio laptop of Yahoo Messenger photo sharing?

A. Because the program was uninstalled and there was wiping of data, we were not able to tell.

Q. So you tested three versions of Yahoo Messenger?

A. Yes.

Q. Without knowing what version of Yahoo Messenger was running on the Sony Vaio laptop; right?

A. What we did was go to the Internet and found some old applications that were available at roughly the time that—

THE COURT: That's a yes or no.

A. Yes. I'm sorry, sir?

MR. ZERILLO: Let me ask it again. Thank you, Your Honor.

BY MR. ZERILLO:

Q. You tested three versions of Yahoo Messenger without knowing which version was running on the Sony Vaio computer; correct?

A. Yes.

Q. And each of those three versions of Yahoo Messenger behaved slightly differently in their interrelation with Windows Vista Home; right?

A. Correct.

Q. And you don't know for certain which version was running on the Sony Vaio laptop; do you?

A. That's correct.

At this point what I am hoping to do is illustrate problems with the government's distribution theory based on the testing done. Remember, the government argument as to distribution was based entirely on their expert, his testing and his conclusion that he could determine when a file was shared through Yahoo Messenger. If his theory is incorrect, the government cannot establish that there was distribution.

Q. All right, so you tested exchanging files using Yahoo Messenger; right?

A. Yes.

Q. And at first—would you agree with me that you had trouble in your testing determining which way files were going based on what you saw?

A. Yes.

Q. What does it mean when a file is uploaded?

A. I would qualify it as distributed or sent by a user.

Q. Sent from something that user has on their computer?

A. Correct.

Q. And what does it mean when a file is downloaded?

A. A user receives a file or image.

Q. And you had some real concerns as you investigated this that you couldn't determine whether files were being uploaded from the Sony Vaio laptop or downloaded to it, right?

A. Until I conducted further testing, correct.

Q. So as of September of this past year, for example, you had done an investigation; right?

A. Yes.

Q. And at that time you couldn't determine whether files that you were seeing were being uploaded or downloaded; right?

A. That's correct.

Q. And we've already said, I believe, but I'll cover just in case briefly, that when a file is shared that Yahoo assigns it a unique name?

A. Yes.

Q. And you're not sure why that naming convention is what it is?

A. Correct.

Q. So if I sent you a photo called "Tim" through Yahoo photo sharing and you opened it in the Yahoo photo sharing directory, it would have a unique name, not "Tim," right?

A. Correct.

Q. And if you opened that file, that "Tim" file, and you didn't save it on the hard drive, it would automatically be saved in that Yahoo Messenger photo sharing directory; correct?

A. Correct.

Q. So eventually, you reached the conclusion that when the—I want to make sure I'm stating it properly—when a file only has an m.jpeg that all you know is that that file was shared; correct?

A. Correct.

Q. It could have been uploaded or downloaded?

A. Correct.

Q. But when a file is uploaded, you concluded from your testing that there was a t.jpeg and an m.jpeg file; isn't that correct?

A. Correct.

Q. So if a file is in the Yahoo photo sharing directory with only an m.jpeg file, it means that it was only a downloaded file; correct?

A. If it only has an m, it may mean it was either sent or received and the program crashed. The directories are only there if the program crashes.

Q. Okay. We're going to talk about crashing, but assuming no crash, if there is only an m file, that means the image was downloaded only; correct?

A. Correct.

Q. And if there is an m and a t file that means—m.jpeg and t.jpeg file, under your testing, that means that the photo was or the image was uploaded; correct?

A. Correct.

Q. And that was the sole way in which you were able to determine whether files in this case were uploaded or downloaded only; correct?

A. Correct.

Q. These conclusions you have come to are based entirely on the testing you've described?

A. Yes.

Q. There are two dates in which you found that images of Minor A were shared; right?

A. Yes.

Q. Now, when I say shared, I'm including files that—I mean uploaded and/or downloaded; is that how you mean it when you say shared?

A. Yes.

Q. Those two dates are April 27, 2009, and May 11, 2009; isn't that correct?

A. Yes.

Q. So on April 27, 2009, there are three images of Minor A that are shared using Yahoo Messenger; correct?

A. Correct.

Q. Two of the Minor A images shared on 4/27/09 are only m.jpeg files; right?

A. Yes.

Q. Those files, those two files did not have the t.jpeg file?

A. Correct.

Q. The only one with the m.jpeg file and the t.jpeg file is the file with that long name of letters and numbers that ends with qxtq; correct?

A. I believe so.

Q. Okay. So I'm showing you an admitted exhibit, that's Government's Exhibit 18A; do you see that there?

A. Yes.

Q. And the file name ending in this case was qxtq; is that correct?

A. That's correct.

Q. And this was the file on April 27, 2009, that had the m.jpeg and the t.jpeg; correct?

A. Correct.

Q. The other two files that were shared and were admitted into evidence only had the m.jpeg; is that correct?

A. Correct.

Q. Now, on May 11, 2009, which is the other sharing date of the Minor A images; correct?

A. Correct.

Q. You found three files of Minor A were shared; right?

A. Yes.

Q. And all three files had the m.jpeg only; correct?

A. Correct.

Q. None had the t.jpeg?

A. Correct.

Q. Your determination was that the three files on May 11th were shared, but you couldn't determine if the images were uploaded or downloaded; correct?

A. Correct.

Q. And the same goes for the files on April 27, 2009, except for the qxtq file; correct?

A. Yes, correct.

Q. You would agree with me that the evidence that you've presented related to file sharing of the images of Minor A does not relate to file creation; is that correct?

A. Correct. The information we have is just about Yahoo photo sharing.

Q. And you don't have evidence as to creation dates, as you said before, of the images of Minor A; correct?

A. That's correct.

Q. And what you're saying is that he uploaded—that Randy uploaded at least one file, the qxtq file, on April 27, 2009; correct?

A. Correct.

Q. And that's the only one of the Minor A images that you can determine in your testing that was, in your view, certainly uploaded; right?

A. Correct.

Q. I want to illustrate that a little further.

MR. ZERILLO: May I have permission to approach?

THE COURT: Yes.

BY MR. ZERILLO:

Q. I'll hand you a blank file and I want you to imagine that—I want you to imagine that you and I are using Yahoo Messenger photo sharing; okay? And I'm going to send you an invitation to this file that is called sunset. Now, you take that file and once you open it, what is—is there an m file on the computer then, m.jpeg?

A. Yes.

Q. There is no m and t.jpeg file then?

A. Not on my computer, no.

Q. And if you then decide you don't like my picture of the sunset and you just get rid of it, then the m.jpeg file of the picture that I sent you will be downloaded into the Yahoo photo sharing directory automatically; correct?

A. It still stays there, yes.

Q. And that stays there as soon as you open that file; right?

A. Correct.

Q. If you take that file and you send it to the Assistant U.S. Attorney Mrs. Pros, at that point there is an m.jpeg and a t.jpeg on your computer; correct?

A. Correct.

Q. But you did not create the image of the sunset picture; correct?

A. That's correct.

Q. I would have created it; right?

A. Yes.

§13:99   Crash Reports

Here's some more cross of this Agent related to his recovery of crash reports and its interrelation to his conclusions.

Q. All right. Let's talk about some of these crash reports. Your contention is that, if I've heard you correctly, that on 4/27/2009, that the two images of Minor A that only are m.jpeg files—well, they didn't have the t.jpeg files, two had just m files only; right?

A. Correct.

Q. And you're saying that sometimes that the system crashes before the t.jpeg file is created; right?

A. Correct.

Q. And when a computer crash occurs, a crash report is generated; right?

A. Not necessarily for Yahoo Messenger.

Q. But crash reports are generated often when computer crashes occur; right?

A. Yes.

Q. The image that I showed you previously, the qxpq file, Government's Exhibit 18A, was created on 4/27/2009 at 11:41 a.m.; correct?

A. Yes.

Q. And there were crash reports for that day, 4/27/2009; isn't that correct?

A. Yes.

Q. But the crash report that you have for that day were at 11:01 a.m.; right?

A. Correct.

Q. And the files that were shared, the one that had the m.jpeg and the t.jpeg and the two other files without the t.jpeg were shared between 11:41 a.m. and 11:44 a.m. on April 27th, 2009; isn't that correct?

A. Correct.

Q. You have absolutely no evidence from crash reports that there was a termination of the computer operation during the time you say that the Minor A photographs were shared; isn't that right?

A. That's correct.

Q. You have only the crash reports from 40 minutes earlier; correct?

A. Those crash reports were from an iPhone application, not from the computer.

Q. But that's the only crash report you have; right?

A. That is correct.

Q. So you're speculating that there was a crash on 4/27/2009; correct?

A. The research supports it.

Q. You don't have any crash reports to support it; correct?

A. That's correct.

Q. Now, on May 11, 2009, we said there were three images of Minor A shared; correct?

A. Yes, correct.

Q. They are only m.jpeg files; right?

A. I believe so.

Q. So we don't know whether they were merely downloaded; is that correct?

A. Correct.

Q. And there are no crash reports associated with the May 11th, 2009, sharing; isn't that right?

A. That's correct.

I filed a motion *in limine* to exclude the file names of the empty files. I lost. The Government, of course, raised the file names multiple times in their case, because they are so prejudicial to my client. So, I want to counter by having their "expert" agree that the file name is indicative of nothing, really.

Q. You reviewed the registry keys for the names of the files that you did not recover? (I.e., the files that were not recovered, but had titles indicative of child pornography.)

A. Correct.

Q. You searched the allocated space of all the computers in this case for those files?

A. Yes.

Q. And you didn't find them?
A. I did not find them.
Q. You searched the unallocated space of all the computers involved with those files; right?
A. I can't determine the content of the file from the file name so we recovered files, but I don't know what the file name would be.
Q. You didn't recover the images other than in the Yahoo Messenger photo sharing directory?
A. Correct.
Q. And you carved those files; right?
A. From Yahoo Messenger?
Q. No. You carved—for GigaTribe, for example, files?
A. Yes.
Q. And the WinRAR files, you carved them; correct?
A. There was no way that I carved that because all I can recover from those things would be the file names, so I couldn't recover the files.
Q. So carving though, because I should define that, is a special recovery method that can find files that are deleted; right?
A. Correct. I would only find the file itself with no idea what the name of that file would have been.
Q. Okay, and sometimes in carving, you can recover a portion of the file, it may not be a complete file; is that right?
A. Correct.
Q. The names of the files are created by the person who puts them out there on the Internet; isn't that right?
A. That is correct.
Q. It doesn't mean that the names of the files actually contain child pornography?
A. That is correct.
Q. You don't know what the files we discussed, leaving aside the Yahoo photo sharing files, actually contain for the other file names you discussed on direct; do you?

(There were lots of files names with nothing in them with titles indicative of child pornography; the prosecution used that to show that Randy had child pornography on his computer and probably later erased it.)

A. That is correct.
Q. And there are all sorts of different types of images out there on the Internet that purport to be child pornography but are not; isn't that true?
A. That is correct.
Q. There are morphed images; right?
A. Yes.
Q. There are cartoon images; right?
A. Correct.
Q. So what's in the file name does not necessarily mean that's what was actually in the file; is that fair to say?
A. That's correct.
Q. And you don't know what was contained in the GigaTribe or WinRAR files we discussed; right?
A. No.

Details are important. You need to work to find favorable details. There is no way around it. Here I discovered in my research an interesting, and perhaps inconsequential fact, but maybe not. The user name Shadow registered himself as living in Cleveland, Ohio. This is the user name for the chat programs previously discussed. I noticed that the Shadow user information sheet that was used when signing up the name also had a space for a zip code. When I looked up the zip code, it actually was a Cleveland zip code. So, my client in Maine would have had to look up a Cleveland zip code when setting up the Shadow account. This seemed like a lot of extra effort to me.

Q. Showing you what's already been admitted as Government's Exhibit 29C, you see what appears to be a black and white box with a black and white photo in there; is that what we call an avatar?
A. Yes.
Q. And this was the avatar you discovered for Shadow?
A. Yes.
Q. That box contained in Government's Exhibit 29C is the avatar you were discussing?

A. Yes.
Q. You received evidence from Yahoo that the Shadow account was from Cleveland, Ohio?
A. Well, looking at the Yahoo subpoena that was given to Detective Local and passed on to me, the city indicated was Cleveland, Ohio, but you could have just have put in anything.
Q. Anyone could have made up a location?
A. Yes.
Q. And Randy never lived in Cleveland as far as you know.
A. As far as I know.
Q. You don't have any info that he's ever been there.
A. No, but like I say—
Q. Did you check the zip code there that was included?
A. No.
Q. You didn't see that this zip code was actually a Cleveland, Ohio zip code?
A. No.
Q. You didn't check that?
A. Nope.
MR. ZERILLO: That's all I have. Thank you.

[§§13:100-13:109 Reserved]

C. Closing Argument

§13:110 My Approach

Randy has a difficult case. Amanda, the mother of the child allegedly in the Minor A photos, has identified the child depicted as hers. She identified the fingers spreading the vagina of the child as Randy's fingers. She identified the baby blanket as having been given to her by her Aunt Jane.

In such a case, I am just trying to poke holes in the government's case. I hope to poke enough holes to deflate the case. Here, I do that by attacking the viability of the evidence compared to the reasonable doubt standard.

In this sample closing, I attack the underpinning of the government's testing of Yahoo Messenger. I try to do this not only through argument related to the facts of the case, but also through stories to elucidate our point of view.

For closing argument tips, see Ch. 2.

§13:111 Sample Closing Argument

Thank you, Your Honor. May it please the Court.

Imagine you took a cat and put it in a box and then for whatever reason (it doesn't make any difference to this story) you put a mouse in the same box. Then you tied up the box, left for a half hour and came back. You look in the box and you see one happy cat and no mouse. That would be circumstantial evidence that the cat ate the mouse.

Now, let's do that again. You put the cat in the box, you put the mouse in the box, you put the lid on, you put the string on, you tie it up, leave for a half hour, you come back, you open the box and there is a cat but no mouse. You look carefully in the box and in the corner you see a tiny hole, just big enough for a mouse to fit through. That hole is reasonable doubt. And there are holes all through the Government's case here that I want to talk to you about.

There are three crimes charged here: sexual exploitation of a child, possession of child pornography, distribution of child pornography. Each crime needs to be proven beyond a reasonable doubt, and each element of each crime needs to be proven beyond a reasonable doubt.

As I told you in opening, this case is about whether or not the forensic evidence fits. This is like Humpty Dumpty. Remember Humpty Dumpty? All the king's horses and all the king's men couldn't put Humpty Dumpty back together again. You remember that from when you were a kid. Well, this is the same story, a man trying to put a computer back together again, but he cannot do it. All the king's horses and all the king's men can't do it.

This slide illustrates a variety of different types of proof that don't make it beyond a reasonable doubt. If you suspect that Randy is guilty, you must acquit him. If you think he's probably guilty, you must acquit him. If you think he is likely guilty, you must acquit him. That is not proof beyond a reasonable doubt. All of the images of child pornography were found in the same space. The Yahoo Messenger photo sharing directory on the laptop. So, let me clarify.

You've heard about a bunch of computers. You heard about a desktop or a tower. No child pornography found. You've heard about an old Gateway laptop, no child pornography found. An iphone. No child pornography found. The issues are on a Sony Vaio laptop computer that was Amanda's laptop and within that computer, there was one specific space in which the child pornography was found. That space is the Yahoo Messenger photo sharing directory.

One of the things that the Government needs to prove beyond a reasonable doubt is that Randy knew that there was child pornography within that Yahoo Messenger photo sharing directory. I disagree with what Mrs. Pros just said to you. An act is done knowingly if it's done without mistake or accident or for another innocent reason. The Government has told you that the photo sharing directory is a hidden directory. All these files are in a secret and hidden directory. How could Randy have knowingly possessed them?

I'll tell you again, they are in a secret and hidden directory and yet, the Government wants you to find beyond a reasonable doubt that he knowingly possessed them. If he wiped the hard drive because he was trying to hide child pornography, he didn't do a very good job because he didn't wipe this hidden directory which would go to show that he didn't know it was there; right? He couldn't have wiped the Yahoo Messenger photo sharing section because he didn't know it was there to begin with!

The Government wants to have it both ways. Randy is really smart with computers, the Government is telling you, but he doesn't wipe the portion of the hard drive in which the child pornography is contained. On one hand, the Government says Randy is leading a double life. He is on the computer, he is Shadow, they tell you. On the other hand, he's on vacation with a laptop full of child pornography going through airport security and that laptop doesn't even have a password on it. On one hand, he's hiding things in a secret directory on the laptop and on the other hand, the laptop is not password protected, as I said, and his wireless network is unsecured.

That is not proof beyond a reasonable doubt. There is another explanation for why he is going through airports with an un-password protected computer full of child pornography and not attempting to hide it. That reason is he does not have consciousness of guilt. He doesn't think he needs a password to protect it. He doesn't think he is under any threat when going through an airport with this child pornography allegedly on his wife's computer.

Now, I have to talk to you about Special Agent Frank's testing. There is such a thing as computer science, but the testing that was done here is not it.

The entire explanation that the prosecutor just gave to you is based upon Special Agent Frank's testing. It all comes down to Agent Frank's testing, but we know he tested three different versions of Yahoo Messenger photo sharing. Each of them behaved differently when he tested them. He doesn't know which version of Yahoo Messenger photo sharing was on the Sony computer. So if each of the three versions behaved differently, he could be testing versions that were never on that computer and he can't tell you what was on that computer.

He also used a Home version of Windows Vista instead of the Business version of Windows Vista, which the operating system actually on the laptop. Again, he can't tell you how that would have changed the operation of this computer, especially as it interrelates with Yahoo Messenger. Remember, this is the foundation upon which the entire Government case is built. He agreed with me, if the testing is incomplete or it's wrong, his theory could be flawed. Here the conclusions are flawed.

So imagine with me for a second you're on an airplane and people are jumping out of the airplane. It seems crazy to me to jump out of a perfectly good airplane, but some people are thrill seekers. Maybe some of you have done it.

So you're jumping out of an airplane and somebody hands you a backpack with a parachute to put on and you say "Did you check this parachute? I want to make sure before I jump out." And they reply to you, "Well, I didn't check that one, but I checked one just like it." Even the biggest thrill seeker on this jury wouldn't jump.

Would you jump? Would you trust your own life to that? Because this is what we are dealing with here, Randy's life. Would you trust your own life with that chute?

If Frank is right, and I have significant argument that he is not, but if he's right, let's just deal with this theoretically. Remember, Frank testified that assuming no crash, if there is only an m.jpeg file, that means the image was downloaded only; And if there is an m and a t.jpeg file that means that the image was uploaded. Only one of the Minor A images, Government's 18A has an m.jpeg file and a t.jpeg file. Yet Frank says that Randy shared three images of Minor A on May 11, 2009, but none of them have the t.jpeg file and the two other images that he claims that Randy shared on April 27th do not have the t.jpeg file.

How could this be? Randy is downloading images from the Internet that the Government is contending he created. That makes no sense, right? And I would submit to you that Special Agent Frank in his testing, he might be a very nice man, but he was taking shortcuts.

He didn't test the right versions of Yahoo Messenger, he didn't test the right versions of Windows Vista and that might be good enough for some Government work, but it's not good enough beyond a reasonable doubt. So the Government's explanation is there's a computer crash and this t.jpeg file didn't have time to be created and because the computer crashed, there was no t file. This is complete speculation. This is not proof beyond a reasonable doubt. There is one crash report we have from April 27, 2009, and it is from 40 minutes before the first file Special Agent Frank tells you was sent on the 10th.

How about May 11th, there must have been a crash report then; right? May 11th, 2009, the time the Government says Randy sent three more images, zero, no crash reports. Okay, so now the explanation for that is "Well, Yahoo Messenger doesn't generate crash reports." They're guessing; aren't they? They can't ask you to guess, folks. This is too important. They can't ask you to guess. They can't ask you to base your decision, each of your individual votes, on guesswork.

Because there's no crash, the Government's explanation is nonsensical and again, if you believe Special Agent Frank's testimony, Randy would be downloading the images, the very images of Minor A that they're claiming he created!

I want to remind you of one more thing because I don't want you to forget it. There is no metadata. I know that sounds like a word out of like "Transformers" or, you know, "The Avengers" or something like that. It sounds like a cartoon character.

But what it means is, if I take a picture as I said in opening, there is embedded data in that picture from the camera or the phone I used. There is no metadata for the Minor A images. So as a result, again, they are asking you to guess and to speculate.

They are also making an argument that the presence of the m and the t files or lack thereof may explain Count 1, the production count, the sexual exploitation of a minor, but that doesn't work either.

We have Aunt Jane who made a baby blanket and gave it to Amanda for Randy and Amanda's daughter. She wasn't asked to identify the blanket in the images of Minor A, Government's 18A, B and C and she can't identify the blanket in them beyond a reasonable doubt as the blanket she made. She can't establish how many identical blankets were sold. In fact, I asked Detective Amy right there and by the way, I'll say that, you know, sometimes juries think the defense is the only side that has a stake in the outcome of these cases, that's not true. I think you can see that by some of these people who are present in the courtroom today like Detective Amy right over there. Anyway, Detective Amy said look, I don't know where this fabric came from. I didn't look into it. It could be sold anywhere worldwide. I don't know how many there are out there. It just doesn't get beyond a reasonable doubt.

Amanda is an upset mom who is shown images and led to believe that those images might be of her daughter. Look, I know many of you have children. You lose objectivity when it comes to them. You lose objectivity and she was upset and she may have said what she thought, but it's not proof beyond a reasonable doubt.

So they get—they take the photographs that they believe are of Minor A and that has no special significance, by the way. We're calling them Minor A because I have to call them something. The Government pulled these three photographs out of the 314 that they found. That's all that means and then they started to focus on them. That's all that means, but they start to focus on them and in the one photograph in which the one finger appears, Amanda gives this identification. Then they take 17 photographs of Randy's hand. I didn't take those pictures, Detective Amy's office took them. She took pictures of his hands, close-ups, posed in different directions, measured, all sorts of different things and they took them down to a consultant and the consultant could not match the hands in the photos that they took to the finger in the photo of the Minor A photograph, Government's Exhibit 18A.

That's the only finger that appears in any of those photographs. How can they expect you to find its Randy's finger beyond a reasonable doubt then when their expert consultant cannot? How do they expect you to do it? Amanda said she's certain that's his finger and the Government has made this argument that she was married to him for 11 years and that means she is certain that this finger is his finger. But Detective Amy has told you she's desperate to prove that Randy produced these images and Amanda believes she had been shown images of child pornography of her daughter. She's upset, she's angry with Randy, I think that's clear and she wants to protect her daughter. That does not make for an identification beyond a reasonable doubt.

Now, additionally, it is after Amanda's identification of the finger that the Government agent decided to hire an expert consultant to make the identification, to make the match and as you know, the consultant couldn't do it. But yet they want you to. The Government's resources are virtually unlimited. Have they provided you an expert on this issue? No. They want you to do it with that blurry one finger when their expert consultant couldn't.

And why try to hire the consultant after Amanda made the identification? If Amanda's identification was so rock-solid, why bother?

Because they didn't think Amanda's identification was good enough. And it isn't.

I noted earlier that the m and the t.jpeg files do not prove sexual exploitation of a minor, which is production. I started to do this in my examination of Special Agent Frank with a file I handed him. I send a picture of a sunset to Special Agent Frank and Special Agent Frank receives the picture, he doesn't see what's in the photograph or doesn't see the images until he accepts it. He accepts it and the moment he accepts it, it's downloaded immediately into that Yahoo Messenger photo sharing directory and at that time, that's when the m.jpeg file is in this secret hidden directory.

Then let's say that he takes that photo of a sunset and he sends it off to the Assistant U.S. Attorney. At that point, he has the m and the t file in his Yahoo Messenger directory, but that does not mean that he created the image of the sunset. I created it. So I just want to make that point because there is a distinction here and it's been muddied, I think.

A few more things to clear up. Myrtle Beach, South Carolina, May 20th and 21st, 2009. They are claiming during that period of time Randy was sharing images of child pornography in his hotel room with Amanda and with his daughter. I asked what time the last sharing was. According to Special Agent Frank, it was 6:17 a.m. on May 21st, 2009. You can question as the jury whether or not that seems reasonable, whether or not that adds up. As Randy told you when he testified, they did have the Internet connection, but it was very spotty and they had tried to upload vacation images on Facebook.

Also, I want to talk to you a little bit about viruses and Trojan Horses that were brought up. What Special Agent Frank told you and, first of all, you have to consider the source, was that he had to admit that Trojan files and viruses can be put as malware or malicious ware on somebody's computer and they're hidden. Those viruses can be used to control somebody's desktop and control the hard drive and control what goes on in the computer and it can be done remotely. There are legitimate programs, software programs, you hear advertisements all the time that can do that, but it can be done maliciously as well. To say that it's impossible then to upload or download images of child pornography remotely just isn't true because Special Agent Frank told you it could be done. He told you. He had to acknowledge that it could be done.

Then the Government tried to clean that up by asking well, have you ever seen it? Well, he's a special agent with the Secret Service. Consider the source. He said he'd never seen it, but you have to know that it can be done and that it can be done remotely. It just can be. Now, there was wiping of software on portions of the hard drive of the computer and I also asked him could that have wiped off any viruses or Trojan Horses and he said that it could, so that's something else you need to consider.

Of course, then, the Government has argued well, why would anyone ever do that? Why? Because this stuff is illegal. Somebody who is collecting child pornography may not want it on their computer and so if they have an ability to use somebody else's computer as a storage bin, that might be why they want to do it. That might be why. To stay out of this court might be why. Detective Amy, she's desperate to find images of child pornography created by Randy. She's got an extreme level of bias against Randy. I would submit to you, frankly, that even though she's the lead detective on this case that you should disregard her testimony because of this bias. She had to admit on cross, even though she did not want to, that she was planning on holding an arrest warrant and, in fact, did so she could try to get him to spend the weekend in jail. That is not a detective being impartial about the evidence and this is dangerous, folks. This is very, very dangerous stuff.

I always wonder if you think there must have been some precipitous event that caused Randy to be here in front of you, but when the Government trains its microscope on you, they rarely move it. They trained their microscope on Randy and then Special Agent Frank got involved and they said okay, now find out everything you can find out about this guy. But it doesn't make it right and it certainly doesn't make it right beyond a reasonable doubt.

You heard from Randy. I'm not saying that there aren't warts in his testimony because he did admit to you that he hid the laptop on that day and he did admit to you he said things to Amanda that he regrets. You have to consider the amount of pressure that this person is under. Have any one of you ever been under this amount of pressure? Your entire life at stake based upon this one incident? Your job, your child, your wife, your freedom?

Look, at the time this is allegedly going on, Randy is working full-time second shift, working on nuclear subs at the Portsmouth Naval Shipyard. Then he's got a full course load during the day pre-med at UNE. He denies any knowledge of child pornography on that computer. He denies that he distributed child pornography. He denies that he created images of child pornography using his daughter and he was asked, I don't know if you could see it, before I asked. He got upset on the stand when I showed him those images of 18A, B, C and D and he's a pretty reserved guy. I don't know that I've ever seen him that upset.

He said to one of us, either the Assistant U.S. Attorney or myself, I frankly can't remember, but one of us asked him if he thought those images were of his daughter. He said "I hope not". I think that's a really honest answer. He hopes that those images aren't his daughter, but he told you unequivocally, unequivocally that he didn't do it. That reminds me yet again of the burden of proof. Because as it says in the instructions, the presumption of innocence alone is sufficient to acquit him if the burden of proof is not met. Remember, this is not a contest as to who has the most witness, okay? It's not a contest who has the most exhibits.

This is the last time I get to address you and as I said to you in the opening, there are very subtle things that happen in the course of a trial that reflect the Government's burden of proof. One of those things is the fact that their counsel table is closer to you than my counsel table. One of the things is that the Government gets to have a rebuttal at the end, gets to have the last word. When you think about that, you have to remember that's because of the heavy burden of proof that they bear, not because of anything else.

I would suggest that they are going to appeal to your emotions in rebuttal. I've not seen Mrs. Pros PowerPoint, but if she has one in rebuttal, there will be an image of Randy's daughter on there. She is a cute kid and I suggest to you that your job, as the Judge told you in his instruction, is to not make your opinion on personal likes, dislikes, opinions, prejudice or sympathy. You have a duty to be businesslike, and I like the term "duty." As the judge said, it's your duty to acquit Randy, if you have a reasonable doubt, and that's in those instructions that you have as well.

Sometimes people think the role of a jury is to find somebody innocent or find them guilty. I think that the way they do it in Scotland actually is more representative of what your real role is. They have a three verdict system in Scotland. In Scotland, you can return a vote of guilty, not guilty or not proven. Here, in the U.S. what we do is we fold not proven into not guilty. So your vote for not guilty can actually be that you think Randy is innocent of this or it can just mean that the Government has not proven the charges beyond a reasonable doubt.

You know, I took—I'll show this to the Assistant U.S. Attorney and the Court. I just took this print it off my wall in my office before I came here. It's a Norman Rockwell painting. It's called "The Hold Out" and I like it. I've had it for years. It shows a woman seated in the jury room. I note that there are 11 men and those 11 men are arguing with her and she is sitting there in a pose that to me suggests that she has her mind made up and she is not going to change it no matter what those 11 men do. I like to think that she's sitting there applying the very hard and very difficult concept of reasonable doubt to a criminal jury.

When you're in the jury room, you may have people attempt to persuade you to come to their side, but what I ask of you is that while you listen to people, you do not give up your own strongly held belief related to reasonable doubt because that is important. While you should listen to people, you should not give up your own individual belief and I would ask you to apply that belief to reasonable doubt.

Since I already covered Scotland, I'll travel to another part of the British Isles now. Let's go to Ireland. The reasonable doubt concept comes from Ireland. The English are credited with it, but it actually really emanates from Ireland. Of course, the Irish had to apply English law for a long period of time when they were occupied by England which meant that they had to sit on juries of their clansmen. Even though they had their own laws, they had to apply English law and in those days, there were no women allowed on the jury; it was just men.

Eventually, the Irish revolted against this and they said look, if we have to apply the law, it has to be strong enough that it's beyond a reasonable doubt. Now, I point that out because you've heard the term reasonable doubt a million times, and you probably think it's just for Randy. It's not just for Randy. It's for you too. Because eventually, somewhere down the line in your lives, you'll think about this case.

As you walk by a mirror and you'll look at yourself in the mirror and you'll want to know that anything you did, if you convicted him, is beyond a reasonable doubt. You'll want to know that you applied that standard correctly. Applying the standard correctly here would mean that you acquit him.

You know, when you walk into this courtroom, we all watch you. We try to read your minds. When you walk in the next time, if any one of you passes a glance this way, you're going to see me with my hand on Randy's shoulder. I want you to keep that image in your mind as you deliberate. When you walk back out, my hand will be on his shoulder. And we're going to be hoping that you are applying the standard of beyond a reasonable doubt appropriately. And that you saw the hole in the back of the box where the mouse once was for what it is. A sign that this case has not been proven beyond a reasonable doubt.

Thank you.

[§§13:112-13:119 Reserved]

VI.   FEDERAL SENTENCING ISSUES

§13:120   Many Defendants Will Face Sentencing

Let's face it, a lot of defendants in federal child porn cases face sentencing. This federal sentencing is extremely complicated and extremely harsh. While sentencing has not been the focus of this book, if you handle federal child porn cases you will be handling sentencings. I would be remiss not to address it.

I am hoping that in the intervening time between my writing of this book and you reading it that Congress will do something about these sentencing schemes. They are completely and totally unfair and, without reason, unduly harsh. For now and the foreseeable future, however, we have to deal with them.

During the time I drafted this chapter, the United States Sentencing Commission issued its report to Congress. In doing so, the Commission essentially rejected the structure of the child pornography guidelines in non-production cases.

While not much new seems to have happened while these Commission recommendations have languished in the legislature, there does seem to be some small movement. For example, January 8, 2016, the Commission proposed an amendment to Congress to require that the Government establish knowing distribution of images over a P2P network before a defendant receives a distribution enhancement. As of this writing, the Fifth, Tenth and Eleventh Circuits, and to some degree the Eighth Circuit, do not require knowledge of distribution for the enhancement to apply. If adopted, this revision would require proof that the defendant "knowingly distributed" the contraband over a P2P network.

The changes are certainly coming slowly, but they are coming. Here's hoping that by the time this Chapter is in print, that Congress has acted to abrogate or outright destroy these unfair and corrupted guidelines.

§13:121   Guidelines for Possession

Let's use our case examples here to examine the federal sentencing guidelines. Let's start with Parker's Guideline calculations. Parker, as you may remember from the scenario at the beginning of the chapter (see §13:04) was charged with possession of child pornography.

Guideline Provision	Description	Offense Level
USSG §2G2.2	Base Offense Level for possession child pornography	18
USSG §2G2.2(b)(2)	Minors under 12 enhancement	+2
USSG §2G2.2(b)(4)	Sadistic and masochistic images enhancement	+4
USSG §2G2.2(b)(6)	Use of Computer Enhancement	+2
USSG §2G2.2(b)(7)(D)	More than 600 Images Enhancement	+5
USSG §3E1.1(a-b)	Acceptance of Responsibility	−3
Criminal Hx Category 1	**Total**	**Level 27 (78-97 months)**

Parker's Guideline calculations capture the very common Guideline provisions. The minors under 12 enhancement, the use of a computer enhancement are present in almost every child porn possession case I have.

Sadistic and masochistic images enhancements are also very common. USSG §2G2.2(b)(4) is the relevant Guideline, which states:

> If the offense involved material that portrays sadistic or masochistic conduct or other depictions of violence, increase by 4 levels.

The circuit courts have generally found that penetration by an adult male on a child is inherently sadistic. *See United States v. Hoey*, 508 F.3d 687 (1st Cir. 2007) *citing cases omitted*. This is a significant 4 level enhancement that you will frequently find in your cases.

§13:122   Guidelines for Sexual Exploitation (i.e., Production and Distribution)

So, let's watch the already crazy Guidelines fly out of control in a sexual exploitation of a minor charge for Randy's case.

Guideline Provision	Description	Offense Level
USSG §2G2.1	Base Offense Level for sexual exploitation of a minor	32
USSG §2G2.1(b)(1)(A)	Minors under 12 enhancement	+4
USSG §2G2.1(b)(2)(A)	Sexual contact	+2
USSG §2G2.1(b)(3)	Distribution of images	+2
USSG §2G2.1(b)(5)	Parent of minor	+2
USSG §3C1.1	Obstruction of justice	+2
Criminal Hx Category 1	**Total**	**Level 44 (off the chart)**

You will note that Randy's production offense literally flies off the Sentencing Guideline Table, which only goes to a Level 43 (which is life).

You can see how easily the enhancements can lead to a long sentence and why I said at the beginning of this Chapter that these offenses can be punished more than cold blooded murder in many cases.

§13:123   Argue that The Guidelines Should Not Apply to Possession Cases

Once again, I hope that by the time you read this book, that these Guidelines will have been rolled back as the Sentencing Commission suggests. Until then, make sure to argue that the Sentencing Guidelines should not apply at sentencing.

Kimbrough v. United States, 552 U.S. 85 (2007). a case involving the disparity between the sentencing guidelines for crack and powder cocaine, effectively opens the door to arguments that the Sentencing Guidelines should not be followed when sentencing your child porn client. In *Kimbrough*, the Supreme Court held that it is not "an abuse of discretion for a district court to conclude when sentencing a particular defendant that the crack/powder disparity yields a sentence 'greater than necessary' to achieve §3553(a)'s purposes, even in a mine-run case."

Kimbrough notes that the Sentencing Commission varied from its usual practice of employing an "empirical approach based on data about past sentencing practices." Instead it adopted the "weight-driven scheme" used in the 1986 Anti-Drug Abuse Act, maintaining the 100-to-1 quantity ratio throughout the drug table. The Court also pointed out that the Commission had subsequently criticized the ratio, quoting from the various Commission reports to Congress on the issue, and discussed Congress's previous responses to Commission actions and recommendations.

Kimbrough holds that "while the Guidelines are no longer binding, closer review may be in order when the sentencing judge varies from the Guidelines based solely on the judge's view that the Guidelines range 'fails properly to reflect §3553(a) considerations' even in a mine-run case." The Court held that the crack cocaine guidelines, however, "do not exemplify the Commission's exercise of its characteristic institutional role" and noted the Commission's opinion that the crack cocaine guidelines produce "disproportionately harsh sanctions." In light of this, "it would not be an abuse of discretion for a district court to conclude when sentencing a particular defendant that the crack/powder disparity yields a sentence 'greater than necessary' to achieve §3553(a)'s purposes, even in a mine-run case." *Id.*

Circuit Courts around the country have been attacking the efficacy of the Guidelines in child pornography cases for several years now. *See e.g., U.S. v. Rodriguez*, 527 F.3d 221 (1st Cir. 2008); *U.S. v. Henderson*, 649 F.3d 955 (9th Cir. 2011); *U.S. v. Grober*, 624 F.3d 592 (3d Cir. 2010); *U.S. v. Dorvee*, 616 F.3d 174 (2d Cir. 2010). As the Second Circuit noted: "The irony of the court's conclusion in this area…[is] that the Guidelines actually punish some forms of direct sexual contact with minors *more leniently* than possession or distribution of child pornography." *U.S. v. Tutty*, 612 F.3d 128 (2d Cir. 2010).

The Circuit Court's rejection of the Guidelines in child pornography cases is not a random act of kindness directed toward the most despised defendants in the criminal justice system. Rather, it results from the hue and cry among scholars and judges who have deconstructed the harsh child pornography Guidelines. *See e.g.* Troy Stabenow, AFD, "*Deconstructing the Myth of Careful Study: A Primer on the Flawed Progression of the Child Pornography Guidelines*" (rev. Jan. 1, 2009) [online at *http://www.fd.org/docs/Select-Topics---sentencing/child-porn-july-revision. pdf*]. I don't know of any Circuit Court decision that has opined that USSG §2G2.2 is sound or comports with the overarching sentencing mandate of §3553(a).

As the Court of Appeals for the Ninth Circuit stated, "an unduly deferential application of §2G2.2 will lead to the vast majority of offenders being sentenced to near the maximum statutory term." *United States v. Henderson*, 649 F.3d 955, 965 (9th Cir. 2011) *citations omitted*. As Judge Merritt of the Sixth Circuit Court of Appeals observed in a dissenting opinion, "The problem in this pornography case is the gross disparity, inequality, and unfairness that exists in sentencing generally, but even more so in these child pornography viewer cases. It illustrates the continued sad dependence of federal judges on a harsh sentencing grid created by a distant bureaucracy." *United States v. Overmyer*, 663 F.3d 862, 866 (6th Cir. Dec. 20, 2011) (Merritt, J., dissenting).

The February 27, 2013 FCPO Report, representing a decade-long study of child pornography sentencing, including a special coding project for child pornography offenses beginning in 2010, disavows the entire structure of child pornography sentencing for non-production cases.[12] The Commission found:

> The current sentencing scheme in §2G2.2 places a disproportionate emphasis on outdated measures of culpability regarding offenders' collecting behavior and insufficient emphasis on offenders' community involvement and sexual dangerousness. As a result, penalty ranges are too severe for some offenders and too lenient for other offenders. The guideline thus should be revised to more fully account for these … factors and thereby provide for more proportionate punishments.

FCPO at xviii (emphasis added).

In light of these inherent flaws in USSG §2G2.2, the Commission recognizes and is concerned by "widespread inconsistent application" of USSG §2G2.2 *Id.* at xxi. Accordingly, the Commission is "request[ing] Congress to provide the Commission with authority to *revise the entire guideline structure.*" *Id.* at 322 (emphasis added).

The FCPO Report concludes:

> As illustrated by this report, child pornography offenses result in substantial and indelible harm to the children who are victimized by both production and non-production offenses. However, there is a growing belief among many interested parties that the existing sentencing scheme in non-production cases fails to distinguish adequately among offenders based on their degrees of culpability and dangerousness. Numerous stakeholders—including the Department of Justice, the federal defender community, and the Criminal Law Committee of the Judicial Conference of the United States Courts — have urged the Commission and Congress to revise the non-production sentencing scheme to better reflect the growing body of knowledge about offense and offender characteristics and to better account for offenders' varying degrees of culpability and dangerousness.

> The Commission believes that the current non-production guideline warrants revision in view of its outdated and disproportionate enhancements related to offenders' collecting behavior as well as its failure to account fully for some offenders' involvement in child pornography communities and sexually dangerous behavior. The current guideline produces overly severe sentencing ranges for some offenders, unduly

---

[12] The FCPO Report indicates that the Commission will be monitoring production cases.

lenient ranges for other offenders, and widespread inconsistent application. A revised guideline…would better promote proportionate sentences and reflect the statutory purposes of sentencing. Such a revised guideline, together with a statutory structure that aligns the penalties for receipt and possession, would reduce much of the unwarranted sentencing disparity that currently exists.

FCPO at Ch. 12, pp. 330-331.

In light of what the Commission has said in its FCPO Report, you should argue that the child pornography possession guidelines have now been effectively deleted. *See United States v. Booker*, 543 U.S. 220, 263 (2005) ("The Sentencing Commission will continue to collect and study appellate court decision-making. It will continue to modify its Guidelines in light of what it learns, thereby encouraging what it finds to be better sentencing practices.").

§13:124 Argue That the Guidelines Should Not Be Applied to Your Client

The purpose of the Guidelines is for the Court to impose a sentence sufficient, but not greater than necessary, to comply with the purposes of sentencing. The United States Supreme Court has summarized factors those purposes as the "(1) offense and offender characteristics; (2) the need for a sentence to reflect the basic aims of sentencing, namely (a) just punishment (retribution), (b) deterrence, (c) incapacitation, (d) rehabilitation; (3) the sentences legally available; (4) the Sentencing Guidelines; (5) Sentencing Commission policy statements; (6) the need to avoid unwarranted disparities; and (7) the need for restitution." *Rita v. United States,* 127 S.Ct. 2456, 2463 (2007).

Always argue that your client should not be given a Guideline sentence here because of the above factors. There are always reasons to argue a §3553 variance. Surely your client has done something right in their life.

Remember, however, issuing a variant sentence for the above reasons does not relieve the Court of its obligation to consider your argument that the Guidelines should not apply for the reasons discussed above. *See, e.g., United States v. Zauner*, 688 F.3d 426, 431 (8th Cir. 2012) (Bright, J., concurring) ("And where the guidelines are out of line and increasingly disregarded by sentencing judges, the mere fact of a downward departure should not insulate the district court's sentence from any type of meaningful review.").

§13:125 FORM 13-70 Sentencing Memorandum—Child Pornography

UNITED STATES DISTRICT COURT
FOR THE DISTRICT OF MAINE

UNITED STATES OF AMERICA,	)	
	)	
Plaintiff,	)	
	)	
v.	)	Criminal No. 2:12-210-001
	)	
PHILLIP KLIENT,	)	
Defendant.	)	

DEFENDANT'S SENTENCING MEMORANDUM

Defendant Phillip Klient, pursuant to Federal Rule of Criminal Procedure 32(b)(2), and by and through Undersigned Counsel, respectfully submits the following Sentencing Memorandum, and states as follows:

I. FACTUAL BACKGROUND

A.   Case Background

Mr. Klient took his laptop computer to the Best Buy store in South Portland, Maine for repair. He was attempting to retrieve personal family photos that had become corrupted. While repairing the computer, a Best Buy technician recovered child pornography and alerted law enforcement.

On January 24, 2013, Mr. Klient pleaded guilty to an Information charging him with possession of 600 or more images of child pornography. He did not contest bail, and was remanded into custody, where he has remained ever since.

B. Defendant's Personal Information

Mr. Klient is 64 years old. He was born on February 3, 1948 in Long Bow, New Mexico. Prior to his incarceration, he lived in Sleepy Hollow, Maine in retirement with his wife, Cynthia Klient.

According to the Social Security Administration, Mr. Klient has a life expectancy of 17.92 years. *See www.ssa. gove/oact/Stats/table4c6.html.* This estimate does not take into account the obvious negative effects of incarceration.

C. Defendant's Criminal History

Defendant has no criminal convictions.

D. Family Background

Mr. Klient has an active and involved family. He is one of five children. His Father, Gregory, is deceased. His Mother, Dolly, splits her time each year between Florida and Maine. Mr. Klient's four siblings are all living, and several of them live in Maine.

Mr. Klient married his wife, Cynthia in 1974. They have a child, Amelia, who is an adult and resides in Maine. She is close to her Father.

Despite his incarceration and the imposition of horrendous charges, Mr. Klient's family has supported him. There is no indication that such support will diminish in the future. Letters of support from Mr. Klient's family and friends will be provided to the Court in advance of sentencing.

E. Defendant's Employment History

Probation Officer Varner noted that the Defendant had a strong employment history, and is now retired. *See Amended PSIR.* There can be no doubt that Mr. Klient is a hard worker who strived for achievement. He retired from Boeing in Washington in 2010, and moved back to Maine, where he grew up, with his Wife, Cynthia.

F. Defendant's Educational History

Mr. Klient is a 1967 graduate of Algonquin High School. He went on to Bowdoin College, where he graduated in 1971. He received a Master's Degree in Business Administration from Cal State Fresno in 1981.

G. Defendant's Mental Health History

Mr. Klient has no mental health history, save the treatment he sought for the instant offense. During his time of release, for nearly approximately a year and a half, Mr. Klient treated with Dr. Jonas Bourne in South Portland, Maine. Dr. Bourne found Mr. Klient to present a very low risk of re-offending, and a very low risk of danger to the community. It is anticipated that Dr. Bourne will be available to speak at Mr. Klient's sentencing.

ARGUMENT

In imposing sentence, a district court must consider the factors set forth in 18 U.S.C. §3553(a). These factors include: (1) the nature and circumstances of the offense and the history and characteristics of the defendant; (2) the need for the sentence imposed—(A) to reflect the seriousness of the offense, to promote respect for the law, and to provide just punishment for the offense; (B) to afford adequate deterrence to criminal conduct; (C) to protect the public from further crimes of the defendant; and (D) to provide the defendant with needed educational or vocational training, medical care, or other correctional treatment in the most effective manner; (3) the kinds of sentences available; (4) the advisory guideline range; (5) any pertinent policy statements issued by the Sentencing Commission; (6) the need to avoid unwarranted sentence disparities; and (7) the need to provide restitution to any victims of the offense. 18 U.S.C. §3553(a). The statute further provides that the court shall, on considering these factors, impose a sentence that is "sufficient, but not greater than necessary to comply with the purposes set forth" in subsection (a)(2): just (or proportional) punishment, deterrence, protection of the public, and rehabilitation of the defendant. 18 U.S.C. §3553(a).

In making this determination, the district court may not presume that the guideline sentence is the correct one. *See Nelson v. United States*, 555 U.S. 350, 352 (2009). Indeed, the guidelines merely provide a "rough approximation" of an appropriate sentence. *Rita v. United States*, 551 U.S. 338, 350 (2007). Ultimately, this Court must make an independent determination as to the appropriate sentence, taking into account the types of sentences available, the relevant §3553(a) factors, and the arguments of the parties. *See Gall v. United States*, 552

U.S. 38, 49-50 (2007). The Court must then explain the chosen sentence in order to promote the perception of fair sentencing and to allow an appellate court a meaningful opportunity to review the record. *Id*. at 50.

II. THE GUIDELINE CALCULATIONS AND REQUESTED DEPARTURES

In Section III *infra*, Mr. Klient argues that the Guideline Calculations should not be employed by this Court in light of the United States Sentencing Commission's February 27, 2013 report entitled *Federal Child Pornography Offenses* (hereafter "FCPO"). Since the FCPO report is a rejection by the Commission of the structure of the child pornography guidelines, Mr. Klient argues in Section III *infra* that they should not be employed in his case. Counsel calculates the Guidelines for the Court's use regardless.

A.   The Guideline Calculation

The following calculations are applicable to Mr. Klient's sentence:

Guideline Provision	Description	Offense Level
USSG §2G2.2	Base Offense Level for possession child pornography	18
USSG §2G2.2(b)(2)	Minors under 12 enhancement	+2
USSG §2G2.2(b)(4) (Disputed by Government)	**Sadistic and masochistic images enhancement**	**+4**
USSG §2G2.2(b)(6)	Use of Computer Enhancement	+2
USSG §2G2.2(b)(7)(D)	More than 600 Images Enhancement	+5
USSG §3E1.1(a-b)	Acceptance of Responsibility	-3
	Undisputed Total	23 (51-63 months)
	Disputed Total	**27 (78-97 months)**

B.   Disputed Guideline Calculation Issues—Sadistic and Masochistic

i.   There Is No Evidence That the Video Shows Adults Engaging in Sexual Acts

The video at issue is alleged to be a pre-pubescent minor being sodomized by a penetrating male. The penetrating male's face cannot be seen, and it is impossible to tell whether he is a teenager or an adult.

USSG §2G2.2(b)(4) is the relevant Guideline, which states:

> *If the offense involved material that portrays sadistic or masochistic conduct or other depictions of violence, increase by 4 levels.*

To be sure, the First Circuit and other Circuits have generally found that penetration by an adult male on a child is inherently sadistic. *See United States v. Hoey*, 508 F.3d 687 (1st Cir. 2007) *citing cases omitted*. Here, the Government's burden of proof that there is an adult penetrating a child cannot be carried. There is no way to establish the same. Counsel is unaware of caselaw indicating that a child penetrating another child is inherently sadistic. Since the burden of establishing the age cannot be carried, the four level increase should not be applied.

ii. The Video Is Not Remotely Characteristic of the Images and Videos Obtained Otherwise

The contraband seized from Mr. Klient's computer is not remotely like the short video the Court will see. The images and videos in Mr. Klient's computer were nearly all soft core child pornography. This one hard core pornography clip sticks out like a sore thumb. The other images are primarily nudes, and videos of nude girls dancing or bathing, etc…This video is an aberration.

Just as relevant conduct can be used to enhance a sentence, the same concept should apply here as the court considers an enhancement. This very short video is not like the other images or videos possessed by Mr. Klient. We ask the Court to not apply the enhancement as a result.

C. Requested Departures

The Guidelines require that there be a mitigating circumstance requiring departure that has not been considered by the Sentencing Commission, which should result in a different sentence from that described. USSG 5K2.0(b). The entire structure of the Guidelines, however, has been rejected by the Sentencing Commission. *See Section III(b) infra.* As a result, the following departures should be considered either as Guideline departures, or as other mitigating grounds at sentencing.

i. Age Departure

This Court has the ability to depart from the Guideline range based on Mr. Klient's age pursuant to §5H1.1. In considering such a departure, the Sentencing Guidelines state:

Age (including youth) may be relevant in determining whether a departure is warranted, if considerations based on age, individually or in combination with other offender characteristics, are present to an unusual degree and distinguish the case from the typical cases covered by the guidelines.

U.S.S.G. §5H1.1.

Older offenders are less likely to recidivate then younger offenders. In 2004, the Sentencing Commission found that within 2 years of their release, an offender over the age of 50, with a criminal history Category I, had a 6.2% chance of committing a new criminal offense following release. United States Sentencing Commission, *Measuring Recidivism: The Criminal History Computation of the Federal Sentencing Guidelines* (May 2004). A person under the age of 21 with a criminal history Category I had a 29.5% chance of committing a new criminal offense following release. *Id.* The Sentencing Commission's report supports the premise that the older a person gets, the less likely he or she will recidivate.

The other underlying issue with offenders similar in age to Mr. Klient is the stress of prison and the impact it has on their future. Prisons have problems managing elderly[13] inmates because of their "vulnerability to abuse and predation, difficulty in establishing social relationships with younger inmates, need for special physical accommodations in a relatively inflexible physical environment." B. Jaye Anno et al., *Correctional Health Care: Addressing the Needs of Elderly, Chronically Ill, and Terminally Ill Inmates*, Washington, DC: U.S. Department of Justice, National Institute of Corrections, pp 9-10, 2004. As of August 25, 2012, the average age of the inmate populations in the Federal Bureau of Prisons was 39 years old. Bureau of Prisons, *http://www.bop.gov/news/quick.jsp.*

This age-based departure is especially important in a case such as this one, where the Defendant's convictions make him extremely susceptible to violence. Sex offenders, and particularly child pornography offenders, are extremely susceptible to violence by prison populations. As a result, prison will be a much harder road for Mr. Klient than for someone convicted of a more innocuous offense, making the age-based departure that much more critical.

---

[13] There is no bright-line definition of an "elderly" person. The U.S. Census Bureau defines "elderly" as a person 65 and older; while the National Commission on Correctional Health Care defines "elderly" as a person 55 years or older. Tina Chiu, *It's About Time: Aging Prisoners, Increasing Costs, and Geriatric Release*, New York: Vera Institute of Justice, 2010 (*Citation Omitted*). We are not alleging that Mr. Klient, or any 64 year old, is elderly. We are simply pointing out that he is coming into an age range where incarceration becomes problematic.

ii. Departure Due To Susceptibility of Abuse in Prison

Mr. Klient suggests the nature of his offense, combined with his age, makes him susceptible to abuse in prison. Such a concern is grounds for a departure: "[a] defendant's unusual susceptibility to abuse by other inmates while in prison may warrant a downward departure." *United States v. Parish*, 308 F.3d 1025, 1031 (9th Cir. 2002); *see also United States v. Redemann*, 295 F. Supp. 2d 887, 896 (E.D. Wisc. 2003) ("For a defendant who faces more onerous conditions of confinement than the typical defendant, the court can impose a shorter prison sentence and obtain the same punitive effect.").

The danger of abuse to Mr. Klient is very real. Child pornography defendants are at extreme risk, and here is such a Defendant who is 64 years old. Consider *United States v. Kelly*, 868 F. Supp. 2d 1202 (D.N.M. June 20, 2012), wherein Judge Bruce Black noted that, in deciding to impose the statutory minimum 5-year term of imprisonment, the defendant before him would "be subject to serious danger in prison," and that "[t]he last defendant this Court was required to sentence to the mandatory five-year prison term for receipt of child pornography, a 72-year old retired attorney, was beaten to death within days of arriving at the federal penitentiary." *Id.* at 1204.

III. THE GUIDELINES SHOULD NOT BE APPLIED AS THEY ARE INEQUITABLE, ARE NOT BASED ON EMPIRICAL DATA OR STUDY AND HAVE BEEN RECENTLY REJECTED BY THE SENTENCING COMMISSION

A. The Rebellion in the Courts Leading Up to the Sentencing Commission FCPO Report

In *Kimbrough v. United States*, 552 U.S. 85 (2007), the Supreme Court held that it is not "an abuse of discretion for a district court to conclude when sentencing a particular defendant that the crack/powder disparity yields a sentence 'greater than necessary' to achieve §3553(a)'s purposes, even in a mine-run case." The Court observed that, in creating the drug guidelines, the Sentencing Commission varied from its usual practice of employing an "empirical approach based on data about past sentencing practices," instead adopting the "weight-driven scheme" used in the 1986 Anti-Drug Abuse Act, and maintaining the 100-to-1 quantity ratio throughout the drug table. The Court also pointed out that the Commission had subsequently criticized the ratio, quoting from the various Commission reports to Congress on the issue, and discussed Congress's previous responses to Commission actions and recommendations.

The Court then discussed the Commission's ongoing role in determining sentencing ranges, noting that "while the Guidelines are no longer binding, closer review may be in order when the sentencing judge varies from the Guidelines based solely on the judge's view that the Guidelines range 'fails properly to reflect §3553(a) considerations' even in a mine-run case." The Court held that the crack cocaine guidelines, however, "do not exemplify the Commission's exercise of its characteristic institutional role" and noted the Commission's opinion that the crack cocaine guidelines produce "disproportionately harsh sanctions." In light of this, "it would not be an abuse of discretion for a district court to conclude when sentencing a particular defendant that the crack/powder disparity yields a sentence 'greater than necessary' to achieve §3553(a)'s purposes, even in a mine-run case." *Id.*

Kimbrough effectively opens the door to the arguments made in this Memorandum, that the Sentencing Guidelines should not be followed when sentencing Mr. Klient. Circuit Courts around the country have been attacking the efficacy of the Guidelines in child pornography cases for several years now. *See e.g., U.S. v. Rodriguez*, 527 F.3d 221 (1st Cir. 2008) (Sentencing courts have discretion to consider items such as fast-track disparity in considering requests for variant sentences because the fast-track departure scheme does not "exemplify the (Sentencing) Commission's exercise of its characteristic institutional role." *Kimbrough*, 128 S. Ct. at 575. For example, the Commission has "not take[n] account of empirical data and national experience" in formulating them. Thus, guidelines and policy statements embodying these judgments deserve less deference than the sentencing guidelines normally attract."); *U.S. v. Henderson*, 649 F.3d 955 (9th Cir. 2011) (case remanded for district court to consider whether it disagrees with pornography Guidelines because "similar to the crack cocaine Guidelines, district courts may vary from the child pornography Guidelines, §2G2.2, based on policy disagreement with them, and not simply based on an individualized determination that they yield an excessive sentence in a particular case" in part because "the child pornography Guidelines are, to a large extent, not the result of the Commission's "exercise of its characteristic institutional role,"); *U.S. v. Grober*, 624 F.3d 592 (3d Cir. 2010) (where Guidelines in child pornography case were 234 to 293 months, district court did not err in granting variance to mandatory minimum of 60 months given that the child pornography Guidelines were too severe and not based on empirical studies); *U.S. v. Dorvee*, 616 F.3d

174 (2d Cir. 2010) (where defendant pled guilty to distribution of pornography and was sentenced to 240 months the sentence was vacated as unreasonable in part because "the Commission did not use this empirical approach in formulating the Guidelines…(and) often openly opposed these Congressionally directed (increases)… The §2G2.2 sentencing enhancements cobbled together through this process routinely result in Guidelines projections near or exceeding the statutory maximum, even in run-of-the-mill cases." The child pornography guideline is beset with "irrationality" and "unless applied with great care, (this Guideline) can lead to unreasonable sentences that are inconsistent with what §3553 requires." By "concentrating all offenders at or near the statutory maximum, (this guideline) eviscerates the fundamental statutory requirement in §3553(a) that district courts consider 'the nature and circumstances of the offense and the history and characteristics of the defendant' and violates the principle, reinforced in *Gall*, that courts must guard against unwarranted similarities among sentences for defendants who have been found guilty of dissimilar conduct." The child pornography Guideline is an "eccentric Guideline of highly unusual provenance which, unless carefully applied, can *easily* generate unreasonable results." "The irony of the court's conclusion in this area…[is] that the Guidelines actually punish some forms of direct sexual contact with minors *more leniently* than possession or distribution of child pornography."); *US v. Tutty*, 612 F.3d 128 (2d Cir. 2010) (where Defendant pleaded guilty to one count of receiving child pornography and was sentenced to 168 months, sentence vacated in part because district court erred "when it held, relying on outdated law, that it did not have the authority to impose a non-Guideline sentence based on policy considerations applicable to all defendants. Moreover, as we recently recognized in *United States v. Dorvee*, 604 F.3d 84 (2d Cir. 2010), the child pornography Guidelines present important policy considerations, and unless they are "carefully applied," they "can easily generate unreasonable results.").

The Circuit Court's rejection of the Guidelines in child pornography cases is not a random act of kindness directed toward the most despised defendants in the criminal justice system. Rather, it results from the hue and cry among scholars and judges who have deconstructed the harsh child pornography Guidelines. *See e.g.* Troy Stabenow, AFD, "*Deconstructing the Myth of Careful Study: A Primer on the Flawed Progression of the Child Pornography Guidelines*" (rev. Jan. 1, 2009) [online at *http://www.fd.org/docs/Select-Topics---sentencing/child-porn-july-revision. pdf*]. The Undersigned knows of no Circuit court decision that has opined that USSG §2G2.2 is sound or comports with the overarching sentencing mandate of §3553(a).

The Circuit Courts do not stand alone. District Courts are equally rejecting these Guidelines. This assertion is supported by nationwide sentencing data collected and published post-Booker by the U.S. Sentencing Commission in Table 14 of its *Sourcebook of Federal Sentencing Statistics* (2006-2011). As the series of charts below illustrate, federal judges are rejecting Guideline sentences in child pornography cases to a frequency and degree unparalleled in federal criminal law.

The first chart below illustrates the percentage of child pornography sentences that were imposed within USSG §2G2.2's advisory range (blue line), and those that were imposed below the range either as a result of a government motion (red line) or a court's decision to depart or vary downward (green line).

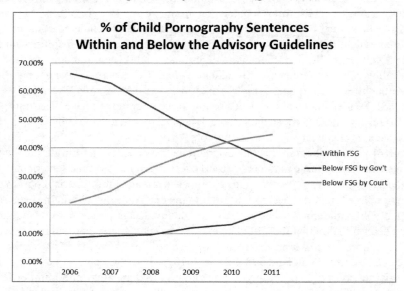

When compared to the other major offense categories (which together with child pornography offenses, collectively make up over 85% of all federal offenses), see *U.S. Sentencing Comm'n, Sourcebook of Federal Sentencing Statistics 2011*, Fig. A., available at http://www.ussc.gov/Data_and_Statistics/Annual_Reports_and_Sourcebooks/2011/FigureA. pdf, it is apparent that the situation for child pornography sentences is unique, as the following series of charts show.

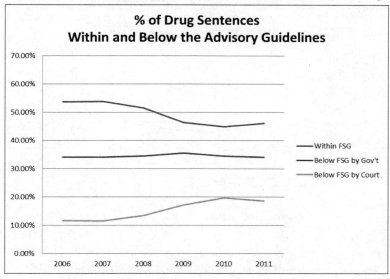

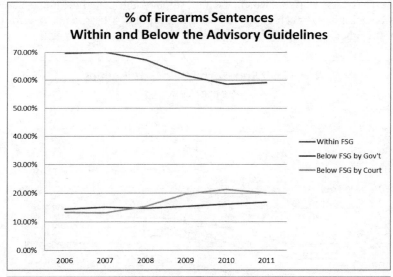

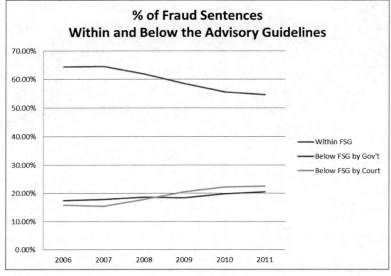

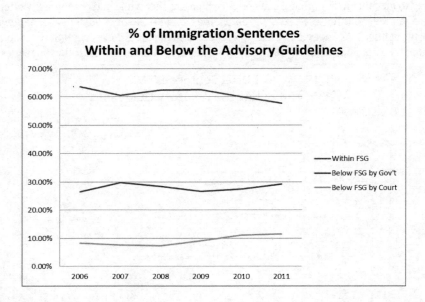

Below is a comparison chart showing the percentage of sentences imposed below USSG §2G2.2, by major offense category, as a result of a downward departure or variance. The chart below simply is a comparison of the green lines in the above charts. As clearly indicated, the imposition of non-government-sponsored below guidelines sentences has always been higher—much higher, and has increased at a far greater rate for child pornography sentences, than any of the other major offense categories.

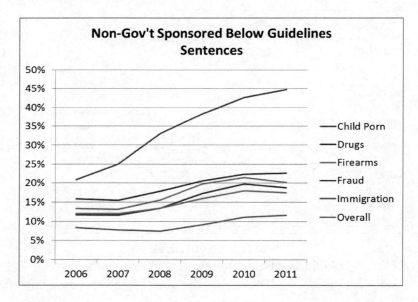

Finally, the chart below shows when imposing a nongovernment-sponsored below guidelines sentence, the median months below the bottom of the applicable Guidelines range such sentences are imposed. In other words, the chart below shows the degree of variance below guidelines sentences.

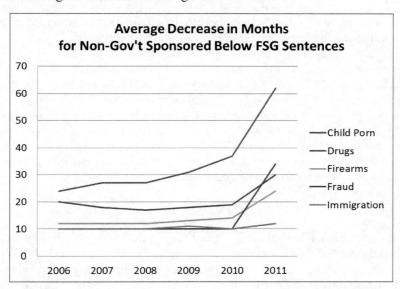

Child pornography cases are a class unto themselves. As the Court of Appeals for the Ninth Circuit stated, "an unduly deferential application of §2G2.2 will lead to the vast majority of offenders being sentenced to near the maximum statutory term." *United States v. Henderson*, 649 F.3d 955, 965 (9th Cir. 2011) *citations omitted*. As Judge Merritt of the Sixth Circuit Court of Appeals observed in a dissenting opinion, "The problem in this pornography case is the gross disparity, inequality, and unfairness that exists in sentencing generally, but even more so in these child pornography viewer cases. It illustrates the continued sad dependence of federal judges on a harsh sentencing grid created by a distant bureaucracy." *United States v. Overmyer*, 663 F.3d 862, 866 (6th Cir. Dec. 20, 2011) (Merritt, J., dissenting).

B. The Sentencing Commission has Rejected the Guidelines for Child Pornography Offenses and This Court Should Reject the Guidelines As Well

The February 27, 2013 FCPO Report, representing a decade-long study of child pornography sentencing, including a special coding project for child pornography offenses beginning in 2010, disavows the entire structure of child pornography sentencing. The Commission found:

> *The current sentencing scheme in §2G2.2 places a disproportionate emphasis on outdated measures of culpability regarding offenders' collecting behavior and insufficient emphases on offenders' community involvement and sexual dangerousness. As a result, penalty ranges are too severe for some offenders and too lenient for other offenders. The guideline thus should be revised to more fully account for these ... factors and thereby provide for more proportionate punishments.*

FCPO at xviii (emphasis added).

In light of these inherent flaws in USSG §2G2.2, the Commission recognizes and is concerned by "widespread inconsistent application" of USSG §2G2.2 *Id.* at xxi. Accordingly, the Commission is "request[ing] Congress to provide the Commission with authority to *revise the entire guideline structure.*" *Id.* at 322 (emphasis added). The FCPR Report concludes:

> *As illustrated by this report, child pornography offenses result in substantial and indelible harm to the children who are victimized by both production and non-production offenses. However, there is a growing belief among many interested parties that the existing sentencing scheme in non-production cases fails*

to distinguish adequately among offenders based on their degrees of culpability and dangerousness. Numerous stakeholders — including the Department of Justice, the federal defender community, and the Criminal Law Committee of the Judicial Conference of the United States Courts — have urged the Commission and Congress to revise the non-production sentencing scheme to better reflect the growing body of knowledge about offense and offender characteristics and to better account for offenders' varying degrees of culpability and dangerousness.

The Commission believes that the current non-production guideline warrants revision in view of its out-dated and disproportionate enhancements related to offenders' collecting behavior as well as its failure to account fully for some offenders' involvement in child pornography communities and sexually dangerous behavior. The current guideline produces overly severe sentencing ranges for some offenders, unduly lenient ranges for other offenders, and widespread inconsistent application. A revised guideline...would better promote proportionate sentences and reflect the statutory purposes of sentencing. Such a revised guideline, together with a statutory structure that aligns the penalties for receipt and possession, would reduce much of the unwarranted sentencing disparity that currently exists.

FCPO at Ch. 12, pp. 330-331.

In light of what the Commission has said in its FCPO Report, the child pornography possession guidelines have now been effectively deleted. *See United States v. Booker*, 543 U.S. 220, 263 (2005) ("The Sentencing Commission will continue to collect and study appellate court decision-making. It will continue to modify its Guidelines in light of what it learns, thereby encouraging what it finds to be better sentencing practices."). USSG §2G2.2 no longer remains a viable Guideline in light of the Commission's findings. Just as it is error to impose a sentence based upon an improper guideline calculation or a belief that the Guidelines are mandatory, it is also error for a sentence to be based on the rejected USSG §2G2.2. This is so irrespective of whether a variance is ultimately imposed. *See, e.g., United States v. Zauner*, 688 F.3d 426, 431 (8th Cir. 2012) (Bright, J., concurring) ("And where the guidelines are out of line and increasingly disregarded by sentencing judges, the mere fact of a downward departure should not insulate the district court's sentence from any type of meaningful review."). As the Guideline itself has been disavowed, no calculation can ever be considered proper. *See, e.g., United States v. Langford*, 516 F.3d 205, 215 (3d Cir. 2008) ("We submit that the improper calculation of the Guidelines range can rarely be shown not to affect the sentence imposed.").

...

This Court now has the statutory authority and the Supreme Court's blessing to refuse to apply the Guidelines when it disagrees with the policy, or how that policy applies to a particular case. *United States v. Kimbrough*, 552 U.S. 85, 101 (2007) (citing *Rita v. United States*, 551 U.S. 338, 351 (2007)); *Spears v. United States*, 555 U.S. 261, 264 (2009). This discretion is most broad when the Guideline is not based on the Sentencing Commission's characteristic institutional role. *United States v Williams*, 517 F.3d 801, 809-10 (5th Cir. 2008) ("courts may vary [from Guidelines ranges] based solely on policy considerations, including disagreements with the Guidelines."). Further, the Sentencing Commission itself is leading a rallying cry against the child pornography Guidelines, especially for possession only cases, such as this one.

The facts above cry out for an outright rejection of the Guidelines in this case.

IV. A GUIDELINE SENTENCE PROVIDES FOR AN UNRESONABLE SENTENCE AS IT RELATES TO MR. KLIENT

The purpose of the Guidelines is for the Court to "impose a sentence sufficient, but not greater than necessary, to comply" with the purposes of sentencing set forth in the second paragraph of the statute. The United States Supreme Court has summarized factors set forth in the second paragraph of the statute: the "(1) offense and offender characteristics; (2) the need for a sentence to reflect the basic aims of sentencing, namely (a) just punishment (retribution), (b) deterrence, (c) incapacitation, (d) rehabilitation; (3) the sentences legally available; (4) the Sentencing Guidelines; (5) Sentencing Commission policy statements; (6) the need to avoid unwarranted disparities; and (7) the need for restitution." *Rita v. United States,* 127 S.Ct. 2456, 2463 (2007).

Probation indicated that this may be an appropriate case for a variant sentence under §3553 due to Mr. Klient's lack of criminal history, strong work and educational history and the severity of the Guidelines. Mr. Klient's age, long marriage, strong family support, education, gainful employment until his retirement and successful therapy support the conclusion that he is most unlikely to re-offend. While a small minority of defendants convicted of possessing child pornography may again view child pornography and an even smaller minority may molest children, Mr. Klient is not one of them. All of the evidence indicates that Mr. Klient will never view child pornography again. Supervised release with appropriate conditions is more than sufficient to ensure that he never does. Counsel urges the Court to apply a variant sentence under §3553 to reflect those positive personal characteristics. A variant sentence is what is needed to balance the Defendant's personal history with the crimes convicted.

V. CONCLUSION

Counsel understands the severity of the charges for which the Defendant has been convicted. Justice must be tempered with mercy. Here, the Guideline sentences are far too long, are not based on empirical study and do not take into account Mr. Klient's life other than as charged.

The dangers of prolonged incarceration are very real to Mr. Klient. Child Pornography offenders have an extreme susceptibility to abuse in prison. There is a high likelihood that he will be housed in solitary/protective custody. He will be a target for violence by other inmates. To protect him, he will be housed in solitary confinement, which will have an irreversible impact on his mental health. The sentences suggested below offer a chance at life.

When considering these potential sentences, Counsel would be remiss to not mention the cost of incarceration. This Court is well aware of the costs of incarceration in general. Beyond that, the cost of incarcerating prisoners age 50 and older has been estimated to be two to four times that of the general inmate population. U.S. Dep't of Justice, National Institute of Corrections, *Correctional Health Care: Addressing the Needs of Elderly, Chronically Ill, and Terminally Ill Inmates,* at 11 (2004) (*Addressing the Needs of Elderly, Chronically Ill, and Terminally Ill Inmates*), *available at* http://www.nicic.org/pubs/2004/018735.pdf

Counsel suggests two alternative sentences. Our favored sentence is a sentence in which home monitoring is a component of the sentence. Mr. Klient asks this court to impose a sentence of four months in custody, credit for time served, a period of home detention with electronic monitoring that is significant in this Court's judgment and ten years of supervised release with the conditions that he register as a sex offender and undergo any further treatment deemed necessary by the Probation Officer. Unlike the advisory Guideline range, this requested sentence is "sufficient, but not greater than necessary" to serve sentencing purposes under §3553(a).

The alternative and more traditional sentence we would request is a sentence of 18 months, with credit for time served. This would give Mr. Klient a little over a year in BOP custody to serve.

Dated this 15th Day of April 2013 in Portland, Maine.

Respectfully submitted,

_____

Timothy E. Zerillo
Attorney for Defendant
ZERILLO LAW FIRM, LLC

See Ch. 2 for more on sentencing memoranda.

(This page intentionally left blank.)

INDEX

A

- AN -

C

- CH -

- CH -

- CL -

- CR -

- DO -

E

EBay scammer
Theft offenses, §4:80

Emails in response to defendant-inquiries
Generally, §1:10
Sample response, §1:11, Form 1–10

Embezzlement
Accountants (forensic), §4:72
Client set up by another employee, §4:73
Client's financial situation, §4:70
Common scenarios, §§4:61, 4:62
Elements of, §4:60
Padding payroll, §4:61
Points-of-sale, §4:62
Release and Settlement Agreement, §4:71, Form 4–30
Sentencing for
Generally, §4:74
Sentencing memorandum, §4:75, Form 4–40
Strategies and tactics, §§4:40–4:75
Victims, contacting before client is charged, §4:70

Entrapment
Robbery cases, §5:143

Evidence
Admissibility. See **Admissibility of evidence**
Burden of proof. See **Burden of proof**
Child pornography cases. See **Child pornography**
Child sexual-assault cases. See **Child sexual-assault cases**
Closing Argument(s), §2:141
Criminal threatening cases, §6:33
Exculpatory. See **Exculpatory evidence**
Impeachment, §2:83
Opening Statement(s), §2:112
Preservation of. See **Preservation of evidence**
Suppression of. See **Suppression of evidence/statements**

Exculpatory evidence
Impeachment evidence as, §2:83
Prosecutor's duty to disclose
Bagley error, §2:82
Bagley-Kyles standard(s), §§2:81–2:85
Collective consideration of evidence's impact, §2:84
Generally, §2:80

Impeachment evidence, §2:83
Truth of paramount concern, §2:85

Exhibits
Robbery cases, §5:155

Experts
Aggravated-felony assault/battery cases, §3:173
Chemist(s)
Drug possession cases, hiring in, §7:32
State chemist. See **Drunk driving cases**
Child pornography cases. See **Child pornography**
Child sexual-assault cases
Defense experts, use of, §12:17
Government experts, interviewing, §§12:50, 12:51, Form 12–50
Cross-examination, §2:131
Retaining, §1:33

Eyewitness(es)
Identifications. See **Eyewitness identification(s)**
Simple assault/battery cases, cross-examination in, §3:32

Eyewitness identification(s)
Forcible rape by stranger, §11:41
Motions to suppress
Drug sales and trafficking cases, §7:86, Form 7–90
Robbery cases, §§5:132, 5:133, Form 5–60
Robbery cases. See **Robbery**

F

Family violence. See Domestic assault/battery

Federal Kidnapping Act
Generally, §10:10
Parental exclusion, §10:11

Federal theft offenses
Computer fraud, §4:81
Credit card fraud
Generally, §4:82
Sentencing memorandum, §4:85, Form 4–50
EBay scammer, §4:80
Mail fraud, §4:81
Sentencing guidelines
Amount of loss, impact of, §4:83
Economic reality theory, departure from guide-

Breath machine operator's credentials (drunk
    driving cases), request for
    Request for, §8:31, Form 8–30
    Response to request for, §8:32
Closing Letter(s)
    Leaving the client feeling good about a bad
        situation, §1:50
    Sample letter, §1:50
Date rape cases, preservation of surveillance video
    in, §11:142, Form 11–50
Drug crimes, letters in support of diversion for,
    §§7:05–7:07, Forms 7–10 to 7–30
Drunk driving cases
    Letter requesting credentials of breath machine
        operator. Breath machine operator's cre-
        dentials (drunk driving cases), request
        for
    Letter to state chemist requesting testing and
        calibration records of breath test ma-
        chine, §8:86, Form 8–50
Dumb kids burglary cases, letter to prosecutor in,
    §§5:11, 5:12, Form 5–10
Fee-agreement follow-up letters
    Sample letter #1, §1:44, Form 1–80
    Sample letter #2, §1:45, Form 1–90
Initial meeting with client, letter confirming,
    §1:18, Form 1–30
Prosecutor(s)
    Dumb kids burglary cases, §§5:11, 5:12, Form
        5–10
    Initial letter to, §2:41, Form 2–50
Social media warning, new client letter with,
    §1:35, Form 1–50
Surveillance video, preservation of
    Date rape cases, §11:142, Form 11–50
Theft offense cases
    Letter from therapist to prosecutor, §4:11
    Letter to prosecutor transmitting letter from
        therapist, §4:12, Form 4–10
Trial risk letter, §2:92, Form 2–100

Lie detector tests. See Polygraph examinations

Lineup(s)
Robbery cases. See **Robbery**

M

Mail fraud
Theft offenses, §4:81

Marijuana cultivation
Cross-examination of officer at suppression hear-
    ing, §7:142
Search warrants
    Defective affidavit, memorandum on defen-
        dant's motion to suppress for, §7:141,
        Form 7–110
    Lack of probable cause, §7:140
Suppression of evidence/statements
    Cross-examination of officer at suppression
        hearing, §7:142
    Memorandum on defendant's motion to
        suppress for defective search warrant
        affidavit, §7:141, Form 7–110

Medical records
Child sexual-assault cases, gathering evidence in,
    §§12:68, 12:69, Form 12–80

Meeting with client(s)
Face-to-face meeting, setting up, §1:17
Initial meeting
    Drunk driving defendants, with, §8:10
    Letter confirming, §§1:18, Form 1–30
    Trust building at, §1:30

Memoranda
Felony conviction, effect of, §2:93, Form 2–110
Law enforcement's failure to preserve evidence,
    motion to dismiss for, §2:24, Form 2–30
Sentencing. See **Sentencing memoranda**

Mens rea
Criminal threatening, §6:30

Military personnel
Firearms possession (domestic violence cases),
    §9:04

Minors. See Child(ren)

Motions
Bail, amendment of. See **Bail**
Bill of particulars, for (drug conspiracy cases),
    §§7:120, 7:121, Form 7–100

- OP -

- RE -

- RE -

V